FOR USE
IN
LIBRA
ONLY
D0948236

WORLD WAR II: THE EUROPEAN AND MEDITERRANEAN THEATERS

WARS OF THE UNITED STATES
(Editor: Richard L. Blanco)
Vol. 2

GARLAND REFERENCE LIBRARY
OF SOCIAL SCIENCE
Vol. 217

WARS OF THE UNITED STATES
(Richard L. Blanco, General Editor)

1. *The War of the American Revolution: A Selected, Annotated Bibliography of Published Sources*
   by Richard L. Blanco

2. *World War II: The European and Mediterranean Theaters: An Annotated Bibliography*
   by Myron J. Smith, Jr.

WORLD WAR II: THE EUROPEAN AND MEDITERRANEAN THEATERS

An Annotated Bibliography

Myron J. Smith, Jr.

GARLAND PUBLISHING, INC. • NEW YORK & LONDON
1984

Library of Congress Cataloging in Publication Data

Smith, Myron J., Jr.
World War II, the European and Mediterranean theaters.

(Wars of the United States ; vol. 2) (Garland reference library of social science ; vol. 217)
Includes indexes.
1. World War, 1939–1945—Campaigns—Western—Bibliography. 2. World War, 1939–1945—Campaigns—Mediterranean Region—Bibliography. I. Title. II. Title: World War 2, the European and Mediterranean theaters. III. Series: Wars of the United States ; v. 2. IV. Series: Garland reference library of social science ; v. 217.
Z6207.W8S573 1984 [D756] 016.94054'21 83-49086
ISBN 0-8240-9013-6 (alk. paper)

Cover design by Laurence Walczak

Printed on acid-free, 250-year-life paper
Manufactured in the United States of America

For my father and his brother who served in World War II
Myron J. Smith, Sr.
82nd Airborne Division
in memory of
Elmer J. Smith
156 Signal Photographic Co.

CONTENTS

PREFACE

In his *World War II: The European and Mediterranean Theaters*, Myron J. Smith, Jr. presents a fine bibliographic study of Western Europe's greatest military struggle in modern times. The war by the United States and her Allies against Germany, Italy, and their satellite nations was a decisive point in history. Millions of Americans served in the European Theater of Operations and innumerable veterans of the conflict inevitably reminisce about aspects of the titanic effort to crush the Nazi and Fascist dictatorships. Judging by the burgeoning output of books, articles, and films about the fighting, public interest in the 1940–1945 epic remains high.

To enable a broad reading audience to select the best books, articles, and essays from the enormous literature in English about the war, Professor Smith has written a concise, imaginative, annotated bibliography of over 2,800 items published through 1983. Whether the reader is a high school student, a college undergraduate, a graduate student or scholar, a military history "buff," or part of a larger audience curious about America's biggest war, he or she can easily find ample citations in this work on virtually every phase of the struggle in Europe. The author has organized his study into six broad categories—Reference Works, Special Studies, The War in the Air, The War on Land, The War at Sea, and a Film Guide. Within each category are numerous subdivisions about individual soldiers, sailors, and airmen, on campaigns and battles, unit histories, weaponry, and provocative essays about the conduct of the war, in addition to innumerable other relevant subjects. To enhance the value of this thoughtful study, Professor Smith has provided crisp, concise descriptions about the relative merits of each entry, a bibliographic technique that should enable the reader to find with ease the most reliable information on a particular subject.

This study, the second volume to be published in the Wars of the United States series, is a highly useful work by a famed specialist in military, naval, and aviation history that will be an invaluable reference tool. Students, professional historians, and general readers alike can learn much about the impact of total war on society by perusing this stimulating book.

Richard L. Blanco
General Editor

FOREWORD

History is the Gibraltar of the learned. Those who seek knowledge are indebted to historians and bibliographers. Professor Myron J. Smith, Jr., has performed a selfless and indelible service. He provides here a signpost to enlightenment and truth. His effort is a contribution to scholars of the Second World War everywhere.

E. R. Quesada, Lt. Gen. U.S.A.F. (Ret.)

In view of the continuing avid interest by readers—and thus by writers and publishers—in the events of World War II, thirteen years between definitive bibliographies is a long time. Almost every month several new and important titles appear, and translations and reprints are numerous.

Yet it was just over thirteen years ago, in 1971, that the first—and until now, the final—definitive bibliography of works on World War II in the English language appeared: Janet Ziegler's *World War II: Books in English, 1945–1965*. That time span adds to the importance of this new work by Professor Myron J. Smith, Jr., a distinguished bibliographer and the first American to receive the *Richard Franck Preis* from the *Bibliothek für Zeitgeschichte*. Professor Smith's earlier works on the air, naval, and intelligence aspects of World War II constitute the definitive bibliographies on those topics.

By limiting the scope of this bibliography to the Europe and Mediterranean theaters (other theaters will be covered by another work in this series), Professor Smith has been able to provide comprehensive coverage, not only of books but also of important articles, documents, dissertations, and 16 mm. motion picture films.

Here is no simple listing of authors, titles, publishers, and publication dates. Every major section begins with a brief, but informative introduction, which puts the listings that follow in proper context. Of even greater value are the annotations to each entry. Those eliminate the problem of sometimes unrevealing or even misleading titles by noting briefly what the book, article, film, etc., is about and the nature of the presentation: campaign history, case study, contemporary film footage, or whatever. Cross-references are extensive and helpful, and the indexing is comprehensive.

Whoever turns to this new work—whether student, researcher, writer, or librarian—will quickly become aware of the lasting value of this important and definitive bibliography.

Charles B. MacDonald
Arlington, Virginia

World War I ended the nineteenth century, its leisurely ways and opulent art, as well as the small-scale power politics of the Europeans who were, essentially, the makers of its history. It left an enormous body of literature even though it was a world war more in name than in fact.

World War II was both to an unimagined degree, bursting the bounds of every effort and every horror mankind had ever known and opening the door to a new age on a grander scale for good and ill. New medicines saved and prolonged life—and caused a population explosion. New weapons and new technology made the globe vulnerable and small. Over all this, as the fallout from an information explosion, hangs a fog of fact to be penetrated by those who want to understand and draw conclusions from what happened between 1939 and 1945 to launch and direct a new era. Details were piled up in sound and film as well as in print—more truth and falsehood (as well as the cunning or accidental combination of the two) and more records, memoirs, reports and analyses than ever before.

Those who grope their way through this profusion need help. A map leading them directly to their goal is too much to expect. Enough that something marks the many ways among which they must choose. A good bibliography is such a guide—to be read with care and followed with profit.

Richard C. Hottelet

INTRODUCTION

BACKGROUND

With the fall of France and the Battle of Britain in the summer of 1940, the foreign policy of the United States with regard to the war in Europe was shifted by American leaders. Strict neutrality and complacency diminished as the President, Congress, military services, and civilian population realized that a stalemate was not likely; Nazi victories awoke the country to the need to prepare for the likely possibility of war.

By the following summer of 1941, America, now helping to supply Britain and Russia by Lend Lease, had begun rebuilding its military establishment, occupied Greeland and Iceland, and established a "neutral zone" far out in the Atlantic. As U.S. naval vessels escorted convoys in the zone, incidents between destroyers and German submarines, called "U-boats," placed the governments of Roosevelt and Hitler in the position of conducting an undeclared naval war as the "Arsenal of Democracy" moved closer to open belligerency. As the situation in the Far East also deteriorated, the Americans assured the British, with whom they had been conducting secret talks, that, in the event of an open two-front conflict, a Europe-first strategy would be followed. The Nazis, with their greater technological and industrial base, were acknowledged to be a greater military threat than the Japanese.

The Japanese attack on Pearl Harbor and the German-Italian declarations of war brought the United States into the now-world conflict by mid-December of 1941. Prime Minister Churchill and his advisors came to Washington and in a conference over the bleak Christmas holidays obtained a reaffirmation from American leaders of the Europe-first strategy and Roosevelt's vague acceptance of England's outline for conducting the strategy of the two countries' coalition war. After due consideration and debate within the American establishment and between the two allies, the first fruits of the Europe-first approach appeared in 1942 with the buildup of the VIII U.S. Bomber Command in Britain, the renewed emphasis on winning the supply battle in the Atlantic against the U-boat, and the invasion of Vichy North Africa in November, which led to the Axis defeat in Tunisia the following spring.

Despite the North African victory, it became politically necessary for President Roosevelt and his advisors to move away from the British idea of defeating Germany via the Mediterranean. The pressure from public opinion and the demand from U.S. Pacific commanders for a stepping-up of the conflict with Japan brought a realization that the "crusade" in Europe must be completed as quickly as militarily possible in order that the country's full strength might be thrown against that most hated of the Axis, the empire of the Rising Sun. To this end from late 1942 onward, America, now providing much of the material without which the defeat of the Reich would be impossible, insisted on a direct approach to the Continent through northern France. The peripheral Mediterranean strategy favored by the British would be sanctioned only in so far as it supported an attack through northwest Europe by tying down Axis forces and allowing for preparations to be completed in Britain. Although he protested in some of his finest prose, Churchill gave way to a spirited cooperation, knowing that an implied U.S. threat to abandon the Europe-first plan could all too easily be implemented.

As planning and organization for the "second front" progressed through 1943 and into 1944, the Allies did, indeed, move in the Mediterranean, not wanting to abandon the possibility of pressure which their forces there provided. Sicily was captured, Mussolini's government fell, and a foothold was established on the Italian peninsula. Elsewhere, the Battle of the Atlantic had turned in favor of the Allies and the "round the clock" Combined Bomber Offensive made its weight felt, particularly after the U.S. air forces received long-range escort fighters to help defeat the Luftwaffe in the air and safeguard the B-17's and B-24's in their daylight attacks on strategic targets.

The D-Day invasion of France in June 1944, following the

liberation of Rome, was one of the most extraordinary acts of coalition military coordination in history. With the war at sea now virtually over, Germany, for all intents fighting alone, faced land and air juggernauts from east and west which she could only hope to slow, not stop. As the Anglo-American armies broke out of their Normandy beachhead, invaded from the Riviera ("Anvil-Dragoon"), and sped deep into France, and Soviet armies pushed into Poland, Hungary, and Rumania, many in Germany outside of Hitler's circle knew that their nation was trapped in a vise.

Weather, terrain, logistical problems, and stiffening German resistance contributed to a slowing of the Anglo-American campaign as 1944 slipped away. In Italy, Field Marshal Kesslring's soldiers continued a magnificent defense, made easier by that country's many mountains. To the north, an Eisenhower–Montgomery dispute over approach strategy was finally settled in favor of the former and a strategic airborne assault ("Market-Garden") planned by the latter met disaster in Holland. In late December, the Germans attempted to move through the Ardennes to Antwerp in a desperate gamble to cut the Allied armies off from one another and block their logistical influx. After initial success, this final Nazi counteroffensive in the west was crushed by Allied soldiers and airmen.

As the Battle of the Bulge ended, troops of the United Nations pushed at Germany in strength. In Italy, the final campaign led to the Po Valley and a negotiated surrender ("Sunrise") on April 29, 1945. Millions of Soviet soldiers battered the Reich from the east while by early April, U.S., British, Free French, and Canadian forces were across the Rhine, the last great natural barrier to the heart of the Fatherland. Spreading out, they shoved their way through light opposition into northwestern, central, and southern Germany, linking up with Allied soldiers in the Brenner Pass and Russian troops on the Elbe. Following Hitler's suicide on April 30 and the surrender of Berlin to the Soviets on May 2, Grand Admiral Karl Dönitz, Hitler's heir, surrendered the remnants of the Third Reich at 2:41 A.M. on May 7, 1945. V-E (Victory in Europe) Day was proclaimed the next morning and the second American military campaign in Europe within a 27-year period came to a close.

OBJECTIVES

The difficulties in bibliographic control seem to exist on all fronts for English-language sources to the Second World War. One reason for this is, undoubtedly, the sheer mass of material available. Another seems to be that despite much interest, so little has actually been accomplished bibliographically in America over the past generation that beginning now is like sinking a battleship with a "burp" gun. It is difficult to believe that our non-English speaking colleagues are so much further along this road than we, but such is the case.[1]

This is not to say that nothing is being accomplished. The American Committee on the History of the Second World War has been working on this problem for over a decade while other devoted scholars have attempted to deal with it.

Although much has been included, it was necessary to draw a line somewhere and omit certain kinds of information which, while helpful, would either take up too much space or be too difficult for the average person to obtain. Excluded materials include: newspaper articles, the majority of the popular periodical titles found in the *Readers Guide to Periodical Literature*, book reviews, poetry, research projects, and fiction, a subject which I have addressed in three other efforts.[2] What is here is not offered strictly as an aid in correcting deficiencies in our knowledge of certain sources, though as such it may serve, but primarily as a means of control. Towards this end, annotations may, in some cases, be a bit critical, but for the most part they simply clarify the content of references. Because of the mass of material available in English and the excellence of foreign-language bibliographies, especially those published by the Bibliothek für Zeitgeschichte in Stuttgart, it was early decided to

[1]Janet Ziegler, *World War II: Books in English, 1945–1965* (Stanford, Calif.: Hoover Institution Press, 1971), pp. xii–xvii.

[2]*War Story Guide: An Annotated Bibliography of Military Fiction* (Metuchen, N.J.: The Scarecrow Press, 1980); *Cloak-and-Dagger Fiction: An Annotated Guide to Spy Thrillers* (2nd ed.; Santa Barbara, Calif.: Clio Books, 1982); and, with Robert C. Weller, *Sea Fiction Guide* (Metuchen, N.J.: The Scarecrow Press, 1976).

limit coverage to items written in English. This may seem a folly to some, but I suspect that the majority of this work's readers will accept this restriction without concern.

Years ago, Martial wrote to a friend concerning a volume then being compiled. It was suggested that the tome be enlarged and more information included. The learned man replied that he must call a halt: "Otherwise, dear Avitus, there would be no book." This same problem confronts many authors today, most especially bibliographers. To keep abreast of new works as they concern our topic, the user will find it necessary to continuously consult the reference works provided in Section I.

ARRANGEMENT

The five main sections in the table of contents form, with their subsections, something of a classified subject index to this guide and the key to the manner in which the book is laid out. Within the text, each section and many subsections have introductions which include information on further references designed to guide the reader to related information.

Each citation has an entry number. These entry numbers run consecutively throughout the guide. Author and subject indexes keyed to entry numbers are provided.

ACKNOWLEDGMENTS

For their advice, assistance, or encouragement in the formulation, research, and completion of this endeavor, the following persons and libraries are gratefully acknowledged.

Mr. Robert B. Lane, Director, U.S.A.F. Air University Library, Maxwell AFB, Alabama

Mrs. Dianne S. Tapley, Head, Public Services Section, U.S. Army Infantry School Library, Fort Benning, Georgia

Mr. Lester L. Miller, Jr., Supervisory Librarian, Morris Swett Library, U.S. Army Field Artillery School, Fort Sill, Oklahoma

Mr. Ray Merriam, International Graphics Corp., Bennington, Vermont

RAdm. John D. H. Kane, USN (Ret.), Director of Naval History and Curator for the Navy Department, Washington, D.C.

Dr. M. Joyce Baker, Director of Educational Services, American Bibliographical Center, Santa Barbara, California

Col. Donald P. Shaw, Director U.S. Army Military History Institute, Carlisle Barracks, Pennsylvania

Mr. Stanley Kalkus, Director, Navy Department Library, Washington, D.C.

Mr. Charles von Luttichau, Office of the Chief of Military History and the Center of Military History, Department of the Army, Washington, D.C.

Dr. Dean C. Allard, Head, Operational Archives, Knox Historical Center, Department of the Navy, Washington, D.C.

VAdm. Peter Gretton, Royal Navy (Ret.), London, England

LTG Mark W. Clark, U.S. Army (Ret.), Charleston, S.C.

LTG Ira Eaker, U.S. Air Force (Ret.), Washington, D.C.

Dr. Richard D. Burns, Director, Center for the Study of Armament and Disarmament, California State University, Los Angeles.

Dr. Jürgen Rohwer, Director, and the staff of the Bibliothek für Zeitgeschichte, Stuttgart, West Germany

MG John W. Huston, U.S.A.F., and Dr. B. Franklin Cooling, III, Office of Air Force History, Department of the Air Force, Washington, D.C.

Dr. Arthur Funk, Chairman, American Committee on the History of the Second World War

West Virginia University Library, Morgantown, West Virginia

U.S. Coast Guard Academy Library, New London, Connecticut

U.S. Naval Academy Library, Annapolis, Maryland

U.S. Military Academy Library, West Point, New York

Clarksburg-Harrison Public Library, Clarksburg, West Virginia
Wayne County Public Library, Wooster, Ohio
Ashbrook Library, Ashland College, Ashland, Ohio

Special appreciation is reserved for my colleagues at Salem College, without whose backing and aid this project would remain undone. President Ronald E. Ohl and Provost Gary S. McAllister provided continuous support and the encouragement to proceed. Margaret Allen, Jacqueline Isaacs, Sara A. Casey, and Janet Underwood of the Benedum Learning Resources Center staff provided support and interlibrary loan assistance.

Finally, hearty thanks is due to series editor Dick Blanco for his support, guidance, and kind words.

Myron J. Smith, Jr.
Salem, West Virginia
1 September 1983

World War II:
The European and
Mediterranean Theatres

I. REFERENCE WORKS

The purpose of this section is twofold. First and foremost is our desire to present tools that should prove useful in updating this guide and for additional research into the complexities of the American role in Europe during World War II. Second, we seek to point out those titles that have, in different ways, a general impact either on the topic or on the formation of background knowledge useful to those who wish to deal with it.

A. BIBLIOGRAPHIES

Introduction: The control of World War II literature has been a continuing battle for bibliographers for most of the past forty years. The sources cited in this section offer significant assistance to those who would attempt to keep up with the barrage of material appearing annually on history's greatest conflict. Unfortunately, as with the tactics and hardware of World War II, many offerings are made obsolete almost as soon as they are published and become period pieces as surely as a Stuart tank by the fact that they are not updated.

1. American Historical Association. *Recently Published Articles.* Washington, D.C., 1976--. v. 1--.

   This series replaces the section by that title found in quarterly issues of the *American Historical Review* before 1976; while containing references to the American war effort in Europe, this tool's lack of an index makes digging necessary.

2. ———. *Writings on American History.* Washington, D.C.: U.S. Government Printing Office, 1947-1960.

   An extremely useful series containing a large number of citations relative to the American war effort, many from military journals such as *Military Review.* Continued by the Dougherty work cited below (item 22).

3. Bayliss, Gwyn. *Bibliographic Guide to the Two World Wars: An Annotated Survey of English-Language Reference Materials.* New York: R.R. Bowker, 1977. 578p.

   A useful guide to reference materials such as dictionaries, encyclopedias, biographies, periodical indexes, directories, atlases, etc., as well as private and official publications, postwar official reports, archival collections, and unit histories. Indexed by author, title, geographical region, and subject.

4. Besterman, Theodore. *A World Bibliography of Bibliograhpies and of Bibliographical Catalogues, Calendars, Abstracts, Digests, Indexes, and the Like*. 4th ed., rev. 5 vols. Lausanne, Switzerland: Societas Bibliographia, 1965-1966.

The world's most famous and largest bibliography of bibliographies lists 117,000 citations, including many on World War II and military affairs.

5. *Bibliographic Index: A Cumulative Bibliography of Bibliographies*. New York: H.W. Wilson Co., 1942--. v. 5--.

Arranged by subject, this series supplements Besterman and includes not only independently published bibliographies, but those found in monographs and periodicals. Bibliographies relating to the 1939-1945 conflict can be found under the subject entry "World War, 1939-1945" and its subdivisions, and under the names of countries and individuals.

6. Bivins, Harold A. *An Annotated Bibliography of Naval Gunfire Support*. Washington, D.C.: Headquarters, U.S. Marine Corps, 1971. 10p.

A brief collection of citations drawn from military periodicals, few of which are relative to the war in Europe.

7. Bloomberg, Marty, and Hans H. Weber. *World War II and Its Origins: A Selected Annotated Bibliography of Books in English*. Littleton, Colo.: Libraries Unlimited, 1975. 311p.

This annotated guide contains a select list of 1,603 titles in a classified listing and is useful for commentary on the major military titles on the subject.

8. Bohanan, Robert D., comp. *Dwight D. Eisenhower: A Selected Bibliography of Periodical and Dissertation Literature*. Abilene, Kans.: U.S. General Services Administration, Dwight D. Eisenhower Library, 1981. 162p.

Includes 741 postwar periodical articles and 558 dissertations; the periodical citations receive brief annotations while those for dissertations do not. Completed by an author index.

9. *Book Review Digest*. New York: H.W. Wilson Co., 1942--. v. 37--.

A digest and index of about 5,000 general fiction and nonfiction books published annually as the result of titles being reviewed in several sources; with a title and subject index, it is issued monthly with semiannual and annual cumulations.

10. Burns, Richard D., ed. *Guide to American Foreign Relations Since 1700*. Santa Barbara, Calif.: Clio Books, 1983. 1,311p.

Prepared under the auspices of the Society for Historians of American Foreign Relations, the 40 chapters of this impressive work include nearly 9,000 annotated citations to both diplomatic and military affairs; extremely useful commentary is contained in chapters 22 and 23 relative to titles dealing with U.S. involvement in World War II.

11. Carroll, Berenice A., Clinton F. Fink, and Jane E. Mohraz. *Peace and War: A Guide to Bibliographies*. War/Peace Bibliographies Series, no. 16. Santa Barbara, Calif.: Clio Books, 1982. 550p.

    Arranged in three main sections and 34 major subject categories, this guide provides 1,351 descriptive annotations to bibliographies from 31 nations; more convenient than Besterman for military items.

12. Cochran, Alexander S., Jr. "Magic, Ultra, and the Second World War: Literature, Sources, Outlook." *Military Affairs*, XLVI (April 1982), 88-92.

    Perhaps the best guide to materials on the newest area of World War II historical interest--signal or communications intelligence.

13. Coletta, Paolo E., comp. *A Bibliography of American Naval History*. Annapolis, Md.: U.S. Naval Institute, 1981. 453p.

    Unannotated for the most part, this paperback guide does provide fairly complete coverage of the secondary literature on the naval aspects of the World War II U.S. effort in Europe.

13a. Controvich, James T., comp. *United States Army Histories: A Reference and Bibliography*. Manhattan, Kans.: Military Affairs/Aerospace Historian, 1983. 591p.

    This massive spiral-bound reproduction from Xerox copy contains 6,672 titles, with chronologies, lists of commanding generals, campaign credits, orders of battle, etc.; compare with Dornbusch and Pappas.

14. Cooling, B. Franklin, 3rd, and Alan Millett. *Doctoral Dissertations in Military Affairs: A Bibliography*. Bibliography Series, no. 10. Manhattan: Kansas State University Library, 1972. 153p.

    The most important source for Ph.D. dissertations in military affairs yet, this work provides data on papers relating to the various aspects of the American campaigns in the European Theater; annually updated since 1973 in the April, then February, issue of *Military Affairs*.

15. *Cumulative Book Index*. New York: H.W. Wilson Co., 1942--. v. 44--.

    A comprehensive international bibliography of books published in English, with citations entered by author, title, or subject; does not include government documents, small pamphlets, and most other forms of ephemeral publication. Use the subject heading "World War, 1939-1945" and its subdivisions as well as such headings as "Airplanes," "Warships," "Tanks," etc.

16. Dornbusch, Charles E. *The G.I. Stories*. New York: New York Public Library, 1950. 7p.

    Lists 53 publications by the Paris office of *Stars and Stripes*, most of which are Army division histories, a number of which are noted in Section IV:D below.

17. ———. *Histories of American Army Units, World War II and Korean Conflict, with Some Earlier Histories.* Washington, D.C.: Library and Service Club Branch, Special Services Division, Office of the Adjutant General, Department of the Army, 1956. 310p.

Still regarded, as with others from this compiler's pen, as the bible of unit history bibliographies, Dornbusch's guide covers not only major units such as divisions, but smaller ones like battalions.

18. ———. *Histories, Personal Narratives, United States Army: A Checklist.* Cornwallville, N.Y.: Hope Farm Press, 1967. 400p.

A typescript guide to 2,742 items arranged by unit, including works of limited edition and some journal articles. Useful annotations.

19. ———. *Postwar Souvenir Books and Unit Histories of the Navy, Marine Corps, and Construction Battalions.* Washington, D.C.: Office of Naval History, Department of the Navy, 1953. 14p.

A brief guide to naval "cruise books" for ships, USMC units, and the hundreds of "Seabee" construction groups.

20. ———. *Unit Histories of the United States Air Force, Including Privately Printed Personal Narratives.* Hampton Bay, N.Y.: Hampton Books, 1958. 56p.

Listing squadrons and other groups, this guide contains 230 World War II items arranged by unit number.

21. ———. *Unit Histories of World War II: United States Army, Air Force, Marines, Navy, Reproduced in Collaboration with the New York Public Library.* Washington, D.C.: Office of Military History, Department of the Army, 1950. 141p.

A 50-page supplement was issued in 1951. All of the Dornbusch titles are extremely rare, but, except for the Pappas contribution cited below, they remain the most important tool available on World War II unit history.

22. Dougherty, James T., *et al.* *Writings on American History, 1962-1973: A Subject Bibliography of Articles.* 4 vols. New York: Kraus for the American Historical Association, 1975.

A valuable guide to a decade of scholarly and popular production with only one major flaw--lack of annotation, which often hinders indication of title contents. Updated by annual volumes since 1976.

23. Dougherty, William J. "Cumulative Listing of Bibliographical and Archival Resources Collated from Publications of the American Committee on the History of the Second World War Since 1975." *ACHSWW Newsletter*, no. 25 (Spring 1981), 1-187.

A cut-and-paste listing of new books and archival sources taken from various issues of the *Newsletter* and arranged in a classified format; annotations vary from substantial to reproduction of Library of Congress MARC cataloging data.

24. Enser, A.G.S. *A Subject Bibliography of the Second World War: Books in English, 1939-1974*. Boulder, Colo.: Westview Press, 1977. 592p.

Alphabetically arranged under subject, the citations receive no annotation and reflect a heavy British emphasis; important for its listing of material published during the war years.

25. Estep, Raymond. *An Aerospace Bibliography*. 3 vols. Maxwell AFB, Ala.: Air University, 1962-1967.

Covers the material published between World War II and 1966, including many relevant and well-annotated titles on the aircraft and air campaigns of the European Theater.

26. *The Foreign Affairs 50-Year Bibliography: New Evaluations of Significant Books on International Relations, 1920-1970*. New York: R.R. Bowker, 1972. 936p.

The entries chosen for this compilation's section on World War II were taken from the review sections of *Foreign Affairs* magazine and were selected for their scholarship and importance in having stood the test of time; each entry includes a long, critical annotation.

27. *Forthcoming Books*. New York: R.R. Bowker Co., 1966--. v. 1--.

A quarterly which provides users with data on books soon to be published in fields of interest; easy access is provided through the companion publication, *Subject Guide to Forthcoming Books*.

28. Funk, Arthur L., comp. *The Second World War: A Bibliography, a Select List of Publications Appearing Since 1968*. Gainesville, Fla.: American Committee on the History of the Second World War, 1972. 32p.

Compiled from the ACHSWW *Newsletter*, 1968-1972, and designed to update Ziegler (q.v.), this brief unannotated guide features a classified arrangement; largely superseded by William J. Dougherty's work, cited above.

29. Higham, Robin, ed. *A Guide to the Sources of British Military History*. Berkeley: University of California Press, 1971. 630p.

A select bibliography with six chapters relating to World War II; a bibliographic essay by a recognized expert is followed in each by a listing of several hundred titles. Also suggests untouched areas for further research and explains how to gain access to special collections and private archives.

30. ———. *A Guide to the Sources of United States Military History*. Hamden, Conn.: Archon Books, 1975. 559p.

A select bibliography arranged in the same essay/listing format as noted in the last entry. Extremely useful for the commentary and access tips; a 416-page *Supplement I* was issued by the same firm in 1981.

31. ———. *Official Histories: Essays and Bibliographies from Around the World*. Manhattan: Kansas State University Library, 1970. 644p.

Official military histories from over 50 nations are covered, with each nation having an essay on the origins and preparation of its studies under discussion. Many of these official histories concern a given country's World War II participation.

32. Kuehl, Warren F., comp. *Dissertations in History: An Index to Dissertations Completed in History Departments of United States and Canadian Universities, 1873-1970*. 2 vols. Lexington: University Press of Kentucky, 1972.

Lists some 13,500 dissertations by author; the work has a subject index.

33. Liddell-Hart, Basil H., and Hugh M. Cole. "World War II." In: American Historical Association. *Guide to Historical Literature*. New York: Macmillan, 1961, pp. 810-815.

An annotated listing of some 130 titles selected by two authorities within an extremely limited scope; largely superseded by other works cited in this section.

34. Mariners' Museum, Newport News, Va. *Dictionary Catalog of the Library*. 9 vols. Boston: G.K. Hall, 1964.

Reproduces catalog cards of the library's file; extremely useful as this repository cataloged articles from various marine/naval journals, many covering the World War II period.

35. Miller, Samuel D., comp. *An Aerospace Bibliography*. Washington, D.C.: U.S. Government Printing Office, 1978. 341p.

The official bibliography of the Office of Air Force History, this guide provides a wealth of citations on the aircraft, personalities, and actions of the U.S.A.F. and its predecessor organization, the U.S.A.A.F.

36. Millett, John D. "World War II; The Post-Mortem Continues." *Political Science Quarterly*, LXIII (March 1948), 125-133.

An early round-up and review of titles produced detailing various aspects of the American participation in the conflict, including the military campaigns in Europe.

37. Morehead, Joseph. "Personal Reminiscences of World War II Prisoners of War." *Bulletin of Bibliography*, XXV (May-August 1968), 143+.

Provides information on 118 titles, including some by Americans held captive by the Germans.

38. Morton, Louis. "World War II: A Survey of Recent Writings." *American Historical Review*, LXXV (December 1970), 1987-2008.

An extended bibliographic essay built around 28 titles.

39. ———. *Writings on World War II*. Washington, D.C.: Service Center for Teachers of History, 1967. 54p.

A brief bibliographic essay on those primary and secondary sources most suitable for use at the high school and college undergraduate level; includes a number on the military campaigns.

40. *Paperbound Books in Print*. New York: R.R. Bowker, 1955--. v. 1--.

A useful tool for determining original paperback titles (and the countless reprints of hardbacks) available on the various military aspects of the war, including hardware; some of the lesser publishers (e.g., Squadron/Signal) are not included.

41. Pappas, George S. *United States Army Unit Histories*. Special Bibliography, no. 4. Carlisle Barracks, Pa.: U.S. Army Military History Institute, 1971. 405p.

Lists unit histories at Carlisle, including books, pamphlets, manuscripts, and mimeographed studies, omitting articles; arranged by unit with cross-references, it updates, and sometimes supersedes, Dornbusch. A two-volume supplement was issued in 1978, but is, in fact, a revised edition.

42. Powe, Marc B. "The History of American Military Intelligence: A Review of Selected Literature." *Military Affairs*, XXXIX (October 1975), 142-145.

A brief bibliographic essay which includes analysis of titles relating to World War II.

42a. Showalter, Dennis E. *German Military History, 1648-1980: A Critical Bibliography*. New York: Garland Publishing, Inc., 1983. 375p.

Organized chronologically, this guide provides an overview of readings in major themes in German military history; the archival sources, military periodicals, dissertations, and monographs cited include professional as well as popular literature and campaign memoirs. The section on World War II should be seen by users of this guide-in-hand.

43. Smith, Myron J., Jr. *Air War Bibliography Series, 1939-1945: English-Language Sources*. 5 vols. Manhattan, Kansas: Military Affairs/Aerospace Historian, 1977-1982.

All of the volumes in this set are valuable to our topic as each contains "parts" providing information relative to the European Theater; each volume is indexed. Unannotated citations.

44. ———. *The Secret Wars: A Guide to Sources in English, Vol. I--Intelligence, Propaganda and Psychological Warfare, Resistance Movements and Secret Operations, 1939-1945*. War/

Peace Bibliography Series, no. 12. Santa Barbara, Calif.: Clio Books, 1980. 250p.

Contains 2,539 citations to books, journal articles, documents, and papers; includes a few citations. Author and title index.

45. ———. *World War II at Sea: A Bibliography of Sources in English.* 3 vols. Metuchen, N.J.: The Scarecrow Press, 1976.

This set contains over 10,000 mostly unannotated citations, with the bulk of those relating to the European Theater found in Volume I; each volume contains an author/subject index with a comprehensive author/subject index in Volume III.

46. Spier, Henry O., ed. *World War II in Our Magazines and Books, September 1939-September 1945: A Bibliography.* New York: Stuyvesant Press, 1945. 96p.

A classified list of some 1,500 unannotated books and journal articles; useful as all of the citations were written during the war.

47. Strong, Russell. *Bombers: A Preliminary Bibliography of the Bomber Offensive of the U.S. Eighth Air Force, 1942-1945.* Dayton, Ohio, 1975.

A little-known but useful guide to the aircraft, men, and campaigns of the VIII Bomber Command, 1942-1945; superseded by Smith above and Werrell below.

48. *Subject Guide to Books in Print.* New York: R.R. Bowker, 1957--. v. 1--.

A subject bibliography of books published in the United States which can stand apart from its parent volume, *Books in Print*; entries on the war can be found not only under the heading "World War, 1939-1945," but under the names of individuals, nations, and weapons, e.g., "Warships."

49. *The Two World Wars: A Selective Bibliography.* New York: Pergamon Press, 1964. 246p.

Contains 466 entries to books, only a few of which were published in English; the major feature of this guide--and what continues to make it useful--are several sections on photographs, records, films, and transparencies.

50. United States. Air Force. Air Force Academy Library. *Air Power and Warfare.* Special Bibliography Series, no. 59. Colorado Springs, 1978. 101p.

Designed for Academy cadets and faculty, this guide is useful for all who are interested in the air power aspects of World War II, including the strategic bombing campaign in Europe.

51. ———. Coast Guard. *United States Coast Guard Annotated Bibliography.* Washington, D.C.: U.S. Government Printing Office, 1982. 148p.

A well-annotated bibliography of books, official histories, and journal articles on Coast Guard history, which updates the 1972 guide compiled by Truman R. Strobridge; World War II is covered in the final section of this classified guide which also features an author index.

52. ———. Department of the Army. Center of Military History. *A Guide to the Study and Use of Military History*. Washington, D.C.: U.S. Government Printing Office, 1979. 507p.

An extremely useful guide which employs the "Higham approach" of bibliographic essays followed by lists of materials; the analysis of World War II by the noted military historian Charles B. MacDonald (pp. 225-251) is not limited to hardware or campaigns but encompasses the entire war effort.

53. ———. ———. Military Academy Library. *Bibliography of Military History*. Compiled by Alan C. Aimone. Library Bulletin, no. 14B. West Point, N.Y.: U.S. Military Academy, 1982. 151p.

Aimone's excellent rendering concentrates on reference books, with full annotations provided for almost every citation; the classified arrangement allows two dozen pages for World War II and finishes with an author index.

54. ———. ———. Military History Institute. *The Era of World War II*. Special Bibliography Series, no. 16. 4 vols. Washington, D.C.: U.S. Government Printing Office, 1977-1978.

As this guide lists (mostly without annotation) only materials held by this facility, one can readily imagine the wealth of information available at Carlisle for the study of the European Theater of World War II. Much of the information cited is mimeographed or other limited format, but the scope is worldwide and the indexes useful.

55. ———, Library of Congress. *Books: Subjects--A Cumulative List of Works Represented by Library of Congress Printed Cards, 1950--*. Washington, D.C.: U.S. Government Printing Office, 1955--.

A listing by subjects of the books cataloged by LC or cooperating library, regardless of language. Books on the war are listed under the heading "World War, 1939-1945" and its subdivisions, and under the names of individuals, nations, and hardware, e.g., "Airplanes." Valuable due to the comprehensiveness of the library's collection and because of the large number of foreign-language items cited.

56. ———. ———. Legislative Reference Service. *The Conduct of the War (April 1941-May 1943)*. 3 vols. Washington, D.C., 1942-1943.

A classified, annotated guide to 4,218 wartime items, including books and articles; it is a pity that the work was not extended beyond 1943!

57. ———. Navy Department. Naval Historical Center. *United States Naval History: A Bibliography.* 6th ed. Washington, D.C.: U.S. Government Printing Office, 1972. 91p.

A brief classified guide to American naval history, the citations in which receive, in certain cases, brief annotation; a 7th edition is presently being compiled. Author index.

58. Werrell, Kenneth P. *8th Air Force Bibliography: An Extended Essay and Listing of Published and Unpublished Materials.* Manhattan, Kans.: Military Affairs/Aerospace Historian, 1981. 291p.

A comprehensive, descriptive, and critical guide to materials on the U.S. Eighth Air Force arranged in a bibliographical essay/listing format; extremely useful not only for the insight the commentary provides but also for the large number of unpublished items brought to light, some for the first time.

59. ———. "The U.S.A.A.F. Over Europe and Its Foes: A Selected, Subjected, and Critical Bibliography." *Aerospace Historian*, XVI (Winter 1978), 231-243.

A preliminary version of the previous citation; naturally somewhat smaller in scope, but no less useful.

60. *World War II from an American Perspective: An Annotated Bibliography.* Santa Barbara, Calif.: Clio Books, 1982. 448p.

An alphabetically arranged listing of over 1,100 detailed abstracts drawn from 2,000 journals published worldwide from 1971 through 1981 complete with a subject index. No more useful guide exists to annotated periodical articles on this topic for the years covered, unless it be the Clio abstracts from which these references were drawn.

61. Wynar, Bohdan S., ed. *American Reference Books Annual.* Littleton, Colo.: Libraries Unlimited, 1970--. v.1--.

As this annual reviews virtually every new reference book published in English, it is especially useful; presented in a classified format, together with an author-title-subject index, this work is easy to employ. Military items (mostly hardware) are covered in the final section.

62. Ziegler, Janet. *World War II: Books in English, 1945-1965.* Stanford, Calif.: Hoover Institution Press, 1971. 223p.

A comprehensive 4,519 title non-selective, unannotated bibliography distinguished for its breadth, introductory summary, and contents pages (which form a classified index); provides a valuable introduction to the multitude of books published on World War II in the first 20 years of the postwar period and serves as the basis from which the American Committee on the History of the Second World War advances its bibliographic coverage.

B. ABSTRACTS/INDEXES

Introduction: Abstracts and indexes are an important group of reference tools which assist readers in keeping up with the flood of World War II material, with the former having the advantage of commentary and the latter that of succinctness. The sources cited in this section include not only periodical indexes, but abstracting services such as *America: History and Life* and indexes to newspapers.

63. *Abstracts of Military Bibliography*. Buenos Aires, Argentina: Instituto de Publicaciones Navales, 1967--. v.1--.

This English-Spanish guide provides some coverage of World War II items, but concentrates mainly on current affairs.

64. *Access: The Supplementary Index to Periodicals*. Syracuse, N.Y.: Gaylord Professional Publications, 1975--. v. 1--.

An index to those periodicals not usually covered in other indexes such as *Reader's Guide*; divided into a lengthy author index followed by a subject index, to which users should refer first.

65. *America: History and Life*. Santa Barbara, Calif.: ABC-Clio, 1964--. v. 1--.

An extremely successful service which has grown over the years from its mission as a guide to periodical literature; Part A, *Article Abstracts and Citations*, provides a survey of articles published on the history of the U.S. and Canada, while Part B, *Index to Book Reviews*, Part C, *American History Bibliography (Books, Articles, and Dissertations)*, and Part D, *Annual Index*, all fulfill a needed function and in total make this as close to a perfect historical bibliography tool as we are likely to get; the military history of World War II in the European Theater is well covered with Part A which now provides many more foreign-language citations than earlier.

66. *Applied Science and Technology Index*. New York: H.W. Wilson Co., 1958--. v. 1--.

Supersedes the *Industrial Arts Index* noted below; extremely useful for citations on military hardware, especially aircraft.

67. *Biography Index: A Cumulative Index to Biographical Material in Books and Magazines*. New York: H.W. Wilson Co., 1946--. v. 1--.

An index to data in books and over 1,500 selected journals published in English arranged under the names of biographees; the index is by occupation, so users look under such headings as "Generals, American" or "Air Force Officers, American" for information on individuals (important to the study of the U.S. European war effort) before referring back to the main body of the index.

68. *Book Review Index*. Detroit: Gale Research, 1965--. v. 1--.

An author listing with alphabetical citations to reviews; published bimonthly with annual cumulation.

69. *Comprehensive Dissertation Index*. 37 vols. Ann Arbor, Mich.: University Microfilms, 1973.

A computer-generated index that attempts to list all U.S. (and some foreign) dissertations accepted between 1861 and 1972; Volume XXVIII is devoted to history and includes titles relative to World War II in Europe.

70. *Dissertation Abstracts International*. Ann Arbor, Mich.: University Microfilms, 1969--. v. 1--.

A compilation of abstracts of Ph.D. dissertations submitted to UM by cooperating universities; those seeking dissertations on history should employ the "A" Schedule which covers the Humanities and Social Sciences.

71. *Historical Abstracts: Schedule B, Twentieth Century Abstracts (1914 to the Present)*. Santa Barbara, Calif.: ABC-Clio, 1955--. v. 1--.

The first of Clio's successful historical abstracting services and the father of *America: History and Life*, this guide provides a survey of articles published on 20th-century world history (excluding the U.S. and Canada after 1964) with close attention paid to military matters; the service presently abstracts almost as many (in some cases more) articles on the military aspects of World War II Europe published in foreign languages as in English. The international scope of this tool makes it important to those who would employ more than the usual U.S. or British secondary sources.

72. *Humanities Index*. New York: H.W. Wilson Co., 1974--. v. 1--.

Broken off from the old *Social Sciences and Humanities Index* when that ceased publication in 1974, this tool covers more scholarly journals than many other Wilson indexes and it is here that the user will find the majority of that firm's current indexing of historical periodicals.

73. *Index to Legal Periodicals*. New York: H.W. Wilson Co., 1942--. v. 34--.

Published for the American Association of Law Libraries in annual cumulations, this index is useful for citations to legal materials relative to our topic, e.g., the law of air warfare.

74. *Index to U.S. Government Periodicals*. Chicago: Infordata International, 1975--. v. 1--.

The first periodical index to provide full coverage to the large number of U.S. government magazines, including those published for the military; useful as a supplement to the *Air University Library Index to Military Periodicals* as the AUL publication does not index all of the journals covered by the Infordata service.

75. *Industrial Arts Index*. New York: H.W. Wilson Co., 1942-1958. v. 30-58.

Superseded by the *Applied Science and Technology Index* cited above and, like it, *IAI* is extremely useful for the location of articles on military hardware.

76. *Masters Abstracts: Abstracts of Selected Masters Theses on Microfilm*. Ann Arbor, Mich.: University Microfilms. 1962--. v. 1--.

Presents abstracts of a selected list of masters theses, from various institutions, available for sale on microfilm; theses on World War II in Europe are usually found under the heading "History."

77. *New York Times Index*. New York: Times, 1942--. v. 29--.

An alphabetical subject index to the contents of the *New York Times* with entries listed chronologically under each subject, some of which provide brief summaries of the articles; use the main heading "World War, 1939-1945," the names of individuals, nations, and various hardware and remember that the censors were very careful about what appeared in U.S. newspapers during the war.

78. Public Affairs Information Service. *Bulletin*. New York, 1942--. v. 27--.

A subject index to books, periodical articles, pamphlets, and government documents with a few entries annotated; popularly known as *PAIS*, this tool can be searched by the same headings employed for the *New York Times Index* and other indexes discussed in this section.

79. *The Reader's Guide to Periodical Literature*. New York: H.W. Wilson Co., 1942--. v. 37--.

The first modern periodical index, *Reader's Guide* indexes about 140 popular, non-technical magazines; arranged by authors and subjects, with cross-references. As with most periodical indexes (and most popular periodicals) coverage of World War II has slipped with the passing of years, but continues to exist with such journals as *American Heritage* and *American History Illustrated* offering at least a couple of articles per year. An *Abridged Reader's Guide to Periodical Literature* is available and is often found in school libraries.

80. *Social Sciences and Humanities Index*. New York: H.W. Wilson, 1942-1974.

Discontinued in 1974, this Wilson index was for years the scholar's choice of this firm's offerings for historical articles; even today the old issues are useful to the student of modern military history as one of the few places citing the defunct but valuable *Infantry Journal*. Known until 1965 as the *International Index*; this tool is arranged in the same fashion as *Reader's Guide*.

81. *Times of London. Index to the Times.* London, Eng.: The Times, 1942--. v. 35--.

Known during the war years as the *Official Index*, the indexing style of this tool has changed with almost every issue, forcing users to study a volume's usage instructions; a valuable source for articles, maps, and statistics as well as for a study of the British reaction to America and Americans (especially troops) during World War II.

82. *Transdex: Bibliography and Index to the United States Joint Publication Research Service (J.P.R.S.) Translations.* New York: C.C.M. Information Corp., 1961--. v. 1--.

Transdex is extremely valuable to those who would like to have English-language translations of material appearing in foreign journals, especially those from Russia, France, and Germany. The J.P.R.S. has long made available its translations and many of these, say for Russian materials, provide a goldmine of information and views on the prosecution of the war in Europe.

83. United States. Air Force. Air University Library. *Abstracts of Student Research Reports.* Maxwell AFB, Ala., 1949--. v. 1--.

A guide to the research undertaken at the Air War College or the Air Command and Staff College by students advancing their careers as officers; many of the reports center around the lessons of history, and a large number of World War II-related reports have been prepared in the past 40 years.

84. ———. ———. ———. *Air University Library Index to Military Periodicals.* Maxwell AFB, Ala., 1949--. v. 1--.

Simply put, this is the single most important military journal index in existence and no solid student of World War II can proceed far without reference to it. Arranged by subjects, many headings are applicable, e.g., "Armored Warfare," but the first consulted should, as in most other indexes, be "World War II."

85. ———. National Technical Information Service. *Government Reports Announcements.* Springfield, Va., 1946--. v. 1--.

An index to those many reports published by the government and not listed in the GPO catalog, including many prepared under contract with outside firms; a classified arrangement with indexing, users will want to consult the heading "Military Science" for titles, of which at least two dozen per year are devoted to World War II.

86. ———. Naval Institute. *United States Naval Institute Proceedings, Cumulative Index, 1874-1977.* Annapolis, Md., 1982. 377p.

A guide to the contents of this naval journal; valuable in that the *AUL Index to Military Periodicals* does not begin its

USNIP coverage until 1949, leaving the *Industrial Arts Index* as the single commonly-available index to carry coverage for the war years.

C. ENCYCLOPEDIAS/HANDBOOKS/DICTIONARIES

Introduction: A large number of handbooks, encyclopedias, and dictionaries have been written exclusively on military topics and World War II. Expecially of late, there seems to be almost a competition in the production of World War II encyclopedias. The sources cited in this section include those dictionaries, handbooks, and encyclopedias judged to be the most helpful to students of the American war effort in Europe. It should be noted that a few guides calling themselves encyclopedias and devoted exclusively to a certain kind of military operation or hardware are listed below in the appropriate sections, III-IV.

87. Barnes, Gladeon M. *Weapons of World War II.* Princeton, N.J.: Van Nostrand, 1947. 317p.

    An early postwar effort which pales in comparison with today's glossy, oversize, "coffee-table" products, but which may still be of interest due to the large number of drawings; covers mostly offensive hardware such as airplanes and tanks with only brief coverage of such technical items as radar.

88. Baudot, Marcel, ed. *The Historical Encyclopedia of World War II.* Translated from the French. New York: Facts on File, Inc., 1980. 548p.

    Originally published in France as *Encyclopédie de la Guerre, 1939-1945*, this alphabetically arranged work contains almost 900 entries on various facets of the conflict, ranging in size from 2 lines to 28 pages; black and white photographs, a chronology, a 4-page bibliography, and no index. Extremely pro-European, especially French, in outlook.

89. Benford, Timothy B. *The World War II Quiz and Fact Book.* New York: Harper & Row, 1982. 230p.

    An interesting trivia book and handy guide to those little-known points that occasionally crop up between buffs and wargamers.

90. Bradley, John. *The Illustrated History of the Third Reich.* New York: Bison Books, 1981. 254p.

    A well-illustrated "coffee-table" British import which tells the story of Nazi Germany's political and military exploits from the beginning to 1945.

91. Carmon, W.Y. *A Dictionary of Military Uniforms.* New York: Scribners, 1977. 140p.

    A nicely illustrated, oversize title which provides information on the military uniforms of various nations in history; a section describes the clothing, etc., of soldiers in World War II, including those of the United States.

92. Cary, Norman M., Jr., comp. *A Guide to U.S. Army Museums and Historic Sites*. Washington, D.C.: U.S. Government Printing Office, 1975. 116p.

With maps and photographs, this Center of Military History publication lists and describes the museums in the U.S. Army Museum System as well as other federal and non-federal museums having significant military collections; the listing also contains a useful introductory discussion of various information sources on military museums. Of value to those who would visit these sites to see the actual equipment employed by the U.S. in its World War II battles in Europe.

93. Chandler, David G., ed. *A Traveller's Guide to the Battlefields of Europe*. 2 vols. Philadelphia, Pa.: Chilton Books, 1965.

Covers military history of all periods with the first volume reporting on battlefields in Western Europe and the second covering those of Central and Eastern Europe; for each engagement, readers will find not only a historical narrative, but also a guide to nearby accommodations and suggested readings. Compare with Denfeld, cited next.

94. Denfeld, Duane. *A Guide to World War II Museums, Relics, and Sites in Europe*. Manhattan, Kans.: Military Affairs/Aerospace Historian, 1979. 222p.

Arranged by nation and facility, this tool does for Europe what Cary (above) has done for the U.S.; should be obtained by all who travel to Europe with an eye toward visiting such historic sites as the Normandy beaches and Britain's Imperial War Museum.

95. Diagram Group. *Weapons, an International Encyclopedia from 5,000 B.C. to 2,000 A.D.* New York: St. Martin's, 1981. 320p.

A basic source for beginners interested in military hardware not only related to our topic but also throughout history; well illustrated with diagrams and line drawings of the various implements employed in land, sea, and air warfare.

96. Dupuy, R. Ernest and Trevor N. *The Encyclopedia of Military History from 3,500 B.C. to the Present*. Rev. ed. New York: Harper & Row, 1977. 1,464p.

The chapters in this important work are arranged alphabetically with each beginning with general discussions of trends in strategy, generalship, and technology followed by geographical subdivisions that outline regional military history in chronological order. Illustrated with drawings, maps, and photographs; indexed. Our period is covered in the section "World War II in the West."

97. Emeed, Vic, ed. *The Encyclopedia of Military Modeling*. London: Octopus Books, 1983. 192p.

Provides information on all aspects of military modeling, including research relevant to this section. Subjects include figures, weapons, tanks and AFV, and soft-skinned vehicles, with emphasis on the World War II years. Illustrated with over 240 full-color illustrations and photographs.

98. Fitzsimons, Bernard, ed. *The Illustrated Encyclopedia of 20th Century Weapons and Warfare*. 24 vols. New York: Columbia House, 1977.

Almost any weapon used in substantial numbers by regular armed forces during this century is found in these volumes with nearly every entry illustrated with photographs, diagrams, color illustrations, or a combination; arranged in alphabetical order, this British work, which draws heavily on the Purnell and Profile sources and drawings, lists certain weapons under their official or unofficial names--e.g., P-51 is cross-referenced to Mustang--rather than their numerical designations; each volume contains a final section providing detailed data on artillery; the index is contained in Volume XXIV.

99. Gaynor, Frank. *The New Military and Naval Dictionary*. Westport, Conn.: Greenwood Press, 1969. 295p.

First published in 1951, this alphabetically arranged dictionary provides information on the terminology, technical phrases, and U.S. forces' slang employed by the American military in the period of and just after World War II.

100. Greet, William C. *World Words, Recommended Pronunciations*. 2nd ed., rev. and enl. New York: Columbia University Press, 1948. 608p.

An expansion of the author's earlier *War Words*, this work lists about 12,000 names, places, battles, air force objectives, and geographic terms (and their pronunciations) associated with World War II.

101. Harbottle, Thomas B. *Dictionary of Battles*. Rev. and updated by George Bruce. New York: Stein and Day, 1971. 333p.

A comprehensive, alphabetically arranged work providing basic data on all of the great (and some of the not-so-great) engagements of history, including the major battles of World War II in Europe.

102. Heflin, Woodford A., comp. *The United States Air Force Dictionary*. Princeton, N.J.: Van Nostrand, 1956. 578p.

An alphabetically arranged guide to the technical and slang expressions employed in the U.S.A.F. in the 1950's and before; much more aerial emphasis than users will find in other military dictionaries, e.g., Gaynor above.

103. Heinl, Robert D., Jr. *The Dictionary of Military and Naval Quotations*. Annapolis, Md.: U.S. Naval Institute, 1978. 395p.

Categorized by subject and arranged under alphabetical subheadings, this work provides over 5,500 quotations from the writings and speeches of military and political leaders, philosophers, and commentators over the past 200 centuries; rubrics range from action to weapons and make this a useful source for those looking for such famous quotations as General McAuliffe's Battle of the Bulge surrender reply: "Nuts."

104. Keegan, John, ed. *Rand McNally Encyclopedia of World War II.* Chicago: Rand McNally, 1977. 256p.

Includes over 1,000 articles, 300 illustrations, 64 pages of color plates, and many maps and photos to describe the fighting and hardware of the conflict; especially strong on weaponry and somewhat weaker in the biographical sketches of leading figures. Compare with the Simon and Schuster product edited by Parrish, cited below.

105. Kirk, John, and Robert Young. *Great Weapons of World War II.* New York: Walker, 1961. 347p.

Similar to the earlier effort by Barnes (q.v.), this over-size work includes information on the major weapons systems employed by the Axis and United Nations forces on land, sea, and air.

106. McCombs, Don. *World War II Super Facts.* New York: Warner, 1983. 659p.

A massive alphabetically arranged dictionary of trivia and detail concerning all aspects of the 1939-1945 conflict.

107. Parkinson, Roger. *The Encyclopedia of Modern War.* New York: Stein and Day, 1976. 238p.

The scope of this work is the years 1793-1975 with three main threads--battles, weapons, and personalities--providing the substance for most of the entries. Includes 22 pages of maps.

108. Parrish, Thomas. *The Simon and Schuster Encyclopedia of World War II.* New York: Simon and Schuster, 1978. 767p.

A massive reference, arranged alphabetically, which contains 700,000 words in 4,000 entries backed up by 200 maps and photographs on the men, strategy, campaigns, hardware, conferences, and issues of World War II. With the late Brig. Gen. "SLAM" Marshall as chief consultant editor and over 100 U.S. and foreign contributors ranging from Barrie Pitt of Britain, Hasso von Manteuffel of Germany, and Charles B. MacDonald of the U.S., Parrish has assembled what Gen. Matthew B. Ridgway has endorsed as "an unparalleled source." Compare with Baudot and Keegan cited above. Oversized and well indexed.

109. Partridge, Eric, ed. *A Dictionary of Forces' Slang, 1939-1945.* Freeport, N.Y.: Books for Libraries, 1970. 212p.

First published in 1948, this work is divided into three main sections: "Naval Slang," by Wilfred Granville; "Army Slang," by Frank Roberts; and "Air Force Slang," by Eric Partridge. More complete than Gaynor on slang, but, as the title suggests, omits more technical terms.

110. Reid, Alan. *A Concise Encyclopedia of the Second World War.* Reading, Eng.: Osprey, 1974. 232p.

Divided into five parts, all of which emphasize the European Theater and all of which reflect a British bias: chronology; chronological outline of major campaigns; alphabetical who's who; a survey of the opposing armed forces; and a review of the civilian wartime experience. Indexed.

111. Rosignoli, Guido. *Ribbons of Orders, Decorations and Medals.* Translated from the Italian. New York: Arco, 1977. 165p.

A brief introduction to the world's military orders and military decorations, especially those of the World War II period, including those of the United States. Well illustrated with photographs and color illustrations.

112. Ruffner, Frederick G., and Robert C. Thomas, eds. *Code Names Dictionary: A Guide to Code Names, Slang, Nicknames, Journalese, and Similar Terms.* Detroit, Mich.: Gale Research, 1963. 555p.

A valuable tool for locating information on the many official code names used during World War II; alphabetically arranged, the work also illuminates the various unofficial nicknames used for military operations and geographic areas, e.g., "The Bulge."

113. Snyder, Louis L. *Louis L. Snyder's Historical Guide to World War II.* Westport, Conn.: Greenwood Press, 1982. 750p.

Snyder's book considers not only leaders and weapons, but emphasizes the economic, social, and political aspects in far greater detail than Baudot, Keegan, Parrish, or Reid (q.v.); little details such as codenames or the work of spies are not overlooked. Each of the alphabetically arranged entries is concluded with a brief bibliography. Indexed.

114. Sobel, Eli. "U.S. Naval Jargon and Slang, 1942-1945." *Southern Folklore Quarterly*, XIII (December 1949), 200-205.

A brief guide to American Navy jargon employed during the war; nowhere near as complete as Gaynor or Partridge.

115. Taylor, Anna M., comp. *The Language of World War II.* Rev. and enl. ed. New York: H.W. Wilson Co., 1948. 265p.

A guide to abbreviations, captions, quotations, slogans, titles, and other phrases which attempts comprehensiveness in its alphabetically arranged coverage.

116. Young, Peter, ed. *The Marshall Cavendish Illustrated Encyclopedia of World War II: An Objective, Chronological, and Comprehensive History of the Second World War.* Text by Eddy Bauer. 11 vols. Freeport, N.Y.: Marshall Cavendish, 1981.

Originally published in 1966 in over 20 small volumes by Purnell, this lavishly illustrated work, penned by Bauer, the noted Swiss historian, has been supplemented by American historians to amplify events of interest to Americans, especially in the Pacific theater. The 178 chapters cover both military and political events and are grouped chronologically and geographically by major military campaign or theater of operation. The final volume, produced especially for this set, is perhaps the most valuable, dealing as it does with military organization, armed forces, weapons, and uniforms. The index is divided into general and thematic sections. Far less concise than, for example, Keegan or Parrish.

117. ———. *The World Almanac Book of World War II*. Englewood Cliffs, N.J.: Prentice-Hall, 1981. 514p.

Published simultaneously by the paperback firm of Ballantine Books, this work has three main sections: a daily chronology of events, 1939-1945; a description of weapons and equipment; and a biographical dictionary of important leaders, political and military; includes maps, drawings, and over 100 photographs. Compare with Keegan and Parrish.

118. ———, with Michael Calvert. *A Dictionary of Battles, 1816-1976*. London: New English Library, 1977. 600p.

An alphabetically arranged guide to important battles by land, sea, or air fought in the period after Napoleon and which are placed in the context of their historical, technical, and political importance. Good use of cross-references from battles to campaigns; European emphasis.

D. ANNUALS/YEARBOOKS

Introduction: The five citations below represent the best of a large number of annuals and yearbooks which appeared during and after the war years; all should be of some value to those who need a quick contemporary reference or, more important, who wish to follow the flow of events as they occurred. Much of the chronological information is repeated in and amplified upon in the next part, Atlases/Chronologies.

119. *The Annual Register of World Events: A Review of the Year*. New York: Longmans, Green, 1941--. v. 182--.

Arranged alphabetically by nation, this annual general review of world events includes summaries of events and developments; a British publication, the work features particularly good coverage of England and the Commonwealth. The volumes for the war years are helpful.

120. *Facts on File Yearbook: The Indexed Record of World Events*. New York: Facts on File, Inc., 1941--. v. 1--.

Brings together the convenient weekly summaries of major news events, domestic and foreign, presented in the service's *Facts on File: A Weekly Digest.* Issues for the war years suffer from the same problem as newspapers and general-circulation magazines such as *Time*; namely, the pleasure of the censor.

121. *Keesing's Contemporary Archives.* London: Keesing's Publications, Ltd., 1941--. v. 10--.

This weekly looseleaf publication consists of reports, arranged by country, and based on data selected, translated, condensed, or summarized from newspapers, official publications, periodicals, and news agencies; the war issues suffered from the same censorship problem as *Facts on File*, its American counterpart.

122. *The Statesman's Yearbook: Statistical and Historical Annual of the States of the World.* New York: St. Martin's, 1941--. v. 77--.

Provides detailed information about significant events and the governments of most countries; data include judicial, political, population, defense, industrial, and commercial facts.

123. *World Almanac and Book of Facts.* New York: World Telegram, 1942-66; Doubleday, 1970--. v. 76--.

One of the best-known ready-reference titles in the world, this work is especially useful for its chronology of events in the preceding year and its list of world leaders.

E. ATLASES/CHRONOLOGIES

Introduction: Atlases have long been recognized as valuable educational tools; by following the action of a given event over its geographical features, one can learn much about the success or failure of an undertaking. Chronologies, likewise, are valuable, perhaps more for the minutiae they preserve than for the learning possibilities they offer. The sources in this section reflect both of these tools as they relate to World War II. It should be noted that maps and chronologies, like bibliographies, appear in many titles and the user should watch for them as he employs the sources noted in the other sections of this guide.

124. Argyle, Christopher. *Chronology of World War II: The Day-by-Day Illustrated Record, 1939-1945.* London and Freeport, N.Y.: Marshall Cavendish Corp., 1981. 200p.

A British "coffee-table" offering which chronicles events on each day of the war worldwide, though European bias is present. Tables of facts and figures, 20 detailed maps, photos, and reproductions of newspaper headlines, cartoons, and posters add emphasis. As events described and biographies given are not restricted to military events, this tool is helpful for obtaining the "Big Picture."

125. Banks, Arthur. *A World Atlas of Military History, 1861-1945.* New York: Hippocrene, 1978. 160p.

An indexed guide to major conflicts from the U.S. Civil War through World War II, with black and white maps and strong charts; unfortunately, little explanatory commentary is provided for either the maps or charts.

126. Brown, Ernest F. *The War in Maps: An Atlas of the New York Times Maps.* 4th ed., rev. New York and London: Oxford University Press, 1946. 197p.

A useful compilation of maps drawn from wartime issues of America's "newspaper of record," all in black and white.

127. Carter, Kit C., and Robert Mueller. *The AAF in World War II: Combat Chronology.* Washington, D.C.: U.S. Government Printing Office, 1975. 991p.

A well-indexed chronology arranged by geographical region; this Office of Air Force History production might well be considered as the final volume in the Craven & Cate official AAF history, cited below.

128. "Chronology of World War II." *Current History*, New Series VIII (June 1945), 492-496.

A brief chronological overview of the war's events through VE-Day.

129. Goodenough, Simon. *War Maps: World War II from September 1939 to August 1945--Air, Sea, and Land, Battle-by-Battle.* New York: St. Martin's Press, 1983. 192p.

An oversize volume which details every crucial engagement in full-color spreads, displaying the deployment of men and equipment in the course of a battle or campaign; the author's text backgrounds and chronicles the stages of each confrontation as further illumination to the maps. Containing 232 color maps and hundreds of photos and illustrations, this is a worthy competitor to Brigadier Young's offering, cited below.

130. Goralski, Robert. *World War II Almanac, 1931-1945: A Political and Military Record.* New York: Putnam, 1981. 486p.

The title is somewhat misleading as this is in fact a chronology, mostly of combat, day-by-day from 1931 through VJ-Day; what makes this different from Argyle, cited above, is the heavy reliance on anecdotes and vignettes of forgotten or overlooked personal triumphs and defeats interlaced into the daily records. Contains some 300 photos, maps, charts, and statistical tables.

131. Hopkins, John A.H. *Diary of World Events: Being a Chronological Record of the Second World War.* 54 vols. Baltimore, Md.: National Advertising Co., 1942-1948.

An interesting but rare item comprised entirely of reproduced American and British newspaper dispatches; suffers the same problems of accuracy found in contemporary newspaper accounts.

132. Husted, H.H. *Thumb-Nail History of World War II.* Boston, Mass.: Bruce Humphries, 1948. 442p.

Another early chronological effort which has long since been eclipsed; data provided are both military and political.

133. Leonard, Thomas M. *Day-by-Day: The Forties.* New York: Facts on File, Inc., 1977. 1,051p.

Culled almost exclusively from *Facts on File: A Weekly Digest*, this work provides data on both the American homefront and the battles in Europe.

134. Lloyd, Christopher. *Atlas of Maritime History.* New York: Arco, 1976. 144p.

The maps provided cover a larger segment of history than just World War II; the accompanying text provides explanatory backgrounds for each map. Useful for those following the naval war.

135. Rohwer, Jürgen, and Gerhard Hummelchen. *Chronology of the War at Sea.* Translated from the German. 2 vols. New York: Arco, 1973-74.

An extremely detailed source covering the activities of over 8,000 warships and 3,000 named participants in major and minor actions, down to the extent of covering AAF raids on German U-boat facilities and the names of ships in various Atlantic convoys. Presented in diary format with comprehensive indexing in the second volume, this work will remain perhaps the most complete chronology of events (general or specific) to appear on the war for some time to come. Few photos.

136. Salmaggi, Cesare, and Alfredo Pallavisini, eds. *2194 Days of War: An Illustrated Chronology of the Second World War.* Translated from the Italian. New York: Mayflower Books, 1979. 756p.

An ambitious attempt to bring together all of the political, economic, and strategic backgrounds in an effort to help highlight the "human" dimensions of the war, this work relates the military and non-military events of every theater on a daily basis. Oversize, with 700 photos and 80 maps. Reviewers have caught a number of factual errors in some of the daily summaries, which cast a pall over what is otherwise a very handsome offering.

137. Smith, Myron J., Jr. *Air War Chronology, 1939-1945.* 5 vols.+ Manhattan, Kans.: Military Affairs/Aerospace Historian, 1977--.

A complete and comprehensive look at every major aspect of the World War II sky war arranged by theater of operations, beginning with Northern Europe. The five volumes to date cover the conflict through mid-1943; one must wonder, along with the compiler, if, because of the increased tempo of aerial combat in 1944-1945, the project can ever be finished.

138. Stembridge, Jasper H. *The Oxford War Atlas*. 4 vols. New York and London: Oxford University Press, 1941-1946.

A detailed collection of contemporary maps useful for locating place names mentioned in newspaper accounts or *Saturday Evening Post* stories.

139. United States. Department of the Army. Military Academy, Department of Military Art and Engineering. *The West Point Atlas of American Wars*. Edited by Vincent J. Esposito. 2 vols. New York: Praeger, 1977.

First published by this firm in 1959. The section on World War II is found in Volume II and encompasses 168 maps, devoted exclusively to land warfare. A unique feature of this work is the descriptive text on one page with one or more maps on the opposite page.

140. ———. Navy Department. Naval History Division. *United States Naval Chronology, World War II*. Washington, D.C.: U.S. Government Printing Office, 1955. 214p.

A valuable if brief USN World War II bibliography important for its appendices of principal civilian officials, navy officers, and ship losses; important in its day, now overshadowed completely by Rohwer and Hummelchen, cited above.

141. ———. War Department. General Staff. *Atlas of the World Battle Fronts in Semimonthly Phases*. Washington, D.C.: U.S. Army Map Service, 1945. 101p.

An extremely rare item which was issued as a supplement to General Marshall's annual reports.

142. Williams, Mary H., comp. *Chronology, 1941-1945*. U.S. Army in World War II: Special Studies. Washington, D.C.: U.S. Government Printing Office, 1960. 660p.

Devoted primarily to tactical events from December 7, 1941, to September 2, 1945, with emphasis on the ground action of U.S. armed forces, particularly the Army, this regionally arranged chronology considers, within the scope of space limitations, air and naval cooperation, combat actions of foreign units--both Allied and Axis--and general political events. Features a voluminous index. As an official product, Williams' work exceeds the Naval History Division's pioneer outing cited above and is on a level with Carter and Mueller's aerial chronology, also cited above.

143. "World War II, 1939-1945." *Air Force*, XL (August 1957), 147-163.

Emphasizes aerial activities; the most helpful AAF chronology until the appearance of Carter and Mueller.

144. Young, Peter. *Atlas of the Second World War*. New York: Berkley Publishing Corp., 1977. 288p.

An oversize volume first published by the London firm of Weidenfeld and Nicolson in 1973, this reference is divided into sections correspondong to the major theaters or campaigns; within these, the individual battles or phases of battles each have a double-page spread with a selection of black-and-white-and-red maps. Accompanying the maps are short explanatory texts and a variety of photo illustrations. Each section begins with an introduction filling in the backgrounds of campaigns. The emphasis of this atlas is European and the section on the air war receives only six pages. Compare with Goodenough, cited above.

145. Zijlstra, Gerrit. *Diary of an Air War.* New York: Vantage, 1977. 487p.

An amateur attempt to provide a chronology of the air war over Western Europe which, unlike Smith's effort, has the advantage of being finished, but which still does not measure up to the work of Carter and Mueller.

F. COLLECTIVE BIOGRAPHY

Introduction: The study of biography brings a human-interest element into a subject and is a valuable method for interesting students in a given topic. Over the years, this pedagogical idea has had an important, often self-motivated, place in the study of or introduction to World War II. The sources cited in this part are all collective and within their pages bring together the lives of many individuals who influenced or participated in the World War II American crusade in Europe. Biographies of individuals, be they generals or privates, admirals or seamen, are found below in the various "operational" sections, II-IV, and above in the assorted handbooks and encyclopedias covered in part C.

146. *Current Biography.* New York: H.W. Wilson Co., 1940--. v. 1--.

A monthly publication which provides short biographies of prominent or newsworthy personages, this work contains almost 2,400 biographies of wartime personalities in its annual cumulations; each sketch usually includes a portrait and bibliographical references. Be sure to check later volumes, as some men who rose to higher positions have their stories fleshed out even more, e.g., Gen. Creighton Abrams, wartime leader of the Thirty-Seventh Tank Batallion, which broke through to Bastogne, later Army Chief of Staff.

147. DeWeerd, Harvey A. *Great Soldiers of World War II.* New York: W.W. Norton, 1945. 316p.

Sketches of eleven leaders which were criticized on the basis of biographies selected/omitted and the fact that the war was not over at publication time; "At least," wrote reviewer Herman Beukema in his April 1945 *American Historical Review* assessment, "it marks a long advance over the snap judgments which characterize the day-by-day appraisals offered the reading public by the commentators of the Press" (p. 50).

148. *Facts on File*, Editors of. *Obituaries on File*. 2 vols. New York: Facts on File, Inc., 1979.

Drawn from newspapers around the nation, these pieces provide excellent career summaries for U.S. military leaders who died between 1940 and 1978.

149. Garraty, John A., and Jerome L. Sternstein, eds. *Encyclopedia of American Biography*. New York: Harper & Row, 1974. 1,241p.

A quick reference tool containing concise sketches of prominent people in U.S. history, including some military leaders; available in many public and school libraries.

150. Hirsch, Phil, ed. *Fighting Generals*. New York: Pyramid Books, 1960. 192p.

This slim paperback reprints articles from *Man's Magazine* on various 20th-century U.S. military leaders; those included from World War II Europe include Clark, Patton, Eisenhower, and Doolittle.

151. *International Who's Who*. London: Europa, 1942--. v. 7--.

This annual is a basic biographical source for information on current world leaders; the volumes for the war years reflect a heavy Allied emphasis.

152. Keegan, John. *Who Was Who in World War II*. New York: Crowell, 1978. 224p.

Covers only subjects prominent during the war years and only their wartime achievements and activities; personalities surveyed are both major and minor (and the entries correspond in size to that perception). Many biographees are shown in color or black and white photographs; contains no index, which is really not needed due to alphabetical arrangement of references.

153. ———, and Andrew Wheatcroft. *Who's Who in Military History, From 1492 to the Present Day*. New York: William Morrow, 1976. 367p.

Alphabetically arranged; useful for fleshing out the careers of major World War II figures and thus serves as a companion volume to the previous entry.

154. Kemp, Anthony, and Angus McBride. *Allied Commanders of World War II*. Men at Arms, no. 120. London: Osprey, 1982. 120p.

Provides brief biographical portraits of Anglo-American military leaders with photos and color plates showing the biographees in their typical uniforms--from the subdued Field Marshal Alexander to the gaudy General George S. Patton.

155. McHenry, Robert, ed. *Webster's American Military Biographies*. Springfield, Mass.: G. & C. Merriam, 1978. 548p.

Brief biographical sketches of prominent military personnel from all periods of American history, including World War II; includes mostly those of flag rank or those who received notice in the popular press. Compare with the Marquis entry, *Who Was Who in American History: The Military*, cited below.

156. Mason, David. *Who's Who in World War II*. Boston, Mass.: Little, Brown, 1978. 363p.

A nicely illustrated biographical guide to some 350 major military, political, and scientific personalities of the war years, arranged alphabetically; few of the entries concern secondary personalities and, like most of these World War II biographical collections, contains very little bibliographical information.

157. *New York Times Obituary Index, 1858-1968*. New York: New York Times Co., 1970. 1,136p.

Fulfills the same purpose as the *Facts on File* entry above; however, for the most part, obituaries here are fuller.

158. *Newsweek*, Editors of. *The Generals and the Admirals: Some Leaders of the United States Forces in World War II*. New York: Devin-Adair, 1945. 62p.

A selection of 35 brief, non-critical biographical sketches designed to satisfy the immediate postwar public search for heroes.

159. *Times of London*, Editors of. *Obituaries from "The Times," 1961-1970*. Reading, Berkshire: Newspaper Archive Developments, 1976. 952p.

With a natural British emphasis, this work does provide information on prominent foreign military leaders who died during the sixties, especially those like Eisenhower who had a strong identification with the war years.

160. Tunney, Christopher. *Biographical Dictionary of World War II*. New York: St. Martin's Press, 1973. 216p.

Provides over 400 biographies for a variety of personalities associated with the war effort, including not only military brass but also scientists, journalists, politicians, conscientious objectors, and others; reflects an Allied bias.

161. United States. Congress. Senate. Committee on Veterans' Affairs. *Medal of Honor Recipients, 1863-1978*. 96th Cong., 1st sess. Washington, D.C.: U.S. Government Printing Office, 1979. 1,113p.

Lists by conflict every American recipient of the Congressional Medal of Honor together with biographical (brief) data and the texts of citations; useful for finding out who won America's highest military honor during World War II and for what.

162. *Who Was Who in American History: The Military.* Chicago: Marquis Who's Who, 1975. 652p.

Some 90,000 entries on deceased Americans, 1607-1974, based on information in the *Who Was Who in America* basic set and recent additions; much of the data came from the volumes of *Who's Who in America* and was directly supplied by the biographees. A useful source for personal information not easily available elsewhere.

163. Windrow, Martin, and Francis K. Mason. *Concise Dictionary of Military Biography.* New York: Beekman Publishers, 1975. 337p.

Published simultaneously by the London firm of Osprey, this guide focuses entirely on 200 significant leaders in land warfare from the 10th to the 20th century; the military achievements of an individual are highlighted rather than his personality, and only a few Americans are considered, regardless of century. Still useful, however, for the data provided on Axis and Allied leaders.

G. DOCUMENT/MANUSCRIPT GUIDES AND COLLECTIONS

Introduction: Historians in particular have always sought to practice their craft by dealing as much as possible in the primary sources of documents and unpublished papers, of states and individuals. For a number of years following World War II, neither type of information, especially the latter, was available in other than official publications. Now, with the passage of time (and a large number of prominent leaders) since 1945, these sources are becoming accessible. The dramatic revelation of "Ultra" in 1974 and the renewed interest in secret dealings occasioned by the CIA hearings of 1975-1976 have led to the opening of vast new areas of study and entire collections to historians and others with an interest in unpublished materials. The sources in this section are all concerned with the presentation or location of published or unpublished documents and papers; some are collections, others are guides or bibliographies. In common, they all foster our search into primary data, the stuff from which the best citations in the other sections of this guide are built.

164. Allard, Dean C., Martha L. Crawley, and Mary W. Edmison, comps. *U.S. Naval History Sources in the United States.* Washington, D.C.: U.S. Government Printing Office, 1979. 235p.

Provides information on manuscripts, archives, and other special collections of papers and documents for officers, men, and civilian Navy officials in 250 depositories around the country.

165. Bilstein, Roger C. "Sources in Aerospace History: The Oral History Collection at Columbia University." *Aerospace Historian*, XXII (March 1975), 46-47.

A brief introduction to the famous Columbia collection of oral history, and a note on which airmen have deposited all or part of their verbal reminiscences there.

166. Buchanan, Albert R., comp. *The United States and World War II: Military and Diplomatic Documents.* Columbia: University of South Carolina Press, 1972. 303p.

A sampling of documents illustrating the military and diplomatic phases of the war arranged in sections, each of which is preceded by an introduction describing, in general, the events of the period covered.

167. *The Declassified Documents Quarterly Catalog.* Washington, D.C.: Carrollton Press, 1976--. v. 1--.

A guide to both the printed and microfiche collections handled by this firm; arranged in two parts: abstracts and a cumulative subject index. Of significant importance for federal material, especially that relating to the intelligence agencies.

168. Detwiler, Donald S., ed. *World War II German Military Studies.* 24 vols. New York: Garland, 1980.

Following the war, many German officers prepared studies on Nazi military campaigns for the Army's historical division in Europe; known as *Foreign Military Studies*, only a few copies of these items were available. Detwiler, the new president of the Association for the Bibliography of History, has drawn together some of the more interesting and significant titles for inclusion in this set. The introductions provide background on the campaigns and battles fought and the process by which the documents were prepared.

169. Floyd, Dale E., and Timothy K. Nenninger. "U.S. Government Documentation." In: Robin Higham, ed. *A Guide to the Sources of United States Military History: Supplement I.* Hamden, Conn.: Archon Books, 1981, pp. 287-300.

Explains the record-keeping process and locations of federal documents on military history with special attention to the National Archives; includes a list of addresses for repositories.

170. Great Britain. Public Record Office. *The Second World War: A Guide to Documents in the Public Records Office.* London: H.M. Stationery Office, 1972. 303p.

A guide to the official records of Great Britain's role in the war, many of which have only recently been made public and are not included in this guide; operating under a 30-year secrecy rule, the British have released many items bearing on American involvement in the European Theater which have not yet been made public in the U.S.

171. Haight, David J., and George H. Curtis. "Abilene, Kansas and the History of World War II: Resources and Research Oppor-

tunities at the Dwight D. Eisenhower Library." *Military Affairs*, XLI (Fall 1977), 195-200.

Discusses the possibilities for researchers at the Eisenhower Library, especially the collection designated "U.S. Army, Unit Record 1940-1950" and that nicknamed the "sixteen-fifty-two file," Eisenhower's pre-Presidential papers, 1916-1952.

172. Hamer, Philip M. *A Guide to Archives and Manuscripts in the United States*. New Haven, Conn.: Yale University Press, 1961. 775p.

Prepared under the auspices of the U.S. National Publications Commission, this guide is arranged by depositories and includes a detailed index covering 20,000 collections of papers in 1,300 depositories; now superseded by *Directory of Archives and Manuscript Repositories*, cited below (item 189).

173. Hasdorff, James C. "Sources in Aerospace History: The USAF Oral History Collection." *Aerospace Historian*, XXII (Summer 1976), 103-104.

Briefly describes the Air Force's oral history collection, housed in the Albert Simpson Historical Research Center in the Air University Library, Maxwell AFB, Alabama; users should note that the U.S. Naval Institute at Annapolis maintains a useful, if somewhat smaller, oral history collection of the reminiscences of certain naval officers who figured in the history of our topic.

174. Hayes, John D. "The Papers of Naval Officers: Where They Are." *Military Affairs*, XX (Summer 1956), 102-103.

A still-useful introduction to this topic which describes the holdings at Library of Congress, University of North Carolina, Duke University, New York Public Library, etc. A better guide is Allard's *U.S. Naval History Sources*, cited above.

175. Heimdahl, William C., and Edward J. Marolda, comps. *Guide to U.S. Naval Administrative Histories of World War II*. Washington, D.C.: U.S. Naval Historical Center, Operational Archives, 1976. 219p.

Describes 173 unpublished narratives compiled during and just after the war, a significant number of which are useful for the USN contribution to the war in Europe, and all of which are housed in the Center's Operational Archives in the Washington Navy Yard.

176. Jacobsen, Hans-Adolf, and Arthur L. Smith, Jr., comps. *World War II: Policy and Strategy, Selected Documents with Commentary*. Santa Barbara, Calif.: Clio Books, 1979. 505p.

A chronologically arranged collection of 214 documents dating from March 1939 to August 1945 with background commentary on their significance; many are political and a few are military, with the scope worldwide. Includes an annotated chronology, a glossary, maps, charts, and photographs. Albert R. Buchanan, cited above, has not been superseded here due to his emphasis on U.S. documents.

177. Langsam, Walter C., ed. *Historic Documents of World War II.* Princeton, N.J.: Van Nostrand, 1958. 192p.

A useful collection of 47 political and military documents issued between 1938 and 1955, each preceded in the text by a short paragraph placing it in historical context.

178. Mayer, S.L., and W.J. Koenig. *The Two World Wars: A Guide to Manuscript Collections in the United Kingdom.* New York: R.R. Bowker, 1977. 317p.

A survey of the more important collections accessible to the public, excepting those in the Public Records Office; arranged alphabetically by locale and then subdivided into sections on World War I and World War II. For the PRO, see the PRO guide cited under Great Britain above.

179. Meckler, Alan M., and Ruth McMullin, comps. *Oral History Collections.* New York: R.R. Bowker, 1975. 344p.

Many interviews of prominent World War II military leaders and diplomats have been conducted by such universities as Duke and Columbia, to say nothing of the military services themselves. These oral histories can be located through this guide, which also contains valuable data on the access restrictions (if any) and the size of collections of the various repositories.

180. O'Neill, James E., and Robert W. Krauskopf. *World War II: An Account of Its Documents.* National Archives Conference, no. 8. Washington, D.C.: Howard University Press, 1976. 269p.

A collection of 18 papers designed to acquaint potential users with the collections of NA; especially useful are those chapters on "Military Biography" and "Major Resources of the National Archives and Records Service for Research on the Second World War." Also included is an unannotated bibliography of NA resource materials.

181. Russell, J. Thomas. *Preliminary Guide to the Manuscript Collection of the U.S. Military Academy Library.* West Point, N.Y.: U.S. Military Academy Library, 1968. 260p.

Over the years, a number of prominent military leaders have donated their papers to West Point, their alma mater; this guide describes the Academy's collection in an A-Z arrangement.

182. Sommers, Richard J. *Manuscript Holdings of the Military History Research Collection.* Carlisle Barracks, Pa.: U.S. Army Military History Institute, 1972. 156p.

As with West Point, Carlisle has become a center for the collection of papers from former military personnel, not necessarily either Army or officers; this guide describes 250 collections and is updated by a supplement which was issued in 1975.

183. *The Ultra Documents.* 104 reels of microfilm. New York: Clearwater, 1979.

Some 52,000 signals, extracted from the main series of military signals and assembled by the British Public Record Office, are here available.

184. United States. Congress. Senate. Committee on Foreign Relations. *A Decade of American Foreign Policy: Basic Documents, 1941-49.* 81st Cong., 1st sess. Washington, D.C.: U.S. Government Printing Office, 1959. 1,381p.

A selective compilation of 313 items which serves as a convenient source for wartime documents on interallied negotiations.

185. ———. Department of State. *Foreign Relations of the United States.* Washington, D.C.: U.S. Government Printing Office, 1941--.

A huge official series begun in 1862 which prints materials from the Department's archival files; each volume is individually titled for the subject, country, or area covered and there are volumes for each of the great wartime Allied conferences. For a useful introduction to the 1943-1946 volumes, see Richard W. Leopold's "The Foreign Relations Series Revisited: One Hundred Plus Ten," *Journal of American History*, XLIX (Fall 1973), 935-957.

186. ———. Library of Congress. *The National Union Catalog of Manuscript Collections.* Hamden, Conn.: Shoe String Press, 1962. 1,061p.

Reproduced catalog cards compiled by LC from reports sent from various repositories; annotated with extensive indexing. An annual until 1971, this series, very useful for the location of papers on military figures and an indication of their microfilm availability, shows cards for 29,000 collections in 850 repositories.

187. ———. National Archives and Records Service. *Federal Records of World War II.* 2 vols. Detroit, Mich.: Gale Research, 1982.

First printed by NA in 1950-1951, this set indexes the available records of federal agencies in the Archives; Volume I records the material of civilian agencies and Volume II, those of the military.

188. ———. ———. *Guides to German Records Microfilmed at Alexandria, Va.* Washington, D.C., 1958--. v. 1--.

Now running in excess of 70 oversize volumes, this collection is in fact an inventory of the tons of captured German documentation brought to the U.S. after World War II; many of the volumes deal with Wehrmacht and Luftwaffe units which were engaged against American forces in the Mediterranean and Western Europe and are thus helpful in showing historians where to obtain primary source material showing life "on the other side of the hill."

188a. ———. ———. *Historical Materials in the Dwight D. Eisenhower Library*. Abilene, Kans.: Eisenhower Library, 1974. 45p.

A useful description of the various collections in the DDE collection which, for those seeking World War II items, should be supplemented by reading Haight and Curtis's "Abilene, Kansas and the History of World War II" cited above.

189. ———. National Historical Publications and Records Commission. *Directory of Archives and Manuscript Repositories*. Washington, D.C.: U.S. National Archives and Records Service, 1978.

A comprehensive finding aid to the holdings of 3,200 repositories, this work virtually replaces most of the non-military guides cited here, including Hamer above. Includes lists showing types of repositories and a name-subject index.

190. ———. Naval Historical Foundation. *Manuscript Collections: A Catalog*. Washington, D.C.: Library of Congress, 1974. 136p.

Describes collections for 254 individuals housed in LC, including the papers of wartime CNO Admiral Ernest J. King.

191. ———. Navy Historical Center, Operational Archives. *U.S. Navy Partial Checklist: World War II Histories and Historical Reports*. Washington, D.C.: U.S. Navy Historical Center, 1972. 226p.

An annotated list of declassified official reports of USN wartime operations and administration housed in the Operational Archives at the Washington Navy Yard; includes a number of unit histories directly related to American naval involvement in Europe.

192. ———. Superintendent of Documents. *Monthly Catalog of United States Government Publications*. Washington, D.C.: Government Printing Office, 1941--. v. 46--.

An index and bibliography to U.S. government publications which excludes most restricted, administrative, and "processed" (e.g., mimeographed) materials, published monthly with an annual cumulation. Issued as *United States Government Publications: A Monthly Catalog* from 1940 to 1950, the guide describes papers from all government agencies, with most relating to the war found under the heading "World War, 1939-1945." GPO published in 1948-1949 a three-volume supplement covering the years 1941-1946.

193. ———. War Department. International Military Tribunal. *Trial of the Major War Criminals Before the International Military Tribunal, Nuremberg, 14 November 1945-1 October 1946*. 42 vols. Nuremberg, 1947-1949.

Covers the trials of two dozen persons, including some who testified on atrocities, campaigns, or reactions to U.S. military operations; can be supplemented by *Nazi Conspiracy and Aggression* (8 vols.; 1946), which includes evidence gathered by the prosecutors, and the 15 volumes of *Trials of War Criminals Before the Nuremberg Military Tribunals Under Control Law 10* (1949-1953).

194. ———. ———. Joint Chiefs of Staff. *Records of the Joint Chiefs of Staff, Part I: 1942-1945*. 50 reels of microfilm. Frederick, Md.: University Publications of America, 1982.

A large collection of various documents detailing JCS work; of interest to users of this guide are the 14 reels covering the European Theater, 7 reels on meetings of the JCS with the Allied Combined Chiefs of Staff, and 13 reels detailing Strategic Issues.

195. "V-E Unconditional Surrender: Text of Reims Surrender Act and Addresses." *Vital Speeches of the Day*, XI (May 15, 1945), 450-454.

An easily available source for the basic terms of the German surrender and statements by Allied leaders.

196. Wile, Annadel, ed. *The Declassified Documents: Retrospective Collection*. 3 vols. Arlington, Va.: Carrollton Press, 1976-1977.

This basic collection of secret American documents is updated by the *Declassified Documents Quarterly Catalog*, cited above.

197. Zobrist, Benedict K. "Resources of Presidential Libraries for the History of the Second World War." *Military Affairs*, XXXIX (April 1975), 82-85.

Describes the collections in the Hoover, Roosevelt, Truman, Eisenhower, and Kennedy libraries relative to World War II.

H. GENERAL WAR HISTORIES

Introduction: The sources cited below are general worldwide accounts of not only military, but also political and economic events of World War II. Most contain fairly complete discussion of American military actions in Europe with a number offering both chronological narrative and analysis. Several are largely illustrated accounts. The various encyclopedias of World War II covered in part C above might as easily have fit here and should not be neglected by readers. Bibliographic information is often noted within these studies. Additional general studies relating to land, sea, or air events will be found listed in the appropriate sections below.

198. Adams, Henry H. *1942: The Year That Doomed the Axis*. New York: David McKay, 1967. 544p. Rpr. 1973.

Part of a four-volume series covering military operations around the globe; of interest to our topic is this book's discussion of the operations of the Allied landing in North Africa.

199. ———. *Years of Deadly Peril: The Coming of the War, 1939-1941*. New York: David McKay, 1969. 559p.

Part of a four-volume series covering military operations around the globe, this volume gives considerable space to a discussion of America's prewar diplomatic position and does not neglect the undeclared U.S.-German naval war in the Atlantic.

200. ———. *Years of Expectation: Guadalcanal to Normandy*. New York: David McKay, 1973. 430p.

Part of a four-volume series covering military operations around the globe, Adams' work portrays U.S. forces in action on land, sea, and air in 1942-mid-1944; coverage relating to this guide's topic includes the invasions of Sicily, Italy, and Normandy and the strategic bombing campaign. Diplomatic events are not neglected.

201. ———. *Years to Victory*. New York: David McKay, 1973. 507p.

The last in a four-volume series covering military operations around the globe, this work portrays U.S. forces in action on land, sea, and air from summer 1944 through V-J Day; coverage relating to this guide's topic includes the Allied ground battle through France and into the heart of the Third Reich. Taken together, Adams' set, indexed and illustrated with maps and photos, is a useful starting place for those who would read in some detail of the events of the conflict.

202. Arnold-Foster, Mark. *The World at War*. New York: Stein & Day, 1973. 340p.

An overall account of the global conflict published as accompaniment for a 26-part BBC television series of the same title; includes maps, illustrations, photos, and biographical notes on key leaders, but, like the television series, is European oriented.

203. Baillie, Hugh. *Two Battlefronts: Dispatches Written by the President of the United Press Covering the Air Offensive Over Germany and the Sicilian Campaign During the Summer of 1943*. New York: United Press, 1943. 139p.

Entered here for the diversity of topics covered; this contemporary commentary on the two events described suffers from lack of complete access to the facts. Interesting reading, but neither informative nor controversial in light of later research.

204. Bauer, Eddy. *The History of World War II.* Freeport, N.Y.: Marshall Cavendish Corp., 1981. 680p.

Extolled for the objective stance taken by Bauer, a noted Swiss military historian, this work is essentially a one-volume edition of the multi-part Marshall Cavendish World War II encyclopedia as it was before being edited by Young (cited above in I:D). Oversize with some 860 black and white/color photographs, this title is now being offered by many "remainder" book dealers in America and is a good bargain, despite its European emphasis.

205. Bliven, Bruce. *From Casablanca to Berlin: The War in North Africa and Europe, 1942-1945.* Landmark Books. New York: Random House, 1965. 180p.

An introductory survey of military operations from "Operation Torch" to V-E Day, this work is suited to the younger reader.

206. Blore, Trevor. *Turning Point--1943.* New York and London: Hutchinson, 1945. 128p.

An early review of events of that year emphasizing the military/naval actions in the Mediterranean Theater and the Atlantic; British bias.

207. Buchanan, Albert R. *The United States and World War II.* New American Nation Series. 2 vols. New York: Harper & Row, 1964.

A general survey of the military, political, and economic events of the war caused by or impacting on America; although the bibliographic essay is now somewhat dated, this is still a useful--and easily available--starting place for students.

208. Calvocoressi, Peter, and Guy Wint. *Total War: The Story of World War II.* New York: Pantheon, 1972. 959p.

A well-balanced and comprehensive survey of the war which pays attention to military, political, economic, and social aspects of the conflict during the prewar and wartime years; enhanced by good maps and illustrations, this work provides almost equal coverage of Europe and the Far East.

209. Churchill, Winston L.S. *The Second World War.* 6 vols. Boston, Mass.: Houghton Mifflin, 1948-1953.

Long considered essential reading for anyone interested in the war, the British Prime Minister's record is included here due to its broad scope. These volumes (*The Gathering Storm*, *Their Finest Hour*, *The Grand Alliance*, *The Hinge of Fate*, *Closing the Ring*, and *Triumph and Tragedy*) offer good, British-oriented, coverage of grand strategy and the personalities of military and political leaders, to say nothing of campaigns and minutiae. An important source probably for years to come, Churchill's memoirs are undoubtedly the finest penned by any major World War II figure. For an interesting essay on the publication history of this work, see pages 351-356 of the 2nd, rev. edition of Frederick Woods' *A Bibliography of the Works of Sir Winston Churchill* (Toronto, Canada: University of Toronto Press, 1969).

210. ———, and *Life Magazine*. *The Second World War: A History Combining New Selections from the Greatest Chronicles of the War and the Most Memorable Illustrations of the Men Who Took Part in It.* 2 vols. New York: Time, Inc., 1959.

The narrative text is drawn from Churchill's *The Second World War* while many of the hundreds of photographs and maps (some in color) appeared first in the wartime issues of *Life*. Special captions were written, where needed, to explain the photos' backgrounds. A most enjoyable reference.

211. Collier, Basil. *The Second World War: A Military History from Munich to Hiroshima*. New York: William Morrow, 1967. 640p.

A well-written military history with some British bias, the majority of which is devoted to the conflict in Europe; includes some 60 maps and appendices which show the composition of the various land forces.

212. Congdon, Don. *Combat: The War with Germany*. New York: Dell, 1963. 384p.

Each section in this paperback anthology is preceded by an introductory essay which explains the event described and places it within its historical context; excerpts include Wolff's account of the Ploesti bombing raid, Morison on the Salerno landings, Oliver St. John on the hedgerow fighting in Normandy, and Chester Wilmot's account of the Arnhem airborne fiasco.

213. Davies, J.B., ed. *Great Campaigns of World War II*. New York and London: Phoebus Publications, 1980. 320p.

An oversize, heavily illustrated British import which details the wartime operations of significance in Europe (mostly) and the Far East; among those of interest are the Normandy campaign and the Battle of the Bulge.

214. Davis, Kenneth S. *Experience of War: The United States in World War II*. Garden City, N.Y.: Doubleday, 1965. 704p.

Perhaps the best popular, general survey of the role of the U.S. in the war and the impact of the conflict on America; items treated include social, political, economic, and military events. Enhanced by maps and a lengthy bibliographic survey of books, this is a splendid introduction to the United States at war.

215. Dupuy, R. Ernest. *World War II: A Compact History*. New York: Hawthorn Books, 1969. 224p.

A simple, readable survey of the military events of the war which concentrates on the European Theater; while this account offers standard interpretation, certain episodes stand out, including the preparations for the Normandy invasion and the intelligence failures surrounding the Battle of the Bulge. Suffers from poor maps.

216. Flower, Desmond, and James Reeves, eds. *The Taste of Courage: The War, 1939-1945.* New York: Harper, 1960. 1,120p.

With maps and bibliography, this remains one of the best anthologies of war narrative, drawing as it does on accounts by participants from all the leading combatants in each period and all theaters.

217. Fuller, John F.C. *The Second World War, 1939-45: A Strategical and Tactical History.* New York: Meredith Press, 1968. 431p.

First published by the New York firm of Duell, Sloan and Pearce in 1948, this primarily military history was written shortly after the war's conclusion, when access to unpublished primary sources was very difficult; Fuller, whose work continues to rank as an important British analysis, had little use for either Churchill, Roosevelt, or their grand strategy.

218. Gardner, Brian. *The Year That Changed the World--1945.* New York: Coward-McCann, 1964. 356p.

A journalistic chronicle of the events of 1945 surrounding the end of the war in Europe and the Far East, the formation of the U.N., and the loss of FDR to death and Churchill to the British electorate; includes a few insights into the period of the German surrender. Maps and bibliography are included.

219. Groth, John. *Studio: Europe.* New York: Vanguard Press, 1945. 282p.

Photographs of and commentary on the war in Europe; introduction by Ernest Hemingway. Interesting, but not vital.

220. *Greatest Battles of World War II.* London: Galahad Books, 1981. 220p.

Another British "coffee-table" presentation sold in America by publishers' "remainders" distributors, this work covers such European campaigns as the Battle of Britain, Normandy, and the Battle of the Bulge; a visual treat, this work includes more than 600 photos, charts, and maps of which more than half are in full color.

221. Heiferman, Ronald. *World War II.* Secaucus, N.J.: Derbibooks, 1973. 256p.

An oversize British import which covers the causes of and execution of World War II in Europe and the Far East; illustrated with 99 color and 350 black and white photos and 16 maps.

222. Herridge, Charles. *Pictorial History of World War II.* London and New York: Hamlyn, 1975. 253p.

Illustrated with hundreds of charts, maps, and photos, this outing is not much different from Heiferman in concept or layout.

223. Hoyle, Martha B. *A World in Flames: A History of World War II.* New York: Atheneum, 1970. 356p.

A solid general survey of political, social, economic, and military events which includes a few maps and photos and a helpful bibliography.

224. Irving, David. *Hitler's War.* New York: Viking Press, 1977. 926p.

A noteworthy chronicle of events "on the other side of the hill" by a controversial British historian who based his narrative on captured German documents and the papers of Hitler's contemporaries; includes coverage of German successes and failures on both the Western and Eastern Fronts, a few maps, and photographs.

225. Jones, James. *World War II.* New York: Grosset & Dunlap, 1975. 272p.

An almost personal account of the war, this oversize pictorial by the distinguished late novelist is illustrated with dozens of little-known drawings and photographs.

225a. Leasor, James. *The Clock with Four Hands.* New York: Reynal, 1959. 314p.

Based on the experiences of Gen. Sir Leslie Hollis, Secretary of the Joint Planning Commission of the Chiefs of Staff, this account tells of the underground London nerve center from which the Allied war was run.

226. Leopard, Donald D. *World War II: A Concise History.* Prospect Heights, Ill.: Waveland Press, 1982. 155p.

A brief narrative outline of events around the globe designed for use as an introductory college text, this paperback includes a few maps and recommended readings.

227. Liddell-Hart, Basil H. *History of the Second World War.* New York: Putnam, 1970. 768p.

The late commentator, famous as one of England's foremost armor exponents before the war, provides a well-written and comprehensive military history of the war in its various theaters; more than a standard survey, this work provides penetrating analysis of the important military engagements and offers judgments on controversial strategic decisions. If Hart's comments sound less British than one might expect, it is probably because he was often in disagreement with Churchill's grand strategy.

228. ———. "The Second World War." In: C.L. Mowat, ed. *The Shifting Balance of World Forces, 1898-1945.* Vol. XII of *The New Cambridge Modern History.* 2nd ed. Cambridge, Eng.: At the Clarendon Press, 1968, pp. 735-797.

An uncontroversial, straightforward summary which might be said to foreshadow his *History of the Second World War* cited above.

229. *Life*, Editors of. *Picture History of World War II.* New York: Time, Inc., 1950. 368p.

An excellent single-volume picture history which includes a text outlining the war and explanatory paragraphs for the photographs, portraits, or paintings; contains appendices with notes on various personalities.

230. ———. *Life Goes to War: A Picture History of World War II.* Boston, Mass.: Little, Brown, 1977. 304p.

Better categorized, this work is similar to the 1950 edition (above) in that it contains text, excellent captions, and hundreds of photographs which originally appeared in *Life* during the war years.

231. Marshall, George C., Henry H. Arnold, and Ernest J. King. *The War Reports of General of the Army George C. Marshall, Chief of Staff, General of the Army H.H. Arnold, Commanding General, Army Air Forces, and Fleet Admiral Ernest J. King, Commander-in-Chief, United States Fleet and Chief of Naval Operations.* Philadelphia, Pa.: Lippincott, 1947. 801p.

A compilation of the periodical reports of the heads of the U.S. military to the Secretaries of War and Navy on the progress of the war which, due to wartime restrictions, left out much that was questionable or not successful; still a valuable source on war planning and execution at the top levels of military command.

232. Martin, Ralph G. *The G.I. War, 1941-1945.* Boston, Mass.: Little, Brown, 1968. 402p.

A former correspondent for the military newspapers *Yank* and *Stars and Stripes* has, from interviews, personal experience, and a variety of other sources, assembled almost 600 vignettes; each story is designed to show a moment in the life or death of an American soldier and is supplemented by photos or cartoons.

233. Maule, Henry. *The Great Battles of World War II.* Chicago: Henry Regnery, 1973. 448p.

Of the thirteen battles surveyed, only two--Anzio and Normandy--are relevant to the topic of this guide; contains photographs and maps.

234. Meyer, Robert J. *The Stars and Stripes Story of World War II.* New York: David McKay, 1960. 504p.

Built around excerpts which appeared in the official Army newspaper *Stars and Stripes* from April 1942 to September 1945 and held together by the author's running commentary; Meyer was a *Stars and Stripes* correspondent in the Mediterranean during the war and his comments, like those in the articles included, evoke much human interest. Compare with Martin above.

235. Michel, Henri. *The Second World War*. Translated from the French. New York: Praeger, 1975. 947p.

Long-time editor of the respected *Revue d'Histoire de la Deuxième Guerre Mondiale*, Michel provides an encyclopedic general history that not only covers the standard military, diplomatic, economic, and social aspects of the conflict, but also pays more than casual attention to German occupation and national resistance movements; extensive bibliography, maps, and some photographs.

236. Middleton, Drew. *Crossroads of Modern Warfare: Sixteen 20th Century Battles That Shaped Contemporary History*. Garden City, N.Y.: Doubleday, 1983. 334p.

The former AP war correspondent and noted *New York Times* military analyst examines turning points in modern warfare, pointing out technological improvements which rendered older forms of warfare obsolete and political ramifications which helped to change the world map; of the World War II engagements of interest to users of this guide, the Normandy landing is best covered. Includes 18 maps.

237. ———. *Our Share of Night: A Personal Narrative of the War Years*. New York: Viking Press, 1946. 380p.

Impressions of the war's six years and a chronicle of people under stress; Middleton's sensitive insights on the war's European defeats and triumphs include angry notes on the political "mess" surrounding the North African invasion, an account of the victory march through France into Germany, and strong statements on the weakness of Anglo-American occupation policies. Useful details and snatches of conversation are included as drawn from his reporter's notebook.

238. ———. *Where Has Last July Gone?: Memoirs*. New York: Quadrangle Books, 1974. 284p.

In part recounts the author's wartime correspondent career through diaries and notes, especially his service in North Africa and Sicily (1942-1943) and in Northwest Europe (1944-1945) where he divided his time between SHAPE headquarters and the U.S. First Army.

239. Moorehead, Alan. *Eclipse*. New York: Coward-McCann, 1946. 309p.

A noted *London Daily Express* reporter's account of the European war from the Sicilian invasion through D-Day, the Rhine crossing, and the liberation of Denmark; reflecting a strong British bias, this chronicle contains useful observations and much attention to color, personality, and details personally observed.

240. Pitt, Barrie, ed. *Great Battles of the 20th Century*. London: Phoebus Books, 1977. 384p.

Drawing heavily on the Purnell publications, this guide to land, sea, and air battles is heavily illustrated with hundreds of maps and photographs.

241. Pratt, Fletcher. *War for the World*. Chronicles of America Series. New Haven, Conn.: Yale University Press, 1950. 364p.

A concise examination of the war from an American viewpoint, covering the years from Pearl Harbor to VJ-Day; primarily a military rendering which explores each theater of war in the air, on land, and at sea--especially the latter.

242. Preston, Anthony, ed. *Decisive Battles of Hitler's War*. London and New York: Hamlyn, 1977. 256p.

Another oversize British contribution which illustrates the war on the Western and Eastern Fronts with hundreds of maps and photographs, many in color; among the battles of interest here are those in North Africa, Normandy, and the Bulge.

243. *Reader's Digest*, Editors of. *The Reader's Digest Illustrated History of World War II*. Pleasantville, N.Y.: Reader's Digest Association, 1969. 528p.

Reflecting a strong American bias, this anthology of articles and personal narratives, many drawn from the pages of *Reader's Digest*, is illustrated with a number of excellent photographs and maps.

244. Rothberg, Abraham. *The Eyewitness History of World War II*. 4 vols. New York: Bantam Books, 1971.

An anthology of writings from a variety of sources backed up with an unusually large selection of photographs for a paperback set.

245. Shirer, William L. *The Rise and Fall of the Third Reich: A History of Nazi Germany*. New York: Simon and Schuster, 1960. 1,245p.

Although given bad reviews by a number of historians, Shirer's monumental popular history of the social, political, and military history of Hitler's Germany has achieved the status of "classic"; the military history presented is primarily that of the command level with little detail on individual battles.

246. Shugg, Roger W., and Harvey A. DeWeerd. *The World at War, 1939-1944*. Washington, D.C.: Infantry Journal Press, 1945. 416p.

An interesting work given that it was published before the war's end, this title covers events from September 1939 to November 1, 1944, in a chronological/campaign arrangement; includes maps and statistical appendices.

247. Snyder, Louis L. *The War: A Concise History, 1939-1945*. New York: Julian Messner, 1960. 579p.

A general survey of the political, military, social, and economic events of the war years worldwide, Snyder's work is noted for its readability; includes a bibliography and chronology.

248. Stokesbury, James L. *A Short History of World War II.* New York: William Morrow, 1980. 352p.

Stokesbury, like Snyder, has given users a readable survey of worldwide military, social, political, and economic events, taking into account the latest information and interpretations; illustrated with maps and a few photos, the book also contains a bibliography.

249. Sulzberger, Cyrus L., *et al. The American Heritage Picture History of World War II.* New York: American Heritage Publishing Co., 1966. 640p.

Except for the *Life* magazine books cited, no better U.S.-produced pictorial on the war years exists; explanatory information and text accompanies over 700 color and black and white reproductions of drawings, photos, maps, and artwork. This visual treat is well known and in the collection of most public libraries.

250. Taylor, Alan J.P. *The Second World War: An Illustrated History.* New York: Putnam, 1975. 234p.

A short pictorial survey which covers both the political and military aspects of the six-year conflict; perhaps the most controversial of the pictorials in that its author contends that Hitler, Stalin, Churchill, and Roosevelt shaped and directed the war's course and that Russia defeated Germany almost without U.S./British ground assistance.

251. *Time*, Editors of. *Time Capsule: History of the War Years, 1939-1945.* 7 vols. in 1. New York: Bonanza Books, 1967.

Excerpts from the actual prose of the *Time* war years pieces are presented in categorized fashion with editorial direction showing where errors existed in the original coverage.

252. Turner, Arthur G. "The U.S. in World War II." *Current History*, LVII (July 1969), 13-17, 51.

A capsule review of America's economic, social, military, and political involvement, especially the latter.

253. United States. Department of the Army. Chief of Staff. *General Marshall's Report: The Winning of the War in Europe and the Pacific--Biennial Report, July 1, 1943 to June 30, 1945, to the Secretary of War.* New York: Published for the War Department by Simon and Schuster, 1945. 123p.

A succinct report and outline beginning with the attack on Sicily; includes maps and an order of battle for each campaign; the commercially available combined report of Marshall, Arnold, and King is cited above.

254. ———. ———. Office of the Chief of Military History. *World War II: A Concise Military History of America's Great All-Out, Two-Front War.* Edited by Maurice Matloff. New York: David McKay, 1980. 160p.

Adapted from the Center of Military History's textbook *American Military History*, this succinct account of the ground war is well illustrated with maps and charts.

255. ———. War Department. *Our Army at War: The Story of American Campaigns in World War II, Told in Official War Department Photographs*. New York: Harper, 1944. Unpaged.

A few short narratives accompany the 482 photos, which depict U.S. ground and air action in, mainly, the Mediterranean, Pacific, and Great Britain. Compare with the Army photo histories cited in the appropriate theater sections below.

256. Welsh, Douglas. *The U.S.A. in World War II: The European Theater*. Americans at War Series. New York: Galahad Books, 1982. 64p.

A heavily illustrated volume in a British pictorial series depicting action in America's post-1775 conflicts; includes coverage of events and hardware in the Mediterranean and Northwest Europe areas.

257. Wright, Gordon. *The Ordeal of Total War, 1939-1945*. New York: Harper & Row, 1968. 315p.

A valuable analysis of the history and impact of the war in Europe which emphasizes the economic, psychological, cultural, and scientific as well as the usual military and political aspects of the conflict; maps and extensive bibliography.

258. Wykes, Alan. *1942: The Turning Point*. London: Macdonald, 1972. 194p.

A well-illustrated brief review of events (mostly military) around the globe in 1942, particularly in Europe and North Africa; compare with Henry Adams' title on the same period cited above.

259. Young, Peter. *Great Battles of World War II on Land, Sea, and Air*. Northbrook, Ill.: Quality Books International, 1981. 320p.

A worldwide review of noteworthy ground, aerial, and naval battles with several, such as North Africa, Normandy, and the Bulge, of interest here; illustrated with hundreds of maps and photographs, this oversize British import is distinguished for its text.

260. ———. *World War, 1939-1945: A Short History*. New York: Crowell, 1966. 447p.

A concise, readable survey which emphasizes military events and which is arranged into 38 small chapters, each headed by a chronology; with maps and bibliography, this work demonstrates a heavy British bias.

261. ———. *World War II*. London and New York: Hamlyn, 1980. 249p.

Similar in many respects to the author's *Great Battles* cited above; British emphasis with hundreds of photographs, maps, and charts.

II. SPECIAL STUDIES

Introduction: The sources in this section do not always fit conveniently into operational categories, be they military or otherwise. Here are items related to the war's grand strategy, diplomacy, Lend Lease, intelligence, U.S. support for European resistance movements, medicine, POW's, logistics, engineering, and communications.

A. THE DIPLOMACY, STRATEGY, AND ECONOMICS OF COALITION WARFARE

Introduction: Even prior to the official American entry into World War II, the U.S. government was leaning toward the British and Soviets in their hours of need. Although many Americans hoped their nation could remain free of the fighting, in the Atlantic an active, if undeclared, naval war took place with Germany. Meanwhile, U.S. and British military leaders met secretly and drew up a plan to deal with Germany should the country be plunged into the war. With Pearl Harbor, any pretense of neutrality ended.

The leap from preliminary covert planning to participation in a full-scale coalition with England and Russia was not particularly easy for the U.S.; after all, we entered the conflict with little combat experience and an "Arsenal of Democracy" not yet in full gear. Steadily, however, through sometimes noisy military and civilian diplomacy and growing arms production and distribution, the United States found itself an important, often dominant, member of that group of allies collectively known as the United Nations.

The matter of dealing with Germany was not as simple as many make it sound; aside from the strictly military requirements, the political in-fighting between the Allies as to how and where the Reich should be battled forced intricate agreement and cooperation. The overall direction of the war, in the hands of the politicians and most commonly noticed by decisions at the great international conferences, had to be implemented by soldier-politicians faced with diverse opinions from above and below.

In addition to the strategic, political, and diplomatic considerations of a wartime coalition, much attention must be given to the economic basis. Even before December 7, 1941, many Americans found themselves working overtime to build war items for the use of forces from friendly governments as well as their own. The delivery of these materials to the war zone of Europe was politically expedited by the famous Lend Lease Act and operationally by determined sailors in the Battle of the Atlantic, soldiers in Iran, or airmen in Alaska.

The sources in this section examine the complexities of coalition diplomacy, America's entry into the European conflict, the planning of grand strategy for the reconquest of Europe, and the idea of Lend Lease. For an in-depth review, readers are directed to Forrest C. Pogue's "Wartime Diplomacy, 1941-1945," a strong essay appearing in

Richard D. Burns (ed.), *Guide to American Foreign Relations Since 1700* (Santa Barbara, Calif.: Clio Books, 1983), pp. 663-698.

262. Ambrose, Stephen E. "Applied Strategy of World War II." *Naval War College Review*, XXII (September 1970), 62-70.

Attacks the myth that America had only a military policy during the war and lacked a political one, pointing out that by V-J, the U.S. exerted pressure on or controlled four of the five major industrial areas of the world.

263. Armstrong, Anne. *Unconditional Surrender: The Impact of the Casablanca Policy Upon World War II*. New Brunswick, N.J.: Rutgers University Press, 1961. 304p.

A detailed view of the unconditional surrender concept as applied to the European war; the author, who first wrote her paper under this title as her 1961 Columbia University Ph.D. dissertation, examines the concept behind and the adoption of this policy, which she believes served to prolong the war by forcing an adverse German reaction.

264. Baldwin, Hanson. *Great Mistakes of the War*. New York: Harper, 1950. 114p.

A somewhat simplistic essay by a noted military critic which suggested that American leaders failed to keep their political goals in mind while waging the war and that the grand strategy adopted was wrong, particularly with regard to the unconditional surrender policy.

265. ———. "Invasion: The Five Great Problems." *New York Times Magazine* (May 14, 1944), 5-7+.

Baldwin here looks at the military-strategic considerations of an Anglo-American invasion of the continent, expressing many concerns then nearly, if not already, resolved by the planners at SHAPE.

266. Balfour, Michael. "Another Look at 'Unconditional Surrender.'" *International Affairs* (London), XLVI (October 1970), 719-736.

Like Armstrong and Baldwin, Balfour also finds much wrong with the policy, but bows to its political necessity in view of the Allied need to convince the Soviets of Western intentions.

267. ———. "The Origin of the Formula: 'Unconditional Surrender' in World War II." *Armed Forces and Society*, V (Winter 1979), 281-301.

Repeats somewhat the previous citation in thesis and emphasis, with additional attention to the "crusade" idea in U.S. history.

268. Beitzell, Robert E. *The Uneasy Alliance: America, Britain, and Russia, 1941-1943*. New York: Alfred A. Knopf, 1972. 404p.

Focusing on the Quebec, Moscow, Cairo, and Tehran conferences, Beitzell examines the official versions of the major negotiations with regard to the problem of grand strategy and the relationship of the major Allied powers as they fought the war and planned the peace. Accuses FDR of appeasing Stalin and fighting an unnecessary war.

269. Brady, Lawrence K. "Marshall's Strategy." *Army Quarterly and Defence Journal*, CIII (January 1972), 52-62.

A British view of Gen. Marshall's role in the creation of Allied strategy which is critical of the American for his perceived underestimation of the dynamic elements in Fascism and Soviet Communism.

270. Brewer, John C. "Lend-Lease: Foreign Policy Weapon in Politics and Diplomacy, 1941-1945." Unpublished Ph.D. dissertation, University of Texas at Austin, 1974.

A review of the use or threat of use of the flow of supplies from America to Europe as a political club by the Roosevelt administration to get its way on strategic matters.

271. Brinton, Irving B., Jr. *Buying Aircraft: Material Procurement for the Army Air Forces*. U.S. Army in World War II: Special Studies. Washington, D.C.: U.S. Government Printing Office, 1964. 625p.

Making up nearly a third of the wartime U.S. Army's purchases, aircraft production and its expansion was a major problem overcome from 1942 on.

272. Burns, James M. *Roosevelt: The Soldier of Freedom*. New York: Harcourt Brace Jovanovich, 1970. 722p.

Second of a two-volume work, this study focuses on FDR's wartime leadership; in warm and intimate detail, Burns shows the President to have been bold in idea and cautious in implementation, which led to serious repercussions in the world political arena.

273. Butler, James R.M., ed. *Grand Strategy*. History of the Second World War: United Kingdom Military Series. 6 vols. London: H.M. Stationery Office, 1956-1976.

Beginning in volume two covers the war with interpretations favorable to Britain, but not to an extent where bias overcomes value; this official history is unmatched by anything of this size produced in the United States except the Matloff volumes on coalition warfare in the Army's official series.

274. Chamberlain, William H. *America's Second Crusade*. Chicago: Henry Regnery, 1950. 372p. Rpr. 1962.

Analyzes the reasons behind America's entry into the war, and like Beitzell concludes that Roosevelt fought a needless conflict.

275. Cline, Ray S. *Washington Command Post: The Operations Division*. U.S. Army in World War II: The War Department. Washington, D.C.: U.S. Government Printing Office, 1951. 413p.

Useful on the development of coalition strategy between America and Britain, Cline's study considers the Army's Operations Division, that section charged with responsibility "in the strategic planning direction of operations in World War II."

276. Coakley, Robert W. "The Persian Corridor as a Route for Allied Aid to the U.S.S.R." In: Kent R. Greenfield, ed. *Command Decisions*. Washington, D.C.: U.S. Government Printing Office, 1960, pp. 225-253.

Considers relations with Iran, Russia, and Britain in the establishment and operation of the major route for Lend Lease aid to the Soviets.

277. Compton, James V. *The Swastika and the Eagle: Hitler, the United States, and the Origins of World War II*. Boston: Houghton Mifflin, 1967. 297p.

Examines Nazi policies and mistakes regarding the U.S. before the war and argues that evidence shows no German intention of attacking the Americans before Pearl Harbor.

278. Connery, Robert H. *The Navy and the Industrial Mobilization in World War II*. Princeton, N.J.: Princeton University Press, 1951. 527p.

A comprehensive review of the problems of the USN in its efforts to organize the acquisition of the huge amounts of war material required for its war effort.

279. Cuff, Robert D., and J.L. Granatstein. *Canadian-American Relations in Wartime: From the Great War to the Cold War*. Toronto, Canada: A.M. Hakkert, Ltd., 1965. 205p.

A review of the close wartime relations between Canada and her neighbor which nevertheless manages to find and discuss points of difference.

280. Dallek, Robert. *Franklin D. Roosevelt and American Foreign Policy, 1932-1945*. New York and London: Oxford University Press, 1979. 657p.

Finds Roosevelt purposeful and farsighted in the conduct of his prewar and wartime diplomacy and contends that he was the principal architect of the basic decisions by the Western allies for the war's prosecution.

281. ———, ed. *The Roosevelt Diplomacy and World War II*. New York: Holt, Rinehart and Winston, 1970. 125p.

A paperback anthology of readings designed for college students and drawn from the writings of well-known FDR scholars; a useful introduction to the various aspects of prewar and wartime diplomacy.

282. Davis, Vernon E. *The History of the Joint Chiefs of Staff in World War II*. 2 vols. Washington, D.C.: U.S. Government Printing Office, 1972.

Examines the creation of the JCS and its role in early and later Allied planning for the coalition war and the execution of its responsibilities in seeing that the agreed-upon plans were executed.

283. Deane, John R. *The Strange Alliance: The Story of Our Efforts at Wartime Cooperation with Russia*. New York: Viking Press, 1947. 344p.

U.S. secretary of the Combined Chiefs of Staff and head of a 1943 military mission to the U.S.S.R., Deane describes the strains in wartime collaboration and contends that the Soviets had no plans to cooperate with America during or after the conflict.

284. Divine, Robert A. *Roosevelt and World War II*. Baltimore, Md.: Johns Hopkins University Press, 1969. 107p.

By emphasizing FDR's pragmatism and realism, Divine's four essays challenge the usual interpretation of the President as an idealistic internationalist and show him as a conservative isolationist.

285. Dougherty, James J. *The Politics of Wartime Aid: American Economic Assistance to France and French North Africa, 1940-1946*. Contributions in American History, no. 7. Westport, Conn.: Greenwood Press, 1978. 264p.

Examines the decisions that led to the assistance program, the problems encountered by all the parties, and the long-range results of the U.S. help.

286. Dunn, Walter S. *Second Front Now--1943*. Tuscaloosa: University of Alabama Press, 1980. 318p.

Argues that the failure of the Western Allies to undertake D-Day before 1944 allowed Russia to end the war strongly placed in Central Europe; contends that the invasion of France should and could have been undertaken in 1943 had the landing forces been concentrated in England rather than being scattered around the Mediterranean.

287. Dziuban, Stanley W. *Military Relations Between the United States and Canada, 1939-1945*. U.S. Army in World War II: Western Hemisphere. Washington, D.C.: U.S. Government Printing Office, 1959. 432p.

A detailed account of the positive actions taken by the two neighbors to cast their collective resources into the effort to tip the scale against the Axis; compare with the Canadian sentiments expressed by Cuff and Granatstein cited above.

288. Eden, Anthony. *The Memoirs of Anthony Eden, Earl of Avon: The Reckoning*. Boston, Mass.: Houghton Mifflin, 1965. 716p.

Memoirs of the British Secretary of State for Foreign Affairs (1940-1945), which offer great insight into the men and events which dominated Allied diplomacy during the conflict.

289. Eisenhower, John S.D. *Allies: Pearl Harbor to D-Day*. Garden City, N.Y.: Doubleday, 1982. 500p.

Focuses on the human elements in the Anglo-American military alliance prior to Normandy, an integration which evolved into political and economic partnership; basing his work on an unfinished manuscript by his father, Eisenhower enhances the Supreme Commander's role by showing his resistance to British efforts to undercut U.S. interests while contributing to the maintenance of allied unity.

290. Elliott, Peter. "The Lend-Lease 'Captains.'" *Warship International*, IX (Fall 1972), 255-269.

On the transfer of 78 destroyer escorts to England in 1943-1945.

291. Emerson, William. "Franklin D. Roosevelt as Commander-in-Chief in World War II." *Military Affairs*, XXIV (Fall 1958), 181-207.

Suggests FDR was very sensitive to the political aspects of the war; controlled his military advisors and not the reverse, as sometimes charged; and planned his grand strategy on the basis of political motives.

292. Fabyanic, Thomas. "A Critique of U.S. Air War Planning, 1941-1944." Unpublished Ph.D. dissertation, St. Louis University, 1973.

An analysis of the work of the AAF Air War Plan Division and its concepts and ideas for fighting the large-scale air war in Europe.

293. Fehrenbach, T.R. *FDR's Undeclared War, 1939-1941*. New York: David McKay, 1967. 344p.

Concerned primarily with America's unneutral position toward Britain as opposed to the undeclared naval war with Germany; supporting Roosevelt's policy, the author illuminates the obstacles to it.

294. Feis, Herbert. *Churchill, Roosevelt, Stalin: The War They Waged and the Peace They Sought*. Princeton, N.J.: Princeton University Press, 1957. 692p.

Long the standard work on high-level World War II diplomacy, this chronological account focuses on the three leaders and pursues the complex tale of their conferences, diplomatic moves, and agreements from 1940 to 1945; still a valuable summary, even in the light of new sources and analyses.

294a. Fodor, Denis J. *The Neutrals*. World War II Series. Alexandria, Va.: Time-Life Books, 1983. 208p.

A review of the "unroles" of the neutral nations of Switzerland, Sweden, Spain, Turkey, and the Irish Republic in World War II, with emphasis on their policies toward the combatants, both Allied and Axis. Many of the hundreds of photographs herein were originally taken by *Life* Magazine photographers on the scene.

295. Friedlander, Saul. *Prelude to Downfall: Hitler and the United States, 1939-1941*. Translated from the French. New York: Alfred A. Knopf, 1967. 238p.

Based on research in German, British, and U.S. archives, this study, first published in France, traces the impact of American policy on German decision-making with emphasis on Roosevelt's dealings with Hitler in the period before and during the undeclared Atlantic naval war.

296. Funk, Arthur L. *Charles DeGaulle: The Crucial Years, 1943-1944*. Norman: University of Oklahoma Press, 1959. 336p.

Follows the Free French leader's attempts to establish a position for his country relative to the Big Three and his role at the Casablanca conference; an interesting account of DeGaulle at the North African summit can also be found in the account by the U.S. Counsel General there, Russell M. Brooks, in his "Casablanca--The French Side of the Fence," published in *U.S. Naval Institute Proceedings*, LXXVII (1951), 909-925.

297. Gaston, James C. *Planning the American Air War: Four Men and Nine Days in 1941--an Inside Narrative*. Washington, D.C.: National Defense University Press, 1982. 121p.

The August 1941 preparation of the strategy AWPD-1 by Colonels Harold George and Kenneth Walker and Majors Haywood Hansell and Laurence S. Kuter of the AAF's Air War Plans Division; compare with Fabyanic cited above and Hansell in our section on the strategic bombing campaign below (III:C:3).

298. Gavin, James M. "Back Door to Normandy: Airborne Plans and Counterplans for the Invasion of Europe." *Infantry Journal*, LIX (November 1946), 8-19.

The wartime boss of the U.S. 82nd Airborne Division here discusses the various plans for use of the Allied airborne divisions on D-Day, taking into account earlier, less successful operations and the chances of failure.

299. Goodhart, Philip. *Fifty Ships That Saved the World: The Foundation of the Anglo-American Alliance*. Garden City, N.Y.: Doubleday, 1965. 267p.

Examines the destroyers-for-bases deal between the U.S. and Britain in 1940 which shows how FDR oversold the value of the Newfoundland and Caribbean bases and Churchill overestimated the value of the old four-stacker escort ships.

300. Gormley, Daniel J. "From 'Accadia' to Casablanca: The Formation of a Military-Political Policy, December 1941-January 1943." Unpublished Ph.D. Dissertation, Georgetown University, 1978.

Analyzes the Anglo-American military and political relationship as it evolved from the FDR-Churchill meeting off Canada in 1941 through the North African landings in late 1942 showing the compromise and growing integration of staffs between the two allies.

301. Greenberg, Daniel S. "U.S. Destroyers for British Bases--50 Old Ships Go to War." *U.S. Naval Institute Proceedings*, LXXXVIII (November 1962), 70-83.

An examination of the 1940 "Destroyer Deal" which marked a distinct change in American policy toward the European conflict.

302. Greenfield, Kent R. *American Strategy in World War II: A Reconsideration*. Baltimore, Md.: Johns Hopkins University Press, 1963. 145p.

Although small, this title remains one of the most useful scholarly interpretations of U.S. war strategy, its formulation, controversy, and operation; among topics analyzed by the former Chief Historian of the Department of the Army are the Anglo-American strategic disputes, FDR's role as Commander in Chief, the role of airpower, and the basic differences between the U.S. and British military approaches to war. Among the best discussions is that of the weight and timing of the cross-channel attack against German forces in Normandy.

303. Grigg, John. *The Victory That Never Was*. New York: Hill and Wang, 1980. 254p.

Like Walter S. Dunn above, this British author advances the thesis that Allied forces could have successfully invaded France in 1943; the reason they did not, he contends, was the political decision-making process and bickering of Churchill and Roosevelt, including U.S. attention to the Pacific war.

304. Grow, Robert W. "The U.S. Military Mission with the Iranian Army." *Armored Cavalry Journal*, LVIII (March-April 1949), 24-26.

A brief review of Army work with the Shah's forces in 1943-1946, especially as they related to the expedition of Lend Lease goods to the Soviets.

305. Harrison, Donald F. "United States-Mexican Military Collaboration During World War II." Unpublished Ph.D. Dissertation, Georgetown University, 1976.

The only English-language study of the role of the U.S. in training and equipping Mexican military forces and the role our southern neighbor was expected to play in Western Hemisphere defense and on foreign battlefields.

306. Hewitt, Henry K. "Planning 'Operation Anvil Dragoon.'" *U.S. Naval Institute Proceedings*, LXXX (July 1954), 730-745.

The American naval boss of the southern France landing describes the reason for the invasion and the intricate planning that went into it.

307. Higgins, Trumbull. "The Problems of a Second Front: An Interpretation of Coalition Strategy Before and During the Turning Point of the Second World War." Unpublished Ph.D. Dissertation, Princeton University, 1952.

This dissertation forms the basis for the author's two books cited below.

308. ———. "The Anglo-American Historians' War in the Mediterranean, 1942-1945." *Military Affairs*, XXXIV (Fall 1970), 84-88.

A balanced and comprehensive review of the dispute between U.S. and British historians, and among historians in England and America, over the British approach to victory via the Mediterranean vs. the American desire for a cross-channel attack.

309. ———. *Soft Underbelly: The Anglo-American Controversy Over the Italian Campaign, 1939-1945*. New York: Macmillan, 1968. 275p.

Complementing the next entry, this work evaluates British aims and methods in the Italian campaign and the long-lasting dispute over the Channel vs. Mediterranean path to victory; Higgins comes down hard on Churchill and the entire British desire for victory via the Middle Sea.

310. ———. *Winston Churchill and the Second Front, 1940-1943*. New York and London: Oxford University Press, 1957. 281p.

Complementing the preceding entry, this title examines British ideas for northern Europe and the dispute over the Channel vs. Mediterranean approach waged between U.S. and British planners; again, Churchill's position is criticized as is the entire compromise strategy which emerged, one which allowed for both an Italian campaign and a Channel landing.

311. Howard, Michael. *The Mediterranean Strategy in the Second World War*. New York: Praeger, 1968. 83p.

A slim analysis of the British idea for a Balkan invasion which suggests that Italy was chosen for invasion as the Allies needed an "easy" theater after North Africa and could not allow their momentum in Europe to cease.

312. Jackson, William G.F. *Overlord--Normandy, 1944*. Policy and Strategy of the Second World War Series. Newark: University of Delaware Press, 1980. 250p.

Focuses on the arguments and controversies at the highest Allied and German levels and on the questions of both offensive and defensive misplanning; wonders what might have happened if the Allies had moved into the Balkans at the same time they invaded France.

313. Kecskemeti, Paul. *Strategic Surrender: The Politics of Victory and Defeat*. Stanford, Calif.: Stanford University Press, 1958. 287p.

An analysis of the unconditional surrender policy of the Allies with four case studies (France, Italy, and Germany in Europe) seeking to find that point at which it was clear to all concerned that the war was lost.

314. Kimball, Warren F. "Churchill and Roosevelt: The Personal Equation." *Prologue*, VI (Fall 1974), 169-182.

After a review of their correspondence, Kimball finds that relations between the Prime Minister and the President were usually amicable, but where disagreements existed, they were fundamental.

315. ———. *The Most Unsordid Act: Lend-Lease, 1939-1941.* Baltimore, Md.: Johns Hopkins University Press, 1969. 281p.

An analysis of the U.S. legislative process relating to the enactment of the legislation and the roles and concerns of foreign and domestic participants in the intricate maneuvering required.

316. ———, ed. *Churchill and Roosevelt: "A Righteous Comradeship"--Their Complete Correspondence, 1939-1945.* Princeton, N.J.: Princeton University Press, 1981.

A complete compilation of the wartime correspondence between the British and U.S. leaders which shows that their attention was turned to postwar planning after mid-1943; includes some interpretative essays and headnotes.

317. Kuter, Laurence S. *Airman at Yalta.* New York: Duell, Sloane and Pearce, 1956. 180p.

The Assistant Chief of Plans of the AAF sat in for Gen. Arnold at Yalta; while recounting the main facts of the conference, he devotes a large portion of his volume to contrasting the AAF view of the war with those held by leaders of the U.S. Army and Navy.

318. Langer, William L. *Our Vichy Gamble.* Hamden, Conn.: Archon Books, 1965. 412p.

First published in 1947, this history examines U.S. relations with and opportunistic policy toward the collaborationist Vichy French government from 1940 to "Operation Torch," listing somewhat unconvincing reasons for the approach taken.

319. Lash, Joseph P. *Roosevelt and Churchill, 1939-1941: The Partnership That Saved the West.* New York: W.W. Norton, 1976. 528p.

A White House resident during the Roosevelt era, Lash paints a fascinating picture of FDR's path to intervention and the evolution of the hesitantly begun cooperation between the U.S. and Britain.

320. Leahy, William D. *I Was There: The Personal Story of the Chief of Staff to Presidents Roosevelt and Truman, Based on His Notes and Diaries Made at the Time.* New York: Whittlesay House, McGraw-Hill, 1950. 527p.

In early 1942, FDR appointed this former Admiral, CNO, and Ambassador to Vichy France as his personal chief-of-staff; from his vantage point, Leahy recounts day-to-day activities and reacts to those planning and diplomatic events in which he participated.

321. Leighton, Richard M. "OVERLORD Revisited: An Interpretation of American Strategy in the European War, 1942-1944." *American Historical Review*, LXVIII (Fall 1963), 919-937.

A major reinterpretation which contends that U.S. strategy in the E.T.O. was not that different from Britain's; the policy of both, he argues, was peripheral, flexible, and pragmatic.

322. ———. "OVERLORD Versus the Mediterranean at the Cairo-Tehran Conference." In: Kent R. Greenfield, ed. *Command Decisions*. Washington, D.C.: Department of the Army, Office of the Chief of Military History, 1960, pp. 255-285.

A review of the controversy between England and America over the merits of invading France in 1943, a discussion which led to a compromise agreement to invade Sicily-Italy instead.

323. ———. "The Planning for Sicily." *U.S. Naval Institute Proceedings*, LXXXVIII (January 1962), 90-101.

To a large extent, a repetition of the previous citation with some additional attention to the military requirements of "Husky."

324. Leutze, James R. *Bargaining for Supremacy: Anglo-American Naval Collaboration, 1937-1941*. Chapel Hill: University of North Carolina Press, 1977. 266p.

The work recounts four years of diplomatic sparring in which the Europe-first strategy of America was allowed to gain the upper hand, making the U.S. the major Atlantic power and the USN the chief naval force.

325. ———. "Technology and Bargaining in Anglo-American Naval Relations, 1938-1946." *U.S. Naval Institute Proceedings*, CIII (June 1977), 50-66.

Examines the stumbling blocks placed by those who did not accept the Churchill-Roosevelt agreements for the free exchange of technical data between the two allies.

326. Lewis, John M. "Franklin Roosevelt and United States Strategy in Workd War II." Unpublished Ph.D. Dissertation, Cornell University, 1978.

A careful review of the role played by the President in the direct and indirect formulation of American military strategy.

327. Loewenheim, Francis L., Harold D. Langley, and Manfred Jones, eds. *Roosevelt and Churchill: Their Secret Wartime Correspondence*. New York: Saturday Review Press, 1975. 805p.

Preceded by three chapters describing the two leaders' relationship, this anthology prints 548 documents out of 1,700 messages and letters between them, the majority of a military nature; the work is arranged chronologically from September 1939 to April 1945 and contains extensive footnotes to identify persons referred to.

328. Longmate, Norman. *The G.I.'s: The Americans in Britain, 1942-1945.* New York: Scribners, 1975. 416p.

A BBC journalist who experienced the Yank influx captures, through anecdotal stories, the collision of the two cultures, their mutual correction of misconceptions, and gradual blending.

329. McCann, Frank D., Jr. "Brazil, the United States, and World War II: A Commentary." *Diplomatic History*, III (Winter 1979), 59-76.

Distilled from the next citation.

330. ———. *The Brazilian-American Alliance, 1937-1945.* Princeton, N.J.: Princeton University Press, 1973. 527p.

A thoroughly researched account of the mutually advantageous political-military-economic developments which fostered the close ties evidenced during the war years.

331. Macmillan, Harold. *The Blast of War, 1939-1945.* New York: Harper & Row, 1968. 623p.

Britain's chief political advisor in the Mediterranean details decisions and actions in that theater from Africa to Italy; following Churchill's views, Macmillan, who later became England's Prime Minister, chides the Americans for their policy toward Gen. Giraud and the undertaking of "Operation Anvil" in southern France.

332. Matloff, Maurice. "Franklin D. Roosevelt as War Leader." In: Harry L. Coles, ed. *Total War and Cold War: Problems in Civilian Control of the Military.* Columbus: Ohio State University Press, 1962, pp. 42-65.

A balanced assessment which justifies FDR's policies, particularly unconditional surrender, but criticizes him for underestimating Soviet ambitions and the postwar repercussions of wartime military decisions.

333. ———. "Prewar Military Plans and Preparations, 1939-1941." *U.S. Naval Institute Proceedings*, LXXIX (July 1953), 740-748.

A preamble to the following works which trace the growing American preparation, especially naval, for the possibility of entering the conflict.

334. ———, and Edwin M. Snell. *Strategic Planning for Coalition Warfare, 1941-1944.* U.S. Army in World War II: The War Department. 2 vols. Washington, D.C.: U.S. Government Printing Office, 1953-1959.

A comprehensive accounting of U.S. strategic planning, within the context of the Grand Alliance, from the pre-Pearl Harbor days to the final international conference; the first volume concentrates on defensive planning and the second on offensive planning.

335. Meyer, Leo. "The Decision to Invade North Africa ('Torch')." In: Kent R. Greenfield, ed. *Command Decisions*. Washington, D.C.: Department of the Army, Office of the Chief of Military History, 1960, pp. 173-198.

Meyer examines why the Allies chose to invade Vichy Africa in an essay the main thoughts of which were later much expanded upon by others, especially the need to put U.S. soldiers into ground action in Europe as quickly as possible for political reasons.

336. Morgan, Frederick E. *Overture to Overlord*. Garden City, N.Y.: Doubleday, 1950. 302p.

The author, deputy chief-of-staff at SHAEF, provides valuable insights into the planning of the cross-channel attack; many of the ideas which his planning group proposed were incorporated into the final plan, and this is a fair evaluation of British and American contributions to that great D-Day undertaking.

337. Morison, Samuel Eliot. *Strategy and Compromise*. Boston, Mass.: Little, Brown, 1958. 120p.

A brief and brisk review of Allied strategy which stresses differences between the Western allies and criticizes their compromises without offering possible alternatives.

338. Morton, Louis. "Germany First." In: Kent R. Greenfield, ed. *Command Decisions*. Washington, D.C.: Department of the Army, Office of the Chief of Military History, 1960, pp. 11-47.

Follows the 1921-1941 basic development of U.S. strategy which provided that, in any war with enemies in both Europe and Asia, those in Europe, especially Germany, should be defeated first as they were likely to be the most technologically advanced.

339. Motter, T.H. Vail. *The Persian Corridor and Aid to Russia*. U.S. Army in World War II: The Middle East Theater. Washington, D.C.: U.S. Government Printing Office, 1952. 545p.

The official account of the Lend-Lease pipeline to Russia via Iran which provides full details of the difficulties encountered in cooperation with not only the Shah's people, but also the British and Soviets.

340. Murphy, Robert D. *Diplomat Among Warriors*. Garden City, N.Y.: Doubleday, 1964. 470p.

The well-written reminiscences of FDR's representative in North Africa (1942-1943) and Eisenhower's political advisor in northwest Europe, which relate events in which he participated, especially as they related to the invasions of North Africa, Italy, and France-Germany and the diplomacy of coordinating those events with the British and Free or Vichy French.

341. ———. "'Operation Torch.'" *Foreign Service Journal*, XLIV (November 1967), 28-31, 53.

Reviews the author's role in the political deal with Darlan which made the invasion a success.

342. Nelson, Donald M. *Arsenal of Democracy: The Story of American War Production*. New York: Harcourt, Brace, 1946. 439p.

The chairman of the U.S. War Production Board describes the nations' achievement in supplying its own and the needs of the Allies and the difficulties involved in converting America from a peace to war economy.

343. Nelson, James, ed. *General Eisenhower on the Military Churchill*. New York: W.W. Norton, 1970. 96p.

In a conversation with Alistair Cooke, Eisenhower reminisces about his wartime relationship with the British Prime Minister, particularly the latter's constant interest or interference in military matters.

344. Norman, Albert. *Operation Overlord, Design and Reality: The Allied Invasion of Western Europe*. Harrisburg, Pa.: Military Service Publishing Co., 1952. 230p.

An analysis of the problems in diplomacy, strategy, and military preparation behind the D-Day landings first presented that year as the author's Clark University Ph.D. Dissertation, "The Allied Invasion of Northwestern Europe: Design and Reality, 1940-1944."

345. O'Connor, Raymond G. *Diplomacy for Victory: FDR and Unconditional Surrender*. New York: W.W. Norton, 1971. 143p.

A brief summary of the controversial Casablanca-announced policy which concludes that it was an intelligent approach which offered a convenient manner for avoiding inter-Allied disharmony over political issues while getting about the business of fighting the war against Germany and Japan.

346. Oldfield, Barney. "'Operation Eclipse.'" *Aerospace Historian*, XV (Summer 1968), 52-53+.

347. ———. "A 'Might-Have-Been': 'Operation Eclipse.'" *Armed Forces Journal International*, CXIII (May 1976), 20+.

These basically similar articles provide details on the proposed Western Allied airborne assault on Berlin planned for early spring 1945.

348. Pendar, Kenneth W. *Adventure in Diplomacy: Our French Dilemma*. New York: Dodd, Mead, 1945. 280p.

Considers the difficulties faced by the U.S. politically in dealing first with Darlan and then with DeGaulle.

349. Pogue, Forrest C. "Political Problems of a Coalition Command." In: Harry L. Coles, ed. *Total War and Cold War: Problems in Civilian Control of the Military.* Columbus: Ohio State University Press, 1962, pp. 108-128.

Considers Eisenhower's difficult job of counteracting Allied personal and national pride and political interests within his SHAEF command.

350. ———. "SHAEF: A Retrospect on Coalition Command." *Journal of Modern History*, XXIII (December 1951), 329-335.

Reviews the difficulties and progress made under Eisenhower's leadership in welding a coordinated command composed of diverse officers from both Britain and America.

351. ———. *The Supreme Command.* U.S. Army in World War II: European Theater of Operations. Washington, D.C.: U.S. Government Printing Office, 1954. 607p.

A detailed examination of the activities and structure of the Supreme Headquarters, Allied Expeditionary Forces which devotes about a third to planning and organization for D-Day and the remainder to issues and events following the landing to VE-Day; details are provided on the German leaders and command system to provide a contrast between the Allied and enemy command systems.

352. Randall, L.V. *Bridgehead to Victory: Plans for the Invasion of Europe.* Garden City, N.Y.: Doubleday, Doran, 1943. 183p.

Presents various proposals for the liberation of Europe and considers not only possible landing sites but the necessary factors of manpower, air- and naval-power.

353. Riess, Curt. *The Invasion of Germany.* New York: Putnam, 1943. 206p.

Suggests possible ways in which Germany might be captured once her troops are cleared from western and southern Europe.

354. Roberts, Martha B. "Reluctant Belligerent: The United States Enters World War II." *American History Illustrated*, XVII (November 1982), 20-29.

An illustrated review of the diplomatic and military background of U.S. entry into the conflict with emphasis on the diplomacy between England and the U.S. government and the undeclared naval war in the Atlantic.

355. Russett, Bruce M. *No Clear and Present Danger: A Skeptical View of the United States Entry into World War II.* New York: Harper & Row, 1972. 111p.

A major revisionist view that argues that the Axis posed no threat to the U.S. in 1941, that American participation in the war had little effect on its outcome, and that Roosevelt could have kept the country aloof from the fighting, supplying arms to England and Russia.

356. Sainsbury, Keith. *The North African Landings, 1942: A Strategic Decision.* Politics and Strategy of the Second World War Series. Cranbury, N.J.: University of Delaware Press, 1981. 216p.

Examines the delay in the Soviet-desired opening of a second front in 1942, the long arguments between Washington and London as to a proper strategy, and, once the decision was made for North Africa, the Anglo-American difficulties in dealing with Vichy leaders prior to the landings.

357. ———. "'Second Front in 1942': Anglo-American Differences over Strategy." *British Journal of International Studies*, IV (Spring 1978), 47-58.

Assesses disagreements between the Anglo-U.S. strategists over the proposed assaults codenamed "Sledgehammer" and "Round-up," both of which would have put the Western Allies ashore in France long before "Overlord."

358. Sas, Anthony. "Military Campaigns--Strategy in the Mediterranean." *Military Review*, XLVI (October 1966), 3-7.

Reviews the Anglo-American differences over which targets to assault in the months following the Tunisian victory.

359. Sayre, Joel. *Persian Gulf Command: Some Marvels on the Road to Kajvin.* New York: Random House, 1945. 140p.

Describes the trials and accomplishments of the Persian Gulf Command, that U.S. Army group charged with getting Lend Lease material to Russia via Iran; includes many anecdotes and a history of Iranian politics. Compare with T.H. Vail Motter's official history cited above.

360. Sherwen, Douglas S. *The Persian Corridor: The Little-Known Story of the Signal Corps in the Middle East During World War II.* Hicksville, N.Y.: Exposition Press, 1979. 232p.

Examines the work of the Signal Corps in setting up the communications network necessary to expedite the flow of U.S. Lend Lease aid to the Soviets; the author was a member of the 883rd Signal Service Company, U.S. Army, in Iran.

361. Sherwood, Robert E. *Roosevelt and Hopkins: An Intimate History.* Rev. ed. New York: Harper, 1950. 1,002p.

The author, a friend of both FDR and Harry Hopkins, explains the relationship between the President and his advisor and the role of the latter in the formulation of the grand coalition between the Big Three, among which he served as Roosevelt's liaison.

362. Smith, Gaddis. *American Diplomacy During the Second World War, 1941-1945.* New York: John Wiley, 1965. 194p.

A review of the policies, problems, and events in U.S. wartime diplomacy from the viewpoint of what American leaders thought significant at the time.

363. Snell, John L. *Illusion and Necessity: The Diplomacy of Global War, 1939-1945*. Boston, Mass.: Houghton Mifflin, 1963. 229p.

A compact, generally well-rounded survey of diplomacy worldwide, which compares the policies of the major powers and reveals the mixture of illusion and reality which governed their interactions.

364. Speer, Albert. *Inside the Third Reich: Memoirs*. Translated from the German. New York: Macmillan, 1970. 596p.

Reminiscences of Hitler's architect and minister of war production which provide intimate portraits of the Nazi hierarchy and, more important to this guide, a look at German perceptions of Allied military successes.

365. Stathis, Stephen W. "Malta: Prelude to Yalta." *Presidential Studies Quarterly*, IX (Fall 1979), 469-482.

Yielding to Churchill's demands, FDR agreed to a meeting of the chiefs of staff on Malta in January 1945 prior to the Yalta Conference; lest Stalin be antagonized, only military matters such as the Rhine crossing were discussed.

366. Steele, Richard W. *The First Offensive, 1942: Roosevelt, Marshall, and the Making of American Strategy*. Bloomington: Indiana University Press, 1973. 182p.

The 1942 strategic debate within the American command system and between the U.S. and Britain is examined; Steele finds that political factors outweighed military ones at the top and that General George Marshall's 1942 cross-channel plan conflicted with FDR's on political grounds.

367. ———. "Political Aspects of American Military Planning, 1941-1942." *Military Affairs*, XXXV (April 1971), 68-74.

Considers the debate over North Africa as outlined in the previous citation as well as the never-effected cross-channel invasion of 1943, Operation "Bolero-Roundup."

368. Stettinius, Edward R. *Lend Lease, Weapon for Victory*. New York: Macmillan, 1944. 358p.

A contemporary look at the Lend Lease program by its administrator, who believed that its monetary value was offset by the contributions of the Allies in blood on the battlefield; explains the origins and progress of the program from 1940 to publication date and gives an accounting of whom it assisted. Includes a variety of photographs, charts, and epigrams.

369. Stoller, Mark A. *The Politics of the Second Front: American Military Planning and Diplomacy in Coalition Warfare, 1941-1943*. Westport, Conn.: Greenwood Press, 1977. 244p.

First presented as the author's 1971 University of Wisconsin Ph.D. Dissertation, this title centers on the diplomatic dispute between England and America and contends that FDR's domestic situation called for the early opening of such a front while

Britain wanted the Mediterranean-Middle East secure for future economic goals; argues that U.S. military leaders did not ignore the politics of coalition warfare, did want to defeat Germany first, but did not want other national interests, such as the Pacific war, to suffer meanwhile.

370. ———. "The 'Second Front' and American Fear of Soviet Expansion, 1941-1943." *Military Affairs*, XXXIX (October 1975), 136-141.

Contends the U.S. pushed the cross-channel assault over the British Mediterranean position as a way of both aiding and blocking the Soviets and explains how in 1943 Washington drew up three "Rankin" plans to insure the presence of U.S. forces in a defeated Germany. The Soviets long believed the capitalist British and American allies were slow in opening a second front due to their desire to see the Nazis and Russians bleed each other, a charge made most specifically in V. Sekistov's "Why the Second Front Was Not Opened in 1943," which appeared in the English-language version of *Soviet Military Review*, no. 8 (August 1972), 50-52.

371. Strange, Joseph L. "The British Rejection of 'Operation Sledgehammer': An Alternative Motive." *Military Affairs*, XLVI (February 1982), 6-14.

Suggests the British wanted to proceed through the Mediterranean because their army simply could not suffer the losses the emergency cross-channel attack plan called for.

372. Strange, Russell P. "The Atlantic Conference: The First Roosevelt-Churchill Meeting." *U.S. Naval Institute Proceedings*, LXXIX (April 1953), 388-397.

Describes events surrounding the meeting of the two leaders aboard warships in the North Atlantic in 1941, including FDR's visit aboard H.M.S. *Prince of Wales*.

373. Trefousse, Hans L. *Germany and American Neutrality, 1939-1941*. New York: Octagon Books, 1969. 247p.

First published by Bookman Associates in 1951, this work argues that Hitler did, indeed, seek the domination of the U.S. under a time-table of U.S.-German neutrality, but FDR's refusal to be frightened forced the Fuehrer to advance the timing of his attempted subjugation.

374. United States. Department of State. *The Conference at Cairo and Tehran, 1943*. Washington, D.C.: U.S. Government Printing Office, 1961. 932p.

375. ———. ———. *The Conference at Quebec, 1944*. Washington, D.C.: U.S. Government Printing Office, 1972. 527p.

376. ———. ———. *The Conference at Washington and Quebec, 1943*. Washington, D.C.: U.S. Government Printing Office, 1970. 1,382p.

377. ———. ———. *The Conference at Washington, 1941-1942, and Casablanca, 1943.* Washington, D.C.: U.S. Government Printing Office, 1970. 1,382p.

These four volumes contain the official records of the conferences named as well as archival material relating to political and military decisions taken at them.

378. Vigneras, Marcel. *Rearming the French.* U.S. Army in World War II: Special Studies. Washington, D.C.: U.S. Government Printing Office, 1957. 444p.

Outlines the discussions between Roosevelt and Giraud at Casablanca and the later negotiations between French representatives and the War Department on arms and reviews the process whereby the U.S. aid to the Free French resulted in the resurgence of a historic ally.

379. Viorst, Milton. *Hostile Allies: FDR and Charles DeGaulle.* New York: Macmillan, 1965. 280p.

Focuses on the wartime relationship between the two leaders and stresses that their differences came not so much from personality clashes as from opposing viewpoints on national interests; includes considerable commentary on DeGaulle's rise and the failure of the U.S. to break off its dealings with Vichy leaders.

380. *The War Against Hitler: Military Strategy in the West.* New York: Hippocrene Books, 1983. 273p.

An overview of Allied operations in Africa, Italy, and Northwest Europe taken from the pages of *Strategy and Tactics* magazine; based on secondary sources, this title neglects sea and air operations but does provide some preliminary background on the strategy behind the land campaigns.

381. Watson, Mark S. *Chief of Staff: Prewar Plans and Preparations.* U.S. Army in World War II: The War Department. Washington, D.C.: U.S. Government Printing Office, 1950. 551p.

Examines the Army and General Marshall's response to U.S. unpreparedness in the years immediately preceding Pearl Harbor; surveys prewar training, rearmament, strategic planning, and covert coordination with Great Britain.

382. Weigley, Russell F. "The Strategic Tradition of U.S. Grant: Strategists of the European War." In: his *The American Way of War: A History of United States Military Strategy and Policy.* New York: Macmillan, 1973, pp. 312-362.

A review of the U.S. strategy for fighting the war in Europe which argues that Civil War strategies, aimed at eliminating enemy men and materiel, led to a history of "unconditional surrender" thinking which persisted through World War II.

383. Werner, Max, pseud. *Attack Can Win in '43.* Boston, Mass.: Little, Brown, 1943. 216p.

Asserts that 1943 was the decisive year for Allied action against the Axis and contends that a second front in 1943 was necessary before Germany grew stronger.

384. Wilson, Theodore A. *The First Summit: Roosevelt and Churchill at Placentia Bay, 1941*. Boston, Mass.: Houghton Mifflin, 1969. 344p.

First presented as the author's 1967 Indiana University Ph.D. dissertation, "The Meeting at Argentia," this work is a comprehensive account of the Atlantic Conference, the style and negotiations of its participants, and the birth of the Atlantic Charter.

385. Woodward, Ernest Llewelyn. *British Foreign Policy in the Second World War*. 5 vols. London: H.M. Stationery Office, 1970-1976.

A chronologically arranged review of British foreign policy (1939-1945) as seen from and conducted by the Foreign Office; carefully avoids criticism of British policy and serves as a helpful source for those who would understand our ally's position on the various matters of coalition strategy.

B. INTELLIGENCE AND RELATED ACTIVITIES

Introduction: Interest in the intelligence aspects of World War II has enjoyed a considerable boost over the past decade by the revelation of the Anglo-American communications--or signal--process codenamed "Ultra." This spectacular form of information gathering was not, however, the only major facet of "the game" to gain new emphasis as histories of human espionage efforts by the U.S. Office of Strategic Services (O.S.S.) and military deception/concealment came from the presses. The sources in this part consider the various aspects of intelligence as it related to the American war effort in Europe, as well as such related subjects as support for resistance movements, military concealment, and prisoner of war experiences. For additional insight into these topics, readers should consult the various bibliographies noted in the opening part of this guide, I:A.

386. Alcorn, Robert H. *No Banners, No Bands: More Tales of the OSS*. New York: David McKay, 1965. 275p.

A former officer in the OSS writes about spies and saboteurs who operated behind German lines in Italy, Norway, and France; sequel to the next title.

387. ———. *No Bugles for Spies: Tales of the OSS*. New York: David McKay, 1962.

A popular history of various OSS espionage and sabotage operations in both the European and Far Eastern theaters; presents a flattering picture of OSS boss General "Wild Bill" Donovan.

388. Alsop, Stewart J.O., and Thomas Braden. *Sub Rosa: The OSS and American Espionage.* New York: Harcourt, Brace, 1964. 264p.

First published in 1946, this is an exciting journalistic account of the organizing of resistance groups, sabotage, spying, and parachute jumps which offers little analysis and is much more "gung ho" in its coverage than Alcorn above.

389. Ambrose, Stephen E. "Eisenhower and the Intelligence Community in World War II." *Journal of Contemporary History*, XVI (January 1981), 153-166.

Examines the extent to which the Supreme Commander was involved with and sponsored the various intelligence operations which operated in the European Theater during the war.

390. ———. "Eisenhower, the Intelligence Community, and the D-Day Invasion." *Wisconsin Magazine of History*, LXIV (Summer 1981), 261-277.

Similar in content to the previous citation with special emphasis on those aspects of intelligence surrounding the Normandy invasion.

391. ———. *Ike's Spies: Eisenhower and the Espionage Establishment.* Garden City, N.Y.: Doubleday, 1981. 368p.

The author traces Eisenhower's involvement with intelligence gathering and covert operations from his discovery of Ultra and his handling of the Darlan affair during his Supreme Commander period through his approval of the U-2 operations during his presidency.

392. Babington-Smith, Constance. *Air Spy: The Story of Photo Intelligence in World War II.* New York: Harper, 1957. 266p.

Recounts the role of photo intelligence, particularly that sponsored by the British for whom the author worked, in the European Theater, including that surrounding the Normandy invasion and the battle against Hitler's V-weapons.

393. Baldwin, Hanson W. "The Battle of the Bulge as a Case History: Battlefield Intelligence." *U.S. Army Combat Forces Journal*, III (February 1953), 30-41.

Comments on the reasons behind the German success in the 1944 Battle of the Ardennes and the reasons why U.S. Army intelligence failed to learn of the counteroffensive before it happened.

394. Barber, Charles H. "Some Problems of Air Intelligence." *Military Review*, XXVI (August 1946), 76-78.

A brief review of some of the problems arising in World War II Europe in the processing of intelligence data related to the strategic bombing campaign.

395. Bell, Ernest L. *An Initial View of Ultra as an American Weapon.* Keene, N.H.: T.S.U. Press, 1977. 110p.

A lithographed typescript produced from as much of three Ultra-related documents as the author was able on Freedom-of-Information Act appeals to get the National Security Agency to declassify: (1) an order on American use of Ultra in the ETO signed by General Marshall on March 15, 1944; (2) the "Synthesis of Experiences in the Use of Ultra Intelligence by U.S. Army Field Commands in the European Theater of Operations"; and (3) "Use of CX/MSS Ultra by the United States War Department."

396. Bennett, Ralph. "Ultra and Some Command Decisions." *Journal of Contemporary History*, XVI (January 1981), 131-151.

A review of the impact of the signal intelligence on the decisions of certain field commanders, including General Patton.

397. ———. *Ultra in the West: The Normandy Campaign, 1944-1945.* New York: Scribners, 1979. 336p.

Illuminates the role of Ultra in the Allied campaigns in Northwest Europe from before Normandy until victory, and claims, among other points, that the Allies had foreknowledge of the German panzer divisions near Arnhem before the launching of "Operation Market-Garden." The author served on the staff of Hut 3 at Bletchley Park during 1944-1945 decoding the messages which are at the heart of his narrative.

398. Blumenson, Martin. "Will Ultra Rewrite History?" *Army*, XXVIII (August 1978), 42-48.

A noted American military historian's assessment of the revelation of the signal intelligence coup; contends that some reputations may change slightly.

399. Boyle, Robert D. "History of Photo Reconnaissance in North Africa, Including My Experiences with the 3rd Photo Group." Unpublished Ph.D. Dissertation, University of Texas at Austin, 1949.

A personal reminiscence of the dangers involved in flying unarmed aircraft over enemy lines on photo reconnaissance runs and the value of the work of his group to the successful prosecution of the North African conflict from November 1942 to May 1943; it is somewhat surprising that this has not yet been published commercially.

400. Brill, C.B.F. "Camouflage in 'Operation Flashpoint.'" *Military Engineer*, XLII (July-August 1950), 260-264.

A discussion of the concealment of bridges and embarkation points during the Allied crossing of the Rhine in March 1945.

401. Calvocoressi, Peter. *Top Secret Ultra.* New York: Pantheon Books, 1980. 132p.

A participant in the Bletchley Park operation, the author tells of the beginning, growth, and use of Ultra; note especially the final two chapters where the writer concludes that this signal intelligence was sometimes peripheral, often supportive, and occasionally decisive.

402. Campbell, Rodney. *The Luciano Project: The Secret Wartime Collaboration of the Mafia and the U.S. Navy*. New York: McGraw-Hill, 1977. 299p.

This account, based on the 1954 New York investigation headed by William Herlands, tells of how the Mafia, working from its New York waterfront base, helped the Navy protect the northeast coast against Nazi saboteurs and suggests that the Sicilian arm of the Mafia helped pave the way for the 1943 "Husky" invasion.

403. Carey, Arthur T. *The Effect of Ultra on the World War II North African Campaign*. Study Project. Carlisle Barracks, Pa.: U.S. Army War College, 1982. 62p.

A study of how the Allies made use of the signal data in seven key ways which shows that both errors and excellence were shown in its handling; concludes that the best of intelligence is no substitute for good command strategy and tactics.

404. Caskey, Edward A. "Baloney Barrage." *Infantry Journal*, LXV (December 1949), 20-23.

The use of psychological warfare in the U.S. Army attack on Geilenkirchen, Germany, in November 1944.

405. Cave-Brown, Anthony. *Bodyguard of Lies*. New York: Harper & Row, 1975. 947p.

Examines the Anglo-American intelligence, counterintelligence, deception, and various clandestine activities aimed at Germany after 1942 all leading up to "Operation Bodyguard," the huge scheme designed to mislead the Nazis as to the location and timing of the Normandy invasion; a noted and controversial source--the first to back up Winterbotham's account of Ultra--which should be checked against later works.

406. ———, ed. *The Secret War Report of the O.S.S.* New York: Berkley Publishing Co., 1976. 572p.

Prepared in 1946-1948 and declassified in 1976, the first 2 chapters describe the structure and organization of the Office of Strategic Services while the remaining 19 detail its operations around the world.

407. Coles, Harry L., and Albert K. Weinberg. *Civil Affairs: Soldiers Become Governors*. U.S. Army in World War II: Special Studies. Washington, D.C.: U.S. Government Printing Office, 1964. 930p.

The only documentary volume in the Army series, this work illustrates the evolution of civil affairs policy in the U.S. and its application in the Mediterranean and European Theaters before the surrender of Germany.

408. Collier, Basil. *Hidden Weapons: Allied Secret or Undercover Services in World War II*. North Pomfret, Vt., and London: David and Charles, 1982. 386p.

A review of the work of the American OSS and British Special Operations Executive in Europe which employs the latest declassified information.

409. Collier, Richard. *Ten Thousand Eyes*. New York: E.P. Dutton, 1958. 320p.

Looks at how the Free French intelligence service under Col. André Dewavrin ran and coordinated the work of 10,000 French civilian "amateur" spies who gathered bits and pieces of data on German defenses during the two years prior to D-Day.

410. Colvin, Ian G. *The Unknown Courier*. London: Kimber, 1953. 208p.

Major Martin, "the man who never was"; Colvin's book, a breach of the British Official Secrets Act, resulted in the publication of Edwin Montagu's title, cited below.

411. Cotton, F. Barrows. "How We Fight with Photographs." *National Geographic Magazine*, LXXXVI (September 1944), 257-280.

A contemporary report on the wartime uses of photography in intelligence and invasion preparation; illustrated.

412. Creal, Richard. "The History of Reconaissance in World War II." *Tactical Air Reconnaissance Digest*, II (February 1968), 14-18.

A brief overview of the work of the AAF photo recon squadrons around the world; illustrated.

413. Cruickshank, Charles. *Deception in World War II*. London and New York: Oxford University Press, 1979. 248p.

Using previously classified documents and photographs, the author reveals the story of the brilliant successes and pathetic failures of deception strategy used by the Allies to mislead the enemy about the invasions of North Africa and Normandy; offers much detail on how this practice, when employed with the work of the XX Committee as described by Masterman below, created a grand tactic of confusion.

414. Downes, Donald. *The Scarlet Thread: Adventures in Wartime Espionage*. London: Derek Verschoyle, 1973. 207p.

A wartime OSS agent recalls his activities in North Africa and Italy, as well as his work as a trainer of spies.

415. Edwards, Morris O. "A Case Study of Military Government in Germany During and After World War II." Unpublished Ph.D. Dissertation, Georgetown University, 1956.

Examines the practices before the German defeat and after; compare with Coles and Weinberg, cited above.

416. Farago, Ladislas. *Burn After Reading: The Espionage History of World War II*. New York: Walker, 1961. 319p.

A popular and by now dated general account of wartime espionage around the world which is concerned with telling the stories of the work of national intelligence bureaus, such as the Abwehr and OSS, resistance movements, and spy networks; the author, noted also as a biographer of General Patton, was a former Chief of Research and Planning in the Special Warfare Branch of the U.S. Navy.

417. Flammer, Philip M., ed. "Dulag Luft: The Third Reich's Prison Camp for Airmen." *Aerospace Historian*, XVIII (June 1972), 58-65.

A history of Stalag Luft III where captured American airmen were housed.

418. Ford, Corey. *Donovan of OSS*. Boston, Mass.: Little, Brown, 1970. 366p.

An admiring biography of Gen. William ("Wild Bill") Donovan, creator and wartime head of the Office of Strategic Services; weak on the theory and use of intelligence, this work does contain a good description of OSS organization.

419. Friedrich, Carl J., ed. *American Experiences in Military Government in World War II*. New York: Rinehart, 1948. 436p.

A review of the U.S. experience in military government which contrasts the American policies with those of the Axis; includes details on operations and Allied coordination in Italy, France, Germany, and Austria.

420. Funk, Arthur L. "American Contacts with the French Resistance, 1940-1943." *Military Affairs*, XXXIV (February 1970), 15-21.

Examines the covert contacts between U.S. representatives and leaders of the various resistance movements from before Pearl Harbor.

421. ———. "Churchill, Eisenhower, and the French Resistance." *Military Affairs*, XLVI (February 1981), 29-33.

Something of a sequel to the above reference, this piece examines the politics behind the Anglo-American approach to the use of the Maquis in the liberation of France.

422. Harris, C.R.S. "Allied Military Administration of Italy, 1943-1945." *U.S. Naval Institute Proceedings*, LXXV (February 1959), 119-121.

A quick overview of the development of civil government application in the first of the Axis partners to be defeated.

423. Hart, Henry C. "U.S. Employment of Underground Forces." *Military Review*, XXVI (March 1947), 50-56.

Examines U.S. employment of resistance forces in Europe with special attention to relations and leadership of the French Maquis.

424. Haswell, Chetwynd J.D. *D-Day: Intelligence and Deception.* New York: Times Books, 1980. 216p.

Another British study of events surrounding the Normandy invasion as they applied to intelligence gathering, counter-intelligence, and deception as employed in "Operation Bodyguard"; employs more recent sources and is more concise than Anthony Cave-Brown's study cited above.

425. Hinsley, F.H., *et al.* *British Intelligence in the Second World War: Its Influence on Strategy and Operations, Part II.* Cambridge, Eng., and New York: Cambridge University Press, 1981. 850p.

The second in an ongoing official series on the wartime history of British intelligence, this volume covers the period from July 1941 to the summer of 1943; while decidedly pro-British, the work does cover in the greatest detail yet the use of Ultra in the North African and Atlantic naval campaign; in the latter the role of signal intelligence came its closest to playing the decisive part.

426. Holborn, Hajo. *American Military Government: Its Organization and Policies.* Washington, D.C.: Infantry Journal Press, 1947. 243p.

A study of U.S. military government during the war which is helpful in its description of the difficulties found in co-ordinating the various Allied occupation policies.

427. Humphreys, R.H. "The Use of 'U' in the Mediterranean and Northwest African Theaters of War." *ACHSWW Newsletter*, no. 26 (Fall 1981), 58-76.

A reprint of the report in National Archives Record Group 457 (National Security Agency), SRH-037, "Reports Received by the U.S. War Department on the Use of Ultra in the European Theater, World War II."

428. Hyde, Harford M. *Room 3603: The Story of the British Intelligence Center in New York During World War II.* New York: Farrar, Straus, 1963. 257p.

A biography of William Stephenson ("Intrepid") and his activities as director of the British Security Coordination office in the U.S., which included "dirty tricks" aimed at destroying American neutrality by fraud and counterfeit. Much more reliable, if somewhat duller, than William Stephenson's *A Man Called Intrepid.*

429. Hymoff, Edward. *The OSS in World War II.* New York: Ballantine Books, 1972. 405p.

This paperback offers an episodic account of clandestine operations which focuses on the suspenseful and the bravado; based on interviews, secondary sources, and the author's own wartime experiences as an agent in Italy, Greece, and Yugoslavia.

430. Joswick, Jerry J. *Combat Cameraman.* New York: Pyramid Books, 1962. 157p.

This little paperback records the services of an Army sergeant who took Signal Corps photographs in North Africa, Omaha Beach, the Battle of the Bulge, and Rhine crossing; in addition, he was the only one of six cameramen along to survive the 1943 Ploesti air raid--his photographs remain the only official pictures of the event.

431. Kahn, David. *The Codebreakers: The Story of Secret Writing.* New York: Macmillan, 1967. 1,164p.

A comprehensive history of cryptology which contains large chapters on World War II; combines a helpful narrative with technical sections on the development of codes and codebreaking.

432. Kauffman, George R. "Intelligence in Heavy Bombardment." *Military Review*, XXVI (November 1946), 20-28.

Reviews the process of obtaining intelligence for target selection, bombing raids, and post-bombing attack assessments of damages caused.

433. Kirkpatrick, Lyman B., Jr. *Captains Without Eyes: Intelligence Failures in World War II.* New York: Macmillan, 1969. 303p.

A former intelligence agent, now a Brown University professor, Kirkpatrick looks at five major battles in which intelligence "failed"; those of interest to users of this guide include the airborne assault on Arnhem and the Battle of the Bulge. One of the best reviews on the subject, Kirkpatrick's work offers reasons for the failures (inefficient, uncoordinated operations, human prejudices, poor organization, and a blindness of leaders on every level to verified facts) and suggestions on how they might have been prevented.

434. Kittredge, Tracy B. "A Military Danger: The Revelation of Secret Strategic Plans." *U.S. Naval Institute Proceedings*, LXXXI (July 1955), 731-743.

On the German use of unofficial secret defense studies published in an American newspaper in 1941.

435. Koch, Oscar W., and Robert G. Hays. *G-2: Intelligence for Patton.* New York: Whitemore Publishing Co., 1972. 167p.

The former Third Army assistant Chief of Staff, Intelligence (G-2), reveals his methods for gathering battlefield intelligence and producing estimates; includes a look at how Patton employed Koch's data in his famous European operations.

436. Lerner, Daniel. *Skyewar: Psychological Warfare Against Germany, D-Day to V-E Day.* New York: George W. Stewart, 1949. 436p.

A look at the work of the Psychological Warfare Division of SHAEF from June 1944 to May 1945 including the use of everything from misinformation to battlefield loudspeakers.

437. Lewin, Ronald. "The Signal Intelligence War." *Journal of Contemporary History*, XVI (July 1981), 501-512.

The most useful and concise overview of the role of Ultra in the European war yet available; based to a large extent upon the data in the next citation.

438. ———. *Ultra Goes to War: The First Account of World War II's Greatest Secret Based on Official Documents*. New York: McGraw-Hill, 1978. 398p.

A review of the development of the Ultra signal intelligence process in England and its operational role in Allied successes and disasters, including the battles of Kasserine Pass, Arnhem, the Bulge, Falaise Gap, Normandy, and the scattering of PQ-17. Based on a review of 700,000 Ultra intercepts and interviews with codebreakers and commanders, the work is especially helpful in showing how the data were obtained, evaluated, passed on, and utilized in the field.

439. MacCloskey, Monro. *Secret Air Missions: Counterinsurgency Operations in Southern Europe*. New York: Richard Rosen, 1966. 159p.

Reviews the operations of the AAF's 885th Bombardment Group (Heavy--Special) in support of covert and resistance movements in Italy, Southern France, and Yugoslavia, 1944-1945.

440. McCormick, Donald. *The Silent War: A History of Western Naval Intelligence*. By Richard Deacon, pseud. New York: Hippocrene Books, 1978. 288p.

This British analysis provides a number of chapters on World War II at sea, especially the signal war involving Ultra, the German Naval High Command, and the Battle of the Atlantic.

441. McGovern, James. *Crossbow and Overcast*. New York: William Morrow, 1964. 279p.

Examines the Allied intelligence effort which resulted in effective countermeasures against German V-weapons ("Operation Crossbow") and the top-secret Anglo-American effort to locate German scientists and extradite them to the U.S. ("Operation Overcast").

442. Maginnis, John J. *Military Government Journal*. Amherst: University of Massachusetts Press, 1971. 371p.

Recollections of a civic affairs officer with the U.S. 101st Airborne Division and his role in the capture and administration of the French town of Carentan during the Normandy invasion and later as a member of the First Army in its move into Germany.

443. Mahoney, Leo J. "A History of the War Department Scientific Intelligence Mission (ALSOS), 1943-1945." Unpublished Ph.D. Dissertation, Kent State University, 1981.

A scholarly review of the American effort to locate German scientists and scientific developments for extradition to the U.S.

444. Masterman, John C. *The Double-Cross System in the War of 1939 to 1945.* New Haven, Conn.: Yale University Press, 1972. 203p.

An official "internal memorandum" first written in 1945 which describes the British apparatus whereby German spies captured in Great Britain were induced to serve the Allied cause by becoming double agents and presenting misinformation to the Nazi intelligence agencies; this most successful British counterintelligence operation was, as noted in the annotations to other titles cited above, also used in connection with the safeguarding and use of Ultra.

445. Michel, Henri. *The Shadow War.* Translated from the French. New York: Harper & Row, 1972. 416p.

A comprehensive history which shows the development and operations of European resistance movements, including their relationship to the occupying Germans and to the Allies.

446. Montagu, Edwin. *Beyond Top Secret Ultra.* New York: Coward, McCann, 1977. 192p.

The only title to date which uses Ultra as a means of checking various actions as they occurred; particularly useful for the coordination of Ultra and the XX System. Compare with Lewin's work above.

447. ———. *The Man Who Never Was.* Philadelphia, Pa.: Lippincott, 1954. 160p.

The author, who was involved in this "Operation Mincemeat," describes the process of planting a corpse with fake official papers, one "Major Martin," on the Germans, via the Spanish, in a successful effort to deceive the Nazis on the invasion of Sicily. See Ian G. Colvin's work cited above for another account.

448. Paddock, Alfred H., Jr. *U.S. Army Special Warfare, Its Origins: Psychological and Unconventional Warfare, 1941-1962.* Washington, D.C.: National Defense University Press, 1982. 220p.

The first two chapters present the most comprehensive history of Army psychological warfare and covert operations (in connection with the OSS) during World War II yet available.

449. Peaslee, Budd J. "Air Scouts of the 8th Bomber Command." *Flying*, LX (February 1957), 32-34+.

An account of the work of the Eighth Air Force photo recon pilots charged with obtaining verification of the effects of strategic bombing raids.

450. Perrault, Giles. *The Secret of D-Day.* Translated from the French. Boston, Mass.: Little, Brown, 1965. 249p.

The organization of tight Allied security measures and the cat-and-mouse spy/counterspy efforts of German and Allied agents before the Normandy invasion are recounted in a volume made nearly obsolete by the revelation of the XX System.

451. Persico, Joseph E. *Piercing the Reich: The Penetration of Nazi Germany by American Secret Agents During World War II.* New York: Viking Press, 1978. 376p.

To obtain information on events in Germany late in the war, the OSS dispatched about 200 agents into the crumbling Reich; based on papers from the OSS files and some 86 interviews, this undocumented account concentrates on the more daring adventures.

452. Pforzheimer, Walter. "Code Breaking: The Ultra Story." *Marine Corps Gazette*, LXIV (July 1980), 76-80.

A brief history of the techniques and impact of Ultra by a noted intelligence authority.

453. Reit, Seymour. *Masquerade: The Amazing Camouflage Deceptions of World War II.* New York: New American Library, 1980. 263p.

Provides a captivating look at the astounding disguises and deceptions developed by the Allies, many as a part of the "Bodyguard" ruse before D-Day; here are stories of dummy tanks and landing craft, smoke screens and special nets which could make naval vessels seem to disappear, and the manufacture of whole communities from wood, paint, and canvas.

454. Rosengarten, Adolph G., Jr. "The Bulge: A Glimpse of Combat Intelligence." *Military Review*, XLI (June 1961), 29-33.

An analysis of the 1944 German counterattack, preparations for which were missed by Allied intelligence; compare with Kirkpatrick's work cited above.

455. ———. "With Ultra from Omaha Beach to Weimar, Germany: A Personal View." *Military Affairs*, XLII (October 1978), 127-133.

Recollections of the War Department Special Branch representative to the U.S. First Army on the influence of Ultra on the battlefield.

456. Russell, Jerry C. *Ultra and the Campaign Against the U-boats in World War II.* Study Project Report. Carlisle Barracks, Pa.: U.S. Army War College, 1980. 45p.

A chronological history of the use of Ultra by the U.S. Navy in the Battle of the Atlantic which stresses that signal intelligence was only one of the factors responsible for the defeat of the German submarine.

457. Smith, Richard Harris. *OSS: The Secret History of America's First Central Intelligence Agency.* Berkeley: University of California Press, 1972. 458p.

A former CIA agent's account of the origins, organization, and growth of the Office of Strategic Services which vividly portrays the people, politics, and operations of the group; based on secondary sources and interviews with 360 OSS veterans named in the bibliography, this is not a flattering account.

458. Spiller, Roger J. "Assessing Ultra." *Military Review*, LIX (August 1979), 13-23.

An attempt to assess the value of Ultra to the war effort, especially as the data generated were employed by American officers.

459. Stanley, Roy M., 2nd. *World War II Photo Intelligence*. New York: Scribners, 1981. 374p.

The first major history of World War II photo intelligence, especially its role in strategic bombardment and enemy troop location; the author details the planes, cameras, and missions and provides a selection of over 500 photographs from the 100,000 10" high cans of exposed film he had access to from World War II recon missions.

460. Strong, Kenneth. *Intelligence at the Top: The Recollections of an Intelligence Officer*. Garden City, N.Y.: Doubleday, 1969. 366p.

Eisenhower's intelligence chief in North Africa and Europe provides a useful view of SHAEF, Anglo-American coordination, the use and role of Allied intelligence in military and political planning, and the disputes between the Supreme Commander, Montgomery, and others.

461. Toliver, Raymond F. *The Interrogator*. Fallbrook, Calif.: Aero Publishers, 1975. 384p.

The story of Hanns Joachim Scharff, master German interrogator of pilots captured and held in POW camps, whose "psychic" methods broke down barriers so effectively that after the war the U.S. Air Force invited him to lecture in America.

462. United States. Army Air Forces. *Ultra and the History of the United States Strategic Air Forces in Europe vs. the German Air Force*. Frederick, Md.: University Publications of America, 1981. 240p.

Combines a narrative of AAF operations with hundreds of Ultra messages in an effort to show how signal intelligence shaped the strategy and actions of the American bomber forces.

463. Vietor, John A. *Time Out*. New York: Richard R. Smith Publisher, 1951. 192p.

A history of captured American airmen at the German POW camp Stalag Luft I.

464. Wallace, Warrach. "Report on [War Department Special Representative] Assignment with the Third United States Army, 15 August

to 18 September 1944." *ACHSWW Newsletter*, no. 26 (Fall 1981), 50-76.

The major's report on Ultra and Patton is reprinted from the document in National Archives RG 457, SRH-108, "Reports Received by the War Department on the Use of Ultra in the European Theater, World War II."

465. Warren, Harris G. *Special Operations: AAF Aid to European Resistance Movements, 1943-1945*. USAAF Historical Study, no. 121. Washington, D.C.: Headquarters, Army Air Forces, 1947. 259p.

Largely concerned with supply drops and agent movements; for the activities of one group, see MacCloskey's *Secret Air Missions* above.

466. White, William L. "They Fight with Cameras." *American Mercury*, LVII (November 1943), 529-542.

Based on an interview with Col. Karl Polifka, this article details the work of photo recon pilots in the Mediterranean and North Africa; reprinted in *Reader's Digest*, XLIII (November 1943), 91-94, as "Fliers Who Fight Without Guns."

467. Wilt, Alan F. "The Intelligence Wave." *Air University Review*, XXXI (May-June 1980), 114-118.

Comments on the revelations of the 1970's on wartime intelligence, including Ultra and the XX System.

468. Winterbotham, Frederic W. *The Ultra Secret*. New York: Harper & Row, 1974. 199p.

The noted account of how the British came to obtain the German Enigma signal machine and how once it was made to perform at Bletchley Park, material from it was sent to and employed by the Combined Chiefs of Staff and the major Allied air, sea, and ground commanders in Europe. Some of the statements of impact are controversial and this work needs to be employed with later accounts, such as those by Ralph Bennett, Peter Calvocoressi, and Ronald Lewin, cited above.

469. Wynne, Barry. *Count Five and Die*. New York: Ballantine Books, 1958. 152p.

A brief history of "Operation Stampede," the attempt to deceive the Germans concerning the timing and location of the Normandy invasion; made obsolete by later works detailing the XX System, Ultra, and "Operation Bodyguard."

C. TECHNICAL SUPPORT: MEDICINE/LOGISTICS/ENGINEERING/COMMUNICATIONS

Introduction: As with intelligence, the four subjects covered in the references in this part are all vital, if unglorious, to the success of armies, navies, and air forces in war. While the technology of these support services has improved, the need for adequate medical help, food and supplies, bridges, and communications was just as great in World War II as it is today or for that matter as it was when Napoleon made his famous statement about armies traveling on their stomachs. In addition to information in the citations here, readers should note that many of the operational histories cited below also contain references to ground, sea, and air support.

470. Albrecht, F.M. "Engineer Aspects of 'Operation Bolero.'" *Military Engineer*, XLII (March-April 1950), 116-120.

On the role of engineers in creating the bases and facilities to handle the American buildup in England, 1942-1944.

471. "The Anatomy of Loading and Supply: The Logistics of Invasion." *Fortune*, XXXI (April 1945), 124-131.

On the various techniques of loading invasion vessels for invasions, including the technique of figuring out what is needed most and loading it last.

472. Anderson, T.S. "Munitions for the Army, 1940-1945." *Infantry Journal*, LIX (October 1946), 8-16; LX (January 1947), 42-48.

Special emphasis on the housing and transportation of munitions and their delivery to troops in the field, especially in Europe.

473. Archard, Theresa. *G.I. Nightingale: The Story of an American Army Nurse*. New York: W.W. Norton, 1945. 187p.

Recollections of a head nurse in a surgical hospital who went ashore with the troops in North Africa and served the next 15 months through the Tunisian and Sicilian campaigns; reveals a sense of humor amid the red tape, mud, supply delays, and death.

474. Armfield, Blanche B., ed. *Organization and Administration in World War II*. U.S. Army in World War II: Medical Department. Washington, D.C.: U.S. Government Printing Office, 1963. 613p.

Covering the prewar emergency period as well as the war, this book describes the expansion which occurred in the U.S. Army Medical Department within a relatively short period of time, the organizational and administrative problems which followed, and the broad uniformity of activities achieved in the various theaters of operation despite the difficulties encountered. No other volume in the Medical Department series gives so complete a picture of worldwide organization.

475. *Army Times*, Editors of. *A History of the U.S. Army Signal Corps*. New York: Putnam, 1961. 192p.

An episodic general review covering the years 1861-1961; includes several chapters on World War II which emphasize human achievements.

476. Ballantine, Duncan S. *U.S. Naval Logistics in the Second World War*. Princeton, N.J.: Princeton University Press, 1947. 308p.

An interesting background study with insight into the Navy's difficulties in developing supply sources and delivering the goods where needed--"that limbo between the factory and the beachhead in which economic and military considerations are inextricably woven together." Has little to say about actual logistical operations in the Atlantic, Mediterranean, or northwest Europe. First presented as the author's 1947 Princeton University Ph.D. Dissertation.

477. Bauchspies, Rollin L. "The Courageous Medics of Anzio." *Military Medicine*, CXXII (January 1958), 53-65; (February 1958), 119-128; (March 1958), 197-207; (April 1958), 267-272; (May 1958), 338-359; (June 1958), 429-448.

Recounts the exploits of medical personnel serving with the U.S. Army Sixth Corps in Italy between January 22 and May 23, 1944.

478. Beebe, Gilbert W., and Michael E. DeBakey. *Battle Casualties: Incidence, Mortality, and Logistical Considerations*. Springfield, Ill.: C.C. Thomas, 1952. 277p.

Based on records of the U.S. Army Medical Department, 1941-1945, this work, which includes comparisons to earlier American wars, was one of the first and remains one of the best summaries of wartime wounded. Coauthor DeBakey later became a noted heart surgeon.

479. Bell, Jasper N. "Air-Head Logistics." *Air University Quarterly Review*, II (Winter 1948), 39-47.

On the airborne resupply of troops; examples from Sicily and Northwest Europe.

480. Billard, Tony. "The Red Ball Express." *Translog*, VII (October 1976), 14-15+.

A brief history of the express motor route which kept supplies moving up to Patton's Third Army.

481. Birdsell, Dale. "United States Army Chemical Warfare Service Logistics Overseas, World War II." Unpublished Ph.D. Dissertation, University of Pennsylvania, 1962.

On the transport and delivery of the various non-lethal chemicals, such as that for making smoke, employed by the Army, especially in the European Theater.

482. Blank, Jonas L. "The Impact of Logistics on Strategy." *Air University Review*, XXIV (March-April 1973), 2-21.

A general survey which includes instances in World War II Europe where the logistical situation impacted upon the movement of troops, e.g., Third Army dash.

483. Bowman, Waldo G. *American Military Engineering in Europe from Normandy to the Rhine*. New York: McGraw-Hill, 1945. 102p.

A brief review of the road construction and bridging operations of U.S. Army engineers in France and the Low Countries with emphasis on construction under fire.

484. Brophy, Leo P., Wyndham D. Miles, and Rexmond C. Cochrane. *The Chemical Warfare Service: From Laboratory to Field*. U.S. Army in World War II: The Technical Services. Washington, D.C.: U.S. Government Printing Office, 1959. 498p.

The R & D phase and that of procurement and supply of both offensive and defensive material are covered.

485. Butterton, Meredith L. *Metric 16*. Durham, N.C.: Moore Publishing Co., 1981. 496p.

An account of the support of First Army by its ordnance soldiers during five campaigns in northwest Europe.

486. Bykofsky, Joseph, and Harold Larson. *The Transportation Corps: Operations Overseas*. U.S. Army in World War II: The Technical Services. Washington, D.C.: U.S. Government Printing Office, 1957. 671p.

Recounts the deficiencies as well as the accomplishments of the corps in the performance of its overseas task, only part of which was the massive deployment of men (7,293,354) and material (126,787,875 measurement tons) from the U.S. to the various theaters.

487. Camelio, Paul, and Christopher F. Shores. *Armée de l'Air: A Pictorial History of the French Air Force, 1937-1945*. Carrollton, Tx.: Squadron/Signal Publications, 1976. 64p.

Includes a look at the massive American-sponsored rebuilding of the Free French air fleet, with arms and training, in the period after the invasion of North Africa in 1942.

488. Cannon, Michael W. "The Red Ball Express." *Armor*, LXXXIX (May-June 1980), 8-10.

A quick review of the special measures taken to get supplies to Patton.

489. Carter, Worrall R., and Elmer E. Duvall. *Ships, Salvage, and Sinews of War: The Story of Fleet Logistics Afloat in Atlantic and Mediterranean Waters During World War II*. Washington, D.C.: U.S. Navy Department, 1954. 533p.

In this official history, the authors demonstrate the vital importance of logistics to modern naval warfare in the Atlantic and Mediterranean, particularly to those forces involved in support of the various invasions in those theaters. Much more complete on the topic than Ballantine, cited above, the work includes chapters on Atlantic/Caribbean bases, war changes in fleet organization, service forces, the Rhine crossing, and over-the-ramp landing from North Africa to southern France.

490. Cave, Hugh B. *Wings Across the World: The Story of Air Transport Command*. New York: Dodd, Mead, 1945. 175p.

A brief review of the work of the AAF's ATC in transporting men and vital war supplies within the various theaters and between them and the U.S.

491. Churchill, Edward D. *Surgeon to Soldiers*. Philadelphia, Pa.: Lippincott, 1972. 490p.

An examination of the medical precautions taken in the European Theater as reflected in the diary and records of the surgical consultant to SHAEF headquarters.

492. Cleveland, Reginald M. *Air Transport at War*. New York: Harper, 1946. 324p.

A detailed history of the ATC of the AAF which is more complete than Cave above; includes references not only to the flying of men as passengers and supplies but to airborne operations as well.

493. Coakley, Robert W., and Richard M. Leighton. *Global Logistics and Strategy, 1943-1945*. U.S. Army in World War II: The War Department. Washington, D.C.: U.S. Government Printing Office, 1969. 889p.

This study stresses the changing character of the logistical-strategic problem faced by the Washington high command in the last two years of the war and shows how the "Arsenal of Democracy" gave allied forces material superiority over their enemies and the U.S. a growing dominance in the councils of the western partners. This is a continuation of Leighton and Coakley, cited below.

494. Colton, F. Barrows. "Winning the War of Supply." *National Geographic Magazine*, LXXXVIII (December 1945), 705-736.

An illustrated account of American logistical movements during the war.

495. Daniel, Hawthorne. *For Want of a Nail: The Influence of Logistics on War*. New York: Whittlesey House, McGraw-Hill, 1948. 296p.

A historic overview which concentrates on World War II; included are details on the buildup of supplies in Europe before the Normandy invasion.

496. Darnall, Joseph R. "Digging in at Cheltenham." *Military Surgeon*, CIV (June 1949), 418-424.

A look at U.S. medical services in England from May 1943 to January 1944.

497. ———. "Hospitalization in ETO, U.S. Army, World War II." *Military Surgeon*, CIII (December 1948), 426-439.

Reviews the organization and administration of Army hospitals in Europe from 1943 through 1945.

498. ———. "Mediterranean Medical Cruise--February 1944." *Military Surgeon*, CII (April 1948), 251-265.

Recalls the situation with regard to hospitals in the Italian Theater during the Anzio invasion.

499. ———. "Sidelights on the Hospital Program, European Theater of Operations." *Military Surgeon*, CIV (January 1949), 21-29.

Reminiscences, 1943-1945, by the former Chief of Hospitalization, Office of the Chief Surgeon, ETO.

500. Davis, Franklin M., Jr., and Thomas T. Jones, eds. *The U.S. Army Engineers--Fighting Elite*. New York: Watts, 1967. 181p.

A brief history of the Army Engineers which includes several chapters on World War II, all emphasizing the fighting and building concept.

501. Dohmann, George W. "A Medic in the Normandy Invasion." *American History Illustrated*, IV (June 1969), 8-17.

The photo-illustrated recollections of one corpsman who went ashore on Omaha Beach on D-Day.

502. Ely, Robert L., Jr. "'Give Us This Day....'" *Quartermaster Review*, XXVIII (November 1948), 30-31; (December 1948), 94, 97-98.

Concerns the activities of the Third Army's Quartermaster bakery companies.

503. Epstein, Laurence B. "Army Aviation Logistics in Evolution, 1940-1953." *U.S. Army Aviation Digest*, XXV (June 1979), 5-11.

A review of the history of logistics in the AAF during the war.

504. Foisie, Jack. "The Angels of Anzio." *New York Times Magazine* (January 25, 1959), 30+.

The work of U.S. Army nurses in caring for the wounded on the Anzio beachhead in 1944.

505. French, Herbert E. *My Yankee Paris*. New York: Vanguard Press, 1946. 260p.

A light-hearted look at the author's non-combat experiences as a lieutenant in the Army Quartermaster Corps in Normandy and Paris; dwells to a large extent on the author's contact with French civilians.

506. Furtos, Norma C. "The Navy Is My Career." *American Medical Women's Association Journal*, XIV (June 1959), 516-517.

Since 1944.

507. Garland, E. Blair. "Radar in ETO Air-Ground Operations." *Signal*, III (March-April 1949), 5-11.

On its use to coordinate armored and tactical air operations in western Europe from 1942 to 1945.

508. Goldberg, Alfred. "Air Logistics: Its Role in the European Theater in World War II." Unpublished Ph.D. Dissertation, Johns Hopkins University, 1950.

Records the growth, organization, and administration of the AAF's Air Transport Command in Europe as well as its operations.

509. Hall, Duncan H., and C.C. Wrigley. *Studies in Overseas Supplies*. History of the Second World War: United Kingdom Civil Series, War Production Series. London: H.M. Stationery Office, 1956. 537p.

An account, from British records only, which is strong in detail on how and to what effect the broad Anglo-Allied policies of supply were translated into action.

510. Harris, Murray G. *Lifelines to Victory*. New York: Putnam, 1942. 160p.

A brief study of worldwide communication lines designed to show that no "second front" could be opened until the trade routes were secure.

511. Heavy, William F. *Down Ramp: The Story of the Army Amphibious Engineers*. Washington, D.C.: Infantry Journal Press, 1947. 272p.

A history of those Army engineers assigned to invasion forces whose duty it was to get out onto the beach quickly and clear obstacles.

512. Henning, Berthel H. "The Air Holding." *Military Surgeon*, CIV (April 1949), 253-259.

The Army's Seventh Field Hospital in France, Belgium, and Germany from July 1944 to June 1945.

513. Houston, H.N. "Sam." *The Hooligan Navy*. New York: Vantage Press, 1973. 150p.

Memories of a USN officer concerning amusing events, often the result of battles with naval supply, which helped to relieve the pressures faced by men serving aboard minor ships; sort of a factual *Mr. Roberts*.

514. Huston, James A. "The Logistics of Global Warfare." In: his *The Sinews of War: Army Logistics, 1775-1953*. Washington, D.C.: U.S. Government Printing Office, 1966. Part IV.

A record of the Army's experience in developing a workable and effective logistical system against the background of changing conditions, which sets forth the means and methods and emphasizes the reasons for changes.

515. Irgang, Frank J. *Etched in Purple*. Caldwell, Idaho: Caxton Printers, 1949. 241p.

Recollections of the author's experiences as a medic in the Normandy invasion and his later service as an infantryman in the battles across Western Europe; his flat style describes combat and medical procedures in stark detail.

516. Jeffcott, George F. *Dental Service in World War II*. U.S. Army in World War II: The Medical Department. Washington, D.C.: U.S. Government Printing Office, 1955. 362p.

Traces the history of the Army Dental Corps and discusses the administrative, logistical, and clinical problems encountered in providing dental care to some eight million men and women during World War II.

517. Johnson, Lucius W. "The Dark Side of Sanitation." *U.S. Naval Institute Proceedings*, LXXIV (December 1948), 1216-1223; LXXV (January 1949), 97-99.

World War II medical and sanitary affairs in the U.S. Navy.

518. Kendrick, Douglas B., ed. *Blood Program in World War II*. U.S. Army in World War II: The Medical Department. Washington, D.C.: U.S. Government Printing Office, 1964. 922p.

The story of lives saved by prompt and adequate hemotherapy, this work discusses administrative problems and procedures developed during the war for the collection, transportation, and storage of blood and the developmental work with plasma and so-called blood substitutes.

519. Kerwin, George D. "Petroleum Goes to War." *U.S. Naval Institute Proceedings*, LXXI (September 1945), 811-813.

A brief review of the Navy's role in the transport and distribution of oil products during the war.

520. Knox. Walter K. *Darken Ship*. New York: Vantage, 1966. 180p.

The author's recollection of service with the cargo ships of the U.S. Army Transportation Corps during the war.

521. Lees, Hannah. "Seagoing Surgery: The Best Medical Skill Looks After Our Navy in Hospitals That Follow the Fleet." *Collier's*, CX (September 26, 1942), 22-23+.

A description of the Navy's hospital ships, their cases and personnel; reprinted in William H. Fetridge, ed. *The Navy Reader* (Indianapolis: Bobbs-Merrill, 1943), pp. 99-109.

522. Lehman, Milton. "Supplying the Seventh Army." *Infantry Journal*, LVI (February 1945), 29-30.

A brief review of the problems involved.

523. ———. "We Learned in Tunisia and Sicily." *Infantry Journal*, LIV (February 1944), 11-14.

A review of logistical operations in those two campaigns.

524. Leigh, Randolph. *48 Million Tons to Eisenhower: The Role of Services of Supply in the Defeat of Germany.* Washington, D.C.: Infantry Journal Press, 1946. 179p.

Based on material gathered by the Historical Division, U.S. Army Europe, this work details the problems and successes of SOS in forwarding supplies to the advancing American armies in France, the Low Countries, Italy, and Germany.

525. Leighton, Richard M. "Preparation for Invasion: The Problem of Troop and Cargo Flow Before D-Day." *Military Affairs*, X (Spring 1946), 2-39.

Provides details on the difficulties of assembling men and materiel in England for the Normandy invasion.

526. ———, and Robert W. Coakley. *Global Logistics and Strategy, 1940-1943.* U.S. Army in World War II: The War Department. Washington, D.C.: U.S. Government Printing Office, 1955. 780p.

U.S. Army logistics, primarily of ground forces, in relation to global strategy during the period of American preparation for the conflict and the first 18 months of participation is treated in this comprehensive study which shows the great complexity of the planning operations behind the great campaigns; the story is told from the viewpoint of the central administration in Washington, including the Joint and Combined Chiefs of Staff, the General Staff, and the Army's Services of Supply. The story is continued by Coakley and Leighton in their account of operations 1943-1945, cited above.

527. LeVacon, Yves. "Allied Logistics in Europe." *Military Review*, XLVI (April 1966), 89-98.

An examination of wartime logistics translated from the French journal *Revue Militaire Générale*.

528. Lutes, LeRoy. "Supply Reorganization for World War II." *Quartermaster Review*, XXXII (September-December 1952), 4-5, 147-148, 151-152, 155-156, 159; 24-25, 148, 151-152, 155-156, 159.

On the changes in the Army service system and the development of Services of Supply, 1942-1946, more comprehensively told by Leighton and Coakley above.

529. McClellan, Willard C. "A History of American Military Sea Transportation." Unpublished Ph.D. Dissertation, American University, 1953.

Includes several chapters on the transportation of men and cargo during World War II.

530. McIntosh, Kenneth C. "Ships and Shoes and Sealing Wax." *U.S. Naval Institute Proceedings*, LXXV (February 1949), 135-147.

A description of naval logistics during the war with emphasis on the fleet's necessity for waterborne transfer of all sorts of goods.

531. McMinn, John H., and Max Levin, eds. *Personnel in World War II*. U.S. Army in World War II: The Medical Department. Washington, D.C.: U.S. Government Printing Office, 1963. 548p.

Examines the problems of a rapid buildup of medical personnel and the steps taken to assure the best use of personnel assignments for optimum medical care of the troops.

532. McNamara, Andrew T., and Raymond F. McNally. *Quartermaster Activities of II Corps Through Algeria, Tunisia, and Sicily and First Army Through Europe*. Fort Lee, Va.: U.S. Army Quartermaster School, 1955. 179p.

Examines the stockpiling and distribution of goods and the problems encountered with a corps rapidly on the march.

533. Maisel, Albert Q. *The Wounded Get Back*. New York: Harcourt, Brace, 1944. 230p.

Written to reassure the public, this work reviews the transport of wounded by the Army, Navy, and AAF.

534. Mayo, Lida. *Of Beachhead and Battlefront*. U.S. Army in World War II: The Ordnance Department. Washington, D.C.: Government Printing Office, 1968. 523p.

The story of how America's munitions reached U.S. and Allied troops and of how Ordnance soldiers stored, maintained, supplied, and salvaged materiel in the various theaters.

535. Miller, Everett. *United States Army Veterinary Services in World War II*. U.S. Army in World War II: The Medical Department. Washington, D.C.: U.S. Government Printing Office, 1961. 779p.

Discusses the work of Army veterinarians in the war, including food inspection and the health of many animals, including 56,000 horses and mules, 10,000 guard dogs, and 55,000 carrier pigeons.

536. Millett, John D. *The Organization and Role of the Army Service Forces*. U.S. Army in World War II: Army Service Forces. Washington, D.C.: U.S. Government Printing Office, 1954. 494p.

Told from the viewpoint of the ASF commanding general, this account of a controversial administrative experiment explores the various opinions on the effectiveness of this organization.

537. Milner, Samuel. "Establishing the 'Bolero' Ferry Route." *Military Affairs*, XI (Winter 1947), 213-222.

On the ferrying of 8th Air Force aircraft across the Atlantic in 1942 for the establishment of AAF presence in England.

538. Morriss, Mack. "Hospital Ship." In: Editors of *Yank*. *The Best from Yank, the Army Weekly*. New York: E.P. Dutton, 1945, pp. 223-231.

On the care of soldiers on board hospital ships, particularly those wounded in the European Theater.

539. Mossman, B.C., and M.W. Stark. *The Last Salute: Civil and Military Funerals, 1921-1969*. Washington, D.C.: U.S. Government Printing Office, 1971. 429p.

This Army-produced history presents accounts of funerals conducted for civil and military officials and for the unknown soldiers of World Wars I and II and the Korean conflict.

540. Nicholas, William H. "Heroes' Return." *National Geographic Magazine*, LXXXVII (March 1945), 333-352.

On the return of wounded servicemen from Europe to the U.S.

541. Oman, Charles M. *Doctors Aweigh: The Story of the United States Navy Medical Corps in Action*. Garden City, N.Y.: Doubleday, Doran, 1943. 231p.

On the organization and activities of USN doctors and hospital ships; the only action covered due to this book's early publication is that in the Pacific and North Africa.

542. Osmanski, Frank A. "The Logistical Planning of 'Operation Overlord.'" *Military Review*, XXIX (November 1949), 31-40; (December 1949), 40-48; (January 1950), 50-62.

Describes the immense complexity of assembling men and war materiel in England prior to the Normandy invasion and the resupply of troops in France after D-Day.

543. Owen, W.V. "Transportation and Supply in Anzio." *Infantry Journal*, LVIII (March 1946), 32-38.

On the difficulty of logistical work under fire on that Italian beachhead in early 1944.

544. Palmer, Catherine B. "Flying Our Wounded Veterans Home." *National Geographic Magazine*, LXXXVII (September 1945), 363-384.

An illustrated look at the medivac work of the AAF's Air Transport Command and the USN Naval Air Transportation Service.

545. Parks, Robert J. "The Development of Segregation in U.S. Army Hospitals, 1940-1942." *Military Affairs*, XXXVII (December 1973), 145-150.

On the separation of the races as official Army practice.

546. ———. *Medical Training in World War II*. U.S. Army in World War II: The Medical Department. Washington, D.C.: U.S. Government Printing Office, 1974. 292p.

Records the problems of training doctors, nurses, and enlisted medical personnel for a department which at peak strength numbered 700,000 individuals--more than three times the strength of the entire Regular Army in 1939.

547. Rafferty, J.A. "Casualties of the U.S. Eighth Air Force in World War II." *Military Surgeon*, CV (July 1949), 225-227.

Enumerates the different kinds of casualties taken between January 1943 and June 1945.

548. Raymond, Allen. "The Wounded Will Live." *Saturday Evening Post*, CCXVI (January 1, 1944), 16-17+.

On medical care provided wounded Fifth Army soldiers in Italy.

549. Reichers, Louis T. *The Flying Years*. New York: Henry Holt, 1956. 384p.

Memories of a wartime lieutenant colonel in the AAF Ferry Command which emphasizes his missions and adventures in North Africa and Europe, 1941-1945.

550. Reister, Frank A., ed. *Medical Statistics in World War II*. U.S. Army in World War II: The Medical Department. Washington, D.C.: U.S. Government Printing Office, 1975. 1,215p.

A valuable reference for medical planners, researchers, and historians, this statistical volume is derived from over 18 million individual World War II medical records and includes various breakdowns on casualties and how they were incurred.

551. Richardson, Eudora R., and Sherman Allen. *Quartermaster Supply in the European Theater in World War II*. 10 vols. Fort Lee, Va.: U.S. Army Quartermaster School, 1948-1950.

The most comprehensive narrative history on the topic ever printed, these volumes detail the logistical support of American armies, particularly in northwest Europe, from 1942 to 1946.

552. ———. *Quartermaster Supply in the Fifth Army in World War II*. Fort Lee, Va.: U.S. Army Quartermaster School, 1950. 181p.

A review of logistical support for the Fifth Army in Italy from 1943 to 1945.

553. Risch, Erna, and Chester L. Kieffer. *Organization, Supply, and Services*. U.S. Army in World War II: The Quartermaster Corps. 2 vols. Washington, D.C.: U.S. Government Printing Office, 1953-1955.

These two volumes cover the activities of the corps in the U.S., including its role in supply planning for the war and its contribution to cutting supply demands through conservation and salvage.

554. Ross, Irwin. "Trucks and Trains in Battle." *Harpers*, CXC (January 1945), 126-132.

The role of the Army Transportation Corps in France.

555. Ross, William F., and Charles F. Romanus. *Operations in the War Against Germany*. U.S. Army in World War II: The Quartermaster Corps. Washington, D.C.: U.S. Government Printing Office, 1965. 798p.

The QM establishment in Europe became the largest organization in history for feeding and clothing military people and providing other services to U.S. and Allied forces; this work recounts those experiences in England, the Mediterranean, and on the Continent.

556. Ruppenthal, Roland G. "Ammunition Supply in the Battle for Brest." *Military Review*, XXX (December 1950), 39-46.

The problems of getting sufficient cannon ammunition to VIII Corps artillery battling the stout defense of the German 2nd Paratroop Division.

557. ———. *The Logistical Support of the Armies, May 1941 to May 1945*. U.S. Army in World War II: European Theater of Operations. 2 vols. Washington, D.C.: U.S. Government Printing Office, 1953-1959.

Volume I describes how U.S. armies under Eisenhower were built up in the United Kingdom for the Normandy invasion of 1944 and how they were supplied during the first three months of operations on the Continent; Volume II carries the story to the end of hostilities. Throughout both volumes, emphasis is placed on the influence that logistical support--or the lack of it as a result of the Allies' headlong dash across the Continent after the breakout--had on the planning and conduct of combat operations by the field armies.

558. ———. "Logistics and the Broad-Front Strategy." In: Kent R. Greenfield, ed. *Command Decisions*. Washington, D.C.: Department of the Army, Office of the Chief of Military History, 1960, pp. 419-427.

Analyzes the impact of logistics on and the impact on logistics of Eisenhower's decision to build up his forces along the Rhine River through the whole length of the Western Front before launching the final drive into the heart of Germany.

559. Scott, Michael R. "The Redball Express: Patton's Fast-Moving Supply Line." *Translog*, I (September 1970), 22-23.

Emphasizes the smoothness of the supply operation.

560. Sondern, Frederick, Jr. "The Great Bridge of Ships to France: Landing Men, Guns, and Supplies on the Beaches of Normandy." *Reader's Digest*, XLV (October 1944), 59-62.

Recounts in general details on the logistical support of the Allied armies over the Normandy beaches after D-Day.

561. Strong, Paschal N. "An Invasion Is Jeopardized." *U.S. Army Combat Forces Journal*, IV (November 1953), 29-33.

Comments on the excessive rigidity of logistical arrangements in southern England before and during the Normandy invasion.

562. Sykes, H.F., Jr. "Logistics and World War II Army Strategy." *Military Review*, XXXV (February 1956), 47-54.

A brief review of the role of logistics and materiel/personnel buildups in anticipation of invasions.

563. Terrett, Dulany. *The Emergency (to December 1941)*. U.S. Army in World War II: The Signal Corps. Washington, D.C.: U.S. Government Printing Office, 1956. 383p.

Descriptions are given of the corps' role in developing, procuring, and furnishing such signal equipment as radar and frequency modulation, which all but revolutionized the use of tanks.

564. Thompson, Clary, ed. *Unsung Heroes!: Your Service Forces in Action--A Photographic Epic of Army Service Force Operations in World War II*. New York: Wise, 1949. 385p.

A heavily illustrated review of ASF services around the globe, including those provided in the Mediterranean and European Theaters.

565. Thompson, George R., and Dixie R. Harris. *The Outcome (Mid-1943 Through 1945)*. U.S. Army in World War II: The Signal Corps. Washington, D.C.: U.S. Government Printing Office, 1966. 693p.

The first part describes the activities of the corps as a service and combat arm in the theaters of operation while the second carries the administrative story to the end of the war.

566. Thompson, George R., Pauline M. Oakes, and Dulany Terrett. *The Test (December 1941 to July 1943)*. U.S. Army in World War II: The Signal Corps. Washington, D.C.: U.S. Government Printing Office, 1957. 621p.

In addition to an account of the corps' expansion and combat operations, this work provides an interesting account of Signal Corps engineers and technicians who were engaged in a desperate game of wits with the enemy in the race to produce electronic weapons and counterweapons.

567. Thomson, Harry C., and Lida Mayo. *Procurement and Supply*. U.S. Army in World War II: The Ordnance Department. Washington, D.C.: U.S. Government Printing Office, 1960. 504p.

Describes how the department and industry manufactured the huge quantities of munitions required by the Army and how its Field Service stored, cataloged, maintained, and distributed the munitions.

568. Thornber, Hubert E. "The Supply and Distribution of Petroleum Products in the European Theater of Operations." *Quartermaster Review*, XXVII (March-June 1948), 33-35, 113-114; 10-12, 90, 93-94.

Discusses procedures in ETO from February 1944 to September 1945.

569. United States. Department of the Army. Quartermaster School. *Storage and Distribution of Quartermaster Supplies in the*

European Theater of Operations in World War II. Fort Lee, Va., 1962. 291p.

A comprehensive survey of the maintenance, storage, and distribution of Army goods from 1943 to 1945.

570. ———. ———. Transportation Corps. *Report of the Chief of Transportation, Army Service Forces, World War II.* Washington, D.C.: U.S. War Department, 1945. 125p.

An account of the role played by transportation, including trains and trucks, in delivering goods to American field armies; includes some mention of the famous "Red Ball Express."

571. Van Creveld, Martin. *Supplying War: Logistics from Wallenstein to Patton.* Cambridge, Eng., and New York: Cambridge University Press, 1977. 284p.

An analysis of the role of logistics on modern war which is both thorough and controversial. The author's sharpest criticism is aimed at the Allied invasion of France, where he believes the Anglo-Americans were overly cautious in their use of overwhelming materiel support.

572. Walker, Charles L. "Preparation for Invasion." *Harpers*, CLXXXVIII (February 1944), 246-252.

Considers the logistical preparations for the U.S. campaign in North Africa.

573. Wardlow, Chester. *Movements, Training, and Supply.* U.S. Army in World War II: The Transportation Corps. Washington, D.C.: U.S. Government Printing Office, 1956. 564p.

Deals with troop and supply movements in the U.S. and to the overseas commands and points up the problems involved in setting up the new Army Service Forces organizations after the war had already begun and making it operate smoothly.

574. Whipple, William. "Logistical Bottleneck at the Ports: Why Patton Couldn't Get to the Rhine in '44." *Infantry Journal*, LXII (March 1948), 6-14.

Critical of the shipping problems in the ports along the English Channel.

575. Williams, Grant A. "First Army's ETO Signal Operations." *Signal*, II (March-April 1944), 5-11.

Communications of the U.S. First Army in France, the Low Countries, and Germany, 1944-1945.

576. Wiltse, Charles M. *Medical Service in the Mediterranean and Minor Theaters.* U.S. Army in World War II: The Medical Department. Washington, D.C.: U.S. Government Printing Office, 1966. 664p.

This work deals with the Atlantic and Persian Gulf non-combat theaters and with the North Africa, Sicily, southern France, and Italy campaigns and narrates the methods of evacuating the wounded and the successful efforts to control disease in those areas. An appendix gives an account of the German medical service in the African and European Theaters covered by the volume, which is useful for comparison.

577. Ziel, Ron. *Steel Rails to Victory*. New York: Hawthorn Books, 1970. 288p.

A pictorial history of railroad operations during the war, with special emphasis on American operations in France.

III. THE WAR IN THE AIR

Introduction: The references in this section of our guide are devoted to the Army Air Forces in Europe during World War II. Here will be found information on officers and heroes, campaigns and battles in the Mediterranean and European Theaters as well as the U.S. strategic bombing campaign against the Third Reich, accounts of specific units, and information on aircraft, uniforms, warplane weapons, camouflage, and markings. Readers should note that additional information is also available in the encyclopedias and handbooks cited in Section I, as well as the various general and illustrated war histories.

A. GENERAL WORKS

Introduction: Although aircraft had been employed on a limited, almost experimental basis, in World War I, it was World War II that saw the flying machine become an important, perhaps decisive, element in victory or defeat. In Europe, the powerful air arms of both Germany and Great Britain had been engaged for over a year before the first American units saw action. During that time much was learned about operations under fire, some of it seen by U.S. observers and the remainder to be learned in the AAF's early missions. The citations in this section reflect those works written over the years which have dealt with the air-war phase of World War II as a whole. While almost all contain information on the American effort, all contain information on the operations of foreign air forces as well, be they German, British, Italian, French, Russian, etc. A review of these can be useful for comparison as well as for an understanding as to exactly how the U.S. aerial contribution made a difference in the final victory in Europe.

578. *Air Power.* London: Phoebus Books, 1979. 392p.

A history of military aircraft, especially bombers and fighters, and air warfare from World War I to the present; this oversize volume contains over 720 photographs and drawings, including more than 400 in full color.

579. Anderton, David. "World War II." In: his *The History of the United States Air Force.* New York: Crescent Books, 1981, pp. 49-130.

Examines the role of the AAF in the various war theaters in a heavily illustrated "coffee-table" book first published in England.

580. Angell, Joseph W., Jr., *et al.* *United States Air Force Tactical Operations: World War II and Korean War.* Washington, D.C.: Office of Air Force History, Department of the Army, 1962. 178p.

A review of AAF operations in support of ground operations, including, with regard to the European conflict, the role of the fighter bomber and of "carpet bombing" by strategic aircraft.

581. "The Army Air Forces' Tactics and How They Worked." *Flying*, XXXVIII (January 1946), 52-74.

A review of the AAF's role in the defeat of Germany, including strategic bombing and the destruction of the flying Luftwaffe.

582. Arnold, Henry H. "The Air War in Europe." *Aero Digest*, XLVII (November 11, 1944), 51-55.

A brief review of AAF successes both in strategic bombing and in tactical operations.

583. ———. "Army Air Forces Report." *Flying*, XXXVI (May 1945), 24-27+; (June 1945), 43-45+.

Excerpts from the AAF Commanding General's report to the Secretary of War on the use of airpower around the globe during the war.

584. Bailey, Ronald H. *The Air War in Europe.* World War II Series. Alexandria, Va.: Time-Life Books, 1979. 208p.

A heavily illustrated account of the entire air war over western Europe, including bombing raids, fighter combats, photo recon, etc. Includes eight "picture essays," which, like other photographic renderings in the book, feature photographs which originally appeared in the wartime issues of *Life* magazine.

585. Bartz, Karl. *Swastika in the Air: The Struggle and Defeat of the German Air Force, 1939-1945.* Translated from the German. 2nd ed. London: Kimber, 1956. 204p.

A general account of the Luftwaffe's battles which some critics have called superior to the history by General Galland cited below.

586. Baumbach, Werner. *The Life and Death of the Luftwaffe.* Translated from the German. New York: Coward-McCann, 1960. 224p.

A history by the former commander of the Luftwaffe's bomber arm that has been praised for its technical accuracy, but questioned on its "facts."

587. Berenbrok, Hans D. *The Luftwaffe War Diaries.* By Cajus D. Bekker, pseud. Translated from the German. Garden City, N.Y.: Doubleday, 1968. 399p.

A German version of the Luftwaffe's role and final defeat which covers the actions in the east, Mediterranean, and over western Europe; based on official German Air Force war diaries, interviews, and the papers of former Luftwaffe officers.

588. Bowyer, Chaz. *Air War Over Europe, 1939-1945.* London: Kimber, 1974. 532p.

A large, illustrated account which is comprehensive from a British viewpoint.

589. ———. *Guns in the Sky: The Air Gunners of World War II.* New York: Scribners, 1979. 182p.

Reviews the service of British and American gunners who shot at attacking German fighters from their often-cramped positions aboard Allied bombers; well illustrated, the volume is fair in its handling of U.S. crewmen.

590. Carlisle, Norman V., *et al.*, eds. *Air Forces Reader: Army and Navy Air Forces.* Indianapolis: Bobbs-Merrill, 1945. 406p.

An anthology which presents pictures of the USA and USN air arms in training and battle; its sections are: (1) *Wings for Victory*; (2) *Prelude to Command*; (3) *Battle in the Skies*; (4) *Of Men and Planes.* The book's appendixes include plane data and a glossary of aviation language.

591. Chant, Christopher. *The Illustrated History of the Air Forces of World War I and World War II.* London and New York: Hamlyn, 1979. 287p.

An oversize history of air warfare which provides an illustrated look at the globe's battling air forces, including the AAF of World War II in Europe.

592. ———. *The Mechanics of War: Ground Attack.* Warren, Mich.: Squadron/Signal Publications, 1976. 72p.

A heavily illustrated account of close air support as practiced by the warring air forces in support of ground operations; published simultaneously by the London firm of Almark.

593. Craven, Wesley F., and James L. Cate, eds. *The Army Air Forces in World War II.* 7 vols. Chicago: University of Chicago Press, 1948-1958.

These volumes constitute the official history of the Army Air Forces in the various theaters. The volumes of interest to users of this guide include: (1) *Plans and Early Operations, January 1939 to August 1942*; (2) *Europe: Torch to Pointblank, August 1942 to December 1943*; and (3) *Europe: Argument to VE-Day, January 1944 to May 1945.* Volume 6, *Men and Planes*, and Volume 7, *Services Around the World*, are important technological studies of aircraft production, troop training, and a variety of necessary support services.

594. Dank, Milton. *The Glider Gang: An Eyewitness History of World War II Glider Combat.* Philadelphia, Pa.: Lippincott, 1977. 273p.

The first concentrated English-language study of Allied glider pilots who flew Horsa and Waco gliders into combat, climbed out, and fought their way back to fly again; based on hundreds of interviews. This labor of love appears objective in its analysis of the planning and direction of the campaigns in which gliders were used.

595. Fitzsimons, Bernard, ed. *Warplanes and Air Battles of World War II*. Beekman History of the Wars Library. New York: Beekman House, 1973. 160p.

First published in Purnell's History of the Second World War series, this oversize British import is noteworthy not only for its illustrations and photographs, but also for its commentary by such leading air historians as Noble Frankland. Decided British bias in opinions and coverage.

596. Ford, Corey, and Alastair MacBain. *The Last Time I Saw Them*. New York: Scribners, 1946. 244p.

An anthology which relates the wartime combat experiences of AAF personnel around the world.

597. Fricker, John, and Edward H. Sims. "Airwar, 1939-1945." *Flying*, CI (September 1977), 185-199.

An overview of the global aerial campaigns with major emphasis on the operations of the USAAF.

598. Friendly, Alfred. *Guys on the Ground*. New York: Duell, Sloane and Pearce, 1944. 170p.

A collection of articles and anecdotes about AAF ground crews, concentrating on the men and their ingenuity and difficulty in repairing damaged aircraft, particularly in England.

599. Futrell, Robert F. "Air Power Lessons of World War II." *Air Force and Space Digest*, XLVIII (September 1965), 42-50+.

A review of the lessons learned by American air leaders as to the effectiveness of U.S. air activities in strategic and tactical situations.

600. Galland, Adolf. "Defeat of the Luftwaffe: Fundamental Reasons." *Air University Quarterly Review*, VI (Spring 1953), 18-36.

The former Inspector General of German fighter aviation traces the decline and fall of the Nazi air force giving major reasons, as he perceived them, for its defeat.

601. ———. *The First and the Last: The Rise and Fall of the German Fighter Forces, 1938-1945*. Translated from the German. New York: Henry Holt, 1954. 368p.

An autobiographical history of the German fighter arm which, like the article by the General cited above, presents a strong case against Luftwaffe leaders and their concept of air power. One of the most widely read and frequently reprinted accounts of the air war.

602. Gilster, Herman L. "Air Interdiction in Protracted War: An Economic Evaluation." *Air University Review*, XXVIII (May-June 1977), 2-18.

A review of the protracted AAF mission against German lines of communication and selected industrial targets, particularly in 1944-45.

603. Gurney, Gene. *The War in the Air*. New York: Crown, 1962. 352p.

A well-known illustrated history of the aerial conflict from 1939 to 1945 which devotes considerable space and many photographs to the AAF campaigns in Europe and the Mediterranean.

604. Huston, James A. "The Tactical Use of Air Power in World War II: The Army Experience." *Military Review*, XXXII (July 1952), 32-49.

The impact on troop movements on the ground made by fighter bombers in the sky, especially the role of the U.S. Ninth Air Force over western Europe, 1944-1945.

605. *Impact*. 8 vols. Marion, Ohio: National Historical Society, 1980.

Reproduces the heavily illustrated 380 articles contained in the formerly classified wartime AAF intelligence magazine.

606. Jablonski, Edward. *Air War*. 4 vols. Garden City, N.Y.: Doubleday, 1971-1972.

An extremely popular illustrated history of the air campaigns around the world available in most public libraries; based on secondary sources, a revised one-volume (259 pages) edition was issued by the same firm in 1979 and contains 761 black and white photos.

607. ———. *America in the Air War*. Epic of Flight Series. Alexandria, Va.: Time-Life Books, 1982. 176p.

Similar in some respects (photo sources, for example) to the Bailey title cited above, this work examines the aerial campaigns with an eye to the work of the AAF.

608. Jackson, Robert. *Aerial Combat: The World's Great Air Battles*. New York: Galahad Books, 1976. 160p.

American imprint of the British title published by Weidenfeld and Nicolson, London, this nicely illustrated work covers the history of air combat after 1914. Chapters 7, "Mediterranean Air War," and 9, "The Battle of Germany," provide a basic introduction.

609. ———. *Fighter: The Story of Air Combat, 1936-1945*. New York: St. Martin's Press, 1980. 168p.

A concise review of the combats and tactics of fighter pilots in the air forces of the major warring powers, written by a noted aviation journalist and student of fighter tactics.

610. McKee, Philip. *Warriors with Wings.* New York: Crowell, 1947. 266p.

An anthology of 20 combat stories, some drawn from personal interviews, of AAF men in action around the world.

611. Mason, Herbert M., Jr. *Duel for the Sky: Fighter Planes and Fighting Pilots of World War II.* Adventures in Flight Series. New York: Grosset and Dunlap, 1970. 148p.

Emphasizes the great aces and their important battles and aircraft; little on tactics or organization.

612. Mrazek, James E. *The Glider War.* New York: St. Martin's Press, 1975. 304p.

Details both the Allied and Axis glider-borne operations of 1940-1945 demonstrating the significant ETO role of the wooden, unengined troop transports. Compare with Milton Dank's work above.

613. Murray, Williamson. *Strategy for Defeat: The Luftwaffe, 1933-1945.* Maxwell AFB, Ala.: Air University Press, 1983. 365p.

Employing the latest declassified documents and research in German, British, and American archives, Murray provides the best recent study of the rise and fall of the German Air Force; for the U.S. contribution to this organization's decline, see especially Chapters 5 through 7.

614. Overy, R.J. *The Air War, 1939-1945.* London: Europa Publications, 1980. 263p.

Not a combat history but a general account which covers all the warring powers, the military campaigns, strategy, economic mobilization, the recruitment of science, production, and the nature and training of leadership; in nine chapters, the author concludes that the Allies' "general air strategy" helped them to win the air war, in the narrower sense of the contest between the air forces, and that the strategic bombing campaign really was much more important to the achievement of overall victory than many recent histories have been prepared to concede.

615. Parsons, Iain, ed. *The Encyclopedia of Air Warfare.* New York: Crowell, 1975. 256p.

A "coffee-table" British history, well illustrated and with a major amount of data relative to our topic; contributors include Christopher Chant, Richard Humble, and William "Bill" Gunston.

616. Pearl, Jack. *Aerial Dogfights of World War II.* Derby, Conn.: Monarch Books, 1962. 138p.

A brief overview of the actions of the great aces, especially Americans, over the world's battlefronts from 1939 to 1945. This paperback is nowhere near as complete as Jackson, cited above.

617. Philpott, Bryan. *Fighters Defending the Reich.* World War II Photo Album, no. 16. New York: E.P. Dutton, 1980. 96p.

A book of photographs, with captions, showing Luftwaffe units in action against Allied bombers; these wartime photos were all taken from the files of the West German Bundesarchiv.

618. Price, Alfred. *The Bomber in World War II.* New York: Scribners, 1979. 150p.

A useful introduction to the warplanes and great missions of the war, particularly in Europe, with information on U.S. British and German countermeasures, escort, successes and failures.

619. ———. *World War II Fighter Conflict.* New York: Hippocrene Books, 1980. 160p.

Part One concerns the evolution of fighter aircraft; Part Two, a comparison of famous fighters; and Part Three, an outline of the tactics employed by the various air forces. This volume, like Price's citation above, was first published in Great Britain.

620. Quesada, Elwood R. "Tactical Air Power." *Air University Quarterly Review*, I (Spring 1948), 37-45.

A review of its World War II application by the wartime boss of the U.S. IX Fighter Command.

621. Sears, Stephen W. *Air War Against Hitler's Germany.* American Heritage Junior Library. New York: American Heritage Publishing Co., 1964. 151p.

A well-illustrated introduction to the difficulties faced by the AAF in Europe as it battled the Reich through strategic bombing and tactical operations.

622. Siefring, Thomas A. *U.S. Air Force in World War II.* Rev. ed. Secaucus, N.J.: Chartwell Books, 1981. 197p.

A detailed history of the AAF from the 1930's to 1945 which concentrates on operations and warplanes; an oversize "coffee-table" import from England first released here in 1977, Siefring's work contains over 300 photos and technical drawings.

623. Silsbee, Nathaniel F. "The American Doctrine of Air Power." In: Karl W. Detzer, ed. *The Army Reader.* Indianapolis, Ind.: Bobbs-Merrill, 1943, pp. 157-170.

A contemporary explanation of the manner in which AAF leaders expected to employ their warplanes and the results of same anticipated; reprinted from *Aviation*, XLII (February 1943), 112+; (March 1943), 96+.

624. ———, ed. *Bombs Away!: Your Air Force in Action.* New York: Wise, 1948. 386p.

A photographic record of worldwide AAF operations with supplementary text on the various campaigns written by various generals; a list of AAF Congressional Medal of Honor winners in World War II is found on pp. 363-364.

625. Sims, Edward H. *Fighter Tactics and Strategy, 1914-1970*. Fallbrook, Calif.: Aero Publishers, 1980. 266p.

Covers the how and why of fighter tactics and recounts thrilling fighter combat stories from World War I through Vietnam, many in the words of the aces who fought the battles. Useful for attention to the strategy behind the use of the aircraft and the tactics of combat.

626. Straubel, James H., ed. *Air Force Diary*. New York: Simon and Schuster, 1947. 492p.

Contains 111 stories from *Air Force* which, while poorly written and unpolished, convey a sense of the AAF airman's battle aloft and on the ground.

627. Sunderman, James F., ed. *Europe*. Vol. II of *World War II in the Air*. New York: Watts, 1963. 345p.

An anthology of writings and anecdotes concerning AAF operations in Europe and over the Mediterranean drawn from a variety of books, articles, and reminiscences.

628. Tantum, William H., 4th, and E.J. Hoffschmidt, eds. *The Rise and Fall of the German Air Force, 1933-1945*. Old Greenwich, Conn.: WE, Inc., 1969. 422p.

First published as British Air Ministry Pamphlet No. 238 in 1948, this work, based on captured German materials and British intelligence sources, remains the best single book on the subject even after nearly 40 years; includes charts and a few photographs, but, unfortunately, no footnotes or bibliography.

629. Taylor, John W.R., *et al*. *Air Facts and Feats*. Rev. ed. New York: Sterling, 1978. 240p.

Covers the history of aviation with attention to the noted airmen, warplanes, and missions of World War II Europe.

630. Taylor, Michael J.H., comp. *Jane's Encyclopedia of Aviation*. 5 vols. London and Boston, Mass.: Jane's, 1980.

Taylor, son of John W.R. Taylor cited above, has compiled an excellent illustrated encyclopedia which covers all facets of flight from its beginning; presented in alphabetical order, the topics cover airmen, aircraft, designers, companies, air forces, and, of interest here, many of the great combat operations of the air war in Europe.

631. United States. Army Air Forces. Historical Office. *The Official Pictorial History of the A.A.F.* New York: Duell, Sloane, and Pearce, 1947. 213p.

A photo history of the AAF which includes accompanying text; many of the illustrations for the World War II period were taken by combat cameramen assigned to bombers and by wing-cameras on fighter planes.

632. Warren, John C. "War in Europe." In: Alfred Goldberg, ed. *A History of the United States Air Force*. New York: Arno, 1974, pp. 57-74.

First published by Van Nostrand in 1957, Warren's work encompasses the whole of the AAF war effort in Europe and the Mediterranean in an excellent, concise overview. Includes a few photographs.

633. Wilbur, Edwin L., and Estelle R. Schoenholtz. *Silver Wings: True Action Stories of the United States Air Force*. New York: Appleton, 1948. 281p.

An anthology of human interest stories concerning AAF personnel in combat around the world during World War II; many of the first-person accounts are taken from previously published sources.

634. *Wings*. 40 pts. London: Orbis, 1976-1977.

A comprehensive aviation encyclopedia which emphasizes not only aircraft but also airmen and military air campaigns; oversize, the alphabetically arranged parts are heavily illustrated.

635. Wood, Tony, and William "Bill" Gunston. *Hitler's Luftwaffe: A Pictorial History and Technical Encyclopedia of Hitler's Air Power in World War II*. New York: Crescent Books, 1977. 248p.

An oversize British import; Part One is a 120-page history of the rise and fall of the Luftwaffe, 1918-1945, and Part Two is a review of Nazi aircraft. The appendixes include the Luftwaffe chain of command and a useful glossary of terms. Heavily illustrated with black and white and color photographs and line drawings.

B. OFFICERS AND HEROES

Introduction: An interesting way to look at the air war in Europe, particularly for younger readers, is through the biography of its participants, leaders and airmen. The citations in this section are arranged in two parts. Part 1 is a collection of general biographies which concern two or more individuals; Part 2 concerns individuals and is arranged alphabetically by the last name of the biographee. It should be noted that additional biographical information is available in the handbooks and encyclopedias, biographical sources, and general war histories cited in Section I, the general aerial histories cited in Part A above, and in the campaign and unit histories noted in Parts C and D below.

1. Collective Biography

636. Andrews, Allen. *The Air Marshals: The Air War in Western Europe*. New York: William Morrow, 1970. 299p.

The development and use of the air power used in Europe during the war is reflected through the lives and roles of six air leaders--four British, Marshal Goering, and General Arnold.

637. Dupre, Flint O. *U.S. Air Force Biographical Dictionary*. New York: Watts, 1965. 273p.

A guide to the biographies of living (in 1965) and deceased AAF/USAF personnel, including generals and those of lesser rank.

638. Fogerty, Robert P. *Selected Air Force Case Histories*. USAF Historical Study, no. 91. Washington, D.C.: Office of Air Force History, Department of the Air Force, 1953.

A biographical study of 541 general officers, 1917-1952; the entries are longer than those appearing in Dupre, but contain more errors.

639. Grinsell, Robert. *Aces Full: Pilots and Fighter Aircraft of World War II*. Granada Hills, Ca.: Sentry Books, 1974.

A pictorial history of warplanes and the great aces from all the warring powers who flew them, including several from the AAF in Europe.

640. Gurney, Gene. *Five Down and Glory: A History of the American Air Ace*. Edited by Mark P. Friedlander, Jr. New York: Putnam, 1958. 302p.

Biographies of those U.S. flyers who shot down five enemy aircraft and became "aces"; includes a large number of important fighter pilots from the European and Mediterranean theaters.

641. Hess, William N. "A.A.F. Aces in a Day." *American Aviation Historical Society Journal*, XI (Summer 1966), 93-101.

Profiles those fighter pilots who shot down five enemy aircraft in one day.

642. ———. *The American Aces of World War II*. New York: Arco, 1968. 64p.

Provides individual combat histories and a compilation of American aces; illustrated with 52 photographs.

643. ———. *The American Fighter Aces Album*. Dallas, Tx.: Taylor, 1978.

A collection of ace sketches, mostly autobiographical, of all services in all wars, 1914 through Vietnam. Illustrated.

644. Hirsch, Phil, ed. *Fighting Aces*. New York: Pyramid Books, 1965. 173p.

Man's Magazine pieces on various U.S. aces, including several who fought in Europe during World War II.

645. Jackson, Robert. *Air Heroes of World War II: Sixteen Stories of Heroism in the Air*. New York: St. Martin's Press, 1978. 175p.

A collection of stories about air crewmen, many aboard AAF bombers over Europe, who performed heroic acts or flew great missions.

646. ———. *Fighter Pilots of World War II.* New York: St. Martin's Press, 1976. 176p.

Fourteen smoothly presented capsule biographies of noted pilots from all the warring powers, including the AAF's Robert S. Johnson and the Luftwaffe's Eric Hartman and Adolf Galland.

647. Loomis, Robert D. *Great American Fighter Pilots of World War II.* Landmark Books. New York: Random House, 1961. 208p.

Chapters 4, 5, 7, and 10 concern noted AAF pilots of the Mediterranean and European Theaters, men like Philip Cochran, Don Blakeslee, and Don Gentile.

648. Puryear, Edgar F., Jr. *Stars in Flight: Studies in Air Force Leadership.* San Rafael, Calif.: Presidio Press, 1981. 310p.

A look at the backgrounds, careers, and responsibilities surrounding the first five USAF Chiefs-of-Staff, Generals Henry Arnold, Carl Spaatz, Hoyt S. Vandenberg, Nathan F. Twining, and Thomas D. White, aimed at discovering why they were great leaders; during the war, Arnold commanded the whole AAF, Spaatz led the U.S. Air Forces in Europe, Vandenberg led the Ninth Air Force, and Twining the Fifteenth.

649. Shores, Christopher F. "Air Combat the World Over, 1932-1945." In: his *Fighter Aces.* London and New York: Hamlyn, 1975, pp. 48-136.

A worldwide review of the exploits of great aces in the air forces of all the warring powers with air forces; well illustrated with black and white and color photographs and reproductions of paintings.

650. Sims, Edward H. *American Aces in Great Fighter Battles of World War II.* New York: Harper, 1958. 256p.

An excellent introduction to the noted U.S. fighter pilots of the AAF and USN in worldwide service; includes all of the major personalities who achieved fame in the European Theaters.

651. Stafford, Gene B., and William N. Hess. *Aces of the Eighth: Fighter Pilots, Planes, and Outfits of the Eighth Air Force.* Carrollton, Tx.: Squadron/Signal Publications, 1978. 63p.

Covers 13 Eighth Air Force aces, their units, planes, codes and markings; includes extensive illustrations, especially of aircraft.

652. Toliver, Raymond F., and Trevor J. Constable. *Fighter Aces of the U.S.A.* Fallbrook, Calif.: Aero Publishers, 1979. 400p.

The only aces book noted here to fully employ official USAF victory credit lists, Toliver and Constable's pictorial cavalcade of 1,300 aces from five wars (World War II through Vietnam) is a goldmine of data which includes interviews and pilot reports; rather poorly organized, the work nevertheless features nearly 700 photographs of the men and their aircraft, including some 684 pilot portraits. Includes a detailed list of all known aces.

653. Turley, Edward. "Mr. Inside and Mr. Outside: In the Skies Over Western Europe." *American Aviation Historical Society Journal*, XXV (Winter 1980), 260-267.

Focuses on the friendship between AAF aces Francis Gabreski and Robert S. Johnson.

654. United States. Air Force. Office of Air Force History. *U.S.A.F. Credits for the Destruction of Enemy Aircraft, World War II*. USAF Historical Study, no. 85. Washington, D.C.: U.S. Government Printing Office, 1978.

An important source which assigns the officially recognized "kills" to every AAF fighter pilot in World War II; employed by Trevor and Constable in their noteworthy *Fighter Aces of the U.S.A.*, cited above.

2. Individuals

Frederick Anderson

655. Kantor, McKinley. "The Boss Bombardier: General Frederick Anderson." *Saturday Evening Post*, CCXVI (January 22, 1944), 16-17+.

Anderson was the commanding general of the VIII Bomber Command under General Doolittle and, later, the Deputy Commander for Operations at Headquarters, U.S. Strategic Air Forces in Europe under General Spaatz. It was Anderson who made the critical decision to launch the August 17, 1943, Schweinfurt-Regensburg Mission.

Frank Andrews

656. Eaker, Ira C. "Airpower Pioneers: LtGen. Frank M. Andrews." *Air Force Magazine*, LXIII (September 1980), 102-104.

A brief recollection by a leading AAF combat general who knew Andrews well.

657. Hart, John W. "A Reputation for Courage." *Aerospace Historian*, XVI (Summer 1969), 6-7.

Andrews became boss of U.S. forces in the European Theater in February 1943; a command pilot, he was killed in a crash in Iceland in May 1943. Andrews Air Force Base in Washington, D.C., was named in his honor in June 1949.

Henry H. "Hap" Arnold

658. *Army Times*, Editors of. "Hap Arnold." In: their *Famous American Military Leaders of World War II*. New York: Dodd, Mead, 1962, pp. 93-101.

A brief biography of the man who prior to and during World War II directed air activities for the nation's global war against the Axis.

659. Arnold, Henry H. *Global Mission.* New York: Harper, 1949. 626p.

Ghostwritten, like the memoirs of General Omar Bradley, cited below, this reminiscence covers the author's entire career, with over half the book devoted to his experience in leading the AAF in World War II. Offers insight into the personalities, conferences, and issues of the war and the development of coalition strategy, with particular emphasis on the role of air power. Employ with caution, as some sequences of events and dates are in error. Arnold's papers are in the Library of Congress.

660. Coffey, Thomas. *Hap: The Story of the U.S. Air Force and the Man Who Built It, General Henry H. "Hap" Arnold.* New York: Viking Press, 1982. 415p.

As much a history of the development of the AAF in the 1930's and 1940's as a biography of Arnold, this work also makes clear the contributions of others (e.g., Carl Spaatz and Ira Eaker) to Arnold's efforts to build U.S. military aviation. An important recent source which may stand as *the* Arnold biography for some time to come. Employs primary as well as secondary sources.

661. DuPre, Flint O. *Hap Arnold.* New York: Macmillan, 1972. 144p.

An adulatory biography of America's only five-star airman, aimed primarily at a juvenile audience.

662. Eaker, Ira C. "Hap Arnold: The Anatomy of Leadership." *Air Force Magazine*, LX (September 1977), 83-86+.

A detailed look at the reasons for Arnold's successful wartime leadership of the AAF by a noted general and friend of the commanding general who knew the biographee well.

663. ———. "Memories of Six Air Chiefs, Part II: Westover, Arnold, and Spaatz." *Aerospace Historian*, XX (December 1973), 188-196.

General Eaker's memories of Hap Arnold remained very fond after many years.

664. Hurd, Charles. "Pilot-in-Chief of the Air Arm." In: Karl W. Detzer, ed. *The Army Reader.* Indianapolis: Bobbs-Merrill, 1943, pp. 149-153.

A brief, somewhat fluffy, biography which is reprinted from the *New York Times Magazine* (January 3, 1943), pp. 11+.

665. Kuter, Laurence S. "How Hap Arnold Built the AAF." *Air Force Magazine*, LVI (September 1973), 88-93.

General Kuter, who worked with Arnold at AAF Headquarters, knew the commanding general well and here writes of his unceasing attempt to build U.S. military air power.

666. Parrish, Noel F. "Hap Arnold and the Historians." *Aerospace Historian*, XX (Fall 1973), 113-115.

Parrish, who also knew the commanding general well, tells of how Arnold sought the aid of a historians' committee to help him make strategic wartime decisions.

667. Pearse, Ben. "Hap Arnold--It's Still His Air Force." *Air Force*, XXXIX (August 1956), 256-261.

A view of the manner in which Arnold's egoism enabled him to win his battles for AAF employment during World War II.

668. Puryear, Edgar F., Jr. "Hap Arnold." In: his *Stars in Flight: Studies in Air Force Leadership*. San Rafael, Calif.: Presidio Press, 1981, pp. 3-46.

Puryear examines the various facets of Arnold's personality and practice which enabled him to provide dynamic wartime leadership to the AAF. A similar, but more concise, appraisal of Arnold's leadership is John W. Huston's "The Wartime Leadership of 'Hap' Arnold," which appears in Alfred F. Hurley and Robert C. Ehrhart's *Air Power and Warfare: The Proceedings of the 8th Military History Symposium, U.S.A.F. Academy 18-20 October 1978* (Washington, D.C.: Office of Air Force History, Department of the Air Force, 1979).

Duane Beeson

669. Fry, Garry L. "'Boise Bee': The Duane Beeson Story." *American Aviation Historical Society Journal*, XXIII (Winter 1978), 242-259.

Biography of a 4th Fighter Group 17-victory ace who was shot down and captured.

Lewis H. Brereton

670. Brereton, Lewis H. *The Brereton Diaries: The War in the Air in the Pacific, Middle East, and Europe, 3 October 1941 to 8 May 1945*. New York: William Morrow, 1946. 450p.

Leaving the Pacific, Brereton became commander of the U.S. Middle East Air Force (later Ninth Air Force) in 1942, boss of the Ninth in Europe in 1943, and chief of the First Allied Airborne Army in August 1944. This volume, obviously compiled with an eye toward publication, provides firsthand accounts of various military incidents in Europe and the Mediterranean as well as comments on his fellow senior officers.

671. Whitney, Cornelius V. *Lone and Level Sands*. New York: Farrar, 1951. 314p.

The author served on General Brereton's Ninth Air Force staff both in the Mediterranean and Europe and offers insight into his boss's leadership style.

Leonard "Kit" Carson

672. Carson, Leonard "Kit." *Pursue and Destroy*. Granada Hills, Calif.: Sentry Books, 1978. 175p.

A poorly organized but fascinating account of fighter combat, complete with pilot reports, facts and figures, and 256 photos; Carson examines not only his own victories, but also the aircraft and groups of the VIII Fighter Command.

673. Stafford, Gene B. "Mustang Ace: Kit Carson." *Airpower*, V (November 1975), 12-19.

An illustrated biography of a 19-victory 357th Fighter Group ace.

James H. Doolittle

674. *Army Times*, Editors of. "General Jimmy Doolittle." In: their *Famous American Military Leaders of World War II*. New York: Dodd, Mead, 1962, pp. 111-121.

Noted aviation pioneer and leader of the April 1942 Tokyo raid from the carrier *Hornet*, Doolittle was sent to Europe, first as boss of the Twelfth Air Force in North Africa, and from 1943 commander, in succession, of the North African Strategic Air Forces, the Fifteenth Air Force, and the Eighth Air Force, ending his wartime service as a lieutenant general.

675. Doolittle, James H. "'I Am Not a Very Timid Type': An Interview." *American Heritage*, XXV (April 1974), 49-57+.

Recollections of pioneering flights, the Tokyo raid, and the European air war.

676. Glines, Carroll V. *Jimmy Doolittle*. New York: Macmillan, 1972. 183p.

Like the DuPre biography of Arnold cited above, this work is aimed at a younger audience and has relatively little to say about Doolittle's service in Europe.

677. Mosely, Leonard. *Jimmy Doolittle*. New York: Nelson, 1960.

Mosely, who has written on such other aviation leaders as Lindbergh and Goering, does not slight Doolittle's work in the Mediterranean and northwest Europe air theaters.

678. Reynolds, Quentin J. *The Amazing Mr. Doolittle: A Biography of Lieutenant General James H. Doolittle*. New York: Arno, 1972. 313p.

First published by Appleton in 1953, Reynolds' biography was, for years, the standard journalistic account of Doolittle's career.

679. Shoemaker, Robert H., and Leonard A. Paris. "General James Harold Doolittle." In: their *Famous American Generals*. New York: Crowell, 1946, pp. 173-184.

A capsule biography with adequate coverage of Doolittle's European tour.

680. Thomas, Lowell, and Edward Jablonski. *Doolittle: A Biography*. Garden City, N.Y.: Doubleday, 1976. 368p.

Supersedes Reynolds as the preferred journalistic account; a careful biography which devotes considerable space to the general's wartime service in the Mediterranean and Europe. The late Lowell Thomas was a noted exponent of aviation while coauthor Jablonski has written a number of aviation titles cited elsewhere in this guide.

Sholto Douglas

681. Douglas, Sholto. *Combat and Command: The Story of an Airman in Two World Wars*. New York: Simon and Schuster, 1966. 806p.

Memoirs of a British air marshal who held a number of responsible commands during the war (RAF Middle East Commander, Coastal Command boss) entered here for the author's recollections and opinions of the Americans he worked with at the command level.

William R. Dunn

682. Dunn, William R. *Fighter Pilot: The First American Ace of World War II*. Lexington: University Press of Kentucky, 1982. 234p.

The author served in the RAF Eagle Squadron before Pearl Harbor and was the first American to down a German warplane; later, he transferred to the AAF and became America's first, if long unrecognized, ace of the European conflict. This memoir reads well and pulls no punches.

Ira C. Eaker

683. Sears, Betty M. "Ira C. Eaker--Aviator." *Red River Valley Historical Review*, III (Summer 1978), 66-78.

A noted aviation pioneer like Doolittle, Eaker was sent to England to organize the VIII Bomber Command and led its first raid, rising to command all U.S. air forces in England by late 1943; in 1944, Eaker was shifted to the Mediterranean to command the Mediterranean Allied Air Forces, during which tour he flew the first Italy-to-Russia shuttle mission. A major figure, it is a pity that he has been no better treated by biographers and somewhat surprising that he has not written his own autobiography, which, as a noted postwar syndicated national columnist, he might easily do.

Francis Gabreski

684. George, James A. "Aerospace Profile: A Salute to America's Top Living Ace." *Aerospace Historian*, 15 (Spring 1968), 4+.

The top-ranking ace of World War II, Gabreski flew 166 missions in 56th Fighter Group P-47's and shot down 31 Luftwaffe aircraft, adding another 6 1/2 credits for air victories in Korea. He rose to the rank of general in the postwar air force, and it would be helpful if Gabrewski, like Eaker, would publish memoirs.

685. Hess, William N. "Francis Gabreski." In: his *American Aces of World War II*. New York: Arco, 1968, pp. 28-29.

The briefest of capsule biographies.

686. Tregaskis, Richard. "Gabreski, Avenger of the Skies." *Saturday Evening Post*, CCXXV (December 13, 1952), 17-19+.

Tregaskis, noted author of *Guadalcanal Diary*, recounts Gabreski's World War II service in an article designed to note his accomplishments in the Korean conflict.

Donald S. Gentile

687. Gentile, Don S., as told to Ira Wolfert. *One Man Air Force.* New York: L.R. Fisher, 1944. 55p.

In 182 4th Fighter Group missions, Gentile downed just a few percentage points less than 20 German aircraft; this slim volume of the pilot's personal reflections are recounted by a noted journalist who recorded them during a time when the two were bunkmates in England.

John T. Godfrey

688. Godfrey, John T. *The Look of Eagles.* New York: Random House, 1958. 245p.

Memoirs of the 4th Fighter Group 16.3-victory ace who sometimes flew as Gentile's wingman, winning the envy of Goering and praise from Roosevelt, Churchill, and Arnold; shot down and captured in August 1944, Godfrey escaped his German POW camp and finally reached Allied lines near Nürnberg in April 1945.

Ralph K. Hofer

689. Rust, Kenn C. "The Last of the Red Hot Pilots." *American Aviation Historical Society Journal*, IX (Summer 1964), 116-128.

A biography of 15-victory 4th Fighter Group ace Ralph Hofer, the highest scoring Eighth Air Force fighter pilot lost in air-to-air combat during the war.

James H. Howard

690. Carnes, Cecil. "Mustang Whip: Major James H. Howard." *Saturday Evening Post*, CCXVI (April 22, 1944), 22-23+.

The story of how 6-victory 356th Fighter Squadron (354th Fighter Group) commander Howard single-handedly beat off 30 Luftwaffe Me-109's attacking B-17's near Oschersleben on January 11, 1944, and won the Congressional Medal of Honor.

Bernard L. Hutain

691. Hutain, Bernard L. "Liberator Pilot." *American Aviation Historical Society Journal*, IX (Winter 1964), 46-53.

Recollections of a 446th Bombardment Group (H) pilot's B-24 missions from December 1943 through June 1944.

Jack Ilfrey

692. Ilfrey, Jack, with Max Reynolds. *Happy Jack's Go-Buggy: A World War II Fighter Pilot's Personal Documents.* Hicksville, N.Y.: Exposition Press, 1979. 167p.

First written in 1946 but not published until 1979, Ilfrey records his Mediterranean and European missions, during which time he downed 8 German aircraft, rose to command the 79th Fighter Squadron (20th Fighter Group), and force landed his P-38 in Portugal and escaped--the only U.S. pilot to avoid internment when caught in a neutral country.

Robert S. Johnson

693. Johnson, Robert S. *Thunderbolt*. New York: Rinehart, 1958. 305p.

A well-written memoir of the author's training and combat service with the 56th Fighter Group of the Eighth Air Force; flying P-47's, the author shot down 28 German aircraft to rank just behind Gabreski as the top AAF ace in Europe.

694. Tregaskis, Richard. "Hot Pilot Cools Off." *Saturday Evening Post*, CCXVIII (March 23, 1946), 17+.

A brief review of Johnson's wartime exploits; the title stems from the fact that the ace was ordered home after May 1944 to boss an operational training unit in Texas until war's end.

John R. "Killer" Kane

695. Kane, John R. "The War Diary of John R. 'Killer' Kane, Out in the Blue." Edited by Kenn C. Rust. *American Aviation Historical Society Journal*, XXVII (Fall 1982), 223-233; (Winter 1982), 263-272; XXVIII (Spring 1983), 32-40.

Recounts the author's service in North Africa in 1942-1943, including his leadership of the B-24's of the 98th Bombardment Group (H), "The Pyramiders," on the August 1, 1943, raid on Ploesti, for which he was awarded the Congressional Medal of Honor. Kane returned to the U.S. in February 1944 and finished the war commanding air bases in Idaho and Nebraska.

Laurence S. Kuter

696. Hansell, Haywood S. "Airpower Pioneers: General Laurence S. Kuter." *Air Force Magazine*, LXIII (June 1980), 95-97.

697. ———. "General Laurence S. Kuter, 1905-1979." *Aerospace Historian*, XXVII (June 1980), 91-94.

Deputy Chief of Air Staff at AAF Headquarters in early 1942, Kuter was posted to Europe to command the 1st Bomb Wing of VIII Bomber Command and in 1943 to North Africa as chief of the Allied Tactical Air Forces in the Tunisian campaign; returned to America by Arnold's direct order, Kuter continued his work on the air staff and participated in international conferences, including the Yalta and Malta conferences as Arnold's representative. Kuter's memoirs, *Airman at Yalta*, are cited above in Section II:A on diplomacy. A brief obituary, "An Air Force General," by Irving B. Holley, Jr. appears in the June 1980 issue of *Aerospace Historian*.

Curtis E. LeMay

698. *Army Times*, Editors of. "General Curtis E. LeMay." In: their *Famous American Military Leaders of World War II*. New York: Dodd, Mead, 1962, pp. 59-67.

A brief biography of the colorful, hard-driving, cigar-chewing leader. Another, contemporary, concise account is Bernard W. Crandell's "'Iron Ass' ... Was the Name," which appeared in the August 1943 issue of *Air Force*.

699. LeMay, Curtis E. *Mission with LeMay*. Garden City, N.Y.: Doubleday, 1965.

These well-written memoirs cover the author's entire career through his retirement as USAF Chief-of-Staff in 1965. During World War II, LeMay organized and led the 305th Bombardment Group (H) of VIII Bomber Command in England, where he used it to devise tactics for the improvement of bombing accuracy; promoted to command the B-17's of the 3rd Bomb Division, LeMay led the Regensburg raid of October 1943. In March 1944, LeMay was transferred home to direct B-29 strikes in the Pacific, the service for which he is best remembered.

Walker M. "Bud" Mahurin

700. Mahurin, Walker. *Honest John: The Autobiography of Walker M. Mahurin*. New York: Putnam, 1962. 313p.

Flying P-47's with the 56th Fighter Group, the author had 19.75 victories before being shot down in March 1944; escaping back to England with the help of the French underground, Mahurin was transferred to the Pacific where he added one more victory.

701. Powell, Hickman. "What It Takes to Be a Thunderbolt Ace." *Popular Science*, CXLIV (May 1944), 56a-56h.

An account of Mahurin's victories written (but not published) before his loss.

George E. Preddy, Jr.

702. Beaman, John R. "The Unknown Ace: Major George E. Preddy, Jr." *American Aviation Historical Society Journal*, XIV (Winter 1969), 242-245.

A brief account of the 26.83-victory 352nd Fighter Group ace who was shot down by *American* AA fire on December 25, 1944, while chasing a German aircraft.

703. Noah, Joseph W. *Wings God Gave My Soul*. Annandale, Va.: Charles Baptie Studios, 1974. 209p.

A competent biography of the ace by his cousin.

Carl A. "Tooey" Spaatz

704. Barnett, Lincoln. "General 'Tooey' Spaatz." *Life*, XIV (April 19, 1942), 72-76.

Very little, surprisingly, has been written on Spaatz, who, like Arnold, Eaker, and Doolittle, was a major prewar aviation pioneer. This contemporary portrait is pure fluff.

705. Cook, Don. "Tactician of the War Skies: Carl A. Spaatz." In: his *Fighting Americans of Today*. New York: E.P. Dutton, 1944, pp. 55-57.

Chief of the AAF Combat Command, he was posted to England in July 1942 to command the Eighth Air Force and all U.S. air forces in Europe; leaving Eaker in command, he departed for North Africa in December 1942 to organize and run the Northwest African Air Force. After the invasion of Italy, Spaatz became Deputy Commander of the Mediterranean Allied Air Forces, a post he held until named to boss the U.S. Strategic Air Forces in Europe in January 1944. He finished the war supervising B-29 raids on Japan.

706. Eaker, Ira C. "General Carl A. Spaatz, U.S.A.F., June 28, 1891-July 14, 1974." *Air Force*, LVII (September 1974), 43-53.

Eaker knew Spaatz very well and in this obituary summary presents a fine combination recollection-appreciation-biography; Eaker's other comments on Spaatz are contained in his piece on Westover, Arnold, and Spaatz, cited under Arnold above.

707. Goldberg, Alfred. "General Carl A. Spaatz." In: Michael Carver, ed. *War Lords: Military Commanders of the 20th Century*. Boston, Mass.: Little, Brown, 1976, pp. 568-581.

This brief contribution is probably the best-balanced account of Spaatz's role as a combat commander in World War II. The papers of General Spaatz, like those of Generals Arnold and Eaker, are in the Library of Congress.

708. Lee, John. "General Tooey." *Flying*, XXXVIII (May 1946), 32-33+.

A brief review of the general's wartime career.

709. Middleton, David. "Boss of the Heavyweights: Lt. Gen. Carl Spaatz." *Saturday Evening Post*, CCXVI (May 20, 1944), 18-19+.

An examination of Spaatz's contribution, especially in Africa and as boss of the strategic bombing campaign after January 1944.

710. Puryear, Edgar F., Jr. "Carl Spaatz." In: his *Stars in Flight: Studies in Air Force Leadership*. San Rafael, Calif.: Presidio Press, 1981, pp. 47-98.

An excellent examination of those qualities and traits of the general's command style which ranks with Goldberg's piece, cited above, as an important starting place for study of Spaatz's service.

711. Shoemaker, Robert H., and Leonard A. Paris. "General Carl A. Spaatz." In: their *Famous American Generals*. New York: Crowell, 1946, pp. 185-196.

A brief, non-critical review of Spaatz's wartime service.

James Stewart

712. Lay, Beirne. "Jimmy Stewart's Finest Performance." *Saturday Evening Post*, CCXVIII (December 8, 1945), 18-19+; (December 15, 1945), 20+.

A detailed overview of the noted actor's wartime service with the 445th and 453rd Bombardment Groups (H) in Europe.

Arthur W. Tedder

713. Goldsmith, R.F.K. "The Development of Air Power in Joint Operations: Lord Tedder's Contribution to World War II." *Army Quarterly and Defence Journal*, XCIV (July 1967), 192-201; XCV (October 1967), 254-261.

This British Air Chief Marshal, whose techniques for air-ground cooperation saw sterling application in the Western Desert campaign, was appointed Air C-in-C Mediterranean in 1943 and thereafter began a partnership with General Dwight D. Eisenhower which would carry through to the end of the war. His policy for the use of air power independently or in support of ground/sea forces was continued after Tedder became Deputy Supreme Commander under Eisenhower in Europe.

714. Owen, Robert. *Tedder*. London: Collins, 1952. 320p.

A career biography of the British airman which emphasizes his contributions both to air power and to the execution of the war strategy which brought victory to the Allies in western Europe.

715. Tedder, Arthur W. *With Prejudice: The War Memoirs of Marshal of the Royal Air Force Lord Tedder*. Boston, Mass.: Little, Brown, 1967. 692p.

An honest review of the author's wartime service, especially his duties as Deputy Supreme Commander; includes insights into the war in the Mediterranean and northwest Europe and into the Allied high command, certain members of which, notably General Montgomery, come in for criticism.

Richard E. Turner

716. Turner, Richard E. *Big Friend, Little Friend: Memoirs of a World War II Fighter Pilot*. Garden City, N.Y.: Doubleday, 1969. 176p.

A useful recollection by an 11-victory 354th Fighter Group ace of air combat and bomber escorts during the winter of 1943-1944.

C. CAMPAIGNS AND BATTLES

Introduction: The citations below reveal details on some of the most intensive combat of World War II. Here is combat of both a strategic and tactical nature, divided into three parts: events in the Mediterranean Theater, events in the European Theater, and those concerned with the Combined Bomber Offensive. In addition to these references, however, readers should be aware that many of the handbooks/

encyclopedias and general war histories noted in Section I above, as well as those covered in the other parts of this section and those in Section IV, The War on Land, and Section V, The War at Sea, below, provide information on the AAF's great air campaigns and battles.

1. Mediterranean Theater

716a. Blumenson, Martin. "The Bombing of Monte Cassino." *American Heritage*, XIX (August 1968), 18-23, 84-89.

Believing the Germans to be using the Benedictine abbey on this mountain which dominated the fighting lines some 90 miles southeast of Rome, the Allies leveled the ancient building in a massive February 15, 1944, bombing attack. Blumenson examines the arguments for and against the raid and the question of German occupancy.

717. Coles, Harry L. *The Ninth Air Force in the Western Desert Campaign to 23 January 1943.* USAAF Historical Study, no. 30. Washington, D.C.: Headquarters, U.S. Army Air Forces, 1945. 134p.

Created from the U.S. Middle East Air Force on November 12, 1942, the Ninth, under General Brereton and consisting of B-24's, B-25's, and P-40's, assisted the British in their push west from Egypt.

718. ———. *Participation in the Ninth and Twelfth Air Forces in the Sicilian Campaign.* USAAF Historical Study, no. 37. Washington, D.C.: Headquarters, U.S. Army Air Forces, 1945. 246p.

Brereton's Ninth and Spaatz's Twelfth, then part of the Allied Northwest African Air Forces, attacked targets in Italy and Sicily from bases in Africa in support of the Anglo-American invasion "Husky."

719. Davis, Frank. "How to Conquer the Continent: Our Smashing Air Offensive in Tunisia." *Saturday Evening Post*, CCXVI (July 24, 1943), 20-21+; (July 31, 1943), 20-21+.

In essence, a review of the tactical operations of the Twelfth Air Force in support of Allied ground troops, including the destruction of German aircraft in the air and on the ground and the bombing of ports and roads employed by the retreating Nazis. Suggests that the same tactics would work well in northwest Europe.

720. Ethell, Jeffrey L. "Lightning over Africa: The Story of America's Versatile and Durable P-28 During World War II Action over North Africa." *Aviation Quarterly*, V (Spring 1979), 88-104.

Discusses the aircraft and its campaigns in North Africa.

721. ———. "Lightning Pilots." *American Aviation Historical Society Journal*, XVII (Fall 1972), 11-17.

A pictorial examination of the role of the P-38's in "Operation Torch," the invasion of French North Africa.

722. Gervasi, Frank. "Air Power Did It: British and American Planes Averted Disaster in Egypt." *Collier's*, CX (October 17, 1942), 13+.

Includes a discussion of how the B-24's of General Brereton's Middle East Air Forces hit Rommel's bases at Tobruk and Benghazi.

723. ———. "Air Power Is Winning." *Collier's*, CXII (August 21, 1943), 13+.

A look at the campaigns of General Spaatz's Northwest African Allied Air Forces against the Germans in Tunisia, and Axis bases in Italy and the Mediterranean islands.

724. ———. "Rommel Meets the AAF." *Collier's*, CX (November 21, 1942), 13-14+.

More on the role of the Middle East Air Forces, with special attention to the El Alamein battle.

725. Guedalla, Philip. *Middle East, 1940-1942: A Study in Air Power.* London: Hodder and Stoughton, 1944. 237p.

A contemporary account of the strategy and use of aircraft in the Middle East, including North Africa, Greece, Crete, Iraq, Syria, Iran, and Malta told from a British viewpoint.

726. Hoelle, William J. "Lightnings in Africa." *Flying*, XXXII (May 1943), 24-25+.

A contemporary look at the battles of the P-38's similar in vein to Ethell's studies above.

727. Kuter, Laurence S. "'Goddammit, Georgie!'" *Air Force Magazine*, LVI (February 1973), 51-56.

Examines Patton's failure to make full use of Twelfth Air Force air support in the Tunisian campaign.

728. McClendon, Dennis E. *"The Lady Be Good": Mystery Bomber of World War II.* New York: Stein and Day, 1962. 208p.

A somewhat padded account of a B-24 which failed to return to its Libyan base from a raid over Naples and which was presumed lost in the Mediterranean, only to be discovered 16 years later by an oil exploration 440 miles away in the desert. Reconstructs the aircraft's last flight, the plight and death of its men after the crash, and the location of the plane and crew.

729. MacCloskey, Monro. *"Torch" and the Twelfth Air Force.* New York: Richard Rosen, 1971. 192p.

Provides background on the strategy and execution of the aerial phase of the North African landings and the formation and role of General Doolittle's new command, the Twelfth.

730. Maycock, Thomas. *The Air Phase of the North African Invasion.* USAAF Historical Study, no. 105. Washington, D.C.: Headquarters, U.S. Army Air Forces, 1948. 112p.

An official review of the support given "Operation Torch" by the newly formed Twelfth Air Force, with some comment on the aerial roles of the RAF, USN, and Royal Navy. This title, and the next, are more succinctly summarized by MacCloskey, cited above.

731. ———. *The Twelfth Air Force in the North African Winter Campaign, November 11, 1942 to the Reorganization of February 10, 1943.* USAAF Historical Study, no. 114. Washington, D.C.: Headquarters, U.S. Army Air Forces, 1946. 219p.

Reviews the work of Doolittle's 500 aircraft in support of Eisenhower's invasion of French North Africa and the first part of the Tunisian campaign.

732. Norstad, Laures. "Airlock in Italy." *Air Force*, XXVIII (January 1945), 31-36, 60.

The one-time operations director for the Mediterranean Allied Air Forces and later NATO Supreme Commander discusses "Operation Strangle," begun in 1944 with the objective of smothering German operations in central Italy from the air.

733. Rodgers, Edith C. *The A.A.F. in the Middle East: A Study of the Origins of the Ninth Air Force.* USAAF Historical Study, no. 108. Washington, D.C.: Headquarters, U.S. Army Air Forces, 1945. 190p.

Reviews the wandering Halverson Detachment of B-24's which were absorbed into General Brereton's Middle East Air Forces, which, in turn, supported British operations in the Western Desert until being redesignated the Ninth on November, 12, 1942.

734. ———. *The Reduction of Pantelleria and Adjacent Islands, 8 May-14 June 1943.* USAAF Historical Study, no. 52. Washington, D.C.: Headquarters, U.S. Army Air Forces, 1947. 115p.

Following the Allied victory in North Africa, this Italian island base, some 150 miles from Malta, was pounded by AAF and RAF bombers until the defenders were forced to surrender.

735. Rust, Kenn C. "The Ninth Air Force in the Desert." *American Aviation Historical Review*, IX (Winter 1964), 274-279.

A review of Brereton's force in support of the British.

736. Sallager, F.M. *"Operation Strangle," Italy, Spring 1944: A Case Study of Tactical Air Interdiction.* Santa Monica, Calif.: RAND Corporation, 1972. 95p.

A review of the Allied air campaign against German lines of communication in central Italy which reveals that the Nazis were, indeed, hampered but were able to hang on by impressing local food and trucks and moving at night. What was learned in

"Strangle" was later employed by the U.S. against the Ho Chi Minh trail in Indochina--with pretty much the same results.

737. Schmaltz, Robert E. "The Uncertainty of Predicting Results of an Interdiction Campaign." *Aerospace Historian*, XVII (December 1970), 150-153.

A brief review of the difficulties involved with the planning and execution of "Operation Strangle."

738. Schweinfurt, William. "African Combat Diary." *Air Classics*, XVI (December 1980), 14-26; XVII (January 1981), 14-19, 76-82.

The 50-mission diary of a B-17 crewman from the 2nd Bombardment Group (H) which flew missions over Tunisia, Italy, and the Mediterranean in 1943.

739. Shores, Christopher F., ed. *Pictorial History of the Mediterranean Air War.* 3 vols. London: Ian Allan, 1972-1980.

A well-illustrated account of the work of RAF and AAF aircraft over the Western Desert, in Tunisia, Italy, and over the Mediterranean; does not neglect the operations of Luftwaffe and Regia Aeronautica warplanes.

740. ———, and Hans Ring. *Fighters over the Desert.* New York: Arco, 1969. 256p.

741. ———, and William N. Hess. *Fighters over Tunisia.* New York: International Publications Service, 1975. 500p.

These two volumes constitute probably the most useful available on the air war over North Africa from June 1940 to July 1943. The narrative is organized as a daily journal which provides data on the combat operations of Allied/Axis squadrons down to the locations, times of day, and names of pilots involved. Readable, without national bias, and illustrated with maps and photographs, the works' only major failing is lack of indexing.

742. Simpson, Albert F. *Air Phase of the Italian Campaign to 1 January 1944.* USAAF Historical Study, no. 115. Washington, D.C.: Headquarters, U.S. Army Air Forces, 1946. 405p.

A detailed review of AAF operations over Italy from Salerno to just before the Anzio invasion which includes discussion of strategy, logistics, and execution of missions both in support of troops and against Axis targets such as communications lines. This study, like all of the AAF Historical Studies cited here, is available in the Albert F. Simpson Historical Research Center at Air University.

743. Stigler, Franz. "The Palm Sunday Massacre." *Air Classics*, XII (February 1976), 16-21, 80-81.

A 28-victory Luftwaffe ace describes the April 1943 destruction of German transports en route to Tunisia by Twelfth Air Force P-40's.

744. Thruelson, Richard, and Elliott Arnold. *Mediterranean Sweep: Air Stories from El Alamein to Rome*. New York: Duell, Sloane, and Pearce, 1944. 278p.

An anthology of 50 true stories, collected at the urging of General Eaker, covering the exploits of Anglo-American airmen in the Mediterranean Allied Air Forces; length for stories varies from many pages to brief anecdotes.

745. United States. Army Air Forces. *The AAF in Northwest Africa*. Wings at War, no. 6. Washington, D.C.: Headquarters, U.S. Army Air Forces, 1945. 67p.

A brief, popularly written overview of Twelfth Air Force operations in the North African invasion and Battle of Tunisia.

746. ———. ———. *The AAF in the Invasion of Southern France*. Wings at War, no. 1. Washington, D.C.: Headquarters, U.S. Army Air Forces, 1945. 60p.

Similar to the last entry; presents a popular history of support for the "Dragoon" invasion by the Mediterranean Allied Air Forces.

747. Watling, Geoffrey. "Mission to Fatha: The 443rd Bombardment Group (M), 24 February 1944." *American Aviation Historical Society Journal*, XVIII (Summer 1973), 96-108.

A Twelfth Air Force B-26 raid on a Luftwaffe airfield near Rome.

2. European Theater

748. Ackerman, Robert W. *Employment of Strategic Bombers in a Tactical Role, 1941-1951*. USAF Historical Study, no. 88. Washington, D.C.: Office of Air Force History, Department of the Air Force, 1953. 183p.

Includes a review of the use of some 1,500 Eighth Air Force B-17's and B-24's to drop bombs on a narrow patch of German positions near St. Lô, France, on July 25, 1944, in preparation for the breakout from the Normandy beachhead.

749. Arnold, Henry H. "The Isolation of the Battlefield by Air Power." *Military Review*, XXIV (July 1944), 3-8.

A discussion of the Allied disruption of German lines of communication and resupply in preparation for the D-day invasion.

750. Browne, Roger J. "'Eggcup' Was the Call Sign." *Infantry Journal*, LXIII (July 1948), 29-32.

On the cooperation of Ninth Air Force fighter bombers with tanks of the U.S. Fourth Armored Division, June 1944-March 1945.

751. Collier, Basil. *The Battle of the V-Weapons, 1944-1945*. New York: William Morrow, 1965. 191p.

A popular British account of the actions taken to defeat the German vengeance rockets, including bombing by U.S. heavy and medium bombers; the author concludes that the only effective solution to the problem was for Allied soldiers to overrun the launching sites on the ground.

752. Ethell, Jeffrey L. "Deadly Interception." *Air Classics*, XIII (May 1977), 74-81.

U.S. 359th Fighter Group P-51's vs. an Me-163 of I/KG 400 on August 16, 1944.

753. George, Robert H. *Ninth Air Force, April-November 1944*. USAAF Historical Study, no. 36. Washington, D.C.: Headquarters, U.S. Army Air Forces, 1944. 376p.

An almost contemporary report of operations rather than a historical analysis, this work details the Ninth, moved to England from Africa as a tactical air force, and its medium bombers, fighters, and transports in support of the Allied invasion and race across France.

754. Havener, J.K. "The Mediums Were Also Out." *Aerospace Historian*, XXIX (December 1982), 218-226.

Recollections of the author's service with the B-26's of the 344th Bombardment Group (M) over France in December 1944.

755. Hennessy, Juliette A. *Tactical Operations of the Eighth Air Force, 6 June 1944 to 8 May 1945*. USAF Historical Study, no. 7. Washington, D.C.: Office of Air Force History, Department of the Air Force, 1952. 285p.

An extremely detailed review of the use of the B-17's and B-24's to "carpet bomb" small areas in support of Allied ground troops and the destruction of German bunkers, gun emplacements, and dumps behind the lines during Allied offensives.

756. Hutton, Bud, and Andrew A. Rooney. *Air Gunner*. New York: Farrar, 1944. 236p.

Human interest stories of air gunners on medium- and heavy-bombers on ETO operations, both tactical and strategic, by two sergeants, the second of whom went on to become a television writer and "60 Minutes" commentator.

757. Jacobs, William A. "Tactical Air Doctrine and AAF Close Air Support in the European Theater, 1944-1945." *Aerospace Historian*, XXVII (March 1980), 35-49.

A review of the development of the strategy and tactics of close-air support for ground troops as employed by the tactical air commands of the U.S. Ninth Army Air Force.

758. Johnson, John E. "Seven League Boots." In: his *Full Circle: The Tactics of Air Fighting, 1914-1964*. New York: Ballantine Books, 1964, pp. 221-234.

The noted 38-victory British ace's recollections of U.S. Eighth and Ninth Air Force fighter operations and combat tactics.

759. Kingston-McCloughry, E.J. *War in Three Dimensions: The Impact of Airpower Upon the Classical Principles of War.* London: Cape, 1949. 159p.

A study resulting from this British Air Vice Marshal's experiences in helping to plan the Normandy campaign as Chief Operational Planner to Air Chief Marshal Sir T.L. Mallory at Headquarters, Allied Expeditionary Air Force.

760. Kuter, Laurence S. "D-Day." *Air Force Magazine*, LXII (June 1979), 96-101.

A review and reminiscence of U.S. air operations in support of the June 6, 1944, invasion of Normandy.

761. Leigh-Mallory, Trafford. "Air Operations by the Allied Expeditionary Air Force in Northwest Europe from November 15, 1943 to September 30, 1944." Supplement 37839, *London Gazette*, January 2, 1947.

The boss of the AEAF, in a report originally given in November 1944, describes Allied air attacks on German lines of communications, supply dumps, marshalling yards, gun emplacements, troop concentrations, etc., before, during, and after the Normandy invasion.

762. Maycock, Thomas J. "Tactical Uses of Air Power in World War II: Notes on the Development of AAF Tactical Doctrine." *Military Affairs*, XIV (Winter 1950), 186-191.

A brief review of the development of strategy and tactics of close-air support for troops in Europe during World War II.

763. O'Doherty, John K. "Tactical Air Power and the Battle of France." *Airman*, VIII (June 1964), 42-48.

An overview of Ninth Air Force operations during the summer of 1944.

764. Olsen, Jack. *Aphrodite: Desperate Mission.* New York: G.P. Putnam, 1970. 228p.

A report of the Allied "Aphrodite" project: guiding radio-controlled explosives-laden bombers into German vengeance weapons launching sites. Reviews the origins and execution of the plan, the technical details involved, and the generally unsuccessful results, including the loss of Lt. Joseph Kennedy, Jr.

765. Parker, Ben L. "Air Power in a Tactical Role." *Military Review*, XXVI (August 1946), 47-53.

An examination of the impact made by Ninth Air Force close-air support for Allied soldiers and tanks in France, the Low Countries, and Germany.

766. Perkins, J.W. "The Use of Heavy Bombers on Tactical Missions." *Military Review*, XXVI (May 1946), 18-21.

Details the concept of "carpet bombing" in support of Allied ground troops, especially at St. Lô in July 1944.

767. Ramsey, John F. *The Ninth Air Force in the European Theater of Operations, 16 October 1943 to 16 April 1944.* USAAF Historical Study, no. 32. Washington, D.C.: Headquarters, U.S. Army Air Forces, 1945. 229p.

A detailed review of the transfer of this air arm to England and of its designation as a tactical arm of the Allied Expeditionary Air Force; examines its operations against Luftwaffe airfields and other communications and manufacturing targets in preparation for the Normandy landings.

768. ———. *The War Against the Luftwaffe: AAF Counterair Operations, April 1943 to June 1944.* USAAF Historical Study, no. 110. Washington, D.C.: Headquarters, U.S. Army Air Forces, 1945. 257p.

An examination of the concentrated Allied plan to neutralize the German air force before the Normandy invasion by seeking it out and engaging it in massive air battles and pounding its airfields, supply points, and those factories which manufactured warplanes.

769. Rust, Kenn C. "Lightnings at War." *American Aviation Historical Society Journal*, VIII (Summer 1963), 128-131.

The role of the P-38 as bomber escort and close support aircraft in the ETO, 1943-1945.

770. ———, and William N. Hess. "The German Jets and the United States Army Air Force." *American Aviation Historical Society Journal*, VIII (Fall 1963), 155-184.

A report on the design and development of the Luftwaffe's Me-163 and 262 and their combats with fighters of the Eighth and Ninth Air Forces.

771. Schmaltz, Robert E. "The Impact of Allied Air Interdiction on German Strategy for Normandy." *Aerospace Historian*, XVII (December 1970), 153-155.

A quick analysis which shows German planners were confused as to how to reinforce the Normandy area.

772. United States. Army Air Forces. *Air-Ground Teamwork on the Western Front.* Wings at War, no. 5. Washington, D.C.: Headquarters, U.S. Army Air Forces, 1945. 50p.

A popular record of the XIX TAC in supporting Patton's advance in August 1944.

773. ———. ———. *Sunday Punch in Normandy.* Wings at War, no. 2. Washington, D.C.: Headquarters, U.S. Army Air Forces, 1945. 32p.

A small popular account of the tactical use of heavy bombers in the Normandy invasion and breakout.

774. Wilkerson, Lawrence B. "Low-Level Mass Tactical Operations." *Military Review*, LXI (July 1981), 24-32.

Recalls the swarms of Allied fighter bombers which gave close-air support to American soldiers in northwest Europe.

775. Yexall, John. "Air and the Rhine Crossing." *Flight*, XLVII (April 12, 1945), 388-391; (April 19, 1945), 416-419; (April 26, 1945), 444-447.

A report on Ninth Air Force fighter bomber and troop transport operations in support of the U.S. Army's crossing of the Rhine River into Germany in early 1945.

3. Combined Bomber Offensive

776. Ardery, Philip. *Bomber Pilot: A Memoir of World War II*. Lexington: University Press of Kentucky, 1978. 226p.

Reminiscences of a 389th Bombardment Group (H) B-24 pilot during the period July 6, 1943, to June 6, 1944; this well-written account recalls a number of noted missions, including those to Ploesti, Vegesack, Gotha, and Berlin. Includes some of the author's philosophy and lots of action.

777. Item deleted.

778. Bamford, Hal. "Priority Target." *Airman*, III (October 1959), 44-47.

A popular rendering of the famous August 1, 1943, attack on the refineries at Ploesti, Rumania, by 177 B-24's from Africa, with mention of later attacks by Fifteenth Air Force bombers.

779. Bendiner, Elmer. *The Fall of Fortresses*. New York: G.P. Putnam, 1980. 258p.

A 397th Bombardment Group (H) B-17 navigator presents a memoir and generalized look at the concepts of strategic bombing, life in wartime Britain, and recollections of a number of raids, including the first two Schweinfurt missions as witnessed from his aircraft, the "Tondelayo." Includes the author's philosophy and much action; a valuable complement to Philip Ardery's work cited above.

780. Bidinian, Larry J. *The Combined Bomber Offensive Against the German Civilian, 1942-1945*. Lawrence, Kans.: Coronado Press, 1976. 284p.

An examination of the impact of the various raids on the lives and livelihoods of German civilians; presents a picture of suffering which at some points is horrible to contemplate.

781. Bottomley, Norman. "The Strategic Bomber Offensive Against Germany." *Journal of the Royal United Service Institute*, XCIII (May 1948), 224-239.

An overview of the Combined Bomber Offensive with special attention to RAF night raiding; the author was an Air Chief Marshal who served as Deputy Chief of Air Staff in 1943-1945 and succeeded Sir Arthur Harris as chief of Bomber Command in 1945.

782. Bowman, Marvin S. "Stopping Over at Ivan's Airdrome." *Air Force Magazine*, LV (April 1972), 51-55.

A report by a participant on one of the AAF shuttle bombing missions to Russia; shuttle bombing was the process of departing one base, bombing a target, and landing at another airfield beyond.

783. Bradley, Mark E. "The P-51 over Berlin." *Aerospace Historian*, XXI (Fall 1974), 129-138.

A record of the escort fighters' attempt to protect the heavies as they attacked the German capital in March and April 1944.

784. Brodie, Bernard. *Strategic Air Power in World War II*. Rand Memorandum RM-1866. Santa Monica, Calif.: RAND Corporation, 1957. 45p.

An examination of the effectiveness of strategic bombing against Germany (and Japan) during the war which concluded that while effective, the process was not decisive.

785. Brooks, Jim. "The Day the 31st Fighter Group Won Its Unit Citation." *Air Force Magazine*, LV (October 1972), 73-75.

A former P-51 pilot recalls the April 21, 1944, escort of Fifteenth Air Force B-17's and B-24's to Ploesti.

786. Caidin, Martin. *Black Thursday*. New York: E.P. Dutton, 1960. 320p.

The best popular account of the second VIII Bomber Command attack on the ball-bearing plants at Schweinfurt, Germany, which cost the Americans 60 bombers and 600 aircrew lost and created a controversy over the idea of daylight strategic bombardment and the need for adequate escort fighters.

787. ———. "The Forts Come Home." *Air Force and Space Digest*, XLVI (October 1963), 72-74+.

A capsule view of the second Schwenfurt raid.

788. ———. *The Night Hamburg Died*. New York: Ballantine Books, 1960. 158p.

The attacks on this German city in the summer of 1943 were principally an RAF Bomber Command show, although the Eighth Air Force mounted a few daylight attacks as a way of keeping the pressure on; Caidin tells the story in all its excruciating detail.

789. Cameron, William R. "Ploesti." *Air Force Magazine*, LIV (August 1971), 57-63.

Another overview of the August 1, 1943, and later attacks on the Rumanian oil facilities.

790. Carnahan, Burrus M. "The Law of Air Bombardment and Its Historical Context." *Air Force Law Review*, XVII (Summer 1975), 39-60.

Looks for legality in the massive World War II Axis and Allied raids on civilian population centers--and finds little.

791. Clodfelter, Mark A. "Culmination Dresden, 1945." *Aerospace Historian*, XXVI (September 1979), 134-147.

Frequently noted as an example of aerial overkill and one of the most controversial raids of the war, the February, March, and April 1945 RAF/AAF attacks on this city are said to have killed well over 35,000 people.

792. Coffey, Thomas M. *Decision over Schweinfurt: The U.S. 8th Air Force Battle for Daylight Bombing.* New York: David McKay, 1977. 373p.

This book begins and ends with accounts of the August 17 and October 14, 1943, U.S. raids; in between these action accounts, the work examines the creation of the Eighth Air Force and its subsequent problems, including the British desire for joint night bombing, the lack of a long-range fighter escort, weather, etc. Coffey's journalistic saga is basically uncritical of the AAF daylight precision-bombing doctrine as espoused during the war.

793. Copp, DeWitt S. *Forged in Fire.* Garden City, N.Y.: Doubleday, 1982. 528p.

Follows the U.S. strategic bombing campaign in Europe in anecdotal style which describes the men who directed it and their contributions to it, including Arnold, Andrews, Eaker, Spaatz, LeMay, Kuter, and Hansell, both operationally against the Germans and diplomatically against the British, who long questioned the merits of daylight, unescorted, bombing attacks.

794. ———. "The Pioneer Plan for Air War." *Air Force Magazine*, LXV (October 1982), 74-78.

A look at the prewar AWPD-1 proposal.

795. Crossman, R.H.S. "Apocalypse at Dresden." *Esquire*, LX (November 1963), 149-152+.

This account of the spring 1945 raids is extremely critical of the necessity for them.

796. Dews, Edmund. *POL Storage as a Target for Air Attack: Evidence from the World War II Allied Air Campaigns Against Enemy Oil Installations.* RAND Note N-1523-PA/E. Santa Monica, Calif.: RAND Corporation, 1980. 30p.

Prepared as background material in support of a study of possible vulnerabilities in NATO's rear areas, this pamphlet reviews Allied air raids on Axis petroleum-oil-lubricants installations, points out the great damages done, and suggests a real current vulnerability.

797. Doolittle, James H., and Beirne Lay, Jr. "'*Impact*': Daylight Precision Bombing." *American History Illustrated*, XIV (February 1980), 8-12+.

Reprints an introduction from *Impact*, the confidential AAF pictorial, which provides an interesting look at the doctrine followed by B-17 and B-24 crews in Europe.

798. Drake, Francis V. *Vertical Warfare*. Garden City, N.Y.: Doubleday, 1943. 142p.

An analysis of the Allied strategic bombing campaign against Germany with arguments for its extension; includes 62 pages of black and white photos and interviews with bomber and fighter crews. Dismissed by many reviewers as overenthusiastic "air propaganda."

799. Dugan, James, and Carroll Stewart. *Ploesti: The Great Ground-Air Battle of 1 August 1943*. New York: Random House, 1962. 407p.

One of the best accounts of "Operation Tidalwave," this study is based on documentary research and over 160 interviews with survivors. Well written, detailed, and an excellent companion to Leon Wolff's earlier *Low Level Mission*, cited below.

800. Eaker, Ira C. "The Schweinfurt-Regensburg Raid." In: Stanley M. Ulanoff, ed. *Bombs Away!* Garden City, N.Y.: Doubleday, 1971, pp. 212-216.

The August 17, 1943, "double strike" was against both the Schweinfurt ball-bearing plants and the aircraft factories at Regensburg; the results against both targets are questionable (though not in the author's eyes), and the cost was high: 60 bombers and 600 aircrew lost.

801. ———. "Some Memories of Winston Churchill." *Aerospace Historian*, XIX (Fall 1972), 120-124.

On the author's efforts at the Casablanca Conference to persuade the British leader to accept the AAF daylight bombing strategy which, together with RAF night raids, would allow an "Around-the-Clock" attack on the Reich.

802. Emerson, William R. "Doctrine and Dogma: 'Operation Pointblank' as a Case History." *Army*, XIII (June 1963), 50-62.

"Pointblank" was the codename for the Allied Combined Bomber Offensive, the directive for which was issued at Casablanca on May 14, 1943, following the Churchill-Eaker discussion noted in the last citation; "Pointblank" brought a measure of coordination to the day-night Anglo-American procedures and at the August 1943 Quebec conference was declared to be a primary pre-invasion effort against Germany. This article is drawn from the next citation.

803. ———. *Operation Pointblank: A Tale of Bombers and Fighters*. Colorado Springs, Colo.: U.S.A.F. Academy, 1962. 44p.

A look at the CBO presented as the Fourth Harmon Memorial Lecture.

804. Ethell, Jeffrey L., and Alfred Price. "Raid 250: Target--Berlin." *Air Force Magazine*, LXIII (January 1980), 74-81.

A concise review of the AAF mission of March 6, 1944, during which only a few bombers hit the German capital.

805. ———. *Target Berlin: Mission 250, 6 March 1944*. New York and London: Jane's, 1983. 224p.

A well-written and well-researched account of the first large daylight U.S. raid on the Reich capital which, together with the article above and Ardery's reminiscence, represents the most recent (the only recent) findings on a contest from which 69 American bombers and 11 escort fighters did not return. Illustrated with maps, diagrams, and black and white photos, the story, told from both sides, is based not only on documents, but on interviews with over 160 survivors.

806. Frankland, Noble. *Bomber Offensive: The Devastation of Europe*. Ballantine's Illustrated History of World War II. New York: Ballantine Books, 1970. 160p.

The raids, planes, targeting procedures, and effectiveness of the giant Allied raids are covered in this pictorial which notes the ebb and flow of battle as one side then another gained temporary advantages.

807. ———. "Schweinfurt." In: Noble Frankland and Christopher Dowling, eds. *Decisive Battles of the 20th Century*. New York: David McKay, 1976, pp. 239-250.

A concise recounting of the diasatrous August 17 and October 14, 1943, raids. Frankland, one of Britain's foremost aviation authorities, coauthored the official British history of the CBO, noted below under Charles Webster.

808. Friedheim, Eric. "Beneath the Rubble of Schweinfurt." *Air Force*, XXVIII (June 1945), 4-7.

A report on the damage done to the city as verified by the victorious Americans who occupied the city late in the war.

809. Galbraith, John K. "After the Air Raids." *American Heritage*, XXXII (April-May 1981), 65-80.

A report on the 1945 investigation of the effectiveness of the war-long U.S. raids on German manufacturing.

810. Gervasi, Frank. "Flying Through Hell: How Col. [John R. "Killer"] Kane and His Crew Came Back from the Ploesti Raid." *Collier's*, CXII (October 2, 1943), 11+.

811. ———. "Hitting Hitler's Oil Barrel: The Memorable Achievement of the Ninth [Air Force]." *Collier's*, CXII (September 18, 1943), 34+.

Both of these contemporary accounts of the August 1, 1943, Ploesti mission concentrate on the bravery exhibited by the U.S. aircrews and make no mention of the high losses or little damage caused.

812. Gordon, Arthur. "Three Years over Germany." *Air Force*, XXVIII (September 1945), 33-50.

A brief review designed to give participants an overview.

813. Graham, Burton. "Attack on Schweinfurt." In: his *The Pictorial History of Air Battles*. London: Marshall Cavendish, 1974, pp. 74-83.

An illustrated general review of the August 17 and October 14, 1943, daylight disasters.

814. Hansell, Haywood S., Jr. *The Air Plan That Defeated Hitler*. Atlanta, Ga.: Higgins, McArthur/Longino and Porter, 1974. 278p.

Hansell, an insider and Eighth Air Force 1st Bomb Wing boss, reviews the prewar planning and later execution of the U.S. strategic bombing doctrine of daylight raids, while conceding certain mistakes like the lack of a long-range escort fighter until late in the war.

815. ———. "Balaklava Redeemed." *Air University Review*, XXV (June 1974), 93-106.

Designed as a review of the Jablonski title, cited below, Hansell goes on to argue that the "double strike" would have been more successful if RAF Bomber Command had joined in as originally planned.

816. ———. "The Plan That Defeated Hitler." *Air Force Magazine*, LXIII (July 1980), 106-113.

Hansell's review of prewar planning and wartime execution of AWPD-1.

817. ———. "Strategic Air Warfare." *Aerospace Historian*, XIII (Winter 1966), 153-160.

An overview of the CBO.

818. Harris, Arthur T. *Bomber Offensive*. New York: Macmillan, 1947. 288p.

Recollections of the wartime chief of RAF Bomber Command who believed he could win the war with strategic bombing alone; details the campaigns, especially those against the V-weapons and oil, his command's evolution, and wartime contacts with the Americans.

819. Helmreich, Jonathan A. "The Diplomacy of Apology: U.S. Bombings of Switzerland During World War II." *Air University Review*, XXVIII (May-June 1977), 19-37.

One of the few accounts of accidental attacks on neutral targets, caused most often by faulty navigation and poor weather.

820. Hersey, John. "The Saturation of Hamburg." *Life*, XV (December 27, 1943), 68-71.

Hersey's prose is accompanied by a number of photographs which show the results on the city of the Anglo-American raids of summer 1943.

821. Hicks, Edmond. "Soviet Sojourn: The First Shuttle-Bombing Mission to Russia." *Airpower Historian*, XI (January 1964), 1-5.

Flown from Amendola, Italy, to Poltava on June 2, 1944; the bombers, led by Gen. Eaker, were B-17's of the 97th Bombardment Group (H).

822. Hodges, R.H. "The 'Magic' 1000-Foot Circle." *Military Journal*, I (September-October 1977), 6-11; II (January-February 1978), 30-32.

On the excellent bombing accuracy of VIII Bomber Command mission number 113 against the Marienburg Focke Wulf facility on October 9, 1943.

823. Hopkins, George E. "Bombing and the American Conscience in World War II." *Historian*, XXVIII (Summer 1966), 451-473.

The American consensus favored the CBO and ignored the ethical considerations of bombing German civilians due to a belief that the U.S. was engaged in a "total war."

824. Howard, Fred S. *Whistle While You Wait*. New York: Duell, Sloane, and Pearce, 1945. 188p.

Reprints letters between an Eighth Air Force B-17 pilot and his wife written between early 1943 and mid-1944; the letters are mostly concerned with the human-interest aspects of the air war and life in Great Britain.

825. Hucker, Robert. "Fatal First Mission: The Marauder in Europe." *Air Classics*, XII (November 1976), 44-47.

Of 11 Eighth Air Force B-26's dispatched against the power stations at Ijmuiden and Haarlem, Holland, on May 17, 1943, one aborted and the other 10 were shot down.

826. Huston, James A. "Air Power and the German War Economy." *Marine Corps Gazette*, XXXIV (March 1950), 22-29.

A review of the CBO and its impact on Germany's ability to manufacture war materiel.

827. Infield, Glenn B. *Big Week*. New York: Pinnacle Books, 1974. 218p.

The only book-length study of the series of Eighth and Fifteenth Air Force and RAF raids mounted between February 20-25, 1944, after which the Luftwaffe began a selective defense against Allied air attacks.

828. ———. *The Poltava Affair: A Russian Warning--an American Tragedy*. New York: Macmillan, 1973. 265p.

Describes "Operation Frantic" and recalls the first U.S. shuttle-bombing mission to Russia (as noted in Hicks, above) from Italy; after the U.S. landing, the Poltava airfield was destroyed by German bombers as were most of the B-17's. Infield suggests that the Nazi success was due to a Soviet tip which constituted one of the first acts of the later "Cold War."

829. ———. "Shuttle Raiders to Russia." *Air Force Magazine*, LV (April 1972), 46-50.

A concise retelling of the data in the previous citation, minus the anti-communist undertone.

830. Irving, David J.C. *The Destruction of Dresden*. Rev. ed. London: Transworld, 1966. 287p.

An exciting, if not always accurate, account of the horror of the saturation bombing in February 1945 presented as an antiwar statement.

831. Jablonski, Edward. *Double Strike: The Epic Air Raids on Regensburg-Schweinfurt, August 17, 1943*. Garden City, N.Y.: Doubleday, 1974. 271p.

Analyzes the need for and situation at the time which brought this two-pronged effort, as well as the raids themselves: the approach to, bombing of, and departure from the targets and the loss of 60 U.S. aircraft. Includes a review of the results both for the men in the mission and for the entire U.S. ETO daylight bombing effort as a whole.

832. Jackson, Robert. *Bomber: Famous Bomber Missions of World War II*. New York: St. Martin's Press, 1980. 157p.

A journalistic account of some of the war's major raids, including Ploesti, Schweinfurt, and Berlin from the ETO.

833. Janis, Irving L. *Air War and Emotional Stress: Psychological Studies of Bombing and Civilian Defense*. New York: McGraw-Hill, 1951. 280p.

A study of how people react psychologically to bombing raids, including German civilians exposed to the strategic raids of the AAF.

834. Johnson, Robert E. "Flight to Poltava." *Flying*, XXXVII (July 1945), 24-25+.

An account of an escort mission with U.S. B-17's to Russia.

835. Julian, Thomas A. "'Operation Frantic' and the Search for American-Soviet Military Collaboration, 1941-1944." Unpublished Ph.D. Dissertation, Syracuse University, 1968.

An account of the diplomatic background behind the American effort to get the Soviets to accept U.S. shuttle raids to Russia by aircraft from Britain and Italy as well as an account of the

Eastern Air Command and the several missions actually flown. Draws heavily on the author's 1964 Air University, Air Command and Staff College, study, "The Political Implication of Military Operations and Assignments: The Eastern Command, United States Strategic Air Forces in Europe, 1943-1945--A Case Study."

836. Kennett, Lee. *A History of Strategic Bombing*. New York: Scribners, 1982. 222p.

Covers the period from 1783 through World War II, with emphasis on the 1939-1945 conflict. Contends that, although strategic bombing made a significant contribution to Allied victory, it failed to fulfill its advocates' expectations.

837. Kiley, Eugene. "Twenty-Nine Missions Over Europe." *Air Classics*, XIX (April 1983), 40-41, 58-61; (May 1983), 16-22, 76-78.

The personal diary of a 306th Bombardment Group (H) B-17 radio operator/gunner for the period from late 1943 to mid-1944; among the raids recalled is a January 1944 strike on Frankfurt.

838. Lay, Beirne, Jr. "Human Target over Germany." *Science Digest*, XV (March 1944), 7-11.

Recollections of a 100th Bombardment Group (H) pilot.

839. ———. *I've Had It: The Survival of a Bomb Group Commander*. New York: Harper, 1946, 141p.

Downed over France a month before D-Day, the author describes how he and his B-17 co-pilot escaped with the help of French civilian and resistance personnel.

840. ———. "The Regensburg Mission." In: Stanley M. Ulanoff, ed. *Bombs Away!* Garden City, N.Y.: Doubleday, 1971, pp. 217-223.

Reprinted from the December 1943 issue of *Air Force*, this recollection has been called the best on any mission of the war.

841. Lukas, Richard C. *Eagles East: The Army Air Forces and the Soviet Union, 1941-1945*. Tallahassee: Florida State University Press, 1970. 256p.

Like Julian above, Lukas reveals the little-known story of American attempts to collaborate with the Soviets on shuttle-bombing attacks on Germany, the difficulty of getting planes and supplies to Russia, and the cool reception received from Stalin and his followers; the only commercially published book on the subject except for Infield's, cited above, Lukas' work provides a fair and not overly Cold War-oriented account.

842. ———. "The 'Velvet' Project: Hope and Frustration." *Military Affairs*, XVIII (Summer 1964), 145-162.

"Velvet" was the codename for the Allied proposal, made late in 1942, to provide air assistance to strengthen the southern flank of the Soviets. This article recounts the protracted delay after which the Russians declined the offer.

843. Lytton, Henry D. "Bombing Policy in the Rome and Pre-Normandy Invasion Aerial Campaigns of World War II." *Military Affairs*, XLVII (April 1983), 53-58.

A study of aerial interdiction, the subtitle of which gives away the scope of the study: "Bridge-Bombing Strategy Vindicated--and Railyard Bombing Strategy Invalidated."

844. McCrary, John R., and David E. Scherman. *First of Many: A Journal of Action with the Men of the Eighth Air Force.* New York: Simon and Schuster, 1944. 241p.

An illustrated history of the VIII Bomber Command from its 12-plane raid on Rouen in August 1942 to D-day; includes 128 pages of black and white photographs, 100 contributed by *Life* magazine, and colorful narratives of some of the airmen. Reprinted by Aviation Book Co. in 1981.

845. MacIsaac, David. *Strategic Bombing in World War II: The Story of the United States Bombing Survey.* New York: Garland, 1976.

An account of the operation and organization of the USSBS and a look at its extensive findings and conclusions, which serves as a helpful introduction to the next citation; MacIsaac also reviews the concept and development of U.S. strategic bombing doctrine during the war.

846. ———, ed. *The United States Strategic Bombing Survey.* 10 vols. New York: Garland, 1981.

Reproduces, with illustrations, 30 of the 321 reports deemed to be the most important. The first six volumes contain the following studies relative to operations in the ETO; Nos. 1-4, 31, 40, 53, 59, 61-64, 92, 101, 109, 128, 134, 200, and 205. The original publications are for the most part noted below.

847. Michie, Allan A. *The Air Offensive Against Germany.* New York: Henry Holt, 1943. 152p.

A contemporary plea and indictment which caused a great stir in the American press; employing his knowledge of European air operations, Michie argued that the AAF was holding up the aerial destruction of Germany by its stubborn doctrinal rejection of RAF night bombing methods in favor of daylight strategic bombardment and suggests that if the AAF would join the British in a night blitz, a second front in Europe could be successful in 1943.

848. ———. "Germany Was Bombed to Defeat." *Reader's Digest*, XLVII (August 1945), 77-81.

The rejection of his proposal above did not halt Michie's approval of bombing or his glorification of the results at war's end.

849. ———. "How Much Has Bombing Hurt Germany?" *Reader's Digest*, XLII (January 1943), 3-8.

While the potential for destruction was great, the author finds that its effect in early 1943 was not great.

850. ———. "What's Holding Up the Air Offensive Against Germany?" *Reader's Digest*, XLII (February 1943), 21-28.

Offers the same thesis as in his book noted above--the AAF commitment to daylight strategic bombing.

851. Middlebrook, Martin. *The Battle of Hamburg: Allied Bomber Forces Against a German City, 1943*. New York: Scribners, 1981. 424p.

Employing documents and interviews, British historian Middlebrook, who has also written on the Nuremberg and Penemunde raids, describes RAF Bomber Command's concentrated assault on Hamburg in the summer of 1943; four chapters and other references are given over to the relatively minor involvement (250 sorties) of Eighth Air Force B-17's.

852. Morrison, Wilbur H. *Fortress Without a Roof: The Allied Bombing of the Third Reich*. New York: St. Martin's Press, 1982. 322p.

This is the second of the author's three-volume history of the World War II air war, in which he reveals himself to be a strong advocate of the decisiveness of air forces (and strategic bombing in particular); Morrison argues in his introduction that D-Day would not have been necessary if the CBO had been pushed to its fullest potential and details in his text the vivid history of the bombing campaign, largely through the eyes of the bomber crews.

853. Murphy, Charles J.B. "The Unknown Battle: Five Great Sky Battles, Fought During the 'Big Week' of February, Cleared Europe's Skies for the Invasion." *Life*, XVII (October 16, 1944), 97-102+.

A competent journalistic treatment; illustrated, this article, with the Infield book noted above, is about the extent of "Big Week" coverage commercially available.

854. ———. "The War of the Bombers." *Fortune*, XXXI (January 1945), 114-120+.

A report on attacks on the German ball-bearing and oil facilities based on a month-long visit to AAF headquarters in England and France.

855. Newby, Leroy. *Target Ploesti: View from a Bombsight*. San Rafael, Calif.: Presidio Press, 1983. 326p.

Basing his work in part on a diary kept during his tour, the author recalls the 50 missions he flew as a 460th Bombardment Group (H) B-24 bombardier with the Fifteenth Air Force in 1944 to Ploesti and other targets from bases in Italy. Newby reflects on the terror he felt when his formation was met by flak or Luftwaffe interceptors and on the nerve needed to keep his eye glued to the bombsight as violence whirled around him.

856. Norris, Joe L. *The Combined Bomber Offensive, 1 January to 6 June 1944.* USAAF Historical Study, no. 122. Washington, D.C.: Headquarters, U.S. Army Air Forces, 1947. 310p.

The official study of the U.S. bomber assault during the first six months of 1944, including those raids made directly in support of the pre-invasion gameplan, "Big Week," and the strikes against Berlin.

857. O'Doherty, John K. "A Feather for Yankee Doodle." *Airman*, VIII (August 1964), 39-42.

A brief but useful account of the first VIII Bomber Command raid in which Gen. Eaker, in his B-17 "Yankee Doodle," led a dozen Fortresses against Rouen, France, in summer 1942.

858. Olson, Maneur, Jr. "The Economics of Strategic Bombing in World War II." *Airpower Historian*, IX (April 1962), 121-127.

Examines reasons why strategic bombing failed to stifle the German economy.

859. ———. "The Economics of Target Selection for the Combined Bomber Offensive." *Journal of the Royal United Service Institute*, CVII (November 1962), 308-314.

Essentially the same as the last citation with attention to the methods and reasons behind the Allied planners' choice of certain targets.

860. Palm, John. "A Texan in King Michael's Court." *Collier's*, CXIV (November 25, 1944), 16-17+.

Recollections of the August 1, 1943, raid on Ploesti; Leon W. Johnson, who won the Medal of Honor for his participation, asks "Why Ploesti?" in the August 1971 issue of *Air Force Magazine*.

861. Peaslee, Budd J. "Blood in the Sky." *Aerospace Historian*, XVI (Summer 1969), 16-18+.

The mission commander of the 384th Bombardment Group (H) vividly recalls the October 14, 1943, attack on Schweinfurt.

862. ———. "The Devastation Bombing of Heroya, 24 July 1943." *Aerospace Historian*, XXIX (December 1982), 260-266.

The attack on Norwegian aluminum targets at Heroya by the author's group of B-17's resulted in the fewest losses to any major VIII Bomber Command mission in the war.

863. "Picking the Target." *Popular Mechanics*, LXXXII (September 1944), 28-31+.

Reveals the process of selecting targets for bombing, including aerial recon and economic analysis.

864. "Precision Bombing: A Sample Mission Shows the Details That Make It Work." *Life*, XV (August 30, 1943), 97-105.

An illustrated account of the March 18, 1943, raid on Vegesak.

865. Price, Alfred. *Battle over the Third Reich*. New York: Scribners, 1973. 208p.

A pictorial history of the Allied CBO and corresponding German defensive tactics.

866. Pringle, Henry F. "What Happened at Ploesti." *Saturday Evening Post*, CCXVII (January 6, 1945), 14-15+.

The full extent of American losses and the tragic navigational errors on the August 1, 1943, raid were a long time coming into public view.

867. Rajninec, Juraj L. "Target Pardubice." *American Aviation Historical Society Journal*, XX (Winter 1975), 226-235.

Reviews the 55th Bomb Wing's August 24, 1944, raid on the Fanto oil refineries at Pardubice, Czechoslovakia.

868. Redding, John M., and Harold I. Leyshon. *Skyways to Berlin: With the American Flyers in England*. Indianapolis: Bobbs-Merrill, 1943. 290p.

Two former journalists working for the AAF Washington press office were sent to England in October 1942 to record the story of VIII Bomber Command; the volume contains not only "PR syrup," but non-specific personal accounts and anecdotes by the airmen on their missions and life in England.

869. Rostow, Walt W. *Pre-Invasion Bombing Strategy*. Austin: University of Texas Press, 1981. 166p.

The former White House official examines the options--and politics--of Eisenhower's decisions on how best to use strategic bombing in support of D-Day; suggests the British plan for concentration against transportation targets was a mistake and shows how attention to oil and bridges would have paid greater dividends if adopted earlier than they were.

870. Rumpf, Hans. *The Bombing of Germany*. Translated from the German. New York: Holt, Rinehart and Winston, 1963. 256p.

The wartime German Inspector of Fire Prevention examines Allied bombing strategy and raids against German cities and offers much criticism, including the arguments that bombing only strengthens the victims' will and does not remove the necessity of ground action.

871. Rust, Kenn C. "Black Night at Poltava." *RAF Flying Review*, XIV (September 1959), 16-17+.

On the Luftwaffe's destruction of the bombers of the first U.S. shuttle raid to Russia.

872. ———. "Extreme Danger Mission." *RAF Flying Review*, XVII (July 1962), 24-26.

A capsule review of the May 17, 1943, attack on the power stations at Ijmuiden, Holland, by 322nd Bombardment Group (M) B-26's.

873. Schaffer, Ronald. "American Military Ethics in World War II: The Bombing of German Civilians." *Journal of American History*, LXVII (Spring 1980), 318-334.

Despite AAF policy against the indiscriminate bombing of civilians, restraints were effected not because of ethical objections, but because of concern over image and the known inefficiency of such operations.

874. Seese, R.J. "Ground Level Air War." *Air Classics*, XIX (March 1983), 62-73, 78-82.

This illustrated piece is the most recent telling of the Ploesti raid (August 1, 1943) story.

875. Shaw, S.R. "Wrong Target: A Study of the Use of Strategic Air Power in World War II." *Ordnance*, XXXV (March-April 1951), 471-478.

Basing this article on his study of the USSBS, the author contends that the major Allied employment of strategic air power supplied only an incidental contribution to the actual victory; this view was not popular at the time it was written.

876. Sights, A.P., Jr. "The Day the Forts Hit Hüls." *Air Force Magazine*, LIV (September 1971), 92-96+.

A detailed account of the August 1943 attack.

877. Siler, Tom. "Berlin Post Mortem." *Air Force*, XXVIII (October 1945), 58-62.

An overview of the 19 VIII Bomber Command missions to the German capital in 1944-1945.

878. Simpson, Albert F. "The Attack on Ploesti." *Antiaircraft Journal*, XCIII (January-February 1950), 45-46.

A quick review of the August 1, 1943, raid, with attention to the effectiveness of German antiaircraft fire.

879. Smith, Dale O. "Not So Fond Memories of Oberpfaffenhafen." *Aerospace Historian*, XXVII (Fall 1981), 193-197.

An account of the April 24, 1944, B-17 raid on the Messerschmitt aircraft plants in that city.

880. ———. "The Target Was Marienburg." *Air Force Magazine*, LXV (September 1982), 122-124+.

Recollections of the October 9, 1943, attack on the Focke Wulf plants in that city.

881. ———, and Stephen E. Ambrose. "Was the Bombing of Germany Worth the Cost?" *American History Illustrated*, V (April 1970), 4-9.

Smith argues that World War II in Europe could not have been won without the bombing of Germany, while Ambrose suggests that the money invested and the effort were wasted and should have been employed to build critically needed landing craft.

882. Smith, Melden E., Jr. "The Bombing of Dresden Reconsidered: A Study in Wartime Decisionmaking." Unpublished Ph.D. Dissertation, Boston University, 1971.

883. ———. "The Dresden Raid, the Climax of the Strategic Air Offensive Against Germany." Unpublished MA thesis, Brown University, 1963.

The author exhausts the subject in two detailed analyses of the reasons for the raid and the damages and deaths caused by it.

884. ———. "The Strategic Bombing Debate: The Second World War and Vietnam." *Journal of Contemporary History*, XII (January 1977), 175-191.

Drawing on his own studies and those of others, the author looks to the effectiveness of World War II bombing to analyze contrary views on bombing in the Vietnamese conflict.

885. Spaatz, Carl A. "Strategic Air Power: Fulfillment of a Concept." *Foreign Affairs*, XXIV (April 1946), 385-396.

A discussion of the role of strategic bombing in World War II and a statement of lessons learned from and about it.

886. Spaight, James M. "The Fire Bombing of Cities." *Ordnance*, XL (September-October 1955), 222-226.

Includes a review of Allied World War II attacks on German cities like Hamburg and Dresden.

887. ———. "War on Logistics." *Air Power*, I (Spring 1954), 237-243.

A review of strategic air interdiction against lines of communication.

888. ———. "The War on Oil." *Military Affairs*, XIII (Fall 1949), 138-141.

Recalls the delay in the decision to attack oil installations and the devastating effectiveness of the raids once undertaken in earnest.

889. Steinbeck, John. *Bombs Away!: The Story of a Bomber Team, Written for the Army Air Forces*. New York: Viking, 1942. 185p.

The famed novelist follows six "boys" from civilian life, through training, and into a team as a bomber crew en route to

England. A well-written piece of recruiting propaganda, condensed as "Our Best, Our Fliers" in *New York Times Magazine* (November 22, 1942), pp. 16-17+.

890. Stiles, Bert. *Serenade to the Big Bird.* New York: W.W. Norton, 1952. 216p.

The author was a 23-year-old VIII Bomber Command B-17 pilot who completed this account of his missions, hopes, and fears before his combat death in 1944; the expression of his sensitive and youthfully idealistic thoughts have made this a classic of strategic bombing literature.

891. Stormont, John W. *The Combined Bomber Offensive, April-December 1943.* USAAF Historical Study, no. 119. Washington, D.C.: Headquarters, U.S. Army Air Forces, 1946. 219p.

A history of the buildup and coordination of the Anglo-American strategic air forces and the costly raids of fall 1943 (e.g., Schweinfurt) which almost put the VIII Bomber Command out of business.

892. Sweetman, John. "Oil Interdiction: The Relevance of Past Experience in Rumania." *Royal Air Forces Quarterly*, XVIII (Autumn 1978), 287-291+.

An account of the August 1, 1943, and later attacks on German refineries at Ploesti.

893. ———. *Ploesti: Oil Strike.* Ballantine's Illustrated History of World War II. New York: Ballantine Books, 1974. 160p.

A useful illustrated introduction written in a popular style.

894. ———. *Schweinfurt: Disaster in the Skies.* Ballantine's Illustrated History of World War II. New York: Ballantine Books, 1974. 160p.

Similar to the previous citation; the aerial massacres of August 17 and October 14, 1943, are detailed in text and pictures.

895. Torrey, Volta. "The Nine Lives of Leuna." *Popular Science*, CXLVII (November 1945), 126-128+.

896. ———. "The Rise and Fall of a Chemical Empire." *Popular Science*, CXLVIII (January 1946), 66-69+.

Torrey's first article concerns the repeated bombing of the German synthetic oil plant at Leuna while the second details not only strikes against oil facilities, but chemical plants as well.

897. United States. Army Air Forces. *Target: Germany.* New York: Simon and Schuster, 1943. 121p.

A well-regarded account of the VIII Bomber Command's first year in Europe which records not only heroism, missions, and perceived accomplishments, but the command's team effort on the ground and in the air. Says little about losses and failures; uses fictitious mission and group numbers.

898. ———. Strategic Bombing Survey. *European War.* Washington, D.C.: U.S. Government Printing Office, 1945-1947.

The basis for most assessments of the effectiveness of the U.S. bombing of Germany is the material collected by the USSBS, which employed AAF data, location studies, interrogations of German officials and German documents. The most convenient review of these data is David MacIsaac's work, cited above. The following numbers in the European War series are important, with the first and second almost "must" reading for their authoritative view:

1. *Summary Report.* 18p.
2. *Over-All Report.* 109p.
3. *The Effects of Strategic Bombing on the German War Economy.* 286p.
4. *Aircraft Division Industry Report.* 2nd ed. Various paging.
20. *Light Metals Industry of Germany.* Various paging.
31. *Area Studies Division Report.* 2nd ed. 69p.
32. *A Detailed Study of the Effects of Area Bombing on Hamburg.* Various paging.
33. *A Detailed Study of the Effects of Area Bombing on Wuppertal.* 2nd ed. 105p.
34. *A Detailed Study of the Effects of Area Bombing on Dusseldorf.* 2nd ed. 75p.
37. *A Detailed Study of the Effects of Area Bombing on Darmstadt.* 2nd ed. 35p.
39. *A Brief Study of the Effects of Area Bombing on Berlin, Augsburg, Bochum, Leipzig, Hagen, Dortmund, Oberhausen, Schweifurt, and Bremen.* 2nd ed. Various paging.
40. *Civilian Defense Division Final Report.* 2nd ed. Various paging.
48. *German Electrical Equipment Industry Report.* 2nd ed. Various paging.
50. *Optical and Precision Instrument Industry Report.* 2nd ed. Various paging.
51. *The German Abrasive Industry.* 2nd ed. 95p.
53. *The German Anti-Friction Bearing Industry.* 2nd ed. Various paging.
55. *Machine Tool Industry in Germany.* 2nd ed. 113p.
59. *The Defeat of the German Air Force.* 44p.
60. *V-Weapons (Crossbow) Campaign.* 42p.
63. *A Study of the Bombing Accuracy of the USAAF Heavy and Medium Bombers in the ETO.* 15p.

64a. *The Impact of the Allied Air Effort on German Logistics.* 158p.

64b. *The Impact of Strategic Bombing on German Morale.* 2 vols.

66. *The Coking Industry, Report on Germany.* 29p.
77. *German Motor Vehicles Industry Report.* 2nd ed. 79p.
78. *Tank Industry Report.* 2nd ed. 33p.
101. *Ordnance Industry Report.* 2nd ed. 104p.
109. *Oil Division Final Report.* 2nd ed. 152p.

112. *Underground and Dispersal Plants in Greater Germany.* 176p.
113. *The German Oil Industry, Ministerial Report Team 78.* 89p.
200. *The Effects of Strategic Bombing on German Transportation.* Various paging.
201. *Rail Operations over the Brenner Pass.* 2nd ed. 58p.
202. *Effects of Bombing on Railroad Installations in Regensburg, Nuremberg, and Munich Divisions.* 2nd ed. 80p.
203. *German Locomotive Industry During the War.* 2nd ed. 32p.
205. *German Electric Utilities Industry Report.* 2nd ed. Various paging.

899. Verrier, Anthony. *The Bomber Offensive.* New York: Macmillan, 1969. 373p.

A general review of the CBO told by a British journalist who rates RAF bombers better than American, but acknowledges the P-51 Mustang as a deciding factor in turning the tide after the VIII Bomber Command losses in late 1943; although the author praises the courage of the air crews, he questions the effectiveness of strategic bombing.

900. Walker, Wayne T. "Operation Ball Bearing." *World War II Magazine*, II (July 1973), 6-17.

A pictorial account of the August 17 and October 14, 1943, daylight raids on Schweinfurt.

901. Webster, Charles K., and Noble Frankland. *The Strategic Air Offensive Against Germany.* 4 vols. London: H.M. Stationery Office, 1961.

These books form the official British history of the bomber war, including the CBO which is covered in the second and third volumes: *Endeavor, 1943-44* and *Victory, 1944-45*. The set discusses, frankly, the disagreements between U.S. and RAF leaders and high-level command arrangements, preparations for D-Day, and the effectiveness of the bombing campaign as a whole. The last volume, *Annexes and Appendices*, includes technical information, statistics, and documents.

902. Williams, R.M. "Why Wasn't Auschwitz Bombed?" *Commonweal*, CV (November 24, 1978), 746-751.

Examines Allied reasons for not knocking out the infamous German concentration camp, including disbelief of the extermination stories and the military necessity of employing strategic bombers elsewhere.

903. Wolff, Leon. *Low Level Mission.* Garden City, N.Y.: Doubleday, 1957. 240p.

A well-written account of the August 1, 1943, raid on the Ploesti oil refineries as recorded by a non-flying AAF public relations official.

904. ———. "The Raid That Failed." *RAF Flying Review*, XIII (August 1958), 23-25+.

A brief overview of the Ploesti raid and its results.

905. Wouk, Herman S. "Prelude to D-Day: The Bomber Offensive--The 'Overload' Air Dispute." *Air University Review*, LVII (June 1974), 60-67.

The noted novelist reviews the British-American controversy over which targets, oil or transportation, to attack in the months before the Normandy invasion.

906. Wyman, D.S. "Why Auschwitz Was Never Bombed." *Commentary*, LXV (May 1978), 37-46.

A review of the Allied reasons; less accusatory than the piece by R.M. Williams cited above.

907. Young, John S. "Attack on Ploesti." In: Stanley M. Ulanoff, ed. *Bombs Away!* Garden City, N.Y.: Doubleday, 1971, pp. 205-211.

A view of the August 1, 1943, mission reprinted from the August 1943 issue of *Air Force*.

D. UNIT HISTORIES

Introduction: Many of the AAF units which fought in World War II produced college-yearbook type commemorative books afterwards; in addition, aviation writers and enthusiasts have since 1945 written many titles on the men and actions of specific units. Both of these sources combine to form a valuable body of literature which is often much more specific than any of the more general citations listed in the parts above. Although the number of unit histories produced by the AAF is nowhere near that of those available on the U.S. Army as a whole, the number is considerable. For that reason, the entries in this part are restricted to numbered air forces, wings, divisions, and groups. The references are also selective, due not only to space requirements, but also to the compiler's judgment as to which are most easily accessible for the average user. A fairly complete list of unit histories will be found in Myron J. Smith, Jr., *Air War Bibliography, 1939-1945: English Language Sources, Volume III, Part V, The Air Forces* (Manhattan, Kans.: Military Affairs/Aerospace Historian, 1977), pp. 178-217. The order of arrangement here is: General Works; Fighter Units; Bomber Units; Other Units.

1. General Works

Introduction: The citations immediately following are general, but may be used in connection with those references of a more specific nature below. Users are cautioned that additional general information on AAF units will be found in the works cited in Parts A-C and E of this section.

908. Britton, Tom. "Combat Cargo Groups--World War II." *American Aviation Historical Society Journal*, XXVI (Summer 1981), 175-177.

Lists the units with their numbers and symbols.

909. Francillon, René J. *USAAF Fighter Units, Europe, 1942-1945.* Aircam Airwar Series, no. 8. New York: Arco, 1979. 48p.

A profusely illustrated review of the planes, units, men, missions, and markings.

910. ———. *USAAF Medium Bomber Units, ETO and MTO, 1942-1945.* Aircam Airwar Series, no. 7. New York: Arco, 1979. 48p.

A well-illustrated guide to the units, men, planes, missions, and markings. Both of these titles were originally published by the London firm of Osprey in 1977.

911. Friedheim, Eric, and Samuel Taylor. *Fighters Up: The Story of American Fighter Pilots in the Battle of Europe.* Edited by Arthur Gordon. New York: Macrae Smith, 1945. 275p.

Two AAF authors familiar with the tactics and engineering of American warplanes provide an account of Eighth and Ninth Air Force fighter units from November 1943 through D-Day, concentrating on action, aircraft, and pilots, including some mentioned in a list of aces.

912. Mauer, Mauer. *Air Force Combat Units of World War II.* New York: Arno Press, 1979. 506p.

First published by the GPO in 1961, this reference lists each combat group, together with its insignia, squadrons assigned, commanders, stations, aircraft flown, and campaigns and awards.

913. ———. *Combat Squadrons of the Air Force in World War II.* New York: Arno Press, 1979. 841p.

First published by the GPO in 1963, this companion to the last citation covers all USAAF/USAF combat squadrons, providing the same sort of data provided for groups in the previous entry.

914. Morris, Danny. *Aces and Wingmen: The Men and Machines of the USAAF Eighth Fighter Command, 1943-1945.* London: Spearman, 1972. 488p.

Provides group histories for the VIII Fighter Command, airfield codes, and a list of aces; the text is backed by 511 photos.

915. Scutts, Jerry. *USAAF Heavy Bomber Units, ETO and MTO, 1942-1945.* Aircam Airwar Series, no. 4. New York: Arco, 1977. 48p.

A profusely illustrated guide to units, men, planes, missions, and markings.

916. Shores, Christopher F. *USAAF fighter Units, MTO, 1942-1945.* Aircam Airwar Series, no. 12. New York: Arco, 1980. 48p.

A well-illustrated account of units, planes, men, missions, and markings.

917. United States. Army Air Forces. Personal Narrative Division. *Combat Air Forces of World War II, Army of the United States.* Washington, D.C.: Army Times, 1945. 95p.

A brief history is provided here for each of the numbered U.S. air forces.

918. Weatherhill, David. *Aces, Pilots, and Aircraft of the Ninth, Twelfth, and Fifteenth U.S. Army Air Forces.* Newark, Del.: Kookaburra Technical Publications, 1978. 144p.

Although the Eighth Air Force received most of the glory for the air war in Europe, this book points out that units of the other three deployed U.S. air forces accounted for 1,100 aerial victories and many tons of bombs dropped over the Middle East and Europe. The text is complemented by 237 black and white photos, 21 rare color photos, and 32 color aircraft profiles.

2. Air Forces

Introduction: The following citations deal with the major Army Air Forces deployed in the European and Mediterranean Theaters and are entered under the command number. Readers are reminded that additional information on these forces can be found in other parts of this section.

Eighth Air Force

919. Cate, James L. *Origins of the Eighth Air Force: Plans, Organization, Doctrines to 17 August 1942.* USAAF Historical Study, no. 102. Washington, D.C.: Headquarters, U.S. Army Air Forces, 1944. 143p.

Not an action-oriented study, but one of setting up the command and moving it to Great Britain.

920. "The Eighth Air Force in England." *National Geographic Magazine*, CXXXVII (March 1945), 297-304.

An overview remarkable for its wartime color photographs.

921. Freeman, Roger A. *The Mighty Eighth: A History of the U.S. 8th Air Force.* Garden City, N.Y.: Doubleday, 1970. 311p.

Regarded for most of the past decade as the standard work on the Eighth Air Force and indeed one of the best histories, if not the best, of a numbered air force ever prepared. Although the book does not put the Eaker/Spaatz/Doolittle outfit into the context of the war, it does provide almost every other piece of information anyone would want to know, including short unit histories, lists of aces and medal winners, and information on airfields, aircraft, markings, and missions. Much of the text is based on personal narrative and interesting anecdotes and is backed by 473 black and white photos and color aircraft plates.

922. ———. *The Mighty Eighth War Diary*. London and New York: Jane's, 1981. 240p.

A day-to-day operational record of the largest air striking force ever committed to battle and a sequel to the previous citation; covers in great detail the more than 1,000 missions flown between June 1942 and May 1945 with information on units involved, bomb tonnages, claims and losses. Some 150 narratives of incidents and events are included with over 400 illustrations.

923. Peaslee, Budd J. *Heritage of Valor*. Philadelphia, Pa.: Lippincott, 1966. 228p.

The boss of the 394th Bombardment Group (H) on the Schweinfurt mission follows the Eighth's history from June 1942 through VE-Day.

924. Rust, Kenn C. *Eighth Air Force Story: In World War II*. Glendale, Calif.: Aviation Book Co., 1978. 72p.

A concise picture is given of the Eighth's 55 fighter and bomber groups, their men, machines, and missions; includes 17 tables, 12 pages of profile line drawings, and 110 photographs.

925. Werrell, Kenneth P. "The Tactical Development of the Eighth Air Force in World War II." Unpublished Ph.D. Dissertation, Duke University, 1969.

A scholarly treatment worthy of commercial publication; compare with Cate's study, cited above.

926. Woolnough, John H. *The 8th Air Force Album: The Story of the Mighty 8th Air Force in World War II*. San Angelo, Tx.: Newsfoto Yearbooks, 1978. 224p.

Designed for those who "have any relationship to the epic air war over England and Germany in 1942 through 1945," this work tells the story with over 1,000 captioned photographs which cover every aspect of the Eighth's men, planes, missions, airfields, etc.

Ninth Air Force

927. Gerdy, Robert S. *From the Letters of Robert S. Gerdy, 1942-1945: A Personal Record of World War II*. Philadelphia, Pa.: Dorrance, 1969. 355p.

The author served as a public relations officer for the Ninth and here recalls his unit's service in the Middle East and Europe.

928. "Ninth Air Force Defensive Measures Against German Flak." *Antiaircraft Journal*, XCII (January 1948), 33-37; (February 1948), 68-72.

929. Reed, William D., *et al.* *Condensed Analysis of the Ninth Air Force in the European Theater of Operations.* Washington, D.C.: Headquarters, U.S. Army Air Forces, 1946. 148p.

An official study covering the effectiveness of the command from October 1943 to May 1945.

930. Rust, Kenn C. *The Ninth Air Force in World War II.* Fallbrook, Calif.: Aero Publishers, 1974. 250p.

Regarded as "standard" for the Ninth as Freeman, above, is for the Eighth, this volume puts its subject into the context of the war, describing its deployment in the Middle East and then in Europe as the American tactical air force in the battle of northwest Europe. Details include anecdotes and narratives of units, men, machines, and missions, with the text supplemented by 18 pages of drawings and 270 photographs.

931. ———. *The Ninth Air Force Story: In World War II.* Glendale, Calif.: Aviation Book Co., 1983. 64p.

Providing basically the same information as the previous entry, this paperback provides a concise view of the Ninth's 54 fighter and bomber groups, their men, machines, and missions. Includes maps, tables, and 108 photographs.

Twelfth Air Force

932. Rust, Kenn C. *The Twelfth Air Force Story: In World War II.* Glendale, Calif.: Aviation Book Company, 1975. 64p.

A concise review of the Twelfth's combat history from North Africa to Italy, this paperback includes information on men, units, and aircraft as well as missions and accomplishments. The text is supplemented by aircraft profiles and 107 photographs. Readers should note that other references to the Twelfth can be found in Part C:1 of this section, above.

Fifteenth Air Force

933. Bozung, Jack H., ed. *The Fifteenth over Italy.* Los Angeles, Calif.: AAF Publications, 1947. 40p.

A brief review of the last major aerial command created by the U.S. in Europe.

934. Rust, Kenn C. *The Fifteenth Air Force Story: In World War II.* Glendale, Calif.: Aviation Book Company, 1976. 64p.

Follows the story of this command from its activation in November 1943 to VE-Day, including the shuttle raids to Russia and raids on the oil refineries at Ploesti. Information is provided on units, combat, and aircraft and is backed by 98 photographs.

3. Fighter Units

Introduction: The following citations deal with the various fighter units deployed by the AAF in the European and Mediterranean

Theaters. All are entered by unit number, regardless of whether the outfit concerned was a command, a group, or a wing, and are then arranged alphabetically by author. Readers should note that additional information on these forces are to be found in other parts of this section.

4th Fighter Group

935. "Eagles Switch to the U.S. Army." *Life*, XIII (November 2, 1942), 37-38+.

A pictorial account of the transfer of the RAF Eagle Squadrons, which fought for Britain before Pearl Harbor, to the AAF, where they became the 4th FG.

936. Fry, Garry L. *The Debden Eagles: The 4th Fighter Group in World War II*. Canoga Park, Calif.: Grenadier Books, 1972. Unpaged.

A pictorial tracing the Eagle Squadrons, RAF, later turned over to the AAF and made into the 4th FG, as well as an account of the achievements of the U.S. group from 1942 to 1945.

937. ———, and Jeffrey L. Ethell. *Escort to Berlin: The 4th Fighter Group in World War II*. New York: Arco, 1980. 226p.

A complete history built around the group's operational diary; profusely illustrated with more than 300 photos, 12 in color, this book contains 11 appendices with information on the group's aces, victories, pilots, aircraft, codes and markings, and losses.

938. Hall, Grover C. *1,000 Destroyed: The Life and Times of the 4th Fighter Group*. Fallbrook, Calif.: Aero Publishers, 1978. 384p.

First published by the Montgomery, Ala., firm of Brown Printing in 1946, this record tells of how the 4th scored 1,016 serial victories during the war, more than any of the other 14 VIII Fighter Command groups. A personal account drawn from the author's war diaries and official reports, the work emphasizes the exploits of the individual pilots as seen by a staff officer who knew them all.

939. Haugland, Vern. *The Eagles' War: The Saga of the Eagle Squadron Pilots, 1940-1945*. New York: Ziff-Davis, 1982. 234p.

An account of those Americans who served with RAF Nos. 71, 121, and 133 until taken into the 4th Fighter Group in 1942--men like Blakeslee, Beeson, Goodson, and Gentile, who formed the combat-proven core of the Eighth's highest-scoring group. Includes appendices and 16 pages of photographs.

IX Tactical Air Command

940. *Stars and Stripes*, Editors of. *Achtung Jabos: The Story of IX TAC*. Paris, France: Curial-Archereau, 1945. 32p.

IX TAC was one of three Ninth Air Force commands established especially to provide close-air support to the First Army ground troops in Europe. This booklet reviews its service concisely; "Jabo" was the German term for fighter bombers, much employed by IX TAC.

XIX Tactical Air Command

941. *Stars and Stripes*, Editors of. *Fly, Seek, and Destroy: The Story of XIX TAC.* Paris, France: Desfosses-Neogravure, 1945. 32p.

XIX TAC was one of the other Ninth Air Force commands set up to assist the soldiers on the ground; this story is just as concise as that presented in the previous citation.

20th Fighter Group

942. *King's Cliffe: The 20th Fighter Group and the 446th Air Service Group in the ETO.* Long Island City, N.Y., 1947. 273p.

A pictorial yearbook-type publication detailing the history of this VIII Fighter Command unit, which was equipped with P-38's.

XXIX Tactical Air Command

943. *Stars and Stripes*, Editors of. *Mission Accomplished: The Story of XXIX TAC.* Paris, France: Desfosses-Neogravure, 1945. 32p.

XXIX TAC was the third Ninth Air Force command established to provide close-air support for the troops; this account is just as brief as those of IX and XIX TAC already cited.

31st Fighter Group

944. Lamensdorf, Roland G. *History of the 31st Fighter Group.* Washington, D.C.: Kaufman Press, 1952. 79p.

A pictorial review of the 12th/15th Air Force group; a unit roster can be found on pp. 64-79.

56th Fighter Group

945. Davis, Albert H., *et al.* *The 56th Fighter Group in World War II.* Washington, D.C.: Infantry Journal Press, 1948. 222p.

The P-47 equipped 56th was an VIII Fighter Command group which saw much action and was a close rival of the 4th FG in victories and achievements. This work contains rosters of men and lists of awards, as well as a history of the group from 1943 to 1945.

946. Stafford, Gene B. "D-Day with the 56th Fighter Group." *Air Classics*, IX (January 1973), 10-13, 51-53.

How the group's P-47's, with special invasion stripes painted on their wings, patrolled the Normandy beaches looking for the Luftwaffe.

66th Fighter Wing

947. *The 66th Fighter Wing in Europe: One Story, Two Worlds, Three Enemies, Four Freedoms, May 27, 1943-September 15, 1945.* Cambridge, Eng.: W. Haffer and Sons, Ltd., 1945. 24p.

An extremely brief review of this unit's contribution.

78th Fighter Group

948. *Duxford Diary, 1942-1945.* Cambridge, Eng.: W. Haffer and Sons, 1945. 151p.

A review of the P-47 equipped group's service on bomber escort and in ground attack; includes a roster and list of aces, many photos.

949. Rust, Kenn C. "Above the Foe." *Airpower Historian*, VIII (April 1961), 101-106.

A concise account of the group's history from 1943 to 1945.

79th Fighter Group

950. Woerpel, Don. *A Hostile Sky: The Mediterranean Air War of the 79th Fighter Group.* Marshall, Wisc.: The Andon Press, 1977. 260p.

Woerpel remembers the epic missions and gallant friends of this unit from 1943 to 1945 and illustrates his work with 220 black and white photographs.

82nd Fighter Group

951. Abberger, Thomas J. "The Freedom Fighters." *Air Classics*, XV (October 1979), 57-61; (November 1979), 14-21; XVI (January 1980), 22-29.

Reproduces the diary of a P-38 pilot in this unit and illustrates the story with many black and white photographs.

325th Fighter Group

952. McDowell, Ernest R., and William N. Hess. *The Checkertail Clan: The 325th Fighter Group in North Africa and Italy.* Fallbrook, Calif.: Aero Publishers, 1972. 96p.

This group flew P-40's into North Africa from the carrier *Ranger* and went on to fly P-47's and P-51's in action over Tunisia, Sardinia, Italy, and on to Berlin; includes a full mission list and 77 photographs. Based on the next entry.

953. ———. "Checkertails: History of the 325th Fighter Group." *American Aviation Historical Society Journal*, X (Fall 1965), 155-171; (Winter 1965), 254-265.

An illustrated history covering the period from November 1942 to May 1945; forms the basis of the previous citation.

332nd Fighter Group

954. "The All Black 332nd Fighter Group." *Air Aces*, I (October 1976), 48-56.

A review of the segregated but effective all-Negro unit formed in North Africa which saw action over the Mediterranean.

955. Francis, Charles E. *The Tuskegee Airmen: The Story of the Negro in the U.S. Air Force*. Boston, Mass.: Bruce Humphries, 1956. 225p.

Includes information on the 332nd's actions over the Mediterranean and Europe, 1942-1949.

956. Osur, Alan M. *Blacks in the Army Air Forces During World War II*. Washington, D.C.: U.S. Government Printing Office, 1977. 227p.

Like the previous citation, this work is a general history of Black affairs in the air arm, which includes much information on the formation and deployment of the 332nd.

957. Paszek, Lawrence J. "Separate but Equal: The Story of the 99th Fighter Squadron." *Aerospace Historian*, XXIV (Fall 1977), 135-145.

On the formation and achievements of this major Black element of the 332nd.

958. Rose, Robert A. *Lonely Eagles: The Story of America's Black Air Force in World War II*. Glendale, Calif.: Aviation Book Company, 1980. 160p.

An illustrated history of not only the Black elements of the 332nd FG, but of the 477th Bombardment Group (M) as well.

350th Fighter Group

959. Schiffman, Charles. *An Unofficial and Historical History of the 347th Fighter Squadron, 350th Fighter Group, 12th Air Force, September 1942-October 1945*. Stockton, Calif.: Atwood Printing Co., 1951. 159p.

The 350th, like the 325th abd 332nd, saw action in North Africa and across the Mediterranean to Italy; a picture reminiscence.

960. *The 350th Fighter Group in the Mediterranean Campaign, 2 November 1942 to 2 May 1945*. Milan, Italy: Pizzi a Pizio, 1945. 41p.

A brief, heavily illustrated souvenir book for the men of the unit; includes a roster.

352nd Fighter Group

961. Mayer, Charles B. "Mustang Pilot: The 352nd Fighter Group." *American Aviation Historical Society Journal*, X (Spring 1965), 18-23.

An account of this group which flew its missions from England, as seen by First Lieutenant Harry Barnes.

353rd Fighter Group

962. Rust, Kenn C., and William N. Hess. *The Slybird Group: The 353rd Fighter Group on Escort and Ground Attack Operations.* Fallbrook, Calif.: Aero Publishers, 1971. 96p.

A history of "Bill's Buzz Boys," a noted P-47 equipped VIII Fighter Command unit; includes a full mission list and 53 photos.

354th Fighter Group

963. *History in the Sky: The 354th Pioneer Mustang Fighter Group.* San Angelo, Tx.: Newsfoto Yearbooks, 1946. 166p.

A photo-illustrated souvenir book for the men of the P-51 equipped XIX TAC unit.

357th Fighter Group

964. Olmstead, Merle C. *The Yoxford Boys: The 357th Fighter Group on Escort over Europe and Russia.* Fallbrook, Calif.: Aero Publishers, 1972. 96p.

The first VIII Fighter Command unit equipped with the P-51, the 357th flew on bomber escorts over Germany and in the shuttle raids to Russia in 1944. Includes many photos and a full mission list.

359th Fighter Group

965. *The 359th Fighter Group.* Nashville, Tenn.: Battery Press, 1979. 68p.

First published by the Norwich, Conn., firm of Soman-Wherry Press in 1946, this is a 334-photo view of the VIII Fighter Command group originally designed as a souvenir book for its men.

365th Fighter Group

966. Johnson, Charles R. *The History of the Hell Hawks.* Anaheim, Calif.: Southwest Typesetting, 1975. 623p.

A limited edition of 2,000 volumes covering the history of this fighter bomber group from February 1944 to May 1945. Many photos.

367th Fighter Group

967. Groth, Richard. *The Dynamite Gang: The 367th Fighter Group in World War II.* Fallbrook, Calif.: Aero Publishers, 1983. 192p.

A detailed history of this P-38 equipped unit's history over the ETO with data on operations, planes, pilots, ground support, insignia and markings; illustrated with over 350 photographs and drawings.

968. Moody, Peter R. *The 367th Fighter Group in World War II.* Manhattan, Kans.: Military Affairs/Aerospace Historian, 1979. 75p.

A history of this fighter bomber group in the northwest Europe campaign in 1944-45 reproduced by Xerography.

371st Fighter Group

969. *The Story of the 371st Fighter Group in the ETO.* Baton Rouge, La.: Army and Navy Publishing Co., 1946. 198p.

A photo-illustrated souvenir booklet for the men of this P-47 equipped TAC unit.

406th Fighter Group

970. Matthews, W.L., Jr. "The Stardusters: A History of the 406th Fighter Group." *American Aviation Historical Society Journal*, XXVIII (Spring 1983), 41-50.

Covers the operations of this P-47 equipped unit in Europe from June 1, 1944, to April 30, 1945.

422nd Night Fighter Squadron

971. Pape, Gary, and Ronald Harrison. "Dark Lady: The Ninth by Night." *Wings*, VI (December 1976), 24-40.

A photo-article detailing the history of the P-61 equipped 422nd in the skies over northwest Europe, 1944-1945.

4. Bomber Units

Introduction: The following citations deal with the various bomber units deployed by the AAF in the European and Mediterranean Theaters. All are entered by their unit number, regardless of whether the outfit concerned was a wing, division, or group, and are then arranged alphabetically. Users will find additional information on certain of these forces in other parts of this section, especially C:3 above.

Second Air Division

972. Bowman, Martin W. *Fields of Little America.* Norwich, Eng.: Wensum, 1977.

The Eighth's Second Air Division was, for the most part, equipped with B-24 Liberators. This illustrated work examines the unit's missions, men, and airfields.

Third Air Division

973. Whelan, Paul A. "History of the 3rd Air Division in World War II, 1943-1945." Unpublished Ph.D. Dissertation, St. Louis University, 1968.

A scholarly examination of the organization, doctrine and tactics, and missions of the Eighth's B-17 and B-24 equipped division.

12th Bombardment Group (M)

974. Wilson, Robert E. *The Earthquakers: Overseas History of the 12th Bomb Group.* Tacoma, Wash.: Dammeier Printing Co., 1947. 147p.

A pictorial which tells of this medium bomber unit's campaigns in Egypt, Libya, Tunisia, Sicily, and Italy.

14th Bombardment Wing (H)

975. Taylor, William B., ed. *14th Combat Bombardment Wing (H).* San Angelo, Tx.: Newsfoto Yearbooks, 1945. 66p.

A souvenir pictorial describing the operations of this VIII Bomber Command subdivision.

44th Bombardment Group (H)

976. Marcell, Ursel P. *Liberators over Europe: The 44th Bomb Group.* San Angelo, Tx.: Newsfoto Yearbooks, 1946. 91p.

Describes the operations of this VIII Bomber Command B-24 unit which participated in numerous raids, including the August 1, 1943, Ploesti strike; many photographs.

47th Bombardment Wing (H)

977. Cerra, Frank R., and Herbert L. Stoolman. *47th Bombardment Wing History.* Sioux City, Iowa: Perkins Brothers, 1946. 94p.

A record of this Fifteenth Air Force division's operations from June 1942 to October 1945; many photographs of the wing's men and B-24 Liberators in action.

91st Bombardment Group (H)

978. Freeman, Roger A. "The Ragged Irregulars: A History of the U.S. 91st Bombardment Group." *Air Pictorial*, XXIII (May 1971), 178-180.

A photo-look at this VIII Bomber Command B-17 unit.

92nd Bombardment Group (H)

979. Sloan, John S. *The Route as Briefed.* Cleveland, Ohio: Argus Press, 1946. 320p.

Covers the history of this VIII Bomber Command B-17 group from 1942 through 1945; list of those killed in action, pp. 311-320.

93rd Bombardment Group (H)

980. *The Story of the 93rd Bomb Group.* San Angelo, Tx.: Newsfoto Yearbooks, 1946. 46p.

A pictorial souvenir book for the men of this VIII Bomber Command B-24 unit.

95th Bombardment Group (H)

981. Henderson, David B. *The 95th Bombardment Group (H), United States Army Air Forces.* Cincinnati, Ohio: A.H. Printing Co., 1945. 125p.

A pictorial souvenir book produced for the survivors of this VIII Bomber Command B-17 outfit.

97th Bombardment Group (H)

982. Hicks, Walter E. "The 97th Bombardment Group, World War II." Unpublished Ph.D. Dissertation, University of Kentucky, 1961.

A scholarly review of this pioneer VIII Bomber Command group's B-17 operations over Africa and Europe. This unit was the first in the AAF to complete 400 combat missions.

100th Bombardment Group (H)

983. Bennett, John H., Jr. *Letters from England.* San Angelo, Tx.: Newsfoto Yearbooks, 1945. 142p.

The author commanded the 349th squadron of this group and here provides a recollection of its famous actions.

984. *One Hundred Missions.* San Angelo, Tx.: Newsfoto Yearbooks, 1946. 38p.

A brief pictorial devoted to this VIII Bomber Command B-17 outfit. For additional information on the 100th, readers should note Beirne Lay's citations noted in part C:3 above.

985. Sheridan, Jack W. *They Never Had It So Good.* San Francisco, Calif.: Stark-Rath, 1946. 165p.

A pictorial devoted to the exploits of this group's 350th Bombardment Squadron.

303rd Bombardment Group (H)

986. *The First 300--"Hell's Angels": The 303rd Bombardment Group (H), United States Army Air Forces.* London: Batsford, 1944. 31p.

An overview of this VIII Bomber Command B-17 outfit through D-Day.

305th Bombardment Group (H)

987. Morrison, Wilbur H. *The Incredible 305th: The "Can Do" Bombers of World War II.* New York: Duell, Sloane and Pearce, 1962. 181p.

Examines this important VIII Bomber Command B-17 unit which Curtis LeMay commanded and employed for the trial of new tactics. See also the references to LeMay in B above.

306th Bombardment Group (H)

988. Bove, Arthur P. *First Over Germany: The Story of the 306th Bombardment Group.* San Angelo, Tx.: Newsfoto Yearbooks, 1946. 148p.

A pictorial published for the men of this VIII Bomber Command B-17 group.

319th Bombardment Group (M)

989. Oyster, H.E. and E.M., comps. *The 319th in Action.* Akron, Ohio: The Burch Directory Co., 1976. 296p.

Records the missions of this Twelfth Air Force group's B-26 missions over Italy and southern France, 1943-1944.

376th Bombardment Wing (H)

990. Rust, Kenn C. "First in Combat: The History of the 376th Bombardment Wing." *Airpower Historian*, VIII (July 1961), 161-171.

A look at this Ninth Air Force B-24 unit in Africa.

379th Bombardment Group (H)

991. Robb, Derwyn D. *Shades of Kimbolton.* San Angelo, Tx.: Newsfoto Yearbooks, 1946. 93p.

A pictorial souvenir book concerning an VIII Bomber Command B-17 group.

384th Bombardment Group (H)

992. Owens, Walter E. *Briefed: A Family History of the 384th Bombardment Group.* New York: Edward Stern, 1946. 210p.

An account of the missions and men of this VIII Bomber Command B-17 Group.

388th Bombardment Group (H)

993. *History of the 388th Bomb Group.* San Angelo, Tx.: Newsfoto Yearbooks, 1946. 121p.

An illustrated souvenir history of this VIII Bomber Command B-17 group.

389th Bombardment Group (H)

994. *The 389th Bombardment Group: A Pictorial Review of Operations in the ETO.* San Angelo, Tx.: Newsfoto Yearbooks, 1946. 133p.

A pictorial history of this VIII Bomber Command B-24 group.

390th Bombardment Group (H)

995. *The Story of the 390th Bombardment Group (H).* New York: Eilert Printing Co., 1947. 472p.

An extremely detailed souvenir history of this VIII Bomber Command B-17 outfit.

391st Bombardment Group (M)

996. Charlton, Fred. "The 391st Bomb Group: The 'Black Death' Group." *Military Journal*, I (May-June 1977), 17-20; (July-August 1977), 26-29.

An account of this B-26 outfit's northwest Europe campaign.

392nd Bombardment Group (H)

997. Vickers, Robert E., Jr. *The Liberators from Wendling.* Manhattan, Kans.: Military Affairs/Aerospace Historian, 1981. 286p.

A member of the group provides a day-bay-day account of the action of this VIII Bomber Command unit nicknamed "The Crusaders."

394th Bombardment Group (M)

998. Ziegler, J. Guy. *The Bridge Busters.* New York: Ganis and Harris, 1949. 213p.

A look at the northwest Europe actions of this IX Bomber Command B-26 group.

397th Bombardment Group (M)

999. Beck, Henry C. *The 397th Bomb Group (M): A Pictorial History.* Cleveland, Ohio: Crane Howard, 1946. 61p.

A souvenir history prepared for the men of this IX Bomber Command B-26 unit.

1000. Stovall, Jack D. "Marauder Men." *Air Classics*, XV (June 1979), 48-55.

A photo-illustrated look at the men and machines of this group in action over northwest Europe.

445th Bombardment Group (H)

1001. Birsic, Rudolph J. *The History of the 445th Bombardment Group (H), (Unofficial).* Glendale, Calif.: Griffin-Patterson, 1948. 81p.

This pictorial reveals the story of this Second Air Division B-24 group which was stationed at Tibenham, England.

446th Bombardment Group (H)

1002. Archer, John W. "Prelude to a Mission." *American Aviation Historical Society Journal*, XVIII (Fall 1973), 163-165.

Preparations for a mission by this VIII Bomber Command B-24 unit.

1003. Castens, Edward H., ed. *The Story of the 446th Bomb Group.* San Angelo, Tx.: Newsfoto Yearbooks, 1946. 105p.

A pictorial review for surviving crewmen; includes a roster.

1004. Woolnough, John H. *Attlebridge Diaries: The History of the 446th Bombardment Group (H).* Hollywood, Fla.: 8th Air Force News, 1979. 218p.

A heavily illustrated account of the group's men, machines, and missions.

454th Bombardment Group (H)

1005. *The Flight of the Liberators.* Rochester, N.Y.: The DuBois Press, 1946. 172p.

A photo-illustrated history of this XV Bomber Command B-24 unit.

457th Bombardment Group (H)

1006. Blakebrough, Ken. *The Fireball Outfit: The 457th Bomb Group in the Skies over Europe.* Fallbrook, Calif.: Aero Publishers, 1972. 96p.

A former group pilot recalls missions such as Merseburg and Politz with this unit's B-17's; photos and mission list.

458th Bombardment Group (H)

1007. Reynolds, George A. *The 458th Bombardment Group (Heavy).* Birmingham, Ala., 1974. 64p.

A pictorial which recalls the missions of this VIII Bomber Command B-24 outfit in 1944 and 1945.

467th Bombardment Group (H)

1008. *The 467th Bombardment Group, September 1943-June 1945.* Brattleboro, Vt.: W.L. Hildreth, 1947. 155p.

A photo-illustrated history of this VIII Bomber Command B-24 group; includes a roster.

483rd Bombardment Group (H)

1009. *483rd Bomb Group (H), Italy, 1944-1945.* Rome, Italy: Novissima, 1945. 80p.

A pictorial souvenir book for the men of this XV Bomber Command B-24 group.

487th Bombardment Group (H)

1010. *History of the 487th Bombardment Group, 22 September 1943-7 November 1945.* San Angelo, Tx.: Newsfoto Yearbooks, 1945. 109p.

Another B-24 group's souvenir book, this one for an VIII Bomber Command unit.

490th Bombardment Group (H)

1011. Lightener, Laurence S., and Fred R. Holland, eds. *100 Missions.* San Angelo, Tx.: Newsfoto Yearbooks, 1945. 234p.

A detailed photo-illustrated history of an VIII Bomber Command B-24 unit; includes mission list and roster of crewmen.

491st Bombardment Group (H)

1012. Blue, Allan G. "'The Ringmasters': A History of the 491st Bomb Group (H)." *American Aviation Historical Society Journal*, IX (Spring 1964), 79-95; (Summer 1964), 207-218.

Follows the history of this VIII Bomber Command B-24 group from June 1944 to April 1945.

492nd Bombardment Group (H)

1013. Blue, Allan G. *The Fortunes of War: The 492nd Bomb Group on Daylight Operations*. Fallbrook, Calif.: Aero Publishers, 1967. 96p.

Details the story of this 2nd Bomb Division B-24 group in 1944-1945; includes a full mission list and 57 photographs.

5. Other Units

Introduction: The following citations deal with other AAF units deployed by the AAF in the European and Mediterranean Theaters, including troop carrier and photo reconnaissance. All are entered by unit number, regardless of whether the outfit concerned was transport or spy, group or wing, and are then arranged alphabetically. Users will find additional information on certain of these forces in other parts of this section and in Section IV, "The War on Land," following.

50th Troop Carrier Wing

1014. "Flying Mules of the Army: The 50th Transport Wing, a Freight and Passenger Carrying Section." *Popular Mechanics*, LXXVII (June 1942), 40-43.

1015. *Stars and Stripes*, Editors of. *Invaders: The Story of the 50th Troop Carrier Wing*. Paris, France: Desfosses-Neogravure, 1945. 32p.

Both of these brief references concern an outfit involved in the transport of supplies and troops during the northwest Europe campaign.

53rd Troop Carrier Wing

1016. *Stars and Stripes*, Editors of. *Ever First: The 53rd Troop Carrier Wing*. Paris, France: Desfosses-Neogravure, 1945. 32p.

Another small paperback pamphlet which tells the story of the airborne exploits of this Ninth Air Force unit.

316th Troop Carrier Group

1017. *History*. San Angelo, Tx.: Newsfoto Yearbooks, 1946. 68p.

A souvenir pictorial describing a group which participated in the delivery of airborne troops for D-Day, Arnhem, and the Rhine.

437th Troop Carrier Group

1018. Guild, Frank H. *Action of the Tiger: The Saga of the 437th Troop Carrier Group*. Nashville, Tenn.: Battery Press, 1980. 177p.

First published by Newsfoto Yearbooks in 1950, this book is almost all text with only 13 photographs (not a common event in unit-history publishing) and tells the story of a group which delivered both paratroops and gliders in the Normandy, southern France, Arnhem, and Rhine crossing campaigns.

440th Troop Carrier Group

1019. *DZ Europe*. Indianapolis, Ind.: Hollenbeck Press, 1946. 203p.

The 440th was involved in the same campaigns as the 437th.

441st Troop Carrier Group

1020. *History, August 1, 1943-August 1, 1944*. Taunton, Eng.: E. Goodman, 1944. 48p.

A souvenir book covering the group's history through D-Day.

442nd Troop Carrier Group

1021. Beeson, Colin R. *The Glider Pilot at Home and Overseas*. Manhattan, Kans.: Military Affairs/Aerospace Historian, 1978. 257p.

The author's reminiscences of service with the 303rd Troop Carrier Squadron of this group which delivered gliders during the four major northwest Europe airborne operations.

1022. *The 442nd Troop Carrier Group in Pictures*. Paris, France: Curial Archerea, 1945. 52p.

A pictorial souvenir book for the men of the group; includes a roster.

10th Photo Reconnaissance Group

1023. Ivie, Thomas G. *The 10th Photo Reconnaissance Group in World War II*. Fallbrook, Calif.: Aero Publishers, 1981. 192p.

Based on letters, diaries, and official papers, this history recalls the group's work in mapping the Normandy beach area prior to D-Day and subsequent recon flights and tactical missions over France and Germany in 1944 and 1945. The text is supplemented by over 90 photographs.

E. AIR WEAPONS, UNIFORMS, AND MARKINGS

Introduction: The amount of information available in English about World War II aircraft employed in the European and Mediterranean Theaters is staggering, as are data concerning uniforms, insignia, and aircraft markings. Given that consideration and the need to employ space for references to other sources on the conflict, the citations noted below are selective and, for the most part, concern items made available in the last decade or so. The literature on topics covered in this part has been noted in several of the bibliographies cited in Section I:A above; users will forgive this compiler for pointing out his own as the most comprehensive. *Air War Bibliography, 1939-1945:*

English-Language Sources, Vol. IV--The Aircraft (Manhattan, Kans.: Military Affairs/Aerospace Historian, 1978) contains 2329 citations on World War II aircraft while *Air War Bibliography, 1939-1945: English-Language Sources, Vol. V: Part VII--Aerial Support* (Manhattan, Kans.: Military Affairs/Aerospace Historian, 1982) includes a section on "Awards and Decorations, Insignia and Markings," pp. 89-98. The order of arrangement here is: General Works; Individual Aircraft; Awards, Insignia, and Markings.

1. General Works

Introduction: The works cited below concern the aircraft and their armament. Readers should note that additional data on aircraft are available in the operational parts of this section noted under III:C above.

1024. *Airview*, Editors of. *Airview's Seventy Fighters of World War II*. Tokyo: Kantosha, 1965. 152p.

Covers both Allied and Axis aircraft, including American bombers and fighters. While the text is in Japanese, the photo captions in this pictorial are in English.

1025. Anderton, David. *American Fighters of World War II*. New York: Crescent Books, 1981.

An oversize British import which provides a survey of the most noteworthy U.S. aircraft backed by 120 full-color illustrations and cutaway illustrations of the Lockheed P-38 Lightning, North American P-51 Mustang, Curtiss P-40 Kittyhawk, and Republic P-47 Thunderbolt.

1026. Andrews, John A.C. "The Forty, the Spit, and the Jug." *Aerospace Historian*, XXVI (December 1979), 202-207.

Recollections of flying the P-40, Spitfire, and P-47 by a former pilot of the 315th Fighter Squadron, 324th Fighter Group, Twelfth Air Force.

1027. Angelucci, Enzo, ed. *Rand McNally Encyclopedia of Military Aircraft, 1914-1980*. Translated from the Italian. Chicago: Rand McNally, 1981. 546p.

A massive guide to the warplanes of all nations, including AAF/USN models of World War II; includes numerous photographs, drawings, and color illustrations.

1028. Bavousett, Glenn B. *World War II Aircraft in Combat*. New York: Arco, 1976. 128p.

1029. ———. *More World War II Aircraft in Combat*. New York: Arco, 1981. 144p.

These two volumes, which might be considered as a set, provide a well-researched text and a variety of black and white and excellent color illustrations which tell the story of 83 Allied and Axis warplanes in combat around the globe, including all of the major AAF machines employed in Europe and the Mediterranean.

1030. Block, Geoffrey D.M. *Allied Aircraft Versus Axis Aircraft.* Old Greenwich, Conn.: WE, Inc., 1970. 133p.

First published by the London firm of Hutchinson in 1945 as *The Wings of Warfare*, this introduction is aimed at acquainting readers with those Axis and Allied warplanes which specifically fought in the European/Mediterranean Theaters.

1031. Bowman, Martin W. *The Encyclopedia of U.S. Military Aircraft.* New York: Bison Books, 1982. 224p.

As with the Anderton and Bavousett titles, this is an oversize British import; describes the development of U.S. warplanes from World War II to the present with over 400 photos, specifications, and drawings.

1032. Brown, K.S., and E.F. Heyn. *United States Army and Air Force Fighters, 1916-1961.* A Harleyford Book. Fallbrook, Calif.: Aero Publishers, 1972. 256p.

This British import provides complete technical details on the aircraft mentioned in the title, including specifications and photographs for those employed in the European and Mediterranean Theaters.

1033. Cooper, Bryan, and John Batchelor. *Fighter: A History of Fighter Aircraft.* New York: Scribners, 1974. 153p.

1034. ———. *The Story of the Bomber, 1914-1945.* London: Octopus Books, 1974. 124p.

Both of these volumes contain an engaging text highlighted by Batchelor's noteworthy drawings and color illustrations.

1035. Cooper, Herbert J., and Owen G. Thetford. *Aircraft of the Fighting Powers.* Edited by D.A. Russell. 7 vols. London: Harborough, 1940-1946.

Illustrations and text are provided for 542 Axis and Allied aircraft, with at least one photograph and one 3-view drawing of each; covers all of the operational aircraft employed in the war, including those used by Americans in the European and Mediterranean Theaters.

1036. Cross, Roy. *Military Aircraft, 1939-1945.* Greenwich, Conn.: New York Graphic Society, 1971. 48p.

A pictorial which notes the most important models, both Axis and Allied, and employs many color illustrations.

1037. Freeman, Roger A. *British Aircraft in USAAF Service, 1942-1945.* London: Ducimus Books, 1973. 24p.

A brief guide to those aircraft employed by the AAF, including the Spitfire, Beaufighter, and Horsa. One of the few studies available on the subject.

1038. Green, William. *War Planes of the Second World War.* 10 vols. Garden City, N.Y.: Doubleday, 1968.

Perhaps the most comprehensive illustrated history of the various Allied and Axis aircraft available. Vols. 1-4 concern Fighters; Vol. 5, Flying Boats; Vol. 6, Floatplanes; and Vols. 7-10, Bombers.

1039. ———, and F. Gordon Swanborough. *U.S. Army Air Force Fighters.* World War II Aircraft Fact Files. 2 vols. New York: Arco, 1977.

Specifications of each aircraft type, with variants and sub-types, detailed outline of service use, and comparison are provided in these 64-page pamphlets which are illustrated with drawings and cutaway drawings.

1040. Groth, Richard. *Fifty Famous Fighter Aircraft.* New York: Arco, 1968. 96p.

Mostly from our period, each aircraft is covered in brief text with a photograph; includes the U.S. P-38, P-40, P-47, and P-51.

1041. Gunston, William T. ("Bill"). *The Encyclopedia of the World's Combat Aircraft.* New York: Chartwell Books, 1976. 229p.

A technical directory of major warplanes from World War I to the present; each aircraft is illustrated by a color drawing, camouflage and markings, and brief technical details.

1042. ———. *The Illustrated Encyclopedia of Combat Aircraft of World War II.* New York: Chartwell Books, 1979. 256p.

One of the most beautiful Allied/Axis aircraft directories available; the 150,000 words of text are backed by 200 color profile works, over 100 color action photos, 25 detailed cutaway drawings, and a number of 4-page foldouts with color airbrush work 30 inches long.

1043. ———. *The Illustrated Encyclopedia of the World's Rockets and Missiles.* New York: Chartwell Books, 1980. 245p.

Like the last two entries, this oversize British import is an illustrated technical directory, this time of the missiles and rockets of the 20th century, including those developed in America during the war. Each nation's entry is presented chronologically with photos, cutaway drawings, and text.

1044. ———. *An Illustrated Guide to Allied Fighters of World War II.* New York: Arco, 1981. 160p.

In 40,000 words of text with more than 120 detailed line drawings, 110 action photos (many in color), and 60 color drawings, Gunston describes some 40 aircraft types plus their variants, including all of the U.S. machines employed in the ETO and MTO.

1045. ———. *An Illustrated Guide to Bombers of World War II.* New York: Arco, 1980. 160p.

In 40,000 words of text with more than 140 detailed line drawings, 90 action photos (many in color), and 40 color drawings, Gunston describes some 50 Allied and Axis bomber types plus their variants, including the major U.S. machines employed in the MTO and ETO.

1046. Halvorsen, Dick. *Steeds in the Sky: The Fabulous Fighting Planes of World War II.* Photobook History of World War II, no. 1. New York: Lancer Books, 1971. 176p.

This paperback shows a variety of aircraft types, including the P-40, P-38, P-47, and P-51; marred by many caption errors.

1047. Hatfield, David D. *North American Aviation Product History.* 2 vols. Inglewood, Calif.: Northrop University, 1977.

Presents detailed data on this firm's entire line, including the B-25 Mitchell and P-51 Mustang.

1048. Higham, Robin, Abigail T. Siddall, and Carol Williams. *Flying Aircraft of the U.S.A.A.F.-U.S.A.F.* 3 vols. Ames, Iowa, and Manhattan, Kans.: Iowa State University and Sunflower Books, 1975-1981.

The first two volumes were published by ISUP and the last by Sunflower; each chapter is by a seasoned pilot expert in flying the type of aircraft described, who discusses the technical details of his warbird and its combat effectiveness. Each volume is illustrated with about 100 photographs. All of the major AAP/USN types employed in the European and Mediterranean Theaters are covered.

1049. *Jane's All the World's Aircraft.* London: Various publishers, 1909--.

Still in existence, this "bible" of the world's military aircraft is by far the most useful of all the aircraft compilations cited in this part. Includes full technical details and design, production, and operational histories with photos and illustrations. The wartime volumes, edited by Leonard Bridgman, have been reprinted by the New York firm of Johnson Reprint.

1050. Jones, Lloyd. *U.S. Bombers: B-1 1928 to B-1 1980's.* 3rd ed. Fallbrook, Calif.: Aero Publishers, 1980. 272p.

An anthology of all bomber-type aircraft ever assigned "B" designations in this country; the detailed descriptions include specifications, performance, and design features and each is illustrated by one or more photos.

1051. Mendenhall, Charles. *Deadly Duo.* New York: Specialty Press, 1981. 160p.

Supplemented by 20 pages of line drawings, a data directory, and many photographs, this work details the operations and production history of the North American B-25 and Martin B-26 medium bombers.

1052. Mondey, David. *Concise Guide to American Aircraft of World War II*. London and New York: Hamlyn, 1981. 160p.

This British import details all of the major types employed in the MTO/ETO (133 types) and illustrates them with 84 diagrams, 170 color drawings, and 117 photographs.

1053. Munson, Kenneth. *Aircraft of World War II*. 2nd ed. Garden City, N.Y.: Doubleday, 1972. 272p.

An alphabetically arranged technical guide to the warplanes of all the major and minor powers, each aircraft illustrated with at least one photograph.

1054. ———. *American Aircraft of World War II in Color*. New York: Sterling, 1982. 160p.

This British import reproduces 68 paintings and 11 color and 150 black and white photographs to tell the story of the major U.S. aircraft types, including those prominent in the ETO and MTO.

1055. ———. *Fighters and Bombers of World War II*. London: Burke's Peerage, 1981. 400p.

A single-volume edition of two works on the fighters, attack and training aircraft, bombers, patrol and transport planes of the Allies and Axis; the text is backed by over 300 color illustrations.

1056. Pimlott, John, and H.P. Willmott. *Classic Aircraft of the World*. London and New York: Bison Books, 1982. 400p.

Provides comprehensive coverage of six noted wartime aircraft, including the B-17 and P-51 from the ETO/MTO; the text is backed by full-color cutaway diagrams (one for each plane), and over 60 illustrations, 150 in color.

1057. Profile Publications, Editors of. *American Bombers*. Men and Machines Series, no. 12. Windsor, Eng.: Profile Publications, 1974. 72p.

Profile Publications has long been synonymous with the best in illustrated technical detail on aircraft; this work, which features color drawings and cutaways, and black and white photos, presents information on the B-17, A-20, and B-26.

1058. ———. *American Fighters*. Men and Machine Series, nos. 1 and 10. 2 vols. Windsor, Eng.: Profile Publications, 1974.

Those aircraft covered in No. 1 include the P-39, P-38, and P-61, while of those in No. 10 only the P-40 is relevant to our subject.

1059. Robinson, Anthony, ed. *In the Cockpit: Flying the World's Great Aircraft*. New York: Ziff-Davis, 1979. 304p.

Somewhat similar to the Higham work noted above, this volume gives one expert's opinions on the flying qualities of various aircraft, including several major AAF types employed in the ETO/MTO. Illustrations are both black and white and color.

1060. Sun, Jack K. "Fighter Armament of World War II." *Aerospace Historian*, XXVIII (June 1981), 74-82.

A detailed presentation of the types employed aboard AAF fighters, including an analysis of their effectiveness.

1061. Tallman, Frank. *Flying the Old Planes*. Garden City, N.Y.: Doubleday, 1973. 255p.

Tallman, one of aviation's greatest flyers, takes the reader "into the cockpit" as he describes the flying qualities of 25 historic aircraft, including several relative to this guide.

1062. Taylor, John W.R. *Aircraft of World War II*. London: Longacre Press, 1963. 124p.

Jane's editor Taylor here presents capsule histories of some of the more important Allied and Axis fighters, bombers, transports, and trainers of the war years, including all of the major U.S. types.

1063. ———. *Milestones of the Air: Jane's 100 Significant Aircraft*. New York: McGraw-Hill, 1969. 158p.

Looks at history's most famous aircraft with text and illustrations and features several AAF models, including the P-40, P-51, and B-17.

1064. Wagner, Ray. *American Combat Planes*. Rev. ed. Garden City, N.Y.: Doubleday, 1982. 565p.

Describes all American military aircraft--experimental, operational, sea- or land-based--from 1908 to the present in detailed text backed by 1,400 photographs.

1065. *Warplanes, 1939-1945*. Purnell's History of the World Wars Special. London: Phoebus Books, 1973. 64p.

A full-color guide to the major aircraft of both the Allied and Axis powers which employs cutaway drawings and other illustrations to show the craft, including the major American types employed in Europe.

1066. Waters, Andrew W. *All the U.S. Air Force Airplanes, 1907-1983*. New York: Hippocrene Books, 1983. 413p.

A somewhat-difficult-to-use reference to 622 aircraft; includes photographs and information on designers, commanded organizations (e.g., Eighth Air Force), bases, and enemy warbirds.

1067. Weal, Elke C., comp. *Combat Aircraft of World War II*. New York: Macmillan, 1977. 238p.

Some 890 aircraft from 25 nations are listed alphabetically under manufacturer and then chronologically; includes 426 scale line drawings or reproductions of paintings.

2. Individual Aircraft

Introduction: The citations which follow are to those major American types employed in the European and Mediterranean theaters. They are arranged by type (bomber, fighter, etc.), then by designation (e.g. A-20), and then alphabetically by author. Users will find additional data on these warplanes not only above but in other parts of this section, especially C, "Campaigns and Battles."

a. *BOMBERS*

A-20 Havoc/A-26 Invader

1068. Gann, Harry. *Douglas A-20*. Aircraft in Profile, no. 202. Windsor, Eng.: Profile Publications, 1971. 15p.

A brief technical guide to the Havoc which includes drawings, specifications, and photographs.

1069. Gault, Owen. "The Amazing 'Coconut Bomber.'" *Air Classics*, IX (July 1973), 26-37.

An illustrated overview of the Havoc's worldwide service.

1070. Hess, William N. *A-20 Havoc at War*. New York: Scribners, 1980. 128p.

The story of the Havoc, first used operationally by the British as the "Boston," from 1940 to 1945, told largely in the words of the crews that flew it. Includes a 30-page section on the A-20's descendant, the A-26, and more than 150 photographs.

1071. Mesko, Jim. *The A-20 in Action*. Carrollton, Tx.: Squadron/Signal Publications, 1981. 50p.

A pictorial history which features 101 photos, 4-views, and color art.

1072. ———. *A-26 Invader in Action*. Carrollton, Tx.: Squadron/Signal Publications, 1982. 50p.

Concise text traces the plane's use from late World War II through Vietnam; illustrations include 120 photographs, 20 detailed line drawings, and 12 color profiles.

1073. Powell, Hickman. "Porcupine Squadron: The A-20 Attack Bomber, Famous Abroad as the Boston and Havoc." *Popular Science*, CXL (May 1942), 82-87.

An early account of the Havoc's operations and characteristics.

B-17 Flying Fortress

1074. Andrews, Paul M. "Seventeen Bits and Pieces--Boeing B-17F's and G's Assigned to the Eighth U.S. Army Air Force, August 1942-May 1945." *American Aviation Historical Society Journal*, XXIV (Fall 1979), 202-213; (Winter 1979), 303-312.

An examination of the Forts assigned to the Eighth's First and Third Air Divisions; includes illustrations.

1075. Beall, Wellwood E. "The Boeing B-17 Flying Fortress." *Aviation*, XLIV (January 1945), 121-144.

1076. ———. "Design Analysis of the Boeing B-17 Flying Fortress." *Aviation*, XLIV (January 1945), 233-243.

These two articles by a prominent designer at Boeing familiar with the Fortress describe the plane's creation and offer one of the better design analyses.

1077. Birdsall, Steve. *B-17 Flying Fortress*. New York: Arco, 1965. 56p.

Follows the aircraft's 29-year career in text and illustration, the latter including 170 illustrations, photographs, side- and 3-views. Reprints the pilot-training manual and looks at nose art.

1078. ———. *B-17 in Action*. Warren, Mich.: Squadron/Signal Publications, 1973. 50p.

A concise text traces the plane's design, deployment history, and World War II feats; illustrations include over 100 photographs and various line drawings and color profiles.

1079. ———, *et al*. *Winged Majesty: The Boeing B-17 Flying Fortress in War and Peace*. Glendale, Calif.: Aviation Book Co., 1980. 41p.

Similar to the titles above in that a text is complemented by 177 photographs and illustrations; includes narratives from pilots and crewmen as well as notes on missions flown.

1080. Bowers, Peter H. *Fortress in the Sky*. Granada Hills, Calif.: Sentry Books, 1976. 275p.

A large pictorial on the history of the B-17 backed by many illustrations, photographs, anecdotes; includes famous pilots and missions flown. Compare with the Caidin and Jablonski works noted below.

1081. ———. "A Fortress Is Forever." *Wings*, VII (March 1977), 24-50.

An illustrated history of the B-17 based on the previous citation.

1082. Caidin, Martin. *Flying Forts*. New York: Meredith Books, 1972. 516p.

A well-written journalistic account of the B-17's World War II history, with emphasis on missions flown and results obtained; includes several pages of photographs.

1083. Coker, William S. "America's Most Famous Bomber." *Air University Review*, XVII (July-August 1966), 80-86.

A pictorial salute to the Flying Fortress.

1084. Collison, Thomas. *Flying Fortress: The Story of the Boeing Bomber*. New York: Scribners, 1943. 168p.

Useful for the development of the B-17 and U.S. bombing plans, this wartime book unfortunately does not give a complete history due to its early publication date.

1085. Freeman, Roger A. *B-17 Fortress at War*. New York: Scribners, 1977. 191p.

Takes the interesting approach of discussing the bomber crew station by crew station as well as providing an overall look at its developmental and operational career; the text is backed by 259 photos, many full- or double-page size.

1086. ———. *Boeing B-17G Flying Fortress*. Aircraft in Profile, no. 205. Windsor, Eng.: Profile Publications, 1971. 20p.

A detailed technical and design history illustrated with many color illustrations and black and white photographs. The "G" was a very late model and featured the best in armament.

1087. Holder, William G. "That Tough Old Bird." *Air Classics*, XVIII (July 1972), 42-51.

A technical survey built around the plane's ability to take lots of flak punishment; illustrated.

1088. Jablonski, Edward. *Flying Fortress*. Garden City, N.Y.: Doubleday, 1965. 362p.

Traces the evolution of the plane, describes the concept of strategic bombing, and looks at the operational history of the famous bomber; includes statistical data, over 400 photos, and excerpts from the *Pilot Training Manual*.

1089. Lloyd, Alwyn T., and Terry D. Moore. *B-17 Flying Fortress in Detail and Scale*. 2 vols. Fallbrook, Calif.: Aero Publishers, 1981-1982.

Designed for modelers, this book shows the B-17 in a way not seen before, in dozens of detail photos and drawings, many of cockpit interiors, turrets, gear details, fuselage interior, etc.

1090. Munson, Kenneth, and F. Gordon Swanborough. *Boeing*. Aircraft Album, no. 4. New York: Arco, 1972. 144p.

A substantial history of the Boeing firm which built the Fortress; this paperback includes over 180 photos.

1091. Schreier, Konrad, Jr. "The Boeing B-17E." *Air Classics*, VIII (February 1972), 22-29.

An illustrated look at this early-model Fortress which saw action over Europe and the Mediterranean in 1942-1943.

1092. Thompson, Charles D. *Boeing B17-E & F Flying Fortress.* Aircraft in Profile, no. 77. Windsor, Eng.: Profile Publications, 1966. 15p.

A brief illustrated technical guide to these two early-model B-17's; includes color side-views and black and white photographs.

1093. Willmott, H.P. *B-17 Flying Fortress.* War Planes in Colour, no. 4. London: Leventhal, 1980. 64p.

A brief history noteworthy in that all of the illustrations are in color, including reproductions of wartime photographs.

B-24 Liberator

1094. Birdsall, Steve. *The B-24 Liberator.* New York: Arco, 1968. 64p.

Examines the developments, modifications, and operations of this B-17 rival (1,498 more B-24's than Fortresses were built during the war), including several famous aircraft and missions, such as the August 1, 1943, Ploesti attack; includes 160 photographs.

1095. ———. *B-24 Liberator in Action.* Warren, Mich.: Squadron/Signal Publications, 1976. 50p.

This story of the Liberator details its modifications and operations with the help of 18 line and detail drawings, several 3-views, and 64 photos.

1096. ———. *Log of the Liberators.* Garden City, N.Y.: Doubleday, 1973. 340p.

A design, modification, and especially good operational history enhanced by 250 photographs.

1097. Blue, Allan G. *The B-24 Liberator: A Pictorial History.* New York: Scribners, 1977. 223p.

The story of the AAF/USN Liberators told largely in the words of the crews that flew them; examines both modifications and operations with the help of over 150 photographs.

1098. ———. "Fortress vs. Liberator." *American Aviation Historical Society Journal*, VIII (Summer 1963), 126-128.

A brief "which was best" survey which concludes the latter was.

1099. Bowman, Martin. *B-24 Liberator, 1939-1945.* Chicago: Rand McNally, 1980. 128p.

Similar to Blue's study above, this work examines the plane's design, modification, and operational history with the aid of a variety of illustrations.

1100. Eaker, Ira C. "The Flying Fortress and the Liberator." *Aerospace Historian*, XXVI (June 1979), 66-68.

The former VIII Bomber Command chief examines the pluses and minuses of both the B-17 and the B-24.

1101. Famme, J.H. "Design Analysis of the Consolidated B-24 Liberator." *Aviation*, XLIV (July 1945), 121-143.

An excellent technical discussion helped along by detail illustrations, including cutaways.

1102. Freeman, Roger A. *Consolidated B-24J Liberator*. Aircraft in Profile, no. 19. Windsor, Eng.: Profile Publications, 1965. 12p.

An extremely brief technical history strengthened by color drawings and black and white photographs. The "J" was an extremely late-model Liberator.

1103. Holder, William G., and Clifford Glassmeyer. "B-24: The Liberator." *Aviation Quarterly*, V (Fall 1979), 288-304.

An illustrated history of the plane' development and modifications, operational career, and flying charactersitics.

B-25 Mitchell

1104. Gault, Owen. "Anatomy of a Killer: The Mitchell." *Air Classics*, VIII (December 1972), 32-59.

An illustrated design and operational history of the twin-tailed Mitchell medium bomber employed by the AAF in Europe, almost exclusively in the Mediterranean Theater.

1105. Hansen, Charles J. "Design Analysis of the North American B-25 Mitchell." *Aviation*, XLIV (March 1945), 119-142.

Still one of the best examinations available, this work is aided by sideviews and black and white photographs.

1106. McDowell, Ernest R. *B-25 Mitchell in Action*. Carrollton, Tx.: Squadron/Signal Publications, 1978. 49p.

Like all of the S/S pictorials, this one contains little text; the Mitchell's story is told almost exclusively through 28 captioned drawings and 3-views, reproductions of 13 paintings, and 97 photos.

1107. Mizrahi, J.V. *The North American B-25*. North Hollywood, Calif.: Challenge Publications, 1965. 48p.

An illustrated pamphlet which discusses the flying characteristics and wartime history of the B-25, including the one owned by the publisher.

1108. Wagner, Ray. *North American B-25A-G Mitchell*. Aircraft in Profile, no. 59. Windsor, Eng.: Profile Publications, 1966. 12p.

A brief technical history told through the help of black and white photos and color drawings.

B-26 Marauder

1109. Allen, Franklin. *The Martin Marauder and the Franklin Allens*. Manhattan, Kans.: Military Affairs/Aerospace Historian, 1980. 480p.

A collection of letters between a B-26 pilot and his wife which describe what it was like to test fly and operationally fly the so-called widow maker. Introduction by Donald J. Mrozek; illustrated.

1110. Birdsall, Steve. *B-26 Marauder in Action*. Carrollton, Tx.: Squadron/Signal Publications, 1979. 50p.

This little-text history covers the war's most widely employed medium bomber in line drawings, 100 photos, some 4-views, and reproductions of 13 paintings.

1111. Francis, Devon E. *Flak Bait: The Story of the Men Who Flew the Martin Marauder*. New York: Duell, Sloane, and Pearce, 1948. 331p.

Based on previously published newspaper, periodical, and army reports, this anthology presents an anecdotal account of the B-26 bombers, its specifications, crewmen, and operations.

1112. Freeman, Roger A. *B-26 Marauder at War*. New York: Scribners, 1978. 192p.

Freeman's effort now supersedes Francis as the most useful Marauder account; told from the viewpoint of the flyers, this work stresses the plane's operational characteristics and missions. Illustrated with over 150 photographs.

1113. Moore, Carl H. *Flying the B-26 Marauder over Europe*. Blue Ridge Summit, Pa.: TAB Books, 1980. 176p.

A realistic study based on the recollections of men who flew this much-maligned aircraft; illustrated with 76 photographs, the work also reproduces the Marauder flight manual.

1114. Mundey, Eric. "B-26 Marauder." *Military Journal*, II (Winter 1978-1979), 26-30.

A brief operational history illustrated by drawings.

1115. Wagner, Ray. *Martin B-26B & C Marauder*. Aircraft in Profile, no. 112. Windsor, Eng.: Profile Publications, 1967. 12p.

A brief technical history helped along by black and white photographs and color drawings and illustrations.

b. FIGHTERS

P-38 Lightning

1116. Caidin, Martin. *Fork-Tailed Devil: The P-38.* New York: Ballantine Books, 1971. 369p.

Provides operational and design information on the long-range, twin-engine Lightning, which saw better service in the Pacific than in Europe, but which was nevertheless well regarded in the Mediterranean. Includes several pages of photographs.

1117. Christy, Joe, and Jeffrey L. Ethell. *P-38 Lightning at War.* New York: Scribners, 1978. 144p.

Told from the viewpoint of the pilots, this work stresses the plane's operational characteristics and missions, including its use as a bomber against the Ploesti oil refineries. Illustrated with over 210 photographs.

1118. Gurney, Gene. *P-38 Lightning.* New York: Arco, 1969. 60p.

Differs from Edward T. Maloney's similar title, cited below, by placing more emphasis upon the pilots who flew the aircraft; includes photo recreations of combat maneuvers/fighter tactics and contains 82 photographs.

1119. Maloney, Edward T. *Lockheed P-38 Lightning.* Fallbrook, Calif.: Aero Publishers, 1968. 52p.

Examines the development and deployment of this versatile long-range fighter; includes 4 pages of color profiles and 80 photos.

1120. Rust, Kenn C. "Lightnings at War." *American Aviation Historical Society Journal*, VIII (Summer 1963), 128-131.

Presents a selection of photographs showing the plane in general.

1121. Stafford, Gene B. *P-38 Lightning in Action.* Warren, Mich.: Squadron/Signal Publications, 1976. 50p.

This little-text history covers the famous "fork-tailed devil" in line drawings, over 100 photos, some 4-views, and reproductions of paintings.

1122. "Three Bullets on a Knife." *Air University Review*, XVIII (January-February 1967), 46-59.

A pictorial salute subtitled "Saga of the P-38."

1123. Ward, Richard, and Ernest R. McDowell. *Lockheed P-38 Lightning.* New York: Arco, 1969. 48p.

Using over 200 illustrations, the authors show the noted fighter as it appeared in the AAF and three other Allied air fleets.

P-39 Airacobra

1124. Davidson, Robert S. "Killer Cobra." *Air Classics*, VIII (December 1971), 10-13, 58-60.

Examines the "failure" of the P-39, a radically-engined fighter which was preferred more by Soviet pilots than by American, but which, nevertheless, saw limited service in Europe.

1125. Dial, Jay F. *Bell P-39 Airacobra*. Aircraft in Profile, no. 165. Windsor, Eng.: Profile Publications, 1967. 12p.

A brief technical history built around black and white photographs and color illustrations.

1126. Hudson, James J. "The P-39 in Europe." *Aerospace Historian*, XXIV (September 1977), 129-134.

Perhaps the most useful P-39 piece for users of this volume; examines why the Airacobra did not do very well and was quickly phased out.

1127. McDowell, Ernest R. *P-39 Airacobra in Action*. Carrollton, Tx.: Squadron/Signal Publications, 1980. 46p.

This little-text history covers the poorly received fighter in over 100 photos, line drawings, some 4-views, and reproductions of paintings.

1128. Miller, Edward E. "Design Analysis of the Bell Airacobra from Cannon to Tail." *Aviation*, XLII (May 1943), 126-155.

A comprehensive analysis available at this early date largely because the plane had been phased out of front-line AAF units.

Curtiss P-40 Kittyhawk

1129. Bowers, Peter M. *Curtiss Aircraft, 1907-1947*. London: Putnam, 1979. 604p.

A detailed company history of the firm begun by Glenn Curtiss early in this century; includes an examination of the P-40, one of the most successful Curtiss products.

1130. Christy, Joe, and Jeffrey L. Ethell. *P-40 Hawks at War*. New York: Scribners, 1980. 128p.

Little used in northwest Europe, the P-40 was extensively employed by Allied air forces, including the AAF, in the Mediterranean; this work is told from the viewpoint of the pilots and stresses the plane's operational characteristics and missions. Illustrated with 210 photographs.

1131. Hart, Eric H. "A Study in Longevity: The Curtiss P-40 in World War II." *American Aviation Historical Society Journal*, XIV (Spring 1969), 26-29; (Summer 1969), 130-131.

An illustrated look at the upgrading of this fighter during the progress of the conflict.

1132. Holloway, Bruce K. "The P-40." *Aerospace Historian*, XXV (Fall 1978), 136-140.

The author's personal recollection and appreciation of this well-traveled machine.

1133. McDowell, Ernest R. *Curtiss P-40 in Action*. Warren, Mich.: Squadron/Signal Publications, 1976. 58p.

Follows the aircraft's progress through the Q model with illustrations, including 12 color profiles, 29 detail- and 3-view drawings, and over 100 photographs.

1134. ———. *The P-40 Kittyhawk*. New York: Arco, 1968. 64p.

Outclassed by almost every enemy fighter it met during the war, the P-40, in the hands of Allied airmen, acquitted itself well; this title examines Allied use of the aircraft; illustrated with 80 photos.

1135. Milch, Robert J. "The P-40: Workhorse of the Skies." *American History Illustrated*, II (June 1967), 22-28, 30.

A pictorial covering the aircraft's Allied use, especially in the Mediterranean and China.

1136. Wagner, Ray. *Curtiss P-40*. Aircraft in Profile, no. 35. Windsor, Eng.: Profile Publications, 1965. 12p.

1137. ———. *Curtiss P-40F-N Kittyhawk*. Aircraft in Profile, no. 136. Windsor, Eng.: Profile Publications, 1967. 12p.

These two brief technical histories are enhanced by color illustrations and a variety of black and white photographs.

P-47 Thunderbolt

1138. Dunn, William R. "P-47: The Beautiful Beast." *Air Force Magazine*, LVIII (September 1975), 91-94+.

America's first European ace recalls his service aboard the large and effective P-47, which was, from its shape, nicknamed "the Jug."

1139. Freeman, Roger A. *Thunderbolt: A Documentary History of the Republic P-47*. New York: Scribners, 1979. 152p.

A documentary (but poorly documented) account which includes not only descriptions and statistics of the aircraft, but extensive comments by wartime pilots and a large number of comparison charts, illustrations, and a list of squadrons equipped with the conflict's largest single-engine propellor-driven fighter.

1140. Hess, William N. *P-47 Thunderbolt at War*. New York: Scribners, 1977. 160p.

The story of the successful large aircraft told from the viewpoint of the pilots; stresses the plane's operational characteristics and missions. Illustrated with 212 combat photos.

1141. McDowell, Ernest R., and Richard Ward. *Republic P-47 Thunderbolt*. New York: Arco, 1968. 46p.

Follows the "Jug" as it served in the following Allied air forces: AAF, RAF, Free French, Mexican, Brazilian, etc. Illustrated with 200 photos and drawings.

1142. Maloney, Edward T. *Republic P-47 Thunderbolt*. Fallbrook, Calif.: Aero Publishers, 1966. 50p.

Examines and describes the development and deployment of this versatile and powerful bomber escort and fighter bomber; includes 4 pages of color and some 80 photographs.

1143. Morgan, Len. *The P-47 Thunderbolt*. New York: Arco, 1963. 52p.

Similar to the McDowell and Ward work cited above; includes pilot comments and 87 illustrations.

1144. Rabbets, John B. *Republic P-47D Thunderbolt*. Oxford, Eng.: Aerodata International, 1978. 20p.

A brief overview of this American fighter using 20 photographs and 40 line drawings.

1145. Shacklady, E.G. *The Republic P-47 Thunderbolt*. Aircraft in Profile, no. 7. Windsor, Eng.: Profile Publications, 1965. 11p.

A small but detailed technical history enhanced by black and white photographs and color illustrations.

1146. Stafford, Gene B. *P-47 Thunderbolt in Action*. Warren, Mich.: Squadron/Signal Publications, 1975. 50p.

Follows the aircraft's introduction and successful employment as bomber escort and fighter bomber with a series of illustrations, including color profiles, detail- and 3-view drawings, and over 100 photos.

1147. Ward, Richard. *Republic P-47 Thunderbolt*. New York: Arco, 1970. 64p.

Includes photos and illustrations showing the "Jug's" many color schemes and squadron insignia.

1148. Winchester, James. "Republic's P-47: The Unbreakable Jug." *Air Force*, XL (December 1957), 100-102+.

A tribute to the huge fighter's exploits in the European Theater with comments from former pilots.

P-51 Mustang

1149. Atkins, Richard. *North American P-51B & C Mustang*. Aircraft in Profile, no. 100. Windsor, Eng.: Profile Publications, 1969. 12p.

A brief design history enhanced by the use of black and white photographs and color illustrations.

1150. Boylan, Bernard L. "The Development of the American Long Range Escort Fighter." Unpublished Ph.D. Dissertation, Columbia University, 1955.

Presents the story of the need for and development of the Mustang, first ordered by the British, but with the substitution of an underpowered engine for a better one, held by the Americans to become the war's best strategic fighter.

1151. Davis, Larry. *P-51 Mustang in Action*. Warren, Mich.: Squadron/Signal, 1975. 58p.

Like all S/S publications, this work is short on text and long on illustrations, including 80+ line drawings, 12 color profiles, and 124 action photographs.

1152. ———. *P-51 Mustang in Color*. Carrollton, Tx.: Squadron/Signal Publications, 1982. 36p.

Emphasis is on markings and detail with dozens of color illustrations showing engines, cockpits, gun bays, and fuselages; includes 37 side-view and 3 color 4-view paintings and 45 black and white photos. Both Davis titles mention the A-36 dive-bombing Mustang.

1153. Ethell, Jeffrey L. "The Marvelous Mustang." *Air Force Magazine*, LXIV (September 1981), 144-146+.

A history of and tribute to this most photogenic of AAF fighters, the one which has created a fanatic band of followers and which to many is the one aircraft believed (incorrectly) to have defeated the Luftwaffe.

1154. ———. *Mustang: A Documentary History*. New York and London: Jane's, 1981. 176p.

Based on pilot accounts and recently uncovered documents, Ethell's work is one of the best of many Mustang books, one which expands the accepted aircraft biography and refutes the myths that grew during the war. Illustrated with nearly 200 photographs.

1155. Freeman, Roger A. *Mustang at War*. London: Ian Allan, 1974. 160p.

The story of the sleek escort fighter and sometimes fighter bomber told from the viewpoint of its pilots; stresses the plane's operational characteristics and missions. Illustrated with 210 photos.

1156. Gruenhagen, Robert W. *The Mustang: The Story of the P-51 Fighter*. Rev. ed. New York: Arco, 1980. 252p.

Utilizing archival research, interviews, and secondary sources, the author covers every aspect of this famous fighter from development through combat use in a work only Ethell rivals. Includes a special section on specification and production data and 323 photos and 19 drawings.

1157. Hardy, M.J. *North American Mustang: The Story of the Perfect Pursuit Plane, P-51.* New York: Arco, 1979. 128p.

Presents the fighter's familiar story with a variety of illustrations and photographs; not quite in the same league with Ethell or Gruenhagen.

1158. Hegg, William. *P-51: Bomber Escort.* Ballantine's Illustrated History of World War II. New York: Ballantine Books, 1971. 160p.

A combat pictorial which discusses development but puts most of its emphasis on combat in the skies of Europe.

1159. Hess, William N. *Fighting Mustang: The Chronicle of the P-51.* Garden City, N.Y.: Doubleday, 1970. 198p.

One of the better pre-Ethell/Gruenhagen chronicles, Hess's book follows the aircraft's development and combat career from 1942 to the late 1960's; includes a few pages of photographs and an appendix containing comments by Mustang aces like the 354th FG's Richard E. Turner.

1160. Hillman, Bradford H. "Mustang Roundup: Saga of the P-51." *Air Classics*, VIII (June 1972), 16-25, 64-65; (July 1972), 52-63.

An illustrated history of and tribute to this fine fighter, used today in air racing.

1161. Holder, William G. "The A-36 Dive-Bombing Mustang." *TAC Attack*, XIV (August 1974), 24-27.

One of the few studies devoted exclusively to this subtype of the P-51, which was employed not too successfully in Italy.

1162. Holmes, Harry. *North American P-51D Mustang.* Oxford, Eng.: Aerodata International, 1978. 20p.

A brief overview dominated by 26 black and white photographs and 19 line drawings.

1163. McCorkle, Charles M. "The Number 1 Fighter of World War II?: Spitfire or Mustang?" *Aerospace Historian*, XX (December 1973), 170-177.

Following analysis, the author concludes that both planes were the best--for different reasons!

1164. "Military Mustangs: A Sword Through Freedom's Enemies." *Air Classics Quarterly Review*, I (Spring 1975), 1-116.

In what amounts to a small book, the editors of this journal present the plane's basic biography and list of missions and pilot comments with ample illustration.

1165. Morgan, Len. *The P-51 Mustang.* New York: Arco, 1963. 52p.

A detailed pilot's report on this fighter--its development, uses, and eventual fall from military inventory in the U.S.; illustrated with 78 photographs.

1166. Shacklady, E.G. *North American P-51D Mustang*. Aircraft in Profile, no. 8. Windsor, Eng.: Profile Publications, 1965. 13p.

A brief technical history enhanced by the use of black and white photographs and color illustrations.

1167. Ward, Richard, and Ernest R. McDowell. *North American P-51B/C Mustang*. New York: Arco, 1969. 46p.

A pictorial survey containing over 200 photographs and color illustrations.

c. OTHER AIRCRAFT

1167a. Conley, Manuel. "Silent Squadrons." *American History Illustrated*, XVIII (June 1983), 12-21.

A pictorial review of the kinds of gliders employed by U.S. airborne forces, including those deployed in the MTO/ETO, and such major glider-borne assaults as the landings in Sicily, Normandy, and Arnhem.

1168. Davis, Paul M., and Amy C. Fenwick. *Development and Procurement of Gliders in the Army Air Forces, 1941-1944*. USAAF Historical Study, no. 47. Washington, D.C.: Headquarters, U.S. Army Air Forces, 1946. 208p.

A detailed account of the design and development of such gliders as the Waco for use by American airborne troops, particularly in the European and Mediterranean Theaters. Discusses setbacks as well as successful tests.

1169. Gault, Owen. "Cubs at War." *Air Classics*, IX (March 1973), 18-27.

Examines the use of the L-4 Piper as a liaison aircraft by the U.S. Army, especially in the northwest Europe campaigns of 1944-45.

1170. Glines, Carroll V., and Wendell F. Mosley. *The Grand Old Lady: Story of the DC-3*. Cleveland, Ohio: Pennington Press, 1960. 250p.

An enthusiastic account of the noted airliner which went into AAF service as the C-47 Skytrain, told as a series of anecdotes concerning important missions and pilots. Includes photographs.

1171. Hutton, C.I. "Cubs in Combat." *U.S. Army Aviation Digest*, III (June 1957), 31-38.

Examines the exploits of the L-4 Piper during World War II.

1172. Ingells, Douglas J. *The Plane That Changed the World: A Biography of the DC-3*. Fallbrook, Calif.: Aero Publishers, 1963. 250p.

Similar to the Glines and Mosley entry; includes details of the C-47's use in the major airborne operations in the European and Mediterranean Theaters and many more photos than the Glines outing.

1173. Johnsen, Frederick A. *Darkly Dangerous: The P-61 Black Widow Night Fighter*. Glendale, Calif.: Aviation Book Company, 1981. 29p.

A brief history of the development and European combat of the first U.S. aircraft designed solely as a night fighter; includes 177 photos.

1174. McQuillen, John A., Jr. "American Military Gliders in World War II in Europe." Unpublished Ph.D. Dissertation, St. Louis University, 1975.

Examines the use of Waco and Horsa gliders by the AAF in Europe in support of major airborne operations. Scholarly.

1175. Morgan, Len. *The Douglas DC-3*. New York: Arco, 1964. 56p.

A former pilot tells the story of a great airliner and troop transport; includes 81 photographs and 23 drawings.

1176. Mrazek, James E. *Fighting Gliders of World War II*. New York: St. Martin's Press, 1977. 207p.

This work examines the history of those gliders used by Allied and Axis forces in the European and Mediterranean; heavy on aircraft specifications and data, light on operational use. Photos.

1177. Nicholas, William H. "Gliders--Silent Weapon of the Sky." *National Geographic Magazine*, LXXXVI (August 1944), 149-160.

An illustrated look at training, testing, and use of glider pilots and their aircraft.

1178. Pearcy, Arthur. *The DC-3 Dakota*. Ballantine's Illustrated History of World War II. New York: Ballantine Books, 1975. 160p.

A pictorial which describes the C-47 (called "Dakota" by the British) with regard to both specifications and operations.

1179. ———. *Douglas Dakota Marks I-IV*. Aircraft in Profile, no. 220. Windsor, Eng.: Profile Publications, 1971. 24p.

A brief, detailed technical history enhanced by the use of color illustrations and black and white photographs.

1180. Redman, Rodney. "Observation and Liaison Aircraft: A Pictorial Review of Observation, Reconnaissance, and Liaison Aircraft of the U.S. Army and Air Force, Part II: 1925-1946." *Air Classics*, VIII (November 1971), 53-58.

A pictorial which describes various aircraft in interesting captions.

3. Awards/Insignia/Markings

1181. Andrade, John M. *U.S. Military Aircraft Designations and Serials Since 1909*. London: Midland Counties Publications, 1980. 254p.

A small British import paperback, filled with numbers and facts, covers the aircraft of all the U.S. services; one of the best sources of serial and construction number information.

1182. Bell, Dana. *Air Force Colors, Vol. II: ETO and MTO, 1942-1945*. Carrollton, Tx.: Squadron/Signal Publications, 1980. 96p.

Based on documentary research, this photo history details the camouflage and markings employed on AAF aircraft; includes a large number of color illustrations.

1183. Birdsall, Steve. *Hell's Angels*. Canoga Park, Calif.: Grenadier Books, 1969. 48p.

An illustrated guide to the imaginative and wide-ranging variety of names and markings placed by AAF crews upon their B-17's.

1184. Bowyer, Michael J.F. *Wartime Military Airfields of East Anglia, 1939-1945*. London: Patrick Stephens, 1979. 232p.

A complete look at the RAF/AAF bases in this British county; describes base-building, security, personnel, aircraft housed, and operations from. Illustrated with photographs.

1185. Campbell, J. Duncan. *Aviation Badges and Insignia of the United States Army, 1913-1946*. Tulsa, Okla.: Military Collectors News Press, 1979. 88p.

Covers the origin and development of hundreds of different wing badges and cap, collar, and sleeve insignia; particularly useful for the wartime AAF, this work contains 375 illustrations.

1186. DeSeversky, Alexander P. "Walt Disney: An Airman in His Heart." *Aerospace Historian*, XIV (April 1967), 5-8, 17-19.

Describes the work of the Disney studio in creating aircraft and unit insignia during the war.

1187. Dial, Jay F. *United States Aircraft Camouflage, World War II*. Arlington, Tx.: Scale, 1964. 20p.

A brief study of the camouflage applied to AAF/USN aircraft during the war, including interesting shades of pink employed in Africa. Illustrated with photos and drawings.

1188. Freeman, Roger A. *Airfields of the Eighth: Then and Now*. London: Battle of Britain International, 1967. 240p.

Revisits 69 bases and provides a brief history of each; presents over 400 "then-and-now" comparison photographs and vertical photographs and aerial obliques taken from the Ministry of Defence archives and modern aircraft.

1189. ———. *Camouflage and Markings: United States Army Air Forces.* London: Ducimus Books, 1974. 240p.

A detailed look at the camouflage painting applied to AAF warplanes as well as squadron markings, personal insignia, etc.; illustrated with a considerable number of color drawings and plates.

1190. ———. "U.S. Eighth and Ninth Air Force Aircraft Paintwork." *Air Pictorial* XXVIII (May 1966), 182-184; (June 1966), 214-216; (July 1966), 254-255.

Black and white photographs described with captions; covers national, unit, and personal markings.

1191. "A History of American Aircraft Insignia." *Aerospace Historian*, XVI (Spring 1969), 21-26.

A brief review of the evolution in national and unit markings; illustrated with black and white photographs.

1192. Hubbard, Gerard. "Aircraft Insignia: Spirit of Youth." *National Geographic Magazine*, LXXXIII (June 1943), 710-722.

A look at the personal insignia applied to aircraft by pilots and crews; highly illustrated.

1193. Jones, Robert C. "Marauder Decor." *Scale Modeler*, VIII (May 1973), 337-338.

A quick overview of the kinds of markings employed by wartime B-26 crews.

1193a. Marso, Richard. "Those Garish, Gaudy Liberators." *Air Classics*, IX (February 1973), 24-31, 48.

A look at the markings placed on B-24's by their crews; illustrated, this piece places particular emphasis on those liberators employed to lead formations.

1194. Nield, Henry, and Ian Logan. *Classy Chassy*. New York: A. & W. Visual Library, 1977.

Examines the art--nude and otherwise--which pilots and aircrew had placed upon their aircraft; illustrated with a variety of color plates.

1195. Robertson, Bruce. *Aircraft Camouflage and Markings, 1907-1954.* Edited by D.A. Russell. Letchworth, Eng.: Harleyford Publications, 1957. 212p.

A detailed review of camouflage and national, unit, and personal markings applied to various aircraft in the inventories of the world's air forces from the beginning through the Korean conflict. Illustrated with black and white photographs, drawings, and many color plates.

1196. Rosignoli, Guido. *Air Force Badges and Insignia of World War II*. New York: Arco, 1977. 200p.

A survey of the badges and insignia worn by the airmen of the war's principal belligerents; heavily illustrated, including 80 color plates.

1197. Scutts, Jerry. *U.S.A.A.F. Camouflage of World War II.* Airfax Magazine Guide, no. 18. London: Patrick Stephens, 1964. 64p.

Designed for modelers, this review is heavily illustrated with color plates and drawings, as well as black and white photographs.

1198. Tannehill, Victor G. "Mediterranean Marauder Markings." *American Aviation Historical Society Journal*, XXIV (Winter 1979), 55-67.

A detailed look at those worn by the B-26's of the 42nd Bombardment Wing (M).

1199. Trimble, Robert. "Military Markings of the World: ETO Mustangs." *Air Combat*, III (January 1975), 11-19.

Reviews the national, unit, and personal insignia and markings placed on the P-51's of the Eighth and Ninth Air Forces, 1944-1945, including D-Day stripes.

IV. THE WAR ON LAND

Introduction: The references in this section of our guide are devoted to the U.S. Army in the Mediterranean and European Theaters during World War II. Here will be found information on officers and heroes, campaigns and battles, accounts of specific units, and information on land weapons, uniforms, equipment, and insignia. Readers should note that additional information on segments of the land war are available in the encyclopedias and handbooks and general war histories cited in Section I above, as well as in some of the diplomatic studies noted in II:A.

A. GENERAL WORKS

Introduction: As the result of politics and planning, the U.S. Army was first committed to combat in North Africa late in 1942; later it moved through the Mediterranean and landed in France, pushing the war to victory in Germany in spring 1945. The citations in this section reflect those works which deal with the ground war phase of World War II as a whole. While almost all contain information on the American effort, all contain information on the operations of other Allied and Axis combatants as well. Here too we have placed those general works dealing with airborne operations; readers should, however, be aware that additional data on these exploits are also covered in the general works part of Section III above. A review of these overviews can be useful for comparison as well as for an understanding of the worldwide commitment of the U.S. Army and how its deployment to Europe and the Mediterranean made a difference in the final victory over the Third Reich.

1200. *Airborne Invasions.* Purnell's History of the World Wars Special. London: Phoebus Books, 1976. 64p.

A pictorial which describes the missions and equipment of Allied and Axis (mainly U.S., British, and German) airborne groups during the war; illustrated with drawings and photographs.

1201. Ayling, Keith. *They Fly to Fight: The Story of the Airborne Divisions.* New York: Appleton, 1944. 191p.

A contemporary overview of the U.S. airborne forces, their training and jumping techniques, with information on operations in North Africa and Sicily of a general nature.

1202. Bidwell, Shelford. *The Mechanics of War: Artillery Tactics, 1939-1945.* Warren, Mich.: Squadron/Signal Publications, 1976. 72p.

A pictorial which describes the various artillery pieces and the manner of their use by Allied and Axis forces in the various theaters; illustrated with color plates and black and white photographs.

1203. Bonds, Ray, ed. *The Encyclopedia of Land Warfare in the 20th Century*. New York: Crowell, 1977. 248p.

This oversize British volume, published under an American imprint, covers ground combat from World War I through Vietnam, with the largest section devoted to World War II. Illustrated with color and black and white photographs and color drawings.

1204. Bradford, George. *Great Tank Battles of World War II*. New York: Arco, 1970. 96p.

Illustrated with over 120 action photos, maps, and battle diagrams, this work reviews 40 armored battles in various theaters, including those involving Americans in North Africa and Europe.

1205. Brucer, Marshall, ed. *A History of Airborne Command and Airborne Center*. Williamstown, N.J.: J.M. Phillips, 1978. 58p.

Originally published in 1946 by the Command Club, this pictorial includes a listing of all U.S. Airborne Division action during the war; illustrated with 149 black and white photographs.

1206. Buchanan, A. Russell. *Black Americans in World War II*. Santa Barbara, Calif.: Clio Books, 1977. 148p.

This popular survey examines the role of Blacks in the military through a balanced approach which acknowledges accomplishments and setbacks.

1207. Crookenden, Napier. *Airborne At War*. New York: Scribners, 1978. 160p.

A noted British airborne commander examines the role of airborne troops, Allied and Axis, in the war, their units, equipment, and missions, including "Operation Varsity," the crossing of the Rhine. Illustrated with over 200 black and white photographs.

1208. Culp, Dennis K. *A Comparative Analysis of River Crossing Operations in the Twentieth Century*. Student Essay. Carlisle Barracks, Pa.: U.S. Army War College, 1982. 29p.

An analysis of German, Soviet, and U.S. river-crossing operations in World War II, including the Rapido and the Rhine, which includes organization, equipment, tactics, planning considerations and results.

1209. Dahlen, Chester A. "Defense of a River Line." *Military Review*, XXIX (February 1950), 30-41.

Reviews the crossing of the Meuthe by the Third Division, the Rhine by the Forty-Fifth Division, and the Rapido by the Thirty-Sixth Division.

1210. Detzer, Karl. *The Mightiest Army.* Pleasantville, N.Y.: Reader's Digest Association, 1945. 168p.

An overview of U.S. Army operations around the world, including those relative to this guide; features information on generals, missions, and equipment.

1211. ———, ed. *The Army Reader.* Indianapolis: Bobbs-Merrill, 1943. 469p.

An anthology of excerpts from previously published articles which show the activities of the U.S. Army in camp and combat around the world during the early years of the war.

1212. Devlin, Gerard. *Paratrooper: The Saga of U.S. Army and Marine Parachute and Glider Combat Troops During World War II.* New York: St. Martin's Press, 1979. 734p.

Filled with anecdotes and personal stories, this mammoth history presents, for the first time in one volume, detailed accounts of every air assault or land battle fought during the war by American airborne troops; based on personal interviews, documents, and the author's own service recollections, the work is illustrated with 20 maps and over 200 action photographs.

1213. Ellis, John. *The Sharp Edge: The Fighting Man in World War II.* New York: Scribners, 1980. 396p.

Drawing on a host of secondary sources, this British military historian attempts to show how U.S./U.K. ground soldiers reacted to wartime stimuli, such as battle and weather; suggests that G.I. infantrymen fared poorly in the northwest Europe campaigns.

1214. Farrar-Hockley, Anthony H. *The Mechanics of War: Infantry Tactics, 1939-1945.* Warren, Mich.: Squadron/Signal Publications, 1976. 72p.

A pictorial which describes the various infantry weapons and the manner of their use by Allied and Axis forces in the various theaters; illustrated with black and white photographs and color plates.

1215. Galvin, John R. *Air Assault: The Development of Airmobile Warfare.* New York: Hawthorn Books, 1970. 356p.

A review of airborne operations in World War II and after revealed, according to this author, that vertical envelopment, even with complete control of the air space, failed to produce the expected shock action. The later use of helicopters overcame the major weakness of parachute delivery: unit organizational control during and after the jump.

1216. Garrett, Richard. *Clash of Arms: The World's Great Land Battles.* London: Weidenfeld and Nicolson, 1976. 160p.

History's greatest land battles, including several from the northwest Europe campaign, are here covered in text and an array of photographs, drawings, and color plates.

1217. Gavin, James M. *Airborne Warfare*. Nashville, Tenn.: Battery Press, 1979. 186p.

First published by Infantry Journal Press in 1947, this work details a commander's view of his division (Eighty-Second) as well as other airborne operations of the war in the Mediterranean and northwest Europe. Includes a section of predictions on the airborne as seen from the perspective of the late 1940's. Illustrated with 9 photographs and 23 maps.

1218. Gregory, Barry, and John Batchelor. *Airborne Warfare, 1918-1945*. London: Phoebus Books, 1979. 128p.

A brief overview of the men, equipment, and missions of airborne troops from the end of World War I through World War II; illustrated with black and white photographs and co-author Batchelor's noteworthy color drawings.

1219. Griffith, Paddy. *Forward into Battle: Fighting Tactics from Waterloo to Vietnam*. Chichester, Eng.: A. Bird, 1981. 156p.

An overview of the manner in which generals marched their men into battle from 1815 through 1972, including the use of airborne, artillery, armor, infantry, cavalry, mechanized, and foot soldiers. A useful work if you want to know how to send forward an armored thrust or clean out a town with a squad of infantry.

1220. Gurney, Gene. *A Pictorial History of the United States Army in War and Peace from Colonial Times to Vietnam*. New York: Crown, 1978. 815p.

A mammoth account of the wars, battles, generals, uniforms, medals, weapons, insignia, posters, services, etc., which is encyclopedic in scope and contains a large section on World War II in the Mediterranean and northwest Europe; illustrated with 3,000 black and white reproductions of photographs, art, drawings.

1221. Hickey, Michael. *Out of the Sky: A History of Airborne Warfare*. New York: Scribners, 1979. 288p.

A comprehensive history of the various aspects of airborne warfare which begins in the 19th century, features a large section on World War II, and concludes with a study of postwar airborne and airmobile operations; illustrated with 16 pages of photos and 18 maps.

1222. Hogg, Ian V. *Fortress: A History of Military Defense*. New York: St. Martin's Press, 1977. 160p.

A look at the use of fortifications in modern war and the ease or difficulty in overcoming them, e.g., Battle of Metz. Illustrated with maps, drawings, and photos.

1223. Holmes, Richard. *Epic Land Battles*. London and New York: Octopus Books, 1976. 256p.

Provides descriptive and critical analysis of the decisive battles of modern military history from Yorktown through the

Ardennes; oversize, this British import is illustrated with dozens of photographs, maps, diagrams, and technical drawings.

1224. Hottelet, Richard C. "Orphans of Battle: Replacements." *Saturday Evening Post*, CCXVII (March 17, 1945), 23-28+.

One of the few studies on the subject of how replacement or "fresh" troops were fed into the battle, particularly in northwest Europe, so that tired veterans could get rest and relief.

1225. Hoyt, Edwin P. *Airborne: The History of American Parachute Forces*. New York: Stein and Day, 1979. 228p.

The author, more famous for his naval books, here discusses the development, organization, units, men, equipment, and missions of the Army's airborne troops, especially in the Mediterranean and European Theaters of World War II. The book is written in a popular style and illustrated with a few photographs.

1226. Huston, James A. *Out of the Blue: U.S. Army Airborne Operations in World War II*. West Lafayette, Ind.: Purdue University Studies, 1972. 327p.

An examination of the development and use of U.S. airborne forces during the war, including aircraft and equipment and the training of troops; provides detailed accounts of major airborne battles, including a lengthy study of the 1944 Arnhem drop.

1227. ———. "Thoughts on the American Airborne Effort in World War II." *Military Review*, XXXI (April 1951), 3-14; (May 1951), 18-30.

An examination of the doctrine behind the use of airborne troops, particularly in northwest Europe.

1228. Jacobsen, Hans Adolf, and Jürgen Rohwer, eds. *Decisive Battles of World War II: The German View*. New York: G.P. Putnam, 1965. 509p.

An anthology of ten essays on campaigns and battles of the European war from the German viewpoint, emphasizing Nazi strategy and tactics and Hitler's role in their formulation. All of the authors are German, all are critical of Hitler's influence, but not all of the studies concern ground warfare--several, like co-editor Rohwer's, are on the air and sea efforts.

1229. Jones, Philip D. "U.S. Antitank Doctrine in World War II." *Military Review*, LX (March 1980), 57-67.

From Kasserine to the Bulge, this study examines the ways in which American soldiers handled German tanks, with small arms, artillery, and a variety of armored vehicles.

1230. Kershaw, Andrew, ed. *Infantry at War, 1939-1945*. Purnell's History of the World Wars Special. London: Phoebus Books, 1975. 64p.

A pictorial which describes the missions and equipment of Allied and Axis infantrymen during the war; illustrated with a variety of black and white photographs, drawings, and color plates.

1231. ———. *Tanks at War, 1939-1945.* Purnell's History of the World Wars Special. London: Phoebus Books, 1975. 64p.

A pictorial similar to that described in the last entry which provides information on Allied and Axis armored troops, equipment, and missions; illustrated similarly to other Purnell titles cited in this part.

1232. Kleber, Brooks E., and Dale Birdsell. *Chemicals in Combat.* U.S. Army in World War II: The Chemical Warfare Service. Washington, D.C.: U.S. Government Printing Office, 1965. 673p.

Describes the use of chemical weapons (e.g., smoke) in combat and the CWS's administrative and supply problems overseas; illustrated with photographs, maps, charts, and tables.

1233. *Land Power: A Modern Illustrated Military History.* London: Phoebus Books, 1979. 352p.

Traces the evolution of infantry and artillery forces during the two world wars, emphasizing the shifts in tactics and the equipment employed. Illustrated with 620 photographs and drawings, including 350 in color.

1234. Lee, Ulysses. *The Employment of Negro Troops.* U.S. Army in World War II: Special Studies. Washington, D.C.: U.S. Government Printing Office, 1966. 740p.

A Black scholar tells in detail the story of how the Army employed Black troops before and during the War and describes the combat experiences of Black units in all the theaters, particularly the Mediterranean and northwest Europe.

1235. Lehman, Milton. "'Nothing Ahead But Krauts': The Front Line Infantryman." *Saturday Evening Post*, CCXVII (March 10, 1945), 34+.

A look at the qualities needed to be an effective infantryman in northwest Europe late in the war; it may be recalled that General Patton, for one, did not think highly of *Post* accounts.

1236. MacDonald, Charles B. *Airborne.* Ballantine's Illustrated History of World War II. New York: Ballantine Books, 1970. 160p.

Emphasizing the German landing on Crete and the Allied Arnhem drop, the author briefly describes all of the war's major airborne operations in this pictorial.

1237. ———. *The Mighty Endeavor: American Armed Forces in the European Theater in World War II.* New York and London: Oxford University Press, 1969. 564p.

In what many regard as a synthesis of the Army's official histories ("the green books") and one of the finest one-volume accounts of the European Theater available, the author, a soldier-historian who saw much of the action firsthand, reviews the circumstances behind the U.S. decision to defeat Germany first and then follows the MTO/ETO campaign and its strategy from the Casablanca landings of 1942 through VE-Day; covering ground (mainly), air, and naval aspects of the "endeavor," MacDonald refutes some of the assertions made in Wilmot's pro-British *The Struggle for Europe*, item 1685, and offers forthright judgments upon U.S. and Allied conduct of the war. Illustrated with 20 maps and 75 photographs, this is an excellent starting place for the uninitiated.

1238. ———. *Three Battles: Arnaville, Altuzzo, and Schmidt*. U.S. Army in World War II: Special Studies. Washington, D.C.: U.S. Government Printing Office, 1952. 443p.

"River Crossing at Arnaville" is the story of a battle that started badly and ended in victory; "Objective Schmidt," of a battle that began with easy success and turned into tragic defeat; "Breakthrough at Monte Altuzzo" is an account of how, after a succession of misguided efforts, a small number of men penetrated the formidable Gothic Line in Italy. Arnaville was fought in France; Altuzzo in Italy; and Schmidt in Germany.

1239. Macksey, Kenneth J. *The History of Land Warfare*. New York: Two Continents, 1974. 248p.

A noted British expert in armored warfare here presents a brief overview of history's great campaigns, showing the development of tactics and equipment along the way.

1240. Marshall, Samuel L.A. *Battle at Best*. New York: William Morrow, 1964. 257p.

Eight actions from World War II are well retold, including four from the ETO: a platoon action in the Battle of Best; the self-sacrifice of Pfc. Joe Mann; the fate of the Twenty-Ninth Infantry Division on Omaha Beach; and a surprising memoir of the author's participation with Ernest Hemingway in the Liberation of Paris.

1241. Mayo, Lida, *et al*. *The War Against Germany*. U.S. Army in World War II: The Corps of Engineers. Washington, D.C.: U.S. Government Printing Office, 1981.

This volume covers Army engineer operations during the campaigns in North Africa, Sicily, Italy, and northwest Europe, placing emphasis on engineering problems and solutions.

1242. Messenger, Charles. "The Anglo-American Version and Final German Fling." In: his *The Blitzkrieg Story*. New York: Scribners, 1976, pp. 220-245.

A brief analysis of U.S./U.K. armored and mechanized warfare tactics in the battles in northwest Europe and the German counteroffensive in the Ardennes, winter 1944.

1243. Motley, Mary P. *The Invisible Soldier: The Experiences of the Black Soldier, World War II.* Detroit, Mich.: Wayne State University Press, 1975. 364p.

More valuable, from a strictly military viewpoint, than the Buchanan source cited above, this work is based on extensive interviews with veterans of Black units, combat and support.

1244. Mrazek, James E. "Our Silent Ones: The Combat Gliders." *Aerospace Historian*, X (June 1963), 69-73.

A rather sketchy overview of some aspects of glider employment by airborne forces in the MTO/ETO.

1245. Palmer, Annette. "The Politics of Race and War: Black American Soldiers in the Caribbean Theater During the Second World War." *Military Affairs*, XLVII (April 1983), 59-62.

Problems between the comparatively "rich" Black U.S. G.I.'s and the poverty-stricken local Blacks on the island of Trinidad.

1246. Palmer, Robert R. "Manpower for the Army: Procurement [of Enlisted Men] for World War II." *Infantry Journal*, LXI (July 1947), 6-12; (August 1947), 27-32; (September 1947), 39-43; (October 1947), 40-43; (November 1947), 39-45; (December 1947), 38-45.

Largely eclipsed by and drawn from the following citation.

1247. ———. Bell I. Wiley, and William R. Keast. *The Procurement and Training of Ground Combat Troops.* U.S. Army in World War II: Army Ground Forces. Washington, D.C.: U.S. Government Printing Office, 1948. 696p.

The first three studies deal with the procurement of enlisted men and officers, the next three discuss the policies and problems involved in training individuals (commissioned and enlisted), for their special functions in ground combat, and the last four cover the training of units.

1248. Perrett, Bryan. *Through Mud and Blood: Infantry/ Tank Operations in World War II.* London: Hale, 1975. 272p.

This British study examines the coordination between infantrymen and armored units of the major belligerents during the war, including--but certainly not limited to--those of the U.S. Army in the Mediterranean and northwest Europe Theaters.

1249. Pritchard, Paul W. "Large-Area Screening in the MTO and ETO." *Military Review*, XXX (January 1951), 3-16.

Army Chemical Corps smoke screens in Italy and Normandy, 1943-1944.

1250. Pyle, Ernest T. *Brave Men.* New York: Henry Holt, 1944. 474p.

America's most famous World War II correspondent here offers a series of G.I. sketches told from the infantryman's viewpoint;

based on the author's newspaper dispatches from the U.S. fronts in Sicily and France, this work begins with the "Husky" invasion of June 1943 and continues through the Liberation of Paris in September 1944.

1251. Revie, Alastair. *The Pictorial History of Land Battles.* London: Marshall Cavendish, 1974. 128p.

This title is somewhat misleading in that the major emphasis is on the land engagements of World War II, although several from earlier conflicts are briefly covered. Illustrated with black and white photographs, color plates, maps, and charts.

1252. Roberts, Kent, Robert R. Greenfield, and Bell I. Wiley. *The Organization of Ground Combat Troops.* U.S. Army in World War II: Army Ground Forces. Washington, D.C.: U.S. Government Printing Office, 1947. 540p.

Contains six essays, five of which are relevant to this guide. The first concerns the antecedents of the Army ground forces, covering the years 1940-1942; the next four studies relate the main problems and decisions regarding the size, internal organization, and armament of the ground troops deployed in the war.

1253. Strawson, John. *Hitler's Battles for Europe.* New York: Scribners, 1971. 256p.

Based on secondary sources, this study by a British historian examines those engagements Hitler directly influenced in either concept or execution and explains how the Führer's influence contributed to victory or loss.

1254. Tugwell, Maurice A.J. *Airborne to Battle.* London: Kimber, 1971. 367p.

A British historian looks at the development and use of airborne troops during World War II, including those of Germany, Britain, and the United States; assessments are made of the reasons behind victories and defeats. Illustrated.

1255. ———. "Day of the Paratroops." *Military Review*, XLVII (March 1977), 40-53.

An overview of the use of airborne forces in World War II.

1256. United States. War Department. *Small Unit Actions.* American Forces in Action Series. Washington, D.C.: U.S. Government Printing Office, 1946. 212p.

From the Italian front, this study looks at the exploits of the Three Hundred Fifty-First Infantry at Santa Maria Infanto; from France, accounts of the Second Ranger Battalion at Pointe du Hoe and the Fourth Armored Division at Singling are provided.

1257. Van Greveld, Martin. *Fighting Power: German and U.S. Army Performance, 1939-1945.* Westport, Conn.: Greenwood Press, 1982. 198p.

Employing figures and exact comparisons and after examining the social structures of both societies, the doctrine and principles, leadership and organization of both armies, the author concludes that both offensively and defensively--even in defeat--the Wehrmacht was clearly superior to the U.S. Army in Europe. This controversial study is illustrated with a number of charts and diagrams.

1258. Von Mellenthin, Friedrich W. *Panzer Battles, 1939-1945: A Study of the Emergence of Armor in the Second World War.* Translated from the German. Norman: University of Oklahoma Press, 1956. 371p.

The former general and chief-of-staff of the Fourth Panzer Army provides a detailed study of the use of armor in the ETO, including--and most important for users of this guide--the final "Campaign in the West." The battle and strategy analyses are sound. Excellent maps.

1259. Weeks, John. *The Airborne Soldier.* New York: Sterling, 1982. 192p.

This oversize British import provides an overall view of the use of paratroops in World War II and a review of units, men, leaders, equipment, and specific battles.

1260. Wilbur, W.H. "Infantrymen, the Fighters of War." *National Geographic Magazine*, LXXXVI (November 1944), 513-538.

A pictorial appreciation of U.S. Army ground forces with much on camp life and daily routine.

1261. Wiley, Bell I. "The Building and Training of Infantry Divisions [1942-1945]." *Infantry Journal*, LXII (February 1948), 6-10; (March 1948), 26-30; (April 1948), 41-45; (May 1948), 30-36.

Covers activation procedures, training, obstacles to effective training, and the effects of overseas requirements on training; much of Wiley's material was absorbed into the Palmer/Wiley/Keast "green book" cited above.

1262. Wilmot, Ned. *The Strategy and Tactics of Land Warfare.* London: Marshall Cavendish, 1979. 80p.

Strictly a study of World War II, Wilmot's work concentrates on the use of infantry, armor, and artillery by the major European belligerents and the U.S. Army; illustrated with maps, black and white photographs, and various color material.

B. OFFICERS AND HEROES

Introduction: An interesting way to look at the ground war in the MTO/ETO, particularly for younger readers, is through the biography of its participants. The citations in this section are arranged in two parts. Part 1 is a collection of general biographies which concern two or more individuals; Part 2 concerns individuals and is arranged alphabetically by the last name of the biographee. It should be noted that additional biographical information is available in the handbooks, encyclopedias, biographical sources, and general war histories cited in Section I, the general land histories cited in Part A above, and in the campaign and unit histories noted in Parts C and D below.

1. Collective Biography

1263. Baldwin, Hanson W. "Our Generals in the Battle of Germany." *New York Times Magazine* (October 22, 1944), 10-11+.

Presents concise portraits of eight field commanders, including Bradley, Simpson, Hodges, Patton, Devers, Patch, Collins, and Walker.

1264. Blumenson, Martin. "The Forgotten Corps Commanders." *Army*, XIII (July 1963), 40-45.

Includes capsule biographies of 34 officers, men like Generals A.C. Gillem, Jr., J.B. Anderson, R.S. McLain, J.L. Collins, Troy H. Middleton, James A. Van Fleet, Clarence R. Huebner, Stafford Irwin, Walton H. Walker, Ernest N. Harmon, Hugh J. Gaffey, Frank Milburn, Wade H. Haislip, and Edward H. Brooks, to name a few.

1265. ———. "Ike and His Indispensable Lieutenants." *Army*, XXX (June 1980), 50-54+.

Examines the relationship between Eisenhower, Montgomery, Bradley, Patton, and others.

1266. Honeywell, Roy J. *Chaplains of the United States Army*. Washington, D.C.: U.S. Government Printing Office, 1958. 376p.

An overall history of Army chaplains from the Revolutionary through the Korean war; includes a large section on those who served in the MTO/ETO in World War II.

1267. Parker, William. *Above and Beyond the Call of Duty: Commemorating the 100th Anniversary of the Medal of Honor, 1863-1865*. New York: Macfadden Books, 1963. 176p.

Biographies relative to this guide include those of Captain Bobbie Brown of the First Division (Aachen) and Ninth Division's Sgt. Pete D'Alessandro (Ardennes).

1268. Pogue, Forrest C. "George C. Marshall and His Commanders, 1942-1945." In: U.S. Military History Institute. *Essays in Some Dimensions of Military History*, IV (February 1976), 80-90.

Examines the relationship between Marshall and several of his top commanders, e.g., Eisenhower, Clark.

2. Specific Individuals

Creighton W. Abrams, Jr.

1269. Lang, Will. "Colonel Abe of the 4th Armored Division, Spearhead of Patton's Advances." *Life*, XVIII (April 23, 1945), 47-50+.

Abrams commanded the Thirty-Seventh Tank Batallion, that armored column which broke through the German siege of Bastogne in December 1944.

Harold Alexander

1270. Alexander, Harold. *The Alexander Memoirs, 1940-1945.* Edited by John North. New York: McGraw-Hill, 1962. 210p.

A somewhat thin and disjointed edited collection of the Field Marshal's reflections; Alexander, one of Britain's top commanders, is remembered for his role as Supreme Allied Commander in the Mediterranean.

1271. Hillson, Norman. *Alexander of Tunis.* London: W.H. Allen, 1952. 252p.

An early reminiscence of the Field Marshal which places much emphasis on his leadership qualities and ability to work well with men as diverse as Montgomery and Clark.

1272. Jackson, William G.F. *Alexander of Tunis as Military Commander.* New York: Dodd, Mead, 1972. 344p.

A study of this much-respected British general who led Allied forces in Tunisia, Sicily, and Italy in 1942-1945; Alexander is praised within these pages which, nevertheless, study fairly his contribution to Mediterranean victory. The author was a former member of Alexander's staff.

1273. Nicolson, Nigel. *Alexander: The Life of Field Marshal Earl Alexander of Tunis.* New York: Atheneum, 1973. 346p.

The only real difference between this biography and, say, Jackson's is Nicolson's heavier detail on Alexander's family life and the qualities and limitations of a self-effacing and personally elusive subject.

Walter Bedell Smith

1274. Wertenbacker, Charles C. "Invasion Plan: Bedell-Smith Worked Out the Secret, Closely-Guarded Moves." *Life*, XVI (June 12, 1944), 94-96+.

Attributes much of the D-Day planning to Eisenhower's Chief of Staff, an extremely effective officer about whom surprisingly little has been written.

Omar N. Bradley

1275. *Army Times*, Editors of. "Gen. Omar Bradley." In: their *Famous American Military Leaders of World War II.* New York: Dodd, Mead, 1962, pp. 85-92.

A concise appreciation of the noted general who, in 1981, became the last of America's five-star officers to die.

1276. Bradley, Omar N. "Leadership." *Parameters*, I (Winter 1972), 2-8.

An address to officers at the U.S. Army War College given in October 1971, an edited version of which was reprinted in the same journal, XI (September 1981), 2-7, under the title "On Leadership."

1277. ———. *A Soldier's Story*. New York: Henry Holt, 1951. 618p.

The memoirs, modest, unpretentious, not overly critical, and insightful, of one of the Army's most consistently successful officers--written largely by Bradley's wartime aide, Chester B. Hansen. Bradley was involved in all of America's major operations in North Africa, Sicily, and northwest Europe and here speaks of some of the other officers with whom he worked, including Eisenhower, Patton, Alexander, Collins, Hodges, and the mildly detested Montgomery.

1278. ———, and Clay Blair. *A General's Life*. New York: Simon and Schuster, 1982. 752p.

Although written in the first person, this is, in fact, a biography by Blair, who worked closely with Bradley on it, the latter seeing some 200 pages of the manuscript before his death. The work covers the subject's entire life with the section on the World War II years based on Bradley's personal papers, official documents, interviews, and other sources. A brief excerpt with the same title was published in the *Washington Post Magazine* (February 6, 1983), pp. 12-14.

1279. Garland, Albert N. "A Study in Leadership--One of the Greatest." *Military Review*, XLIX (December 1969), 18-27.

Bradley's leadership qualities as gleaned from the papers of Lt. Gen. Raymond S. McLain, who commanded the U.S. XIX Corps under Bradley in northwest Europe.

1280. "General of the Army Omar N. Bradley, 1893-1981." *Army*, XXXI (May 1981), 16-19.

An obituary-biography written in tribute.

1281. Hansen, Chester B. "General Bradley as Seen Close-up." *New York Times Magazine* (November 30, 1947), 14+.

Recollections of Bradley's wartime service by his wartime aide--and the ghostwriter of his memoirs.

1282. Mansfield, Stephanie. "A General's Wife." *Washington Post Magazine* (February 6, 1983), 15-17.

Covers the married life of Omar and Kitty Bradley, including their separation during World War II.

1283. Middleton, Drew. "The General Who Outblitzed the Nazis." *New York Times Magazine* (September 10, 1944), 5+.

Concerns Bradley's service as commander of the U.S. First Army in the Normandy invasion and breakout.

1284. Pogue, Forrest C. "General of the Army Omar N. Bradley." In: Michael Carver, ed. *War Lords: Military Commanders of the 20th Century*. Boston, Mass.: Little, Brown, 1976, pp. 538-553.

A concise, fair, and insightful look at Bradley's leadership qualities from North Africa to VE-Day, including his relationship with Eisenhower.

1285. Pratt, Fletcher. "Bradley." In: his *Eleven Generals: Studies in American Command*. New York: William Sloane Associates, 1949, pp. 297-355.

Essentially a reprinting of the next entry.

1286. ———. "Infantry Specialist" [and] "The Tactician of the West." *Infantry Journal*, LXI (December 1947), 4-14; LXII (January 1948), 52-56; (February 1948), 19-25.

Almost without criticism, Pratt follows Bradley's wartime career from North Africa through Sicily and especially across northwest Europe, remarking upon those personal qualities that made him the "G.I.'s General."

1287. Reeder, Russell. *Omar Nelson Bradley: The Soldier's General*. Champaign, Ill.: Garrard Publishing Co., 1969. 112p.

A brief overview of the general's life, suitable for younger readers.

1288. Robinson, Donald. "General Bradley." *American Mercury*, LXVII (December 1948), 671-678.

Comments on the soldier's career, and, more important, on his elevation to the position of Army Chief of Staff.

1289. Shoemaker, Robert H., and Leonard A. Paris. "General Omar N. Bradley." In: their *Famous American Generals*. New York: Crowell, 1946, pp. 138-151.

A scant overview of Bradley's wartime accomplishments.

1290. "A Soldier's Story." *Soldiers*, XXXVI (May 1981), 2-3.

A capsule obituary-biography.

1291. Whiting, Charles. *Bradley*. Ballantine's Illustrated History of World War II: War Leaders Book. New York: Ballantine Books, 1971. 160p.

A pictorial which examines not only Bradley's contributions but also the battles and campaigns in which he was a participant.

Alan F. Brooke

1292. Bryant, Arthur. *The Turn of the Tide: A History of the War Years Based on the Diaries of Field Marshal Lord Alanbrooke, Chief of the Imperial General Staff.* Garden City, N.Y.: Doubleday, 1957. 264p.

1293. ———. *Triumph in the West: A History of the War Years Based on the Diaries of Field Marshal Lord Alanbrooke, Chief of the Imperial General Staff.* Garden City, N.Y.: Doubleday, 1959. 438p.

Presents a British view of the war which stresses Anglo-American strategy and shows the increasing dominance of the U.S. after 1942. Brooke, known for his self-discipline, had a great deal to do with running Britain's daily war effort, in addition to his service within the Combined Chiefs of Staff, where he developed an antipathy (mutually shared) for General Marshall which lasted throughout the war. Brooke was extremely disappointed at not becoming Supreme Commander, and perhaps as a result, these memoirs are extremely anti-Churchill and anti-Eisenhower.

Mark W. Clark

1294. Blumenson, Martin, and James L. Stokesbury. "Mark Clark and the War in Italy." *Army*, XXI (May 1971), 49-52.

Dubbed the "American Eagle" by Winston Churchill, Clark was Eisenhower's deputy in the invasion of North Africa and later boss of American forces in the Italian campaign. This piece examines the controversies which surfaced surrounding certain of his decisions in the latter operation.

1295. Bracker, Milton. "Gen. Mark Clark Gets the Tough Jobs." *New York Times Magazine* (September 19, 1943), 9+.

Reviews Clark's North African service and command of the Fifth Army in the Salerno invasion of Italy.

1296. Clark, Mark W. *Calculated Risk: A Personal Story of the Campaign in North Africa and Italy.* New York: Harper, 1950. 500p.

A forthright appraisal of the author's service which, although containing some material on North Africa, concentrates mainly on the Italian campaign. Clark saw Italy as a magnet with which to draw German forces from east and northwest Europe, agreed with Churchill's desire for a Balkan campaign, and comments on the controversies (e.g. Monte Cassino, Rapido River crossing) which arose during his push toward Rome.

1297. Clark, Maurine. *Captain's Bride, General's Lady: Memoirs.* New York: McGraw-Hill, 1956. 278p.

Mrs. Clark relates the story of her life with the noted officer and comments on their time apart during World War II.

1298. Cook, Don. "'I'm Sticking to My Guns': Gen. Mark Wayne Clark." In: his *Fighting Americans of Today*. New York: E.P. Dutton, 1944, pp. 24-41.

An uncritical overview of Clark's Italian command role.

1299. McCardle, M.C. "Lt. Gen. Mark Wayne Clark." In: *These Are the Generals*. New York: Alfred A. Knopf, 1943, pp. 84-97.

A contemporary view of Clark which relates his North African service but, because of its publication date, has little to say about his handling of the Italian Theater.

1300. Shoemaker, Robert H., and Leonard A. Paris. "Gen. Mark W. Clark." In: their *Famous American Generals*. New York: Crowell, 1946, pp. 125-137.

A brief, uncritical report on Clark's wartime service.

Bruce C. Clarke

1301. Ellis, William D., and Thomas J. Cunningham, Jr. *Clarke of St. Vith: The Sergeant's General*. Cleveland, Ohio: Dillon/ Lieder Bach, 1974. 344p.

Recalls the subject's wartime service with the Fourth and Seventh Armored Divisions, particularly his delaying action at St. Vith, Belgium, in December 1944 during the Battle of the Bulge.

J. Lawton Collins

1302. Collins, J. Lawton. *Lightning Joe: An Autobiography*. Baton Rouge: Louisiana State University Press, 1979. 449p.

The author reviews his wartime service when, after service on Guadalcanal where he earned his nickname, he was shifted to Europe to command Seventh Corps, U.S. First Army from Utah Beach to the Elbe River; includes a number of vivid battle recollections, including the drive to Cherbourg and the Second Armored Division counterattack in the Ardennes, December 1944.

1303. Hines, William. "Gen. J. Lawton Collins: Army Chief-of-Staff." *American Mercury*, LXXI (September 1950), 266-273.

A postwar biography with emphasis on the subject's World War II service.

1304. Whitehead, Don. "He Shook Patton Loose: Gen. Collins." *Saturday Evening Post*, CCXVII (November 4, 1944), 18-19+.

How the subject and his corps led the American breakout from the Normandy beachhead.

William O. Darby

1305. King, Michael J. *William Orlando Darby: A Military Biography*. Hamden, Conn.: Archon Books, 1981. 224p.

Based on the author's 1977 Northern Illinois University Ph.D. Dissertation of the same title; explains how this officer formed a special group of shock troops called Rangers which were employed in both the MTO and ETO. Darby was killed in action in Italy shortly before V-E Day.

Francis W. DeGuingand

1306. DeGuingand, Francis W. *Operation Victory.* New York: Scribners, 1947. 488p.

Presents a headquarters view of the war in North Africa, Sicily, and northwest Europe as seen by General Montgomery's chief of staff, who relates only incidents of which he had firsthand knowledge. The work is pro-Monty, even though the diplomatic DeGuingand was well liked by Eisenhower and was often able to resolve misunderstandings between his boss and the Supreme Commander.

Jacob L. Devers

1307. Shoemaker, Robert H., and Leonard A. Paris. "Gen. Jacob L. Devers." In: their *Famous American Generals.* New York: Crowell, 1946, pp. 152-159.

This is about the only substantial piece available on Devers, who served briefly as Commanding General of both the ETO and North Africa Theater, Deputy Supreme Allied Commander, Mediterranean, and after September 1944, boss of the Allied Sixth Army Group.

Dwight D. Eisenhower

1308. Altman, Frances. *Dwight D. Eisenhower, Crusader for Peace.* New York: Denison, 1970. 223p.

A tribute to the former President and Supreme Commander written for younger readers.

1309. Ambrose, Stephen E. "Dwight D. Eisenhower." In: Peter Dennis and Adrian Preston, eds. *Soldiers as Statesmen.* New York: Barnes and Noble, 1976, pp. 113-133.

A study of the former President and Supreme Commander here analyzes his leadership/diplomatic roles both as chief executive and chief Allied soldier.

1310. ———. *Eisenhower: Soldier, General of the Army, President-Elect, 1890-1952.* New York: Simon and Schuster, 1983. 640p.

This is the first volume of what promises to be one of the best Eisenhower biographies, based on original sources, many not employed before. Covers the subject's career from Abilene to the White House, and through a combination of anecdotes, quotations, and text, relates not only incidents of international importance, but also those affecting Eisenhower and those closest to him, including wife, Mamie, son John, and driver-aide Kay Summersby. Ambrose's prose, only occasionally critical of its subject, reveals the general's concerns and feelings toward other leaders and the events in which he participated.

1311. ———. "Fateful Friendship." *American Heritage*, XX (April 1969), 41+.

Eisenhower's career-long relationship with flashy General Patton.

1312. ———. "How Ike Became Supreme Commander." *American History Illustrated*, III (November 1968), 20-26, 30.

A pictorial which relates the story of how Roosevelt and Marshall settled on Eisenhower's appointment.

1313. ———. *Ike: Abilene to Berlin*. New York: Harper & Row, 1973. 220p.

A military biography which concentrates on Eisenhower's wartime career as Supreme Commander; surpassed by the author's multi-volume biography noted above and the next citation.

1314. ———. *The Supreme Commander: The War Years of General Dwight D. Eisenhower*. Garden City, N.Y.: Doubleday, 1970. 732p.

Based primarily on *The Papers of Dwight David Eisenhower*, which the author helped to edit, this work is a scholarly analysis of the subject's 1941-1945 military career which places emphasis on Eisenhower's command decisions relating to North Africa, Overlord, the Ardennes, and other operations. While defending Eisenhower's numerous political-military choices, the author also studies the Supreme Commander's relations with a variety of leaders, including FDR, Churchill, DeGaulle, Brooke, Marshall, Montgomery, and Patton.

1315. American Heritage, Editors of. *Eisenhower: American Hero*. New York: American Heritage Publishing Co., 1969. 144p.

With a narrative by Kenneth S. Davis, this memorial pictorial features an anthology of recollections by some of the general's famous associates, including Montgomery, Bradley, and Mark Clark.

1316. Archer, Jules. *Battlefield President: Dwight D. Eisenhower*. New York: Julian Messner, 1967. 191p.

Covers the subject's entire military-political career; suitable for younger readers.

1317. *Army Times*, Editors of. *The Challenge and the Triumph: The Story of Dwight D. Eisenhower*. New York: G.P. Putnam, 1966. 192p.

A concise biography which concentrates on the military aspects of its subject's career; suitable for younger readers.

1318. ———. "Gen. Dwight D. Eisenhower." In: its *Famous American Military Leaders of World War II*. New York: Dodd, Mead, 1962, pp. 42-50.

A concise account which concentrates on Eisenhower's role as Supreme Commander and his relations with Allied and U.S. Army leaders.

1319. Blumenson, Martin. *Eisenhower*. Ballantine's Illustrated History of World War II: War Leader Book. New York: Ballantine Books, 1972. 160p.

A concise pictorial war biography of the Allied Supreme Commander with some appraisal of his effectiveness as both a diplomat and a military chieftain.

1320. ———. "Eisenhower: Great General or Chairman of the Board?" *Army*, XVI (June 1966), 34-45.

Discusses the merits of the subtitle positions, both of which were ascribed to Eisenhower's leadership pattern.

1321. Butcher, Harry C. *My Three Years with Eisenhower*. New York: Simon and Schuster, 1946. 911p.

Eisenhower's wartime naval aide was directed to keep a diary of his boss's activities, here published in part (the complete diary is in the Eisenhower Library in Kansas); this is a warm and friendly portrait filled with opinions on military operations, strategy, and personalities, some of whom and which the author knew little about.

1322. Churchill, Winston L.S. "General Eisenhower." In: his *Victory: War Speeches*. Boston, Mass.: Little, Brown, 1946, pp. 199-201.

The British Prime Minister's public appreciation of the Supreme Commander is here expressed.

1323. Cook, Blanche W. *Declassified Eisenhower: A Divided Legacy*. Garden City, N.Y.: Doubleday, 1981. 432p.

This biography, like Ambrose's *Eisenhower* noted above, relies to a large extent upon access to newly available documents, particularly concerning the biographee's presidency. Using these and other sources, Cook attempts to point out the successes and failures, good and evil of the general as Supreme Commander and President.

1324. Cook, Dan. "Fighting Kansan: Dwight D. Eisenhower." In: his *Fighting Americans of Today*. New York: E.P. Dutton, 1944, pp. 11-23.

A brief, uncritical overview of Eisenhower's wartime career through D-Day.

1325. ———. "General of the Army Dwight D. Eisenhower." In: Michael Carver, ed. *War Lords: Military Commanders of the 20th Century*. Boston, Mass.: Little, Brown, 1976, pp. 509-537.

A much more balanced view of Eisenhower's Supreme Commander role than the previous entry, here Cook presents an analysis of his subject's military and political successes and failures.

1326. Davis, Kenneth S. *Soldier of Democracy: A Biography of Dwight D. Eisenhower*. New ed. Garden City, N.Y.: Doubleday, 1952. 577p.

Davis, who wrote the American Heritage tribute cited above, presents a detailed summary of Eisenhower's wartime career and his postwar service with NATO, based largely on interviews. This book was read widely during the 1952 presidential campaign.

1327. DeWeerd, Harvey A. "Eisenhower." In: his *Great Soldiers of World War II*. New York: W.W. Norton, 1944, pp. 264-298.

A noted wartime author follows Eisenhower's assignment as Supreme Commander in North Africa, Sicily, and northwest Europe, offering almost no criticism at all.

1328. ———. "General Eisenhower." *American Mercury*, LXI (July 1945), 16-25.

Completes the story begun in the previous citation.

1329. "Dwight D. Eisenhower, 1890-1969." *Newsweek*, LXXIII (April 7, 1969), 18-21.

A pictorial obituary and tribute.

1330. Eisenhower, Dwight D. *At Ease: Stories I Tell My Friends*. Garden City, N.Y.: Doubleday, 1967. 400p.

A volume of informal recollections, mostly from the subject's military days, which are of little historical significance, but do reveal something of the man's inner feelings and character.

1331. ———. *Crusade in Europe*. Garden City, N.Y.: Doubleday, 1948. 559p.

The author's recollections of wartime service as U.S. Army planner and Supreme Commander of SHAEF cover both military and political developments; easily read or quoted (some have said to the point of blandness), Eisenhower's comments are fair, diplomatic, and charitable, and offer some important insights on the special problems of coalition warfare.

1332. ———. *In Review: Pictures I've Kept--A Concise Pictorial Autobiography*. Garden City, N.Y.: Doubleday, 1969. 237p.

The captioned photographs are intermixed with quotations from Eisenhower's other memoirs, including the two noted above.

1333. ———. *Letters to Mamie*. Edited by John S.D. Eisenhower. Garden City, N.Y.: Doubleday, 1978. 282p.

An edited collection of Eisenhower's letters to his wife written before and during the course of the war; the letters reveal a warm but pressured individual devoted to his family and profession. Excerpted in *Ladies Home Journal*, XCIV (June 1977), 185-187+.

1334. ———. *The Papers of Dwight David Eisenhower: The War Years*. Edited by Alfred D. Chandler. 5 vols. Baltimore, Md.: Johns Hopkins University Press, 1970.

A huge collection of well-selected and edited, previously classified notes, telegrams, memos, and letters written or dictated by Eisenhower between 1941 and 1945; including no "routine documents," this primary source is chronologically arranged and definitely not intended for "light reading." The subject's letters to his wife, not included here, are available in the previous citation.

1335. Eisenhower, Mamie D. "My Memories of Ike." *Reader's Digest*, XCVI (February 1970), 69-74.

Written less than a year after the general's death, these recollections record something of the hardship the couple endured during the war and before.

1336. "Eisenhower of Abilene." *Life*, XXXII (April 28, 1969), 112-121.

A pictorial obituary-biography and tribute.

1337. Ferrell, Robert H., ed. *The Eisenhower Diaries*. New York: W.W. Norton, 1981. 445p.

Drawn from the subject's intermittently kept 1935-1967 diary with entries linked by commentary; World War II events noted include Eisenhower's assumption of the Supreme Allied Commandership, D-Day, and the Rhine River crossing.

1338. Field, Rudolph. *Ike: Man of the Hour*. New York: Universal, 1952. 142p.

An extremely pro-Eisenhower campaign biography which deals almost exclusively with the subject's military career, especially during World War II.

1339. Fowler, John G., Jr. "Command Decision." *Military Review*, LIX (June 1979), 2-6.

Explores FDR's decision to give the Supreme Command to Eisenhower rather than Marshall.

1340. Gunther, John. *Eisenhower: The Man and the Symbol*. New York: Harper, 1952. 180p.

A well-respected journalist and wartime correspondent's uncritical biography of the general, widely used by Republicans as a campaign biography.

1341. Hobbs, Joseph P., ed. *Dear General: Eisenhower's Wartime Letters to Marshall*. Baltimore, Md.: Johns Hopkins University Press, 1971. 255p.

A selection of 75 of the 108 letters sent from the Supreme Commander to the Chief of Staff, all of which appeared in Eisenhower's *Papers*, noted above, but which are here treated separately with more analytical detail and fitted logically and chronologically into context. In sum, they show Eisenhower's growth in confidence, his review of Allied relations, and comments on other leading generals and political figures.

1342. LaFay, H. "The Eisenhower Story." *National Geographic Magazine*, CXXXVI (July 1969), 1-38.

A pictorial review which is also a tribute; good use of color photographs.

1343. Longgood, William F. *Ike: A Pictorial Biography*. New York: Time-Life, 1969. 144p.

A pictorial history of Eisenhower's life which is similar to the American Heritage tribute noted above.

1344. Lyon, Peter. *Eisenhower: Portrait of a Hero*. Boston, Mass.: Little, Brown, 1974. 937p.

This full biography is the largest pre-Ambrose study available, the first two-thirds of which deal with its subject's pre-presidential career. Most of the criticism in this work is reserved for the presidential years; Lyon agrees with the manner in which Eisenhower handled his assignment as Allied Supreme Commander.

1345. McKeogh, Michael J., and Richard Lockridge. *Sergeant Mickey and General Ike*. New York: G.P. Putnam, 1946. 185p.

An extremely admiring portrait which describes the war and Eisenhower as both appeared to the young New Yorker who served as the Supreme Commander's personal orderly.

1346. Michie, Allan A. "Great Decisions: Behind the Scenes with Eisenhower." *Reader's Digest*, XLV (August 1944), 112-118.

More atmosphere than substance; Michie was a SHAEF correspondent.

1347. Middleton, Drew. "With Eisenhower at Headquarters." *New York Times Magazine* (October 1, 1944), 9+.

Similar to the Michie piece.

1348. Pogue, Forrest C. "Political Problems of a Coalition Command." In: Harry L. Coles, ed. *Total War and Cold War: Problems in Civilian Control of the Military*. Columbus: Ohio State University Press, 1962, pp. 108-128.

General Marshall's biographer suggests that Eisenhower's contribution as Supreme Commander has been underestimated as his job was complicated by Allied political interests and national prides.

1349. Shoemaker, Robert H., and Leonard A. Paris. "General Dwight D. Eisenhower." In: their *Famous American Generals*. New York: Crowell, 1946, pp. 68-82.

An uncritical overview of the subject's wartime career and responsibilities.

1350. Sixsmith, Eric K.G. *Eisenhower as Military Commander*. New York: Stein and Day, 1972. 248p.

A British general assesses Eisenhower's wartime career from North Africa through D-Day, with some discussion of the post-Normandy strategy for the defeat of the Reich; the assessment is generally favorable and concludes that Eisenhower's "special genius was his skill at management."

1351. Summersby, Kathleen ("Kay"). *Eisenhower Was My Boss.* Edited by Michael Kearns. New York: Prentice-Hall, 1948. 302p.

An adulatory account by a young British W.A.C. who advanced from the position of Eisenhower's driver to secretary/aide; presents a picture of the strains, jealousies, and hardships the Supreme Commander worked under and with during the MTO/ETO campaigns.

1352. ———. *Past Forgetting: My Love Affair with Dwight D. Eisenhower.* New York: Simon and Schuster, 1976. 285p.

Amplifies the above citation and adds the now-familiar charge that the author and Eisenhower were more than professionally related; excerpted in *Ladies Home Journal*, XCIII (December 1976), 121-128+.

1353. Vexler, Robert I., ed. *Dwight D. Eisenhower, 1890-1969: Chronology--Documents--Bibliographical Aids.* New York: Oceana, 1970. 150p.

A useful guide to sources and a helpful chronology are presented here in a convenient reference.

1354. Whitney, David C. *Picture Life of Dwight D. Eisenhower.* New York: Watts, 1968. 56p.

This brief pictorial weaves together images and text for a helpful introduction for younger readers.

James M. Gavin

1355. Biggs, Bradley. *Gavin.* Hamden, Conn.: Archon Books, 1980. 182p.

An admirer's short biography which portrays the high points of the general's career during World War II, but which emphasizes his postwar disagreements with U.S. civilian and military leaders, particularly over Vietnam.

1356. Gavin, James M. *On to Berlin: Battles of an Airborne Commander, 1943-1946.* New York: Viking Press, 1978. 336p.

This analysis of ETO commanders, strategy, and operations, especially as they applied to airborne activities, by the wartime boss of the Eighty-Second Airborne Division is critical of the leadership of both Eisenhower and Montgomery and of the Allied failure to move in on Berlin.

Ernest N. Harmon

1357. Harmon, Ernest N. *Combat Commander: Autobiography of a Soldier.* Englewood Cliffs, N.J.: Prentice-Hall, 1970. 352p.

Harmon led the Second Armored Division in the Tunisian operation and in 1943-44, the First Armored Division in Italy; later he returned to the Second Armored Division and finished the war as boss of the Twenty-Second Corps; the former leader provides interesting details on a number of campaigns, including that at Anzio.

1358. ———, and Milton MacKaye. "A Fighting General Tells His Story." *Saturday Evening Post*, CCXXI (September 19, 1948), 10, 15-17+; (September 25, 1948), 38-39+; (October 2, 1948), 34-35+; (October 9, 1948), 28+.

Emphasis here is on the Italian campaign and the Battle of the Bulge.

Courtney H. Hodges

1359. Hottelet, Richard C. "Victor of Aachen: Lt. Gen. Courtney H. Hodges." *Collier's*, CXIV (December 30, 1944), 17+.

A journalistic profile of the then little-known leader who followed Bradley as chief of the U.S. First Army.

1360. Murray, G. Patrick. "Courtney Hodges: Modest Star of World War II." *American History Illustrated*, VII (September 1973), 12-25.

While Hodges' achievements were not modest, his personal reputation was so slim and lacking in eccentricity that the Supreme Commander at one point had to ask his public relations people to focus on the general in order to obtain recognition for the First Army.

Franklyn A. Johnson

1361. Johnson, Franklyn A. *One More Hill*. New York: Funk and Wagnalls, 1949. 181p.

Reminiscences of service with the Eighteenth Infantry Regiment, U.S. First Army, in North Africa, Sicily, and France, September 1942-October 1944.

Charles E. Kelly

1362. Kelly, Charles E., with Pete Martin. *One Man's War*. New York: Alfred A. Knopf, 1944. 182p. Also published in the *Saturday Evening Post*, CCXVII (July 1, 1944), 9-11+; (July 8, 1944), 20-21+; (July 15, 1944), 24-25+; (July 22, 1944), 20+; (July [?], 1944), 18+.

How this One Hundred Forty-Sixth Infantry Regiment, Thirty-Sixth Division sergeant, nicknamed "Commando Kelly," distinguished himself in action around Altavilla, Italy, in September 1943, killing 40 Nazis and winning the Medal of Honor.

1363. Mayo, Andrew. *No Time for Glory*. New York: Pageant Press, 1955. 69p.

A brief interview and reminiscence with the subject which, like Kelly's book cited above, reflects on North African and Italian service.

Sir John Kennedy

1364. Kennedy, John. *The Business of War: The War Narrative of John Kennedy*. Edited by Bernard Fergusson. New York: William Morrow, 1958. 370p.

These memoirs, resulting from a narrative based on notes taken during the war, portray the work of Brooke's director of military operations and a chief British strategic planner. In addition to a reflection on the strategy of coalition warfare, Kennedy offers insight into the personal relationships between the Allied leaders, including Churchill, Brooke, Eisenhower, and Marshall.

Lesley J. McNair

1365. Cook, Don. "The Chief's Right Hand: Lesley J. McNair." In: his *Fighting Americans of Today*. New York: E.P. Dutton, 1944, pp. 42-54.

Remembered as the man who "trained the Army," McNair moved to England to command the phantom U.S. First Army Group established as part of the misinformation plot aimed at the Germans before D-Day; on July 25, the head of Army Ground Forces was killed by a bomb which fell short of its target during the carpet bombing of "Operation Cobra."

1366. Kahn, Ely J. *McNair, Educator of an Army*. Washington, D.C.: Infantry Journal Press, 1945. 64p.

A brief overview of the general's career with emphasis on his service as head of Army Ground Forces, the man responsible for the entire training cycle.

1367. Whitaker, John T. "Lt. Gen. Lesley James McNair." In: *These Are the Generals*. New York: Alfred A. Knopf, 1943, pp. 123-135.

A career summary through 1942.

George C. Marshall

1368. Ambrose, Stephen E. "George C. Marshall." *American History Illustrated*, III (November 1968), 20-25, 27-30.

An overview of the wartime career of the Army's top-ranking officer and perhaps the most important Allied strategist.

1369. Carter, M.S. "The Unforgettable George C. Marshall." *Reader's Digest*, CI (July 1972), 71-76.

An anecdotal reminiscence and tribute.

1370. DeWeerd, Harvey A. "Marshall, Organizer of Victory." *Infantry Journal*, LIX (December 1946), 8-14; LX (January 1947), 12-18.

An overview of the wartime career of the man Churchill dubbed the "Organizer of Victory," stressing the general's role in coalition diplomacy and in the buildup of the Army prior to Pearl Harbor.

1371. Marshall, George C. *Selected Speeches and Statements of General of the Army George C. Marshall.* Washington, D.C.: Infantry Journal Press, 1945. 263p.

These comments are, in some cases, detailed expositions of the military policies and needs for global victory and represent their author's thinking on his great responsibilities in the years from 1938 to 1945.

1372. Mosley, Leonard. *Marshall: Hero for Our Time.* San Francisco, Calif.: Hearst Books, 1982. 608p.

A sympathetic biography of the wartime Army Chief of Staff, based on original research into a variety of sources, the work stresses Marshall's interaction with military-political leaders. The last part of the volume concerns its biographee's Secretary of State years.

1373. Pogue, Forrest C. *George C. Marshall: Education of a General, 1880-1939.* New York: Viking Press, 1963. 421p.

The first volume in an as-yet unfinished set, this work covers the general's early career, including his service under and friendship with World War I hero Gen. John J. Pershing.

1374. ———. *George C. Marshall: Global Commander.* Harmon Memorial Lectures in Military History. Colorado Springs, Colo.: U.S. Air Force Academy, 1968. 20p.

A brief overview of Marshall's relations with his chief field subordinates during the course of the conflict.

1375. ———. *George C. Marshall: Ordeal and Hope, 1939-1942.* New York: Viking Press, 1966.

The definitive account of Marshall's career from his installation as Army Chief of Staff in mid-1939 through the North African invasion; coverage includes the development of coalition strategy with the British, the Germany-first decision, and the successful "Torch" landings. Readers will find additional data on Marshall's work in inter-Allied strategy in Section II:A above on wartime diplomacy.

1376. ———. *George C. Marshall: Organizer of Victory, 1943-1945.* New York: Viking Press, 1973. 683p.

Looks at the central role of its subject in shaping Allied strategy, U.S. civil-military relations, the great international conferences, and the military command chain, especially with regard to Eisenhower and MacArthur. As Marshall wrote no memoirs (feeling it improper for a military leader to be so self-serving), Pogue's biographies will be perhaps the most important work on the general that we are likely to have for some time to come.

1377. Wilson, Rose P. *General Marshall Remembered.* Englewood Cliffs, N.J.: Prentice-Hall, 1968. 399p.

An uncritical overview of Marshall's wartime and postwar careers, with emphasis on his ability to stand up under pressure and his soft-spoken but firm manner.

William H. ("Bill") Mauldin

1378. "Bill, Willie and Joe." *Time*, XLV (June 18, 1945), 16-18.

A salute to the preeminent U.S. Army artist-cartoonist of the war who saw service in the Mediterranean (mainly) and northwest Europe and whose cartoons, featuring the G.I.'s "Willie and Joe," in *Stars and Stripes* reflected the grim humor of the infantryman's lot.

1379. Lang, Will, and Tom Durrance. "Mauldin." *Life*, XVIII (February 5, 1945), 49-53.

A salute which reprints many of its subject's cartoon pieces.

1380. Mauldin, William H. ("Bill"). *Bill Mauldin's Army*. New York: Sloane Associates, 1951. 383p.

A collection of cartoons showing U.S. Army forces in the U.S., Mediterranean, and northwest Europe between 1942 and 1946.

1381. ———. *The Brass Ring*. New York: W.W. Norton, 1972. 275p.

The author's anecdote-filled autobiography concerns his early life and Army experience to the end of the war when he received the Pulitzer Prize at age 23 for his cartoon book *Up Front*, cited below (item 1600). Mauldin's narrative on the war is one presented in human terms which forsake both politics and passion.

Troy H. Middleton

1382. Price, Frank J. *Troy H. Middleton: A Biography*. Baton Rouge: Louisiana State University Press, 1974. 416p.

General Middleton commanded the Forty-Fifth Division in Sicily and later the First Army's Eighth Corps, from the Normandy breakout through V-E Day. Known as a hard-cusser, Middleton retired just after the war.

Bernard Law Montgomery

1383. Chalfont, Alun. *Montgomery of Alamein*. New York: Atheneum, 1976. 365p.

A former British army officer seeks to reveal the man behind the legend of "Monty." Perhaps the most famous and certainly the most controversial and difficult to work with of Britain's wartime generals, Montgomery took over the British Eighth Army in 1942 and won the Battle of El Alamein; thereafter he commanded Commonwealth troops in the Tunisian, Sicilian, and Italian campaigns, moving to England for the northwest Europe campaign in late 1943. Eisenhower, Bradley, Patton, and other U.S. field commanders argued constantly with the outspoken general over strategy and detail of the ETO operation; his plan for the American landing, though an operational failure, was a bold concept.

1384. Lewin, Ronald. *Montgomery as Military Commander.* New York: Stein and Day, 1972. 288p.

An analysis of the British general's military career and leadership characteristics which suggests that "Monty's" methods prior to the German Ardennes counterattack were sound but turned faulty thereafter. Lewin is almost unique among British commentators in supporting Eisenhower's strategy (vs. Montgomery's) after the Normandy breakout.

1385. Montgomery, Bernard L. *El Alamein to the River Sangro.* New York: E.P. Dutton, 1948. 192p.

An "operational report" rather than a memoir in which Monty details the campaigns of the British Eighth Army in North Africa, Sicily, and Italy from August 1942 to December 1943. Avoiding personal sentiment, the general does, nevertheless, provide an account of planning and coalition cooperation.

1386. ———. *The Memoirs of Field-Marshal the Viscount Montgomery of Alamein.* Cleveland, Ohio, and New York: World Publishing Co., 1958. 508p.

Employing speeches, messages, etc., Montgomery strongly argues for the strategy of a single thrust into Germany which he maintained was superior to American planning for a broad-front push. Providing less detail and analysis of operations than in his works cited above and below, the general uses this work to criticize his opponents, especially Eisenhower and Bradley. Readers will soon find that this work, instead of supporting Monty's case, turns out to be what one reviewer called "a testimonial to the magnificent forbearance of General Eisenhower."

1387. ———. *Normandy to the Baltic.* Boston, Mass.: Houghton Mifflin, 1948. 351p.

An "operational report" rather than a memoir in which Monty details the campaigns of the Twenty-First Army Group in northwest Europe from June 1944 to March 1945; this somewhat muddy narrative, intended to be a straightforward account, does, unfortunately, allow some anti-American sentiment to slip in.

1388. Thompson, Reginald W. *The Montgomery Legend.* London: Allen and Unwin, 1967. 276p.

Published in America the following year by the New York firm of Evans under the title *Churchill and the Montgomery Myth.* The first book-length attack on the achievements of the field marshal by a British writer, this work suggests that Churchill created the legend at a time when British morale needed it, but that other generals such as Auchinleck actually had the North African situation in hand. Similar comments are offered with regard to Monty's role in the Tunisian and Sicilian campaigns, a line of thinking continued into northwest Europe by the following citation.

1389. ———. *Montgomery, The Field Marshal: The Campaign in Northwest Europe, 1944/1945.* New York: Scribners, 1970. 344p.

Although primarily a study of the British/Commonwealth military in the northwest Europe campaign, this work is in fact a critical study of Montgomery's leadership.

Frederick E. Morgan

1390. Morgan, Frederick E. *Peace and War: A Soldier's Life.* London: Hodder and Stoughton, 1961. 320p.

The autobiography of the British general who became Deputy Chief of Staff under Eisenhower in SHAEF in 1944 and who headed the Anglo-American planning staff which designed the technical end of the invasion strategy.

Audie Murphy

1391. Boersema, Jim. "Audie Murphy: The Most Decorated Soldier of World War II." *Soldiers*, XXXV (February 1980), 18-21.

Murphy, who died in 1971, won the Medal of Honor for his heroism during an encounter with the Germans in France in 1945 and, in addition, received 27 other decorations.

1392. Murphy, Audie. *To Hell and Back.* New York: Henry Holt, 1949. 274p.

In one of the better soldier memoirs, Murphy describes his service at Salerno, Anzio, southern France, and in the final drive into Germany. After the war, Murphy became an actor and played the lead in the film version of this book.

1393. Simpson, Harold B. *Audie Murphy: American Soldier.* Hillsboro, Tx.: Hill Junior College Press, 1975. 466p.

The most scholarly look at Murphy's wartime career and also the most detailed; based on interviews, documents, and secondary sources, the work catches the essentials, but not really the flavor, of the man as expressed in his autobiography above.

George S. Patton, Jr.

1394. Ambrose, Stephen E. "George Patton: A Personality Profile." *American History Illustrated*, I (July 1966), 1-13.

Ambrose, who also profiled the Patton-Eisenhower relationship above, examines the qualities of drama, discipline, and outspokenness which were Patton's hallmark.

1395. *Army Times*, Editors of. "Gen. George S. Patton." In: its *Famous American Military Leaders of World War II.* New York: Dodd, Mead, 1962, pp. 68-76.

An overview of Patton's wartime career which deals with (mainly) the general's leadership qualities and campaigns.

1396. ———. *Warrior: The Story of Gen. George S. Patton.* New York: G.P. Putnam, 1967. 223p.

Covers the entire career of the cavalryman-turned-armor-genius from West Point to his death in 1945, with emphasis on the flamboyant World War II years.

1397. Ayer, Frederick. *Before the Colors Fade--Portrait of a Soldier: George S. Patton, Jr.* Boston, Mass.: Houghton Mifflin, 1964. 266p.

A general biography of the sometimes controversial, but always mobile and interesting general; emphasis, as in the last entry, is on the color of the wartime years.

1398. Bell, William G., and Martin Blumenson. "Patton the Soldier." *Ordnance*, XLIII (January-February 1959), 589-596.

Demonstrates insights into Patton's character as revealed by 16 articles he published in the *Cavalry Journal* from 1913 to 1943.

1399. Blumenson, Martin. "Gen. George S. Patton." In: Michael Carver, ed. *War Lords: Military Commanders of the 20th Century.* Boston, Mass.: Little, Brown, 1976, pp. 554-567.

The single most useful concise piece on Patton available, Blumenson follows not only his campaigns, but also explores his leadership qualities and flare for the dramatic which sometimes got him into trouble.

1400. ———. *The Many Faces of George S. Patton, Jr.* Harmon Memorial Lecture in Military History. Colorado Springs, Colo.: U.S. Air Force Academy, 1972. 27p.

A brief transcript of a talk which says much the same as the piece in Carver's work, cited above. Explains how, in North Africa for example, the general, when called upon to be a diplomat, could display strength, charm, and understanding.

1401. ———. "Patton and Montgomery: Alike or Different?" *Army*, XXII (June 1972), 16-22.

Concludes that the two men were very different, with Patton being much the bolder and the two men about equal in colorfulness.

1402. ———. "Patton as Diplomat." *Army*, XXIII (July 1973), 26-30.

Patton fared well as a diplomat in Morocco after the "Torch" landings.

1403. ———, ed. *The Patton Papers, 1940-1945.* Boston, Mass.: Houghton Mifflin, 1974.

Drawing upon and quoting from Patton's diary and correspondence written during the period from the North African invasion through the Third Army advance in France, the author assesses the general's strengths and explains his weaknesses.

1404. Bowen, Vernon. *The Emperor's White Horses.* New York: David McKay, 1956. 147p.

Written for younger readers, this work tells how Patton's men saved the "White Stallions of Vienna" which were trapped in the Soviet zone in Czechoslovakia at war's end.

1405. Clark, Mark W. "Background: 'Patton.'" *TV Guide*, XX (November 11, 1972), 40-42.

Clark, who knew Patton in North Africa and elsewhere, profiles the man and comments on the film then about to be shown on U.S. television.

1406. Codman, Charles R. *Drive.* Boston, Mass.: Little, Brown, 1957. 335p.

After serving as a translator, Codman entered service as Patton's aide-de-camp, a position he held from 1943 to 1945; based on war letters to his wife, the author provides a behind-the-scenes and anecdotal look at the general and his headquarters.

1407. Essame, Hubert. *Patton: A Study in Command.* New York: Scribners, 1974. 280p.

Not so much a biography of the general as a study of his leadership qualities; after careful analysis, this British author renders a very favorable report.

1408. Evans, Medford. "General Patton: Why They Didn't Let George Do It." *American Opinion*, XVIII (September 1975), 11-18+.

Comments on the reasons why Patton did not command the Normandy invasion.

1409. Farago, Ladislas. *Patton: Ordeal and Triumph.* New York: Oblensky, 1964. 885p.

This lengthy biography is supplanted only by the Blumenson-edited *Patton Papers*, cited above. Following the general's entire career, but focusing on the war years, Farago tells of Patton's service in Morocco, with the Second Corps in Tunisia, as head of the Seventh Army in Sicily, and commander of the Third Army in northwest Europe. Although addressing both weaknesses and strengths, the author's interpretation of the general is favorable and came to serve as the basis of the George C. Scott movie "Patton."

1410. Fisher, George J.B. "The Boss of 'Lucky Forward.'" *U.S. Army Combat Forces Journal*, I (May 1951), 20-26.

Reminiscences of Patton's personal habits while in command at Bad Tolz, Bavaria, in 1945.

1411. Gavin, James M. "Two Fighting Generals: Patton and MacArthur." *Atlantic*, CCXV (February 1965), 55-58.

An acquaintance of both generals, the wartime commander of the Eighty-Second Airborne Division contrasts the leadership of the two.

1412. Hatch, Alden. *George Patton: General in Spurs.* New York: Julian Messner, 1950. 184p.

A sympathetic view of the life of the controversial general; Hatch considers both Patton's personal and military life, especially the former.

1413. Mauldin, William H. ("Bill"). "My Confrontation with General Patton." *Life*, LXXI (August 6, 1971), 50-52+.

Willie and Joe's creator remembers a time Patton was not too pleased with his humor.

1414. Mellor, William B. *General Patton, the Last Cavalier.* New York: G.P. Putnam, 1971. 191p.

An overview of the general's life and career written for younger readers.

1415. ———. *Patton, Fighting Man.* New York: G.P. Putnam, 1946. 245p.

One of the first book-length biographies of Patton, Mellor's work relates the familiar story of the general's boldness in an adulatory fashion.

1416. Patton, George S., Jr. "Draughts of Old Bourbon." *American Mercury*, LXXII (January 1951), 127-128.

An address to the men of his Third Army, some of which George C. Scott repeats before a huge U.S. flag at the beginning of the movie "Patton."

1417. ———. *War as I Knew It.* Boston, Mass.: Houghton Mifflin, 1947. 425p.

Consists of personal memories, diary entries, and letters to his wife and to military colleagues, some of which are very critical of those with whom he disagrees; also published, as "General Patton's War Letters," in *Atlantic*, CLXXX (November 1947), 57-61; (December 1947), 33-37; CLXXXI (January 1948), 53-57.

1418. ———. "World War II Diary: Excerpts." *Saturday Evening Post*, CCLXVIII (July 1976), 72-73.

Includes a few entries not printed in the previous citation.

1419. Pearl, Jack. *Blood-and-Guts Patton: The Swashbuckling Life Story of America's Most Daring and Controversial General.* Derby, Conn.: Monarch Books, 1961. 142p.

This paperback concentrates on the more "swashbuckling" aspects of the general's wartime service and adds nothing not considered in most of the other citations covered here.

1420. Perry, Milton F., and Barbara W. Parke. *Patton and His Pistols: The Favorite Side Arms of Gen. George S. Patton, Jr.* Harrisburg, Pa.: Stackpole, 1957. 138p.

This work presents an overview of the general's career, but concentrates mainly on the pearl-handled revolvers he often wore in public.

1421. Randle, Edwin H. "The General and the Movie." *Army*, XXI (September 1971), 17-22.

There was quite a bit of controversy over the portrait of the general presented by George C. Scott in the film "Patton," and this article examines both the man and the film, pointing out differences.

1422. Semmes, Harry H. "Gen. George S. Patton, Jr.'s Psychology of Leadership." *Armor*, LXIV (May-June 1955), 1A-11A.

Semmes examines those points of hardness, toughness, and discipline which Patton considered as his concept of what a good soldier should be. Drawn from the next entry.

1423. ———. *Portrait of Patton*. New York: Appleton-Century-Crofts, 1955. 308p.

The author, who knew the general, presents an overview of his Army career from 1909 to 1945, which stresses not only his color, but his skill as a commander. Still a valuable study.

1424. Sheean, Victor. "The Patton Legend and Patton as He Is." *Saturday Evening Post*, CCXVII (June 23, 1945), 9-10+.

The noted war correspondent suggests that a more thoughtful, scholarly, and gentle man lay beneath Patton's dramatic and colorful exterior.

1425. Shoemaker, Robert H., and Leonard A. Paris. "Gen. George Patton." In: their *Famous American Generals*. New York: Crowell, 1946, pp. 113-124.

A short overview of Patton's wartime service.

1426. South, Betty. "We Called Him 'Uncle Georgie.'" *Quartermaster Review*, XXXIII (January 1954), 28-29; (February 1954), 122-125.

Personal memories of Patton, especially his cussing, ca. 1944.

1427. Taylor, Henry J. "General Patton's Version of the Sicilian Slapping Incident." In: Overseas Press Club of America. *Deadline Delayed*. New York: E.P. Dutton, 1947, pp. 149-158.

The general's version of why he slapped two battle-fatigued men in the hospital in August 1943, an action which created a furor when revealed to the public.

1428. Whiting, Charles. *Patton*. Ballantine's Illustrated History of World War II: War Leader Book. New York: Ballantine Books, 1970. 160p.

Information distilled from a limited number of sources is, nevertheless, woven into an effective analytical and pictorial war biography.

Ernest T. Pyle

1429. Lancaster, Paul. "Ernie Pyle." *American Heritage*, XXXII (February-March 1981), 30-36+.

This Scripps-Howard correspondent was the best-known journalist of the war and a man who told of the tribulations of the common enlisted man while professing his own personal fears. Pyle was killed in the Pacific late in 1945.

Matthew B. Ridgway

1430. "Airborne Grenadier." *Time*, LVII (March 5, 1951), 26-29.

Written upon Ridgway's assumption of the UN command in Korea, this piece also describes his war service in the MTO and ETO.

1431. Alberts, Robert C. "Profile of a Soldier: Matthew B. Ridgway." *American Heritage*, XXVII (February 1976), 4-7, 73-82.

Commander of the Eighty-Second Airborne Division in Sicily and Normandy jumps, Ridgway was succeeded in command of that unit by General Gavin, whose biography is noted above. Just before the liberation of the Netherlands, Ridgway was promoted to command the Eighteenth Airborne Corps. In 1950, this man, who seemed to cherish danger, succeeded MacArthur as commander of all UN troops in Korea.

1432. Michener, James A. "Tough Man for a Tough Job." *Life*, XXXII (May 12, 1952), 103-106+.

Penned in connection with Ridgway's UN assignment, Michener's piece also considers his wartime airborne career.

1433. Ridgway, Matthew B. "Memories of a Simpler War." *Time*, XC (October 20, 1967), 102.

Comparison of World War II and Vietnam.

1434. ———. *Soldier: The Memoirs of Matthew B. Ridgway*. New York: Harper, 1956. 371p.

The airborne general's memoirs recall not only his wartime service and the daring parachute drops into Sicily and Normandy, but serve as a political treatise which rejects the mid-1950's concerns with limited and massive nuclear war in favor of versatile conventional force preparedness.

Karl Rudolf Gerd von Rundstedt

1435. Blumentritt, Günther. *Von Runstedt: The Soldier and the Man*. Translated from the German. London: Odhams, 1952. 288p.

Former General der Infanterie Blumentritt was his subject's chief of staff in OB West and knew von Rundstedt very well. This study examines the Field Marshal's career and personal life, adding insights on his command of German forces which opposed Eisenhower from D-Day until March 1945.

1436. Keegan, John. *Rundstedt*. Ballantine's Illustrated History of World War II: War Leader Book. New York: Ballantine Books, 1974. 160p.

This pictorial details the Field Marshal's wartime career from Poland to the Bulge, including his leadership of the Wehrmacht during the Anglo-American drive across northwest Europe.

William H. Simpson

1437. Shoemaker, Robert H., and Leonard A. Paris. "Gen. William Hood Simpson." In: their *Famous American Generals*. New York: Crowell, 1946, pp. 93-101.

An overview of the service of this Texan as commander of the U.S. Ninth Army from September 1944 through VE-Day, Simpson and his command were occasionally under General Montgomery, with whom he could work perhaps better than any other U.S. army field commander. Of him, Eisenhower later wrote: "If Simpson ever made a mistake as an army commander, it never came to my attention."

1438. Stone, Thomas R. *Never Send an Infantryman Where You Can Send an Artillery Shell*. Study Project. Carlisle Barracks, Pa.: U.S. Army War College, 1980. 61p.

This biographical paper deals with the leadership of Lt. Gen. William H. Simpson, commander of the U.S. Ninth Army, with emphasis on his disagreements with Field Marshal Montgomery as to the Ninth's role in the Rhine River crossing in March 1945; although Simpson's men served as part of the Britisher's Twenty-First Army Group, their tactical differences were, on occasion, great, but nevertheless, the American was better able to work with the temperamental field marshal than most U.S. generals.

Edward D. Slovik

1439. Avins, Alfred. "The Execution of Private Slovik and the Punishment for Short Desertion." *George Washington Law Review*, XX (June 1962), 785-805.

The author finds that courts-martial usually imposed harsh punishments on deserters, but that these sentences were almost always subsequently reduced.

1440. "The Execution of Eddie Slovik." *After the Battle*, no. 32 (1981), 28-43.

One of only two sources I have seen which detail the private's decision to desert, his trial, and execution.

1441. Huie, William B. *The Execution of Private Slovik*. New York: Duell, Sloane, and Pearce, 1954. 247p.

Slovik was a member of the One Hundred Ninth Infantry, Twenty-Eighth Division, before he deserted, was tried, and executed in 1945; hardly a hero, Slovik's significance lies in the fact that, while others also deserted, he was the only one to pay the supreme price, in fact, the only American soldier so killed since 1864.

Maxwell D. Taylor

1442. Taylor, Maxwell D. *Swords and Plowshares*. New York: W.W. Norton, 1972. 434p.

One of the U.S. Army's earlier airborne enthusiasts, the author commanded the Eighty-Second's artillery in Sicily and Italy in 1943 and the One Hundred First Airborne Division during the assaults on Normandy and Arnhem and the defense in the Bulge. His postwar career was one of military and diplomatic assignments lasting into the Vietnam era.

Lucian K. Truscott, Jr.

1443. Lang, Will. "Lucian King Truscott, Jr." *Life*, XVII (October 2, 1944), 96-98+.

A close associate of Eisenhower, Truscott commanded the Sixth Corps in the invasion of southern France and later the Fifth Army; this brief piece profiles his service in the Mediterranean in 1942-1944.

1444. Truscott, Lucian K., Jr. *Command Decisions: A Personal Story*. New York: E.P. Dutton, 1954. 570p.

"Luck plays a part in the life of every man," begins this honest and straightforward reminiscence by the Eisenhower deputy who saw much combat in North Africa, Sicily, Italy, and southern France. Here the subject explains strategy, logistics, tactics, leadership, and command relations, including comments on individuals and the problems of reaching decisions during critical battle situations.

William Weaver

1445. Weaver, William. *Yankee Doodle Dandy*. Ann Arbor, Mich.: Edwards Brothers, 1958. 370p.

This major general's memoirs highlight his service as chief of staff of ETO Services of Supply and commander of the Eighth Infantry Division.

Henry M. Wilson

1446. Wilson, Henry M. *Eight Years Overseas, 1939-1947*. London: Hutchinson, 1950. 285p.

Nicknamed "Jumbo," this British officer became Supreme Allied Commander, Mediterranean Theater, in 1944 and the following year was named to head the British Joint Staff Mission in Washington. The field marshal's memoirs contain a good deal of analysis (by a man many considered to have one of the war's better military minds) and much information on the invasion of southern France.

John S. ("Tiger Jack") Wood

1447. Baldwin, Hanson W. *Tiger Jack*. Fort Collins, Colo.: Old Army Press, 1979. 195p.

An aggressive commander and student of tank tactics, Wood served with the Fifth Armored Division until 1942 and then was promoted to lead the Fourth Armored Division across France in the summer of 1944, earning the praise of General Patton. Wood was relieved for reasons of health in fall 1944 and died in 1966.

C. CAMPAIGNS AND BATTLES

Introduction: The citations below reveal details on some of the great campaigns and most intensive ground combat of World War II. Here is the soldier's war divided into two major parts: Mediterranean Theater and European Theater. Each of these parts is further subdivided. General works, citations to North Africa, and references to the Sicilian, Italian, and southern France campaigns are set out under the Mediterranean Theater while, under the European Theater, parts direct readers to citations on general works, the battle across France, and the Allied drive into Holland, Belgium, and Germany. Users should be aware that many of the handbooks/encyclopedias and general war histories noted in Section I, certain of the aerial citations in Section III, and a number of the sea forces references in Section V also provide information relative to the U.S. Army's offensives in the MTO/ETO.

1. Mediterranean Theater

Introduction: For purposes of this guide, the Mediterranean Theater of Operations encompasses North Africa, the islands of the Mediterranean, Italy, the Balkans, and southern France. During the early part of the Allies' coalition war, considerable debate existed as to the direction the fighting should take in this theater. Citations to those strategic-political differences are covered for the most part in Section II:A on diplomacy, above.

a. GENERAL WORKS

Introduction: Comparatively few studies address the military (i.e., land) campaigns in the Mediterranean as a whole; as users will see, the majority of studies available consider specific campaigns, such as North Africa, Sicily, Italy, or southern France. The citations noted below should be employed in conjunction with those on aerial operations and sea warfare covered in Section III:C:1 above and V:C:1 below. Additionally, many of the memoirs and biographies of U.S. and British officers cited in part IV:B just above contain information on their Mediterranean service.

1448. Gunther, John. *D-Day*. New York: Harper, 1943. 276p.

This title should not mislead readers into believing it concerns the Normandy invasion covered in C:2:b below; rather, this work represents the author's experiences in covering the American ground effort in North Africa and Sicily during the spring and summer of 1943.

1449. Playfair, Ian S.O., *et al*. *The Mediterranean and the Middle East*. History of the Second World War: United Kingdom Military Series. 6 vols. London: H.M. Stationery Office, 1954-1973.

A comprehensive official history of sea, air, and land (mainly) operations in the Mediterranean and Middle East Theaters from 1940 to 1945; each volume is a scholarly and detailed treatment, valuable for an examination not only of British but also of American operations, especially after November 1942.

1450. *The War Against Germany and Italy: Mediterranean and Adjacent Areas*. Compiled by John C. Hatlem and Kenneth E. Hunter. Washington, D.C.: U.S. Government Printing Office, 1951. 465p.

Part of the Army's "green book" series, this work contains some 450 pages of photographs with explanatory text which portray various aspects of the Mediterranean war as a whole and specific campaigns such as those in North Africa, Sicily, Italy, and southern France.

1451. Warren, John C. *Airborne Missions in the Mediterranean, 1942-1945*. USAF Historical Study, no. 74. Washington, D.C.: Office of Air Force History, Department of the Air Force, 1955. 137p.

This documented study is presented as a series of case studies on the background, planning, training for, execution, and impact on doctrine of U.S. airborne operations in the MTO.

1452. Young, Ford E., Jr. *To the Regiment*. Washington, D.C.: National Capitol Publishing Co., 1970. 145p.

A history of the ground war in North Africa and Italy as recalled by men who served in the U.S. Army's Three Hundred Sixth Cavalry Regiment and Three Hundred Sixth Armored Cavalry Corps.

b. NORTH AFRICA

Introduction: Although U.S. Marines had invaded Guadalcanal nearly three months earlier, the U.S. Army landing in French Morocco and Algeria represented the first *major* commitment of American ground strength to the war against the Axis. This landing, the product of a political compromise at the highest level (noted in certain of the citations in Section II:A above), led to the testing of thousands of "green" U.S. troops in a campaign lasting until the surrender of German-Italian troops in Tunisia on May 23, 1943. The citations in this section follow the various aspects of the U.S. land campaign in North Africa in whole and in part; for citations to the air and sea aspects of the six-month operation, readers should see Section III:C:1 above and V:C:1 below. Certain of the biographies and memoirs noted in IV:B above and unit histories covered in IV:D below may also prove helpful.

1453. Akers, Russell F. "Tunisia--Springboard to Victory." *Fellowship*, I (January 1948), 49-58.

A summary of U.S. land operations in the Tunisian campaign from late 1942 through May 1943 with emphasis on the "blooding" of American troops.

1454. Bennett, Lowell. *Assignment to Nowhere: The Battle for Tunisia*. New York: Vanguard, 1943. 316p.

The author's adventures as a war correspondent with American forces in Tunisia are breezily recalled with some comments on the diplomatic background of the campaign and a description of civilian life in Algiers and elsewhere.

1455. Benson, C.C. "Some Tunisian Details." *Field Artillery Journal*, XXXIV (January 1944), 2-7.

Recollections of service with the U.S. First Armored Division in the latter stages of the 1943 Battle of Tunisia.

1456. Betson, William R. "Sidi Bou Zid: A Case History of Failure." *Armor*, XCI (November-December 1982), 38-44.

Located 12 miles west of Faid, Tunisia, this place was the site of victory by German panzers over Second Corps troops during the opening of the Nazi Kasserine Pass counteroffensive on February 14, 1943.

1457. Bidwell, Shelford. "Tunisia, 1943." In: Philip de Ste. Croix, ed. *Airborne Operations: An Illustrated Encyclopedia of the Great Battles of Airborne Forces*. New York: Crescent Books, 1978, pp. 76-83.

Reviews the first use of Allied airborne forces on any scale in wasted, casualty-producing operations which did, however, provide invaluable tactical information.

1458. Bingham, James K.W., and Werner Haupt. *The North African Campaign, 1940-1943*. London: Macdonald, 1969. 160p.

An overview of the Western Desert-French North Africa-Tunisia campaigns illustrated with a number of photographs and drawings.

1459. Blumenson, Martin. "The Agony and the Glory." *Infantry*, LVII (July-August 1967), 47-52.

A concise history of the German Kasserine Pass offensive of February 1943 and, after initial setbacks, the U.S. response to it.

1460. ———. "Command at Kasserine Pass." *Army*, XVII (January 1967), 32-44.

An examination primarily of the perceived failure of Gen. Lloyd R. Fredenhall and his commanders to hold off the German offensive; Fredenhall was replaced by Gen. George S. Patton, Jr.

1461. ———. *Kasserine Pass*. Boston, Mass.: Houghton Mifflin, 1967. 341p.

This remains the premier book-length account of the first major clash between German and American soldiers; the work shows the failures in American command as well as the steps taken to reverse the humiliating if short-lived defeat through a still defense at Thala. Blumenson points out the lessons learned and changes made after the battle was over.

1462. Burba, E.H. "Sidi Bou Zid to Sbeitla, February 14-17, 1943." *Field Artillery Journal*, XXXIV (January 1944), 8-13.

Memories of an artillery battalion (unnamed) during the German counteroffensive near Kasserine in February 1943.

1463. Cairns, Bogardus S. "The Employment of Armor in the Invasion of Oran." *Military Review*, XXVIII (September 1948), 46-56.

Recalls the work of the U.S. First Armored Division in the November 8-10, 1942, capture of this vital Algerian port.

1464. Carvey, James B. "Faid Pass." *Infantry Journal*, LV (November 1944), 8-13.

Records the actions of Five Hundred Ninth Parachute Infantry Regiment airborne troops at this North African hotspot.

1465. Coggins, Jack. *The Campaign for North Africa*. Garden City, N.Y.: Doubleday, 1980. 208p.

Traces the see-saw battles back and forth across this area from fall 1940 to spring 1943 in an introductory text backed by 250 superb maps and hand-drawn illustrations.

1466. Cole, John D. "Situation: Normally Abnormal." *Military Review*, XXIX (September 1949), 34-40.

Traces the route and actions of the U.S. Ninth Division in northern Tunisia during April and May 1943.

1467. Crawford, Kenneth G. *Report on North Africa*. New York: Farrar, 1943. 206p.

This work is a journalist's view of the North African situation based on an April-June 1943 tour of the battle fronts; provides a wealth of economic details in addition to some battle accounts and contends that the Anglo-American decision on prosecuting the war here was correct, despite a displeasure over the deals with Darlan.

1468. Funk, Arthur L. "Eisenhower, Giraud, and the Command of 'Torch.'" *Military Affairs*, XXXV (October 1971), 103-108.

Examines the dispute, which developed almost at the last minute, as to who should call the shots in the North African invasion--Eisenhower or the noted French general.

1469. ———. *The Politics of TORCH: The Allied Landings and the Algiers Putsch, 1942*. Lawrence: University Press of Kansas, 1974. 322p.

Although some account of the landings is made, this work is, in fact, the first study to examine the political aspects of the Anglo-American invasion, including the Giraud flap cited above, from the French, British, and U.S. viewpoints; contains much on the military necessity of the Darlan affair.

1470. Gallagher, Wesley. *Back Door to Berlin: The Full Story of the American Coup in North Africa*. Garden City, N.Y.: Doubleday, 1943. 242p.

An AP correspondent attached to Eisenhower's staff provides a readable contemporary account of the U.S. North African campaign from the beaches to final victory which explains, en route, Allied dealings with Darlan and the Vichy French.

1471. Gardiner, Henry E. "Kasserine Pass." *Armor*, LXXXVIII (September-October 1979), 12-17.

Essentially a repeat of the next entry.

1472. ———. "'We Fought at Kasserine Pass.'" *Armored Cavalry Journal*, LVII (March-April 1948), 8-17.

Relates the experiences of the commander of the Second Battalion, Thirteenth Armored Regiment, before and during the Battle of Kasserine Pass, December 10, 1942-February 25, 1943.

1473. Hines, Paul S. "Gen. Mark Clark's Secret Landing." In: Phil Hirsch, ed. *Fighting Generals*. New York: Pyramid Books, 1960, pp. 7-28.

Reprinted from *Man's Magazine*, this piece recalls how Eisenhower's deputy secretly landed at Algiers prior to the invasion to confer with the French. Clark himself recalls the incident in his memoirs cited in part IV:B above.

1474. Holmes, Julius C. "Eisenhower's African Gamble." *Collier's*, CXVII (January 13, 1946), 14-15+; (January 19, 1946), 27-30.

An account of the pre-invasion negotiations with French leaders which resulted in the Darlan affair.

1475. Howe, George F. *Northwest Africa: Seizing the Initiative in the West*. U.S. Army in World War II: The Mediterranean Theater of Operations. Washington, D.C.: U.S. Government Printing Office, 1957. 748p.

This official history follows the Allied assault on North Africa from the "Torch" landings to victory in Tunisia, describing battles in detail from both Axis and Allied perspectives. The work points out that campaigning in northwest Africa was, for the U.S. Army, a school of coalition warfare and a graduate school of Axis tactics.

1476. Ingersoll, Ralph M. *Battle Is the Pay-Off.* New York: Harcourt, 1943. 217p.

A journalist's attempt to describe a battle from the G.I.'s viewpoint; the fight was that at El Guettar, a village some 12 miles below Gafsa, taken by U.S. troops on March 17, 1943.

1477. ———. "'We Take El Guettar.'" *Infantry Journal*, LIII (November 1943), 16-34.

Based on the last citation.

1478. Jackson, William G.F. *The Battle for North Africa, 1940-1943.* New York: Mason/Charter, 1976. 402p.

Covers the campaign from the British-Italian duels of 1940 through to victory in Tunisia in 1943, with emphasis on Anglo-German operations; this British author agrees that U.S. aid was important to the victory, but chides the green Americans for mistakes such as Kasserine Pass.

1479. Jones, Vincent. *Operation Torch.* Ballantine's Illustrated History of World War II. New York: Ballantine Books, 1972. 160p.

A pictorial review of the Anglo-American landings of November 1942 which covers not only the military action but Allied-French political dealing as well.

1480. Kellett, Donald T. "The Action at Robaa." *Infantry Journal*, LXIII (September 1948), 12-16.

Reminiscences of Thirty-Sixth Brigade operations at this tiny Tunisian outpost on January 31, 1943.

1481. ———. "El Guettar: Victory or Stalemate?" *Military Review*, XXXI (July 1951), 18-25.

A thorough examination of U.S. tactics in the contest won in late March 1943.

1482. Lange, Herman W.W. "The Battle of Thala: A Study of the Factors Which Resulted in a Defeat for Rommel." Unpublished M.A. thesis, George Washington University, 1966.

Held by U.S. soldiers and reinforced by General Alexander's British Sixth Armored Division, Thala was successfully held against the German Tenth Panzer Division.

1483. Larson, William B. "Hill 223." *Infantry Journal*, LV (September 1944), 23-27.

The battle in April-May 1943 for one of a series of hills overlooking a strategic Tunisian valley.

1484. Lunn-Rockliffe, W.P. "The Tunisian Campaign." *Army Quarterly and Defence Journal*, XCVIII (April-May 1969), 109-118; (June-July 1969), 228-235.

An overview of the campaign, especially the role of the British in backing up the relatively untested Americans.

1485. McBride, Lauren E. "The Battle of Sened Station." *Infantry Journal*, LVI (April 1943), 30-33; (May 1943), 54-55.

The station, located on a rail line between Gafsa and Maknassy, Tunisia, was overrun by Rommel's forces in the opening phase of the Kasserine Pass offensive.

1486. Macksey, Kenneth J. *Crucible of Power: The Fight for Tunisia, 1942-1943*. London: Hutchinson, 1969. 325p.

A British tank expert focuses on the Allied attempts to squeeze the Germans into the sea, which finally happened in May 1943; includes material on such battles as Kasserine Pass and the Mareth Line as well as the interaction of political and military goals and their impact on the campaign.

1487. Meyers, Edward H. "The Fragrance of Spring Was Heavy in the Air." *Trail Tales*, no. 35 (1979), 1-82.

A detailed look at the operations of the One Hundred Eighty-Fifth Field Artillery Battalion in the Tunisian campaign, April-May 1943; this journal is published by the Boone County (Iowa) Historical Society.

1488. Middleton, Drew. "The Battle for North Africa." *New York Times Magazine* (November 7, 1982), 48+.

A 40th anniversary overview of the political and military aspects of the campaign by a noted military analyst.

1489. ———. "They Called It Hill 609." In: Frank Brookhouser, ed. *This Was Your War: An Anthology of Great Writings from World War II*. Garden City, N.Y.: Doubleday, 1960, pp. 309-317.

The May 1, 1943, capture of a strategic hill overlooking the wide Tunisian plain.

1490. Moorehead, Alan. *The March to Tunis: The North African War, 1940-1943*. New York: Harper & Row, 1965. 592p.

A trilogy comprising three works first published in 1942-1943: *Mediterranean Front*, *Don't Blame the Generals*, and *The End in Africa*. A journalistic account of merit which offers a contemporary view of the frustrations involved in driving the Germans out of North Africa.

1491. North, John. "Lessons of the North African Campaign." *Military Affairs*, VIII (Fall 1944), 161-168.

Examines the command and logistical lessons of the campaign as well as the tactics employed by the Germans.

1492. Pack, Stanley W.C. *Invasion North Africa, 1942*. New York: Scribners, 1978. 112p.

Examines the Allied landings on the North African coast in November 1942, an operation based on a gamble which turned out to be successful; looks at a variety of lessons learned, both in the tricky techniques of opposed landings and problems of inter-Allied cooperation. Illustrated with 157 photographs.

1493. Page, Douglas J. "El Guettar: March 25-April 8, 1943." *Field Artillery Journal*, XXXIII (September 1943), 645-647.

An examination of a tough battle against hardened German troops.

1494. Painton, Frederick C. "Comeback at Kasserine Pass." *Saturday Evening Post*, CCXV (May 29, 1943), 20-21+.

A journalistic view of the eventual U.S. recovery from the shock of Rommel's offensive.

1495. Philipsborn, Martin, Jr., and Milton Lehman. "The Untold Story of Kasserine Pass." *Saturday Evening Post*, CCXX (February 14, 1948), 23+.

Two well-known war correspondents point out the command and defensive arrangements which allowed Rommel's surprise to be so devastating.

1496. Pyle, Ernest T. ("Ernie"). *Here Is Your War*. New York: Henry Holt, 1943. 304p.

One of the war's best-known books, this is a human-interest account of the North African campaign told from the G.I. viewpoint; in fact, Pyle's narrative is a collection of his newspaper columns in expanded form with pen and ink drawings added.

1497. ———. "They Were Just Guys from Broadway and Main Street." In: Louis L. Snyder, ed. *Treasury of Great Reporting*. New York: Simon and Schuster, 1949, pp. 619-623.

Pyle's tribute to the common soldiers who fought in North Africa, most of whom were recent civilians thrown into their first fight.

1498. Raff, Edson D. *We Jumped to Fight*. New York: Duell, Sloane, and Pearce, 1944. 207p.

Reminiscences of the U.S. lieutenant colonel who led elements of the Five Hundred Third Parachute Infantry in a drop on Oran and on several against targets in Tunisia in November 1942; written in a soldierly manner, the account describes the bluff and skill needed to hold airfields and communication centers against superior German might.

1499. Ramsey, Guy H. *One Continent Redeemed*. Garden City, N.Y.: Doubleday, Doran, 1943. 280p.

A journalistic account of the U.S. role in the North African campaign from "Operation Torch" in November 1942 to victory in Tunisia in May 1943. Military operations are covered in overview.

1500. Raymond, Edward A. "Slugging It Out." *Field Artillery Journal*, XXXIV (January 1944), 14-20.

Recollections of service with an unnamed U.S. artillery battalion during the German Tenth Panzer Division's assault on the U.S. First Infantry Division at El Guettar, late March 1943.

1501. Rutherford, Ward. *Kasserine: Baptism of Fire*. Ballantine's Illustrated History of World War II. New York: Ballantine Books, 1970. 160p.

A pictorial review of the battle which shattered American complacency and led to Patton's receiving an active field command.

1502. Schmidt, Paul K. *The Foxes of the Desert*. By Paul Carell, pseud. New York: E.P. Dutton, 1961. 370p.

A popular account of the German Afrika Corps from a German viewpoint; covers not only the Western Desert campaigns, but the North African landings, the Battle of Kasserine Pass, and the final Nazi defeat in Tunisia in May 1943. Well written, with insight into the difficulties faced by the Axis leaders as they tried to stem defeat.

1503. Strawson, John. *The Battle for North Africa*. New York: Scribners, 1969. 226p.

A British author's brief account of the war which places emphasis rather more on the ordinary soldier's efforts than on his commander's; includes insight into strategy and useful battle descriptions.

1504. Thornton, M.M. "Try the Reverse Slope." *Infantry Journal*, LIV (February 1944), 8-11.

One platoon's experiences in the Battle of El Guettar.

1505. Tute, Warren. *The North African War*. New York: Two Continents, 1976. 220p.

This British writer follows the North African struggle from February 1941 to May 1943, describing Allied strategy in the Mediterranean, the general planning for "Torch," the Darlan affair, and some of the major battles including those in the Western Desert and Tunisia. Heavily illustrated and loaded with eyewitness commentary, this work is similar to Tute's earlier D-Day effort cited below.

1506. United States. War Department. *Lessons from the Tunisian Campaign*. Washington, D.C.: U.S. Government Printing Office, 1943. 70p.

A pamphlet filled with tactical, logistical, and command experiences and passed to officers fighting Germans on other fronts.

1507. ———. ———. *To Bizerte with the II Corps (23 April 1943-13 May 1943)*. American Forces in Action Series. Washington, D.C.: U.S. Government Printing Office, 1946. 80p.

An action-packed pamphlet which describes the actions of Patton's corps in the final weeks of the Tunisian campaign. Still interesting reading.

1508. Westrate, Edwin V. *Forward Observer*. New York: E.P. Dutton, 1944. 179p.

Using disguised names, the author describes the feats of each man in an unnamed U.S. Army forward observer team operating somewhere in Tunisia; useful for flavor and tactics, but not on battle detail.

1509. Yarborough, William P. *Bail out Over North Africa: America's First Combat Parachute Missions, 1942*. Williamstown, N.J.: Phillips Publications, 1979. 220p.

Drawing on his 1943 after-action report, General Yarborough, airborne advisor to Gen. Mark Clark, describes the long flight from England and the drop of the Five Hundred Ninth Parachute Infantry Regiment near Oran in November 1942.

1510. ———. "House Party in Jerryland." *Infantry Journal*, LV (July 1944), 8-15.

Another look at the Five Hundred Ninth's long flight from England and descent near Oran.

1511. Zanuck, Darryl F. *Tunis Expedition*. New York: Random House, 1943. 160p.

An account of U.S. North African operations in November-December 1942, by the Army Signal Corps colonel and noted film producer who directed cameramen in making the documentary film "At the Front."

c. SICILY/ITALY/SOUTHERN FRANCE

Introduction: The Allied campaigns in the Mediterranean islands, on the Italian mainland, and into southern France were all conducted as the result of political decisions covered in certain of the citations in Section II:A above. None of the campaigns was simple and all involved tough fighting against defense-minded German opponents. If anything, the fall of Mussolini's government in Italy made the campaign there all the more difficult for Allied troops, who found the conduct of operations against the stubborn Nazis under Kesselring extremely difficult due to terrain and other factors. The citations in this part follow the various U.S. land campaigns in the Mediterranean Theater outside of North Africa, with emphasis on those conducted in Italy. For references to the air and sea aspects of these operations, users should consult Section III:C:1 above and V:C:1 below. Certain of the biographies and memoirs noted in IV:B above and the unit histories covered in IV:D below may also prove useful.

1512. Adams, Henry M. "Allied Military Government in Sicily, 1943." *Military Affairs*, XV (Fall 1951), 157-165.

Once taken, Sicily provided the Allies with their first sizable laboratory for the conduct of military government; this piece discusses the various aspects of the process and differences in philosophy and direction between the British and Americans.

1513. Adleman, Robert H., and George Walton. *The Champagne Campaign.* Boston, Mass.: Little, Brown, 1969. 298p.

Adleman and Walton provide a look at "Operation Anvil-Dragoon," the Allied invasion of southern France, which was designed to take the pressure off Allied forces in northern France; the authors examine the lengthy and divisive debates in command circles over the wisdom and purpose of the undertaking, including Churchill's desire to have the resources of this "second D-Day" employed in Italy and the Balkans.

1514. ———. *Rome Fell Today.* Boston, Mass.: Little, Brown, 1968. 336p.

Examines the twists and turns of the Allied military campaign in Italy from the Salerno landings in September 1943 through the liberation of Rome in June 1944, centering attention on the greater and lesser personages on both sides, especially Gen. Mark Clark, whose generalship of the controversial operation is defended.

1515. Allen, William L. *Anzio: Edge of Disaster.* New York: Dial Press, 1978. 181p.

Illustrated, and based on documents and eyewitness accounts, this work tells of the planning and execution of these January 22, 1944, landings on the Italian west coast near Rome; the author scores Mjr. Gen. John Lucas's decision to have his troops dig in and await reinforcements and supplies rather than advancing.

1516. Allied Forces. Supreme Allied Commander. *Report of the Supreme Allied Commander, Mediterranean, to the Combined Chiefs of Staff on the Italian Campaign.* 2 vols. London: H.M. Stationery Office, 1946-1948.

Field Marshal Alexander's account stresses Allied unity while describing battles, terrain, and logistical difficulties.

1517. "Anzio and Its Lessons." *Military Review*, XXXI (July 1951), 97-102.

Examines the difficulties which resulted from Lucas's decision to dig in.

1518. Badoglio, Pietro. *Italy in the Second World War: Memories and Documents.* Translated from the Italian. London and New York: Oxford University Press, 1948. 234p.

Marshal Badoglio had opposed Italy's entry into the war and resigned as chief of staff in late 1940. In July 1943 when Mussolini was deposed, Badoglio was called to head the government, which he surrendered to the Allies on September 3 and which declared war on Germany on October 13, achieving "co-belligerent" status for his country. The Germans simply moved in and took over control of the territory which the Allies did not hold. This memoir describes its author's role in the maneuvers described in this annotation.

1519. Baldwin, Hanson W. "The Sicilian Campaign--Strategic Compromise: July 10-August 17, 1943." In: his *Battles Lost and Won: Great Campaigns of World War II*. New York: Harper & Row, 1966, pp. 188-235.

Agreed to at Casablanca, the Sicilian operation, codenamed "Husky," was a short, 38-day effort which cleared the Mediterranean for Allied use and provided the impetus needed to force Mussolini's resignation. Baldwin's account is concise and notes both strategy and battles.

1520. Ball, Edmond F. *Staff Officer with the Fifth Army*. Hicksville, N.Y.: Exposition Press, 1958. 365p.

An officer on Mark Clark's Fifth Army staff recalls the Salerno and Anzio invasions and the hard fighting which lay between; valuable for insights into command operations at times of crisis.

1521. Barker, M.E. "Heavy Mortars in Direct Support." *Infantry Journal*, LV (December 1944), 20-23.

A brief piece describing mortar operations in Italy.

1522. Battillo, Anthony. "Thunder in the Po Valley." *American History Illustrated*, X (February 1976), 22-30.

Breaking the Gustav Line, Allied forces broke through to the Po Valley in northern Italy in late April 1945 and mopped up what remained of the once stubborn German army.

1523. "The Battle of Salerno." *Life*, XV (September 27, 1943), 25-35.

A pictorial which brought many Americans their first views of the Allied landings.

1524. Bernstein, Walter S. *Keep Your Head Down*. New York: Viking Press, 1946. 213p.

A series of articles first published in the *New Yorker* which cover the author's career in the U.S. Army, 1941-1944; four pieces relate his experiences as a sergeant in Sicily/Italy and dwell on the human interest side of the war à la Ernie Pyle and Bill Mauldin.

1525. Bidwell, Shelford. "The Airborne Assault on Sicily." In: Philip de Ste. Croix, ed. *Airborne Operations: An Illustrated Encyclopedia of the Great Battles of Airborne Forces*. New York: Crescent Books, 1978, pp. 84-91.

Sicily was the scene of the first major Allied airborne operation of the war, but lack of experience and forethought resulted in a near disaster redeemed only by the flexibility and courage of the troops and the lack of serious Axis power in the southern part of the island.

1526. Blaxland, Gregory. *Alexander's Generals: The Italian Campaign, 1944-1945.* London: Kimber, 1979. 320p.

Blaxland examines the leadership and direction of the Italian campaign and the men who led it, including Alexander, Clark, Truscott, and various British officers. Mistakes and successes are noted and analyzed.

1527. Blumenson, Martin. "Anzio: Dilemma on the Beachhead." *Army*, XXXIII (March 1983), 38-41+.

An analysis of General Lucas's decision to dig in and await reinforcement and the difficulties met by his successor, General Truscott, in advancing from the beachhead once German forces had pinned the Americans down.

1528. ———. *Anzio: The Gamble That Failed.* Philadelphia, Pa.: Lippincott, 1963. 212p.

Designed to break a stalemate and lead to Rome's capture, Anzio was a nearly disastrous amphibious operation in January 1944, brought on by misunderstanding and a strong German defense. The author examines the political and military reasons for the failure and the men like Alexander, Clark, and Lucas who were responsible.

1529. ———. *Bloody River: The Real Tragedy of the Rapido.* Boston, Mass.: Houghton Mifflin, 1970. 150p.

Told from a command level with little emphasis on actual combat, this work discusses the plan to cross this river in conjunction with the Anzio landings and smash the Gustav Line and the disaster which occurred when the Texas Thirty-Sixth Infantry Division failed, incurring 1,600 casualties and opening a leadership controversy which still lingers. With slightly different conclusions, this work is based on the author's "green book," *Salerno to Cassino*, cited below.

1530. ———. "General Lucas at Anzio." In: Kent R. Greenfield, ed. *Command Decisions.* Washington, D.C.: Office of the Chief of Military History, Department of the Army, 1960, pp. 323-350.

Another look at Lucas's decision to dig in after landing.

1531. ———. *Salerno to Cassino.* U.S. Army in World War II: The Mediterranean Theater of Operations. Washington, D.C.: U.S. Government Printing Office, 1969. 491p.

The story of U.S. Army operations in Italy from the invasion of the mainland near Salerno in September 1943 through the winter fighting and up to the stalemate in the battles for Monte Cassino (including the Rapido River crossing) and in the

Anzio beachhead to May 1944. Includes discussion of terrain, weather, and logistics, along with the Fifth Army's difficulties in fighting German and Italian troops.

1532. ———. "Sicily and Italy: Why and What For?" *Military Review*, XLVI (February 1966), 61-68.

An examination of the political and military reasons for the two campaigns which, like the last citation, generally defends the decision to attack via the so-called soft underbelly.

1533. ———. *Sicily: Whose Victory?* Ballantine's Illustrated History of World War II. New York: Ballantine Books, 1969. 160p.

A balanced pictorial retelling of the Sicily story which concludes that the battle was a strategic Allied victory and a tactical German gain which prolonged the Italian campaign. The last two pages cover the famous Patton slapping incident.

1533a. ———. "The Struggle for Rome." *American History Illustrated*, XVIII (June 1983), 22-31.

An illustrated overview of the spring 1944 Allied effort to move through entrenched German defenses to the liberation of Rome with attention to the generalships of Alexander, Clark, and Kesselring.

1534. ———. "Why Southern France?" *Army*, XIX (September 1969), 37-41.

Analysis of the decision for "Anvil-Dragoon," sought by General Eisenhower as a coordinated effort with the Normandy invasion.

1535. Bohmler, Rudolf. *Monte Cassino*. Translated from the German. London: Cassell, 1964. 314p.

A German author examines the Allied attack on Monte Cassino, a key outpost in the Gustav Line, which held a Benedictine abbey which was bombed as a Nazi observatory; describes the intense fighting which followed the February 15, 1944, air assault and the hill's capture by Polish troops on May 18.

1536. Bond, Harold L. *Return to Cassino: A Memoir of the Fight for Rome*. Garden City, N.Y.: Doubleday, 1964. 207p.

A U.S. Thirty-Sixth Infantry Division veteran recalls the battles for Cassino (including the Rapido River crossing) with sorrow after a return visit made 18 years later.

1537. Butler, Frederic B. "Southern France Exploits of Task Force Butler." *Armored Cavalry Journal*, LVII (January-February 1948), 12-18; (March-April 1948), 30-38.

The story of a provisional armored-mechanized unit drawn from the U.S. Sixth Corps and commanded by the author, August 16-23, 1944.

1538. Cairns, Bogardus S. "The Breakout at Anzio: A Lesson in Tank-Infantry Cooperation." *Military Review*, XXVIII (January 1949), 23-32.

On the coordination between French Expeditionary Corps troops and Fifth Army men in May 1944.

1539. "Cassino: The Fifth Army Finds It a Hard Nut to Crack." *Infantry Journal*, LIV (May 1944), 20-23.

A report on the battles around the town south of Rome in early 1944.

1540. Chandler, Harriette L. "Another View of 'Operation Crossword.'" *Military Affairs*, XLII (April 1978), 68-75.

A review of the secret operation which brought about the May 1945 surrender of German troops in Italy; called "Operation Sunrise" by those who negotiated the move.

1541. Clifton, C.V. "A Gun and a Company." *U.S. Army Combat Forces Journal*, I (August 1950), 8-10.

Operations of the U.S. Six Hundred Ninety-Eighth Field Artillery Batallion near Ponsacco, Italy, in July 1944.

1542. Connell, Charles. *Monte Cassino: The Historic Battle*. London: Elek Books, 1963. 206p.

A British author examines the famous operation in which U.S., French, Polish, and British troops fought for the ruins of the bombed-out Benedictine abbey in May 1944.

1543. Connor, A.O. "On the Defensive." *Infantry Journal*, LV (July 1944), 35-39.

These notes from the Anzio beachhead concentrate on U.S. underground defenses.

1544. Cookley, Peter. "Reflections on Anzio." *Military Review*, XXXIII (October 1953), 96-100.

An overview of the difficulties faced by the defenders once the decision had been taken to dig in.

1545. Curtis, Claire E. "From the Arno to the Winter Line." *Armored Cavalry Journal*, LVII (May-June 1948), 46-49.

Recalls the operations of elements of the U.S. Seven Hundred Sixtieth Tank Batallion in Italy between September 1-November 9, 1944.

1546. Darby, William O., with William H. Baumer. *We Led the Way: Darby's Rangers*. San Rafael, Calif.: Presidio Press, 1980. 198p.

Dictated to his friend General Baumer just a few months before his death in 1944, Darby's memoirs tell of the creation of the Rangers in 1942, training in Scotland, and operations in North Africa, Sicily, and at Salerno and Anzio in Italy. Baumer adds background facts on the war, Darby's life, and a summary of the action of other Ranger units.

1547. Davis, Forrest. "Secret History of a Surrender: German Armies in Northern Italy." *Saturday Evening Post*, CCXVIII (September 22, 1945), 9-11+; (September 29, 1945), 17+.

Davis describes "Operation Crossword/Sunrise" which spymaster Allen W. Dulles helped to direct and which resulted in the surrender of German troops in north Italy in May 1945.

1548. Devers, Jacob L. "Operation Dragoon: The Invasion of Southern France." *Military Affairs*, X (Summer 1946), 3-41.

Devers was Deputy Supreme Allied Commander, Mediterranean, when U.S. and French forces went ashore in southern France in August 1944, an operation here described from firsthand knowledge.

1549. DeVore, Robert. "Paratroops Behind Nazi Lines." *Collier's*, CXII (September 18, 1943), 18-19+.

Avoiding criticism of the drop, the author concentrates on the successful aspects of the U.S. airborne drop on Sicily.

1550. Dulles, Allen W. *The Secret Surrender*. New York: Harper & Row, 1966. 268p.

The author, a leading negotiator/director in "Operation Sunrise," describes the attempts of the SS to speed up the surrender and the unexpected factors on the German side which, in fact, caused the capitulation to be made quicker than Americans anticipated.

1551. Dziubau, Stanley W. "When Engineers Fight as Infantry." *Army*, XIII (September 1962), 68-71.

The story of the amphibious assault on Gela, Sicily, in July 1943 made by the First Battalion, Thirty-Ninth Combat Engineers, and the First and Fourth Ranger Battalions.

1552. Edmonson, Edward M. "Anzio Analysis." *Marine Corps Gazette*, XXIX (January 1945), 22-26.

An almost-contemporary examination of the American decision to halt at the beachhead instead of moving quickly on; Martin Blumenson in his article on "Italy--Operations, 1943-1945" (p. 309) in Thomas Parrish, ed., *The Simon and Schuster Encyclopedia of World War II* (New York: Simon and Schuster, 1978) presents a view of General Lucas's decision not available even when he wrote of Anzio in the citations noted above: "Learning through the ULTRA intelligence reports of Hitler's intention, Clark advised Lucas not to head for the Alban Hills but to dig in and prepare to meet the inevitable German counterattack."

1553. Essame, Hubert. "A Controversial Campaign: Italy, 1943-1945." *Army Quarterly and Defence Journal*, XCV (1968), 219-224.

Defends the British push for the operation on the basis of its impact on the total ETO war effort.

1554. Featherstone, Donald. *A Wargamers' Guide to the Mediterranean Campaigns, 1943-1945.* Tank Battles in Miniature, no. 4. Cambridge, Eng.: Patrick Stephens, 1977. 152p.

Examines the strategy, operations, men, equipment, and vehicles employed by Allied and Axis forces in the battles for Sicily and Italy; contains 12 illustrations, 12 maps, and a variety of diagrams. The work is equally useful for historians and board gamers.

1555. Fehrenbach, T.R. *The Battle of Anzio: The Dramatic Story of the Major Engagement of World War II.* Derby, Conn.: Monarch Books, 1962. 160p.

An overview of the campaign from the January 1944 landing to the final breakout in May, with emphasis on the defense of the beachhead by besieged American G.I.'s.

1556. Ffrench-Blake, R.L.V. "Armor in Italy." In: Bernard Fitzsimons, ed. *Tanks and Weapons of World War II.* New York: Beekman House, 1973, pp. 101-105.

First published in the multi-part Purnell's History of the Second World War, this overview comments on the difficulties of operating tanks in Italy's mountainous terrain.

1557. Finch, J.R.G. "The Second Battle of Cassino: 'Operation Revenge.'" *Journal of the Royal United Service Institute*, CX (February 1965), 68-72.

Discusses the mid-March 1944 bombing of the town of Cassino and the failure of Allied troops to take this point on the Gustav Line.

1558. "First Pictures of the Sicily Invasion." *Life*, XV (August 2, 1943), 13-25.

Still a useful pictorial piece.

1559. Fisher, Ernest F., Jr. *Cassino to the Alps.* U.S. Army in World War II: The Mediterranean Theater of Operations. Washington, D.C.: U.S. Government Printing Office, 1977. 584p.

Continues the account of operations in Italy begun by Blumenson above; covers "Operation Diadem," the capture of Rome plus the pursuit of the Germans to the Arno, the Gothic Line battles, the last offensive, the pursuit across the Po Valley, and the negotiations for the surrender of German armies in Italy.

1560. Ford, Corey. "Cloak-and-Dagger--Espionage and Secret Intelligence Service of the O.S.S.: Germans in Italy." *Collier's*, CXVI (October 27, 1945), 30+.

An account of the O.S.S. role in the negotiations for the German surrender.

1561. "Forgotten Front: The U.S. Fifth Army Fights a Plodding War in Italy." *Life*, XVIII (April 16, 1945), 79-87.

Still a useful pictorial piece.

1562. Fry, James C. "The Bloody Ridge at Volterra." *Infantry Journal*, LXVII (July 1950), 12-17.

Follows the operations of the Three Hundred Fiftieth Infantry Regiment, Eighty-Eighth Division in July 1944, as American forces pushed the Germans toward their Gothic Line.

1563. ———. *Combat Soldier*. Washington, D.C.: National Press, 1968. 368p.

The commanding general of the Three Hundred Fiftieth Infantry recalls his unit's service in Italy, including the incidents noted in the preceding and next entries.

1564. ———. "One Week in Hell." *Saturday Evening Post*, CCXXI (June 25, 1949), 36-37+.

The Three Hundred Fiftieth's stubborn stand against the German counteroffensive at this point near Salerno in September 1943.

1565. Garland, Albert N., and Howard M. Smyth. *Sicily and the Surrender of Italy*. U.S. Army in World War II: The Mediterranean Theater of Operations. Washington, D.C.: U.S. Government Printing Office, 1965. 609p.

Operations, including airborne and amphibious, in the invasion and conquest of Sicily in July-August 1943 are described; a second story, one of military diplomacy, covers the negotiations leading to Italy's surrender.

1566. Gavin, James M. "Jump into Sicily." *American Heritage*, XXIX (April 1978), 46-61.

A noted participant describes the failure of the paratroop landings behind German lines on the island's south coast, a failure caused largely by inexperience and high winds.

1567. ———. "Paratroops over Sicily." *Infantry Journal*, LVII (November 1945), 25-33.

A more concise telling of the details noted in the last entry.

1568. Gellhorn, Martha. "Cracking the Gothic Line." *Collier's*, CXIV (October 28, 1944), 24+.

A famous lady combat correspondent presents an overly optimistic report on the Fifth Army's fall progress; although "cracked" just a bit, the Gothic Line was not overcome until the spring of 1945.

1569. Gervasi, Frank. "'At Last You Have Come Home." *Collier's*, CXIV (October 30, 1944), 15+.

A look at the southern French invasion with emphasis on the U.S. supported First French Infantry and Third Algerian Divisions.

1570. ———. "Battle at Cassino." *Collier's*, CXIII (March 18, 1944), 20+.

Describes the attempts to capture Monte Cassino and the leveling of the Benedictine abbey.

1571. ———. "Victory at Volturno." *Collier's*, CXII (December 11, 1943), 31+.

Describes the U.S. Fifth Army's assault crossing of this river north of Naples in mid-October 1943.

1572. Graham, Dominick. *Cassino*. Ballantine's Illustrated History of World War II. New York: Ballantine Books, 1971. 160p.

A pictorial review of the static bloodletting which resulted in the Allies' Pyrrhic victory at the site of the devastated Benedictine abbey.

1573. Graham, Frederick. "Out of the Skies by Glider and 'Chute.'" *New York Times Magazine* (June 4, 1944), 11+.

Puts a good face on the costly U.S. paradrop on Sicily.

1574. Harpur, Brian. *The Impossible Victory: A Personal Account of the Battle for the River Po*. New York: Hippocrene Books, 1981. 202p.

A then-junior British officer describes the grim realities of Italian fighting which began at Cassino and continued through the bitter winter of 1944-45 to the climactic battle in April 1945 which saw the German defenders crumble under ceaseless Allied attack; on a different level, the author analyzes the tensions and controversies among the high command on the basis of postwar interviews with Generals Clark and Wladyslaw Anders and Field Marshal Alexander.

1575. Harr, William ("Bill"). *Combat Boots, Tales of Fighting Men--Including the "Anzio Derby."* Hicksville, N.Y.: Exposition Press, 1952. 232p.

The author recalls his service in the U.S. Forty-Fifth Division and the bloody fighting in Italy, including Anzio.

1576. Hassler, Elizabeth V. "The Capitulation of Italy, 1943: A Study of the First Application of the Unconditional Surrender Formula." Unpublished M.A. thesis, Pennsylvania State University, 1966.

Examines the military diplomacy and negotiations surrounding the surrender of Marshal Badoglio's government to the Allies in September 1943.

1577. Hayman-Joyce, Robert J. "Salerno: D. Plus 26 Years--Retracing the Steps of Battles Past." *Armor*, LXXX (March-April 1971), 4-7.

An overview of the nearly disastrous Allied landing south of Naples in September 1943.

1578. Hibbert, Christopher. *Anzio--The Bid for Rome.* Ballantine's Illustrated History of World War II. New York: Ballantine Books, 1970. 160p.

Summarizes the nearly disastrous Allied amphibious attempt to outflank German forces on the Italian boot below Rome; in words and pictures, portrays the bitter fighting and missed opportunities.

1579. Hills, Robert F. "What a Beating Our Gliders Took." *Saturday Evening Post*, CCXXII (November 5, 1949), 36-37+.

Discusses the high winds and American AA fire which caused so many casualties among gliderborne troops at Sicily.

1580. Hunter, S.J. "The Capture of Mount Frassino." *Infantry Journal*, LVIII (April 1946), 27-30.

Recalls the taking of a hill near Cassino in spring 1944.

1581. Hussa, Norman. "Action at Salerno." *Infantry Journal*, LIII (December 1943), 23-29.

Details the Allied landing in September 1943 and the breakout toward Naples.

1582. "The Invasion of Italy." *Military Review*, XXXI (April 1951), 80-85.

Recalls the politics and military operations surrounding Salerno.

1583. "The Italian Campaign." *Military Review*, XXXI (May 1951), 101-105; (June 1951), 103-105.

A brief overview of the bitter fighting between 1943 and 1945.

1584. Jackson, William G.F. *The Battle for Italy.* New York: Harper & Row, 1967. 372p.

A clear and fairly comprehensive retelling of the Italian campaign story as a whole, with particular attention to the origins of and differences in Allied strategy; with useful maps, Jackson explains the various battles, often finding fault with the policies of such leaders as Alexander and Clark. Illustrated with maps and photographs.

1585. ———. *The Battle for Rome.* New York: Scribners, 1969. 224p.

A senior British officer in Italy recalls "Operation Diadem," the Allied effort in Italy to tie down as many German divisions as possible during the Normandy invasion while weakening Reich morale by taking the rich prize of Rome; although generally fair, Jackson reserves most of his praise for Marshal Alexander and his chief of staff, General Harding. Includes over 40 maps and photographs.

1586. Kesselring, Albert. *Kesselring: A Soldier's Record*. Translated from the German. New York: William Morrow, 1954. 381p.

Kesselring, who led the Luftwaffe in the French and Russian campaigns, took over as Commander-in-Chief, South, in late 1941. It was he who led the Nazi defense of Sicily and Italy against the Allies until an injury put him out of action in October 1944. In this memoir, the author explains how he made such extraordinary use of terrain and his own resourcefulness to conduct the long, slow retreat up the peninsula that kept the Allies from quick and sure victory early on.

1587. Komer, R.W. "Assault Along the Ridges." *Infantry Journal*, LXVII (July 1945), 16-20.

An overview of fighting conditions in the areas overlooking the Po River plain.

1588. Liddell-Hart, Basil H. "How the Allies Got Back into Europe--Through Sicily." *Marine Corps Gazette*, XLI (February 1957), 24-29.

An overview of the July-August 1943 "Husky" campaign told by a noted British military historian.

1589. ———. "Italy--The Tumbled Opportunity." *Marine Corps Gazette*, XLI (August 1957), 44-49.

The noted historian examines Allied missed opportunities in Italy, especially the Anzio invasion of January 1944.

1590. Linklater, Eric. *The Campaign in Italy*. London: H.M. Stationery Office, 1951. 480p.

A "popular" official British history which covers Allied operations from Salerno to the German surrender at Caserta in May 1945; largely superseded by the British and American official histories cited elsewhere in this section.

1591. McBee, Frederick. "The Invasion of Italy." *World War II Magazine*, II (February 1972), 34-44.

A pictorial piece on the Salerno undertaking.

1592. McBride, Lauren E. "Crossing the Volturno." *Infantry Journal*, LV (September 1944), 14-17.

Examines the assault crossing made by Fifth Army troops of the stream above Naples in mid-October 1943.

1593. Macksey, Kenneth. *Kesselring: The Making of the Luftwaffe*. New York: David McKay, 1978. 262p.

The title is misleading as this is a full biography of the Luftwaffe general and field marshal turned Nazi defender of Italy; the work is extremely flattering to its subject. Dr.

Rainer Kess, Kesselring's son, cooperated with Macksey in the completion of the work.

1594. Majdalany, Fred. *The Battle of Cassino.* Boston, Mass.: Houghton Mifflin, 1957. 309p.

A detailed study of the four months in early 1944 when the Allies attempted to capture Monte Cassino, break the Gustav Line, relieve the Anzio beachhead, and open the road to Rome; analyzes the various battles, the destruction of the Benedictine abbey, and the commanders on both sides, including Kesselring and Clark.

1595. ———. *The Monastery.* Boston, Mass.: Houghton Mifflin, 1946. 148p.

An early review of the wisdom of destroying the ancient abbey atop Monte Cassino.

1596. Mason, David. *Salerno--Foothold in Europe.* Ballantine's Illustrated History of World War II. New York: Ballantine Books, 1972. 160p.

The beachhead battle of September 1943 which was nearly won by the defending Germans is recalled in this pictorial, but sometimes repetitious, account.

1597. Mathews, Sidney T. "General Clark's Decision to Drive on Rome." In: Kent R. Greenfield, ed. *Command Decisions.* Washington, D.C.: Office of the Chief of Military History, Department of the Army, 1960, pp. 351-363.

An analysis of the two options facing Clark at the end of May 1944: to attempt to block retreating German troops or take the Italian capital. Doubting his ability to perform the former task, Clark attempted both but succeeded only at the latter.

1598. Matloff, Maurice. "The ANVIL Decision: Crossroads of Strategy." In: Kent R. Greenfield, ed. *Command Decisions.* Washington, D.C.: Office of the Chief of Military History, Department of the Army, 1960, pp. 383-400.

Churchill, wanting resources for Italy and the Balkans, opposed the invasion of southern France, but Eisenhower saw it as a way of drawing German pressure away from Normandy.

1599. ———. "Was the Invasion of Southern France a Blunder?" *U.S. Naval Institute Proceedings*, LXXXIV (July 1958), 35-45.

Suggests that given the scope of the Normandy victory, German forces in southern France would probably have withdrawn without a second invasion and posed little threat to Allied forces in the north; nevertheless, Eisenhower and his planners did not know this before the second D-Day was unleashed.

1600. Mauldin, William ("Bill"). *Up Front.* Cleveland, Ohio, and New York: World Publishing Co., 1945. 228p.

One of the classic books of the war, in which "Willie and Joe," the author's cartoon G.I.'s, offer commentary on the lives of common U.S. soldiers in Italy.

1601. Mitchell, Donald W. "Triumph in Sicily." *Current History*, V (September 1943), 13-17.

A day-to-day chronicle of the Allied July-August 1943 campaign.

1602. Morison, Samuel E. "Elba Interlude." *Military Affairs*, XXI (Winter 1957), 182-187.

Recaptured from the Germans in an amphibious landing by Free French troops, June 17-19, 1944.

1603. Morrow, Norman P. "The Employment of Artillery in Italy." *Field Artillery Journal*, XXXIV (August 1944), 499-505.

Army cannon played a major role in the Italian campaign, especially in the early months of 1944 at Anzio and Cassino.

1604. Nofi, Albert A. "The Race for Messina, 10 July-17 August 1943." *Strategy and Tactics* (November-December 1981), 9-17.

Recounts the unofficial but real contest between troops of Generals Montgomery and Patton on Sicily.

1605. Orgill, Douglas. *The Gothic Line: The Italian Campaign, Autumn 1944*. New York: W.W. Norton, 1967. 257p.

After examining the conflict between Anglo-American planners, this British journalist, who was an Allied tank commander at the time, narrates accounts of the various ground efforts to break the Gothic Line; although concentrating on British actions, the author relates some of the American experiences, including the flanking of Futa Pass and the taking of Mount Altuzzo.

1606. Pack, Stanley W.G. *Operation Husky: The Allied Invasion of Sicily*. New York: Hippocrene Books, 1977. 186p.

Using pictures and research based on documents and interviews, the author reconstructs the Anglo-American invasion of the island in July-August 1943, including the difficulties of the paratroops, naval support, and the unofficial "race for Messina."

1607. Painton, Frederick C. "Dirty Work on the Road to Rome." *Saturday Evening Post*, CCXVI (February 19, 1944), 12-13+.

Reviews the work of U.S. Army combat engineers in lifting German land mines, building bridges and roads, and firing their guns when necessary.

1608. Perry, George S. "Beachhead." *New Yorker*, XIX (August 14, 1943), 46+.

An eyewitness report on the establishment of the Allied invasion in Sicily, including naval support.

1609. ———. "First Wave Touchdown." *Saturday Evening Post*, CCXVII (September 30, 1944), 20+.

Reconstructs the landing of the U.S. Seventh Army in southern France on August 15, 1944.

1610. Piekalkiewicz, Janusz. *The Battle for Cassino*. Indianapolis: Bobbs-Merrill, 1981. 192p.

Using documentary evidence, a detailed day-to-day narrative, and over 150 photographs and maps, the noted documentary film-maker illuminates the savage, controversial, and frustrating Allied campaign.

1611. "Planning the Assault in Sicily." *Military Review*, XXX (February 1951), 73-79; (March 1951), 87-94.

A detailed examination of the factors considered by Allied planners preparing for "Operation Husky."

1612. Pond, Hugh. *Salerno*. Boston, Mass.: Little, Brown, 1962. 269p.

A chronological account of the first large-scale landing in Europe which provides details on battles and command strategy.

1613. ———. *Sicily*. London: Kimber, 1962. 224p.

A somewhat briefer entry than the last, but arranged similarly, i.e., a chronological day-by-day account interspersed with battle narrative and command analysis.

1614. Powers, John L. "Crossing the Rapido." *Infantry Journal*, LVI (May 1945), 50-53.

A brief discussion of the costly Thirty-Sixth Division failure on January 20, and the successful, but not followed-up, crossing by a regiment of the Thirty-Fourth Division on January 25.

1615. Pyle, Ernest T. ("Ernie"). "Fifth Army Fights It Out on the Winter Line." In: Henry S. Commager and Alan Nevins, eds. *Heritage of America*. Boston, Mass.: Little, Brown, 1949, pp. 1170-1174.

1616. ———. "Sicily Landing." In: Karl Detzer, ed. *The Army Reader*. Indianapolis: Bobbs-Merrill, 1943, pp. 439-441.

Two previously published pieces describing the lot of the common soldier in the two undertakings described.

1617. Raymond, Edward A. "A Fight." *Field Artillery Journal*, XXXV (March 1945), 156-160.

Stresses the role of Forty-Fifth Division cannon in the Battle of Salerno.

1618. Reynolds, Quentin. "Bloody Salerno." *Collier's*, CXII (October 16, 1943), 13+; (October 23, 1943), 20+.

The famed correspondent watched the landings from a USN ship and comments on the confusion which almost led to tragedy.

1619. ———. "Sicily Wasn't Easy." *Collier's*, CXII (September 11, 1943), 20-21+.

An overview of "Operation Husky" which stresses the opposition to and danger of the undertaking.

1620. Robbins, Charles. "The Nazis Loved Monte Cassino." *Saturday Evening Post*, CCXVIII (January 19, 1946), 36-37+.

An attempt to justify the abbey based on the use made of the ruins of the place after its destruction.

1621. Robichon, Jacques. *The Second D-Day*. Translated from the French. New York: Walker, 1969. 314p.

A French journalist carefully examines the planning, development, and tactical operations of the invasion of southern France in August 1944 detailing the activities of German and Allied forces in a style reminiscent of Cornelius Ryan.

1622. Ryder, William T. "Action on Biazza Ridge." *Saturday Evening Post*, CCXVI (December 22, 1943), 14, 49-54.

Airborne operations in Sicily, September 9/10, 1943.

1623. Seymour, William. "Anzio." In: his *Yours to Reason Why: Decision in Battle*. New York: St. Martin's Press, 1982, Chap. 10.

In a book of battles designed to give readers a chance to experience the problems facing generals in battle, Anzio is the only engagement of World War II chosen. Setting the battle in its historical context, with details on terrain and the forces involved, the author looks at the German and Allied commanders, their personal qualities of leadership and their weaknesses. The battle is then developed, pausing at decisive stages to provide the options open to the generals and a chance for the reader to decide for himself which option to choose. A highly original approach--could you have won Anzio?

1624. Shadel, W.F. "Street Fighting in Cassino." *Infantry Journal*, LIV (June 1944), 24+.

Describes the inconclusive March 1944 house-to-house combat.

1625. Sheehan, Fred. *Anzio, Epic of Bravery*. Norman: University of Oklahoma Press, 1964. 239p.

Another retelling of the familiar story of invasion, missed opportunity, and stiff German defense told with an emphasis on the bravery of the Allied soldiers besieged within the beachhead.

1626. Shepperd, Gilbert A. *The Italian Campaign, 1943-1945: A Political and Military Re-Assessment*. New York: Praeger, 1968. 450p.

A retired British army officer presents a good review of the Italian campaign from Salerno to May 1945, including a critical analysis of political decisions and an even stronger look at military strategy and tactics. Military operations are covered from unit level, omitting individual exploits, stressing the international composition of the Allied forces and the stiff German defense.

1627. Shoemaker, John J. "Breaking Through of the Gothic Line." *Military Review*, XXX (September 1950), 9-18.

How the renewed Fifteenth Army Group broke the line in spring 1945 and rapidly captured Bologna.

1628. Smith, Bradley F., and Elena Agrossi. *Operation Sunrise: The Secret Surrender*. New York: Basic Books, 1979. 192p.

Employing declassified O.S.S. documents, the authors debunk revisionist claims that the Bern negotiations for the surrender of German troops in Italy were an act of perfidy, showing, instead, that the American participants were concerned more with the military situation than politics.

1629. Smith, Charles W. "SS General Karl Wolff and the Surrender of the German Troops in Italy, 1945." Unpublished Ph.D. Dissertation, Southern Mississippi University, 1970.

Wolff, an SS general in northern Italy and military governor, was a close friend of Heinrich Himmler; seeing the war was lost, he opened negotiations with the Americans in spring 1945, leading to the surrender of his troops in May. Smith comments on the general's motives as well as the political-military situation in Italy at the end of the conflict.

1630. Smith, E.D. *The Battles for Cassino*. New York: Scribners, 1976. 192p.

A then-young Ghurka officer recalls and analyzes the four major operations which made up the Cassino battle, commenting on difficulties encountered, leadership, German defense, etc.

1631. ———. "The Rapido Fiasco." *Army Quarterly and Defence Journal*, CII (Fall 1972), 483-495.

"The verdict of history must be that the Rapido fiasco was an unnecessary attack, that the conditions made it impossible for the 36th Division to succeed, and that the result was not only tragic and inevitable but contributed nothing."

1632. ———. "Why Was the Monastery at Cassino Bombed?" *Army Quarterly and Defense Journal*, XCVIII (July 1969), 220-224.

Because Allied general Bernard Freyberg considered it a key to German defenses and because British and American air force chiefs elected to use it as a way of showing the effectiveness of air power.

1633. Smyth, Howard M. "The Armistice of Cassibile." *Military Review*, XII (Spring 1948), 12-35.

Discusses operations near this Sicilian town, August 19-September 9, 1943.

1634. Stokesbury, James L. "1943 Invasion of Italy." *American History Illustrated*, XII (August 1977), 26-37.

Reviews the political reasons for the invasion and the extremely active defense at the Salerno beachhead by Kesselring's troops.

1635. Stuart, James. "Attack by Glider." *Flying*, XXXIII (November 1943), 26-27+.

Recalls the airborne landings and the difficulties and casualties taken by Allied gliderborne forces.

1636. "They Stopped Us at Cassino." *Life*, XVI (April 10, 1944), 27-33.

Still a useful pictorial piece.

1637. Tidyman, Ernest. *The Anzio Death Trap*. New York: Belmont Books, 1968. 155p.

An overview of the Allied defense of the Anzio beachhead against a strong and determined German enemy working to crush it; retells the familiar story without adding anything new.

1638. Tregaskis, Richard W. *Invasion Diary*. New York: Random House, 1944. 245p.

The author of *Guadalcanal Diary* provides an account of the invasions of Sicily and Italy which examines both from the heights of strategy to the depths of actions by common soldiers; the last portion of the book describes his experiences as a casualty after receiving a head wound in November 1943, relating it to the experiences of other G.I.'s.

1639. Trevelyan, Raleigh. *The Fortress: A Diary of Anzio and After*. New York: St. Martin's Press, 1957. 221p.

A participant recalls the landings and defense of the Anzio beachhead, the breakout, and the push to Rome in a chronologically arranged sequence of thoughts and details.

1640. ———. *Rome '44: The Battle for the Eternal City*. New York: Viking Press, 1982. 366p.

Follows the military operations from Anzio to the Eternal City's liberation in June as well as the maneuvering of Italy's political factions and other interested parties, including the Germans, the Vatican, and the Resistance. The military coverage concentrates on Anzio (including the removal of General Lucas), the battles for Cassino and the bombing of the abbey, and the German evacuation of Rome.

1641. United States, Congress. Committee on Military Affairs. *The Rapido River Crossing: Hearings*. 79th Cong., 2nd sess. Washington, D.C.: U.S. Government Printing Office, 1946. 46p.

The commander of the U.S. Thirty-Sixth Division charged General Clark with recklessness and bad judgment concerning the crossing and these inconclusive hearings looked into who was to blame for the disaster.

1642. ———. War Department. Historical Division. *Anzio Beachhead (22 January-25 May 1944)*. American Forces in Action. Washington, D.C.: U.S. Government Printing Office, 1947. 122p.

A popularly written account of the besieged beachhead, illustrated with maps and photographs.

1643. ———. ———. ———. *Fifth Army at the Winter Line (15 November 1943-January 1944)*. American Forces in Action Series. Washington, D.C.: U.S. Government Printing Office, 1945. 117p.

A popularly written account of the stalemate at the Bernhard and Gustav Lines, illustrated with maps and photographs.

1644. ———. ———. ———. *From the Volturno to the Winter Line (6 October-15 November 1943)*. American Forces in Action. Washington, D.C.: U.S. Government Printing Office, 1944. 119p.

Actions of the U.S. Fifth Army in fall 1943 are covered in this popularly written account, illustrated with photographs and maps.

1645. ———. ———. ———. *Salerno: American Operations from the Beaches to the Volturno (9 September-6 October 1943)*. American Forces in Action. Washington, D.C.: U.S. Government Printing Office, 1944. 95p.

The invasion of Italy and capture of Naples are reviewed in this popularly written work, illustrated with maps and photographs.

1646. Von Senger und Etterlin, Fridolin R. "The Battles of Cassino." *Journal of the Royal United Service Institute*, CIII (May 1958), 208-214.

Recollections of the author's service as commander of the Fourteenth Panzer Corps in the battles.

1647. ———. *Neither Fear Nor Hope: The Wartime Career of General Fridolin R. von Senger und Etterlin*. Translated from the German. London: Macdonald, 1963. 368p.

Memoirs of the German general who commanded Nazi troops in Sicily and later the Fourteenth Panzer Corps in Italy; provides insight into German leadership in Italy from the Führer level down.

1648. Wagner, Robert L. *The Texas Army: A History of the 36th Division in the Italian Campaign*. Austin, Tx., 1972. 285p.

This privately printed work is a combat record of the Thirty-Sixth Division from Salerno to its relief north of Rome in June 1944; the bulk of the work is taken up with a challenge to official reports and interpretations of the Rapido River crossing as a diversion to Anzio and a military necessity.

1649. Walker, Fred L. *From Texas to Rome: A General's Journal.* Dallas, Tx.: Taylor Publishing Co., 1969. 448p.

The author commanded the Thirty-Sixth Division from Salerno to Rome and it was he who raised charges of foul play against Mark Clark after his unit suffered 1,000 casualties in the Rapido River crossing in spring 1944. This work examines not only those charges but the unit's participation in the long fight up the Italian boot to the liberation of the Eternal City.

1650. ———. "My Story of the Rapido Crossing." *Army*, XIII (September 1962), 52-60.

An in-depth examination of the reasons for the crossing and the failure of the author's division to obtain a foothold.

1651. Wallace, Robert. *The Italian Campaign.* World War II Series. Alexandria, Va.: Time-Life Books, 1978. 208p.

This pictorial presents a clear and concise overview of the difficulties of the campaign and the military-political strategy and leadership behind it. Many of the photographs were taken by *Life* magazine reporters and cameramen during the actions described.

1652. Walters, James W. "Artillery and Air Support of a Ground Attack: Cassino, March 1944." *Military Review*, XXVI (January 1947), 52-58.

Despite air and cannon bombardment, the ground assault of mid-March was inconclusive.

1653. Werstein, Irving. *The Battle of Salerno.* New York: Crowell, 1965. 152p.

This is a concise overview of the September 1943 landings and the German near-victory, suitable for younger readers.

1654. White, Margaret Bourke. *They Called It Purple Heart Valley: A Combat Chronicle of the War in Italy.* New York: Simon and Schuster, 1944. 182p.

The noted *Life* correspondent provides, in text and pictures, a closeup view of the Italian front from the Salerno invasion through the liberation and restoration of Naples.

1655. White, William L. "Some Affairs of Honor: Operatives of the O.S.S. Hastened the German Collapse in Italy." *Reader's Digest*, XLVII (December 1945), 136-154.

Describes the negotiations between Dulles' and Wolff's people for the surrender of German forces in Italy in May 1945.

1656. Wilt, Alan F. *The French Riviera Campaign of August 1944.* Carbondale: Southern Illinois University Press, 1981. 208p.

Primarily a background study of the concept, planning, Anglo-American debate over, and execution of "Operation Anvil-Dragoon," which concludes that the invasion did not detract from either the Normandy or Italian campaigns.

1657. Worth, Alexander M., Jr. "Supporting Weapons and High Ground: The Rangers at Salerno." *Infantry Journal*, LVI (May 1945), 33-34.

A brief overview of the work of Colonel Darby's people in helping to secure the Salerno beachhead.

2. European Theater

Introduction: For purposes of this guide, the European Theater of Operations encompasses the nations of northwest Europe, including Britain, France, Holland, Belgium, Denmark, and Germany proper. During the early part of the Allies' coalition war, considerable debate existed as to the direction fighting should take in this theater. Citations to those strategic-political differences and the call for a "Second Front Now" are covered for the most part in Section II:A on diplomacy, above.

a. *GENERAL WORKS*

Introduction: A few studies address the military (i.e., land) campaign in northwest Europe as a whole; as users will see, however, the majority of works available consider specific campaigns such as the Normandy invasion and the Battle of the Bulge. The citations noted below should be employed in conjunction with those on aerial operations and sea warfare covered in Section III:C:2 and 3 above and V:C:2 below. Additionally, many of the memoirs and biographies of U.S. and British officers cited in part IV:B above contain information on their northwest Europe service.

1658. Allied Forces. SHAEF. *Report by the Supreme Commander to the Combined Chiefs of Staff on the Operation in Europe of the Allied Expeditionary Force, 6 June 1944 to 8 May 1945.* Washington, D.C.: U.S. Government Printing Office, 1946. 122p.

General Eisenhower's report of Allied campaigns in northwest Europe from the Normandy invasion to VE-Day.

1659. Baldwin, Hanson W. *Battles Lost and Won: Great Campaigns of World War II.* New York: Harper & Row, 1966. 532p.

An analysis of 11 major campaigns considered decisive with explanations as to what happened, why, and the effects. Those of the ETO considered are D-Day and the Battle of the Bulge.

1660. CBS, Inc. *From D-Day Through Victory in Europe.* New York, 1945. 314p.

Reprints accounts of the battles and campaigns in Europe as told by CBS News correspondents on the air.

1661. DeGaulle, Charles. *War Memoirs.* 5 vols. New York: Viking Press, 1955-1960.

The wartime leader of the Free French describes his services from 1940 to 1946, including his relations with Allied leaders and the liberation of his country from the Germans.

1662. DeLattre de Tassigny, Jean. *The History of the First French Army.* Translated from the French. London: Allen and Unwin, 1952.

An operational history of the Free French Army's campaigns in France and Germany, including the southern France landings, the Rhone Valley campaign, the battles in the Vosges, the Rhine crossing, and the drive into Germany.

1663. Dupuy, R. Ernest, and Herbert L. Bregstein, comps. *Soldiers' Album.* Boston, Mass.: Houghton Mifflin, 1946. 173p.

A pictorial history of the ETO from D-Day through VE-Day.

1664. Eisenhower, Dwight D. *Eisenhower's Own Story of the War.* New York: Arco, 1946. 122p.

The Supreme Commander's report (the GPO version is identical and cited above, item 1658) written in simple and concise language, but, as one might expect in such a document, it glosses over the differences between the British and Americans on points of strategy. Eisenhower's *Crusade in Europe* is cited in IV:B above.

1665. Ellis, Lionel F., *et al. Victory in the West.* History of the Second World War: United Kingdom Military Series. 2 vols. London: H.M. Stationery Office, 1962-1968.

The two volumes in this official British history are: *The Battle for Normandy* and *The Defeat of Germany.* The former surveys the planning and landing in Normandy and operations through the liberation of Paris in September 1944 while the second covers the campaign to May 1945. The works are relatively unbiased and provide information on U.S. Army efforts.

1666. Freidin, Seymour, and William Richardson, eds. *The Fatal Decisions.* New York: Sloane Associates, 1956. 302p.

A collection of essays by former German officers on six major campaigns in the ETO, including the Battle of France and the Ardennes counteroffensive. Lack of troops, supplies, and effective leadership (including Hitler's) are given most often as the reasons for defeat.

1667. Giles, Henry. *The G.I. Journal of Sergeant Giles.* Compiled and edited by Janice H. Giles. Boston, Mass.: Houghton Mifflin, 1965. 399p.

Comprised of the diary and letters home of Weapons Sgt. Giles of the Two Hundred Ninety-First Combat Engineer Battalion, who helped the U.S. Army build its way from France to the heart of Germany; the human element is high as Giles reveals his emotional and intellectual responses to war, death, and his fellow soldiers.

1668. Henderson, Ian. "The G.I.'s in Ireland." *After the Battle*, no. 34 (1981), 1-41.

One of the few studies available on the U.S. soldiers who landed in Northern Ireland en route to England in 1943.

1669. Houston, Robert J. *D-Day to Bastogne: A Paratrooper Recalls World War II*. Hicksville, N.Y.: Exposition Press, 1980. 182p.

The author, a sergeant in the One Hundred First Airborne Division, recalls his service in the D-Day and Arnhem paradrops and the defense of Bastogne; a human interest account, Houston's book tells of gallant actions by men whose names are unknown to history.

1670. Hunter, Kenneth E. *The War Against Germany: Europe and Adjacent Areas*. Washington, D.C.: U.S. Government Printing Office, 1951. 448p.

The "green book" pictorial history of the Army in ETO, including the buildup in England and the campaigns from D-Day to VE-Day; each of the photographs receives an explanatory caption.

1671. Ingersoll, Ralph. *Top Secret*. New York: Harcourt, 1946. 373p.

A controversial book at the time of its publication. After Africa, the author was assigned to the SHAEF staff and performed liaison work between the staffs of Eisenhower, Bradley, and Montgomery. The author presents a story of secret planning, military politics, and personality conflicts which, although detailed by Irving and Weigley, both below, were generally condemned as impossible in the light of Allied unity in 1946. This work, which is very critical of the British, particularly Montgomery, provides accounts of the Normandy landing, the race across France and Germany, and the liberation of the concentration camps.

1672. Irving, David. *The War Between the Generals*. New York: St. Martin's Press, 1981. 446p.

This British historian places his emphasis on the major Allied military personalities of the ETO, particularly Eisenhower, Montgomery, and Patton. He suggests that a bitter personal and ideological rivalry existed in the Allied SHAEF between Eisenhower and Montgomery, providing details on "Monty's" irritation with the Supreme Commander's vacillation and caution. Woven throughout are details on the supposed Eisenhower-Summersby and Patton-Jean Gordon romances. Compare with Weigley's *Eisenhower's Lieutenants*, cited below.

1673. Kays, Marvin D. *Weather Effects During the Battle of the Bulge and the Normandy Invasion*. Report, no. ERADCOM/ASL-TR-0115. White Sands Missile Range, N.M.: Atmospheric Sciences Lab, Army Electronics Research and Development Command, 1982. 34p.

Examines how the adverse weather and lack of timely surface observation caused the German generals not to suspect D-Day on June 6 while adverse weather played into their hands during the Ardennes counteroffensive in December 1944. Weather-related instances on the battlefield are noted.

1674. Maginnis, John J. *Military Government Journal: Normandy to Berlin*. Edited by Robert A. Hart. Boston: University of Massachusetts Press, 1981. 351p.

A day-to-day record of the Civil Affairs/Military Government (CA/MG) function of the U.S. Army in those places in northwest Europe liberated by the Americans.

1675. Martin, Robert G. "The G.I.'s: Their War in Europe." *Look*, XXVII (February 26, 1963), 72-76.

Examines the lot of enlisted soldiers and junior officers in the U.S. Army during the campaign in northwest Europe.

1676. Millis, Walter. *The Last Phase: The Allied Victory in Western Europe*. Boston, Mass.: Houghton Mifflin, 1946. 130p.

A concise review of the D-Day to VE-Day military campaign of the Western Allies prepared for the Bureau of Overseas Publications of the U.S. Office of War Information and intended for distribution, in translation, in conquered Germany.

1677. Moorehead, Alan. "Montgomery's Quarrel with Eisenhower." *Collier's*, CXVIII (October 5, 1946), 12-13+.

Their conflict was officially over the strategy of a narrow thrust into Germany (Monty) vs. a broad-front strategy (Eisenhower).

1678. Pogue, Forrest C. "The Supreme Allied Command in Northwest Europe, 1944-1945." In: Dwight E. Lee and George E. McReynolds, eds. *Essays in History and International Relations in Honor of George Hubbard Blakeslee*. Boston, Mass.: Clark University Press, 1949, pp. 171-192.

The noted biographer of General Marshall discusses the difficulties faced by Eisenhower and his staff in running a coalition war; for further information, see Pogue's other writings on the Supreme Command in Section II:A above.

1679. Rooney, Andrew A. *The Fortunes of War: Four Great Battles of World War II*. Boston, Mass.: Little, Brown, 1962. 236p.

Based on episodes of the CBS television series "The 20th Century"; two of the four engagements took place in the ETO: Normandy and the Bulge. Straightforward text, no criticism.

1680. Smith, Walter B. *Eisenhower's Six Great Decisions: Europe, 1944-1945*. New York: Longmans, Green, 1956. 237p.

Eisenhower's wartime chief of staff analyzes and sympathetically reviews the following decisions made by his boss: (1) the date for the Normandy invasion; (2) the encirclement of German forces in Normandy; (3) the Battle of the Bulge; (4) the destruction of German forces west of the Rhine; (5) the encirclement of the Ruhr; and (6) the pursuit of German forces far into Germany and the decision not to capture Berlin. Smith's assertions are based on firsthand knowledge and experience.

1681. "Symposium: Who Was Right?--Monty or Ike?" *U.S. News and World Report*, XLVI (June 22, 1959), 78-84.

Examines the strategic positions of both Allied leaders in light of the 15th anniversary of D-Day.

1682. Wardlaw, Frederick C., ed. *Missing in Action: Letters of a Medic*. Raleigh, N.C.: Sparks Press, 1979. 111p.

Letters home of T5 Charles W. Wardlaw, Jr., a medic with the U.S. First Division in the campaigns across northwest Europe; captured by German troops in November 1944, Wardlaw was released from his POW camp with the collapse of the Reich, only to die in a French hospital in June 1945 as the result of his wounds and pneumonia.

1683. Warren, John C. *Airborne Operations in World War II: European Theater*. USAF Historical Study, no. 97. Washington, D.C.: Office of Air Force History, Department of the Air Force, 1956. 239p.

A documented study of the planning and execution of the U.S. airborne operations in northwest Europe from 1944 to 1945, including the Normandy, Arnhem, and Rhine River missions; provides insight concerning the impact of these operations on airborne doctrine.

1684. Weigley, Russell F. *Eisenhower's Lieutenants: The Campaigns of France and Germany, 1944-1945*. Bloomington: Indiana University Press, 1981. 800p.

This huge study of the American-led campaign in northwest Europe from D-Day through VE-Day provides an analysis of command at both the strategic and tactical levels which has already become something of a classic of American military history. Weigley asserts that the U.S. Army and its leaders entered the ETO campaign with a small-war heritage and came of age in northwest Europe, often as the result of mistakes and hard lessons learned at great cost. The portraits of Montgomery, Bradley, Devers, Hodges, Patton, Patch, Simpson, Collins, Ridgway, and others are the first extended treatments some of these men have received.

1685. Wilmot, Chester. *The Struggle for Europe*. New York: Harper, 1952. 766p.

Written from a pro-British viewpoint, this work was long considered the best single-volume history of the military aspects of the northwest Europe campaign, 1944-1945; eclipsed to some degree by Kenneth Davis' *Experience of War*, cited above (item 214), and other recent studies, Wilmot still provides a valuable introduction.

1686. Wilt, Alan F. *The Atlantic Wall: Hitler's Defenses in the West, 1941-1944.* Ames: University of Iowa Press, 1976. 244p.

A study of the planning, building, operation, and significance of the German fortifications along the French coast, which includes not only architectural information, but detail on how the Allies learned the secrets of the wall and prepared to defeat it in the "second front" landings.

1687. Wright, Gordon. *The Ordeal of Total War, 1939-1945.* New York: Harper & Row, 1968. 315p.

A comprehensive synthesis of Europe during the war years; includes information on the political, social, scientific, military and psychological aspects of the conflict which make the study a useful introduction for beginning students.

b. D-DAY THROUGH FRANCE

Introduction: The Allied campaign in France was conducted at least partially as the result of political decisions covered in certain of the citations noted in Section II:A above. The citations in this part follow the U.S. land campaign in northern France from June 6, 1944, into the fall, including the D-Day landings, the breakout from Normandy, Patton's dash across France, and the liberation of Paris. For references to the air and sea aspects of these operations, users should consult Section III:C:2 and 3 above and V:C:2 below. Certain of the biographies and memoirs cited in IV:B above and the unit histories covered in IV:D below may also prove helpful.

1688. Ahearn, J.L. "D-Day, June 6, 1944." *Look*, XXVIII (June 16, 1964), 21-23.

A pictorial 20th anniversary look back.

1689. Alden, Robert. "The Silence of Omaha Beach." *New York Times Magazine* (May 27, 1962), 15+.

Eighteen years later, the author looks back at the difficulties of U.S. troops in attacking this heavily fortified position on D-Day.

1690. Ambrose, Stephen E. "Ike's Decision to Go." *American History Illustrated*, IV (May 1969), 4-11.

After considering the weather and impact of not attacking, Eisenhower made the decision to proceed with the Normandy invasion.

1691. ———. "They Were There: D-Day, 1944." *American History Illustrated*, IV (June 1969), 4-7.

A 25th anniversary account of the bravery, daring, and resourcefulness which marked the Normandy invasion.

1692. Anderson, Henry H., Jr. "The 920th Field Artillery Battalion in Action at Metz, November, 1944." *Military Collector and Historian*, XXX (Fall 1978), 148-157.

Traces the actions of one Third Army unit in the November 19-23 attack on a group of old forts surrounding the old capital of Lorraine.

1693. *Army Times*, Editors of. *D-Day: The Greatest Invasion*. New York: G.P. Putnam, 1969. 192p.

A casual history of the D-Day undertaking, more than half of which is a collection of photographs, many previously published.

1694. Aron, Robert. *France Reborn: The History of the Liberation, June 1944-May 1945*. Translated from the French. New York: Scribners, 1964. 490p.

Based on documents and interviews and first published in France in 1959, this pro-DeGaulle story of the Battle of France covers the period from D-Day through the clearing of the last pockets of German resistance within the country; critical of both Montgomery and the Americans, Aron concentrates on the operations of the Resistance and the Free French Army.

1695. Assmann, Kurt. "Normandy, 1944." *Military Review*, XXXIV (February 1955), 86-93.

A recollection of the Allied landing and the June-July 1944 battle in Normandy by a former German officer.

1696. Baldwin, Hanson W. "As Eisenhower Sees It Two Years After." *New York Times Magazine* (June 2, 1946), 7-9+.

A distinguished correspondent portrays the views of the wartime Supreme Commander on the problems of the Normandy invasion.

1697. ———. "D-Day: This Is the Way It Was." *New York Times Magazine* (May 31, 1959), 7-9+.

Baldwin retells the familiar story of the landings 15 years after the invasion.

1698. ———. "The Greatest Martial Drama in History: D-Day Remembered." *Army*, XXX (June 1980), 18-25.

An updated version of the piece done for the *New York Times Magazine* in 1959 and cited above.

1699. ———. "The Invasion and Battle of France." *Foreign Affairs*, XXII (July 1944), 521-531; XXIII (October 1944), 1-15.

The first article details as much as was known about the Normandy invasion while the second provides information on the breakout and Patton's drive deep into France. Gives away no military secrets.

1700. ———. "Normandy: The Beginning of the End." In: his *Battles Lost and Won: Great Campaigns of World War II*. New York: Harper & Row, 1966, pp. 256-284.

A concise retelling of the planning for and execution of the D-Day invasion.

1701. Balish, Harry. "The Battle of Nancy." *Military Review*, XXIX (January 1950), 16-23.

Recalls the virtually unopposed occupation of this town in eastern Lorraine by Patton's Third Army on September 15, 1944.

1702. Balkoski, Joseph. "Patton's Third Army: The Lorraine Campaign, 8 November to 1 December 1944." *Strategy and Tactics* (January-February 1980), 4-15.

Follows the Third Army into eastern France where logistical difficulties slowed the advance.

1703. "Battle of the Hedgerows: New U.S. Offensive in Normandy." *Life*, XVII (August 7, 1944), 17-23.

Still a useful pictorial piece.

1704. "Battlefields Revisited: Normandy's Beaches 25 Years After D-Day." *Time*, XCIII (May 30, 1969), 30-37.

A pictorial "then-and-now" presentation with excerpts from the reminiscences of veterans.

1705. "Beachheads of Normandy: The Fateful Battle for Europe Is Joined by Sea and Air." *Life*, XVI (June 19, 1944), 25-37.

Still a useful pictorial piece.

1706. Belchem, David. *Victory in Normandy*. London: Chatto and Windus, 1981. 192p.

The former head of Montgomery's operations and planning staff details the Allied invasion from the formulation of the master plan through the route of the German Seventh Army at Falaise; the author occasionally indulges in a defense of his chief's tactical decisions and opinions.

1707. Belfield, Eversley M.G., and Hubert Essame. *The Battle for Normandy*. Philadelphia, Pa.: Dufour, 1965. 239p.

Two Englishmen who fought in the actions described cover the British battle for Normandy from June 7 to August 22, 1944, including the contest for Caen and the Falaise Gap and excluding the D-Day landings. The work contains an analysis of the differences in Anglo-American strategy, and the effects those differences had on the outcome of the campaign.

1708. Bidwell, Shelford. "The Airborne Assault in France." In: Philip de Ste. Croix, ed. *Airborne Operations: An Illustrated*

Encyclopedia of the Great Battles of Airborne Forces. New York: Crescent Books, 1978, pp. 92-105.

This operation made daring and large-scale use of paratroops and gliders which, despite the serious handicaps of a night drop and considerable dispersion, mostly achieved the goals of their mission.

1709. Blakeley, H.W. "Artillery in Normandy." *Field Artillery Journal*, XXXIX (March-April 1945), 52-54.

Asserts that U.S. Army field artillery was not useful during the Normandy operation.

1710. Bliven, Bruce. *The Story of D-Day, June 6, 1944*. Landmark Books. New York: Random House, 1956. 180p.

A brief introduction to the planning and execution of the Allied invasion suitable for younger readers.

1711. Blumenson, Martin. *Breakout and Pursuit*. U.S. Army in World War II: The European Theater of Operations. Washington, D.C.: U.S. Government Printing Office, 1961. 748p.

The operations of the U.S. First Army from July 1-September 10, 1944, and of the U.S. Third Army from August 1 to 21, 1944, are recounted in a work which is critical of both German and Allied strategy and which is especially hostile to General Montgomery. The action covers the hedgerow fighting, the Mortain counterattack, the reduction of Brest, and the liberation of Paris, ending at the Siegfried Line and the Meuse River. Includes maps and photographs.

1712. ———. "Coordination and Muscular Movement in the Hedgerows." *Army*, VII (May 1957), 42-47.

A discussion of the difficulty of Allied movement in Normandy and Brittany caused by the dense fencelike rows of tree-covered mounds which offered protection to the defending Germans.

1713. ———. *The Duel for France, 1944*. Boston, Mass.: Houghton Mifflin, 1963. 432p.

A popular history based on the author's "green book," *Breakout and Pursuit*, cited above; presents a month-by-month chronicle of the fighting.

1714. ———. "General Bradley's Decision ar Argentan (13 August 1944)." In: Kent R. Greenfield, ed. *Command Decisions*. Washington, D.C.: Office of the Chief of Military History, Department of the Army, 1960, pp. 401-417.

Concerns the failure to close the Falaise-Argentan "gap" before more than 35,000 German troops had escaped it.

1715. ———. "The Genesis of Monty's Master Plan." *Army*, IX (January 1959), 29-33.

Discusses the differences between Montgomery and Eisenhower over plans and their execution for D-Day and the Normandy fight, June 1-July 31, 1944.

1716. ———. *Liberation.* World War II Series. Alexandria, Va.: Time-Life Books, 1978. 208p.

A pictorial account of the battle for France and the liberation of Paris; many of the photographs are from the archives of *Life* magazine.

1717. ———. "Mortain." *American History Illustrated*, V (February 1970), 12-21.

Describes the German counterattack of August 7, 1944, undertaken against the U.S. First Army in an effort to cut off its armored spearheads and retake Avranches; the effort was a failure.

1718. ———. "The Mortain Counterattack: Future Portent?" *Army*, VIII (July 1958), 30-32+.

Retells the story of the Mortain counterattack and suggests that a similar operation could be undertaken in any future conflict.

1719. ———. "Normandy, 1944." In: Noble Frankland and Christopher Dowling, eds. *Decisive Battles of the 20th Century.* New York: David McKay, 1976, pp. 265-276.

A concise account of the Normandy campaign, including the fighting from D-Day through the breakout. Assigns significance to it.

1720. Boussel, Patrice. *D-Day Beaches Pocket Guide.* Garden City, N.Y.: Doubleday, 1966. 218p.

Extremely valuable for the tourist wanting to revisit or see for the first time the actual scene of the D-Day invasion; includes pictures, maps, accounts of the landing, and information on the countryside in the area.

1721. Bovee, D.E. "Hedgerow Fighting." *Infantry Journal*, LV (October 1944), 8-18.

Describes the difficulties of operating in the hedgerow country of Normandy and Brittany before the July 1944 breakout.

1722. "Breakthrough in France." *Life*, XVII (August 14, 1944), 19-25.

Still a useful pictorial piece on the Normandy breakout.

1723. Burgett, Donald. *Currahee! We Stand Alone: A Paratrooper's Account of the Normandy Invasion.* London: Hutchinson, 1967. 192p.

Recollections of the June 5/6 mission by a member of the Five Hundred Sixth Parachute Infantry Regiment, One Hundred First Airborne Division.

1724. Carlson, Robert H. "Surprise Opportunity Applied." *U.S. Army Combat Forces Journal*, I (December 1950), 18-20.

A brief overview of the Normandy operations of the Thirty-Eighth Infantry Regiment, Second Division, on July 11, 1944.

1725. Cawthorn, Charles R. "July 1944: St. Lô." *American Heritage*, XXV (April 1974), 4-11, 82-88.

A discussion of the campaign leading to the July 18, 1944, capture of this fortress town on the Vire River in northwestern France.

1726. ———. "The Plan Beyond the Assault." *Army*, VII (December 1958), 28-34.

Examines Allied plans for the Normandy campaign after the initial landings.

1727. ———. "Pursuit: Normandy, 1944--An Infantryman Remembers." *American Heritage*, XXIX (February 1978), 80-91.

A former sergeant who joined the battle on July 28, 1944, recalls how Patton's Third Army poured through a gap at Avranches.

1728. Chandler, Stedman. "The Fire Power of Company J." *U.S. Army Combat Forces Journal*, I (December 1950), 22-24.

Recalls the service of a unit of the Three Hundred Fifty-Ninth Regiment, Ninetieth Infantry Division, on the Moselle River front, November 9-13, 1944.

1729. Chaplin, William W. *52 Days: An NBC Reporter's Story of the Battle That Freed France*. Indianapolis: Bobbs-Merrill, 1944. 215p.

Records events during the 52 days after D-Day as seen by a radio reporter who broadcast to the U.S. from J.E.S.Q., a mobile radio truck in Normandy; includes reprints of actual communiques and anecdotes on the difficulties encountered in keeping the station operational.

1730. Cherniss, Ruth. "St. Lô: The Resurrection of a Dead City." *Saturday Review of Literature*, LII (July 5, 1969), 11-15+.

Comments on the great battle which took place 25 years earlier as well as the city's postwar rebuilding.

1731. Cole, Hugh M. *The Lorraine Campaign*. U.S. Army in World War II: The European Theater of Operations. Washington, D.C.: U.S. Government Printing Office, 1950. 657p.

The campaign waged in this part of France during the period September 1-December 18, 1944, is detailed, with the story of command decision at higher headquarters told only when it has a direct bearing on the campaign. The focus is on the tactical operations of Patton's Third Army and its subordinate units. The maps help the reader through a somewhat complex narrative.

1732. ———. "The Tank Battles in Lorraine." *Military Review*, XXIX (November 1949), 3-16.

Focuses on engagements between German tanks and Patton's armor during the operations of the Third Army in this part of France.

1733. Collins, Larry, and Dominique Lapierre. *Is Paris Burning?* New York: Simon and Schuster, 1965. 376p.

A Cornelius Ryan-like telling of the liberation of Paris in August 1944 with emphasis on the German failure to follow Hitler's order to destroy the city, the role of the French Resistance and Free French Army and the decisions and diversions of the U.S. Army and its leaders.

1734. ———. "The Story Behind the Liberation of Paris, A Quarter Century Ago." *New York Times Magazine* (September 7, 1969), 46-47+.

A succinct presentation of the information presented in the last entry.

1735. Cottingham, L.B. "Smoke over the Moselle." *Infantry Journal*, LXIII (August 1948), 14-19.

Follows the operations of the Eighty-Fourth Chemical Smoke Generator Company, U.S. Army, on the Moselle River, September 9-21, 1944, in the first ETO employment of smoke generators by the Allies in support of an assault river crossing.

1736. Courtney, William B. "Breakthrough for Paris." *Collier's*, CXIV (September 16, 1944), 14+.

A contemporary telling of the story so well done by Collins and Lapierre above.

1737. Critchell, Laurence. "Air Drop in Normandy." In: Frank Brookhauser, ed. *This Was Your War: An Anthology of Great Writings from World War II*. Garden City, N.Y.: Doubleday, 1960, pp. 107-112.

An account of the airborne drop behind German lines on the night of June 5/6, 1944.

1738. Crookenden, Napier. *Dropzone Normandy: The Story of the American and British Airborne Assault on D-Day, 1944.* New York: Scribners, 1976. 304p.

After a brief pre-Normandy history of U.S./U.K. parachute forces, this British general-participant analyzes the controversy surrounding the use of the airborne in Normandy and follows the actions of the major Allied and gliderborne and paratroop units in France on D-Day in a factual, if anecdotal, style.

1739. Davies, Arthur. "Geographical Factors in the Invasion and Battle of Normandy." *Geographical Journal*, XXXVI (October 1946), 613-631.

Examines such natural obstacles as beaches, tides, currents, hedgerows, etc.

1740. "D-Day in Europe." *Time*, LXXIII (June 8, 1959), 22-26.

A pictorial 15th anniversary tribute.

1741. *D-Day: The Normandy Invasion in Retrospect*. Lawrence: University Press of Kansas, 1971. 254p.

A collection of essays by former commanders and scholars, such as Omar Bradley and Martin Blumenson, which consider and evaluate such factors in the landings as planning, weather, logistics, equipment, gunfire support, air support, etc.

1742. Deveikis, Casey. "The 'Eager Beavers' Come to War." *Military Engineer*, XLI (September-October 1949), 373-377.

Recalls the work of the U.S. Thirteen Hundred Third Engineer Regiment in France between July and September 1944.

1743. Dupuy, R. Ernest. "A Morning to Remember." *Army*, VIII (June 1957), 42-45.

A reprinting of Eisenhower's famous D-Day broadcast.

1744. Dupuy, Trevor N., *et al*. "'Operation Cobra': The Allied Breakthrough in Normandy, 1944." In: their *A Study of Breakthrough Operations*. Dun Loring, Va.: Historical Evaluation and Research Organization, 1976, Chap. 8.

A narrative covering the background, plans, and execution of the Normandy breakout with conclusions on the effectiveness of the operation.

1745. Eisenhower, Dwight D. "General Eisenhower Describes the Great Invasion." In: Henry S. Commager and Alan Nevins, eds. *Heritage of America*. Boston, Mass.: Little, Brown, 1949, pp. 1174-1178.

A concise review by the Supreme Commander which is general and rather lacking in detail.

1746. ———. "The Significance of the Allied Landing in Normandy: Statement, June 5, 1954." *Department of State Bulletin*, XXX (June 21, 1954), 959.

The American President speaks of the freedom brought by the operation.

1747. Essame, Hubert. *Normandy Bridgehead*. Ballantine's Illustrated History of World War II. New York: Ballantine Books, 1970. 160p.

A pictorial review of the fighting in Normandy from D-Day, through the hedgerow combat, and onto the breakout for Paris.

1748. Field, Eugene J. "The 4th Cavalry Group in Combat." *Armored Cavalry Journal*, LVII (January-February 1948), 62-63.

In Normandy from D-Day through D-Day + 7.

1749. "The First Week in the Battle for France." *Military Review*, XXIX (October 1949), 95-104.

Consolidation of the Normandy beachhead and the beginning of the push inland.

1750. Florentin, Eddy. *The Battle of the Falaise*. Translated from the French. New York: Hawthorn Books, 1967. 362p.

First published in France in 1966, this account of the August 1944 destruction of German troops and equipment in the Argentan-Falaise Gap is based on war diaries, official histories, and the testimony of 700 battle participants.

1751. Foley, Cederic J. *Battle of the Falaise Gap*. Translated from the French. London: Elek Books, 1965. 336p.

Similar in certain respects to the preceding citation; describes the Anglo-American attacks on the German Seventh Army's escape route and wonders how so many Nazis managed to escape the trap.

1752. Fowler, John G., Jr. "Command Decision." *Military Review*, LIX (June 1979), 2-6.

Concerns Eisenhower's decision to "go" with the D-Day invasion.

1753. Fussell, Paul. "My War." *Harpers*, CCLXIV (January 1982), 40-48.

The author's recollections of service with the One Hundred Third Infantry Division in France in 1944.

1754. Gaskill, Gordon. "Bloody Beach: The Assault on Normandy." *American Magazine*, CXXXVIII (September 1944), 26-29+.

An eyewitness description of the difficulties on Omaha Beach on D-Day.

1755. ———. "The Day We Saved Chartres Cathedral." *Reader's Digest*, LXXXVII (August 1965), 102-107.

U.S. Seventh Armored Division action on August 16, 1944.

1756. Grow, Robert W. "Mobility Unused." *Military Review*, XXXII (February 1953), 18-24.

Activities of Twentieth Corps, Third Army during the Lorraine campaign.

1757. Hall, William C. "Bridging at Thionville." *Military Engineer*, XL (April 1948), 169-173.

Activities of the Thirteen Hundred Sixth Engineer General Service Regiment on the Moselle Rover, November 10-14, 1944.

1758. Harding, Thomas C., Jr. "The Shortest Way Home." *Armor*, LXXIII (January-February 1964), 46-47.

On the capture of Nancy by the Twelfth Corps, Third Army.

1759. Harrison, Gordon A. "Airborne Assault in Normandy." *Military Review*, XXIX (July 1949), 8-22.

Digested from Chapters 5 and 7 of the next entry's manuscript.

1760. ———. *Cross Channel Attack*. U.S. Army in World War II: The European Theater of Operations. Washington, D.C.: U.S. Government Printing Office, 1951. 519p.

An introduction to the tactical volumes in the "green book" series on the ETO, this volume covers in seven chapters the prelude to the June 6 assault--the preparations and discussions of strategy on both the Allied and German sides from 1941 to 1944--and describes in three chapters the combat operations of the First Army in Normandy from D-Day to July 1, 1944. The work is concerned primarily with the role of American forces, and Allied activities are covered only insofar as they relate to U.S. participation. Although new information has come to light on the political and intelligence backgrounds of D-Day, this work remains one of the best studies of "Operation Overlord."

1761. ———. "Hitting the Beaches." *Armor*, LX (January-February 1951), 14-21.

Digested from the above entry; describes the assault landings on Omaha and Utah Beaches on D-Day.

1762. ———. "Was D-Day a Mistake?" *Harpers*, CCIII (August 1951), 77-81.

Examines the political-military-strategical background of "Overlord."

1763. Hastings, Max. *Das Reich: The March of the 2nd SS Panzer Division Through France*. New York: Holt, Rinehart and Winston, 1982. 264p.

Based on documentary research and interviews, this work follows the movement of a German panzer unit from southwest France to Normandy in June 1944; held up by the French Resistance and Allied fighter bombers, Das Reich's attempt to save the Nazi position in Normandy was a failure.

1764. Haupt, Werner, and Uwe Feist. *Invasion D-Day, June 6, 1944*. Buena Park, Calif.: Feist Publications, 1968. 50p.

A pictorial which covers the first 24 hours of the Allied assault.

1765. Heysek, Thomas R. "The Battle of Metz, France, 1944." Unpublished Ph.D. Dissertation, University of Georgia, 1980.

Records the encirclement of the old capital of Lorraine in mid-November 1944 by the U.S. Thirteenth Corps (Third Army), the reduction of the old forts on the city's outskirts, and the town's capture on November 23.

1766. Hine, Al. *D-Day: The Invasion of Europe*. American Heritage Junior Library. New York: American Heritage, 1962. 153p.

A pictorial review of the planning for and execution of the Normandy invasion which may be the best starting place for young readers interested in the topic.

1767. Hogan, Pendleton. "Incident in Lorraine." *U.S. Army Combat Forces Journal*, I (May 1951), 31-33.

How Lt. Frederick D. Titterington cleared German mines from a bridge over the Nied Française River on November 11, 1944.

1768. Howarth, David A. *D-Day, the 6th of June*. New York: McGraw-Hill, 1959. 255p.

Basing his work on 30 interviews and other sources, the British journalist covers the invasion from the human interest viewpoint of junior officers and common soldiers who tell what it was like to be in the assault waves or the German defenses. Surprisingly, no mention is made of Omaha Beach. Compare with Cornelius Ryan below.

1769. ———. "D-Day, the Sixth of June." *Saturday Evening Post*, CCXXXI (March 14, 1959), 19-21+; (March 21, 1959), 42-43+; (March 28, 1959), 28-29+; (April 4, 1959), 32-33+; (April 11, 1959), 36+.

Serialized version of the last entry.

1770. Hunt, Robert, and David Mason. *The Normandy Campaign*. New York: Hippocrene Books, 1976. 158p.

A review of Allied landings and operations in Normandy, June-July 1944, with emphasis on the British effort to capture Caen; illustrated with 161 photographs.

1771. "Invasion, June 6, 1944." *Life*, XVI (June 12, 1944), 27-37.

Still a useful pictorial piece.

1772. Jackson, William G.F. *"Overlord": Normandy, 1944*. Cranbury, N.J.: University of Delaware Press, 1981. 256p.

Part of the "Politics and Strategy of the Second World War" series edited by Noble Frankland and Christopher Dowling. Portrays the hard-fought Anglo-American debates on invasion strategy alongside the equally bitter struggles within the German High Command as to how "Overlord" should be met and defeated. Examines the military factors governing the debates and looks at the Allied campaign of June 6 in detail.

1773. Johns, Glover S. *The Clay Pigeons of St. Lô*. Harrisburg, Pa.: Military Service Publishing Company, 1958. 256p.

Recollections of the commander of the First Batallion, One Hundred Fifteenth Infantry Regiment, Twenty-Ninth Infantry Division in the Normandy campaign from D-Day to the capture of St. Lô on July 18, 1944. Reprinted in 1979.

1774. Keegan, John. *Six Armies in Normandy*. New York: Viking Press, 1982. 365p.

Probing to discover a sense of the common infantryman's experience, the author analyzes the impact of the battle for Normandy on the participating armies of Germany and five Allied nations, including the U.S.

1775. Kemp, Anthony. *The Unknown Battle: Metz, 1944*. New York: Stein and Day, 1980. 250p.

Relying to a large extent on Cole's *The Lorraine Campaign*, cited above, this British fortifications expert examines Patton's drive to cross the Moselle River and capture the old capital of Lorraine, which was defended by a series of forts impervious to air and artillery bombardment; firsthand accounts liven the author's criticism of the many U.S. tactical errors which sent men on futile attacks against the dug-in Germans and of the Nazis for not conducting a more "active defense."

1776. Koskimaki, George E. *D-Day with the Screaming Eagles*. Kalamazoo, Mich.: 101st Airborne Division Association, 1977. 431p.

First published in 1970, this work is a collection of eyewitness narratives by 518 participants in the One Hundred First Airborne Division's night attack, ranging from division-command personnel to the troopers themselves; chronicles the series of events leading up to the loading of the planes, the emotions of the paratroopers en route, and the reactions of the individuals during the period shortly after landing. Acclaimed by "SLAM" Marshall as the best, most detailed account of D-Day ever written from the airborne soldier's standpoint.

1777. Lambert, J.C. "Armored Rescue." *Armored Cavalry Journal*, LVIII (January-February 1949), 36-45.

Follows the operations of the Fourteenth Armored Division in the Hatten-Rittershoffen campaign in Alsace, December 24, 1944, to January 20, 1945.

1778. Larrabee, Eric. "On the Far Shore: The Normandy Invasion." *American Heritage*, X (October 1959), 73-75.

A brief pictorial on the D-Day landings.

1779. Liebling, Abbott J. *Normandy Revisited*. New York: Simon and Schuster, 1958. 243p.

A review of the planning for and execution of "Operation Overlord," as seen by a noted correspondent aboard a Coast Guard LCI and recalled many years later as the 15th anniversary approached.

1780. ———. *The Road Back to Paris*. London: Joseph, 1944. 260p.

Liebling follows the U.S. and British campaigns in France from D-Day through the liberation of Paris with details on large battles and the work of common soldiers.

1781. Lord, John. "The Longest Wait: American Forces Before the Normandy Invasion." *American Heritage*, XX (June 1969), 4-15+.

Describes the waiting and tension among U.S. forces in England preparing for the invasion, including those loaded on the ships during that first week in June.

1782. Lucas, James S., and James Barker. *The Battle of Normandy: Falaise Gap*. New York: Holmes and Meier, 1978. 176p.

Making extensive use of German documents and diaries, the authors tell of the Allied trapping of 80,000 Wehrmacht soldiers in a large pocket in August 1944 and how nearly 35,000 escaped; the British authors' anti-American bias displayed toward the actions of U.S. troops is persistent and undocumented.

1783. McAdoo, Richard B. "Guns at Falaise Gap." *Harpers*, CCXVI (May 1958), 36-45.

Recounts the story of the Falaise pocket and the efforts of Allied troops and aircraft to ensure the total destruction of German units therein.

1784. MacDonald, James. "When the Tanks Strike in France." *New York Times Magazine* (August 20, 1944), 5+.

A general piece on the armored push of Patton's Third Army.

1785. McKee, Alexander. *Last Round Against Rommel: Battle of the Normandy Beachhead*. New York: New American Library, 1966. 336p.

The U.S. edition of the British title *Caen: Anvil of Victory*; reconstructs the British phase of "Operation Overlord" from June to mid-August 1944, including the Eisenhower-Montgomery debate on strategy and tactics.

1786. Macksey, Kenneth J. *Anatomy of a Battle*. New York: Stein and Day, 1974. 205p.

British author and tank expert Macksey analyzes the Normandy fighting from all sides, catching mistakes and missed opportunities as well as opportunities made and exploited.

1787. Majdalany, Fred. *The Fall of Fortress Europe*. Garden City, N.Y.: Doubleday, 1968. 442p.

An overview of the German development of and attempt to defend "Fortress Europe" between 1941 and the end of the Normandy campaign in 1944; includes a large number of biographical sketches of German officers ordered to hold the Atlantic Wall against the Allies.

1788. Marrin, Albert. *Overlord: D-Day and the Invasion of Europe*. New York: Atheneum, 1982. 177p.

This slim volume is the latest retelling of the D-Day story; describes events and strategy on both sides prior to, during, and after the landings. A useful introduction for beginning students.

1789. Marshall, Samuel L.A. "Affair at Hill 30." *Marine Corps Gazette*, XXXII (February 1948), 8-15; (March 1948), 20-25.

Recalls the experiences of the Third Battalion, Five Hundred Eighth Parachute Infantry Regiment, during the Normanday invasion, June 5/6-9, 1944.

1790. ———. "The First Wave at Omaha Beach." *Atlantic*, CCLXV (November 1960), 67-72.

Describes the stiff German resistance met on this Normandy beach by elements of Fifth Corps, U.S. First Army, on D-Day.

1791. ———. "How 'Papa' Liberated Paris." *American Heritage*, XIII (April 1962), 4-7, 92-101.

The author's experiences with Ernest Hemingway during the Liberation of Paris are recalled. For many, this will be Marshall's most interesting war story.

1792. ———. *Night Drop: The American Airborne Invasion of Normandy*. Boston, Mass.: Little, Brown, 1962. 425p.

Employing many interviews and other sources, Marshall recreated the story of the Eighty-Second and One Hundred First Airborne Division drops behind the German lines in Normandy just hours before the invasion, and their efforts to establish a foothold.

1793. ———. "The 111th Field Artillery Battalion on D-Day." *Field Artillery Journal*, XXXV (January 1945), 13-16.

Discusses the unit's difficulties in offloading and setting up.

1794. Mason, David. *Breakout: Drive to the Seine*. Ballantine's Illustrated History of World War II. New York: Ballantine Books, 1969. 160p.

A pictorial survey detailing the breakout of Allied forces from the stalemated Normandy beachhead through the hedgerows to victory over the retreating Germans in the Falaise pocket.

1795. Maurey, Eugene. "Close Support at Kaltenhouse." *Field Artillery Journal*, XXXV (April 1945), 205-207.

Artillery aspects of the capture of Kaltenhouse, Alsace, by the Seventy-Ninth Infantry Division on December 10, 1944.

1796. Michie, Allan A. "Great Decision: Behind the Scenes with Eisenhower." In: *Reader's Digest*, Editors of. *Thirtieth Anniversary Reader's Digest Reader*. Garden City, N.Y.: Doubleday, 1951, pp. 19-25.

Drawn from the next entry; Eisenhower's decision to "go" with the invasion.

1797. ———. *The Invasion of Europe: The Story Behind D-Day.* New York: Dodd, Mead, 1964. 203p.

Michie, a correspondent attached to SHAEF headquarters, reconstructs the strategy and problems behind the Allied invasion of Normandy in the summer of 1944; in addition to coverage of the landings, the author provides details on the pre-invasion reconnaissance, bombing, and deception efforts.

1798. Middleton, Drew. "Normandy Beachhead, One Year After." *New York Times Magazine* (June 3, 1945), 8+.

The author returns to the scene of the great landings and tells not only of the invasion but of the general backwater which Normandy had become.

1799. Morawetz, Francis E. "The Accuracy of the 8-inch Howitzer." *U.S. Army Combat Forces Journal*, I (May 1951), 36-37.

A brief look at the use of this huge cannon by the Nine Hundred Ninety-Seventh Field Artillery Battalion in Normandy during July 1944.

1800. *The Nancy Bridgehead.* Fort Knox, Ky.: U.S. Army Armor School, 1946. 29p.

A brief review of the role of the U.S. Fourth Armored Division in opening this key position.

1801. Nichols, W.J. "Where Is the Enemy?" *Military Review*, XXX (May 1950), 55-62.

Operations of the Seven Hundred Forty-Fifth Tank Battalion when it was attached to the U.S. First Infantry Division in September 1944.

1802. Norris, Frank W. "In France with the Mediums." *Field Artillery Journal*, XXXV (March 1945), 171-176.

The actions of the U.S. Nineteenth Division's artillery from Utah Beach to Metz, 1944.

1803. Nye, Robert O. "The Falaise-Argentan Pocket." *Army Quarterly and Defence Journal*, XCIII (January 1967), 168-176.

Examines the controversy engendered among Allied officers over the escape of 35,000 Germans from this gap in August 1944.

1804. Persons, Howard P., Jr. "St. Lô Breakthrough." *Military Review*, XXX (December 1950), 13-23.

Describes the "Cobra" operation of July 25, 1944; after carpet bombing, U.S. Seventh Corps Infantry held the shoulders of the penetration while armored and motorized infantry poured through the gap.

1805. Prados, John. "'Cobra' and Patton's 1944 Summer Offensive in France." *Strategy and Tactics*, no. 65 (November-December 1977), 4-14.

Examines the Normandy breakout and the rush of the U.S. Third Army across France.

1806. Pyle, Ernest T. ("Ernie"). "Ernie Pyle Describes Hedgerow Fighting in Normandy." In: Henry S. Commager and Alan Nevins, eds. *Heritage of America*. Boston, Mass.: Little, Brown, 1949, pp. 1178-1182.

Still one of the most interesting portraits of the difficulties of combat in Normandy prior to the breakout; told from the G.I. standpoint.

1807. ———. "The Toughest Beachhead in the World." *Science Digest*, XVI (September 1944), 13-14.

A brief review of the invasion at Omaha Beach.

1808. Renaud, Alexandre. *Saint-Mère Eglise: First American Bridgehead in France, 6th June 1944*. Translated from the French. Monaco: Pathé, 1964. 198p.

A tribute by the people in this Normandy crossroads town inland of Utah Beach; when captured by the men of the Eighty-Second Airborne Division early on D-Day, the town became the first in France to be liberated by the U.S.

1809. Roberts, Palmer W. "D-Day: Europe, 1944." *Navy Civilian Engineer*, XX (Summer-Fall 1979), 15-18.

A brief accounting of the actions of U.S. Navy Seabee construction teams on Omaha and Utah Beaches during and just after the landings.

1810. Rohmer, Richard. *Patton's Gap: An Account of the Battle of Normandy, 1944*. New York: Beaufort Books, 1981. 240p.

Canadian general Rohmer, who flew a P-51 over the D-Day beaches, examines here not only the role of reconnaissance in the campaign, but the far larger and more controversial question of who was responsible for allowing over a third of the Germans trapped in the Falaise Gap to escape. After considering the evidence, responsibility for this costly command blunder, which left open an avenue of escape, is not laid, as the title suggests, upon George Patton, but, rather, upon the British general Montgomery. Certainly one of the most controversial books listed in this part.

1811. Ryan, Cornelius. "Background: The Longest Day." *TV Guide*, XIX (November 13, 1970), 20-23.

A concise telling of the D-Day story as preparation for viewers of the television presentation of the film made from the next entry.

1812. ———. *The Longest Day, June 6, 1944*. New York: Simon and Schuster, 1959. 350p.

Far and away the most popular "popular" history cited in this part, this work by a wartime correspondent is based on research in primary sources and, more important, hundreds of interviews with participants from both the Allied and German sides. The story is told not only from the viewpoint of leaders and generals, but also from the human interest angles of common German, British, and American soldiers. This anecdotal work, which was serialized in *Reader's Digest* and made into a popular film, was published the same year and in competition with David Howarth's record, cited above.

1813. ———. "Untold Stories from the Longest Day." *Reader's Digest*, CIV (June 1974), 73-79.

Includes additional anecdotes on D-Day not published in the last entry.

1814. Schmidt, Paul K. *Invasion--They're Coming!: The German Account of the Allied Landings and the 80 Days' Battle for France.* By Paul Carrel, pseud. Translated from the German. New York: E.P. Dutton, 1963. 288p.

Acting as something of a natural follow-up to Ryan and employing the same technique of anecdotal presentation based on hundreds of interviews, Schmidt tells the story of D-Day from the German viewpoint and recounts the unsuccessful efforts to contain the Normandy breakout and escape, among other traps, the one created by the Falaise Gap.

1815. Seaman, Jonathan O. "The Reduction of the Colmar Pocket." *Military Review*, XXXI (October 1951), 37-40.

The Colmar Pocket was a holdout position of the German Nineteenth Army on the west bank of the Rhine around this Alsatian city which defied French advances for two months; late in December 1944 in "Operation Northwind" the Nazis roared north out of the pocket to attack Strasbourg but were stopped by a renewed French drive assisted by the U.S. Twenty-First.

1816. Soffer, Lewis R. "An M-12 Battalion in Combat." *Field Artillery Journal*, XXXV (January 1945), 29-31.

Reviews the service of the U.S. Nine Hundred Ninety-First Field Artillery Battalion, which employed self-propelled 155mm guns in France from the Normandy landing through the battle of Falaise.

1817. Speidel, Hans. *Invasion 1944: Rommel and the Normandy Campaign.* Translated from the German. Chicago: Regnery, 1950. 176p.

The author was chief of staff to, successively, German field marshals Rommel, Kluge, and Model and tells of the surprise of the landings and the vain German effort to contain them, including Hitler's refusal to release for action nearby reserve panzer units.

1818. Stagg, James M. *Forecast for Overlord, June 6, 1944.* New York: W.W. Norton, 1972. 128p.

Written by the (British) chief meteorologist to SHAEF and based on his diary, this story describes the plans, preparations, and bureaucratic infighting surrounding weather forecasting for D-Day; also includes an assessment of the impact of weather on the invasion, both with regard to Eisenhower's decision to "go" and to the great storm which nearly destroyed the artificial harbor supporting the invasion beaches.

1819. Thompson, P.W. "D-Day on Omaha Beach." *Infantry Journal*, LVI (June 1945), 34-48.

A first anniversary review of the difficulties faced by U.S. troops in capturing this heavily defended Normandy real estate.

1820. ———. "Why Normandy?" *Infantry Journal*, LVIII (February 1946), 8-14.

The choice of Normandy was based on a deception laid on to convince the Germans the invasion would be made elsewhere.

1821. Thompson, Reginald W. *D-Day: Spearhead of Invasion*. Ballantine's Illustrated History of World War II. New York: Ballantine Books, 1968. 160p.

The first battle book in this popular series offers a pictorial review of the Allied invasion on June 6 and the German defense.

1822. Thornton, Willis. *The Liberation of Paris*. New York: Harcourt, Brace, and World, 1962. 231p.

Describes the August 1944 rising of the French Resistance within the city, the limited defense and evacuation of the Germans, Eisenhower's initial decision to bypass the city, and his change of heart which allowed the French Second Armored and U.S. Fourth Infantry Divisions to enter the city on August 25; finishing with an account of DeGaulle's triumphant entry, this work should be compared to the account by Collins and Lapierre cited above.

1823. Tobin, Richard L. *Invasion Journal*. New York: E.P. Dutton, 1944. 223p.

An anecdotal human interest account of this reporter's passage to England aboard a U.S. transport, the D-Day invasion as seen from H.M. battleship *Warspite*, and his exploits ashore covering American troops in the hedgerow fighting and "Cobra" breakout.

1824. Toole, John H. *Battle Diary*. N.p., 1978. 177p.

Recollections of a company commander in the U.S. Fifteenth Infantry Regiment during the U.S. Third Division's battle for France in 1944; includes anecdotes about the lives and exploits of enlisted G.I.'s.

1825. Tozer, Elizabeth. "How Eisenhower Gambled on History's Most Fateful Weather Forecast." *Popular Science*, CLXX (June 1957), 72-76+.

Explains the importance of weather to a successful D-Day invasion and Eisenhower's decision to "go" based on weather data he obtained from Stagg, cited above, on probable weather patterns for June 6.

1826. Turner, John F. *Invasion '44: The First Full Story of D-Day in Normandy*. New York: G.P. Putnam, 1959. 248p.

Published the same year as Howarth and Ryan, to which this work should be compared, this undocumented popular account considers the plans, preparations, and events of the invasion; told with a pro-British bias which concentrates on the massiveness of the operation (few G.I./Tommy anecdotes), the work concludes with information on such special projects as "Operation PLUTO" and the Mulberry harbors.

1827. Tute, Warren, John Costello, and Terry Hughes. *D-Day*. New York: Macmillan, 1974. 256p.

Employing extracts from diaries and memoirs as well as a number of rare photographs (some in color), the authors reconstruct the planning for and execution of the Normandy invasion as seen from both the Allied and German viewpoints.

1828. United States. War Department. Historical Division. *Omaha Beachhead (6 June-13 June 1944)*. American Forces in Action. Washington, D.C.: U.S. Government Printing Office, 1945. 167p.

Employing maps, photographs, and annexes, this paperback reconstructs the assault on and consolidation of Omaha Beach by units of the U.S. First Army.

1829. ———. ———. ———. *St. Lô (7 July-19 July 1944)*. American Forces in Action. Washington, D.C.: U.S. Government Printing Office, 1947. 128p.

Employing photographs, maps, and annexes, this popularly written account tells of the battle for and capture of this communications center in July 1944.

1830. ———. ———. ———. *Utah Beach to Cherbourg (6 June-27 June 1944)*. American Forces in Action. Washington, D.C.: U.S. Government Printing Office, 1947. 213p.

This popularly written paperback, using maps, photographs, and annexes, describes the First Army campaign and capture of this Cotentin Peninsula port city in the weeks immediately after D-Day.

1831. Wertenbaker, Charles C. "D-Day." In: Margaret C. Scoggin, ed. *Battle Stations: True Stories of Men in War*. New York: Alfred A. Knopf, 1953, pp. 187-210.

An account of the landings drawn from the next entry.

1832. ———. *Invasion*. New York: Appleton-Century-Crofts, 1944. 168p.

A reporter's chronicle of the D-Day invasion from its planning stages to the occupation of Cherbourg on June 27, 1944; illustrated with a number of interesting photographs taken by Robert Capa of *Life* magazine.

1833. West, Arthur L., Jr., and Crosby P. Miller. "Troyes--An Armored Attack." *Armor*, LXXII (November-December 1963), 4-9.

Concerns the capture of this French town by the Third Army on August 25-26, 1944.

1834. Wolfert, Ira. "Beachhead Panorama: Going Ashore with the Troops." *Reader's Digest*, XLV (August 1944), 122-128.

1835. ———. "The Invasion: A Great Event in History." *Reader's Digest*, XLV (August 1944), 112-121.

Two accounts of the D-Day landings (the first eyewitness) which describe for the home folks the planning and execution of history's largest amphibious undertaking.

1836. Wright, Charles E. "Moselle River Crossing at Cattenom." *Armored Cavalry Journal*, LVII (May-June 1948), 50-53+.

A study in coordination, October 15-November 19, 1944.

1837. Young, Peter. *Great Battles of World War II: D-Day*. Northbrook, Ill.: Quality Books International, 1981. 160p.

A reconstruction of the landings and beachhead securement, including the author's recollections of service as a British commander; includes some 100 photographs and maps, over half of which are in color.

c. HOLLAND/BELGIUM/GERMANY

Introduction: The Allied campaign to liberate the Low Countries and move to victory on the ground inside Germany was nowhere near as mobile as the dash across France. Not only did the weather and terrain stiffen as the Anglo-Americans approached and entered the Fatherland, but so too did Nazi resistance, stiffened, some believe, by Joseph Goebbels' skillful use of propaganda concerning Allied war aims and unconditional surrender, topics covered in Section II:A above. The citations in this part follow the U.S. land campaign in Holland, Belgium, and Germany from the late fall of 1944 through VE-Day in May 1945. Here readers will find references to two of the most controversial battles of the war: the Ardennes counterattack (popularly called the Battle of the Bulge) and the preceding Allied airborne effort to capture a bridgehead across the Rhine at Arnhem. For references to the air and sea aspects of these operations, users should consult Sections III:C:2 and 3 above and V:C:2 below. Certain of the biographies and memoirs cited in IV:B above and the unit histories in IV:D below may also prove helpful.

1838. Allen, Peter. *One More River: The Rhine Crossings of 1945*. New York: Scribners, 1980. 318p.

The great natural German defense barrier and largest and strongest water obstacle in the Western Theater, the Rhine was first crossed by the Ninth Armored Division, First Army, at Remagen on March 7, 1945. Later in the month, U.S. airborne forces joined those of Great Britain in a paradrop behind German lines on the eastern side while ground troops were ferried across. Allen provides information on the difficulties faced by the Allies in fording this water barrier as well as maps and photographs which help readers to follow the text.

1839. "Allied Armies Vault the Rhine." *Life*, XVIII (April 2, 1945), 21-27.

Still a useful pictorial piece.

1840. Ambrose, Stephen E. *Eisenhower and Berlin, 1945: The Decision to Halt at the Elbe*. New York: W.W. Norton, 1967. 119p.

The British believed it important to postwar dealing with the Soviets that the Western Allies reach the German capital first and the U.S. chiefs of staff left the decision to the Supreme Commander; Eisenhower, in turn, elected not to attempt the Berlin capture on the basis that the casualties taken could not justify the event, which he knew would soon be nullified by a withdrawal to previously agreed upon occupation zones.

1841. Baldwin, Hanson W. "Our Greatest Battle." *New York Times Magazine* (December 15, 1946), 7-9+; (December 29, 1946), 18+.

A full report on the Battle of the Bulge written a year after the event by a leading military analyst.

1842. Balkoski, Joseph. "'Operation Grenade': The Battle for the Rhineland, 23 February-5 March 1945." *Strategy and Tactics* (January-February 1981), 4-15.

An overview of the American battles along the approaches to the Rhine River in early 1945.

1843. Baron, Richard, Abe Baum, and Richard Goldhurst. *Raid!: The Untold Story of Patton's Secret Mission*. New York: G.P. Putnam, 1981. 283p.

During the last weeks of the war, General Patton authorized a task force under co-author Baum to liberate the POW camp at Hammelburg where a suspected 200 U.S. captives would be found; the entry to the camp was easy, but instead of 200 men, the soldiers found 1,500 including co-author Baron and Patton's son-in-law. Then came the nightmarish search for a route back. Well written and dramatic.

1844. "Battle of Huertgen Forest." *Life*, XVIII (January 1, 1945), 33-36.

Still a useful pictorial piece on the bitter fighting in the dense terrain which covered roughly the triangle of Aachen-Dueren-Monschau.

1845. *The Battle of St. Vith, Belgium, 17-23 November 1944*. Fort Knox, Ky.: The U.S. Army Armor School, 1965. 33p.

The activities of the U.S. Seventh Armored Division in the contest for this town waged against the Wehrmacht from December 16 to 21, 1944, the group's withdrawal, and later recapture of the Belgian village on January 23, 1945.

1846. The Battle of the Bulge. *After the Battle*, no. 3 (1974), 1-56.

A pictorial review of the great December 1944 German counteroffensive in the Ardennes.

1847. Bell, Paul B. "Tank Destroyers in the Roer River Crossing." *Field Artillery Journal*, XXXV (August 1945), 497-499.

Actions of the Second Tank Destroyer Group with the U.S. Twenty-Ninth and Thirtieth Divisions beginning on February 23, 1945.

1848. Blumenson, Martin. "The Hammelburg Affair." *Army*, XV (October 1965), 16-18+.

1849. ———. "The Hammelburg Mission." *Military Review*, XXXV (May 1955), 26-31.

Blumenson presents two pieces which contain the outline of the controversial chase after Patton's son-in-law, so well covered by Baron and company in the above citation.

1850. Blumentritt, Günther. "The Battle of the Bulge." *Collier's*, CXXXI (January 3, 1945), 16-25.

The former German General der Infanterie commanded the German Fifteenth Army during the Ardennes counteroffensive and recalls the mistakes made on both sides.

1851. Boesch, Paul. *Road to Huertgen: Forest in Hell*. Houston, Tx.: Gulf, 1962. 254p.

A U.S. infantryman recalls the horror of fighting in the dense, dark forest just inside the German border; the account is told from the viewpoint of a common soldier without a large amount of attention to the activities of generals or strategy behind the campaign.

1852. Bortz, Abe. "The First Army Jumps the Rhine." *Military Engineer*, LIV (September-October 1962), 342-347.

Describes "Operation Varsity," the dropping of the British Sixth and U.S. Seventeenth Airborne Divisions of the First Allied Airborne Army east of the river in the most successful paradrop of the Allies' northwest Europe campaign.

1853. Breuer, William B. *Bloody Clash at Sadzot: Hitler's Final Strike for Antwerp*. St. Louis, Mo.: Zeus Publishers, 1981. 240p.

Tells how on December 17-18 during the Battle of the Bulge, Mjr. Paul J. Solis with a small task force denied a crucial fuel depot to the spearhead of the German Sixth Panzer Division by pouring gasoline into a road cut near this small Belgian town on the Amblève River.

1854. Briggs, Richard A. *The Battle of the Ruhr Pocket*. West Point, N.Y.: Tioga Book Press, 1957. 84p.

A brief recollection of how the U.S. First and Ninth Armies met on the east side of the Ruhr industrial area on April 1, 1945, trapping German Army Group B and part of Army Group H which surrendered 325,000 men.

1855. Brownlow, Donald C. *Panzer Baron: The Military Exploits of General Hasso von Manteuffel*. West Hanover, Mass.: Christopher Publishing House, 1975. 176p.

This dynamic General der Panzertruppen saw service not only in Tunisia and on the Eastern Front, but commanded the Fifth Panzer Army during the Ardennes counteroffensive in December 1944. This work follows his entire wartime career with emphasis on his use of mobility, ending with his surrender to the U.S. Eighth Infantry Division on May 3, 1945.

1856. "The Capture of Burgelin." *Armored Cavalry Journal*, LIII (September-October 1949), 34-39.

Provides details on how this city in the Ruhr was taken by the U.S. Seventh Armored Division in spring 1945.

1857. Chandler, David G. "The Bridge at Remagen, March 7, 1945." *History Today*, XXIX (March 1979), 194-197.

A pictorial outline piece explaining how men of the U.S. Ninth Armored Division captured this strategic Rhine River bridge and the subsequent impact of the capture on German forces east of the barrier.

1858. Chang, Ronnie C. "Bridge at Remagen." *Engineer*, IX (Winter 1979), 8-11.

Describes not only the bridge's capture, but the efforts of U.S. Army engineers to keep it standing after it was damaged by German sappers; the bridge collapsed ten days after its capture, but not before other bridges had been built across the Rhine and many men had crossed.

1859. Chant, Christopher. "The Defense of Bastogne." In: Philip de Ste. Croix, ed. *Airborne Operations: An Illustrated Encyclopedia of the Great Battles of Airborne Forces*. New York: Crescent Books, 1978, pp. 128-133.

Resting after the rigors of the Arnhem operation, the U.S. One Hundred First Airborne Division acquired an enviable reputation for dour defensive fighting during the Battle of the Bulge.

1860. ———. "The Rhine Crossings." In: Philip de Ste. Croix, ed. *Airborne Operations: An Illustrated Encyclopedia of the Great Battles of Airborne Forces*. New York: Crescent Books, 1978, pp. 134-140.

An overview of the Allies' most successful ETO airborne mission, "Operation Varsity."

1861. Chase, Francis, Jr. "The Rhine Was 1,000 Miles Wide." *Saturday Evening Post*, CCXVII (May 5, 1945), 20+.

On the ferrying of U.S. troops from the west to east banks of the Rhine River in March 1945.

1862. Chuikov, Vasilii I. *The Fall of Berlin*. Translated from the Russian. New York: Holt, Rinehart and Winston, 1968. 261p.

Mixing in only a limited amount of propaganda, Marshal Chuikov, hero of the Soviet defense of Stalingrad, provides a candid personal account, filled with detail and analysis, on the last great battle in the ETO as conducted by his Eighth Guards Army. The author plays down the contributions of the Western Allies. His account, written under the Khruschev regime when the marshal's star was at its height, was later attacked by Russian historians as a falsification.

1863. Clarke, Bruce C. "The Battle for St. Vith: Armor in the Defense and Delay." *Armor*, LXXXIII (November-December 1974), 39-40.

The wartime commander of the U.S. Seventh Armored Division describes his use of tanks in a delaying action which upset the German advance during the Battle of the Bulge.

1864. Cole, Hugh M. *The Ardennes: Battle of the Bulge*. U.S. Army in World War II: The European Theater of Operations. Washington, D.C.: U.S. Government Printing Office, 1965. 720p.

The official Army history of the German winter counter-offensive from its jump-off on December 16, 1944, until Allied armies were ready to eliminate the bulge in their lines in early January 1945 is here related with German planes and Allied reaction described in detail. The coverage of the battle action is based on official sources and numerous interviews with Nazi and Allied participants, especially U.S. commanders and troops. The maps are helpful in understanding the text.

1865. ———. "The Origins of the Battle of the Bulge." *Army*, XV (December 1964), 22-30.

A discussion of German aims and strategy and the Allied failure to uncover them before the attack started.

1866. Colon, William. "Crossing the Rhine." *Infantry*, LXXII (July-August 1982), 30-33.

A brief outline piece on how the U.S. armies overcame the largest and final barrier to the heartland of the Reich.

1867. Cooper, P.W. *Rhine Crossing*. Ballantine's Illustrated History of World War II. New York: Ballantine Books, 1968. 160p.

In addition to "Operation Varsity," the airborne mission, this pictorial describes the lift-over of more than 50,000 troops and thousands of vehicles and pieces of ordnance in one 72-hour period in late March 1945.

1868. Creel, George. "Patton at the Pay-Off." *Collier's*, CXV (January 13, 1945), 24-25+.

Describes how the U.S. Third Army was taken out of line and rushed to the defense of Americans caught in the Ardennes counteroffensive.

1869. Cress, J.B. "Bridging the Rhine at Wesel." *Military Engineer*, XXVIII (November-December 1949), 433-436.

Follows the work of the Ten Hundred Fifty-Sixth Engineer Group, a U.S. Ninth Army outfit, at a town on the Rhine directly above Duisburg.

1870. Crookenden, Napier. *The Battle of the Bulge, 1944*. New York: Scribners, 1980. 160p.

A British airborne expert describes the concept and execution of the German Ardennes counteroffensive and the defense put up by the U.S. One Hundred First Airborne Division in Bastogne; illustrated with maps and a large number of photographs.

1871. Dalrymple, John C. "Engineer Combat Group in the Rhine Crossing." *Military Review*, XXVIII (August 1945), 42-52.

Describes the actions of the Eleven Hundred Seventeenth Engineer Group at Wesel in March 1945; compare with Cress's article, cited above.

1872. David, Lester. "Christmas in Bastogne." *American Legion Magazine*, CXI (December 1981), 16-17, 44-48.

Recalls in detail the defense of the One Hundred First Airborne Division in the besieged Belgian town, especially how its members spent Christmas in combat.

1873. Davis, Franklin M., Jr. *Across the Rhine*. World War II Series. Alexandria, Va.: Time-Life Books, 1980. 208p.

A description of the Allied effort in March-April 1945 to cross the last great barrier cutting them off from an invasion of the central Reich; includes discussion of the Remagen bridge, "Operation Varsity," and the manner in which troops were ferried over. Includes a large number of photographs, many taken by *Life* magazine cameramen.

1874. ———. *Breakthrough, the Epic Story of the Battle of the Bulge--The Greatest Pitched Battle in American History*. Derby, Conn.: Monarch Books, 1961. 159p.

Davis tells the familiar story of the German counteroffensive and the stout defense thrown up by scattered American units with emphasis on the greater fighting quality of U.S. troops.

1875. Dawley, Jay P. "Combat Across the Roer." *Military Engineer*, XLVII (January-February 1955), 32-39.

Follows U.S. First Army (Seventh Corps) bridgebuilding operations during its February 1945 crossing of the Roer River.

1876. *The Defense of St. Vith, Belgium.* Fort Knox, Ky.: Army Armored School, 1949. 47p.

An overview of the role of the Seventh Armored Division at this town during the Battle of the Bulge.

1877. Deveikis, Casey. "Building Patton's Rhine River Bridge." *Military Engineer*, XL (February 1948), 71-74.

Its March 27-April 16, 1945, construction by the Thirteen Hundred Third Engineers at Mainz, Germany.

1878. "Did Eisenhower Lose the War?" *Collier's*, CXVIII (August 3, 1946), 74.

A review of the Supreme Commander's decision not to take Berlin.

1879. Dollinger, Hans. *The Decline and Fall of Nazi Germany and Imperial Japan: A Pictorial History of the Final Days of World War II.* Translated from the German. New York: Crown, 1968. 432p.

Over half of this excellent pictorial is devoted to the Allied conquest of the Reich from January through May 1945; detail is particularly strong as to the impact of the Allied advance on German troops and civilians. Includes photostats of official orders and pages from the Allied German-language propaganda newspaper "News for the Troops."

1880. Draper, Theodore. "The Battle of the Bulge: Classic Offensive Campaign in the Ardennes." *Infantry Journal*, LVI (May 1945), 8-17.

One of the first accounts in a military journal of the full extent of the German planning for and execution of their Ardennes counteroffensive as well as the initial confusion caused in Allied circles. Based on item 1882 below.

1881. ———. *The 84th Infantry Division in the Battle of Germany, November 1944-May 1945.* New York: Viking Press, 1946. 260p.

Based on official records and personal interviews with men during the fighting or just returned from the front, this work follows a U.S. Ninth Army division from France, through the Ardennes, to the Ruhr and central Germany in text accompanied by useful photographs and maps.

1882. ———. *The 84th Infantry Division in the Battle of the Ardennes, December 1944-January 1945.* New York: Viking Press, 1945. 260p.

Follows this unit of the Eighth Corps in the counterattack from the western edge of the Bulge toward Bastogne.

1883. Duncan, W.D. "Tanks and Infantry in Night Attacks." *Armored Cavalry Journal*, LVII (January-February 1948), 56-61.

Action of the U.S. Thirtieth Infantry Division and two attached units in the vicinity of Lich, Oberembt, and Kirchtroisdorf from February 25 to 27, 1945.

1884. Dupuy, R. Ernest. "The Incredible Valor of Eric Wood in the Battle of St. Vith." *Saturday Evening Post*, CCXX (December 29, 1947), 26+.

Examines the actions of one U.S. infantryman in the defense against the German Ardennes counteroffensive.

1885. ———. "Parker's Crossroads." *Infantry Journal*, LXII (April 1948), 14-16.

Activities of the Five Hundred Eighty-Ninth Field Artillery Battalion of the One Hundred Sixth Infantry Division in the Ardennes, December 19-23, 1944.

1886. Edmonson, Ross. "He Waited His Turn to Die." *Military Journal*, II (Winter 1978-1979), 20-21, 49.

Recollections of a Two Hundred Eighty-Fifth Field Artillery Observation Battalion survivor of the December 17, 1944, Malmedy Massacre.

1887. Eisenhower, Dwight D. "Americans Seize a Bridge at Remagen and Cross the Rhine." In: Henry S. Commager and Alan Nevins, eds. *Heritage of America*. Boston, Mass.: Little, Brown, 1949, pp. 1182-1185.

The Supreme Commander recalls his reactions to news of the bridge's capture and records the crossing which followed.

1888. ———. "My Views on Berlin." *Saturday Evening Post*, CCXXXIV (December 9, 1961), 19-29.

The former President and Supreme Commander defends his decision not to capture the German capital.

1889. Eisenhower, John S.D. *The Bitter Woods: The Dramatic Story, Told at All Echelons, from Supreme Command to Squad Leader, of the Crisis That Shook the Western Coalition--Hitler's Surprise Ardennes Offensive*. New York: G.P. Putnam, 1969. 506p.

The Supreme Commander's son, who saw 30 months' service with the U.S. First Army in World War II, tells the whole story of the ETO campaign after D-Day with particular emphasis on the strategy and tactics of the Battle of the Bulge; basing his work on interviews, visits to the battlefields, and primary and secondary sources, Eisenhower covers command decisions and small unit actions. Includes useful photographs, but the mapwork is inadequate to guide readers through the textual detail.

1890. Ellison, Marvin C. "Landing Craft in River Crossings." *U.S. Naval Institute Proceedings*, LXXII (January 1946), 121-123.

A brief review of the role of U.S. Navy landing craft in the ferrying of men across the Rhine in spring 1945.

1891. Elstob, Peter. *Bastogne: The Road Block*. Ballantine's Illustrated History of World War II. New York: Ballantine Books, 1968. 160p.

Examines the importance of the Belgian town to the Germans during their counteroffensive and the stubborn defense and famous relief of the place by U.S. forces. Part of a noted pictorial series.

1892. ———. "The Battle of the Bulge: The Last Gasp, Belgium, 1944." In: Bernard Fitzsimons, ed. *Tanks and Weapons of World War II*. New York: Beekman House, 1973, pp. 126-131.

An account of the role of German and American armor in the Ardennes contest, first published in Purnell's *History of the Second World War*.

1893. ———. *Hitler's Last Offensive*. New York: Macmillan, 1971. 413p.

First published in England, this detailed survey of the Battle of the Bulge is well organized and written, covering the story from both the German and Allied standpoints from command to small unit, but is devoid of new information. Compare with John Eisenhower's effort noted above.

1894. Essame, Hubert. *The Battle for Germany*. New York: Scribners, 1969. 228p.

A former member of Montgomery's staff views the conquest of northwest Europe, especially Germany, in 1944-1945; attempting fairness, the author nevertheless sides with his former boss in his discussions of those strategic and tactical arguments between Monty, Eisenhower, and Bradley.

1895. Exton, Hugh M. "The Guards Armored Division in 'Operation Market Garden.'" *Armored Cavalry Journal*, LVII (May-June 1948), 2-8.

The September 17-25, 1944, Holland operations of the British tank unit of Thirtieth Corps, Second Army, in relation to its effort to relieve the U.S. Eighty-Second Airborne Division at Nijmegen.

1896. Featherstone, Donald. *Wargaming Airborne Operations*. New York: International Publications Service, 1977. 250p.

Designed for students of board wargames, this work presents a detailed analysis of the Allied airborne attempt to capture the bridges at Arnhem-Nijmegen, Holland, in September 1944 and the German countermoves which prevented the "Market-Garden" operation's success.

1897. Fox, Frederic. "The Battle of the Bulge as Seen from Headquarters." *New York Times Magazine* (December 12, 1954), 14-15+.

A recollection of the confusion existing at Allied HQ during the initial phase of the German counteroffensive and the gradual reaction of the "brass" designed to contain it.

1898. Frank, Stanley B. "The Glorious Collapse of the 106th: The Battle of the Bulge." *Saturday Evening Post*, CCXIX (November 9, 1946), 32-33+.

In the most serious reverse to American arms in the MTO/ETO, the German Fifth Panzer Army surrounded the One Hundred Sixth near St. Vith and captured two of its regiments--8,000 men.

1899. Friedheim, Eric. "Rhineland Rendezvous." *Air Force*, XXVIII (May 1945), 4-7.

An overview of "Operation Varsity," the paradrop of the First Allied Airborne Army beyond the Rhine in March 1945.

1900. Frost, John. *A Drop Too Many*. London: Cassell, 1980. 254p.

The British commander who tried to hold Arnhem bridge during the "Market-Garden" operation reviews the great airdrops and battles of that campaign, including the U.S. Eighty-Second Airborne descent upon Nijmegen.

1901. Fuller, John F. "'Market Garden'--The Operation That Failed." *Airlift Operations Review*, II (October-December 1980), 24-28.

An overview of the disastrous Allied airborne attempt to capture bridges over the Rhine River in Holland in September 1944.

1902. Gallagher, Richard. *The Malmedy Massacre*. New York: Paperback Library, 1964. 158p.

In the worst atrocity of the ETO involving U.S. troops, some 86 of 100 U.S. Two Hundred Eighty-Fifth Field Artillery Observation Battalion prisoners were machine-gunned to death by the Germans near this Belgian town on December 17, 1944.

1903. Ganz, A. Harding. "Breakthrough to Bastogne." *Armor*, XC (November-December 1981), 12-18.

After briefly describing the siege of the One Hundred First Airborne Division in the city during the German Ardennes counteroffensive, this work concentrates on the relief mission of the U.S. Fourth Armored Division, which broke through to the defenders on December 26.

1904. Gavin, James M. "The Airborne Army's First Test." *Infantry Journal*, LXII (January 1948), 22-30; (February 1948), 39-46.

A detailed look at operations by the U.S. Eighty-Second and One Hundred First Airborne Divisions in "Operation Market-Garden" in Holland, September 10-26, 1944.

1905. ———. "Bloody Huertgen: The Battle That Should Never Have Been Fought." *American Heritage*, XXXI (December 1979), 32-44.

Examines the nightmare of fighting in this dark forest just inside the German border and criticizes U.S. leaders for sending their troops into it.

1906. "German Press Comments on the Ardennes Breakthrough." *Military Review*, XXV (October 1945), 87-92.

Examines Joseph Goebbels' account of the Allied campaign in the Ardennes in late fall 1944, before the German counterattack.

1907. Goolrick, William K., and Ogden Tanner. *The Battle of the Bulge*. World War II Series. Alexandria, Va.: Time-Life Books, 1979. 208p.

The text, with accompanying photographs, many taken by *Life* magazine reporters during the events described, provides information on the planning and execution of the German Ardennes counteroffensive and the Allied reaction to it. A useful introduction.

1908. Gorman, James B. "Narrow Is the Way." *Armor*, LXXIV (September-October 1965), 13-16.

On the difficulties of crossing over the newly captured Rhine River bridge at Remagen.

1909. Greene, Michael J.L. "Contact at Houffalize." *Armored Cavalry Journal*, LVIII (May-June 1949), 36-44.

Follows the operations of the Forty-First Cavalry Reconnaissance Squadron of the U.S. Eleventh Armored Division in the Bastogne area, January 15-16, 1945.

1910. Gun, Nerin E. *The Day of the Americans*. New York: Fleet, 1966. 317p.

Recollections of the Nazi concentration camps liberated by U.S. troops in the spring of 1945, including the overrunning of Dachau by the Forty-Second and Forty-Fifth Infantry Divisions.

1911. Hamel, George F. "The Crailsheim Operation of the 10th Armored Division." *Armored Cavalry Journal*, LVIII (March-April 1949), 34-45.

Operations in south-central Germany, April 1-10, 1945.

1912. Hanlon, John. "The Bell Rings in Hemroulle." *Reader's Digest*, LXXXI (December 1962), 102-106.

Records a touching moment during the Battle of the Bulge.

1913. Harmon, Ernest N., and Milton McKay. "We Gambled in the Battle of the Bulge." *Saturday Evening Post*, CCXXI (October 2, 1948), 34-35+.

The former Second Armored Division chief recalls the thin defense available at the start of the German counteroffensive and the dash by other armored columns to contain the Nazi onslaught.

1914. Heckler, Kenneth W. *The Bridge at Remagen*. New York: Ballantine Books, 1957. 238p.

The definitive account of the U.S. Ninth Armored Division capture of this Rhine River crossing point on March 7, 1945, the efforts made by U.S. engineers to keep it standing under constant German air and artillery fire, and the collapse of the structure into the river ten days later.

1915. ———. "Some Men Who Were at Remagen." In: Frank Brookhauser, ed. *This Was Your War: An Anthology of Great Writings from World War II.* Garden City, N.Y.: Doubleday, 1960, pp. 402-408.

An extract from the last citation.

1916. Heiberg, Harrison H.D. "12th Army Group Plans and Operations for the Rhine Crossing and the Closing of the Ruhr Pocket." *Military Review*, XXXI (September 1951), 26-37.

A detailed review of General Bradley's plans and operations during late March and early April 1945.

1917. Heinz, Wilfred C. "After 20 Years: The G.I.'s War Fades Away." *Saturday Evening Post*, CCXXXVII (December 12, 1964), 22-30+.

On the dimming remembrances of the Battle of the Bulge and the cold, hard fighting by U.S. troops against Hitler's last offensive.

1918. Hibbert, Christopher. *The Battle of Arnhem.* New York: Macmillan, 1962. 224p.

An analysis of Montgomery's war-winning game plan, the failed execution of the plan during the ground phase of "Market-Garden," and a speculation upon ways in which the tragedy might have been avoided.

1919. Hottelet, Richard C. "Bastogne: How We Stopped Von Rundstedt." *Collier's*, CXV (February 10, 1945), 16-17+.

Describes the stubborn Christmas-week defense of the Belgian town by the U.S. One Hundred First Airborne Division.

1920. ———. "The Big Jump into Germany." *Collier's*, CXV (May 5, 1945), 13+.

An eyewitness account of "Operation Varsity," and the part played in this Rhine River paratroop operation by the Seventeenth Airborne Division.

1921. "How Berlin Got Behind the [Iron] Curtain." *Time*, LXXVIII (September 29, 1961), 18-19.

At the height of the Berlin Crisis, the newsmagazine examines General Eisenhower's decision in 1945 not to capture the German capital.

1922. Huston, James A. "The Air Invasion of Holland." *Military Review*, XXXII (August 1952), 37-57; (September 1952), 13-27.

A detailed overview of the Allied attempt to capture the Rhine River bridges and the German counterattack which stopped the effort.

1923. Hyde, John F. "Armored Bridgehead Operation." *Armored Cavalry Journal*, LVIII (July-August 1949), 34-42, 48.

The U.S. Ninth Armored Division in the capture and maintenance of the Ludendorff Bridge at Remagen, March 7-17, 1945.

1924. Infield, Glenn B. *Skorzeny: Hitler's Commando.* New York: St. Martin's Press, 1981. 266p.

A biography of "Hitler's favorite commando" and the man who, during the Battle of the Bulge, organized "Operation Greif" to infiltrate English-speaking Germans in U.S. uniforms behind Allied lines.

1925. Irwin, Theodore. "The Combat Snafu of 'Blood-and-Guts' Patton." In: Phil Hirsch, ed. *Fighting Generals.* New York: Pyramid Books, 1960, pp. 47-58.

Reprinted from *Man's Magazine*; an account of the Hammelburg mission.

1926. Jesse, William R. "Bastogne: An Artillery Classic." *Field Artillery Journal*, XXXV (December 1945), 718-720.

A brief accounting of the role of artillery in the U.S. defense and the German offensive at Bastogne, Belgium, 1944.

1927. Johnson, Gerald K. "The Black Soldier in the Ardennes." *Soldiers*, XXXVI (February 1981), 16-19.

Many of the troops taken on by German panzers during the Bulge offensive were rear-area types, who were pressed into the American defense and gave a good accounting of themselves.

1928. Kane, Steve. *The 1st SS Panzer Division "Leibstandarte Adolf Hitler" in the Battle of the Bulge.* Military Journal Special, no. 2. Bennington, Vt.: International Graphics Corp., 1982. 36p.

Includes an account of the 2,000-man task force led by Lt. Col. Joachim Peiper that committed the Malmedy Massacre.

1929. Karig, Walter. "One More River to Cross." *U.S. Naval Institute Proceedings*, LXXI (October 1945), 1193-1201.

Outside of Morison's account (item 2445) cited in Section V:C:2 below, this is the best account of the role of U.S. Navy landing craft in the March-April 1945 Rhine River crossing.

1930. Keasey, Charles B. "The Roer River Crossing at Linnich, Germany." *Armored Cavalry Journal*, LVII (May-June 1948), 54-56.

A study of coordination, February 21-24, 1945.

1931. Knowlton, W.A. "Your Mission Is to Contact the Russians." *Reader's Digest*, XLVII (August 1945), 116-128.

How Ninth Army troops met the Soviets on the Elbe River.

1932. Kohutka, George A. "Schmidt, 1944." *Armor*, LXXIV (September-October 1965), 17-22.

The costly and vain effort by the U.S. Twenty-Eighth Infantry Division to capture this town opposite the Huertgen Forest in October 1944.

1933. Kosnett, Phil. "Highway to the Reich: 'Operation Market-Garden,' 17-26 September 1944." *Strategy and Tactics* (March-April 1977), 25-35.

A summary of the First Allied Airborne Army's effort to capture the Rhine River bridges in Holland accompanied by useful maps.

1934. Koyen, Kenneth. "General Patton's Mistake: Third Army's 4th Armored Division and the Hammelburg Affair." *Saturday Evening Post*, CCXX (May 1, 1948), 18-19+.

An early account of the attempt to liberate the POW camp which held the general's son-in-law.

1935. Krivitsky, Alexander I. "Handshake on the Elbe." *Soviet Literature*, no. 4 (April 1980), 110-120.

Recounts from a Russian standpoint the meeting of U.S. and Red Army troops on the Elbe River in May 1945.

1936. Kuzell, Ralph E. "Command and Communication." *Armored Cavalry Journal*, LVII (November-December 1948), 32-40.

Suggests reasons for the defeat suffered by the One Hundred Sixth Division in the Battle of the Bulge, December 16, 1944.

1937. Langston, Joe V. "Night Crossing." *Infantry Journal*, LXIV (June 1949), 21-25.

Subtitled "How the 6th Armored Division Crossed the Our River into Germany in February 1945."

1938. "Last Round: Airborne Landings East of the Rhine." *Life*, XVIII (April 9, 1945), 27-37.

Still a useful pictorial piece.

1939. MacDonald, Charles B. *The Battle of Huertgen Forest*. Philadelphia, Pa.: Lippincott, 1963. 215p.

A review of the terrible fighting just inside the German border which occupied much of the U.S. First Army from September-December 1944; the author is critical of American leadership and maintains that the battle was both unnecessary and avoidable.

1940. ———. *Battle of the Bulge*. New York: William Morrow, forthcoming.

A definitive study employing much unpublished material to provide a detailed treatment; focuses on the intelligence failure during the initial phase of the battle.

1941. ———. "Bridgehead to Victory." *Army Digest*, XXV (March 1970), 30-31.

A quick telling of the Remagen bridge story.

1941a. ———. *Company Commander*. Washington, D.C.: Infantry Journal Press, 1948. 278p.

In something of a classic, a junior officer recalls his problems and opportunities in leading Company I, Twenty-Third Regiment, Second Infantry Division in northwest Europe from October 1944 through July 1945; this candid view recalls not only the trials of combat but the difficulties in the daily lives of U.S. G.I.'s.

1942. ———. "The Decision to Launch 'Operation Market-Garden.'" In: Kent R. Greenfield, ed. *Command Decisions*. Washington, D.C.: Office of the Chief of Military History, Department of the Army, 1960, pp. 429-442.

Ike's decision to proceed with the airborne operation was something of a sop given to Montgomery after the rejection of the field marshal's call for the concentration of all resources on a single thrust to Berlin.

1943. ———. "Horror in the Huertgen Forest." *American History Illustrated*, VII (February 1972), 12-22.

Based on item 1939; concentrates on the enormous casualties suffered by the U.S. Twenty-Eighth Infantry Division. Illustrated.

1944. ———. *The Last Offensive*. U.S. Army in World War II: The European Theater of Operations. Washington, D.C.: U.S. Government Printing Office, 1973. 532p.

Chronologically the last of the ETO "green books," this work follows Allied thrusts into Germany from the Rhine crossing through VE-Day, including the battle of the Ruhr and the link-up with the Russians on the Elbe River. Illustrated with good maps and interesting photographs.

1945. ———. "The Man Who Did Not Capture Leipzig." *Infantry Journal*, LX (June 1947), 47-51.

The author's experiences with the Second Infantry Division during the Third Army's invasion of southern Germany.

1946. ———. *The Siegfried Line Campaign*. U.S. Army in World War II: The European Theater of Operations. Washington, D.C.: U.S. Government Printing Office, 1963. 670p.

Relates the story of the U.S. First and Ninth Armies from the initial crossing of the German border on September 11, 1944, to the German counteroffensive in the Ardennes on December 16; describes the reduction of Aachen, the costly fighting in the Huertgen Forest, and the efforts of the First Allied Airborne Army to capture the Rhine bridges in Holland during the "Market-Garden" operation.

1947. McKee, Alexander. *The Race for the Rhine Bridges*. New York: Stein and Day, 1971. 490p.

Recounts three wartime drives on that barrier: the German in 1940, the Allied push into the Ruhr in 1944, and the U.S./U.K. crossing of 1945; based on interviews with participants from both sides and published sources.

1948. MacKenzie, Fred. *The Men of Bastogne*. New York: David McKay, 1968. 265p.

A day-to-day narrative of the defense of the Belgian town by the One Hundred First Airborne Division during the Battle of the Bulge by the only newsman actually on the scene.

1949. Marshall, Samuel L.A. *Bastogne: The Story of the First Eight Days in Which the 101st Airborne Division Was Closed Within the Ring of German Forces*. Washington, D.C.: Infantry Journal Press, 1946. 261p.

A classic of World War II ETO literature which describes the forming of men from various ground units with the airborne troopers to form a successful defense; the narrative, a product of the Army's ETO postwar historical program, is based on the author's interviews with American soldiers who participated in the Belgian town's defense.

1950. ———. "Christmas Eve at Bastogne." *Infantry Journal*, LVII (December 1945), 8-15.

Examines the manner in which the besieged G.I.'s spent their holiday as the encircling Forty-Seventh Panzer Corps prepared to attack.

1951. ———. "The Christmas Tree Defeat: General Bruce Clarke's Blackest Yuletide." *Army*, IX (December 1958), 22-24.

Concerns the unsuccessful push of the Seventh Armored Division against Manhay, Belgium, on December 25, 1944.

1952. ———. "The Fight at Best." *Marine Corps Gazette*, XXXII (October 1948), 10-17; (November 1948), 14-19; (December 1948), 27-32.

Details the operations of the U.S. Five Hundred Second Parachute Infantry Regiment near Veghel, Holland, September 17-19, 1944, during "Operation Market Garden."

1953. ———. "Men Against Armor." *Armored Cavalry Journal*, LIX (May-June 1950), 4-9.

The gallant operations of the Three Hundred Twenty-Seventh Glider Infantry Regiment at Bastogne on December 25, 1944.

1954. Mattera, James P. "Murder at Malmedy." *Army*, XXXI (December 1981): 32-35+.

Reconstructs the massacre of American prisoners near this Belgian town by troopers of Lt. Col. Joachim Peiper's First SS Panzer Division task force on December 17, 1944.

1955. Merriam, Robert E. *Dark December: The Full Account of the Battle of the Bulge*. New York: Ziff-Davis, 1947. 234p.

Writing from official records and interviews with U.S. and German participants, the author, in this now classic book, describes the Ardennes counteroffensive from both the Nazi and American viewpoints; parts of this work have been superseded by later accounts.

1956. Middleton, Drew. "Into Germany with the First Army." *New York Times Magazine* (October 8, 1944), 5+.

A noted correspondent describes the exploits of patrols which crossed the frontier on September 11, 1944.

1957. Minott, Rodney G. *The Fortress That Never Was: The Myth of Hitler's Bavarian Stronghold*. New York: Holt, Rinehart and Winston, 1964. 208p.

An examination of the basis of 1945 rumors of a last-ditch Nazi stand to be made in a National Redoubt or Alpine Redoubt located in the Bavarian-Austrian mountains and the impact of this incorrect intelligence on Eisenhower's planners, who believed it. This redoubt affair caused the Supreme Commander to divert troops to the Alps and, according to the author, thereby allowed the Soviets to liberate Prague and Berlin.

1958. Montgomery, John H., Jr. "The Remagen Bridgehead." *Military Review*, XXIX (July 1950), 3-7.

A retelling of how the U.S. Ninth Armored Division captured this Rhine River crossing and the exploitation made of it by the Americans.

1959. Muller, Edwin. "How the Rhine Battle Was Planned." *Reader's Digest*, XLVI (June 1945), 27-31.

Discusses Eisenhower's decision to mount a thrust in the north and his assignment of First and Third Army units to the Ninth Army and how the latter, under Montgomery's command, would join the Canadian First Army in making the main drive in February 1945.

1960. Myer, Samuel C. "'Varsity's' Organic Artillery." *Field Artillery Journal*, XXXV (November 1945), 673-677.

How the Seventeenth Airborne Division's artillery was flown into action across the Rhine by gliders.

1961. "The Navy's Watch on the Rhine." *Popular Mechanics*, LXXXIII (June 1945), 1-5+.

The use of USN landing craft to ferry soldiers across the Rhine in March-April 1945 is related.

1962. Neff, J.C. "The Race to the Elbe." *Infantry Journal*, LXI (August 1947), 36-40.

Recounts the April 25, 1945, link-up between the U.S. Sixty-Ninth Division and the Soviet Fifty-Eighth Guards Rifle Division.

1963. Nobécourt, Jacques. *Hitler's Last Gamble: The Battle of the Bulge*. Translated from the French. New York: Schocken, 1967. 302p.

First published in France, this account tells the story of the Ardennes counteroffensive from both the German and American viewpoints.

1964. Oldinsky, Frederick E. "Patton and the Hammelburg Mission." *Armor*, LXXXV (July-August 1976), 13-18.

Examines reasons why the Third Army commander ordered the mission for the rescue of POW's held here and the difficulties of the troopers involved in the mission.

1965. O'Neill, James H. "The True Story of the Patton Prayer." *Military Chaplain*, XIX (October 1948), 1-3; (November 1948), 13.

Recollections by the former chief Third Army Chaplain of the circumstances surrounding Patton's ordering a prayer for "fair weather for battle" in December 1944--and the results. The incident was played up in the film "Patton."

1966. O'Steen, James E. "Artillery Targets Across the Rhine." *Field Artillery Journal*, XXXV (August 1945), 471-479.

Army artillery firing in support of the March-April 1945 Rhine crossings.

1967. Pallud, Jean P. "The Battle of the Bulge--Then and Now." *After the Battle*, no. 37 (1982), 17-22.

A look at the battlefields in the Ardennes as they appeared in 1944 and 1982.

1968. Parrish, Monte M. "The Battle of Aachen: City Fighting Tactics." *Field Artillery Journal*, XLIV (September-October 1976), 25-30.

Describes the house-to-house fighting by units of the U.S. First Infantry and Third Armored Divisions in October 1944.

1969. Patrick, Stephen B. "AAA Protection of a River Crossing." *Antiaircraft Journal*, XCIII (March-April 1950), 29-31.

Explains the defense measures adopted against German planes which were attempting to knock down the newly captured Remagen bridge.

1970. ———. "The Ardennes Offensive: The Battle of the Bulge, December 1944." *Strategy and Tactics*, no. 37 (March-April 1973), 4-21.

An overview of the last great German offensive in the West; includes helpful maps and orders of battle.

1971. ———. "The Battle for Germany: The Destruction of the Reich, December 1944-May 1945." *Strategy and Tactics*, no. 50 (May-June 1975), 4-16.

A summary of the fighting on both the eastern and western fronts, which is greatly helped by battle maps and orders of battle.

1972. ———. "Westwall: Four Battles to Germany." *Strategy and Tactics*, no. 54 (January-February 1976), 3-14.

Helped by good maps, the author explains the 1944 battles of Arnhem, Huertgen Forest, and Bastogne and the 1945 capture of the Remagen bridge.

1973. Peterman, Ivan H. "They Took the Nazis' Sunday Punch." *Saturday Evening Post*, CCXIX (September 28, 1946), 20+.

Describes the casualties taken by the U.S. Twenty-Eighth Infantry Division in the Battle of Huertgen Forest.

1974. Phillips, Robert F. *To Save Bastogne*. New York: Stein & Day, 1983. 283p.

An account of the actions in front of the Belgian city in December 1944 during the German Ardennes counteroffensive; concentrates on the efforts of the soldiers of the U.S. One Hundred Tenth Infantry, Twenty-Eighth Division. Includes photos.

1975. Pickert, Wilhelm. "The Battle of Arnhem-Nijmegen." *Interavia*, VIII (April 1953), 179-183.

A German view of the Allied airborne assault which shows the errors in the U.S./U.K. planning and execution of "Market-Garden."

1976. Pickett, George B., Jr. "The Reinforced Tank Battalion in Exploitation." *Armored Cavalry Journal*, LIX (March-April 1950), 34-39.

Recalls the work of the Fifty-Second Tank Battalion, Eleventh Armored Division, in the drive from the Moselle to the Rhine, March 17-20, 1945.

1977. ———, and Edgar N. Millington. "The Pilsen Story." *U.S. Army Combat Forces Journal*, I (April 1951), 33-36.

Examines the failure of the subunits of the Third Army's Sixteenth Armored Division to cooperate with the Czech partisans who were already holding the town when the American tanks arrived on May 4.

1978. Piekalkiewicz, Janusz. *Arnhem, 1944*. Translated from the German. New York: Scribners, 1978. 111p.

Enhanced by a liberal collection of battlefield photos, maps, and source material, including reprints of official announcements and articles from the *London Times*, Piekalkiewicz evokes the ten dramatic days of Germany's last victory against the western Allies.

1979. Pogue, Forrest C. "The Decision to Halt at the Elbe." In: Kent R. Greenfield, ed. *Command Decisions*. Washington, D.C.: Office of the Chief of Military History, Department of the Army, 1960, pp. 479-492.

Presents evidence that Eisenhower's decision was dictated by "military reasons alone."

1980. ———. "Why Eisenhower's Forces Stopped at the Elbe." *World Politics*, IV (April 1952), 356-368.

An earlier version of the preceding entry.

1981. Pritchard, Tattnall R., Jr. "Crossing the Meuse." *Field Artillery Journal*, XXXVIII (May-June 1948), 128-130.

A quick look at the experiences of Company K, Sixtieth Infantry Regiment, in Belgium, September 3-5, 1944.

1982. Randall, Howard M. *Dirt and Doughfeet: Combat Experiences of a Rifle Platoon Leader*. Hicksville, N.Y.: Exposition Press, 1955. 113p.

In the same vein as MacDonald's *Company Commander* cited above, the author explores the everyday life of G.I.'s from the Eighty-Seventh Infantry Division as they fought their way from Luxembourg to Germany, February-May 1945.

1983. Raymond, Allen D., III. "The Battle of St. Vith." *Armor*, LXXIII (November-December 1964), 5-11.

How the men of the Seventh Armored Division joined single regiments from the One Hundred Sixth and Twenty-Eighth Infantry Divisions and a combat command from the Ninth Armored Division in forming a horseshoe-shaped defense of this Belgian town during the opening phases of the Battle of the Bulge.

1984. Reeves, Joseph R. "Artillery in the Ardennes." *Field Artillery Journal*, XXXVI (March 1946), 138-142, 173-184.

Except in the Normandy campaign, U.S. First Army artillery units fired more ammunition between December 16-27 than at any other time during the war; an average of 800 weapons fired over 750,000 shells.

1985. Richard, Duke. "Bastogne Revisited." *Army Digest*, XXIV (December 1969), 15-21.

Briefly describes the impact of the battle on the Belgian town and shows how it recovered during the postwar years.

1986. Ryan, Cornelius. *A Bridge Too Far*. New York: Simon and Schuster, 1974. 670p.

Written while the author was dying of cancer, this acclaimed account details the concept and execution of Montgomery's "Market-Garden" plan to end the ETO war in fall 1944 through a massive U.S./U.K. airborne operation in Holland designed to capture five bridges and open a small corridor to the Rhine for an armored push. Written in the same fashion as the successful and popular *The Longest Day*, cited above (item 1812), Ryan's account relies on primary and secondary sources and, most important, interviews with hundreds of German and Allied participants of both high and low rank. Made into a successful motion picture directed by Richard Attenborough.

1987. ———. "A Bridge Too Far." *Reader's Digest*, CV (October 1974), 258-311; (November 1974), 236-289.

Serialized version of preceding entry.

1988. ———. *The Last Battle*. New York: Simon and Schuster, 1966. 571p.

This popular and readable account of the final three weeks of the war on the eastern front and the Battle of Berlin is somewhat shaky in its analysis of the German-Soviet encounter, and should be compared to the many citations on the Berlin fighting cited in my *The Soviet Army: A Guide to Sources in English* (Santa Barbara, Calif.: Clio Books, 1982), pp. 141-146; Ryan does consider the U.S. decision not to tackle the German capital and the meeting of American and Soviet troops on the Elbe River. Based on primary and secondary sources and interviews with hundreds of survivors from all involved sides.

1989. Schorr, David P., Jr. "Airborne Assault Crossing of the Rhine." *Military Review*, XXVIII (June 1948), 48-55.

An overview of the First Allied Airborne Army's parachute and glider operation, "Varsity," of March 1945.

1990. Sears, Stephen W. *The Battle of the Bulge*. American Heritage Junior Library. New York: American Heritage Publishing Co., 1969. 148p.

Explaining the important points of the German Ardennes counteroffensive and the Allied reaction to it, Sears's pictorial is suitable as an introduction for the uninitiated or younger readers.

1991. ———. "Hell's Highway to Arnhem." *American Heritage*, XXII (June 1971), 60-63, 94-99.

A pictorial retelling of the story of "Operation Market-Garden," the Allied airborne attempt to reach the Rhine via bridges in Holland.

1992. Simons, Gerald. *Victory in Europe*. World War II Series. Alexandria, Va.: Time-Life Books, 1983. 208p.

This pictorial is chronologically the last ETO volume in this series and describes the fighting by the western Allies and the Soviets during late March to May 1945, including the Battle of Berlin, the Allied meeting on the Elbe, and the flight west of German civilians and surrendering troops. Many of the photographs were taken by *Life* magazine cameramen on the scene of the events described.

1993. Simpson, Louis. "The Way It Was in the Bulge." *New York Times Magazine* (December 6, 1964), 27-29+.

A 20th anniversary look back at the difficult fight of American G.I.'s caught up in the German Ardennes counter-offensive, December 1944.

1994. Skorzeny, Otto. *Secret Missions: War Memoirs of the Most Dangerous Man in Europe*. Translated from the French. New York: E.P. Dutton, 1951. 256p.

Recollections of the noted German SS commando and dedicated Nazi which are of interest here for his infiltration of English speaking German soldiers behind U.S. lines during the Battle of the Bulge ("Operation Greif") and his setting afloat rumors of an assassination plot against Eisenhower. Use with caution as correct dates and place names suffer in the author's story-telling.

1995. Small, Collie. "Bastogne: American Epic." *Saturday Evening Post*, CCXVII (February 17, 1945), 18-19+.

Details the defense of this Belgian town by the U.S. One Hundred First Airborne Division during the Battle of the Bulge in December 1944.

1996. ———. "How Antwerp Was Saved." *Saturday Evening Post*, CCXVIII (July 21, 1945), 18-19+.

The story of the American counterattack against the Germans, which smashed the bulge in January 1945.

1997. Smith, Helena H. "A Few Men in Soldier Suits." *American Heritage*, VIII (August 1957), 29-31, 104-105.

Highlights the roles of ordinarily noncombatant U.S. troops (e.g., cooks, bakers, stenographers) in the Battle of the Bulge.

1998. Stacey, Charles P. *The Victory Campaign: The Operations in Northwest Europe, 1944-1945*. Ottawa, Canada: Queen's Printer, 1960. 770p.

A volume from the official Canadian war history which provides insight into and analysis of the role of the First Canadian Army in the battle for Germany; placed in the context of the overall Allied push, this work is basically unbiased and provides much information on the role of the Americans, especially the Ninth Army, with whom the Canadians fought.

1999. Steinert, Marlis G. *23 Days: The Final Collapse of Nazi Germany*. New York: Walker, 1969. 326p.

A history of the Dönitz government which followed Hitler's death and attempted to get as many Germans to the west as possible before the end; provides information on the politics of this government and its peace feelers to the Western Allies, its collapse, and the arrest of its members.

2000. Stevenson, Frank E. "Third Army's Planning for the Crossing of the Rhine River." *Military Review*, XXX (March 1951), 33-42.

Notes Patton's desire to cross the river as quickly as possible after the completion of "Operation Varsity."

2001. Stock, James W. *Rhine Crossing*. Ballantine's Illustrated History of World War II. New York: Ballantine Books, 1973. 160p.

A pictorial which describes not only the airborne crossing, "Operation Varsity," but the ferrying across of the British, Canadian, and American field armies during the last week of March 1945.

2002. Stone, Thomas R. "1630 Comes Early on the Roer." *Military Review*, LIII (October 1973), 3-21.

Why high water forced Gen. William Simpson to postpone his Ninth Army crossing in February 1945.

2003. Strawson, John. *The Battle for Berlin*. New York: Scribners, 1974. 182p.

Beginning in January 1945, this British author describes the battles and political moves which led to the final German collapse, including the Yalta conference, the Rhine River crossings, and Eisenhower's decision not to capture the German capital.

2004. ———. *The Battle for the Ardennes*. New York: Scribners, 1972. 212p.

Pointing out the strategic value of the area, Strawson describes the German counteroffensive and Allied reaction from high command and troop levels, noting errors made by both sides during this Battle of the Bulge.

2005. Sweetser, Warren E. "Dustpan and Broom." *Marine Corps Gazette*, XXXI (August 1947), 8-15.

Life for the men of the Five Hundred Second Parachute Infantry Regiment, One Hundred First Airborne Division, in Bastogne during the German Christmas 1944 siege.

2006. *Tanks Illustrated: The Battle of the Bulge*. London: Arms and Armour Press, 1983. 68p.

Describes the use of armor by German and U.S. forces during the Ardennes counteroffensive of December 1944-January 1945; illustrated with over 100 rare and unusual photographs and four pages of color plates.

2007. Thompson, Reginald W. *The Battle for the Rhineland*. London: Hutchinson, 1958. 242p.

Follows the exploits of the British Twenty-First Army Group, including the U.S. Ninth Army, from the Rhine River crossing through the capture of Cologne; includes analysis of leaders and tactics employed on both sides, German and Allied.

2008. Thompson, W.F.K. "'Operation Market Garden.'" In: Philip de Ste. Croix, ed. *Airborne Operations: An Illustrated Encyclopedia of the Great Battles of Airborne Forces.* New York: Crescent Books, 1978, pp. 106-127.

The airborne part of this gamble was the largest paratroop effort made by the Allies during the war and the only attempt at a semi-strategic operation, but failed in its efforts to secure a Rhine bridge because of poor planning and intelligence.

2009. Toland, John. *Battle: The Story of the Bulge.* New York: Random House, 1959. 400p.

Not a definitive study, Toland's work, like Ryan's and Marshall's cited above, is valuable for the insights it provides into the feelings and emotions of the G.I.'s caught up in the engagement; based on primary and secondary sources and a large number of interviews, the work is short on strategic analysis but delightful and dramatic in its readability.

2010. ———. *The Last 100 Days.* New York: Random House, 1966. 622p.

A massive account of the final three months of the ETO conflict, based on a variety of sources including hundreds of inetrviews with participants from command to troop level; includes much information on the eastern as well as the western fronts, including the Rhine crossing, the battle for Berlin, the U.S.-Soviet meeting on the Elbe, and the surrender ceremonies.

2011. ———. "The Reluctant Warriors." *Look*, XXIII (October 13, 1959), 106+.

Based on item 2009; looks at those ordinarily noncombatant U.S. soldiers (e.g., cooks and bakers) who were pressed into frontline service during the Battle of the Bulge.

2012. Tompkins, Rathvon McC. "The Bridge." *Marine Corps Gazette*, XXXV (April 1951), 36-47; (May 1951), 38-46.

A detailed account of the planning and execution of "Operation Market-Garden," the allied airborne effort in Holland, September 1944.

2013. Tooley, I.P. "Artillery Support at Arnhem." *Field Artillery Journal*, XXXV (April 1945), 202-204.

A brief analysis of the impact of airborne artillery pieces on the outcome of the "Market-Garden" adventure.

2014. Trahan, E.A. "Armor in the Bulge." *Armored Cavalry Journal*, LVII (January-February 1948), 2-11; (March-April 1948), 39-43.

Examines the actions of the U.S. Second Division in the Allied Ardennes counteroffensive from December 16, 1944, to January 16, 1945.

2015. "The Truth About the Berlin Problem." *U.S. News and World Report*, XLVI (May 18, 1959), 63-66+.

A discussion of Eisenhower's decision not to capture the German capital is included in this political piece.

2016. Tumey, Benjamin. *A G.I.'s View of World War II.* Hicksville, N.Y.: Exposition Press, 1959. 64p.

Reprints a private's diary of service as a rifleman with the U.S. Seventy-Ninth Infantry Division in the campaigns in Belgium and Germany in 1945.

2017. United States. Army. Armor School. "The Deliberate River Crossing." *Armor*, LIX (July-August 1950), 34-39.

A study of the U.S. Sixth Armored Division's crossing of the Our River in February 1945.

2018. ———. Army Air Forces. *Assault on Holland.* Wings at War, no. 4. Washington, D.C.: Headquarters, U.S. Army Air Forces, 1945. 57p.

Examines the preparations, execution, and aftermath of "Operation Market-Garden," the Allied airborne effort in Holland, September 1944, with emphasis on the U.S. aspects of the campaign.

2019. ———. National Archives and Records Service. *Germany Surrenders Unconditionally.* Washington, D.C.: U.S. Government Printing Office, 1945. 41p.

A collection of facsimiles of the various documents of the German surrender.

2020. Urquhart, Robert E. *Arnhem.* London: Cassell, 1958. 238p.

The author's recollections of "Operation Market-Garden" in which he served as commander of the British First Airborne Division; includes an analysis of the Allied planning and execution of the effort, including reasons why both failed to meet the military requirements of Montgomery's vast gamble. Fair to U.S. airborne units involved.

2021. Van Bibber, E.M. "Objective: Perfection." *Infantry Journal*, LVIII (April 1946), 36-41.

Reconstructs the planning and execution of the Allied crossing of the Rhine in late March 1945.

2022. Van Horne, Richard W. "Short-Range Firing Against the Siegfried Line." *Field Artillery Journal*, XXXV (February 1945), 75-77.

Action of the self-propelled 155's of the Nine Hundred Ninety-First Field Artillery Battalion (attached to the Ninth Infantry Division), September 14-October 12, 1944.

2023. Von Luttichau, Charles V.P. "The German Counteroffensive in the Ardennes." In: Kent R. Greenfield, ed. *Command Decisions.*

Washington, D.C.: Office of the Chief of Military History, Department of the Army, 1960, pp. 443-459.

Provides details on German planning and operations during their counteroffensive of December 1944 (Battle of the Bulge), an analysis of initial Allied indecision concerning the purpose of the thrust, and the reasons why the German effort collapsed in January 1945.

2024. Webster, David K. "'We Drank Hitler's Champagne.'" *Saturday Evening Post*, CCXIV (May 3, 1952), 25+.

A tale of the One Hundred First Airborne Division during the defense of Bastogne in December 1944.

2025. Weingartner, James J. *Crossroads of Death: The Story of the Malmedy Massacre and Trial.* Berkeley: University of California Press, 1981.

Describes the execution of U.S. soldiers by Lieutenant Colonel Peiper's task force on December 17, 1944, and the postwar trial which convicted the murderers, who were only lightly punished after the U.S. Senate Armed Services Committee questioned the trial procedures; the author suggests such immoral acts will continue whenever or wherever there is a war.

2026. Werstein, Irving. *The Battle of Aachen.* New York: Crowell, 1962. 146p.

Concise telling of the October 1944 battle for this town which, when liberated on October 21, became the first German city to fall to the Western Allies; describes the stubborn German defense and the house-to-house fighting that defense wrought.

2027. Wertenbaker, Charles G. "Americans Battle the German Big Push." *Life*, XVIII (January 8, 1945), 19-23.

Still a useful pictorial piece on the Allied effort to crush the Nazi assault known as the Battle of the Bulge.

2028. Wesneski, Carl. "Name the Commander." *Armor*, LXXIII (March-April 1964), 10-12.

On the failure of the Third Army task force to liberate the POW's at Hammelburg on March 26, 1945.

2029. Whiting, Charles. *The Battle of the Ruhr Pocket.* Ballantine's Illustrated History of World War II. New York: Ballantine Books, 1970. 160p.

A pictorial which describes how the U.S. Ninth and First Armies raced to a juncture on the east side of the Ruhr manufacturing area on April 1, 1945, trapping over 325,000 German soldiers from Army Groups B and H.

2030. ———. *Bloody Aachen.* New York: Stein and Day, 1976. 191p.

The story of the first German city besieged by the U.S. Army during the war and how, according to the author, its fierce defense extended the war and gave Hitler time to mobilize for the Battle of the Bulge. The old imperial town was taken in late October 1944 by the U.S. First Army after costly house-to-house fighting.

2031. ———. *A Bridge at Arnhem.* London: Future Publications, 1974. 264p.

Whiting tells the familiar story of "Operation Market-Garden," the Allied airborne effort to get to the Rhine through a plan to capture bridges in Holland; analyzes the planning, execution, and aftermath of the campaign and the reasons why it failed.

2032. ———. *Death of a Division.* New York: Stein and Day, 1981. 176p.

Successfully conveying the chaos of the fighting, the author describes the collapse of the 16,000 green troops of the U.S. One Hundred Sixth "Golden Lion" Division on the night of December 16, 1944, during the initial phase of the Battle of the Bulge.

2033. ———. *Decision at St. Vith.* New York: Ballantine Books, 1969. 260p.

A somewhat poorly written account of this engagement during the Battle of the Bulge and the historical conflict engendered when the U.S. One Hundred Sixth Infantry Division was destroyed; the preceding citation is an improvement over this one.

2034. ———. *The End of the War in Europe, April 15 to May 23, 1945.* New York: Stein and Day, 1973. 178p.

Examines the Anglo-American military/political debates during the final 39 days of the ETO war, including the British desire to drive east and the American effort to push south, as well as Eisenhower's reasons for not attempting the capture of Berlin, the Nazi capital city.

2035. ———. *48 Hours to Hammelberg.* New York: Ballantine Books, 1970. 199p.

The late March 1945 raid by a task force of Patton's Third Army to free POW's at Hammelberg and the failure of the mission are reconstructed in a somewhat wandering account. Compare with the Baron work cited above.

2036. ———. *Hitler's Werewolves.* New York: Stein and Day, 1972. 208p.

Shows how this short-lived Nazi guerrilla group, created by Himmler in November 1944 to operate behind Allied lines, scared many on the Allied side but never lived up to its boast to fight or die, disbanding without fanfare following only one successful operation. The only book-length study on the subject available in English.

2037. ———. *Massacre at Malmedy.* New York: Stein and Day, 1971. 198p.

Focuses on the activities of the Peiper battle group, including its slaughter of 80 U.S. Army prisoners and its later destruction (loss of 4,200 of 5,000 men) when caught in action by two U.S. divisions; condemned at Nuremberg, Peiper's sentence was reduced due to political interference.

2038. ———. *Siegfried: The Nazis Last Stand.* New York: Stein and Day, 1982. 268p.

Describes the Allied center attacks against the German West Wall, which ran from near Duisburg in the north into Bavaria in the south protecting the Rhineland, from the end of the Ardennes counteroffensive in January 1945 through the seizure of the Remagen bridge in March.

2039. "Why Ike Didn't Capture Berlin: An Untold Story." *U.S. News and World Report*, LXX (April 26, 1971), 70-73.

Discusses the military reasons Eisenhower followed for not taking the German capital, as well as the political one of having to turn over captured territory in accordance with Big Power agreements.

2040. Zarish, Joseph M. *The Collapse of the Remagen Bridge.* New York: Vantage, 1968. 137p.

Amplifying Heckler's work cited above, the author describes not only the capture of the bridge, but also the work of the U.S. Two Hundred Seventy-Sixth Engineer Combat Battalion during the second week of March 1945 in trying to keep it standing; due to battle damage and heavy weight loads, the engineers' efforts were unsuccessful.

2041. Ziemke, Earl F. *The U.S. Army in the Occupation of Germany, 1944-1946.* Washington, D.C.: U.S. Government Printing Office, 1975. 484p.

An examination of the origin, definition, and execution of the Army's military government role in captured German territory from Aachen to June 1946; includes maps, charts, and photographs.

D. UNIT HISTORIES

Introduction: Many of the U.S. Army units which fought in World War II later produced college yearbook-type commemorative histories; in addition, military writers and enthusiasts have, since 1945, written many titles on the men and actions of specific units. These resources combine to form a valuable body of literature which is often much more specific than any of the more general citations listed in the parts above. Since there are hundreds of accounts of U.S. Army units, the entries in this part are restricted to larger organizations: numbered armies, corps, and divisions. The references are also selective, not only because of space requirements, but also based on the compiler's judgment as to those which may be most easily accessible for the average user. More complete lists of unit histories can be found in Section I:A above. The order of arrangement here is: General Works; Armies and Corps; Airborne Divisions; Armored Divisions; Infantry Divisions; and Miscellaneous Units.

1. General Works

Introduction: The citations immediately following are general, but may be used in connection with those references of a more specific nature below. Users are cautioned that additional general information on U.S. Army units will be found in the works cited in Parts A-C and E of this section.

2042. *Army Times*, Editors of. *Combat Divisions of World War II: Army of the United States*. Washington, D.C.: Army Times, 1946. 96p.

A collection of brief divisional histories from all theaters providing information on activation, commanders, campaigns; arranged numerically.

2043. Dupuy, R. Ernest. "War Department Reorganization, August 1941-March 1942." *Military Affairs*, XVI (Spring 1952), 12-29; (Fall 1952), 97-114.

A history of change under Gen. George Marshall which saw the creation of the Army Ground Forces, Army Air Forces, and Services of Supply (later Army Service Forces).

2044. Forty, George. *U.S. Army Handbook, 1939-1945*. New York: Scribners, 1981.

A detailed examination of the wartime army which covers, with charts, diagrams, and illustrations, everything from ranks and formations to rations and rifles to units and overall organization.

2045. Greenwald, Robert J., ed. *Order of Battle of the United States Army, World War II: European Theater of Operations--Divisions*. Paris, France: Order of Battle Sub-Section, Office of the Theater Historian, 1945. 586p.

An exceedingly rare typescript which presents data on the various Army organizations which fought in northwest Europe, including commanders, campaigns, mottos and slogans, etc.; arranged numerically by division number. A circulation copy is available from the U.S. Army Military History Institute, Carlisle Barracks, Pa.

2046. Kahn, Ely J., and Henry McLemore. *Fighting Divisions: Histories of Each U.S. Army Combat Division in World War II*. Washington, D.C.: Zenger Publications, 1979. 238p.

First published by Infantry Journal Press in 1946, this guide provides a concise history of each division in numerical order; includes an 8-page color section of division insignia and ap- appendices providing the order of battle by theater and dates of campaigns plus 18 maps of the various theater battle areas.

2047. Mahon, John K., and Romana Danysh. *Infantry, Part I: Regular Army*. U.S. Army Lineage Series. Washington, D.C.: U.S. Government Printing Office, 1972. 938p.

Opening with a narrative history of the Infantry Branch, this reference contains the lineages, honors, coats of arms, and distinctive insignia of infantry units of the active Army from the Revolution through Vietnam, concentrating on those of regimental size.

2048. Sawicki, James A., ed. *Field Artillery Battalions of the U.S. Army*. 2 vols. Dumfries, Va.: Wyvern, 1979.

Documents the lineage (history), campaigns, decorations, coats of arms, and unit crests of all Army field artillery battalions and includes a glossary.

2049. ———. *Infantry Regiments of the U.S. Army*. Dumfries, Va.: Wyvern, 1981. 696p.

Contains the lineage, heraldry, and honors of all 481 U.S. Army infantry regiments listed on the rolls since World War I; compare with the Mahon and Danysh work cited above.

2050. Stubbs, Mary Lee, and Stanley R. Connor. *Armor-Cavalry: Regular Army and Army National Guard*. U.S. Army Lineage Series. 2 vols. Washington, D.C.: U.S. Government Printing Office, 1969-1972.

Opening with a narrative history of the Armor Branch (Armor and Cavalry units), this work contains the lineages, honors, coats of arms, and distinctive insignia of the regular and guard units from the Revolution through Vietnam, concentrating on those of regimental size.

2051. Treadwell, Mattie E. *The Women's Army Corps*. U.S. Army in World War II: Special Studies. Washington, D.C.: U.S. Government Printing Office, 1954. 841p.

A study of the advent of the women's corps in the midst of a traditionally male service and the women's experiences in the various theaters, including the MTO and ETO; includes charts and photographs.

2052. United States. War Department. Adjutant General's Office. *Units Cited for Battle Participation*. Washington, D.C., 1945. 165p.

Lists those units, division size and smaller, which received special honors for their participation in various World War II campaigns.

2. Armies and Corps

Introduction: In May 1945, the United States had one field Army, the Fifth, in the Mediterranean, which was made up of two corps (Second and Fourth) and six divisions, the Thirty-Fourth, Eighty-Fifth, Eighty-Eighth, and Ninety-Second Infantry Divisions, the Tenth Mountain Division, and the First Armored Division. One infantry division, the Ninety-First, was attached to the British Eighth Army. Both of these Allied armies came under the command of the Fifteenth Army Group, led by Gen. Mark W. Clark.

To the north in May 1945, the American contingent of Gen. Dwight D. Eisenhower's Allied Expeditionary Force comprised two groups, the XII under General Omar N. Bradley (the Central Group of Armies) and the VI under General Jacob L. Devers (the Southern Group of Armies). The Commonwealth contingent of the A.E.F. was made up of the XXI Group led by Field Marshal Sir Bernard L. Montgomery (the Northern Group of Armies) with the attached U.S. Eighteenth Airborne Corps under MG Matthew B. Ridgway, the Eighth Infantry Division, the Eighty-Second Airborne Division, and the Fifth and Seventh Armored Divisions.

General Bradley's central group consisted of four armies, north to south geographically, the Ninth, First, Third, and Fifteenth. The Ninth Army, led by LTG William H. Simpson, comprised three corps (Thirteenth, Sixteenth, and Nineteenth) and 11 divisions: Second, Twenty-Ninth, Thirtieth, Thirty-Fifth, Seventy-Fifth, Seventy-Ninth, Eighty-Third, Eighty-Fourth, Ninety-Fifth, and One Hundred Second Infantry Divisions, Second Armored Division. The First Army, commanded by Gen. Courtney H. Hodges, comprised two corps (Seventh and Eighth) and 9 divisions: Ninth, Sixty-Ninth, Seventy-Sixth, Seventy-Eighth, Eighty-Seventh, Eighty-Ninth, and One Hundred Fourth Infantry Divisions, Third and Sixth Armored Divisions. The Third Army, led by the colorful Gen. George S. Patton, Jr., was at war's end Bradley's largest, comprising four corps (Third, Fifth, Twelfth, and Twentieth) and 18 divisions: First, Second, Fourth, Fifth, Twenty-Sixth, Sixty-Fifth, Seventieth, Seventy-First, Eightieth, Ninetieth, Ninety-Seventh, and Ninety-Ninth Infantry Divisions and Fourth, Ninth, Eleventh, Thirteenth, Fourteenth, and Sixteenth Armored Divisions. The Fifteenth Army, under LTG Leonard T. Gerow, was Bradley's smallest, comprising two corps (Twenty-Second and Twenty-Third) and 5 divisions: Twenty-Eighth, Sixty-Sixth, Ninety-Fourth, and One Hundred Sixth Infantry Divisions and the Seventeenth Airborne Division.

Gen. Devers' southern group consisted of the U.S. Seventh Army and Gen. Jean J. De Lattre de Tassigny's First French Army. The Seventh Army, under LTG Alexander M. Patch, comprised three corps (Sixth, Fifteenth, and Twenty-First) and 13 divisions: Third, Thirty-Sixth, Forty-Second, Forty-Fourth, Forty-Fifth, Sixty-Third, Eighty-Sixth, One Hundredth, and One Hundred Third Infantry Divisions, the One Hundred First Airborne Division, and the Tenth, Twelfth, and Twentieth Armored Divisions.

The citations in this section concern only the numbered field armies and corps within those armies; the arrangement is numerical by army. Only U.S. organizations are considered.

First Army

2053. *A Brief History of the First United States Army from 1918 to 1946*. Fayetteville, N.C.: Worth Publishing Co., 1947. 47p.

A concise review of the army's World War I and II service, which, during the latter conflict, saw it the first ashore in Normandy, the first to break out of the beachhead, the first into Paris, the first across the Seine River, the first across the German frontier, the first across the Rhine River, and the first to contact the Soviets.

2054. Colby, Elbridge. *The First Army in Europe, 1943-1945*. Senate Document 91-25. 91st Cong., 1st sess. Washington, D.C.: U.S. Government Printing Office, 1969. 189p.

Although tough to follow in places, this is an excellent summary of First Army activities from Normandy to the Elbe, including the organization's only temporary setback, the Battle of the Bulge. Illustrated with only one map.

2055. Exton, Hugh M. "Armored and Infantry Cooperation in the Pursuit." *Field Artillery Journal*, XXXIX (July-August 1949), 155-159.

Follows the activities of the infantry and armored divisions of Seventh Corps in France and Belgium, August 25-September 11, 1944.

2056. MacDonald, Charles B. "Why Didn't They Let the First Army Win the War?" *Army*, IX (April 1959), 48-52.

A study of the decision not to thrust toward Berlin.

2057. United States. War Department. First Army. *First United States Army Combat Operations Data: Europe, 1944-1945*. Washington, D.C.: U.S. Government Printing Office, 1948. 283p.

2058. ———. ———. ———. *Report of Operations, 1 August 1944 to 8 May 1945*. 7 vols. Washington, D.C.: U.S. Government Printing Office, 1946.

Taken together, these eight volumes constitute the largest amount of published information available on any American field army in the MTO/ETO; includes charts, tables, and lists.

Third Army

2059. Allen, Robert S. *Drive to Victory*. New York: Berkley Publishers, 1947. 271p.

Similar to the next title in coverage, although not as well known.

2060. ———. *Lucky Forward: The History of Patton's Third U.S. Army*. New York: Vanguard, 1947. 424p.

A detailed history of the Third Army and biography of its boss written by the executive officer of the organization's G-2 operations section. Extremely flattering in almost every instance.

2061. Dyer, George. *XII Corps: Spearhead of Patton's Third Army*. Baton Rouge: Military Press of Louisiana, 1947. 560p.

An extremely detailed look at one of the more important corps and how its armored units made the famous dash across France in 1944; includes charts, tables, graphs, and illustrations.

2062. Forty, George. *Patton's Third Army at War.* New York: Scribners, 1978. 192p.

Although not the largest, this is one of the newest and most readily available histories, which tells the organization's story as a pictorial emphasizing combat at the company level; the text loosely holds the army and the 260 photographs together as the army forges across Europe in 1944-1945. A special section is given over to a biography of George S. Patton, Jr.

2063. Harkins, Paul D., with the Editors of *Army Times. When the Third Cracked Europe: The Story of Patton's Incredible Army.* Harrisburg, Pa.: Stackpole Books, 1969. 95p.

A brief pictorial with its photographs arranged in pairs contrasting the 1944-1945 scene with that of 1969; Harkins, who was Patton's deputy chief of staff, writes a highly personal account of the organization's commander and of its dash from the Channel to Czechoslovakia.

2064. Johnson, Danny M. "The Third Army: Past and Present." *Infantry*, LXXIII (March-April 1983), 7-9.

A brief history of Patton's organization of 1944-1945 is contrasted with the same organization nearly 40 years later.

2065. Metheny, E.A. *History of the Third United States Army, 1918-1962.* Fort McPherson, Ga.: Headquarters, Third Army, 1967. 230p.

This command history, more detailed than most, was written to give new officers and men a feel for the organization's illustrious past; illustrated with drawings and photographs.

2066. Small, Collie. "The Third: Tops in Honors, Casablanca to Nürenberg." *Saturday Evening Post*, CCXVIII (August 11, 1945), 28-29+.

An overview of the organization's campaigns in northwest Europe written for a home-front audience anxious for news of their "boys."

2067. Smith, Francis C. *History of the Third Army.* Study, no. 17. Washington, D.C.: Historical Section, U.S. Army Ground Forces, 1946. 145p.

Covers the organization's history from its creation in France in late fall 1918 through World War II with emphasis not only on its combat but on its organization, logistics, command relationships, etc. Seeks to find and explain why it was such an effective force.

2068. Wallace, Brenton G. *Patton and His Third Army.* Harrisburg, Pa.: Military Service Publishing Co., 1946. 232p.

An examination of the role of the Third Army in the liberation of Europe and a description of General Patton's part in the actual fighting as recalled by a colonel on his staff.

Fifth Army

2069. Forty, George. *Fifth Army at War.* New York: Scribners, 1980. 144p.

A pictorial history which attempts to describe the bitter fighting in Italy from the infantryman's viewpoint; illustrated with 217 photographs and 14 maps plus a special section on Gen. Mark W. Clark. Readers should also note, in connection with the Fifth, General Clark's memoirs, which are cited in IV:B:2 above.

2070. Starr, Chester G. *From Salerno to the Alps: A History of the Fifth Army, 1943-1945.* Nashville, Tenn.: Battery Press, 1979. 530p.

First published by the Infantry Journal Press in 1946, this is considered by many to be one of the finest field army histories and the best chronological and circumstantial account of the Italian campaign; illustrated with 32 photographs and 42 maps.

Seventh Army

2071. Turner, John F., and Robert Jackson. *Destination Berchtesgarden.* New York: Scribners, 1977. 192p.

This pictorial history of the Seventh, which attempts to tell its history from the infantryman's viewpoint, is the only substantial account of the organization available and covers its campaigns from Sicily through southern France to the Rhine crossing and link-up with the Fifth Army; illustrated with some 200 photographs and maps.

Ninth Army

2072. *Conquer: The Story of the Ninth Army, 1944-1945.* Nashville, Tenn.: Battery Press, 1980. 406p.

First published by Infantry Journal Press in 1948, this work details the organization's history and campaigns in France, Belgium, Luxembourg, Holland, and in Germany to within 50 miles of Berlin; illustrated with 52 photographs and 18 maps.

2073. Dean, Gardner A. *One Hundred and Eighty Days: XIII Corps.* Hanover, Pa.: Richard Petersen, 1945. 43p.

An account of this subsection of Ninth Army which on May 7, 1945, comprised the Thirty-Fifth, Eighty-Fourth, and One Hundred Second Infantry Divisions.

2074. *History of the XVI Corps from Its Activation to the End of the War in Europe.* Washington, D.C.: Infantry Journal Press, 1947. 111p.

A review of this subsection's hard fighting in France, Belgium, Holland, and Germany, where on May 7, 1945, it comprised four infantry divisions: the Twenty-Ninth, Seventy-Fifth, Seventy-Ninth, and Ninety-Fifth.

3. Airborne Divisions

Introduction: Following German successes with paratroops early in the war, both England and America completed plans to deploy such airborne soldiers themselves. The Allies saw the value of air-dropped soldiers as shock troops, able to seize points behind the lines and to hold them (it was hoped) until more powerful reinforcements arrived. Four U.S. airborne divisions were sent to the MTO and ETO, the Thirteenth, Seventeenth, Eighty-Second, and One Hundred First, with only the last three seeing combat. The citations in this section examine the literature commonly available on those units.

Thirteenth Airborne Division

2075. Blythe, William J., ed. *History and Pictorial Record of the 13th Airborne Division.* Atlanta, Ga.: Albert Love, 1946. 207p.

This yearbook-like history recalls the men of the "Black Cat Division," so-called because of its August 13, 1943 (Friday) activation, which arrived in the ETO in February 1945 but saw no combat.

Seventeenth Airborne Division

2076. Pay, Don. *Thunder from Heaven: 17th Airborne Division in World War II.* Nashville, Tenn.: Battery Press, 1980. 179p.

First printed in Birmingham, Mich., in 1947, this account tells how the unit arrived in the ETO in time to participate in the Battle of the Bulge and the airborne assault crossing of the Rhine in March 1945; includes brief histories of the regimental units and 22 illustrations.

Eighty-Second Airborne Division

2077. *All American, the Story of the 82nd Airborne Division.* G.I. Stories. Paris, France: Stars & Stripes, 1945. 32p.

A brief overview of the unit's history from Sicily to Arnhem.

2078. Carter, Ross S. *Those Devils in Baggy Pants.* New York: Appleton-Century, 1951. 299p.

Recollections of the training and combat of one of the division's regiments (the Five Hundred Fourth) by one of the three survivors of the author's original platoon; covers combat in Sicily, Italy, Normandy, and Arnhem.

2079. Dawson, W. Forrest, ed. *Saga of the All American.* Atlanta, Ga.: Albert Love, 1946. 191p.

A pictorial yearbook-like souvenir booklet put together for the officers and men of the division; includes scenes not only of combat, but of training and rest camps, in 850 photos and drawings.

2080. *The Devils in Baggy Pants.* Nashville, Tenn.: Battery Press, 1982. 172p.

A pictorial look at the Five Hundred Fourth which complements Carter's work, cited above; first published in Germany in 1945, this souvenir book contains over 300 photographs, some in color. Oversize format.

2081. Gellhorn, Martha. "The 82nd Airborne: Master of the Hot Spots." *Saturday Evening Post*, CCXVIII (February 23, 1946), 22-23+.

An overview of the organization's most significant campaigns from Sicily through Arnhem.

2082. ———. "Rough and Tumble: The 82nd Airborne Division." *Saturday Evening Post*, CCXIV (December 2, 1944), 22+.

A popular presentation of the unit's campaigns in Sicily, Italy, and, particularly, Normandy.

2083. Ospital, John. *We Wore Jump Boots and Baggy Pants.* Nashville, Tenn.: Battery Press, 1977. 118p.

This is a slightly fictionalized reminiscence of the division, which, nevertheless, manages to capture the spirit of the soldiers who fought in it.

2084. Thomas, Charles R. *Hell on Earth.* New York: Vantage, 1980. 152p.

These spicy memories of the leader of Company I, Five Hundred Fourth Parachute Infantry, recall the Eighty-Second's dangerous drops in Sicily, Italy, Normandy, and especially Arnhem, or more precisely, Nijmegen.

One Hundred First Airborne Division

2085. Critchell, Laurence. *Four Stars of Hell.* New York: Ballantine Books, 1968. 320p.

First published by the New York firm of Declan X. McMullen Co. in 1947, these recollections of the Five Hundred First Parachute Infantry of the One Hundred First relive the unit's most famous operations: Normandy, Eindhoven in the "Market-Garden" fiasco, and, of course, the Battle of the Bulge.

2086. Katcher, Philip. *U.S. 101st Airborne Division, 1942-1945.* London: Osprey, 1979. 40p.

A short, profusely illustrated review of the unit's history with emphasis on its uniforms and equipment.

2087. McDonough, J.L., and K.S. Gardner. *Skyriders.* Nashville, Tenn.: Battery Press, 1980. 176p.

A history of the 327/401 Glider Infantry of the One Hundred First which entered combat in Normandy, fought at Eindhoven, and helped defend Bastogne; illustrated with 200 photographs.

2088. *The 101st Airborne Division*. G.I. Stories. Paris, France: Stars & Stripes, 1945. 31p.

A quick overview of the division's most memorable campaigns.

2089. Rapport, Leonard, and Arthur Northwood, Jr. *Rendezvous with Destiny: A History of the 101st Airborne Division*. 2nd enl. ed. Madelia, Minn.: House of Print, 1982. 860p.

The first edition was published in 1948 by the One Hundred First Airborne Division Association. The operations of the division as a whole are set down and then broken down into their smallest possible parts--the operations of platoons, squads, and individuals. Includes almost three-quarters of "SLAM" Marshall's *Bastogne: The First Eight Days* (cited in IV:C:2:c above), over 100 photographs and drawings, and 107 maps.

2090. Shapiro, Milton J. *The Screaming Eagles: The 101st Airborne Division in World War II*. New York: Julian Messner, 1976. 191p.

Follows the combat of the division from Normandy through the Ardennes in a text suitable for younger readers; illustrated with photographs and maps.

2091. Thompson, Francis I. *Look Out Below*. Washington, D.C.: Catholic University of America, 1975. 234p.

Recollections of a Catholic priest who served as a chaplain with the One Hundred First in Europe; includes the author's thoughts on the morality of war as well as on the difficulties of being an airborne soldier. Includes a few photographs.

4. Armored Divisions

Introduction: Tanks and armored vehicles played an important role in the European war from the beginning; indeed, one can say that the drive by Patton's Third across France in 1944 was simply a vast improvement on the air-supported blitzkrieg tactics unleashed by the Germans in 1939-1940. Speaking of the Third, one recalls the argument that it was "top-heavy" with armor. Interestingly, this was not the case. Blessed with armored divisions organized into an "old style," which meant about 100 more tanks, the First Army almost always had more armor than any other U.S. field army, including Patton's. The citations below examine the literature available on the 14 armored divisions which saw service in the MTO and ETO.

First Armored Division

2092. Howe, George F. *The Battle History of the First Armored Division*. Nashville, Tenn.: Battery Press, 1979. 471p.

First published by the Combat Forces Press in 1954, this account tells of the First, organized in 1940 in answer to the Army's demand for a new unit suited to modern war; nicknamed "Old Ironsides," the outfit pioneered U.S. tank gunnery and armored tactics and saw service in the MTO from 1942 to 1945.

Second Armored Division

2093. Houston, Donald E. *Hell on Wheels: The 2nd Armored Division.* San Rafael, Calif.: Presidio Press, 1977. 492p.

A well-written documentary study of this unit which was formed in mid-1940 and landed at Normandy, June 7, 1944; spending most of its next year with the First Army, Second troopers saw action in France, Belgium, Luxembourg, and Germany. Based on the author's 1975 Oklahoma State University M.A. thesis, "The Second Armored Division's Formative Era, 1940-1944."

2094. Katcher, Philip. *U.S. 2nd Armored Division, 1940-1945.* London: Osprey, 1980. 40p.

A profusely illustrated history of the unit which concentrates on the uniforms of its men and the camouflage/markings of its vehicles.

2095. Trahan, E.A., ed. *A History of the 2nd United States Armored Division, 1940-1946.* Atlanta, Ga.: Albert Love, 1946. 89p.

A pictorial yearbook-type souvenir book assembled for the men who served in the organization; includes a roster.

Third Armored Division

2096. Berry, Edward S. "From the Seine to the Siegfried Line." *Armored Cavalry Journal*, LIX (January-February 1950), 35-41.

The diary of a division officer, August 26-September 9, 1944, covering the fighting in the Oise and Aisne regions of France and the Hainaut, Namur, and Liège regions of Belgium.

2097. *"Call Me Spearhead," the Saga of the 3rd Armored "Spearhead" Division.* G.I. Stories. Paris, France: Stars & Stripes, 1944. 36p.

An overview of this First Army unit from late June 1944 to its arrival at Hotton, Belgium, in December.

2098. Henry, Thomas R. "Masters of Slash-and-Surprise; The Third Armored Division." *Saturday Evening Post*, CCXIX (October 19, 1946), 30-31+.

An overview of the unit's combat with special attention to its service in Germany from February to May 1945.

2099. Rock, William R. *Third Armored Division, "Spearhead": A History of the Third Armored Division.* Darmstadt, West Germany: Stars & Stripes, 1957. 69p.

Follows the unit's history from its activation in April 1941 through the war years in northwest Europe to occupation and Cold War duty in Germany; illustrated.

2100. *Spearhead in the West: The Third Armored Division, 1941-1945.* Nashville, Tenn.: Battery Press, 1980. 260p.

This pictorial souvenir book was first published in Germany in 1945 and tells how the unit took the First Army out of

Normandy and across France, closed the Falaise gap, and broke the Siegfried Line to capture Cologne; illustrated with 510 photographs and 53 maps.

Fourth Armored Division

2101. *The Fourth Armored Division from the Beach to Bastogne*. G.I. Stories. Paris, France: Stars & Stripes, 1945. 31p.

An overview of the unit which arrived in France in July 1944 and fought as part of Patton's Third across northern France, relieved the One Hundred First Airborne at Bastogne, and pushed on into Germany.

2102. Small, Collie. "Rat Chase to the Rhine: The Fourth Armored Division." *Saturday Evening Post*, CCXVII (April 28, 1945), 18-19+.

Describes the Fourth's fighting from Bastogne through the Rhineland and into Central Europe.

Fifth Armored Division

2103. *Paths of Armor*. Atlanta, Ga.: Albert Love, 1950. 358p.

A pictorial review of the "Victory" Division as it fought its way from Normandy through northern France, the Ardennes, Alsace, and the Rhineland into central Europe with the Third, First, and Ninth Armies.

2104. *The Road to Germany*. G.I. Stories. Paris, France: Stars & Stripes, 1944. 32p.

An overview which follows the unit from its landing at Utah Beach in July 1944 to the Rhineland in December.

Sixth Armored Division

2105. *Brest to Bastogne, the Story of the Sixth Armored Division*. G.I. Stories. Paris, France: Stars & Stripes, 1945. 31p.

Follows this Third Army tank outfit from the Normandy break-out through northern France to the Ardennes, Rhineland, and central Europe.

2106. Hofmann, George F. *The Super Sixth: History of the Sixth Armored Division in World War II and Its Postwar Association*. Louisville, Ky.: Sixth Armored Division Association, 1975. 512p.

Hofmann's detailed study, with illustrations, portrays the unit's heavy combat across northern France, in the effort to stem the German counteroffensive in the Ardennes, the battles in the Rhineland, the Rhine crossing, and the march into Czechoslovakia.

Eighth Armored Division

2107. Leach, Charles R. *In Tornado's Wake: A History of the Eighth Armored Division*. Chicago: Published for the Eighth Armored Division Association by Argus Press, 1956. 232p.

The Eighth entered combat late, arriving in the Ardennes in January-February 1945. Thereafter it campaigned as a Ninth Army unit in the Rhineland-Westphalia area of Germany until VE-Day.

Ninth Armored Division

2108. *The Ninth, the Story of the Ninth Armored Division.* G.I. Stories. Paris, France: Stars & Stripes, 1945. 31p.

An overview of the campaigns of this unit which saw service with both the First and Third Armies and which is remembered best for its capture of the Remagen Bridge, a story well told by Ken Heckler in Section IV:C:2:c above.

Tenth Armored Division

2109. Nichols, Lester M. *Impact: The Battle Story of the Tenth Armored Division.* New York: Bradbury, Sayles, O'Neill Co., 1954. 325p.

Transferred to the Third Army from the Ninth in October 1944, the "Tiger" Division saw action in the Ardennes, the Rhineland, Baden-Wurttemberg, and Bavaria, Germany.

2110. *Terrify and Destroy, the Story of the 10th Armored Division.* G.I. Stories. Paris, France: Stars & Stripes, 1945. 31p.

An overview of the unit's history from the Ardennes to Bavaria.

2111. *Tiger Tracks.* Atlanta, Ga.: Albert Love, 1944. 36p.

A brief pictorial souvenir book which marks the unit's August-September 1944 service with the U.S. Ninth Army.

Eleventh Armored Division

2112. Steward, Hal D. *Thunderbolts: The History of the Eleventh Armored Division.* Nashville, Tenn.: Battery Press, 1980. 143p.

This oversize book, first published for the division association in 1948, follows the unit's service in central Germany as part of the Third Army during the last four months of the war; illustrated with 225 photographs and 4 maps.

2113. *The Story of the 11th Armored Division, Thunderbolt.* G.I. Stories. Paris, France: Stars & Stripes, 1945. 32p.

An overview of the organization's service in central Germany and its move into Austria beginning May 3, 1945.

Twelfth Armored Division

2114. *Hellcats, the Twelfth Armored Division.* Atlanta, Ga.: Albert Love, 1943. 60p.

This souvenir book covers the unit's activation and training.

2115. *Speed Is the Password.* G.I. Stories. Paris, France: Stars and Stripes, 1945. 32p.

This Seventh Army unit saw combat in eastern France, the Rhineland, and Bavaria between December 1944 and May 1945.

Thirteenth Armored Division

2116. *The Thirteenth Armored Division: A History of the "Black Cats" from Texas to France, Germany, and Austria and Back to California*. Baton Rouge, La.: Army and Navy Publishing Co., 1945. 145p.

This Third Army unit entered combat in early April 1945 and fought through the Rhineland to Bavaria. This is a pictorial souvenir book for the unit's officers and men.

Fourteenth Armored Division

2117. Carter, Joseph. *The History of the Fourteenth Armored Division, World War II*. Atlanta, Ga.: Albert Love, 1946. 394p.

An oversize pictorial souvenir book designed for the officers and men of this Seventh Army unit which entered combat in November 1944 and drove through eastern France to the Rhineland and Bavaria.

Twentieth Armored Division

2118. *Armor in the ETO*. Atlanta, Ga.: Albert Love, 1946. 85p.

A brief pictorial souvenir title designed for the men of this Seventh Army unit which entered combat in late April 1945 in Bavaria, spending only eight days on the line and losing only nine dead.

5. Infantry Divisions

Introduction: The "dogface" infantryman bore the brunt of the fighting in World War II, just as he had/has in every other war before and since. For that reason, more infantry divisions were formed by the U.S. Army in 1940-1945 than any other kind; everyone realized that it was the kid on the ground with the rifle who would, in the end, win the war. The citations below examine the literature available on infantry divisions which fought for America in the MTO and ETO, 1942-1945.

First Infantry Division

2119. *The First: The Story of the First Infantry Division*. G.I. Stories. Paris, France: Stars & Stripes, 1945. 32p.

An overview of the "Big Red One's" service from North Africa to Czechoslovakia.

2120. Hurkala, John. *The Fighting First Division: A True Story*. New York: Greenwich Book Publishers, 1957. 201p.

One of the organization's many sergeants recalls the fighting in North Africa in 1942-1943, evoking scenes made familiar to moviegoers in writer-director Samuel Fuller's 1980 film "The Big Red One," which starred Lee Marvin and Mark Hamill.

2121. Knickerbocker, H.R. *Danger Forward: The Story of the First Division in World War II.* Nashville, Tenn.: Battery Press, 1980. 479p.

First published in 1947, this account follows its subject from November 1942 when it entered combat in North Africa against the Vichy French, through Tunisia and the invasion of Sicily; withdrawn to England, the First landed on Omaha Beach on D-Day and fought through France, Belgium, central Germany, and into Czechoslovakia with the Third Army. Illustrated with 115 photographs and 19 maps.

2122. Small, Collie. "Big Red One Wrote the Book." *Saturday Evening Post*, CCXVIII (February 2, 1946), 14-15+.

An overview of the outfit's service from North Africa to Czechoslovakia.

Second Infantry Division

2123. *Combat History of the 2nd Infantry Division in World War II.* Baton Rouge, La.: Army and Navy Publishing Co., 1946. 202p.

This pictorial souvenir book designed for the unit's officers and men recalls the "Second-to-None" Division's service with the First, Third, and Ninth Armies from Normandy through northern France, the Ardennes, and the Rhineland to Pilsen, Czechoslovakia, in May 1945.

Third Infantry Division

2124. *Blue and White Devils.* G.I. Stories. Paris, France: Stars & Stripes, 1945. 31p.

The "Marne" Division's history is followed with the Seventh Army from the invasion of southern France in August 1944 through its move into Salzburg, Austria, in May 1945.

2125. Taggart, Donald G. *History of the Third Infantry Division in World War II.* Washington, D.C.: Infantry Journal Press, 1947. 574p.

A complete history of this veteran unit was activated in late 1917 for service in World War I, with emphasis on its service with the Seventh Army in the invasion of southern France, combat in eastern France and the Rhineland, and descent upon south-central Germany. Illustrated with maps and photographs.

Fourth Infantry Division

2126. *The Famous Fourth, the Story of the Fourth Division.* G.I. Stories. Paris, France: Stars & Stripes, 1945. 31p.

Another veteran World War I division, the "Ivy," which landed at Normandy on D-Day and remained with the First Army until late December 1944 when it was attached to the Third Army; in 1945 the unit served with both the Third and Seventh Armies, ending the war in Amberg, Bavaria.

Fifth Infantry Division

2127. Barta, Edward J. *Red Diamond's First Fifty: A History of the Fifth Infantry Division, 1917-1967*. Fort Carson, Colo.: Information Office, 1967. 67p.

An overview of the history of this unit from World War I through the early part of the Vietnam era; illustrated with photographs.

2128. *The Fifth Infantry Division in the ETO*. Nashville, Tenn.: Battery Press, 1981. 254p.

First published by Albert Love in 1945 as the unit's souvenir book, the work (oversize and illustrated with 307 photographs) details the Fifth's service with the Third Army in the dash across northern France, the battles at Metz and of the Bulge, and the operations in central Germany.

Eighth Infantry Division

2129. Griesbach, Marc F., ed. *Combat History of the 8th Infantry Division in World War II*. Baton Rouge, La.: Army and Navy Publishing Co., 1945. 98p.

The pictorial souvenir book of the division known as both the "Pathfinder" and "Arrow" Division; landing on Utah Beach in July 1944, the unit served with the Third, First, and Ninth Armies and participated in the campaigns in northern France, the Rhineland, and central Germany.

2130. *"There Are My Credentials," the Story of the 8th Infantry Division*. G.I. Stories. Paris, France: Stars & Stripes, 1944. 31p.

An overview of the unit's fighting in northern France taken from the division motto.

Ninth Infantry Division

2131. Henry, Thomas R. "Avenging Ghosts of the Ninth." *Saturday Evening Post*, CCXIX (July 6, 1946), 24-25+.

A review of the combat service of this First Army unit which landed at Normandy and fought from northern France through the Ardennes and Rhineland to Kothen in Saxony, Germany.

2132. *"Hitler's Nemesis," the 9th Infantry Division*. G.I. Stories. Paris, France: Stars & Stripes, 1944. 32p.

An overview of the unit's service in the battles in northern France, based on the divisional nickname.

2133. Mittelman, Joseph B. *Eight Stars to Victory: A History of the Veteran Ninth U.S. Infantry Division*. Washington, D.C.: Ninth Infantry Division Association, 1948. 406p.

A detailed and pictorial account which follows the unit from its 1940 activation through its service in North Africa, Sicily, England, France, and Germany.

Tenth (Mountain) Infantry Division

2134. Burton, Hal. *The Ski Troops.* New York: Simon and Schuster, 1971. 192p.

A history of the unique U.S. division trained especially for combat in the mountains of Italy; it was with this division that Col. William O. Darby met his death shortly before war's end.

2135. Casewitt, Curtis W. *The Saga of the Mountain Soldiers; The Story of the 10th Mountain Division.* New York: Julian Messner, 1981. 159p.

Based on primary and secondary sources plus interviews, this account follows the training of this organization and its deployment to Italy in late 1944 for combat in the northern mountain regions of that nation.

2136. Govan, Thomas P. *History of the 10th (Alpine) Light Division.* Historical Study, no. 28. Washington, D.C.: Historical Section, U.S. Army Ground Forces, 1946. 14p.

A brief review of the unit's organization, training, and deployment with special attention to unique techniques taught such as skiing.

2137. Harper, Frank. *Night Climb.* New York: Longmans, Green, 1946. 216p.

The first book-length study of the Tenth Mountain Division and its role in the final months of the conflict in northern Italy.

2138. Thruelsen, Richard. "The 10th Caught It All at Once." *Saturday Evening Post*, CCXVIII (December 8, 1945), 26-27+.

An overview of the Mountain Division's service during the last months of the war in northern Italy.

Twenty-Eighth Infantry Division

2139. Colbaugh, Jack. *The Bloody Patch: A True Story of the Daring 28th Infantry Division.* New York: Vantage Press, 1973. 131p.

An account of the First Army unit which landed in Normandy and fought its way across northern France, the Ardennes, and the Rhineland into central Germany, with emphasis on the fighting in Huertgen Forest in fall 1944.

2140. *28 Roll On.* G.I. Stories. Paris, France: Stars & Stripes, 1945. 32p.

Follows the organization from Normandy to Kaiserslautern in the Rhineland.

Twenty-Ninth Infantry Division

2141. Ewing, Joseph H. *"29 Let's Go": A History of the 29th Infantry Division in World War II.* Washington, D.C.: Infantry Journal Press, 1948. 315p.

Nicknamed the "Blue and Gray Division," this unit served with the First Army through September 1944 before transfer to the Ninth; after D-Day, the Twenty-Ninth served in the campaigns across northern France, into the Rhineland, to central Germany, finishing the war at Warendorf, in Hannover.

2142. *"29 Let's Go!"* G.I. Stories. Paris, France: Stars & Stripes, 1945. 31p.

An overview of the unit's history from D-Day to central Germany.

Thirtieth Infantry Division

2143. Apter, Howard. "'Old Hickory': The Saga of the 30th Infantry Division." *Saga* (May 1962), 37-41, 79-83.

Follows the organization from D-Day to central Germany.

2144. Hewitt, Robert L. *Workhorse of the Western Front: The Story of the 30th Infantry Division.* Nashville, Tenn.: Battery Press, 1980. 404p.

First published by Infantry Journal Press in 1946, this account recalls the unit's formation in 1940 and its eleven months of ETO combat from Normandy, the battles in northern France, at the Siegfried Line and in the Ardennes, and on into central Germany.

Thirty-Fourth Infantry Division

2145. Hougen, John H. *The Story of the Famous 34th Infantry Division.* Nashville, Tenn.: Battery Press, 1980. 196p.

This reprint of the 1949 Arlington edition traces the unit's history from Fondouk Gap in North Africa in March 1943 through the hard campaigning in Italy marked by such battles as Cassino.

2146. Lehman, Milton. "The Champion Hard-Luck Division." *Saturday Evening Post*, CCXVIII (October 13, 1945), 18-19+.

An overview of the "Red Bull's" service in Africa and Italy from 1943 to 1945.

Thirty-Fifth Infantry Division

2147. *Attack!* G.I. Stories. Paris, France: Stars & Stripes, 1945. 31p.

An overview of the "Santa Fe" Division, which fought with the Third Army until 1945 when it joined the Ninth.

2148. Faubus, Orval E. *In This Faraway Land.* N.p., 1971. 736p.

A diary of service with the Thirty-Fifth Division's Three Hundred Twentieth Infantry Regiment from Normandy to Magdeburg, Germany, with emphasis on the human interest elements of the conflict as seen from the foxhole.

2149. Huston, James A. *Biography of a Battalion.* Gering, Neb.: Courier Press, 1950. 306p.

This noted military historian provides a detailed study of the Third Battalion, One Hundred Thirty-Fourth Infantry of the Thirty-Fifth Division in the fighting at St. Lô, Nancy, the Ruhr, and meeting the Soviets on the Elbe.

2150. *Presenting the 35th Infantry Division in World War II, 1941-1945*. Atlanta, Ga.: Albert Love, 1946. 122p.

An oversize souvenir book designed for the unit's officers and men; illustrated with hundreds of photos. Contains a roster.

Thirty-Sixth Infantry Division

2151. Huff, Richard A., ed. *A Pictorial History of the 36th "Texas" Infantry Division*. Nashville, Tenn.: Battery Press, 1979. 108p.

First published by Newsfoto in 1946, this oversize souvenir book, illustrated with hundreds of photographs, recalls the service of this unit in Italy (including the Rapido River affair) and later as part of the Seventh Army in the invasion of southern France and the drive through the Rhineland into central Germany.

2152. McDugal, Leila. *Uphill and Down: A History of the Texas National Guard*. Waco, Tx.: Texan Press, 1966. 162p.

An overall account of the guard, including the part played by the Thirty-Sixth Division in Italy and France/Germany, 1943-1945.

2153. *The Story of the 36th Infantry Division*. G.I. Stories. Paris, France: Stars & Stripes, 1945. 32p.

A brief review of this unit's history with emphasis on its Seventh Army service in the ETO.

2154. Walker, Fred L. "The 36th Was a Great Fighting Division." *Southwestern Historical Quarterly*, LXXII (Spring 1968), 40-59.

The unit's one-time commanding officer recalls the organization's service in Italy, including Salerno and the Rapido; for further references to the Thirty-Sixth in Italy, see Section IV:C:1:c above.

Forty-Second Infantry Division

2155. Daly, Hugh C., ed. *The 42nd "Rainbow" Infantry Division: A Combat History of World War II*. Baton Rouge, La.: Army and Navy Publishing Co., 1946. 106p.

Nicknamed the "rainbow" by the unit's Great War chief of staff Col. Douglas MacArthur because it comprised men from 26 states, this unit was reactivated in 1943 and sent with the Seventh Army into the Rhineland and central Germany in early 1945.

Forty-Fourth Infantry Division

2156. *Combat History of the 44th Infantry Division, September 4, 1944-July 20, 1945.* Atlanta, Ga.: Albert Love, 1946. 155p.

Entering combat with the Seventh Army in late fall of 1944, the unit participated in the campaign in the Rhineland and central Germany, finishing the war in Austria.

Forty-Fifth Infantry Division

2157. Bishop, Leo V., ed. *The Fighting 45th: The Combat Record of an Infantry Division.* Baton Rouge, La.: Army and Navy Publishing Co., 1946. 200p.

Reprinted by Battery Press in 1979, this heavily illustrated souvenir book recalls the "Thunderbird Division's" Seventh Army service from the invasion of southern France through the campaign in the Rhineland and on into central Germany. Earlier service in Italy is also covered.

2158. *The 45th.* G.I. Stories. Paris, France: Stars & Stripes, 1945. 31p.

An overview of the unit's history from August 1944 through May 1945.

2159. Longmire, Carey. "The Beachhead Happy Thunderbirds: 45th Division Kept Kesselring's Krauts Always Off Balance." *Saturday Evening Post*, CCXIX (November 30, 1946), 26-27+.

Includes a look at the unit's participation in the Anzio struggle.

2160. Nelson, Guy. *Thunderbird, a History of the 45th Infantry Division.* Oklahoma City, Okla.: 45th Division Association, 1970. 144p.

A well-written look at the unit's service in Italy, including Anzio, and its participation in the invasion of southern France and drive to central Germany.

Sixty-Sixth Infantry Division

2161. *The Black Panthers.* G.I. Stories. Paris, France: Stars & Stripes, 1945. 31p.

An overview of the division's campaigns against St. Nazaire and Lorient, France.

2162. Wessman, Sinto S. *The 66th Infantry Division in World War II.* Nashville, Tenn.: Battery Press, 1978. 175p.

First published by the Army and Navy Publishing Co. in 1946 as *66, a Story of World War II*, this account tells of a 15th Army unit which spent most of its war service besieging the hold-out German defenders in the French coastal cities of Lorient and St. Nazaire. Illustrated with 270 photographs.

Seventieth Infantry Division

2163. *Trailblazers*. G.I. Stories. Paris, France: Stars & Stripes, 1945. 31p.

An overview of this Seventh Army unit which entered combat in early 1945 and participated in the battles for the Rhineland and central Germany.

Seventy-Fifth Infantry Division

2164. *Pictorial History of the 75th Infantry Division, 1944-1945*. Baton Rouge, La.: Army and Navy Publishing Co., 1946. 224p.

This fresh but untested First Army division was rushed into the Ardennes fighting in December 1944 and, as this pictorial souvenir book recalls, later fought under the Seventh and Ninth Armies in the Rhineland and central Germany.

2165. *The 75th*. G.I. Stories. Paris, France: Stars & Stripes, 1945. 30p.

Emphasizes the unit's actions in the Ardennes, the Colmar Pocket, and the battle for the Ruhr.

Seventy-Eighth Infantry Division

2166. *Lightning, the History of the 78th Infantry Division*. Washington, D.C.: Infantry Journal Press, 1947. 301p.

This Ninth Army unit entered combat in the Ardennes in December 1944 and was then transferred to the First Army for combat in the Rhineland and central Germany.

2167. *Lightning, the Story of the 78th Infantry Division*. Paris, France: Stars & Stripes, 1945. 30p.

An overview of this unit's service in the Ardennes and central Germany.

Seventy-Ninth Infantry Division

2168. *The Cross of Lorraine, a Combat History of the 79th Infantry Division, June 1942-December 1945*. Baton Rouge, La.: Army and Navy Publishing Co., 1946. 200p.

This pictorial souvenir book designed for the officers and men of the unit details its service with the Third and Seventh Armies in Normandy, the battles across northern France, the battle of the Rhineland, and the drive into central Germany.

2169. *The Cross of Lorraine Division, the Story of the 79th*. G.I. Stories. Paris, France: Stars & Stripes, 1944. 31p.

An overview of the unit's Third Army service in Normandy and northern France.

2170. McCardell, Lee. "They Wrote Their Story in Blood: The 79th Infantry Division." *Saturday Evening Post*, CCXIX (December 21, 1946), 26-27+.

Perhaps the most easily accessible overview of the Seventy-Ninth's campaigns.

Eightieth Infantry Division

2171. *Forward 80th*. G.I. Stories. Paris, France: Stars & Stripes, 1945. 31p.

A review of the "Blue Ridge Division's" service with the Third Army from the Normandy breakout through the drive into Bavaria.

Eighty-Third Infantry Division

2172. Blumenson, Martin. "With the 83rd Division in Normandy." *American History Illustrated*, II (November 1967), 30-39.

This unit, which operated under the nicknames of the "Thunderbolt Division" and the "Ohio Division," came ashore with the U.S. First Army at Normandy, served under the Third Army for the breakout, and then was traded back and forth between the First, Third, and Ninth Armies, seeing action in northern France, the Ardennes, the Rhineland, and central Germany. This account is limited to the unit's First Army service on D-Day and just after.

Eighty-Fourth Infantry Division

2173. *Railsplitters*. G.I. Stories. Paris, France: Stars & Stripes, 1945. 31p.

Entering combat in November 1944 with the Ninth Army, this unit saw action in the Ardennes, the Rhineland, and central Germany.

Eighty-Fifth Infantry Division

2174. Schultz, Paul L. *The 85th Infantry Division in World War II*. Washington, D.C.: Infantry Journal Press, 1949. 240p.

A detailed review of this unit's service in the U.S. and in Italy under the Fifth Army, April 1942-August 1945.

Eighty-Sixth Infantry Division

2175. Briggs, Richard A. *Black Hawks over the Danube: The History of the 86th Infantry Division in World War II*. Louisville, Ky.: Western Recorder, 1945. 127p.

Entering combat with the Third Army in late March 1945, this unit participated in the drive into Bavaria, serving on the line just 31 days.

Eighty-Seventh Infantry Division

2176. *Stalwart and Strong*. G.I. Stories. Paris, France: Stars & Stripes, 1945. 30p.

This Third Army unit entered combat in mid-December 1944, seeing action in the Ardennes, the Rhineland, and central Germany.

Eighty-Eighth Infantry Division

2177. Delaney, John P. *The Blue Devils in Italy: A History of the 88th Infantry Division.* Washington, D.C.: Infantry Journal Press, 1947. 359p.

A detailed review of this unit's service in the Italian campaign including much of the heavy fighting in and north of the region.

Eighty-Ninth Infantry Division

2178. *The 89th Division, 1942-1945.* Nashville, Tenn.: Battery Press, 1980. 270p.

First published by Infantry Journal Press in 1947, this account of a Third Army unit tells how it entered combat in mid-March 1945 and fought in the Rhineland and central Germany. Includes 287 photographs.

2179. *Rolling Ahead.* G.I. Stories. Paris, France: Stars & Stripes, 1945. 31p.

An overview of the Eighty-Ninth's service in central Germany, March-May 1945.

Ninetieth Infantry Division

2180. Abrams, Joe I., ed. *A History of the 90th Division in World War II, 6 June 1944 to 9 May 1945.* Baton Rouge, La.: Army and Navy Publishing Co., 1946. 89p.

This oversize pictorial souvenir book follows a Third Army unit from the Normandy landing (where it was attached to the First Army), through the breakout and battles across northern France, into the Ardennes, the Rhineland, and central Germany.

2181. Blumenson, Martin. "Re-Assessing a Reputation." *Military Affairs*, XXII (Summer 1958), 95-102.

An analysis of the Ninetieth's impact.

2182. Weaver, William G. *Yankee Doodle Went to Town.* Ann Arbor, Mich.: Edwards Brothers, 1959. 432p.

A detailed reminiscence of the author's service with the Ninetieth Infantry Division from the landings at Normandy to its entry into the Sudetenland of Czechoslovakia on May 7, 1945. Emphasis is laid on the period from late July through November when Weaver was the assistant division commander.

Ninety-First Infantry Division

2183. Robbins, Robert A. *The 91st Infantry Division in World War II.* Washington, D.C.: Infantry Journal Press, 1947. 428p.

Provides a complete review of this unit's combat in Italy in 1944 and 1945 where it completed the war attached to the British Eighth Army.

Ninety-Fourth Infantry Division

2184. Byrnes, Laurence G., ed. *History of the 94th Infantry Division in World War II.* Washington, D.C.: Infantry Journal Press, 1948. 527p.

Entering combat in September 1944, this Ninth Army unit saw action in northern France, the Ardennes, the Rhineland, and central Germany.

2185. *On the Way.* G.I. Stories. Paris, France: Stars & Stripes, 1945. 31p.

An overview of the unit's service in France, the Ardennes, and Germany.

Ninety-Fifth Infantry Division

2186. *Bravest of the Brave.* G.I. Stories. Paris, France: Stars & Stripes, 1944. 29p.

An overview of the division's service in northern France with the U.S. Ninth Army in late October-November 1944.

2187. Fuermann, George M., and F. Edward Dranz. *95th Infantry Division History, 1918-1946.* Atlanta, Ga.: Albert Love, 1947. 211p.

This pictorial souvenir book details the unit's history from World War I through World War II, with emphasis on its combat in northern France, the Rhineland, and central Germany.

Ninety-Ninth Infantry Division

2188. *Battle Babies.* G.I. Stories. Paris, France: Stars & Stripes, 1945. 31p.

An overview of this unit's service from the Ardennes to central Germany.

2189. Lauer, Walter E. *Battle Babies: The Story of the 99th Infantry Division in World War II.* Baton Rouge, La.: Army and Navy Publishing Co., 1951. 351p.

This oversize pictorial souvenir book details this unit's service with the First Army in the Ardennes, the Rhineland, and central Germany from November 1944 through May 1945.

One Hundredth Infantry Division

2190. Bass, Michael A. *The Story of the Century.* Nashville, Tenn.: Battery Press, 1979. 413p.

First published in 1946, this detailed account follows MG Withers A. Burress' unit in Seventh Army action in the Rhineland and central Germany from early November 1944 through May 1945.

2191. *The Story of the Century.* G.I. Stories. Paris, France: Stars & Stripes, 1945. 30p.

An overview of the division's combat in the Rhineland and central Germany, 1944-1945.

One Hundred Second Infantry Division

2192. Mick, Allan H., ed. *With the 102nd Infantry Division Through Germany.* Washington, D.C.: Infantry Journal Press, 1947. 541p.

A detailed review of the "Ozark Division's" service with the Ninth Army in the Rhineland and central Germany from late October 1944 through May 1945.

One Hundred Third Infantry Division

2193. Mueller, Ralph, and Jerry Turk. *Report After Action: The Story of the 103rd Infantry Division in World War II.* Nashville, Tenn.: Battery Press, 1978. 166p.

A reprint of the 1945 edition which details the actions of the "Cactus Division" with the Seventh Army in the Rhineland and central Germany from late November 1944 through May 1945; promoted after the defense of Bastogne, MG Anthony C. McAuliffe became this unit's CO on January 11, 1945.

One Hundred Fourth Infantry Division

2194. Downs, Kenneth T. "Nothing Stopped the Timberwolves." *Saturday Evening Post*, CCXIX (August 17, 1946), 20+.

An overview of this unit's participation in the French and German campaigns from late 1944 through May 1945.

2195. Hoegh, Leo A., and Howard J. Doyle. *Timberwolf Tracks: The History of the 104th Infantry Division, 1942-1945.* Washington, D.C.: Infantry Journal Press, 1946. 444p.

A detailed recounting of this First Army unit's service from northern France to Antwerp, the Rhineland, and central Germany, October 1944-May 1945.

2196. *Timberwolves.* G.I. Stories. Paris, France: Stars & Stripes, 1945. 20p.

An overview of the division's service with the First and Ninth Armies.

One Hundred Sixth Infantry Division

2197. Dupuy, R. Ernest. *St. Vith--Lion in the Way: The 106th Infantry Division in World War II.* Washington, D.C.: Infantry Journal Press, 1949. 252p.

The saga of the "Golden Lion" division of the First Army which lost several regiments in the Ardennes fighting, but went on to participate in the fighting in the Rhineland and central Germany after April 1945. Further references to the One Hundred Sixth in the Ardennes will be found in IV:C:2:c above.

2198. *The 106th.* G.I. Stories. Paris, France: Stars & Stripes, 1945. 31p.

An overview which concentrates on the Ardennes battle of December 1944.

6. Miscellaneous Units

Introduction: The majority of references below deal with the U.S. Army Rangers, the American counterparts to the British Commandos. These troops were involved in surprise raids and intelligence gathering behind German lines as well as actions where they functioned as light infantry. Of the six Ranger battalions organized during the war, five fought in Europe, including North Africa, Sicily, Italy, and northwest Europe. In a unique experiment in international cooperation, a special unit comprised of both Americans and Canadians was raised; serving as the First Special Service Force, these men performed creditably in France. Additional references to the Rangers will be found within the combat sections of IV:C above while noted Ranger leader William I. Darby's biographies are noted in IV:B:2 above.

2199. Adleman, Robert H., and George Walton. *The Devil's Brigade.* Philadelphia, Pa.: Chilton Books, 1966. 259p.

A history of the First Special Service Force and its American/Canadian volunteers who were trained to operate in snow behind enemy lines and provided useful service in France in 1944-1945.

2200. Altieri, James. *The Spearheaders: A Personal History of Darby's Rangers.* Nashville, Tenn.: Battery Press, 1981. 318p.

First published by Bobbs-Merrill in 1960, this is a survivor's affectionate recollection of the organization of the Fourth Ranger Battalion in northern Ireland, its commando training in Scotland, and its role in bloody combat in North Africa, Sicily, and Italy. Illustrated with 19 photos.

2201. Burhans, Robert D. *The First Special Service Force: A War History of the North Americans.* Nashville, Tenn.: Battery Press, 1978. 376p.

First published by Infantry Journal Press in 1947, this was the first major account of the American/Canadian special force which performed well in winter fighting in 1944-1945.

2202. Glassman, Henry S. *"Lead the Way Rangers": The Fifth Ranger Battalion.* Nashville, Tenn.: Battery Press, 1980. 104p.

Examines the training and operations of this unit which came ashore at Normandy on D-Day and soldiered on through the northern France campaign.

2203. Haggerty, Jerome J. "A History of the Ranger Battalions in World War II." Unpublished Ph.D. Dissertation, Fordham University, 1982.

The author considers the need for, the organization and training of, and the combat by the six U.S. Ranger battalions in World War II: based on a variety of sources both primary and secondary, this is the most scholarly treatment of the subject available.

2204. Ladd, James. *Commandos and Rangers of World War II.* New York: St. Martin's Press, 1978. 288p.

Ladd's study concerns not only the British Commandos, but also the U.S. Rangers and shows how their special skills and weapons were employed in beach reconnaissance, sabotage raids, and spearhead invasions. Illustrated with 64 black and white photographs and 34 maps.

2205. Lane, Ronald I. *Rudder's Rangers*. Manassas, Va.: Ranger Associates, 1979. 198p.

A look at the organization and training of the Second Ranger Battalion, as well as its scaling of the cliffs at Normandy on D-Day and later combats in northwest Europe.

2206. Lehman, Milton. "The Rangers Fought Ahead of Everybody." *Saturday Evening Post*, CCXVIII (June 15, 1946), 28-29+.

An overview of the service of the Ranger battalions which fought in Sicily and Italy, 1943-1945.

2207. Murphy, Thomas D. *Ambassadors in Arms*. Honolulu, Hawaii: University of Hawaii Press, 1955. 315p.

Murphy details the history of the separate Japanese-American (nisei) One Hundredth Infantry Battalion from its activation through its combat in the MTO, particularly from Salerno to the Arno River in Italy where the "Buddaheads" became one of the most-decorated units in the U.S. Army.

2208. Sorvisto, Edwin M. *Roughing It with Charlie: The World War II History of "C" Company, 2nd Ranger Battalion*. Williamstown, N.J.: J.M. Phillips, 1978. 80p.

A reprint of the 1945 pictorial souvenir book which briefly details this group's service from Normandy to VE-Day.

2209. Windsor, Joseph. "Rugged and Ready." *Infantry School Quarterly*, XLII (January 1953), 94-103.

A brief history of the Army's Ranger battalions with emphasis on their role in the MTO and ETO during World War II.

E. LAND WEAPONS, UNIFORMS, AND MARKINGS

Introduction: The amount of information available in English about World War II land weaponry, uniforms, insignia, and camouflage/markings is staggering. Given that consideration and the need to employ space for references to other sources on the conflict, the citations noted below are selective and mainly concern items made available in the last decade or so. The literature on topics covered in this part has also been covered in several of the bibliographies cited in Section I:A above. The order of arrangement here is: General Works; Artillery; Tanks and Armored Vehicles; Infantry and Airborne Weapons; Military Vehicles; and Uniforms/Insignia/Markings.

1. General Works

Introduction: The few works noted here are only a sample of the many weapons-uniform books of a general nature available. Readers should note that additional weapons data is provided in the operational parts of this work noted under III:C above.

2210. Hogg, Ian V., and J.B. King. *German and Allied Secret Weapons of World War II.* Secaucus, N.J.: Chartwell Books, 1976. 127p.

A heavily illustrated account of the development of new weapons systems designed to obtain advantage in the air, on land, or at sea; includes land warfare weapons such as tanks and artillery.

2211. Sylvia, Steven W., and Michael J. O'Donnell. *Uniforms, Weapons, and Equipment of World War II.* Orange, Va.: Moss Publications, 1982. 223p.

An in-depth pictorial study of the weapons, gear, and clothing of U.S. G.I.'s based on research and interviews which reveal much about the soldiers' daily lives; oversize and illustrated with hundreds of previously unpublished photographs.

2. Artillery

Introduction: The citations which follow illuminate the major types of artillery employed by the U.S. Army in the European and Mediterranean Theaters. Users will find additional data on these guns not only above, but also in other parts of this section, especially C, Campaigns and Battles.

2212. Binder, Gary. "American Assault Guns of World War II." *World War II Journal*, I (May-June 1975), 84-89; II (July-August 1975), 20-21.

A pictorial piece concerning those heavy American cannon employed in places like the siege of Metz, France, in 1944.

2213. Brown, Frederic J. "Spearhead Artillery." *Field Artillery Journal*, XXXVI (September 1946), 502-510.

Examines the pieces employed by the artillery unit of the U.S. Third Armored Division.

2214. Chamberlain, Peter, and Terry Gander. *Anti-Aircraft Guns.* World War II Fact Files. New York: Arco, 1976. 64p.

A lavishly illustrated study supplemented by separate sections on the technical details of AA guns in use by various nations, including the U.S.

2215. ———. *Heavy Artillery.* World War II Fact Files. New York: Arco, 1975. 64p.

A lavishly illustrated narrative supplemented by separate sections which provide details on the logistics and cannon employed by various nations, including the U.S.

2216. ———. *Infantry, Mountain, and Airborne Guns.* World War II Fact Files. New York: Arco, 1976. 64p.

A lavishly illustrated booklet supplemented by separate sections which provide details on the lightweight cannon employed by infantry, airborne, and mountain troops of the combatant countries, including the U.S.

2217. ———. *Light and Medium Field Artillery.* World War II Fact Files. New York: Arco, 1976. 64p.

A lavishly illustrated study supplemented by separate sections on the technical details and logistics of field guns of both sides, Allied and Axis.

2218. Franzi, Emil A. *Artillery of the Second World War.* Tucson, Ariz.: Weapons Research Institute, 1977. 63p.

Contains brief descriptions and illustrations of cannon employed by both the Axis and the Allies.

2219. Hogg, Ian V. *Artillery in Color, 1923-1963.* New York: Arco, 1980.

The text takes second place to the many color photographs and illustrations of the world's cannon, including those employed by the U.S. Army in the MTO/ETO during World War II.

2220. ———. *Barrage: The Guns in Action.* Ballantine's Illustrated History of World War II. New York: Ballantine Books, 1970. 160p.

A pictorial which describes not only the use of cannon, but also the various types employed by the combatants; written from the perspective of a wartime British artilleryman.

2221. ———. *British and American Artillery of World War II.* New York: Hippocrene Books, 1979. 256p.

Probably the best account of U.S. artillery is contained in this work, first published in England; the study is divided into eight sections corresponding to various cannon types, and for each piece there is a brief history and comments on its development and effectiveness. Illustrated with 350 photographs.

2222. ———, and John Batchelor. *Artillery.* New York: Scribners, 1972. 158p.

This "coffee-table" British import combines a readable text with an array of photographs and drawings to provide a survey of the history of cannon, including those employed by the U.S. in the MTO/ETO during World War II. An expanded 240-page version was published as *A History of Artillery* by the London/New York firm of Hamlyn in 1974.

2223. Jobé, Joseph, ed. *Guns*. Greenwich, Conn.: New York Graphic Society, 1971. 216p.

This illustrated history of artillery is similar to the work by Hogg and Batchelor cited above and is noteworthy for its color prints.

3. Tanks and Armored Vehicles

Introduction: The references below illustrate the various types of tanks and AFV's employed by the U.S. Army in Europe during the war. Readers will find additional information on these vehicles not only in part E:1 above, but in the other parts of this section, especially C, Campaigns and Battles.

2224. Baily, Charles H. "Faint Praise: The Development of American Tanks and Tank Destroyers During World War II." Unpublished Ph.D. Dissertation, Duke University, 1977.

Baily studies the development of U.S. armor from light to medium models as well as the disputes over what kind and how many should be manufactured.

2225. Bonds, Ray. *Illustrated Guide to World War II Tanks and Fighting Vehicles*. New York: Arco, 1981. 160p.

Employs some 40,000 words of text and over 200 photographs, many in color, to show the major tanks and AFV's of both the Axis and Allies; includes line drawings and tables of specifications.

2226. Bradford, George, and Len Morgan. *Fifty Famous Tanks*. New York: Arco, 1967. 96p.

A brief history of tanks employed by the major powers, including the M3 Lee, M4 Sherman, and M5 Stuart tanks of the United States.

2227. Cary, James. *Tanks and Armor in Modern Warfare*. New York: Watts, 1966. 267p.

An overall assessment which focuses on World War II; the author was a wartime tank commander with the U.S. Army Seven Hundred Twelfth Tank Battalion. Illustrated with 32 photographs and maps.

2228. Chamberlain, Peter, and Christopher Ellis. *British and American Tanks of World War II: The Complete Illustrated History of British, American, and Commonwealth Tanks, Gun Motor Carriages, and Special Vehicles, 1939-1945*. New York: Arco, 1970. 222p.

With vehicles grouped by nation, the development and use of each is described in concise detail while appendices provide material on interior layout, guns, smoke devices, engines, and diagrams of U.S. and British vehicles; illustrated with more than 500 photographs and drawings.

2229. ———. *Pictorial History of Tanks of the World, 1915-1945.* Harrisburg, Pa.: Stackpole, 1972. 256p.

A complete and profusely illustrated tank encyclopedia covering armor from World War I through World War II in chronological and geographical order; over 1,000 photographs plus data and notes demonstrate design, production, and performance.

2230. ———. *The Sherman.* New York: Arco, 1969. 80p.

The first but no longer the best book devoted exclusively to the history, development, and employment of the M4 Sherman tank and its variants; illustrated with over 90 photographs, scale drawings, and cutaways.

2231. ———, and John Milson. *Self-Propelled Anti-Tank and Anti-Aircraft Guns.* World War II Fact Files. New York: Arco, 1975. 64p.

A lavishly illustrated study supplemented by separate sections on the technical details on anti-tank and AA platforms mounted on the armored bodies of various mounts from different warring nations.

2232. Conger, Elizabeth M. *American Tanks and Tank Destroyers.* New York: Holt, Rinehart and Winston, 1944. 159p.

Provides a limited amount of detail, drawings, and photographs on wartime U.S. armor, including the M3, M4, and M5, as well as a discussion of their use in North Africa and Sicily.

2233. Crow, Duncan. *American AFV's of World War II.* Garden City, N.Y.: Doubleday, 1973. 293p.

Covers all non-tank U.S. Army armored vehicles from 1919 to the 1960's emphasizing production, developments in evolution, and operations; the final chapter is a comprehensive and valuable account of the history of U.S. armored organization from World War I to 1964. Illustrated with 700+ photographs and drawings.

2234. ———. *U.S. Armor/Cavalry (1917-1967): A Short History.* AFV/Weapons Series, no. 6. Windsor, Eng.: Profile Publications, 1973. 63p.

An overall survey of U.S. armored history from World War I to Vietnam which concentrates on vehicles and their markings; illustrated with black and white and color drawings and photographs of AFV's, unit crests, etc.

2235. ———, and Robert J. Icks. *Encyclopedia of Armoured Cars and Halftracks.* Secaucus, N.J.: Chartwell Books, 1976. 160p.

Arranged by nation, this work describes the armored cars (not widely employed by the U.S. Army) and halftracks of the war's major powers; illustrated with drawings and a large selection of photographs.

2236. ———. *Encyclopedia of Tanks*. London: Barrie and Jenkins, 1976. 300p.

Combines a discussion of the particulars of AFV's and the different kinds of tanks with a listing of summaries concerning the specifications for those used by different nations; illustrated with drawings and photographs.

2237. Culver, Bruce. *Sherman in Action*. Carrollton, Tx.: Squadron/Signal Publications, 1977. 50p.

The text is secondary in this pictorial which details the M4 tank with 85 captioned black and white photographs.

2238. Ellis, Christopher. *Tanks of the World*. New York: Macmillan, 1971. 177p.

This oversize study concentrates on 40 of the most important tanks and AFV's of the war years with each receiving a technical section and some of the 500 full-color scale drawings which fill this model-maker's dream book.

2239. ———, and Peter Chamberlain. *The Great Tanks*. London and New York: Hamlyn, 1975. 176p.

An oversize British import which highlights the best armored vehicles from World War I to the 1970s, including the U.S. M3, M4, and M5 of World War II; illustrated with hundreds of photos and drawings.

2240. Forty, George. *United States Tanks of World War II in Action*. New York: Scribners, 1983. 160p.

Provides an examination of the planning for and construction and operations of the major armored tanks and vehicles of the U.S., backed by 250 wartime photographs and tables of specifications.

2241. Forty, Simon. *American Armor: 1939-1945 Portfolio*. Harrisburg, Pa.: Stackpole, 1981. 96p.

A data file provides specifications for each tank with detailed drawings of most, while the text describes the design, development, and use of U.S. armor, including a table of organization for an armored division. Illustrated with 138 photographs.

2242. Grove, Eric. *World War II Tanks*. London: Orbis Books, 1976. 143p.

Arranged by nation and providing technical detail on each major tank employed, including those of the U.S.; illustrated with a variety of drawings and photographs, some in color.

2243. Halle, Armin. *Tanks*. Greenwich, Conn.: New York Graphic Society, 1971. 175p.

An illustrated history of fighting vehicles from World War I arranged by nation and featuring a large variety of drawings and photographs, a number of which are published in color for the first time.

2244. Hogg, Ian V., and John Batchelor. *The Tank Story*. London: Phoebus Books, 1977. 160p.

Similar to the authors' work on artillery cited in the last subsection; an oversize work which combines a readable historical text with an array of photographs and drawings covering the development of tanks from World War I to the 1970s.

2245. Hunnicutt, R.P. *Pershing: A History of the Medium Tank T20 Series*. San Rafael, Calif.: Presidio Press, 1980. 240p.

A detailed history of the wide-tracked U.S. tank designed in 1942, which saw action in Europe during the closing months of the war; includes detailed data sheets for 23 vehicles and variants and 580 other photographic and artwork illustrations.

2246. ———. *Sherman: A History of the American Medium Tank*. San Rafael, Calif.: Presidio Press, 1978. 576p.

Divided into six major parts designed to produce a complete technical and operational history, this oversize work covers all aspects of the M4 medium tank, which is still in service in some of the world's armies; illustrated with hundreds of photographs and drawings.

2247. *Infantry Journal*, Staff of. *The Armored Forces of the United States*. Washington, D.C.: Infantry Journal Press, 1943. 72p.

Describes not only organization, but also the vehicles employed through the time of the landings in Italy. Illustrated with 35 drawings, some in color, and a few black and white photographs.

2248. Jarrett, George B. *Portrait in Power*. Forest Grove, Ore.: Normount Technical Publications, 1971. 146p.

A pictorial history of U.S. tanks and self-propelled artillery from World War I to the early 1970's, with emphasis on the World War II years; includes technical details for the major models and variants and a variety of illustrations.

2249. Louis, Murray A. "Seek, Strike, and Destroy: Tank Destroyers in the ETO." *Armor*, LXXIV (September-October 1965), 23-26.

A brief history of the operations of these anti-tank armored vehicles, especially in northwest Europe.

2250. Macksey, Kenneth J. "Build-up for D-Day: The Balance of Armour." In: Bernard Fitzsimons, ed. *Tanks and Weapons of World War II*. New York: Beekman House, 1973, pp. 106-118.

First published in Purnell's *History of the Second World War*, this is an analysis of German and Anglo-American armor available for use after the June 6, 1944, invasion.

2251. ———. *Tank Force: Allied Armor in the Second World War.* Ballantine's Illustrated History of World War II. New York: Ballantine Books, 1970. 160p.

A pictorial history of Allied tanks which saw service, mostly in the MTO and ETO, including the M3, M4, and M5 American models; includes general details and several cutaway drawings.

2252. ———. *Tank Warfare: A History of Tanks in Battle.* New York: Stein and Day, 1972. 284p.

With some little attention to technical details, this British armor expert describes the operational use of tanks in combat from World War I to the Six-Day War, with emphasis on German and Allied use during World War II.

2253. ———, *et al.* "The Era of Struggle, 1942-1945." In: their *The Guinness Book of Tank Facts and Feats: A Record of Armoured Fighting Vehicle Achievement.* 3rd ed. London: Guinness Superlatives, 1981, Chap. 5.

Covers the evolution of design and engineering, weapons and armor, tactics and doctrine, and famous commanders and battles; heavily illustrated.

2254. Ogorkiewicz, Richard M. *Armored Forces.* New York: Praeger, 1970. 488p.

First published as *Armor: A History of Mechanized Forces* in 1960, this edition contains a new introduction and 16 pages of photographs; recognized as a classic work on the multitude of facets of armor development, arranged chronologically.

2255. Patrick, Stephen B. "Tank: A Weapon System Survey." *Strategy and Tactics*, no. 44 (March-April 1974), 3-15.

A pictorial piece on the development of armored vehicles by the Germans and Allies during World War II; a useful survey for those who do not want too much information.

2256. Perrett, Bryan. *Allied Tank Destroyers.* London: Osprey, 1980. 40p.

A lavishly illustrated guide to tank destroyers on both sides; concentrates on camouflage, markings, and other detail.

2257. ———. *The [M-5] Stuart Light Tank Series.* London: Osprey, 1980. 40p.

Similar in layout and execution to the preceding entry; both are heavily illustrated, with much color.

2258. Pickett, George B., Jr. "Armored Personnel Carriers." *Armored Cavalry Journal*, LVIII (May-June 1949), 8-12.

The use of the M2, M3, and M5 halftracks in the ETO during the war.

2259. Pugh, Stevenson, ed. *Armour in Profile*. 5 vols. Garden City, N.Y.: Doubleday, 1968-1972.

A series of pamphlets similar to the Aircraft in Profile series cited in Section III:E above are bound together into a single volume; each chapter is, in fact, a 12- to 20-page pamphlet describing one tank or AFV employed by one of the warring powers; illustrated with black and white photographs and color drawings.

2260. Rigg, Robert B. "A Pictorial History of Armor." *Armor*, LXVIII (September-October 1959), 42-53.

Covers the period from World War I to the mid-1950's; limited to American types.

2261. Rogge, R.E. "A Jaundiced View of Tanks." *Armor*, XCI (September-October 1982), 15-17.

A look at the post-Pearl Harbor debate over the building of heavy or lighter tanks.

2262. Steuard, James C., ed. *The Best Articles and Illustrations from Volume One of AFV-G2: An Anthology*. La Puente, Calif.: Baron Publishing Co., 1972. 102p.

AFV-G2, to which we did not have access during the compilation of this guide, is an important tank-enthusiast publication; this work presents a number of articles and drawings of U.S. and foreign tanks employed during the war as seen by scholars, modelers, and buffs.

2263. ———, and Rick Fines. *Halftracks*. La Puente, Calif.: Baron Publishing Co., 1976. 30p.

An illustrated overview of the U.S. M2, M3, and M5, which were employed as armored personnel carriers, AA carriers, and mortar carriers in the MTO/ETO.

2264. Stout, Wesley W. *Tanks Are Mighty Fine Things*. Detroit, Mich.: Chrysler Motor Corporation, 1946. 144p.

An interesting and rare review of tank production in the U.S. and an appreciation of the use of tanks in battle around the world.

2265. Vanderveen, Burt H., ed. *The Observer's Fighting Vehicles Directory: World War II*. Rev. ed. London: Warne, 1972. 370p.

Arranged by nation, this study provides technical detail for each tank and AFV in use with at least one photograph or drawing of each.

2266. White, Brian T. *Tanks and Other Armored Fighting Vehicles, 1942-1946*. New York: Macmillan, 1976. 171p.

An authoritative directory arranged by nation with complete technical details and 160 pages of color drawings; the London firm of Burke's Peerage published a new edition of this work in 1981.

2267. Zaloga, Steve. *Stuart: U.S. Light Tanks in Action*. Carrollton, Tx.: Squadron/Signal Publications, 1979. 49p.

Text is slight in this pictorial which features over 80 captioned black and white photographs on the M5's use around the world.

4. Infantry and Airborne Weapons

Introduction: The citations here illustrate the various types of small arms employed by the U.S. Army in the ETO/MTO. Users will find more data on them not only in part E:1 above, but in the other parts of this section, especially C, Campaigns and Battles.

2268. Barker, A.J. *British and American Infantry Weapons of World War II*. New York: Arco, 1969. 76p.

Provides descriptions and technical details on the many different infantry weapons used by the Anglo-American forces; illustrated with photographs and line drawings.

2269. Burrell, Brian. *Combat Weapons: Handguns and Shoulder Arms of World War II*. New York: Transatlantic, 1974. 112p.

A guide to the pistols, rifles, and submachine guns employed by Allied and Axis forces during the war; illustrated with drawings and photographs.

2270. Carter, J. Anthony. *Allied Bayonets of World War II*. New York: Arco, 1969. 80p.

Complete technical details are provided for the principal bayonets employed by the Allies, including the U.S., from 1939 to 1946; illustrated with some 65 photos and drawings.

2271. Chamberlain, Peter, and Terry J. Gander. *Allied Pistols, Rifles, and Grenades*. World War II Fact Files. New York: Arco, 1976. 64p.

A lavishly illustrated narrative supplemented by separate sections on technical details of weaponry.

2272. ———. *Anti-Tank Weapons*. World War II Fact Files. New York: Arco, 1974. 64p.

A lavishly illustrated text supplemented by separate sections on technical details for such weapons as the U.S. bazooka.

2273. ———. *Machine Guns*. World War II Fact Files. New York: Arco, 1974. 64p.

Each entry treats one of the types employed by one of the warring powers and includes brief history, specifications, and at least one photo. The emphasis is on heavy weapons such as the U.S. .50 calibre.

2274. ———. *Mortars and Rockets.* World War II Fact Files. New York: Arco, 1976. 64p.

A lavishly illustrated narrative supplemented by separate sections on technical details of weaponry. Includes mortars and rockets of both the Axis and Allies.

2275. ———. *Submachine Guns and Automatic Rifles.* World War II Fact Files. New York: Arco, 1982. 64p.

A lavishly illustrated study supplemented by separate sections on technical details; includes the U.S. Thompson and BAR models.

2276. Cox, Roger A. *Thompson Submachine Guns.* Athens, Ga.: Law Enforcement Ordnance Co., 1982. 220p.

The history and use of this famous weapon is covered by the reprinting, under one cover, of five uncut manuals, four from the U.S. Army and one from the British; illustrated with photographs and exploded-view illustrations.

2277. Hatcher, Julian S. *Hatcher's Book of the Garand.* Washington, D.C.: Infantry Journal Press, 1948. 292p.

The most complete source of the M1 rifle; illustrated, this work tells the history of semiautomatic rifles through the M1, details the M1's use in World War II, and provides instruction for use and care.

2278. Hobart, Frank W.A. *Pictorial History of the Sub-Machine Gun.* New York: Scribners, 1975. 224p.

Illustrated with photographs and drawings, this study details the design, development, and use of "burp" guns by both Allied and Axis forces during World War II.

2279. Hoffschmidt, E.J. *Know Your .45 Auto Pistols, Models 1911 and A1.* Southport, Conn.: Blacksmith Corp., 1973. 58p.

A booklet with data on and illustrations of the variations and different contracted pieces of these famous handguns with tables of quantities manufactured and delivered to the U.S. Army, with dates, serial numbers, etc.

2280. ———. *Know Your M1 Garand Rifles.* Southport, Conn.: Blacksmith Corp., 1976. 80p.

A profusely illustrated paperback which details all models and variants with tables of quantities manufactured and delivered to the U.S. Army, with dates, serial numbers, etc.

2281. Hogg, Ian V. *The Encyclopedia of Infantry Weapons of World War II.* London: Bison Books, 1977. 192p.

Illustrated with drawings and photographs, including some in color, this work provides information on rifles, pistols, mortars, machine guns, grenades, bayonets, etc., employed by both Allied and Axis forces.

2282. ———. *Grenades and Mortars.* Ballantine's Illustrated History of World War II. New York: Ballantine Books, 1974. 160p.

Discusses the design, manufacture, and use of these weapons, including a short chapter on the U.S. bazooka; illustrated with photos.

2283. ———. *Military Pistols and Revolvers: The Handguns of the Two World Wars.* New York: Arco, 1970. 79p.

Complete technical details are provided for the principal handguns employed by Allied and Axis forces during World War II, as well as Allied and Central Powers forces in World War I; illustrated with over 50 photographs.

2284. ———, and John Batchelor. *The Complete Machine-Gun, 1885 to the Present.* New York: Hippocrene Books, 1979. 128p.

Traces the entire history of the machine gun and its use, including World War II, with a description of the various principles on which the guns operate and assessments of individual weapons. Illustrated with almost 300 illustrations, half in color.

2285. ———. *The Machine Gun.* Purnell's History of the World Wars Special. London: Phoebus, 1976. 64p.

A brief illustrated look at the major machine guns employed by the warring nations in World Wars I and II, including U.S. models.

2286. Hogg, Ian V., and John Weeks. *Military Small Arms of the 20th Century.* 4th ed. Northfield, Ill.: DBI, 1981. 288p.

Divided into sections covering handguns, submachine guns, machine guns, bolt-action rifles, automatic rifles, anti-tank rifles, and ammunition; oversize and profusely illustrated with drawings and photos.

2287. Kerne, S. Frederick. "The U.S. [Mk. III] 'Pineapple' Grenade." *World War II Journal*, II (September-December 1975), 50.

A brief description with a single illustration.

2288. King, J.B., and John Batchelor. *Infantry at War.* Purnell's History of the World Wars Special. London: Phoebus, 1974. 64p.

Examines infantry weapons with 13 photographs and 106 black and white and color illustrations. Weapons from both the Allied and Axis sides are described with technical details.

2289. McKinney, Leonard L. "European Theater of Operations." In: his *Portable Flame Thrower Operations in World War II.* Washington, D.C.: U.S. Government Printing Office, 1949, Chap. 8.

Examines the use of the portable one-man flamethrower, especially during the battles en route to Germany's heart in 1945.

2290. ———. *Mechanized Flame Thrower Operations in World War II.* Washington, D.C.: U.S. Government Printing Office, 1951. 439p.

Examines the use of flame throwers mounted on tank bodies in Europe and the Pacific from 1943 on.

2291. North, Peter. "Technical Section." In: Philip de Ste. Croix, ed. *Airborne Operations: An Illustrated Encyclopedia of the Great Battles of Airborne Forces.* New York: Crescent Books, 1978, pp. 8-25.

Illustrated with color drawings, this piece describes the weapons, uniforms, and equipment of Allied and Axis airborne troops.

2292. Schreier, Konrad F., Jr. *Guide to United States Machine Guns.* Forest Grove, Ore.: Normount Technical Publications, 1971. 178p.

Covers nearly 50 designs and variations over a 110-year period beginning with the Civil War; illustrated with photos and drawings.

2293. Stephens, Frederick J. *Fighting Knives: An Illustrated Guide to Fighting Knives and Military Survival Weapons of the World.* New York: Arco, 1980. 127p.

Includes sections on American knives, World War II knives, the special knives employed by U.S. Rangers; illustrated with over 600 photographs. Ideal for collectors.

2294. Wahl, Paul. *Carbine Handbook.* New York: Arco, 1964. 80p.

A complete manual on the M1 Garand including its function, design, assembly, and repair; includes 115 illustrations.

2295. Weeks, John. *Airborne Equipment: A History of Its Development.* New York: Hippocrene Books, 1976. 192p.

Explains the development of gliders, weapons, rifles, radios, and other gear used by paratroopers on both sides during the war.

2296. ———. *Infantry Weapons.* Ballantine's Illustrated History of World War II. New York: Ballantine Books, 1971. 160p.

A pictorial review of the rifles, handguns, grenades, mortars, machine guns, etc., employed by Allied and Axis forces; illustrated with photographs and drawings.

5. Military Vehicles

Introduction: The references below illustrate the various military vehicles employed by the U.S. Army in Europe. Readers will find more information on some of these in Part C, Campaigns and Battles, above.

2297. Auerbach, Bill. "The M-31 Tank Recovery Vehicle." *World War II Journal*, II (July-August 1975), 14-17.

2298. ———, and Peter Frandsen. "The M-25 Tank Transporter." *Military Journal*, I (September-October 1977), 16-21.

Two vehicles used for the service of tanks when the latter were not operating under their own power.

2299. Church, John. *Military Vehicles of World War II.* New York: Sterling, 1982. 160p.

Describes many of the nonarmored vehicles employed by Allied and Axis forces during the war, including ambulances, staff cars, cargo haulers, radar trucks, mobile kitchens, bridging vehicles, and so forth. Illustrated with black and white and color photographs, the latter mainly of British vehicles.

2300. Conley, M.A. "The Legendary Jeep." *American History Illustrated*, XVI (June 1981), 18-28.

Discusses the development and use of this U.S. Army quarter-ton 4 x 4 reconnaissance truck, which was produced by the thousands.

2301. Ellis, Christopher. *Military Transport of World War II.* New York: Macmillan, 1971. 177p.

An illustrated review of the various trucks, trailers, and other transport vehicles employed by Allied and Axis forces; illustrated with line drawings and black and white photographs.

2302. Hogg, Ian V., and John Weeks. *An Illustrated History of Military Vehicles.* Englewood Cliffs, N.J.: Prentice-Hall, 1980. 64p.

Recalls military vehicles from the 1890's to the present with emphasis on the multitude of trucks, tractors, and specialized vehicles introduced by the Axis and Allies during World War II; illustrated with 120 photographs, 60 in color. Oversize.

2303. Huffschmidt, Edward J., and William H. Tantum. *U.S. Military Vehicles, World War II.* Boulder, Colo.: Paladin Press, 1972. 160p.

Describes the wide range of vehicles employed by the U.S. during the war--everything from bicycles to huge trucks; illustrated with 450 photographs and line drawings.

2304. Jeudy, J.G., and Marc Tararine. *The Jeep.* N.p.: Editions Vilo, 1981. 272p.

An illustrated, adulatory history of the U.S. 4 x 4 reconnaissance vehicle with emphasis on its background, development, and use by the U.S. Army in World War II.

2305. Pool, Jim, and Bill Auerbach. "The M-19 Tank Transporter." *World War II Journal*, III (March-April 1976), 14-18.

Another truck-trailer combination for hauling tanks.

2306. Vanderveen, Burt H., ed. *Tanks and Transport Vehicles of World War II*. London: Warne, 1974. 64p.

Provides history and specifications for the AFV's and soft-skins of 13 nations; illustrated with black and white photographs and color plates.

2307. Willinger, Kurt, and Jean Guerney. *The American Jeep: In War and Peace*. New York: Crown, 1983. 224p.

A military and civilian history of this Army-developed reconnaissance truck showing its background and use by U.S. forces during the war; illustrated with over 200 photographs.

6. Uniforms/Insignia/Markings

Introduction: The citations in this subpart describe the various uniforms and shoulder and vehicle insignia and markings deployed by the U.S. Army in the ETO/MTO. Users will find more data on these in part D, Unit Histories.

2308. *American Military Camouflage and Markings, 1939-1945*. London: Almark, 1975. 32p.

A guide to the color schemes and markings used on U.S. military vehicles, including formation markings, tactical signs, etc.; profusely illustrated with color drawings and black and white photographs.

2309. Bradford, George. *Armor Camouflage and Markings: North Africa, 1940-1943*. London: Arms and Armour Press, 1979. 160p.

Features 105 color profile paintings covering Allied and Axis vehicles used in the desert war, plus 12 color sections on marking systems and color swatches; includes 90 photographs.

2310. Bragg, R.J., and Roy Turner. *Parachute Badges and Insignia of the World*. New York: Sterling, 1979. 227p.

Describing the development of airborne forces, this work is based on a set of over 1,000 parachutists' qualification brevets. The appendix contains a chronological list of World War II drops; illustrated with 69 plates, 64 of which are in color.

2311. Britton, Jack, comp. *Uniform Insignia of the United States Military Forces*. Tulsa, Okla.: Military Collectors News Press, 1979. 59p.

An identification guide to cap badges, rank insignia, branch of service, breast badges, I.S. badges, wings, etc., for all the U.S. services; each insignia in this oversize work is captioned and, where necessary, information is given as to coloration and usage. Illustrated with over 1,000 black and white illustrations.

2312. ———. *United States Military Medals and Decorations*. Tulsa, Okla.: Military Collectors News Press, 1978. 84p.

An illustrated guide to U.S. medals and decorations, including those for campaigns, heroism, service; 182 awards are covered, with brief histories and notes on ribbon coloration.

2313. ———, and George Washington, Jr. *U.S. Military Shoulder Patches of the United States Armed Forces*. New, 3rd ed. Tulsa, Okla.: Military Collectors News Press, 1980. 80p.

Covers the period from World War I to the present, identifying over 1,550 patches and 157 arcs-tabs in full color and another 150 in black and white from all the services. Useful for buffs and collectors. Much less Army bias than in the second edition, published in 1975.

2314. Campbell, J. Duncan. "Hiding under the Enemy's Nose." *Harpers*, CLXXXVII (August 1943), 254-259.

A look at U.S. military camouflage as applied to vehicles, guns, soldiers, planes, etc., current through the North African campaign.

2315. ———. "Modern Military Buttons and Army Insignia." *Hobbies*, XLVIII (February 1944), 26-34.

Examines clothing buttons and uniform insignia of the U.S. Army through 1943; illustrated with drawings and photographs.

2316. Chandler, Stedman. "Too Much 'Fruit Salad.'" *Army*, IX (November 1958), 68-70.

A review of the system of awarding Army decorations, 1941-1945.

2317. Davies, Howard P. *U.S. Infantry, Europe 1944-1945*. New York: Arco, 1974. 48p.

The uniforms of U.S. troops who participated in the northwest Europe campaign are described; in addition to basic uniform coverage, details are given of the soldiers' equipment, and the color artwork illustrates the various corps and army badges as well as the standard rank and army insignia.

2318. Davis, Brian L. *U.S. Airborne Forces Europe, 1942-1945*. London: Osprey, 1974. 32p.

The uniforms of U.S. paratroops are described as is their equipment; the color artwork illustrates the various army, division, and regiment insignia.

2319. Dilley, Roy. *U.S. Army Uniforms, 1939-1945*. London: Almark, 1972. 80p.

A pictorial guide to the rank emblems, unit insignia, uniforms, and equipment of U.S. soldiers; illustrated with black and white photographs and six pages of color plates.

2320. Emerson, William K. *Chevrons: Illustrated History and Catalog of U.S. Army Insignia*. Washington, D.C.: Smithsonian Institution Press, 1983. 298p.

A useful identification guide to chevrons and service stripes worn by officers and enlisted personnel from the Revolution to date with general information and history of the design, material, and color of Army uniforms. Illustrated with black and white and color photographs of 637 individual chevrons.

2321. Katcher, Philip. *U.S. First Infantry Division, 1939-1945.* Carrollton, Tx.: Squadron/Signal Publications, 1978. 40p.

The text is brief and supportive of the 35 black and white and 5 color photographs which provide details on the soldiers' uniforms, equipment, and insignia.

2322. Laframboise, Leon W. *History of the Artillery, Cavalry, and Infantry Branch of Service Insignia.* Tulsa, Okla.: Military Collectors News Press, 1982. 194p.

Traces designs from inception to the present, including every basic design and its variety based on function and wearer, officer or enlisted man, with attention to detail shown by adherence to Army regulations and other publications; oversize and illustrated with hundreds of photographs.

2323. ———. *History of the Combat Support Branches: Branch of Service Insignia.* Tulsa, Okla.: Military Collectors News Press, 1982. 242p.

Treats the Army Air Force, Engineer, Medical, Military Police, Ordnance, Quartermaster/Commissary, Signal, and Transportation branches in the same fashion as the Artillery, Cavalry, and Infantry, described in the preceding entry; illustrated with hundreds of photographs. Oversize.

2324. Mollow, Andrew. *Armed Forces of World War II: Uniforms, Insignia, and Organization.* New York: Crown, 1981. 312p.

Examines these items for the various land, sea, and air forces of the combatants; oversize, the work is illustrated with 350 specially-commissioned drawings in color, 160 photographs of combatants in action, and 53 plates of insignia.

2325. ———, and Malcolm McGregor. *Army Uniforms of World War II.* New York: Sterling, 1980. 183p.

Presents data on the uniforms of all land powers, 1939-1945, backed by color plates; similar to the World War II section in the next entry.

2326. Mollow, Andrew, and Digby Smith. *World Army Uniforms Since 1939.* New York: Sterling, 1981. 352p.

This oversize British import covers the uniforms, weapons, and personal equipment of the two dozen nations that participated in World War II as well as postwar armies; shows 349 uniformed figures and 50 pieces of equipment, and 132 black and white drawings depicting badges, small arms, headdress, shoes, and other equipment. Includes 96 pages of color plates.

2327. Rosignoli, Guido. *Army Badges and Insignia of World War II.* Translated from the Italian. New York: Macmillan, 1972. 228p.

Lists over 2,000 different insignia of the principal armed forces of the war (most illustrated in full color); a detailed text provides historical background, evolution, and a description of variant types. Illustrated with drawings and 80 pages of full-color artwork.

2328. Smith, Richard W., and Roy A. Petz. *Shoulder Sleeve Insignia of the U.S. Armed Forces, 1941-1945.* Tulsa, Okla.: Military Collectors News Press, 1979. 250p.

Covers combat detail and historical highlights of all U.S. units with authorized shoulder patches, including state guard units; illustrated with 32 full-color plates containing over 600 individual patches.

2329. Windrow, Martin. *Tank and AFV Crew Uniforms Since 1916.* Carrollton, Tx.: Squadron/Signal Publications, 1979. 104p.

The text is brief and supportive of the 50+ black and white and color photographs which provide details on the troopers' uniforms, equipment, and insignia.

2330. ———. *World War II Combat Uniforms and Insignia.* Carrollton, Tx.: Squadron/Signal Publications, 1977. 104p.

Provides basic data for the infantry, armor, and airborne troops of six nations, including the U.S.; the limited text is backed by 125 black and white photographs and 40 color photos/illustrations.

2331. Wise, Terence. *D-Day to Berlin: Armor Camouflage and Markings of the United States, British, and German Armies, June 1944-May 1945.* Carrollton, Tx.: Squadron/Signal Publications, 1979. 96p.

Provides basic data on the coloring and marking of tanks and AFV's; the limited text is supported by 150 black and white and 65 color illustrations plus 51 line drawings.

2332. ———. *Military Vehicle Markings of World War II.* Tucson, Ariz.: Aztec, 1980. 160p.

Describes the sophisticated marking systems employed by both Allied and Axis forces; each country's insignia are described in detail and the work is illustrated with over 1,000 line drawings.

V. THE WAR AT SEA

Introduction: The references in this section of our guide are devoted to the U.S. Navy and Coast Guard in the Atlantic, Mediterranean, and European Theaters during World War II. Here will be found information on officers and heroes, campaigns and battles, accounts of specific ships, and information on naval weapons, uniforms, aircraft, equipment, and insignia. Readers should note that additional information on segments of the sea war is available in the encyclopedias and handbooks and general war histories cited in Section I above, some of the diplomatic studies noted in II:A, and certain of the more general entries in Sections III and IV covering the war in the air and on land.

A. GENERAL WORKS

Introduction: America's military participation in World War II combat began not with Pearl Harbor, but with the actions of convoy escorts in the Atlantic several months earlier. After the Japanese attack of December 7, the naval war in the Atlantic, MTO, and ETO became one of antisubmarine warfare, convoy escort, shore bombardment, and amphibious operations, with the great surface engagements between hostile fleets left to the Pacific. The citations in this part reflect those works written over the years which have dealt with the naval war as a whole. While almost all contain information on the American effort, most contain information on the operations of other Allied and Axis combatants as well. A review of these overviews can be useful for comparison work as well as for understanding the worldwide commitment of the U.S. Navy and Coast Guard and how their deployment in the Atlantic, the Mediterranean, and Europe made a difference in the final victory over the Third Reich and Fascist Italy.

For additional citations to the general aspects of the war at sea in the Atlantic and eastern hemisphere, users might profitably consult my *The European Theater* which is Volume I of *World War II at Sea: A Bibliography of Sources in English* (Metuchen, N.J.: The Scarecrow Press, 1976), pp. 21-37.

2333. Bennett, Geoffrey. "In the Atlantic and Mediterranean." In: his *Naval Battles of World War II*. New York: David McKay, 1957, Part II.

This English author details the great convoy battles and Mediterranean battles of 1940 to 1943 with emphasis on the role of the Royal Navy.

2334. Berry, Erich. *Underwater Warriors: The Story of American Frogmen*. New York: David McKay, 1967. 152p.

2335. Best, Herbert. *The Webfoot Warriors: The Story of UDT, the U.S. Navy's Underwater Demolition Team*. New York: John Day, 1962. 187p.

Both Berry and Best provide information on the operations of U.S. frogmen in scouting and preparing the landing areas for several of the MTO/ETO invasions.

2336. Buchanan, Albert R., ed. *The Navy's Air War*. New York: Harper, 1946. 432p.

Although most of this important work is related to the air war in the Pacific, chapters are provided for the work of USN naval aviation in the Atlantic convoy battles and in support of landings in the Mediterranean and northwest Europe.

2337. Buckley, Robert J., Jr. *At Close Quarters: PT Boats in the United States Navy*. Washington, D.C.: Government Printing Office, 1962. 574p.

For operations, see especially Chapters 6 and 7, "The Mediterranean--Torpedo War" (pp. 277-348) and "The English Channel--D-Day and After" (pp. 349-367).

2338. Creswell, John. *Sea Warfare, 1939-1945*. Rev. and augm. ed. Berkeley: University of California Press, 1967. 343p.

A general history which covers the doctrines and operations of six navies, including that of the United States; useful insights and some coverage of the Atlantic, Mediterranean, and northwest Europe theaters.

2339. Donahue, Joseph A. *Tin Cans and Other Ships: A War Diary, 1941-1945*. North Quincy, Mass.: Christopher Publishing House, 1979. 255p.

The author's day-to-day recollections of service aboard the U.S.S. *Niblack* (DD-424) in the Battle of the Atlantic and the invasions of North Africa, Sicily, Salerno, and Anzio.

2340. Elliott, Peter. *Allied Minesweeping in World War II*. Annapolis, Md.: U.S. Naval Institute, 1979. 132p.

Describes how the U.S./U.K. navies captured or neutralized German mines and provides details on minesweeping in advance of the invasions at Normandy and in the Mediterranean.

2341. Farrar, Arthur. "LCI's Are Veterans Now." *U.S. Coast Guard Academy Alumni Association Newsletter*, VI (December 1944), 1+.

Describes the activities of Coast Guard-manned landing craft in the invasions of Sicily, Salerno, and Normandy.

2342. Fetridge, William H., ed. *The Navy Reader*. Indianapolis: Bobbs-Merrill, 1943. 443p.

An anthology of 50 previously published articles describing USN efforts around the world and designed to help new personnel understand the wartime fleet; illustrated with maps, diagrams, and black and white photos.

2343. ———. *Second Navy Reader.* Indianapolis: Bobbs-Merrill, 1944. 383p.

Similar to the last entry, with another 50 previously published articles describing USN efforts around the world from the date of the first anthology to the publication date of this one; illustrated with black and white photos, maps, and diagrams, this volume also contains a chronology, "Diary of the War at Sea (December 7, 1941-February 20, 1944)."

2344. Hewitt, Henry K. "The Navy in the ETO in World War II." Unpublished paper, Individual Personnel File, U.S. Navy Operational Archives, Knox Historical Center, 1947. 53p.

An overview of USN operations and their significance first delivered as a talk to the Naval War College in January 1947. A useful summary by a leading participant.

2345. Hezlett, Arthur. *Electronics and Sea Power.* New York: Stein and Day, 1975. 318p.

Traces the impact of electricity and electronics on naval warfare, following their accelerating value, particularly during World War II.

2346. Ladd, James D. *Assault from the Sea, 1939-1945: The Craft, the Landings, the Men.* New York: Hippocrene Books, 1976. 256p.

A narrative on the various landings worldwide, including those by the Allies in the MTO/ETO, which is employed as backdrop for a well-illustrated catalog on the various amphibious ships, boats, and craft employed.

2347. Lott, Arnold S. *Most Dangerous Sea: A History of Mine Warfare and an Account of U.S. Navy Mine Warfare Operations in World War II and Korea.* Annapolis, Md.: U.S. Naval Institute, 1959. 322p.

With more American emphasis than Elliott above, Lott describes the role of USN minesweepers and minelayers in the various U.S. theaters, including the MTO/ETO, in a dramatic narrative.

2348. Macintyre, Donald G.F.W. *The Naval War Against Hitler.* New York: Scribners, 1971. 376p.

A history of Allied operations against the Kriegsmarine with discussion of both German and Allied strategy; includes coverage of the Battle of the Atlantic and the landings in the Mediterranean and at Normandy. Illustrated with maps, photographs, and diagrams.

2349. Morison, Samuel E. *History of United States Naval Operations in World War II*. 15 vols. Boston, Mass.: Little, Brown, 1947-1962.

The unofficial USN official history, the appropriate volumes of which are noted in the various subparts of part C below.

2350. ———. *The Two-Ocean War: A Short History of the United States Navy in the Second World War*. Boston, Mass.: Little, Brown, 1963. 611p.

A highly readable popular history which is not a condensation but an independent work based on the official history cited above; includes adequate treatment of the Battle of the Atlantic and the various landings in the MTO/ETO.

2351. "The Navy's Victory in Europe." *All Hands* (May 1946), 11-14.

A brief pictorial overview of the USN role in the MTO/ETO and Battle of the Atlantic written for serving sailors.

2352. Parsons, Iain, ed. *The Encyclopedia of Sea Warfare*. New York: Crowell, 1975. 255p.

A British oversize import which contains a few chapters on the sea war in 1939-1945 which are illustrated with ship profiles, maps, diagrams, and a variety of photographs, some in color.

2353. Potter, Elmer B., and Chester W. Nimitz, eds. *The Great Sea War: The Story of Naval Action in World War II*. Englewood Cliffs, N.J.: Prentice-Hall, 1960. 468p.

Adapted from the editors' *Sea Power: A Naval History*, this popular general history includes sections devoted to the role of the USN and other navies in the ETO/MTO, as well as the Battle of the Atlantic.

2354. Roscoe, Theodore. *United States Destroyer Operations in World War II*. Annapolis, Md.: U.S. Naval Institute, 1953. 581p.

A detailed and spritely look at the exploits of USN "tin cans" around the world, including the Atlantic, MTO, and ETO; includes stories of ships which performed unusual tasks or scored noteworthy victories.

2355. ———. *United States Submarine Operations in World War II*. Annapolis, Md.: U.S. Naval Institute, 1949. 577p.

Similar to the above title which is also based on official USN histories and reports; although most of the emphasis is on the Pacific, submarine operations in the Atlantic are noted.

2356. Roskill, Stephen W. *The War at Sea, 1939-1945*. History of the Second World War: United Kingdom Military Series. 3 vols. in 4. London: H.M. Stationery Office, 1954-1961.

The comprehensive British official history of the sea war with emphasis on the role of the Royal Navy (and its support from and coordination with the USN) in the Atlantic, Mediterranean, and northwest Europe; insightful on high command, strategy, and combined operations.

2357. ———. *White Ensign: The British Navy at War, 1939-1945.* Annapolis, Md.: U.S. Naval Institute, 1960. 480p.

Based on the author's official history cited immediately above, this survey remains perhaps the best single-volume history of the Royal Navy in the war; with emphasis on the Atlantic, MTO, and ETO, the study also points out the British fleet's coordination with the American.

2358. Ruge, Friedrich. *Der Seekrieg: The German Navy's Story, 1939-1945.* Translated from the German. Annapolis, Md.: U.S. Naval Institute, 1957. 440p.

A former Kriegsmarine admiral's dispassionate account of German high seas operations in the Atlantic, MTO, and ETO, with emphasis on the role of the Reich and Italian navies in the Mediterranean and North Africa and the U-boats in the Atlantic.

2359. *Sea Power.* London: Phoebus, 1979. 392p.

A history of navies and naval operations from the 19th century to the end of World War II with emphasis on the 1939-1945 conflict; this oversize title is illustrated with some 720 photographs and drawings, including over 350 in color.

2360. Smith, Stanley E. *The Destroyermen.* New York: Belmont Books, 1966. 156p.

Accounts of "tin can" action reprinted from *Bluebook* and *Man's Magazine*; includes accounts of USN destroyer and USCG cutter actions in the Battle of the Atlantic and the North African landings.

2361. ———, ed. *The United States Navy in World War II: The One-Volume History, from Pearl Harbor to Tokyo Bay.* New York: William Morrow, 1966. 1,049p.

An anthology of carefully selected excerpts and articles which provide human-interest insight into the actions of the USN around the world and are tied together with the editor's contextual commentary; illustrated with 18 maps and several pages of black and white photographs.

2362. United States. Navy Department. Office of Naval Operations. *U.S. Navy at War, 1941-1945.* Washington, D.C., 1946. 305p.

This is the war report of Fleet Admiral Ernest J. King on the development, strategy, and worldwide operations of the USN during the war; illustrated with maps and charts.

2363. Weller, Donald W. "Salvo--Splash!: The Development of Naval Gunfire Support in World War II." *U.S. Naval Institute Proceedings*, LXXX (August-September 1954), 839-849, 1011-1021.

Describes the lessons learned in shore bombardment and how they were applied in succeeding invasions, including those of the MTO/ETO.

2364. Wilmot, Ned. *The Strategy and Tactics of Sea Warfare.* London: Marshall Cavendish, 1979. 80p.

A brief guide to the use of navies by admirals during World War II as well as a study of such tactics as the stalking of U-boats by Allied antisubmarine warfare escorts; illustrated with a variety of photographs, maps, charts, and color drawings.

2365. Winton, John. *Air Power at Sea, 1939-1945.* New York: Crowell, 1977. 187p.

A British author's discussion of British, American, and Japanese naval aviation during the war, including the use of carrier planes in the Battle of the Atlantic and the MTO/ETO landings; illustrated with profiles, photographs, maps, charts, and drawings.

B. OFFICERS AND HEROES

Introduction: An interesting way to look at the war at sea in the Atlantic, MTO, and ETO, especially for younger readers, is through the biography of its participants. Unfortunately, one of the major deficiencies of the English-language literature on the war is biographical coverage of American naval leaders who did not fight in the Pacific. The citations in this section are arranged in two parts. Part 1 reveals the few guides available to the collective biography of USN/USCG officers and heroes. Part 2 concerns individuals and is arranged alphabetically by the last name of the biographee. Certain important leaders cannot be listed as no individual biographical references are available, although some, such as Admiral Hewitt, have left accounts of their service which are scattered through the operational subparts of C below. It should be noted that additional biographical information is available in the handbooks, encyclopedias, biographical sources, and general war histories cited in Section I, the general sea histories cited in Part A above, and in the campaign histories noted in Part C below.

1. Collective Biography

2366. Schuon, Karl. *U.S. Navy Biographical Dictionary.* New York: Watts, 1964. 180p.

Provides brief entries on 800 individuals, including most Medal of Honor winners and all of the important admirals of World War II.

2367. United States. Coast Guard. *Register of Officers and Cadets of the United States Coast Guard in Order of Precedence.* Washington, D.C.: U.S. Government Printing Office, 1941-1946.

Listed by ranks; begun in 1915 and continued today.

2368. ———. Naval Academy. Alumni Association. *Register of Alumni, Graduates, and Former Naval Cadets and Midshipmen.* Annapolis, Md.: The Association, 1941-1946.

Begun in 1886, this became an annual in 1908 and is still published.

2369. ———. Navy Department. Bureau of Naval Personnel. *Register of Commissioned and Warrant Officers of the United States Naval Reserve.* Washington, D.C.: U.S. Government Printing Office, 1941-1946.

Begun in 1921 and still published, particularly helpful in finding data on the war's so-called 90-Day Wonders.

2370. ———. ———. *Register of Commissioned and Warrant Officers of the United States Navy and Marine Corps.* Washington, D.C.: U.S. Government Printing Office, 1941-1946.

Begun in 1798 and still published today under a later title; especially useful for finding basic data on regular officers, including those who held significant posts in Europe.

2. Specific Individuals

Andrew B. Cunningham

2371. Cunningham, Andrew B. *A Sailor's Odyssey: The Autobiography of Admiral of the Fleet, Viscount Cunningham of Hyndhope.* New York: E.P. Dutton, 1951. 715p.

The autobiography of the admiral most consider the outstanding British naval leader of the war. The author explains not only his early life, but also his war service in the Mediterranean through 1941, his work with the Combined Chiefs of Staff in 1942, and his service as Allied naval commander in North Africa, where he met and became close to General Eisenhower. Cunningham became Britain's First Sea Lord in 1943, a post he held through the remainder of the war. An essential work for both MTO/ETO naval operations and the study of Allied strategy.

2372. Hewitt, Henry K. "Admiral of the Fleet Viscount Cunningham." *U.S. Naval Institute Proceedings*, LXXVIII (March 1952), 553-555.

The author commanded U.S. naval forces in the North African invasion under Cunningham and here extends an appreciation of his British superior.

2373. Pack, Stanley W.C. *Cunningham the Commander.* London: Batsford, 1974. 323p.

A sympathetic analysis of the admiral's leadership qualities and his service not only in the great Mediterranean battles, but in the councils of high command.

2374. Warner, Oliver. *Admiral of the Fleet: Cunningham of Hyndhope.* Athens: Ohio University Press, 1967. 301p.

A popular biography of the British leader which follows his career from before World War I through his command positions in World War II.

Karl Doenitz

2375. Dönitz, Karl. *Memoirs: Ten Years and Twenty Days.* Translated from the German. Cleveland, Ohio: World Publishing Co., 1959. 500p.

The memoirs of the German admiral who built up and employed the U-boat arm during the war, became chief of the Kriegsmarine in 1943, and succeeded Hitler as head of the Reich during the last ten days of its existence; this frank memoir of an unrepentant leader considers the undeclared war with the U.S. in the North Atlantic as well as other aspects of German naval strategy and operations.

2376. Seagren, Leonard W. "The Last Fuehrer." *U.S. Naval Institute Proceedings*, LXXX (March 1952), 522-537.

Concentrates on Dönitz's service as head of state and his subsequent arrest and trial.

John L. Hall, Jr.

2377. Godson, Susan H. *Viking of Assault: Admiral John Leslie Hall, Jr., and Amphibious Warfare.* Washington, D.C.: University Press of America, 1982. 237p.

A eulogistic biography of a pioneer USN logistics manager and expert trainer of assault forces who made his reputation as an innovative manager in the major MTO/ETO invasions, especially in training, combat loading, gunfire support, ship-to-shore movement, and beach offloading; by following Hall's career, the author provides an appraisal of the strengths and weaknesses of joint- and combined-amphibious tactics and doctrine. This is only the second biography of a World War II USN amphibious specialist and the first to cover a European expert.

Henry Kent Hewitt

2378. Clagett, John. "Admiral H. Kent Hewitt, USN: High Command." *Naval War College Review*, XXVIII (February 1975), 60-86.

Outside of Hewitt's own writings, this is the most important source on the man who commanded USN forces in the North Africa, Sicily, Salerno, Anzio, and southern France landings. This piece examines his command of forces in "Operation Torch" in November 1942.

2379. Perry, George S. "Why Don't They Write About Hewitt?" *Saturday Evening Post*, CCXVII (December 16, 1944), 22+.

A contemporary profile which is most flattering.

Ernest J. King

2380. Buell, Thomas B. *Master of Sea Power: A Biography of Fleet Admiral Ernest J. King.* Boston, Mass.: Little, Brown, 1980. 512p.

In addition to running the USN as Commander in Chief, United States Fleet and Chief of Naval Operations, King was the blue water representative to the U.S. Joint Chiefs of Staff and the Allied Combined Chiefs of Staff; ambitious, ugly when crossed, and jealous of his perquisites, the admiral, a man who by his own admission was an "S.O.B.," King receives an engrossing if not overly sympathetic biography.

2381. King, Ernest J., and Walter M. Whitehall. *Fleet Admiral King: A Naval Record.* New York: W.W. Norton, 1952. 674p.

A combination memoir and biography which devotes less than half its length to King's World War II service and reveals little about either his impact on the war or its operations which was not known before.

2382. Sanders, Harry. "King of the Oceans." *U.S. Naval Institute Proceedings*, C (August 1974), 52-59.

King's wartime War Plans officer recalls the personality and work ethic of the CINCUS/CNO.

Bertram Home Ramsay

2383. Chalmers, William S. *Full Cycle: The Biography of Admiral Sir Bertram Home Ramsay.* London: Hodder and Stoughton, 1950. 288p.

Brought out of retirement in 1938, Ramsay led the force which saved Allied troops at Dunkirk in 1940, planned the naval aspects of the North African invasion, led the British fleet at Sicily, and served as naval Commander in Chief of the Allied Expeditionary Force in the invasion of Normandy; Ramsay, who worked well with his U.S. subordinates in the D-Day effort, was killed in an air crash in January 1945.

2384. Woodward, David. *Ramsay at War: The Fighting Life of Admiral Sir Bertram Ramsay.* London: Kimber, 1957. 204p.

A somewhat shorter book than the last entry which contains essentially the same information presented in a livelier narrative.

C. CAMPAIGNS AND BATTLES

Introduction: The citations below reveal details on some of the great naval and amphibious campaigns of the war. Here is the sailor's war divided into three major parts: Mediterranean, English Channel, and Battle of the Atlantic. Users should be aware that many of the handbooks/encyclopedias and general war histories noted in Section I, many of the citations in the Campaigns and Battles parts of Sections

III and IV, and data in the other parts of this section are relevant to the Navy-Coast Guard efforts in the Atlantic, the MTO, and the ETO.

1. Mediterranean

Introduction: For purposes of this guide, the Mediterranean is defined as that area encompassing North Africa, the islands of the Mediterranean, Italy, the Balkans, and southern France. During the early part of the Allies' coalition war, considerable debate existed as to the direction the fighting should take in this theater, as noted in the citations in Section II:A above. The navies of Britain and England supported the great invasions in the Mediterranean from late 1942 through mid-1944, including those in North Africa, Sicily, Italy, and southern France, invasions which are also covered in the references in Section III:C:1 and IV:C:1 above. Comprehensive but unannotated bibliographic coverage for publications prior to 1976 is found in my *The European Theater*, which is Volume I of *World War II at Sea: A Bibliography of Sources in English* (Metuchen, N.J.: The Scarecrow Press, 1976), pp. 136-210.

2385. Auphan, Gabriel A., and Hervé Cras. *The French Navy in World War II*. Translated from the French. Annapolis, Md.: U.S. Naval Institute, 1959. 413p.

Details the 1939-1940 and 1942-1945 actions of the French fleet, including the unhappy resistance put up by Vichy naval units to the Allied invasion of Casablanca in November 1942.

2386. Blumenson, Martin. "The Real Achievement at Anzio." *Navy*, IV (March 1961), 12-16.

A noted Army historian pays tribute to the USN effort in the January 1944 landing and resupply of troops at this unhappy beachhead on Italy's west coast near Rome.

2387. Bogart, Charles H. "German Remotely Piloted Bombs." *U.S. Naval Institute Proceedings*, CII (November 1976), 62-68.

Discusses the Luftwaffe's use of HS-293 glide bombs against the Allied invasion fleet off Salerno in September 1943.

2388. Brown, John M. "From the Theater of War: Broadcast on Shipboard to Men Below Decks During the Sicilian Campaign." *Theater Arts*, XXVII (November 1943), 669-673.

Drawn from the next entry.

2389. ———. *To All Hands*. New York: McGraw-Hill, 1943. 236p.

The author was the bridge announcer on the U.S. flagship in the Sicilian invasion and wrote his text as a series of pieces to broadcast over his ship's PA system to inform the crew of events on their vessel, in the convoy, and on the fighting front.

2390. Cope, Harley F. "'Play Ball, Navy!'" *U.S. Naval Institute Proceedings*, LXIX (October 1943), 1311-1318.

An early analysis of the naval aspects of the North African invasion in November 1942.

2391. DeBelot, Raymond. *The Struggle for the Mediterranean, 1939-1945.* Princeton, N.J.: Princeton University Press, 1951. 287p.

A French admiral provides a general history of the naval war in the "Med" discussing both strategy and operations from a French standpoint.

2392. DiPhilip, John. *Gunner's Diary.* Boston, Mass.: Meador, 1946. 111p.

A brief recollection of the Mediterranean naval war by a USN enlisted man; high on human interest, low on command decision.

2393. Ellsberg, Edward. *No Banners, No Bugles.* New York: Dodd, Mead, 1949. 370p.

An account of salvage work in the Mediterranean ports rendered useless by the scuttling of the French fleet and the maintenance of the "Torch" beachheads in November 1942 by the chief USN salvage officer on the scene.

2394. Hendren, Paul, and Wesley Price. "Invasion Sunday Punch." *Saturday Evening Post*, CCXVI (April 1, 1944), 16-17+.

How two USN cruisers and eight destroyers prevented a German tank column from hitting the U.S. First Division on Sicily, July 11, 1943.

2395. Hewitt, Henry K. "The Allied Navies at Salerno: 'Operation Avalanche,' September 1943." *U.S. Naval Institute Proceedings*, LXXIX (September 1953), 958-976.

2396. ———. "Executing 'Operation Anvil-Dragoon.'" *U.S. Naval Institute Proceedings*, LXXX (August 1954), 896-925.

2397. ———. "The Landing in Morocco, November 1942." *U.S. Naval Institute Proceedings*, LXXVIII (November 1952), 1242-1253.

2398. ———. "Naval Aspects of the Sicilian Campaign." *U.S. Naval Institute Proceedings*, LXXIX (July 1953), 704-723.

Taken together, these four references constitute the recollections of the American admiral who commanded the USN components of these operations, Salerno, southern France, North Africa, and Sicily; includes insights into planning and strategy as well as operational aspects of naval support.

2399. Hunn, Max. "Saga of the 'Lucky Ark.'" *Ships and the Sea*, II (January 1953), 38-44.

The author recalls his service aboard U.S.S. *Arcturus* (AKA-1) during the invasion of Sicily in July 1943.

2400. Infield, Glenn B. *Disaster at Bari.* New York: Macmillan, 1972. 301p.

Recounts the German bombing of the Allied supply port at Bari, Italy, on December 2, 1944, which resulted in the destruction of many vessels, including one cargo vessel holding a secret cargo of mustard gas bombs which detonated and caused significant casualties.

2401. Keating, John S. "Mission to Mecca: A Postscript." *U.S. Naval Institute Proceedings*, CIV (April 1978), 74-77.

Sequel to the next entry.

2402. ———. "Mission to Mecca: The Cruise of the *Murphy*." *U.S. Naval Institute Proceedings*, CII (January 1976), 54-63.

Recounts Arabian King Saud's travels aboard DD-603 to meet with President Roosevelt in early 1945.

2403. Kerwin, Paschael E. *Big Men in the Little Navy*. Paterson, N.J.: St. Anthony Guild Press, 1946. 129p.

A brief history of the USN amphibious force in the Mediterranean in 1943-1945, its composition, and participation in the Sicilian and Italian landings; based on the author's recollections and other sources.

2404. Lowry, F.J. "The Naval Side of Anzio." *U.S. Naval Institute Proceedings*, LXXX (January 1954), 22-31.

Describes the USN participation in "Operation Shingle," which, under Admiral Hewitt's command, put the U.S. Sixth Corps ashore on the west side of Italy below Rome.

2405. Macintyre, Donald G.F.W. *The Battle for the Mediterranean*. New York: W.W. Norton, 1965. 216p.

An "account of the struggle from June 1940-May 1943 for control of the supply routes to the opposing armies in North Africa" which is long on strategic/high command analysis and short on battle action; with emphasis on the duel between the Royal Navy and the Luftwaffe, this former British escort commander's story includes some mention of the role of the USN in the Mediterranean.

2406. Mazzella, Donald P. "Seatrain to the War Zone." *Sea Classics*, IV (September 1973), 6-10, 60-61, 66.

The author recollects his service aboard the merchantman SS *Seatrain Texas*, which transported Army tanks to North Africa in 1942-1943.

2407. Melanephy, James P., and John G. Robinson. "*Savannah* [CL-42] at Salerno." *Surface Warfare*, VI (March 1981), 2-11.

Explains the role taken by this light cruiser in shore bombardment and the near fatal hit she took from a Luftwaffe glide bomb.

2408. Morison, Samuel E. "The Landing at Fedhala, Morocco, November 8, 1942." *American Foreign Service Journal*, XX (March 1943), 113-116+.

Describes the USN silencing of Vichy shore batteries and the landing of U.S. troops near Casablanca.

2409. ———. *Operations in North African Waters, October 1942-June 1943.* Vol. II of *History of United States Naval Operations in World War II.* Boston, Mass.: Little, Brown, 1950. 297p.

Employing official reports, interviews, and eyewitness recollections, Morison recreates the USN/USCG participation in the "Torch" landings as well as naval support for the campaign in Tunisia. Illustrated with maps, charts, and photographs.

2410. ———. *Sicily--Salerno--Anzio, January 1943 to June 1944.* Vol. IX of *History of United States Naval Operations in World War II.* Boston, Mass.: Little, Brown, 1954. 413p.

An examination of the preparations for and execution of these major Allied invasions, including support operations begun before the fall of Tunisia; based on official reports, the author's eyewitness recollections, interviews, etc., and illustrated with charts, maps, and photographs.

2411. "The Navy's Job: Sicily Invasion." *Life*, XV (August 23, 1943), 69-72.

Still a useful pictorial piece.

2412. Nofi, Albert A. "North Africa: Sea War." *Strategy and Tactics* (March-April 1971), 17-24.

A concise overview covering the period 1940-1943, with emphasis on the USN/Vichy naval shootout at Casablanca in November 1942.

2413. Norris, John G. "Hellcats over France." *Flying*, XXXVI (January 1945), 53-54+.

How F6F's from four American escort carriers spotted naval gunfire and bombed retreating German troops during the August 1944 invasion of southern France.

2414. Palmer, Fitzhugh L. "The Old Indispensables." *U.S. Naval Institute Proceedings*, CII (August 1976), 61-63.

Operations of the escort carriers *Sangamon* (CVE-26), *Suwanee* (CVE-27), *Chenango* (CVE-28), and *Santee* (CVE-29) in the "Torch" invasion of North Africa in November 1942.

2415. Perowne, Stewart. *The Siege Within the Walls: Malta, 1940-1943.* London: Hodder and Stoughton, 1970. 192p.

Using interviews, official reports, and documentary sources, the author explains the Luftwaffe siege of Malta from 1940 to 1943 as seen by the island's inhabitants; includes the late May 1942 arrival of Spitfires flown off the deck of U.S.S. *Wasp* (CV-7).

2416. Perry, George S. "Forty Hours off a Sicilian Beachhead: Unloading an Ammunition Ship as Axis Planes Bomb It." *Saturday Evening Post*, CCXVI (August 14, 1943), 22+.

Examines the Luftwaffe concentration on USN shipping off the beachhead with emphasis on the defense of one unnamed vessel.

2417. ———. "Sealed Ship: A Transport Loaded with United States Amphibious Troops and Anchored off the Coast of Algeria." *New Yorker*, XIX (July 24, 1943), 50-53.

A human interest story depicting the soldiers' lot aboard ship awaiting the departure of the USN for the invasion of Sicily.

2418. Saunders, D.M. "The Bari Incident." *U.S. Naval Institute Proceedings*, XCIII (September 1967), 35-39.

A brief account of the December 2, 1944, Luftwaffe attack on the Allied supply port at Bari, Italy, and the destruction of a ship carrying mustard gas bombs; more fully told in Infield's *Disaster at Bari*, cited above.

2419. Sollie, Frederick E. "Convoy to Casablanca." *Sea Classics*, VI (July 1973), 42-51.

Follows the U.S. Western Naval Task Force and its convoy from the U.S. to North Africa and discusses the naval battle of Casablanca in November 1942.

2420. ———. "Hottest Target in the Mediterranean." *Sea Classics*, VI (March 1973), 28-31, 65-66.

Recalls the service of the U.S.S. *Delta* (AKA-9) from March 1943 to April 1945.

2421. United States. Coast Guard. Historical Section. *The North African Landings*. The Coast Guard at War. Washington, D.C.: Headquarters, U.S. Coast Guard, 1946. 183p.

2422. ———. ———. ———. *Sicily-Italy Landings*. The Coast Guard at War. Washington, D.C.: Headquarters, U.S. Coast Guard, 1946. 261p.

These two volumes from the official Coast Guard history depict the role of that service in the Mediterranean, with emphasis on strategy and the operations of Coast Guard-manned cutters, escort vessels, transports, and landing craft.

2423. Van Vleet, Clarke. "'Torch.'" *Naval Aviation News* (November 1976), 34-37.

A detailed summary of the operations of the U.S.S. *Ranger* (CV-4) and four escort carriers in the November 1942 invasion of North Africa.

2424. Whipple, A.B.C. *The Mediterranean*. World War II Series. Alexandria, Va.: Time-Life Books, 1981. 208p.

An account of mainly Allied-Axis naval actions in the "Med" from 1940 to 1943 with a decidedly British emphasis which does, however, contain some mention of USN activities. Many of the photographs were taken by *Life* magazine cameramen on the scene.

2425. Williams, Robert C. "Operations Amphibious." *U.S. Army Combat Forces Journal*, I (August and October 1950), 30-33, 36-40.

A useful comparison of Pacific amphibious operations with those conducted in Sicily and southern France.

2426. Wordell, Malcolm T., and Edwin N. Seiler, as told to Keith Ayling. *Wildcats over Casablanca*. Boston, Mass.: Little, Brown, 1943. 309p.

The story of one U.S.S. *Ranger* (CV-4) squadron of F4F's which supported the USN attack at Fedhala and Casablanca in November 1942, told mostly in the words of the pilots who flew the missions; Wordell was shot down while on a bombing run, taken POW, and later released after the cease-fire.

2427. Wright, Jerauld M.P., Jr. "Harbor Clearance: Casablanca to Naples." *American Society of Naval Engineers Journal*, LXIX (May 1957), 319-329.

A recollection of the work of the USN Naval Salvage Service in the Mediterranean from late 1942 through mid-1944.

2. English Channel

Introduction: American naval activity in the channel was undertaken for the most part in support of the Normandy invasion and the Allied campaign through France to the heart of Germany. The diplomacy behind the invasion and northwest Europe campaign is covered in Section II:A above, while the air and ground operations pursuant to them, which incidentally include many references to the naval role, are found in Sections III:C:2 and IV:C:2. Comprehensive but unannotated bibliographic coverage for publications prior to 1976 is found in my *The European Theater*, which is Volume I of *World War II at Sea: A Bibliography of Sources in English* (Metuchen, N.J.: The Scarecrow Press, 1976), pp. 96-135.

2428. Arnold, James R. "N.O.I.C. Utah." *U.S. Naval Institute Proceedings*, LXXIII (June 1947), 671-681.

A recollection of the role of the USN beachmaster, or Naval Officer in Charge, on Utah Beach after the initial D-Day landings.

2429. Ashton, George. "Minesweeping Made Easy." *U.S. Naval Institute Proceedings*, LXXXVII (January 1961), 66-71.

An account of USN minesweeping in the Channel preparatory to the Normandy invasion.

2430. Braynard, Frank O. "The Loss of the *Santa Clara*." *Steamboat Bill of Facts*, VII (March 1950), 5-6.

Sunk en route to Normandy on June 6, 1944, without loss of life.

2431. Brown, John M. *Many a Watchful Night*. New York: McGraw-Hill, 1944. 219p.

After reporting the Sicilian invasion as noted in the last subpart, Lieutenant Brown was assigned to duty aboard a naval vessel of Adm. A.G. Kirk's Western Naval Task Force for the D-Day invasion, which he here reports.

2432. Edwards, Kenneth. *Operation Neptune*. London: Collins, 1946. 319p.

"Neptune" was the codename for the naval side of the D-Day invasion, and came under the direction of British admiral Sir Bertram Ramsay. Edwards details the organization of the great sea effort, including beach preparation (minesweeping, obstacle removal, etc.), escort of the intricately prepared invasion convoy, gunfire support, and the landings.

2433. Ellsberg, Edward. *The Far Shore*. New York: Dodd, Mead, 1960. 381p.

After service in the Mediterranean described in the last subpart, Captain Ellsberg was assigned to "Neptune," which he here describes, giving over a large portion of his title to a description of the "Mulberry" project for the creation and installation of artificial harbors off the Normandy beaches, including the one off Omaha Beach, which was severely damaged by the great June 19-21 Channel storm.

2434. Elsey, George M. "Naval Aspects of Normandy in Retrospect." In: Eisenhower Foundation, ed. *D-Day: The Normandy Invasion in Retrospect*. Lawrence: University Press of Kansas, 1971, pp. 170-197.

An overview of "Operation Neptune" which employs all of the latest information except Ultra in its analysis.

2435. Forester, Cecil S. "History's Biggest Gamble: The Invasion Strategists Staked Everything on the Largest Fleet Ever Assembled." *Saturday Evening Post*, CCXVII (August 12, 1944), 18-19+.

The author of *Captain Horatio Hornblower* and *Sink the Bismarck* here provides a contemporary view of the assembling of the D-Day armada.

2436. Fry, Michael. "Mulberry Harbors." *British History Illustrated*, I (October 1974), 2-15.

Describes the planning for and operation of the Allied harbors which were towed over and sunk off the Normandy beaches following D-Day.

2437. Harrison, Michael. *Mulberry: The Return in Triumph*. London: W.H. Allen, 1965. 286p.

The author explains the concept of the artificial harbors, their construction in Britain, their installation off Normandy, and the impact they made on the logistical support of the invasion.

2438. Hartcup, Guy. *Code Name Mulberry: The Planning, Building, and Operation of the Normandy Harbours*. New York: Hippocrene Books, 1977. 160p.

Another British view of the artificial harbors based on official sources and recollections of those who worked on the project; as with the last two entries, this one is illustrated with photos and drawings.

2439. Hicks, George. "From an American Naval Flagship in the English Channel." In: Louis L. Snyder, ed. *Masterpieces of War Reporting*. New York: Julian Messner, 1962, pp. 344-347.

The transcript of this CBS reporter's radio report on the D-Day landings made from the cruiser *Augusta* (CA-31) on June 6, 1944.

2440. Karig, Walter, and C.L. Freeland. "Rhinos and Mulberries." *U.S. Naval Institute Proceedings*, LXXI (December 1945), 1415-1425.

A discussion of the Mulberry artificial harbors installed at Normandy as well as the Rhino self-propelled ferries designed to carry cargo and vehicles ashore from amphibious ships.

2441. Liebling, Abbott J. "Cross-Channel Trip." *New Yorker*, XX (July 1, 1944), 38+; (July 8, 1944), 34+; (July 15, 1944), 36+.

The author's detailed recollections of service aboard a Coast Guard-manned LCI during the Normandy invasion.

2442. Miller, Max. *The Far Shore*. New York: McGraw-Hill, 1945. 173p.

A view of the Normandy invasion as seen by a USN Lieutenant Commander aboard an LCI; discusses "Neptune's" planning, weather problems, vessel formations in the invasion armada, the landing and gunfire support, and beach securement.

2443. ———. "The Far Shore: The Navy at Omaha and Utah--The Normandy Landings." *Harpers*, CXC (January 1945), 116-125.

Drawn from the previous entry, this piece concentrates on gunfire support and the actual landings.

2444. Moore, Rufus J. "'Operation Pluto." *U.S. Naval Institute Proceedings*, LXXX (May 1954), 647-653.

A description of the planning, building, and operation of PLUTO (Pipe Line Under The Ocean) which took gasoline from England to Normandy after the invasion.

2445. Morison, Samuel E. *The Invasion of France and Germany, 1944-1945*. Vol. XI of *History of United States Naval Operations in World War II*. Boston, Mass.: Little, Brown, 1957. 360p.

Morison, who was present at D-Day, tells of the planning and operation of "Neptune" as well as USN/USCG support for forces ashore after June 6, examples of which include bombardment of the hold-out Nazi forts along the French coast and the ferrying of troops across the Rhine in March-April 1945, naval details of the latter also being covered in Section IV:C:2:c above. Based on official reports and interviews and illustrated with maps, charts, and photographs.

2446. "Normandy Beaches, 1944: The Coast Guard Was There." *U.S. Coast Guard Academy Alumni Association Bulletin*, XLII (May-June 1980), 20-25.

An overview of the CG role in D-Day, including a summary of the participation of its transports and LCI's in the landing.

2447. "'Operation Neptune.'" *U.S. Naval Institute Proceedings*, LXXX (June 1954), 672-685.

A tenth-anniversary pictorial which remains one of the better sources for pictures of the naval aspects of Normandy.

2448. Postus, Craig. "The Storm That Almost Wrecked D-Day." *Battles*, I (Fall 1979), 32-37, 69.

Describes the June 19-21 gale which destroyed the Mulberry off Omaha Beach and created havoc with the invasion shipping and resupply effort.

2449. Ramsay, Bertram H. "The Assault Phase of the Normandy Landings." Supplement 38110, *London Gazette*, October 30, 1947.

Reprints a dispatch from the naval Commander in Chief, Allied Expeditionary Force originally dated October 16, 1944.

2450. Schofield, Brian B. *Operation Neptune*. Sea Battles in Close-Up, no. 10. Annapolis, Md.: U.S. Naval Institute, 1974. 168p.

A British admiral discusses the naval side of "Overlord" and describes the multitude of tasks involved from beach reconnaissance to the landings to the installations of PLUTO and the Mulberries. Includes eleven appendices on specific phases of Neptune; illustrated with maps and a large number of black and white photographs.

2451. Somers, Martin. "The Longest Hour in History." *Saturday Evening Post*, CCXVII (July 8, 1944), 22+.

Describes the gunfire support mission of the destroyer *McCook* (DD-496) whose captain risked grounding in order to deliver close-in call fire to Omaha Beach.

2452. ———. "'Right Hard Rudder! All Hands Below!'" *Saturday Evening Post*, CCXVII (September 16, 1944), 18-19+.

An account of the battleship *Texas*' (BB-35) bombardment of Nazi artillery positions at Cherbourg.

2453. Sondern, Frederick, Jr. "Armada in Action." *Reader's Digest*, XLV (August 1944), 118-122.

An overview of the naval phase of the D-Day landings.

2454. Stanford, Alfred B. *Force Mulberry: The Planning and Installation of the Artificial Harbor off U.S. Normandy Beaches in World War II.* New York: William Morrow, 1951. 240p.

Describes the process of building the artificial harbors, towing them to France, and installing them behind a breakwater of sunken ships; also includes a picture of the June 19-21 storm which damaged the U.S. Mulberry off Omaha Beach, forcing logistic support to come via the more conventional over-the-beach method.

2455. Strobridge, Truman R. "'St. Bernards' of Normandy." *Sea Classics*, VII (January 1974), 62-65.

How 60 Coast Guard 83-foot cutters saved 1,438 men floundering in the water off the beaches on D-Day.

2456. United States. Coast Guard. Historical Section. *Landings in France.* The Coast Guard at War. Washington, D.C.: Headquarters, U.S. Coast Guard, 1946. 310p.

A detailed examination of the CG role in the D-Day invasion which includes not only information on the "St. Bernards," as noted in the preceding entry, but also the work of Coast Guard-manned transports and LCI's. A valuable official history which includes more data on this service's role than is provided in Morison's account, cited above.

3. Battle of the Atlantic

Introduction: As noted in the introduction to this section, World War II action for the U.S. actually began in the Atlantic several months before Pearl Harbor. From the period of this undeclared U.S.-German naval war through early 1944, the conflict against the U-boat went from a period which can only be described as near-defeat to one of mastery over the logistic-killing submarine. The diplomacy behind the savage Atlantic battle, before and after December 7, 1941, is covered in Section II:A above while a few references to the aerial phase of the contest as conducted by land-based warplanes can be found in Section III:C. Readers will note that certain of the encyclopedias and handbooks as well as general war histories referenced in Section I above as well as the sea weapons part below contain information on the most difficult nautical phase to be covered by this guide. Comprehensive but unannotated bibliographic coverage for publications prior to 1976 is found in my *The European Theater*, which is Volume I of *World War II at Sea: A Bibliography of Sources in English* (Metuchen, N.J.: The Scarecrow Press, 1976), pp. 211-272.

2457. Abbazia, Patrick. *Mr. Roosevelt's Navy.* Annapolis, Md.: U.S. Naval Institute, 1975. 520p.

An exceptionally well-done and detailed view of the U.S. Navy in the undeclared naval war with Germany; examines not only the diplomatic background and politics of the extension of U.S. protection to British convoys prior to America's entry into the war, but also useful coverage of the close encounters and actual shooting between German submarines and Yankee escorts. The story is carried on into the dark period of 1942 when

Allied shipping losses off the U.S. east coast and in the Caribbean were very high.

2458. ———. "When the Good Shepherds Were Blind." *U.S. Naval Institute Proceedings*, CI (September 1975), 49-57.

Portrays the hazards of the North Atlantic convoys of early 1942 in which U.S. escorts lacked basic ASW detection equipment.

2459. "Action in the North Atlantic: Subs vs. Convoy Escorts." *Sea Classics*, III (March 1970), 52+.

A photo feature detailing U-boat attacks and depth-charging by convoy escorts.

2460. "The Atlantic Convoy: The Second Front Depends on It." *Life*, XIII (July 27, 1942), 64-73.

Still a useful pictorial piece showing ships in column and the work of escorts.

2461. Bailey, Thomas A., and Paul B. Ryan. *Hitler vs. Roosevelt*. New York: Free Press, 1979. 303p.

The Dean of American diplomatic historians and a former USN captain cover the diplomatic and military aspects of the undeclared U.S.-German naval war of 1939-1941; compare with Abbazia above. The study is wide-ranging, but does include a look at the *Greer* and *Reuben James* episodes.

2462. "Battle of the Arctic Convoy." *Life*, XIII (August 2, 1942), 19-23.

Still a useful pictorial piece showing the effort to get a convoy through to Russia with Lend-Lease materials.

2463. "Battling the Subs--World War II." *All Hands*, no. 495 (April 1958), 59-63.

An overview on Atlantic ASW operations written for serving sailors.

2464. Beecher, John. *All Brave Sailors: The Story of the S.S. Booker T. Washington*. New York: L.B. Fischer, 1945. 208p.

The *Booker T.* was the first sizable U.S. ship captained by a Black with an integrated crew; this work details crew life aboard and the merchantman's first convoy across the Atlantic.

2465. Berry, Robert B. *Gunners Get Glory: The Story of the Navy's Armed Guard*. Indianapolis: Bobbs-Merrill, 1943. 293p.

A contemporary account of the USN sailors who shipped aboard merchantmen to man AAA and ASW defenses; the story, mostly human interest, describes the men's duties and interaction with civilian crews in port and out, during convoy and battle.

2466. Blackman, John L., Jr. "Carrier War in the Atlantic." *U.S. Naval Institute Proceedings*, LXXIV (August 1948), 999-1003.

A look at the 1943 cruise of the escort carrier U.S.S. *Bogue* (CVE-9) and the sinking of three U-boats by the planes of her composite squadron VC-42.

2467. Blond, Georges. *Ordeal Below Zero: The Heroic Story of the Arctic Convoys in World War II.* London: Souvenir Press, 1956. 199p.

A general history of the Allied convoys which departed England and fought their way through U-boats and Luftwaffe bombers up around Norway to the Soviet port of Murmansk; details the strategy behind the convoys, the tactics employed by German and Allied combatants, and the impact of the convoy battles on the men involved.

2468. Bond, Geoffrey. *Laconia.* London: Oldbourne, 1956. 200p.

Tells how survivors of a torpedoed British merchantman were assisted by German U-boats until an AAF B-24 Liberator drove them off; the incident gave Admiral Dönitz a reason for ordering his submarines not to provide aid to the survivors of sinking Allied vessels.

2469. Bowling, R.A. "Escort of Convoy--Still the Only Way." *U.S. Naval Institute Proceedings*, XCV (December 1969), 46-56.

An overview of the success of the convoy system in the Atlantic during World War II with emphasis on lessons learned which are applicable today.

2470. Bowman, Richard C. "Organizational Fanaticism: A Case Study of Allied Air Operations Against the U-boat During World War II." *Air Power Historian*, X (April 1963), 50-53.

A discussion of the drive behind AAF efforts to assist the USN in its war against submarines in 1942 and the resultant squabbles over turf this desire created.

2471. Browning, Miles R. "Convoy Escorts." *Marine Corps Gazette*, XXXII (September 1948), 18-23.

An overview of Atlantic convoy operations, 1942-1945, with emphasis on the work of USN escort vessels.

2472. Buchheim, Lothar-Günther. *U-boat War.* Translated from the German. Annapolis, Md.: U.S. Naval Institute, 1978. Unpaged.

Examines the German side of the Battle of the Atlantic through 205 black and white photographs and a supportive text by the author, a former Kriegsmarine combat artist.

2473. Bunker, John. "The Story of the *Stephen Hopkins*." *U.S. Naval Institute Proceedings*, LXXX (November 1954), 1254-1257.

A U.S. liberty ship defends herself against the German disguised merchant raider *Stier* in the South Atlantic in September 1942.

2474. Busch, Harold. *U-boats at War*. Translated from the German. New York: Ballantine Books, 1955. 176p.

A general history of the organization and operations of the German Navy's U-boat arm during the war with some insight into perceived reasons why the Reich lost the Battle of the Atlantic.

2475. Campbell, Ian, and Donald G. Macintyre. *The Kola Run: A Record of the Arctic Convoys, 1941-1945*. London: Muller, 1958. 254p.

Two former British naval officers examine in detail the Allied arctic convoys and the dangers they encountered while making the passage from Scotland or northern Ireland to Murmansk; emphasis is on British action with some attention to the participation of U.S. merchantmen.

2476. Carr, Roland T. *To Sea in Haste*. Washington, D.C.: Acropolis Books, 1975. 260p.

Basing his work on a supply officer's diary, the author records the activities of the USN corvette *Haste* (PG-92) on ASW and convoy duty on the Eastern Sea Frontier in 1943-1944.

2477. Carse, Robert. *A Cold Corner of Hell*. Garden City, N.Y.: Doubleday, 1969. 268p.

An account of the 1941-1945 Murmansk convoys and the struggle by Allied sailors to get their vessels through the Arctic Ocean against the cold and Germans, with emphasis on the period 1941-1942. The author served aboard convoy merchantmen as a seaman in 1942.

2478. ———. *Lifeline: The Ships and Men of Our Merchant Marine at War*. New York: William Morrow, 1944. 189p.

Describes the ships and their crews, as well as deeds of heroism exhibited during the passage of pre-D-Day convoys; heavy on human interest, light on specific or geographical detail.

2479. ———. *There Go the Ships*. New York: William Morrow, 1942. 156p.

Five months on the Murmansk run as experienced by a writer who enlisted as an able seaman in the U.S. Merchant Marine in order to witness firsthand the action he describes; about half of the book was published in the next entry.

2480. ———. "We Fought Through to Murmansk." *Saturday Evening Post*, CCXV (November 7, 1942), 9-11+; (November 14, 1942), 16-17+; (November 21, 1942), 28-29+.

Excerpted from the previous citation's most action-filled section.

2481. "Convoy HX-166." *U.S. Coast Guard Alumni Association Bulletin*, XXXIX (September-October 1977), 16-21.

Describes the Coast Guard contribution to the defense of this February 1943 convoy.

2481a. Cooke, Henry D. "The Atlantic Convoys." *U.S. Naval Institute Proceedings*, LXXVI (August 1950), 862-869.

A pictorial discussion of the formation and execution of the major Allied convoys from 1942 to 1944.

2482. Cope, Harley F. "... and Sank Same." *U.S. Naval Institute Proceedings*, LXXII (June 1946), 953-961.

Examines the role of USN hunter-killer groups formed around escort carriers in the destruction of the U-boat menace in 1943.

2483. Dear, Wilfred P. "America's Undeclared Naval War." *U.S. Naval Institute Proceedings*, LXXXVII (January 1961), 70-79.

An overview of the naval incidents between the U.S. and Germany during the months before Pearl Harbor, including the *Greer* and *Reuben James* episodes.

2484. Farago, Ladislas. *The Tenth Fleet*. New York: Obolensky, 1962. 366p.

A poorly organized history of the Washington-based USN effort to coordinate the naval war against the U-boat, including the use of intelligence (Ultra is not mentioned, naturally), survivor reports, convoy coordination, etc. Describes the development of processes and tactics, including hunter-killer groups, for the stalking of German submarines.

2485. Ferguson, Arthur B. *The Antisubmarine Command*. USAAF Historical Study, no. 107. Washington, D.C.: Headquarters, U.S. Army Air Forces, 1945. 315p.

A detailed account of the AAF's efforts to use some of its long-range bombers against German U-boats and to offer protection to Atlantic convoys.

2486. Frank, Wolfgang. *The Sea Wolves: The Story of German U-Boats at War*. Translated from the German. New York: Rinehart, 1955. 340p.

A former PR man on Admiral Dönitz's staff provides a chronological record of Kriegsmarine submarine operations in the Atlantic, including data on the development of the technical, scientific, and political aspects of the U-boat arm of the German Navy.

2487. Gallery, Daniel V. *Clear the Decks!* New York: William Morrow, 1952. 243p.

A blunt, often humorous, memoir of the author's wartime service as skipper of the escort carrier *Guadalcanal* (CVE-60) during the Battle of the Atlantic.

2488. ———. "... nor Dark of Night." *U.S. Naval Institute Proceedings*, XCV (January 1969), 85-90.

Describes flight operations from the *Guadalcanal*, often during adverse weather.

2489. ———. *Twenty Million Tons Under the Sea*. Chicago: Regnery, 1956. 344p.

An eyewitness history of the USN Battle of the Atlantic, the formation of the hunter-killer groups and their impact, and the capture, by ships of the author's group, of the Nazi submarine *U-505*.

2490. ———. "We Captured a German Submarine." *Saturday Evening Post*, CCXVIII (August 4, 1945), 9-11+.

How the *Guadalcanal* hunter-killer group took the *U-505*.

2491. Gibson, Charles D., 2nd. *The Ordeal of Convoy N.Y. 119*. New York: South Street Seaport Museum, 1973. 178p.

A chronological record of the mid-1944 Atlantic crossing of non-seagoing Army tugboats, yard tankers, and barges (under USN escort) which were needed in Europe to clear crowded anchorages and keep the supply lines functioning smoothly.

2492. Gnaedinger, L.B.N. "Picket Patrol: Yachts Against Subs." *Motor Boating and Sailing*, CXXX (December 1972), 46-49+.

A look at the Coast Guard's Auxiliary Coastal Picket Service which was designed to guard against U-boats in the dark early days of 1942.

2493. Golovko, Arsenii G. *With the Red Fleet: The War Memoirs of the Late Admiral Arsenii G. Golovko*. Translated from the Russian. London: Putnam, 1965. 247p.

The wartime Soviet Commander in Chief of the Northern Fleet recalls, in a work critical of the Western Allies, the operations of Russian destroyers, submarines, and convoys in the Arctic, the latter including those from Britain. Offers few statistics, but considerable Red propaganda and inaccuracies; nevertheless, interesting because this is one of the few Soviet items available on the naval war in the Atlantic and Arctic.

2494. Greene, Laurence. "'Away All Boarding Parties!': The Flattop *Guadalcanal*." *Coronet*, XXXIV (July 1953), 64-68.

A summary of how the CVE-60 group captured *U-505*.

2495. Grosvenor, Melville B. "Cruise on an Escort Carrier." *National Geographic Magazine*, LXXXIV (November 1943), 513-546.

Still a useful pictorial look at the Atlantic hunter-killer group built around the escort carrier U.S.S. *Card* (CVE-11).

2496. Guerlac, Henry, and Marie Boas. "The Radar War Against the U-Boat." *Military Affairs*, XIV (Summer 1950), 99-111.

Describes the use of radar by Allied escort ships in the Battle of the Atlantic.

2497. Heckman, Hugh M. "The U.S.S. *Block Island* [CVE-21]: One of a Kind." *Sea Classics*, XIV (January 1981), 42-45.

Her service in the Battle of the Atlantic until May 29, 1944, when she was torpedoed and sunk by *U-549*.

2498. Herman, Frederick S. *Dynamite Cargo: Convoy to Russia*. New York: Vanguard Press, 1943. 158p.

An American merchant sailor's account of a convoy to Murmansk and its eight-day battle with Nazi planes and submarines; many passages convey the horror of battle during an Arctic passage.

2499. Herrick, John O. *Subsurface Warfare: The History of Division 6, N.D.R.C.* Washington, D.C.: Research and Development Board, Department of Defense, 1951. 135p.

A report on the researches of the National Defense Research Committee on the use of acoustics in antisubmarine warfare, 1941-1945.

2500. Hersey, John. "The U.S.S. *Borie*'s Last Battle: Lt. [Charles H.] Hutchins Fights His Old Destroyer to a Gallant Finish in Ramming and Sinking a U-boat." *Life*, XV (December 13, 1943), 104-106+.

The noted writer's account, illustrated with drawings, of how DD-215 sank the surfaced *U-405* on November 1, 1943; abridged in *Reader's Digest*, XLIV (March 1944), 58-62.

2501. Hickam, Homer H., Jr. "Day of Anger, Day of Pride." *American History Illustrated*, XVII (January 1983), 30-39.

The hunt for *U-352* off the North Carolina coast.

2502. Hoyt, Edwin P. *The Sea Wolves: Germany's Dreaded U-boats of World War II*. New York: Lancer Books, 1973. 160p.

A brief summary of the operations of Kriegsmarine submarines, particularly in the Atlantic, throughout the course of the war.

2503. ———. *U-boats Offshore!* Chicago, Ill.: Playboy Press, 1980. 288p.

Superior to the last title in detail if not in style, this work concentrates on telling of the "happy hunting" enjoyed by German submarines off the U.S. east coast and in the Caribbean in 1942.

2504. Hughes, Terry, and John Costello. *The Battle of the Atlantic*. New York: Dial Press, 1977. 314p.

The Allied naval struggle against the U-boats was the longest single sustained campaign of World War II and perhaps the most pivotal. Employing official reports, recently declassified documents (including Ultra), interviews with top German leaders like Dönitz, and other sources, the authors sketch the submarine war and explain why it did not reach a successful Nazi conclusion; illustrated with drawings, maps, and 160 black and white photographs.

2505. Ingram, Jonas H. "The Battle of the Atlantic." *U.S. Naval Institute Proceedings*, LXXI (August 1945), 854-859.

The official report (reprinted from the June 1945 issue of *All Hands*) of the ASW effort as told by the American admiral who commanded the U.S. Fourth Fleet in the South Atlantic from 1942 to 1944 and the Atlantic Fleet until war's end.

2506. Karig, Walter. *The Atlantic War*. Vol. II of *Battle Report*. New York: Farrar and Rinehart, 1946. 558p.

A massive early official look at the U.S. Navy in the Battle of the Atlantic from before Pearl Harbor to VE-Day, which is based on Navy reports and illustrated with a variety of maps, drawings, and photos.

2507. ———, Earl Burton, and C.L. Freeland. "Murmansk Run." *U.S. Naval Institute Proceedings*, LXXII (January 1946), 25-33.

Drawn from the above citation; illustrates the hardships suffered by USN escorts assigned to convoys to Russia.

2508. Kemp, Peter. *Decision at Sea: The Convoy Escorts*. New York: Elsevier-Dutton, 1978. 184p.

A concise illustrated history of the Battle of the Atlantic, with emphasis on the role of the convoy escorts, as told by a noted British naval historian.

2509. Kershaw, Andrew, ed. *The Battle of the Atlantic*. Purnell's History of the World Wars Special. London: Phoebus, 1975. 64p.

A pictorial overview of the Atlantic naval war with major emphasis on the battle between the Allied convoys and the German submarines; illustrated with dozens of drawings and photographs, some in color.

2510. Klemmer, Harvey. "Convoys to Victory." *National Geographic Magazine*, LXXXIII (February 1943), 193-216.

The text describes the purpose of convoys while the photographs show one assembled and under escort.

2511. Leighton, Richard M. "U.S. Merchant Shipping and the British Import Crisis." In: Kent R. Greenfield, ed. *Command Decisions*. Washington, D.C.: Office of the Chief of Military History, Department of the Army, 1960, pp. 199-223.

An analysis of how U.S. production responded to Britain's urgent needs by constructing more ships than the German submarines could sink.

2512. Lundeberg, Philip K. "American Anti-Submarine Operations in the Atlantic, May 1943-May 1945." Unpublished Ph.D. Dissertation, Harvard University, 1954.

An early scholarly study of the subject which is concerned not only with convoy protection but with the development of and operations by hunter-killer groups composed of escort carriers and destroyer escorts.

2513. Macintyre, Donald G.F.W. *The Battle of the Atlantic*. New York: Macmillan, 1961. 208p.

The author, a famous British escort commander, writes from experience, his own and that reported by others, Allied and German. His work follows the course of the campaign from 1939 to May 1943, when 40 German submarines were lost, ending the U-boat threat to Allied shipping. Consideration is given not only to operations, but also to U-boat strategy, the convoy system, and the coordination of air and naval forces, Allied and Nazi.

2514. Mason, David. *U-boat: The Secret Menace*. Ballantine's Illustrated History of World War II. New York: Ballantine Books, 1968. 160p.

A somewhat misleading title in that the German submarines were not secret, although the time of their appearance was; a pictorial history which traces the rise of this German menace and the manner by which the Allies ended it.

2515. Mauer, Mauer, and Lawrence J. Paszek. "Origins of the *Laconia* Order." *Air University Review*, XV (March-April 1964), 26-37.

Describes the AAF bombing of *U-156* which was displaying a red cross and attempting to aid the survivors of the British merchantman *Laconia*; the act led Dönitz to forbid his submariners to save torpedo victims. Reprinted in the *Journal of the Royal United Service Institute*, CIX (November 1964), 334-344.

2516. Middlebrook, Martin. *Convoy: The Battle for Convoy SC 122 and HX 229*. New York: William Morrow, 1976. 378p.

A blow-by-blow account of the critical March 1943 North Atlantic convoy battles based on published and unpublished sources, including interviews with 300 participants in the action. Another interesting title, not entered here due to its British emphasis, is Sir Peter Gretton's *Crisis Convoy: The Story of HX 231* (Annapolis, Md.: U.S. Naval Institute, 1975. 182p). Compare with Jürgen Rohwer's study, cited below.

2517. Middleton, Drew. "Killer Groups vs. Wolf Packs." *New York Times Magazine* (October 31, 1943), 15+.

On the antisubmarine successes of American hunter-killer groups composed of escort carriers and destroyer escorts.

2518. Morison, Samuel E. *The Atlantic Battle Won, May 1943-May 1945.* Vol. X of *History of United States Naval Operations in World War II.* Boston, Mass.: Little, Brown, 1956. 399p.

2519. ———. *The Battle of the Atlantic.* Vol. I of *History of United States Naval Operations in World War II.* Boston, Mass.: Little, Brown, 1958. 432p.

Separated by eight years in publication dates, these volumes nevertheless provide, with only the late revelations on signal intelligence to be added, the official and best history of American operations in the Atlantic (North Atlantic, South Atlantic, Caribbean, and U.S. east coast waters) during the war. The ebb and flow of the action and the search for advantage are masterfully told with sufficient charts, maps, and photographs to allow readers to follow the story easily. Definitely the starting spot for all students.

2520. ———. "Hunter-Killers in the Atlantic, October-December 1943." *Atlantic*, CXCVII (March 1956), 42-47.

Drawn from the first Morison title above, this piece recounts the toll of U-boats taken by U.S. escort carrier groups during the period covered.

2521. Mueller, William. "Liberty in the Kriegsmarine Sights." *Sea Classics*, X (March 1977), 6-15.

The SS *Stephen Hopkins* vs. the German disguised merchant cruiser *Stier* in the South Atlantic in September 1942.

2522. Museum of Science and Industry. *The Story of the U-505.* Chicago, 1955. 36p.

A brief pamphlet which describes how Capt. Daniel V. Gallery's *Guadalcanal* group caught the submarine in 1944 and how it later came to rest as a prize exhibit at the museum; illustrated.

2523. Noble, Dennis L., and Bernard Nalty. "The Hooligan Navy." *Sea Classics*, XV (March 1982), 52-57.

How the Coast Guard formed the Auxiliary Coastal Picket Service, employing volunteer yachts to guard against U-boats in early 1942.

2524. Noli, Jean. *The Admiral's Wolfpack.* Translated from the French. Garden City, N.Y.: Doubleday, 1974. 396p.

An episodic history of the U-boat campaign from 1939 to 1945 first published in France in 1970 as *Les Loups de l'Amiral*; based on research in German and British archives, this work adds nothing to Morison, but is illustrated with interesting photographs, and does provide good coverage of submarine strategy and tactics.

2525. Norton, Douglas. "The Open Secret: The U.S. Navy in the Battle of the Atlantic, April-December 1941." *Naval War College Review*, XXVI (April 1974), 63-83.

Shows the undeclared naval war in the Atlantic as a possible infringement on the warmaking powers of Congress, but one which FDR took, despite the *Greer* and *Reuben James* incidents, as a way of helping to save Britain from defeat.

2526. O'Connell, James A. "Radar and the U-boat." *U.S. Naval Institute Proceedings*, LXXXIX (September 1963), 53-65.

A detailed look at the use of radar in the Atlantic ASW campaign by the USN; as this author and Guerlac and Boas above contend, this weapon was considered to be one of the most important technical devices employed--and neither writer knew about Ultra--by the Allies against the Germans in the Atlantic.

2527. Oliver, Edward F. "The *Odenwald* Incident." *U.S. Naval Institute Proceedings*, LXXXII (April 1956), 338-342.

Describes the salvage of the abandoned German blockade runner *Odenwald* off the coast of Brazil in November 1941 by the USN cruiser *Omaha* (CL-4) and the destroyer *Somers* (DD-381).

2528. Peillard, Leonce. *The Laconia Affair*. Translated from the French. New York: G.P. Putnam, 1963. 270p.

A French historian's detailed study of the origin of Admiral Dönitz's directive to his submarines not to rescue the victims of torpedoed Allied ships caused, so the Germans maintained, because an AAF B-24 Liberator bombed a German submarine attempting to help the survivors of the *Laconia*. Compare with the shorter Mauer and Paszek article cited above.

2529. Pitt, Barrie. *The Battle of the Atlantic*. World War II Series. Alexandria, Va.: Time-Life Books, 1977. 208p.

A pictorial history of the Allied-German naval war from 1939 to 1945 which includes coverage not only of the U-boat campaign but also of the destruction of such Nazi surface units as the *Bismarck*; many of the photographs were taken by *Life* magazine cameramen on the scene.

2530. Polmar, Norman. "Protecting the Sea Lanes of Communication." *Sea Power*, CIII (September 1977), 11-16.

A brief overview of the Battle of the Atlantic with emphasis on lessons applicable today.

2531. Pratt, Fletcher. "Caribbean Command." *Harpers*, CLXXXVIII (February 1944), 232-241.

A contemporary look at the Caribbean Sea Frontier, the USN command responsible for patrolling and defense of the area from Cuba to French Guiana.

2532. ———. "The South Atlantic: A Diplomatic Campaign." *U.S. Naval Institute Proceedings*, LXXIV (June 1948), 691-699.

Considers the operations of Vice Admiral Jonas Ingram's U.S. Fourth Fleet from its base at Recife, Brazil, March 1941-July 1945.

2533. Price, Alfred. *Aircraft Versus Submarines.* London: Kimber, 1973. 268p.

Based mostly on the British experience, this is an episodic account of the growth of aircraft employment in ASW since 1912; does cite a few instances of American use in the Atlantic war of 1941-1945.

2534. Rohwer, Jürgen. *The Critical Convoy Battles of March 1943: The Battle for HX 229/SC 122.* Translated from the German. Annapolis, Md.: U.S. Naval Institute, 1977. 256p.

Based on recently declassified U.S. and British documents, including Ultra, this detailed study follows the fate of two convoys from the perspectives of both the submarine and surface forces. Compare with Martin Middlebrook's study, cited above.

2535. Rouse, Parke, Jr. "Under the Cloak of Night." *U.S. Naval Institute Proceedings*, CVIII (June 1982), 74-75.

How the U.S.S. *Roper* (DD-147) sank *U-85* off Cape Hatteras on April 13, 1942.

2536. Sanders, Jacquin. *A Night Before Christmas.* New York: G.P. Putnam, 1963. 320p.

Details the torpedoing of the Belgian liner *Leopoldville* on December 24, 1944, with great loss of life to the soldiers of the U.S. Sixty-Sixth Division.

2537. Schnepf, Edward. "Not for Glory." In: Alden Price, ed. *Sea Raiders.* North Hollywood, Calif.: Challenge Publications, [1965?], pp. 173-191.

The SS *Stephen Hopkins* vs. the German raider *Stier* in the South Atlantic.

2538. ———. "The U.S. Navy Armed Guard in World War II." *Sea Classics*, XVI (January 1983), 44-47, 70-75.

An illustrated piece concerning the USN sailors put aboard merchantmen to operate the AAA and ASW equipment.

2539. Schofield, Brian B. "The Defeat of the U-boats During World War II." *Journal of Contemporary History*, XVI (January 1981), 119-129.

The first major article to detail the role of signal intelligence (Ultra) in the Allied conquest of the German undersea menace.

2540. ———. *The Russian Convoys.* Philadelphia, Pa.: Dufour, 1964. 224p.

A general history of the four-year battle to supply Russia by convoy from Britain to Murmansk, which explains both the German air-and-submarine strategy and the countermeasures taken by the Allies; includes interesting episodes of action in this climatically most inhospitable of war theaters.

2541. *Sea Classics*, Editors of. *Fighting Hitler's U-boats*. Canoga Park, Calif.: Challenge Publications, 1983. 64p.

A pictorial history of the Allied-German war for the Atlantic with emphasis on the role of the convoy escorts; one of the better illustrated efforts.

2542. Seagrave, Sterling. "War at Sea Seared Americans Before Pearl Harbor." *Smithsonian*, XII (November 1981), 100-109.

A pictorial account of the undeclared U.S.-German naval war which includes the *Greer* and *Reuben James* incidents.

2543. Seth, Ronald. *The Fiercest Battle: The Story of North Atlantic Convoy ONS-5, 22nd April-7th May 1943*. New York: W.W. Norton, 1962. 208p.

Tells of the successful passage of a large convoy which took fewer losses than those inflicted on the Germans and was considered as marking the final turning point in the Allied struggle with the U-boats; well written, with maps and illustrations.

2544. Smith, C. Alphonso. "The Battle of the Caribbean." *U.S. Naval Institute Proceedings*, LXXX (October 1954), 976-982.

2545. ———. "Martinique in World War II." *U.S. Naval Institute Proceedings*, LXXXI (February 1955), 168-174.

Admiral Smith recalls the U-boat war in the Caribbean Sea Frontier as well as the guarding of elements of the Vichy Navy which had assembled at this French Caribbean island.

2546. Soeten, Harlan. "Caribbean Convoy." *U.S. Naval Institute Proceedings*, C (July 1973), 78-82.

The author recalls his service on the freighter SS *Kahuku*, which was sunk out of a Caribbean convoy on June 15, 1942.

2547. Sternhell, Charles M., and Alan M. Thorndike. *Antisubmarine Warfare in World War II*. OEG Report, no. 51. Washington, D.C.: Operations Evaluation Group, Office of the Chief of Naval Operations, Department of the Navy, 1946. 193p.

Originally classified, this document describes, with charts and maps, the development of effective USN antisubmarine procedures after mid-1942, including information on the hunter-killer groups.

2548. Taylor, Theodore. *Fire on the Beaches*. New York: W.W. Norton, 1958. 248p.

The story of the U-boat campaign off the U.S. east coast in the months immediately following Pearl Harbor and the USN development of effective inshore convoy and patrol operations to combat the German menace.

2549. Thomas, Charles W. *Ice Is Where You Find It*. Indianapolis: Bobbs-Merrill, 1951. 378p.

Memoirs of the wartime Greenland Patrol by the one-time captain of the Coast Guard icebreaker *Northland* who later commanded the entire operation. Includes insight into the seemingly endless hunt for Nazi weather stations and the impact of Arctic gales on the men under his command.

2550. Thompson, Lawrence R. *The Navy Hunts the CGR-3070.* Garden City, N.Y.: Doubleday, 1944. 150p.

Describes the epic of the converted yacht *Zaida* which was lost in the North Atlantic for 21 days in December 1942; based on the memories of the Coast Guard personnel who survived the ordeal.

2551. "Three Down and One to Go." *All Hands*, no. 477 (May 1954), 2-5.

The story of the noteworthy ASW performance turned in by the destroyer escort *Bronstein* (DE-189) between February and April 1944.

2552. Townsend, Thomas. "Armed Yacht." *Sea Classics*, XII (March 1979), 18-23.

Recollections of the yacht *Avanti*, which served as a member of the Coast Guard's Auxiliary Coastal Picket Service in early 1942.

2553. "War in the Caribbean Basin." *Surface Warfare*, VII (September 1982), 4-7.

An overview of German U-boat attacks on Allied merchant shipping in the Caribbean in 1942 and the efforts taken by the USN to establish effective countermeasures.

2554. Waters, John M., Jr. *Bloody Winter.* Princeton, N.J.: Van Nostrand, 1967. 279p.

An account of the ordeal of the North Atlantic convoys during the winter of 1942-1943 is provided by a Coast Guard captain who served with an escort; graphic accounts of the difficulties of serving and fighting in the awful weather conditions are described, as well as battles surrounding a number of convoys, including SC-118.

2555. ———. "The Saga of Convoy SC-118." *Sea Classics*, XVI (May 1983), 64-70, 83.

Recollections of the March 1943 convoy battle in which eight Allied merchantmen and three German U-boats were sunk; compare with Rohwer and Middlebrook, cited above.

2556. ———. "Stay Tough." *U.S. Naval Institute Proceedings*, XCII (January 1966), 95-105.

A concise remembrance of the ordeal of convoy SC-118 by a participant in its defense.

2557. Watts, Anthony. *The U-boat Hunters*. London: Macdonald and Janes, 1976. 192p.

The Allied ASW war against Germany is retold in a well-illustrated account which pays particular attention to the development of the technology which finally drove Dönitz's wolfpacks from the Atlantic.

2558. Wenzell, Ronald. "'Mined.'" *Sandlapper*, XIII (November 1980), 64+.

Coping with mines dropped by U-boats in the harbor of Charleston, S.C.

2559. Werner, Herbert A. *Iron Coffins*. Translated from the German. New York: Holt, Rinehart and Winston, 1969. 329p.

A straightforward, unromanticized memoir of daily life aboard German submarines in the Battle of the Atlantic by one of the few surviving U-boat commanders; illustrated with interesting black and white photographs.

2560. West, Fred. "Invisible Convoys." *Sea Classics*, XIV (May 1981), 62-64.

Follows the service of the U.S.S. *Roe* (DD-148) in the undeclared U.S. naval war with Germany in the Atlantic during the fall of 1941.

2561. Willoughby, Malcolm F. *The U.S. Coast Guard in World War II*. Annapolis, Md.: U.S. Naval Institute, 1957. 347p.

A specific Coast Guard portrait of its role in the naval war, serving as part of the USN; describes CG domestic and combat operations, especially its work on inshore patrol and convoy escort in the Battle of the Atlantic.

2562. Wise, James E., Jr. "U-boats Off Our Coasts." *U.S. Naval Institute Proceedings*, XCI (October 1965), 84-101.

A pictorial which clearly shows the depredations by German submarines against U.S. east coast shipping in early 1942.

2563. ———. "Victory of the Woolworth Brigade." *Sea Classics*, VIII (September 1975), 48-59.

A description of the role, operations, and impact of USN escort carriers in the Battle of the Atlantic, 1942-1944.

2564. Y'Blood, William T. *Hunter-Killer: U.S. Escort Carriers in the Battle of the Atlantic*. Annapolis, Md.: U.S. Naval Institute, 1983. 288p.

Y'Blood offers a vivid you-are-there narrative and in-depth study of U.S. CVE's vs. Nazi U-boats in the Atlantic, 1942-1945, with emphasis on the conflict in antisubmarine warfare as seen from the cockpit; illustrated with 50 photographs and drawings.

2565. Yeager, Philip B. "The Stormy Romance of the 'Pickleboat.'" *U.S. Naval Institute Proceedings*, XC (January 1964), 66-75.

Portrays the ASW career of the destroyer escort *Fogg* (DE-57), which was torpedoed and sunk in December 1944.

D. SEA WEAPONS, UNIFORMS, AND MARKINGS

Introduction: The amount of information available in English concerning World War II sea weapons, uniforms, insignia, and camouflage/markings is huge. Given that consideration and the need to employ space for references to other sources in the conflict, the citations noted below are selective and, for the most part, concern items made available in the last decade or so. The literature on topics treated in this part has also been covered in several of the bibliographies cited in Section I:A above, especially the three volumes of my *World War II at Sea*. The order of arrangement here is: Warships; Warplanes; Sea Weapons; and Uniforms/Insignia/Markings.

1. Warships

Introduction: Although the U.S. Navy and Coast Guard employed every major and minor class of warship in the Atlantic, MTO, and ETO, a few stand out more than others: cruisers, destroyers and other escorts, and light carriers. The citations below for the most part reflect these ships. Readers should note that additional warship data is available in the other parts of this section.

2566. Alden, John D. *Flush Decks and Four Pipes*. Annapolis, Md.: U.S. Naval Institute, 1965. 107p.

An illustrated history of the famous "four-stack" destroyers built during World War I and which constituted over a third of the tin-cans available to the USN at the time of Pearl Harbor, even after 50 of them were transferred to Britain in 1940.

2567. Bellow, Steve. "Evolution of the Destroyer, 1904-1981." *All Hands*, no. 782 (April 1982), 32-37.

An overview of the different destroyer classes built for the USN, including those employed in World War II; illustrated with black and white photos and some color drawings.

2568. Bunker, John. *Liberty Ships: The Ugly Ducklings of World War II*. Annapolis, Md.: U.S. Naval Institute, 1972. 304p.

An exciting history of the design, development, and operations of these cargo vessels which saw service in the Atlantic, MTO, and ETO; illustrated with hull lines, deck plans, and photographs.

2569. Charles, Roland W. *Troopships of World War II*. Washington, D.C.: U.S. Army Transportation Association, 1947. 374p.

A detailed look at those merchant ships employed by the U.S. Army to carry troops to the MTO and ETO, many of which did not come under the jurisdiction of the U.S. Navy.

2570. Dater, Henry M. "The Development of the Escort Carrier." *Military Affairs*, XII (Summer 1948), 79-90.

Describes the conversion of merchant ships into CVE's and the impact of these small vessels on the Battle of the Atlantic.

2571. Elliott, Peter. *Allied Escort Ships of World War II: A Complete Survey*. Annapolis, Md.: U.S. Naval Institute, 1977. 575p.

Describes the technical and operational history of all classes of Allied escort ships built between 1939 and 1945, including the famous American class called destroyer escorts (DE); illustrated with over 330 photographs and numerous plans.

2572. ———. *American Destroyer Escorts of World War II*. London: Almark, 1974. 128p.

This detailed pictorial shows the evolution of the design and alterations made by the U.S. and British navies.

2573. Evans, Robert L., and Fitzhugh L. Palmer, Jr. "'Cinderella Carriers': A Pictorial." *U.S. Naval Institute Proceedings*, CII (August 1976), 52-63.

Shows CVE's at work in the Atlantic, MTO, and ETO during the war.

2573a. Friedman, Norman. *Modern Warship Design and Development*. London and New York: Mayflower Books, 1980. 192p.

A technical study of the evolution of warship types illustrated with many drawings and photographs.

2574. ———. *U.S. Aircraft Carriers: An Illustrated Design History*. Annapolis, Md.: U.S. Naval Institute, 1983. 488p.

A complete technical history of all American carriers from the *Langley* (CV-1) to the present, including those which fought during World War II; illustrated with hundreds of photos and drawings.

2574a. ———. *U.S. Destroyers: An Illustrated Design History*. Annapolis, Md.: U.S. Naval Institute, 1982. 481p.

A complete technical history of all American destroyer designs from the turn of the century to the present, including those which fought in World War II; illustrated with hundreds of photos and drawings. Friedman's three works cited here are the most detailed studies on carriers and "cans" available.

2575. Gordon, Arthur. "Troopships Are Never Dull." *Infantry Journal*, LXV (August 1949), 9-12.

A look at soldier life aboard the U.S.S. *General A.E. Anderson* (AP-111).

2576. Haislip, Harvey. "A Memory of Ships." *U.S. Naval Institute Proceedings*, CIII (September 1977), 48-59.

A recollection of wartime American destroyers.

2577. Hannon, E.J., Jr. "Destroyers in Their 60th Year." *U.S. Naval Institute Proceedings*, LXXXVIII (November 1962), 138-142.

A brief overview of the development of destroyers since 1902.

2578. Hoyt, Edwin P. *Destroyers: Foxes of the Sea.* Boston, Mass.: Little, Brown, 1969. 151p.

This destroyer history emphasizes operations by the little warships, with major emphasis on World War II and the Battle of the Atlantic.

2579. Land, Emory S. "The 'Wheelhorse' of World War II." *U.S. Naval Institute Proceedings*, LXXXIV (August 1958), 119-122.

A tribute to the effectiveness of the common-design Liberty ship.

2580. Lenton, Henry T. *American Battleships, Carriers, and Cruisers.* Navies of the Second World War. Garden City, N.Y.: Doubleday, 1968. 160p.

Divided into sections by the three classes of warship, this handy little compendium provides brief statistical data, photos, and comparison information.

2581. ———. *American Fleet and Escort Destroyers.* Navies of the Second World War. 2 vols. Garden City, N.Y.: Doubleday, 1971.

These handy little guides, one for DD's and one for DE's, provide brief statistical data, photos, and comparison information.

2582. ———. *American Gunboats and Minesweepers.* World War II Fact Files. New York: Arco, 1974. 64p.

A brief pictorial guide which provides statistical data and comparison information backed by dozens of photos and drawings.

2583. Lyon, Hugh. "United States." In: his *The Encyclopedia of the World's Warships: A Technical Directory of Major Fighting Ships from 1900 to the Present Day.* New York: Crescent Books, 1979, pp. 212-267.

Provides technical information on U.S. battleships, carriers, cruisers, and destroyers which fought in World War II together with a variety of photographs and drawings, many in color.

2584. McMurtrie, Francis E., ed. *Jane's Fighting Ships, 1939.* New York: Arco, 1974. 550p.

2585. ———. *Jane's Fighting Ships, 1944/45.* New York: Arco, 1974. 784p.

These reprints of the finest contemporary warship guides are extremely helpful to those who would have a look at the available information on fighting vessels as seen by those who participated in World War II at sea. Arranged geographically, the work provides valuable statistical and technical data as well as reports on war losses and improvements.

2586. Miller, Richard T. "Sixty Years of Destroyers: A Study of Evolution." *U.S. Naval Institute Proceedings*, LXXXVIII (January 1962), 93-111.

A pictorial which traces the changes and improvements in American destroyers since 1902.

2587. Mound, L.E.H. "The Development of Landing Craft." *U.S. Naval Institute Proceedings*, LXXI (December 1945), 1124-1129.

A brief but still useful study of the development of those craft, few if any of which existed before 1939, for the delivery of troops to shore under combat conditions.

2588. Musgrove, H.E. *U.S. Naval Ships Data Arranged by Hull Classification*. 2 vols. Stoughton, Wisc.: Nautical Books, 1975-1977.

This somewhat rare volume provides technical data on all USN vessels which received hull classifications after 1920.

2589. Niedermair, John C. "As I Recall--Designing the LST." *U.S. Naval Institute Proceedings*, CVIII (November 1982), 58-59.

On the Anglo-American joint design of the Tank Landing Ship.

2590. Polmar, Norman, *et al*. *Aircraft Carriers: A Graphic History of Carrier Aviation and Its Influence on World Events*. Garden City, N.Y.: Doubleday, 1969. 788p.

Both a design and operational history, Polmar's study gives much attention to World War II; illustrated with plans and photographs.

2591. Preston, Antony. *Aircraft Carriers*. London and New York: Hamlyn, 1979. 192p.

A pictorial history of carriers from 1918 to the present with emphasis on the war years 1939-1945; illustrated with drawings and photographs, including many in color. Reflects something of a British bias.

2592. ———. *Aircraft Carriers*. London: Bison Books, 1981. 64p.

A more concise version of the last entry with the same attributes and limitations.

2593. ———. *Destroyers*. Englewood Cliffs, N.J.: Prentice-Hall, 1977. 196p.

Includes technical facts, historical details, and anecdotes on the development and use of "cans" by all navies; illustrated with over 300 photographs, many in color. Reflects something of a British bias.

2594. ———. *Destroyers*. New York: Frederick Fell, 1982. 50p.

A more concise version of the last entry with the same attributes and limitations.

2595. Roberts, Leslie. "Little Ships That Saved the Day." *Saturday Evening Post*, CCXVI (February 12, 1944), 28-29+.

Covers the design and, more important, the Atlantic operations of destroyer escorts through December 1943.

2596. Scheina, Robert L. *U.S. Coast Guard Cutters and Craft of World War II*. Annapolis, Md.: U.S. Naval Institute, 1982. 384p.

Provides building, outfitting, and operational histories of each CG vessel; organized by vessel type with scale line drawings of the major cutter classes and over 300 black and white photographs.

2597. *Sea Classics*, Editors of. *Sea Classics Special Presentation: A Pictorial Monograph of the Fighting Fleet Class Destroyers*. Canoga Park, Calif.: Challenge Publications, 1979. 100p.

A pictorial on U.S. destroyers during World War II, including those employed in the Atlantic, MTO, and ETO. The illustrations are particularly rewarding.

2598. Silverstone, Paul. *U.S. Warships of World War II*. Garden City, N.Y.: Doubleday, 1965. 442p.

A small and handy compendium which is arranged by class and provides technical detail for warships large and small; illustrated with photographs.

2599. Terzibaschitsch, Stefan. *Escort Carriers of the U.S. Navy*. Translated from the German. New York: Rutledge Press, 1981. 224p.

The Federal Republic's leading World War II USN authority here provides an interesting guide to CVE's which concentrates on design and technical development; illustrated with a large number of drawings and photographs, many from the Bibliotek für Zeitgeschichte in Stuttgart.

2600. Thomas, Donald L. "The Four-Stackers." *U.S. Naval Institute Proceedings*, LXXVI (1950), 752-757; LXXVII (1951), 86-87.

Considers the design and deployment of the flush-deck "cans" from World War I through World War II; illustrated with photographs.

2601. United States. Navy Department. Bureau of Ships. "The 'Tin Can' Navy." *Bureau of Ships Journal*, II (October 1953), 2-9.

Details the history of destroyers in the USN from 1890 to 1953, with major emphasis on the war years 1941-1945.

2602. ———. ———. Naval Historical Center. *Destroyers in the United States Navy*. Washington, D.C.: Government Printing Office, 1962. 40p.

A brief pictorial pamphlet which discusses the use of "cans" by the USN from around 1990 to the present; the largest section is on World War II.

2603. ———. ———. ———. *Dictionary of American Naval Fighting Ships*. 8 vols. Washington, D.C.: U.S. Government Printing Office, 1959-1981.

Arranged alphabetically by ship name, this work provides complete information on every warship that ever served in the U.S. Navy after 1775; providing only basic technical detail, the entries concentrate on operational history, history which in number of lines provided grows longer as the work progresses. This is the single best source for operational histories on the majority of combat vessels which fought in the Atlantic, MTO, and ETO during World War II.

2604. White, Robb. "Life on an Oilslick." *Flying*, XXXVII (July 1945), 26-27+.

Details the crew and pilot lives of men who served on CVE's.

2605. Wyckoff, Don P. "'Let There Be Built Great Ships....'" *U.S. Naval Institute Proceedings*, CVIII (November 1982), 50-57.

Examines the Anglo-American conception of various landing craft which were then built in U.S. yards for World War II amphibious invasions.

2606. Yates, Brock W. *Destroyers and Destroyermen: The Story of Our Tin-Can Navy*. New York: Harper, 1959. 207p.

A narrative history of the development of and operations by American destroyers from 1900 to the mid-1950's which emphasizes life aboard and the use of "cans" during World War II.

2. Warplanes

Introduction: The U.S. Navy operated its own air force during World War II, an organization which won considerable glory especially in the Pacific. In the Atlantic, MTO, and ETO, USN aircraft also saw service, flying from small carriers in support of invasions or against U-boats or from land on long patrols over the North and South Atlantic, some of which work was conducted by lighter-than-air blimps. The citations in this part look at some of the Navy aircraft employed relative to the subject of this guide. Additional citations of a general nature can be found in Section III:E:1 above as well as in the bibliographies cited in Section I:A.

2607. Aubuchon, Norbert. "Wildcat: The Lethal Loser." *Flying*, XCII (January 1973), 36-43.

A close look at the F4F, a tubby fighter which saw action from the decks of CVE's in the Atlantic, MTO, and ETO.

2608. "Avenger." *Air Classics*, V (February 1969), 38-54.

A heavily illustrated history of the Grumman TBF torpedo bomber which, in the Atlantic, was fitted with ASW bombs and flown from CVE's.

2609. Bishop, John. "'Dumbo': The Magnificent Navy PBY." *Saturday Evening Post*, CCXVII (August 5, 1944), 12-13+.

A human interest portrait of the Catalina patrol aircraft widely employed during the Battle of the Atlantic.

2610. Cassangneres, Everett. *Consolidated PBY Catalina*. Aircraft in Profile, no. 183. Windsor, Eng.: Profile Publications, 1967. 15p.

A brief design, evolution, and technical history backed by a variety of drawings and photographs, including some in color.

2611. Forbes, Esther H. "Guardians of the Convoys." *Aviation*, XLI (November 1942), 197-199.

A quick look at USN blimps on inshore patrol off the east coast.

2612. Greene, Frank L. "Addendum to the Wildcat Story." *American Aviation Historical Society Journal*, VII (Spring 1962), 46-47+.

2613. ———. *Grumman F4F-3 Wildcat*. Aircraft in Profile, no. 49. Windsor, Eng.: Profile Publications, 1966. 15p.

2614. ———. *The Wildcat Story: History of the Grumman F4F Wildcat*. Bethpage, N.Y.: Grumman Aircraft Engineering Corp., n.d.

These three citations present detailed technical and developmental data on the Wildcat; all are illustrated with drawings and photographs, some in color.

2615. Harkins, Philip. "Blimp Patrols Guard the Coast." *Science Digest*, XIII (January 1943), 91-93.

Concerns the operations of Navy semi-rigid airships in the Battle of the Atlantic; little technical detail.

2616. Huse, Robert E. "Maintaining Sub Killers." *Aviation*, XLII (December 1943), 128-135.

Describes the maintenance effort required to keep USN blimps aloft.

2617. Jackson, Berkeley R., and Thomas E. Doll. *The Grumman TBF/TBM Avenger*. Fallbrook, Calif.: Aero Publishers, 1970. 60p.

A technical and operational history told with a wide-ranging variety of photographs and drawings; provides some attention to TBF/TBM use in the Atlantic.

2618. Johnsen, Frederick A. *Bombers in Blue: PB4Y-2 Privateers and PB4Y-1 Liberators*. Glendale, Calif.: Aviation Book Co., 1979. 28p.

This oversize pictorial paperback is slim on text and wide on the use of photographs to tell the story of these two land-based USN patrol bombers on ocean patrol during World War II.

2619. Mundorff, George T. "The Catalina Patrol Bomber." *Aerospace Historian*, XXIII (December 1976), 217-222.

An appreciation of the capabilities of the PBY on ocean patrol.

2620. Pininich, R.G., Jr. "Blimps on Patrol." *Aero Digest*, XLIII (July 1943), 116-117+.

2621. ———. "Blimps Return to the War: Naval Lighter-than-Air Craft on Submarine Patrol." *Aviation*, XLI (October 1942), 207-210.

A pair of appreciations for the long-range convoy protection afforded by the slow but high-endurance blimps in the Atlantic.

2622. Pratt, Fletcher. "The Blimp, All-American Sub-Fighter." *Reader's Digest*, XLI (September 1942), 63-66.

2623. ———. "Blimps." *Infantry Journal*, LII (February 1943), 34-38.

Two more appreciations of the effectiveness of the blimp in patrol work over convoys off the U.S. east coast and in the Atlantic.

2624. Quinn, D.C. "Confessions of a PBM Pilot." *Air Classics*, XII (May 1976), 72-79.

The author recalls how he flew the Martin Mariner patrol bomber over the Atlantic with squadron VP-214 in 1944; includes information on the aircraft.

2625. Rust, Kenn C. "Army Cats." *Air Classics*, VIII (November 1971), 11-16.

Examines the U.S. Army use of Catalina patrol bombers (OA-10's) for rescue work in the English Channel.

2626. Scarborough, William E. "The Consolidated PBY: Catalina to Canso." *American Aviation Historical Society Journal*, XVI (Spring 1971), 27-38; (Summer 1971), 112-123; (Fall 1971), 200-203.

Examines the design, deployment, and use of the PBY with much attention to technical detail; illsutrated with drawings and photos.

2626a. ———. *PBY Catalina in Action.* Carrollton, Tx.: Squadron/ Signal Publications, 1983. 48p.

In Aircraft No. 62, Scarborough details the history and development of the noted flying boat in a pictorial valuable for its 3-view drawings, marking schemes, and many photographs, some in color.

2627. Settle, T.G.W. "Lighter-than-Air." *Flying*, XXXII (February 1943), 184-186.

Remarks on the performance characteristics of USN blimps which made them excellent patrol and convoy escorts.

2628. Stimson, Thomas E., Jr. "Gas Bags on Patrol." *Popular Mechanics*, LXXIX (June 1943), 34-39.

2629. ———. "Riding the Gas Bag Patrol." *Popular Mechanics*, LXXXIV (July 1945), 65-69.

Provides information on the use of USN blimps and data on what it was like to fly in one during an extended ocean patrol.

2630. Sutherland, Mason. "Aboard a Blimp Hunting U-boats." *National Geographic Magazine*, LXXXIV (July 1943), 79-96.

Similar to the last entry with much human interest material on the crews and a variety of interesting photographs.

2631. Swanborough, F. Gordon, and Peter M. Bowers. *United States Navy Aircraft Since 1911*. 2nd ed. Annapolis, Md.: U.S. Naval Institute, 1977. 545p.

Presents a detailed look at every aircraft examined or employed by the USN after 1911, including many employed in the Atlantic, MTO, and ETO; illustrated with diagrams, drawings, and photographs. The best single-volume source for technical information on the World War II types.

2632. Thorburn, Lois and Donald. *No Tumult, No Shooting: The Story of the PBY*. New York: Henry Holt, 1945. 148p.

A narrative history of the design and more important, the use of the Consolidated patrol bomber in all theaters during the war.

2633. Tillman, Barrett. *Avenger at War*. New York: Scribners, 1980. 128p.

A profile of the versatile Grumman TBF told from the viewpoint of the men who flew it, including anecdotes of its Atlantic service as an ASW aircraft flying off jeep or escort carriers; oversize and illustrated with 176 black and white photographs.

2634. ———. *The Dauntless Dive Bomber in World War II*. Annapolis, Md.: U.S. Naval Institute, 1976. 192p.

A design and operational history of the SBD dive bomber, which was employed operationally by the USN during the "Torch" landings in North Africa; provides comments from air crew and a large variety of illustrations.

2635. ———. *Wildcat in World War II*. Annapolis, Md.: Nautical and Aviation Publishing Co., 1983. 265p.

A design and operational history of the F4F fighter which flew from U.S. escort carriers during several MTO/ETO invasions and was the standard interceptor carried aboard CVE's during the Battle of the Atlantic; illustrated with many photographs.

2636. United States. Navy Department. Bureau of Aeronautics. *Operational History of the Flying Boat, Open-Sea and Seadrome Aspects, Selected Campaigns, World War II.* Prepared by Michael G. Kammen. Washington, D.C., 1959. 133p.

A brief but fairly technical operational history of USN flying boats, including the PBY, in the war, including the operations in the Atlantic and ETO.

2637. ———. ———. ———. Naval Airship Training and Experimental Command, Lakehurst, New Jersey. *"They Were Dependable": Airship Operation, World War II, December 7, 1941 to September 1945.* Trenton, N.J.: Trenton Printing Company, 1946. 56p.

This amounts to the "cruise book" for the airship command; illustrated with a variety of photographs which show the crews of the blimps at work and the gas bags on patrol.

3. Sea Weapons

Introduction: I have chosen to note only two works in this section as both are very complete. Additional information on sea weapons can be found among the citations in the bibliographies noted in Section I:A.

2638. Friedman, Norman. *U.S. Naval Weapons.* Annapolis, Md.: U.S. Naval Institute, 1983. 287p.

A detailed technical history of every gun, missile, mine, and torpedo employed by the USN from 1883 to the present, with appendices which cover fire-control systems amd other items; illustrated with more than 300 drawings, plans, and photographs.

2639. ———, and Peter Hodges. *Destroyer Weapons of World War II.* Annapolis, Md.: U.S. Naval Institute, 1979. 192p.

A detailed comparison of British and U.S. destroyer armament, including guns, mountings, torpedoes, ASW weapons, and electronics; illustrated with 73 line drawings and 150 black and white photographs.

4. Uniforms/Insignia/Markings

Introduction: The citations in this section provide information on the uniforms worn by U.S. sailors during the war and the insignia, camouflage, and markings applied to their aircraft and ships. The list is selective and additional references can be found in certain of the bibliographies cited in Section I:A above, particularly the third volume of my *World War II at Sea*.

2640. Doll, Thomas E., Berkeley R. Jackson, and William A. Riley. *Naval Air Colors.* Carrollton, Tx.: Squadron/Signal Publications, 1983. 96p.

Follows the changes in USN aircraft camouflage and markings during the war years; illustrated with 323 black and white and 6 color photos, 24 charts, and 154 color paintings on 16 pages of color plates.

2641. Mollow, Andrew, and Malcolm McGregor. *Naval, Marine, and Air Force Uniforms of World War II.* New York: Macmillan, 1976. 231p.

Over 320 uniforms of the Allied and Axis powers are described with accompanying color illustrations and action photographs.

2642. Rairden, P.W., Jr. "Campaign and Service Medals." *U.S. Naval Institute Proceedings*, LXXV (May 1949), 515-521.

An illustrated description of the various USN campaign and service medals awarded to officers and seamen during the war.

2643. Riley, David L. *Uncommon Valor: Decorations, Badges, and Service Medals of the U.S. Navy and Marine Corps.* Tulsa, Okla.: Military Collectors News Press, 1979. 88p.

The most complete guide to naval badges and service medals, which includes a design history; illustrated by 113 color and black and white photographs.

2644. Rosignoli, Guido. *Badges and Insignia of World War II: Air Force, Naval, Marine.* Translated from the Italian. London: Burke's Peerage, 1981. 363p.

Over 25,000 color illustrations and the text trace the history of the badges and insignia of the major combatant services during the war.

2645. Sumrall, Robert F. "Ship Camouflage, World War II: Deceptive Art." *U.S. Naval Institute Proceedings*, XCIX (February 1973), 67-81.

This pictorial piece is the best available on the evolution of USN ship camouflage during the war.

VI. 16mm DOCUMENTARY FILM GUIDE

INTRODUCTION

I. Background

Millions of feet of 16mm film were exposed by cameramen during the combat phases of World War II, both for governments and private news organizations. The armed services of all the major combatants sent moviemakers to war in order to obtain and provide material which could be supplied to movie houses as propaganda or "progress reports," and for employment within the military for training purposes. Regardless of motive, these photographic efforts have come down through time to form an extremely valuable visual record of history's greatest conflict.

In both the Mediterranean and European Theaters, Allied cameramen recorded the activities of the United Nations advance, just as German and Italian cameramen shot footage showing their defenses. U.S. Army Signal Corps cameramen, often working with famous directors who had joined "for the duration," produced technically advanced documentaries which created dramatic impact when shown "back home." In addition to Signal Corps' operations on land, combat photographers went aloft with AAF bombers to record the danger of daylight attacks on strategic and tactical targets. Aboard fighter planes, where there was no room for passengers, cameras were often rigged to the warbirds' machine guns, synchronized to operate when those guns fired. Most of the pictures we have of fighters in air-to-air combat were achieved by this method. Meanwhile, at sea, U.S. Navy and Coast Guard cameramen braved the elements to record the difficulties of putting down the U-boat menace in the Atlantic as well as the dramatic incidents surrounding such invasions as North Africa, Sicily, Salerno, Anzio, D-Day, and southern France.

Following the war, the Allies were able to take over the 16mm film collections of Germany and Italy, and thereafter, enterprising documentary makers began the production of documentary films which could tell the history of the war in its various phases. Noteworthy examples are the Navy's "Victory at Sea" series, the Army's "Big Picture" selections, and the Air Force's "Air Power" and "Air Force Story" productions.

II. Purpose and Arrangement

The purpose of this documentary film guide is to provide users with citations to and borrowing information about a select group of 16mm documentary productions available on the land, air, and sea aspects of World War II in the Atlantic, MTO, and ETO. While most references are to official U.S. military films made during the conflict and after, some concern the efforts of private firms which employed official film to make documentaries for television.

Citations are arranged alphabetically, by title, with each receiving a reference number keying the entry into the guide's subject index. Additional information provided includes: producing or sponsoring agency and date (keyed to a Roman numeral which corresponds to the listing of loan/rental agencies in the borrowing information section below), serial number, designation as to color or black and white (b x w), sound, and running time. Each entry is then briefly annotated.

III. Borrowing Information

1. *UNIVERSITIES AND PUBLIC LIBRARIES*

Many universities and public libraries maintain media collections which provide the public free or rental access to 16mm films relative to our subject. Each has different procedures, and potential borrowers are urged to contact the agency closest to them for details. These outlets are usually the best sources for nongovernmental films. Here is a list of selected university media collections which maintain large stocks of films and in some cases produce catalogs:

I.

University of California Extension Media Center, 2223 Fulton Street, Berkeley, Calif. 94720
University of Connecticut Film Library, Storrs, Conn. 06268
Florida State University Regional Film Library, Instructional Support Center, Tallahassee, Fla. 32306
University of Georgia Film Library, Center for Continuing Education, Athens, Ga. 30602
University of Illinois Film Center, 1325 S. Oak, Champaign, Ill. 61820
Southern Illinois University Learning Resources Center, Carbondale, Ill. 62901
Indiana University, AV Center, Bloomington, Ind. 47405
University of Kansas Film Services, 746 Mass St., Lawrence, Kans. 66044
Louisiana State University Film and Materials Library, 137 Himes St., Baton Rouge, La. 70130
University of Minnesota AV Library Service, 3300 University, SE, Minneapolis, Minn. 55414
University of New Hampshire Media Service, Durham, N.H. 03820
Kent State University Educational Film Service, Kent, Ohio 44242
University of South Carolina Film Center, Columbia, S.C. 29208
University of Texas Film Library, Box W, Austin, Tx. 78712
West Virginia University Film Library, Morgantown, W.V. 26505
University of Wisconsin, Bureau of AV Instruction, Box 2093, Madison, Wisc. 53701

A source of free films which might be consulted is:

Modern Talking Picture Service, Inc., 5000 Park St., N, St. Petersburg, Fla. 33709

2. U.S. GOVERNMENT FILM COLLECTIONS

Each of the military services maintains film collections. In addition, many of the films available from the military, and others which are not, are held by the National Audiovisual Center. Differences are noted.

II. U.S. Army

All U.S. Army films should be requested on DA (Department of the Army) form 11-44, available from the nearest large Army facility. If you require help in determining the location of your nearest Army facility, visit your local library, Army recruiter, or National Guard armory. All films may be borrowed from large Army installations, but be sure to book well in advance.

III. U.S. Air Force

All U.S. Air Force films should be requested on Air Force Form 2018, which is available from any U.S.A.F. base or from the central AV library. Requests should be sent in at least three (3) weeks in advance of need. Address all requests to:

Air Force Central Audio-Visual Library
Aerospace Audiovisual Service
Norton Air Force Base, Calif. 92409

If you require help in determining the location of your nearest air force base, visit your local library or Air Force recruiter.

IV. U.S. Coast Guard

All U.S. Coast Guard films are held by the Headquarters, U.S. Coast Guard, Washington, D.C., and many are held in the headquarters of the various Coast Guard districts. For specific ordering instructions, consult those agencies, addresses for which may be had from your local library or Coast Guard recruiter.

V. U.S. Navy

Navy films may be booked without a specific form. Again, they should be ordered early. If you live in states east of the Mississippi River, address your request to:

Commanding Officer
Naval Education and Training Support Center
Atlantic Naval Station, Bldg. Z-86
Norfolk, Va. 23511

If you reside west of the Mississippi River, address your request to:

Commanding Officer
Naval Education and Training Support Center
Pacific Fleet Station, Post Office Bldg.
San Diego, Calif. 92132

VI. National Audiovisual Center

In the event that any of these films is not available at the above military sources, it is still possible to obtain them, although there may be a borrowing fee involved. For details on borrowing (or purchase) consult the GSA's *Reference List of Audiovisual Materials Produced by the U.S. Government* (Washington, D.C.: U.S. Government Printing Office, 1978) and its supplements, available at many libraries, especially those holding government document collections. If it is not available, write directly to:

National Audiovisual Center
National Archives and Records Service
General Services Administration
Reference Section DL
Washington, D.C. 20409

3. PRIVATE FILM COLLECTIONS

A number of private film organizations have produced and marketed their own 16mm documentaries and are willing to rent these to individuals, groups, and schools. For information, write directly to these organizations:

VII. McGraw-Hill Films, Dept. 455
1221 Avenue of the Americas, New York, N.Y. 10020

VIII. Time-Life Video
100 Eisenhower Dr., Box 644, Paramus, N.J. 07652

IX. Encyclopaedia Britannica Educational Corp.
425 North Michigan Ave., Chicago, Ill. 60611

X. CBS, 485 Madison Ave., New York, N.Y. 10022

XI. Sterling Educational Films
241 East 34th St., New York, N.Y. 10016

XII. British Information Service, Film and Publications Division
45 Rockefeller Plaza, New York, N.Y. 10020

XIII. Coronet Instructional Media
65 E. South Water St., Chicago, Ill. 60601

2646. *The Air Force Story: D-Day, June 6, 1944*. US Air Force, 1953, III, VI, SFP-263-19. 16mm, b x w, sd., 13min.

AAF operations in Europe in mid-1944, particularly those surrounding the Normandy invasion.

2647. *The Air Force Story: Expanding Airpower, June 1943*. U.S. Air Force, 1953, III, VI, SFP-263-13. 16mm, b x w, sd., 14min.

Examines the AAF's training program and the bombing of the Italian island of Pantelleria into surrender.

2648. *The Air Force Story: Maximum Effort, October 1943*. U.S. Air Force, 1953, III, VI, SFP-263-16. 16mm, b x w, sd., 14min.

Follows AAF operations in the bombing of German war facilities by the VIII Bomber Command; demonstrates mission planning, preparation and briefing, execution, and debriefing.

2649. *The Air Force Story: North Africa, November 1942-May 1943.* U.S. Air Force, 1953, III, VI, SFP-263-11. 16mm, b x w, sd., 14min.

Covers AAF operations in support of the "Torch" invasion and the campaign in Tunisia.

2650. *The Air Force Story: Ploesti, March-April 1944.* U.S. Air Force, 1953, III, VI, SFP-263-20. 16mm, b x w, sd., 14min.

Describes the bombing of the Rumanian oil facilities by the U.S. Fifteenth Air Force.

2651. *The Air Force Story: Prelude to Invasion, January-June 1944.* U.S. Air Force, 1953, III, VI, SFP-263-18. 16mm, b x w, sd., 14min.

Reviews AAF attacks on German factories, aerodromes, and supply lines in preparation for the Normandy invasion.

2652. *The Air Force Story: Schweinfurt and Regensburg, August 1943.* U.S. Air Force, 1953. III, VI, SFP-263-14. 16mm, b x w, sd., 14min.

A review of the costly double strike made by B-17's of the VIII Bomber Command deep into Germany.

2653. *The Air Force Story: The Road to Rome, September 1943-June 1944.* U.S. Air Force, 1953, III, VI, SFP-263-17. 16mm, b x w, sd., 14min.

A summary of the Twelfth Air Force operations in Italy from the Salerno landings through the fall of Rome.

2654. *The Air Force Story: The Tide Turns, June-December 1942.* U.S. Air Force, 1953, III, VI, SFP-263-10. 16mm, b x w, sd., 14min.

Examines the AAF buildup around the world, including the arrival of heavy bombers in the MTO and ETO.

2655. *The Air Force Story: Victory in Europe, June 1944-May 1945.* U.S. Air Force, 1953, III, VI, SFP-263-22. 16mm, b x w, sd., 14min.

Reviews AAF tactical air support of the advancing U.S. Army, the battles at Arnhem and of the Bulge, and the bombing of German cities. Includes scenes of the German surrender.

2656. *Air Power.* U.S. Air Force, 1949, III, VI, SFP-228. 16mm, b x w, sd., 18min.

Traces the history and development of the AAF from 1917 to 1945.

2657. *Air Power--Conquest of the Air.* U.S. Air Force, 1957, III, VI, SFP-510. 16mm, b x w, sd., 27min.

Explains how heavy losses to VIII Bomber Command B-17's and B-24's in 1943 brought P-51 fighters, equipped with wing-tanks, into the battle.

2658. *Air Power--Schweinfurt.* U.S. Air Force, 1957, III, VI, SFP-509 (DF). 16mm, b x w, sd., 27min.

Reveals the costly daylight raids by which the AAF attempted to destroy Germany's ball-bearing production.

2659. *Air Power--Strangle.* U.S. Air Force, 1957, III, VI, SFP-513 (GX). 16mm, b x w, sd., 27min.

Reviews the Twelfth Air Force attacks on German supply lines in 1944 Italy.

2660. *Air Power--Target Ploesti.* U.S. Air Force, 1957, III, VI, SFP-508 (AW). 16mm, b x w, sd., 27min.

Discusses the AAF attempts to destroy oil refineries in Rumania, 1943-1944.

2661. *Air Power--Victory in Europe.* U.S. Air Force, 1957, III, VI, SFP-518 (FL). 16mm, b x w, sd., 24min.

How the Allied airpower turned the Battle of the Bulge into a victory.

2662. *Air Power--Winning of France.* U.S. Air Force, 1957, III, VI, SFP-516 (JL). 16mm, b x w, sd., 26min.

Shows the coordination between American ground and air forces in their dash across France and the liberation of Paris in 1944.

2663. *Air Siege.* U.S. Air Force, 1947, III, VI, SFP-175. 16mm, b x w, sd., 22min.

Reviews the bombing of Ploesti by Fifteenth Air Force bombers; includes scenes from captured German films.

2664. *Allied Victory.* Encyclopaedia Britannica, 1963, IX. 16mm, b x w, sd., 28min.

A review of key military events from 1943 to 1945 which uses footage from captured, newsreel, and U.S. government film.

2665. *American First Army--Aachen to the Roer River.* U.S. Army, 1948, II, VI, CHR-B-30. 16mm, b x w, sd., 29min.

Examines the First Army advance into Germany with scenes of combat by the First, Ninth, Eighty-Third, and One Hundred Fourth Infantry Divisions and the Third Armored Division.

2666. *American Ninth Army--Aachen to the Roer River.* U.S. Army, 1948, II, VI, CHR-B-29. 16mm, b x w, sd., 31min.

Reviews the work of the U.S. Ninth Army with British Twenty-First Group in the advance into Germany.

2667. *Army in Action, no. 3--Flames on the Horizon.* U.S. Army, 1964, II, VI, TV-636. 16mm, b x w, sd., 28min.

"The Big Picture" review of world events, 1939-1945, including U.S. mobilization.

2668. *Army in Action, no. 4--The Spreading Holocaust.* U.S. Army, 1965, II, VI, TV-637. 16mm, b x w, sd., 28min.

"The Big Picture" recalls military events in 1942, with emphasis on U.S. involvement in Europe and North Africa.

2669. *Army in Action, no. 5--The Slumbering Giant Awakes.* U.S. Army, 1965, II, VI, TV-638. 16mm, b x w, sd., 28min.

"The Big Picture" shows U.S. logistical and tactical operations in North Africa and Europe up to the Sicilian invasion.

2670. *Army in Action, no. 6--Global War.* U.S. Army, 1965, II, VI, TV-639. 16mm, b x w, sd., 28min.

"The Big Picture" examines the war in 1943, including the U.S. landings in Sicily and Italy.

2671. *Army in Action, no. 7--The Tide Turns.* U.S. Army, 1965, II, VI, TV-640. 16mm, b x w, sd., 28min.

"The Big Picture" reveals the war in Europe in 1944, including Allied advances in Italy, France, and Belgium, the liberation of Paris, and early drives into Germany.

2672. *Army in Action, no. 8--The Victory.* U.S. Army, 1965, II, VI, TV-641. 16mm, b x w, sd., 28min.

"The Big Picture" recalls events leading to the German surrender.

2673. *Army Transportation--Key to Mobility.* U.S. Army, 1967, II, VI, TV-719. 16mm, b x w, sd., 28min.

"The Big Picture" examines the role of the Army Transportation Corps in delivering men and equipment to the battlefield, with emphasis on World War II in Europe.

2674. *At the Front in North Africa.* Made for the Office of War Information by the U.S. Army Signal Corps, 1942, VI. 16mm, color, sd., 11min.

American troops are shown en route to Tunisia from Algeria and in action at the Tunisian front in December 1942.

2675. *The Autobiography of a Jeep.* U.S. Office of War Information, 1943, Released by the Office of Education, 1945, VI. 16mm, b x w, sd., 10min.

A lighthearted look at the "All-American" 4 x 4 reconaissance vehicle.

2676. *Away Boarders*. U.S. Navy, 1945, V, VI, MN-9031. 16mm, b x w, sd., 19min.

Reviews the capture of the *U-505* by ships of the U.S.S. *Guadalcanal* hunter-killer group.

2677. *The Baily Bridge in Combat*. U.S. Army, 1945, II, VI, FR-185. 16mm, b x w, sd., 13min.

Shows the construction and use of this bridge in the ETO.

2678. *Battle of Cassino*. CBS News, 1961, X. 16mm, b x w, sd., 27min.

An episode from "The Twentieth Century" which describes the early effort to capture the approaches to Rome and this mountain, key to the Gustav Line; narrated by Walter Cronkite.

2679. *The Battle of Cassino*. Time-Life Video, 1971, VIII. 16mm, b x w and color, sd., 50min.

Employs current location filming and historic archival clips to document this account of a crucial battle on the road to Rome, 1944.

2680. *The Battle of North Africa*. U.S. Army, 1960, II, VI, TV 484/485. 16mm, b x w, sd., 58min.

This "Big Picture" record reviews the military operations in North Africa, 1940-1943, with U.S. action covered on reel two.

2681. *The Battle of Saint Vith*. U.S. Army, 1965, II, VI, TV-648/649. 16mm, b x w, sd., 58min.

"The Big Picture" shows a key engagement which disrupted the overall German plan in the Battle of the Bulge.

2682. *The Battle of Salerno*. U.S. Army, 1958, II, VI, TV-406. 16mm, b x w, sd., 28min.

The Fifth Army landing in Italy in September 1943 as recalled by "The Big Picture."

2683. *The Battle of San Pietro*. U.S. Army, 1945, II, VI, CR-2. 16mm, b x w, sd., 35min.

Written, directed, and narrated by John Huston with an introduction by Gen. Mark Clark, this dramatic documentary describes the fighting for control of Italy's Liri Valley.

2684. *The Battle of San Pietro*. U.S. Army, 1958, II, VI, TV-431. 16mm, b x w, sd., 28min.

With a historical introduction, this "Big Picture" episode is essentially a repetition of the preceding entry.

2685. *The Battle of the Bulge*. Time-Life Video, 1971, VIII. 16mm, b x w and color, sd., 50min.

Uses current location filming and archival clips to document the Battle of the Ardennes, the last great German counter-offensive of the war.

2686. *The Battle of the Bulge.* CBS News, 1960, X. 16mm, b x w, sd., 27min.

This "Twentieth Century" episode documents the phases of the Ardennes fighting, including the Battle of Bastogne, while highlighting Generals McAuliffe, Patton, and the One Hundred First Airborne Division.

2687. *The Battle of the Bulge.* U.S. Army, 1958, II, VI, TV-413. 16mm, b x w, sd., 28min.

A "Big Picture" review of the German counteroffensive which emphasizes the role of the U.S. "citizen-soldier" in its repulse.

2688. *Beachhead--Anzio.* U.S. Army, 1962, II, VI, TV-579. 16mm, b x w, sd., 29min.

Made in cooperation with the USN, this "The Big Picture" shows the establishment of the Anzio beachhead in Italy in January 1944.

2689. *Beyond the Call.* U.S. Army, 1962, II, VI, TV-575/576. 16mm, b x w, sd., 58min.

A "The Big Picture" tribute to the heroic men who won the Medal of Honor; World War II is covered in the second reel.

2690. *The Big Wheel.* U.S. Army, 1950, II, VI, CMF-130-7723. 16mm, b x w, sd., 17min.

A tribute to the ETO combat activities of the Thirty-Fifth Infantry Division.

2691. *Bomber.* U.S. Office of War Information, 1942, Released by the Office of Education, 1945, VI. 16mm, b x w, sd., 10min.

Shows the manufacture, speed, and flight characteristics of the B-26 Marauder; the commentary was written by Carl Sandburg.

2692. *Bombers over North Africa.* U.S. Army Air Forces, 1944, III, VI, TF-1-3337. 16mm, b x w, sd., 19min.

Shows the various steps in preparing for and executing a bombing raid by aircraft of the Northwest African Strategic Air Forces; includes statements by Generals Eisenhower and Doolittle.

2693. *Breakout and Pursuit.* U.S. Army, 1960, II, VI, TV-506. 16mm, b x w, sd., 28min.

"The Big Picture" reveals the manner by which American troops broke out of Normandy in July-August 1944 and moved across France.

2694. *Bridge at Remagen.* U.S. Army, 1965, II, VI, TV-657/658. 16mm, b x w, sd., 56min.

"The Big Picture" details the capture of the Rhine bridge here on March 7, 1945; includes comments by General Eisenhower and others.

2695. *Building a Bomber*. U.S. Office of War Information, 1942, Released by the Office of Education, 1945, VI. 16mm, b x w, sd., 19min.

Explains the technical details of manufacturing a B-26 Marauder.

2696. *Building a Tank*. U.S. Office of War Information, 1942, Released by the Office of Education, 1945, VI. 16mm, b x w, sd., 20min.

Reviews the technical details in manufacturing an M-3.

2697. *Campaign in Sicily*. U.S. Army, 1958, II, VI, CHR-C-1. 16mm, b x w, sd., 20min.

The island's 1943 invasion by the Allied Fifteenth Army Group, including the U.S. Seventh and British Eighth Armies.

2698. *Climb to Glory*. U.S. Army, 1963, II, VI, TV-599/600. 16mm, b x w, sd., 58min.

"The Big Picture" details the U.S. Tenth Mountain Division's breaking of the invincible Gothic Line in Italy.

2699. *Close Air Support*. U.S. Air Force, 1972, III, VI, FR-1328 (NY). 16mm, color, sd., 32min.

Examines the role played by aircraft in the close-air support of ground troops from World War I through World War II.

2700. *Combat America*. U.S. Army Air Forces, 1945, III, VI, WF-104-39. 16mm, color, sd., 55min.

Presents the story of the 351st Bombardment Group (H) from its training in Colorado to a mission over Germany, with emphasis on crews in England and on the mission. Excellent combat footage.

2701. *Combat Bulletin, no. 1*. U.S. Army, 1944, II, VI, CB-1. 16mm, b x w, sd., 13min.

Provides combat shots of Army troops in Italy.

2702. *Combat Bulletin, no. 2*. U.S. Army, 1944, II, VI, CB-2. 16mm, b x w, sd., 14min.

Includes a look at bridging on Italy's Volturno River.

2703. *Combat Bulletin, no. 3*. U.S. Army, 1944, II, VI, CB-3. 16mm, b x w, sd., 20min.

Includes shots of pillbox building in Italy, the embarkation for Anzio, and Capadichine airfield in Italy.

2704. *Combat Bulletin, no. 4*. U.S. Army, 1944, II, VI, CB-4. 16mm, b x w, sd., 19min.

Provides combat footage of the battle for Cassino.

2705. *Combat Bulletin, no. 6.* U.S. Army, 1944, II, VI, CB-6. 16mm, b x w, sd., 23min.

Includes shots of Army combat on the northern France beachheads at Normandy.

2706. *Combat Bulletin, no. 17.* U.S. Army, 1944, II, VI, CB-17. 16mm, b x w, sd., 38min.

Examines the invasion of southern France and Army operations in Normandy before the breakout.

2707. *Combat Bulletin, no. 19.* U.S. Army, 1944, II, VI, CB-19. 16mm, b x w, sd., 21min.

Looks at the expansion of the beachhead in southern France, activities at Leghorn, Italy, and operations in northern France.

2708. *Combat Bulletin, no. 21.* U.S. Army, 1944, II, VI, CB-21. 16mm, b x w, sd., 20min.

Reviews Army progress in southern and northern France and into Belgium.

2709. *Combat Bulletin, no. 22.* U.S. Army, 1944, II, VI, CB-22. 16mm, b x w, sd., 26min.

Shows the U.S. Third and Seventh Armies meeting in Germany and the takeoff of the Allied Airborne Army for Arnhem.

2710. *Combat Bulletin, no. 23.* U.S. Army, 1944, II, VI, CB-23. 16mm, b x w, sd., 26min.

Recalls the battles of the Siegfried Line, the capture of the Rhine bridge at Remagen, the battles in Lorraine, and the cracking of the Gothic Line in Italy.

2711. *Combat Bulletin, no. 24.* U.S. Army, 1944, II, VI, CB-24. 16mm, b x w, sd., 20min.

Examines Channel coast activities, ordnance repairs, German frontier operations, airborne activities at Arnhem, and the situation in Toulon harbor.

2712. *Combat Bulletin, no. 25.* U.S. Army, 1944, II, VI, CB-25. 16mm, b x w, sd., 25min.

Shows resupply of the U.S. First Army and Allied activity near Italy's Po Valley.

2713. *Combat Bulletin, no. 27.* U.S. Army, 1944, II, VI, CB-27. 16mm, b x w, sd., 28min.

A general look at the ETO activities plus the arrival of Brazilian troops in Italy.

2714. *Combat Bulletin, no. 28.* U.S. Army, 1944, II, VI, CB-28. 16mm, b x w, sd., 19min.

Reviews the battle of Holland, a glider pickup at Eindhoven, AAF fighter pilot kills, and the liberation of Greece.

2715. *Combat Bulletin, no. 30.* U.S. Army, 1944, II, VI, CB-30. 16mm, b x w, sd., 22min.

Shows the bombing of the Belgian rail network and how Allied armies faced rain and snow.

2716. *Combat Bulletin, no. 31.* U.S. Army, 1944, II, VI, CB-31. 16mm, b x w, sd., 15min.

Provides nice footage of VIII Fighter Command aerial kills.

2717. *Combat Bulletin, no. 32.* U.S. Army, 1945, II, VI, CB-32. 16mm, b x w, sd., 21min.

Includes a look at the U.S. First and Ninth Armies driving on the Roer River.

2718. *Combat Bulletin, no. 33.* U.S. Army, 1945, II, VI, CB-33. 16mm, b x w, sd., 18min.

Includes shots of the U.S. First and Ninth Armies on the Aachen front.

2719. *Combat Bulletin, no. 34.* U.S. Army, 1945, II, VI, CB-34. 16mm, b x w, sd., 16min.

Portrays activities on the U.S. Ninth Army front and in the port of Antwerp.

2720. *Combat Bulletin, no. 38.* U.S. Army, 1945, II, VI, CB-38. 16mm, b x w, sd., 21min.

Presents footage of the Allied counteroffensive in the Battle of the Bulge.

2721. *Combat Bulletin, no. 40.* U.S. Army, 1945, II, VI, CB-40. 16mm, b x w, sd., 20min.

Shows action on the Alsace front.

2722. *Combat Bulletin, no. 47.* U.S. Army, 1945, II, VI, CB-47. 16mm, b x w, sd., 27min.

Follows the Allied offensive on the Rhine.

2723. *Combat Bulletin, no. 48.* U.S. Army, 1945, II, VI, CB-48. 16mm, b x w, sd., 31min.

Includes footage of Allied tactical air support in northwest Europe.

2724. *Combat Bulletin, no. 49.* U.S. Army, 1945, II, VI, CB-49. 16mm, b x w, sd., 25min.

Includes footage on the defenders of Bastogne.

2725. *Combat Bulletin, no. 50.* U.S. Army, 1945, II, VI, CB-50. 16mm, b x w, sd., 29min.

Depicts U.S. forces driving deeper into Germany.

2726. *Combat Bulletin, no. 55.* U.S. Army, 1945, II, VI, CB-55. 16mm, b x w, sd., 29min.

Presents footage of the German surrender in May 1945.

2727. *Command Decision: The Invasion of Southern France.* U.S. Army, 1962, II, VI, TV-572. 16mm, b x w, sd., 29min.

"The Big Picture" describes the planning and execution of "Operation Anvil-Dragoon."

2728. *The Commanders: Dwight Eisenhower, Supreme Commander of the Grand Alliance.* Time-Life Video, VIII. 16mm, b x w, sd., 56min.

Examines General Eisenhower's leadership of the AEF in North Africa and, more particularly, in northwest Europe.

2729. *Crusade in Europe.* March of Time/McGraw-Hill, 1949, VI. 16mm, b x w, sd., 25min.

A series of 25 motion pictures describing the American war effort in Europe from 1942 to 1945, each with the technical data noted above.

2730. *D-Day.* CBS News, 1955, X. 16mm, b x w, sd., 28min.

Walter Cronkite describes the U.S. landing on Utah and Omaha Beaches in this episode from the "You Are There" series.

2731. *D-Day.* Encyclopaedia Britannica, 1962, IX. 16mm, b x w, 52min.

Examines the planning and execution of "Operation Overlord" using Allied and captured German footage.

2732. *D-Day Anniversary.* U.S. Army, 1968, II, VI, TV-762. 16mm, b x w, sd., 28min.

"The Big Picture's" 25th anniversary look at the sights and sounds of the Normandy beaches, including clips of the landing and battle inland.

2733. *D-Day Convoy.* U.S. Army, 1948, II, VI, CHR-15. 16mm, b x w, sd., 19min.

Describes activities just prior to and including D-Day movements of U.S. troops from all parts of POE's prior to Normandy.

2734. *D-Day Minus One.* U.S. Army Air Forces, 1945, III, VI, SFP-158. 16mm, b x w, sd., 16min.

Records the June 5/6 drop of the U.S. Eighty-Second/One Hundred First Airborne Divisions behind the German lines in Normandy.

2735. *Defense of Antwerp Against the V-1.* U.S. Army, 1947, II, VI, CMF-9-1286. 16mm, b x w, sd., 21min.

The defense of Antwerp against the buzz bomb in late 1944.

2736. *Dragon's Teeth.* U.S. Army, 1962, II, VI, TV-566. 16mm, b x w, sd., 28min.

Gen. J. Lawton Childs tells of the fight to take the Siegfried Line in this "The Big Picture" episode.

2737. *Dwight David Eisenhower.* McGraw-Hill, 1963, VII. 16mm, b x w, sd., 26min.

A biography of the Allied Supreme Commander and later U.S. President narrated by Mike Wallace.

2738. *D-Z Normandy: Employment of Troop Carrier Forces.* U.S. Army Air Forces, 1945, III, VI, TF-1-3711. 16mm, b x w, sd., 95min.

Ninth Troop Carrier Command training and execution of the D-Day drop of the Eighty-Second/One Hundred First Airborne Divisions in Normandy.

2739. *The Earthquakers.* U.S. Army Air Forces, n.d., III, VI, SFP-26133. 16mm, color, sd., 20min.

Reviews the role of the Ninth Air Force 12th Bombardment Group (M) in the North African campaign.

2740. *The 82nd Airborne Division.* U.S. Army, 1948, II, VI, CMF-45-1426. 16mm, b x w, sd., 21min.

Shows the "All American" division's fights and drops in Sicily, Salerno, Anzio, Normandy, Holland, and the Bulge plus the victory parade on New York's Fifth Avenue.

2741. *The 83rd Infantry Division in Europe.* U.S. Army, 1951, II, VI, CMF-45-7814. 16mm, b x w, sd., 20min.

Recounts the outfit's Omaha Beach landing, hedgerow fighting in Normandy, taking of St. Malo, battles in Loire valley and Bulge, and drive to the Elbe River.

2742. *Eisenhower vs. Rommel.* Encyclopaedia Britannica, 1964, IX. 16mm, b x w, sd., 25min.

This episode of the "Men in Crisis" series discusses Eisenhower's D-Day preparations and Rommel's breaking of a code revealing the date of the landings.

2743. *The Enemy Strikes.* U.S. War Finance Division, U.S. Treasury, by U.S. Army Signal Corps, 1945, II, VI. 16mm, b x w, sd., 11min.

Uses captured German film to show the unexpected Ardennes counteroffensive.

2744. *The Famous Fourth.* U.S. Army, 1961, II, VI, TV-546. 16mm, b x w, sd., 29min.

Traces the history of the Fourth Infantry Division in World War II.

2745. *Famous Generals--Arnold.* U.S. Army, 1963, II, VI, TV-595. 16mm, b x w, sd., 28min.

"The Big Picture's" tribute to Hap Arnold and the AAF.

2746. *Famous Generals--Eisenhower.* U.S. Army, 1963, II, VI, TV-590. 16mm, b x w, sd., 28min.

A biography of Eisenhower from Abilene to Nato with emphasis on his service as Supreme Commander of the AEF. A "The Big Picture" episode.

2747. *Famous Generals--Marshall.* U.S. Army, 1963, II, VI, TV-592. 16mm, b x w, sd., 28min.

A biography of the U.S. Army Chief of Staff during the war as recalled by the editors of "The Big Picture."

2748. *Famous Generals--Patton.* U.S. Army, 1963, II, VI, TV-594. 16mm, b x w, sd., 28min.

"The Big Picture's" biography of the controversial and colorful commander of the U.S. Third Army.

2749. *The Famous Third Army.* U.S. Army, 1952, II, VI, CMF-7705. 16mm, b x w, sd., 22min.

A historical review of the Third's advance across France and into Germany, 1944-1945.

2750. *A Fifth Army Report from the Beachhead.* U.S. Army, 1944, II, VI, War Film, no. 1039. 16mm, b x w, sd., 11min.

A report on the Anzio invasion showing the landings, fighting, and evacuation of wounded.

2751. *Fight for the Sky.* U.S. Air Force, 1965, III, VI, SFP-1563. 16mm, b x w, sd., 21min.

Documents the heroism of U.S. escort fighter pilots who guarded VIII Bomber Command B-17's and B-24's en route to German targets and battled the intercepting Luftwaffe.

2752. *The Fighting First.* U.S. Army, 1947, II, VI, CNF-45-1279. 16mm, b x w, sd., 15min.

Shows the combat operations of the First Infantry Division in the Mediterranean and Europe, 1942-1945.

2753. *Film Communique, no. 1.* U.S. War Department, 1943, II, VI, WF-20. 16mm, b x w, sd., 22min.

Shows scenes of Hitler's Atlantic Wall and 5 min. on the Sicily landings.

2754. *Film Communique, no. 2.* U.S. War Department, 1943, II, VI, WF-20-2. 16mm, b x w, sd., 19min.

Eight min. of this film are used to show AAF A-36 dive bombers over Sicily.

2755. *Film Communique, no. 4.* U.S. War Department, 1943, II, VI, WF-15. 16mm, b x w, sd., 17min.

Includes footage of the Fifth Army landing at Salerno in September 1943.

2756. *Film Communique, no. 5.* U.S. War Department, 1944, II, VI, WF-16. 16mm, b x w, sd., 20min.

Shows assembly and testing of P-47's in England in the first 3 min.

2757. *Film Communique, no. 6.* U.S. War Department, 1944, II, VI, WF-17. 16mm, b x w, sd., 19min.

Depicts the impact of mud in Italy, the use of light liaison aircraft ("Grasshoppers"), and the battle record of a bomber named "Stella."

2758. *Film Communique, no. 8.* U.S. War Department, 1944, II, VI, WF-22. 16mm, b x w, sd., 20min.

Portrays an VIII Bomber Command raid on Germany and the Fifth Army's landing at Anzio.

2759. *Film Communique, no. 9.* U.S. War Department, 1944, II, VI, WF-23. 16mm, b x w, sd., 22min.

Examines the Fifteenth Air Force and one of its bombers, "The Blue Streak."

2760. *Film Communique, no. 10.* U.S. War Department, 1944, II, VI, WF-24. 16mm, b x w, sd., 20min.

Includes a look at Fifth Army operations in Italy and a Ninth Air Force B-26 raid on northern France.

2761. *Film Communique, no. 11.* U.S. War Department, 1944, II, VI, WF-35. 16mm, b x w, sd., 21min.

Shows aerial views of Normandy after the landing and fighting in St. Lô.

2762. *Film Communique, no. 16.* U.S. War Department, 1945, II, VI, WF-52. 16mm, b x w, sd., 18min.

Half the film depicts the use of the Mulberry artificial harbors off the Normandy beaches.

2763. *The French Campaign.* McGraw-Hill/March of Time, 1945, XII. 16mm, b x w, sd., 19min.

Describes the 1944 Allied race across France and the liberation of Paris.

2764. *The General Bradley Story.* U.S. Army, 1970, II, VI, TV-786. 16mm, color, sd., 28min.

"The Big Picture's" tribute to the G.I.'s general who led the Twelfth Army Group across France and into Germany.

2765. *George Marshall.* Sterling Educational Films, 1963, XI. 16mm, b x w, sd., 23min.

A biography of the wartime Army Chief of Staff.

2766. *George Patton.* Sterling Educational Films, 1965, XI. 16mm, b x w, sd., 23min.

A biography of the colorful boss of the U.S. Third Army.

2767. *Greyhounds of the Sea.* U.S. Navy, 1967, V, VI, MN-9726. 16mm, b x w, sd., 29min.

A history of destroyers, including their employment in the Battle of the Atlantic.

2768. *A Harbour Goes to France.* British Information Service, 1945, XII. 16mm, b x w, sd., 15min.

The story of Mulberry, the artificial harbor which was built in England and towed across the Channel to Arromaches, Normandy.

2769. *Hell on Wheels.* U.S. Army, 1951, II, VI, CMF-17-7864. 16mm, b x w, sd., 17min.

Covers the highlights of the war service of the Fourth Armored Division, including its role in the Battle of the Bulge.

2770. *Invasion of Sicily.* CBS News, 1964, X. 16mm, b x w, sd., 27min.

This "The Twentieth Century" episode describes the Allied landings on July 10, 1943, and the month-long campaign to liberate the island.

2771. *Invasion of Southern France.* U.S. Army, 1950, II, VI, CHR-C-8. 16mm, b x w, sd., 22min.

Shows the Seventh Army's invasion and later link-up with the Third Army in central France.

2772. *The Joe Mann Story.* U.S. Army, 1960, II, VI, TV-459. 16mm, b x w, sd., 28min.

A "The Big Picture" tribute to a U.S. soldier killed in Holland.

2773. *The Liberation of Paris.* CBS News/McGraw-Hill, 1956, VII, X. 16mm, b x w, sd., 27min.

Walter Cronkite narrates this "You Are There" episode which shows the liberation of the French capital in 1944.

2774. *Medal of Honor--A Team Man.* U.S. Air Force, 1967, III, VI, SFP-1544G. 16mm, b x w, sd., 5min.

Cites Forrest Vosler for self-sacrifice while serving as a gunner during an VIII Bomber Command raid on Bremen, Germany, in 1943.

2775. *Medal of Honor--Burning Ploesti Oil.* U.S. Air Force, 1967, III, VI, SFP-1544C. 16mm, b x w, sd., 5min.

Cites Cols. John Kane and Leon Johnson for bravery during the August 1, 1943, B-24 raid on the Rumanian oil refineries.

2776. *Medal of Honor--Capt. Jay Zeamer.* U.S. Air Force, 1967, III, VI, SFP-1544E. 16mm, b x w, sd., 5min.

Cites Zeamer, a bomber pilot, for heroism during a reconnaissance mission.

2777. *Medal of Honor--Heading Home.* U.S. Air Force, 1967, III, VI, SFP-1544L. 16mm, b x w, sd., 5min.

Cites Capt. William Lawley for bravery during an VIII Bomber Command raid on a European city.

2778. *Medal of Honor--One Man Air Force.* U.S. Air Force, 1967, III, VI, SFP-1544H. 16mm, b x w, sd., 5min.

Cites Col. James H. Howard for his fighter pilot abilities during an VIII Fighter Command escort mission.

2779. *Medal of Honor--Only a Few Returned.* U.S. Air Force, 1967, III, VI, SFP-1544N. 16mm, b x w, sd., 5 min.

Cites B-17 gunner Sgt. Maynard Smith.

2780. *Medal of Honor--Trial by Fire.* U.S. Air Force, 1967, III, VI, SFP-1544K. 16mm, b x w, sd., 5min.

How Sgt. Edward Erwin threw a phosphorous bomb from his aircraft after the missile had caught fire.

2781. *Medal of Honor--With One Hand.* U.S. Air Force, 1967, III, VI, SFP-1544F. 16mm, b x w, sd., 5min.

How Lt. John Morgan flew his bomber single-handedly to target.

2782. *Memphis Belle.* U.S. Army Air Forces, 1944, III, VI, SFP-114. 16mm, b x w, sd., 43min.

Looks at a single VIII Bomber Command B-17 and her crew during a mission over Germany, including preparations, takeoff, bombing of submarine facilities, and return to base.

2783. *Mission Accomplished.* U.S. Office of War Information, 1942, Released by the Office of Education, 1945, VI. 16mm, b x w, sd., 11min.

A photographic record of the first VIII Bomber Command B-17 raid on France in July 1942.

2784. *Naples to Cassino.* U.S. Army, 1948, II, VI, CHR-C-3. 16mm, b x w, sd., 26min.

Shows scenes of fighting during the Fifth Army drive from Naples to Cassino, 1943-1944.

2785. *The Negro Soldier*. U.S. War Department, 1944, II, VI, OF-51. 16mm, b x w, sd., 42min.

Directed by Frank Capra, this film, ignoring discrimination, traces the accomplishment of Black troops from 1775 to 1944.

2786. *The Ninth Division*. U.S. Army, 1968, II, VI, TV-746. 16mm, b x w, sd., 28min.

A "The Big Picture" episode showing this unit in action in North Africa, France, and Germany.

2787. *The Normandy Invasion*. U.S. Coast Guard, 1944, IV, VI. 16mm, b x w, sd., 19min.

Coast Guard record of preparations for and execution of Normandy landings.

2788. *Nurses in the Army*. U.S. Army, 1955, II, VI, MF-8-8564. 16mm, b x w, sd., 27min.

Examines their services in World War II and after, including their work at Anzio and Normandy.

2789. *On Foreign Shores*. U.S. Coast Guard, 1945, IV, VI. 16mm, b x w, sd., 25min.

Reviews CG activities in invasions and the Battle of the Atlantic.

2790. *Paris '44*. U.S. Army, 1963, II, VI, TV-601. 16mm, b x w, sd., 28min.

Shows the liberation of the French capital; part of "The Big Picture" series.

2791. *Patton and the Third Army*. CBS News, 1960, X. 16mm, b x w, sd., 27min.

Walter Cronkite records the Third's battles in France and Germany and its colorful commander for "The Twentieth Century."

2792. *A Place in History*. U.S. National Archives, 1970, VI. 16mm, color, sd., 28min.

A tribute to Eisenhower as Supreme Commander and President.

2793. *Prelude to Victory*. U.S. Navy, 1946, V, VI, MN-9119-d. 16mm, b x w, sd., 40min.

Depicts the work of the U.S. Eighth Fleet during the war.

2794. *The Red Bull Attacks--34th Infantry Division*. U.S. Army, 1950, II, VI, CMF-130-7555. 16mm, b x w, sd., 21min.

Traces the history of the Third Infantry Division from the Civil War through World War II in Europe.

2795. *The Red Diamond*. U.S. Army, 1966, II, VI, TV-693. 16mm, b x w, sd., 28min.

Follows the story of the U.S. Fifth Infantry Division, including its ETO service during World War II; a "The Big Picture" episode.

2796. *Rolling to the Rhine.* U.S. Army, 1945, II, VI, MF-55-1135. 16mm, b x w, sd., 10min.

Examines the role of trucks in maintaining the ETO supply lines.

2797. *Sicily to Naples.* U.S. Army, 1948, II, VI, CHR-C-2. 16mm, b x w, sd., 13min.

Depicts the Fifth Army landing at Salerno and the push to Naples, 1943.

2798. *Target: North Africa.* CBS News, 1965, X. 16mm, b x w, sd., 30min.

In this "The Twentieth Century" episode narrated by Walter Cronkite, we see the planning and execution of "Operation Torch," including U.S. dealings with Vichy leader Darlan.

2799. *That Magnificent Man.* U.S. Air Force, 1970, III, VI, SFP-1906(NP). 16mm, color, sd., 25min.

A biography of Henry A. Arnold.

2800. *The Third Armored Division--The Spearhead.* U.S. Army, 1970, II, VI, TV-795. 16mm, color, sd., 28 1/2min.

A history of the Third Armored, including its ETO service; a "The Big Picture" episode.

2801. *The Third Infantry Division.* U.S. Army, 1970, II, VI, TV-801. 16mm, b x w, sd., 28 1/2min.

A "Big Picture" tribute to the Third, including its ETO service.

2802. *The Thirty-Sixth Infantry Division.* U.S. Army, 1953, II, VI, CMF-130-7931. 16mm, b x w, sd., 21min.

Follows the "Texas Division" through the Italian campaign, including the Rapido River crossing.

2803. *Thunderbolt.* U.S. Army Air Forces, 1946, III, VI, SFP-182. 16mm, color, sd., 43min.

Tells the story of the P-47's involved in the Italian interdiction campaign called "Operation Strangle"; excellent combat footage.

2804. *The Thunderbolts--Ramrod to Emden.* U.S. Army Air Forces, 1943, III, VI. 16mm, b x w, sd., 33min.

Shows the planning for an VIII Fighter Command P-47 escort of B-17's to Emden, scenes of battle, and the post-mission debriefing.

2805. *Tigers on the Loose*. U.S. Army, 1965, II, VI, TV-659/660. 16mm, b x w, sd., 56min.

Combat story of the Tenth Armored Division in fighting at Metz, Bastogne, and into the Brenner Pass, 1944-1945; a "The Big Picture" episode.

2806. *Tried by Fire*. U.S. Army, 1965, II, VI, TV-650/651. 16mm, b x w, sd., 56min.

"The Big Picture" record of the U.S. Eighty-Fourth Infantry Division in fighting for the Siegfried Line and the Bulge, November 1944-January 1945.

2807. *The True Glory*. U.S. Army, 1945, II, VI, M-1211. 16mm, b x w, sd., 85min.

With a script by Peter Ustinov, this winner of the 1945 Academy Award for Best Documentary Feature describes the bravery of the men who fought in the ETO from D-Day through VE-Day in the words of the enlisted soldiers themselves; co-produced with the British Ministry of Information.

2808. *Tunisian Victory*. U.S. Office of War Information, 1943, Released by the Office of Education, 1944, VI. 16mm, b x w, sd., 76min.

The story of the North African campaign from the "Torch" landings of November 1942 through the Axis defeat in May 1943.

2809. *The Twenty-Sixth Infantry Division*. U.S. Army, 1952, II, VI, CMF-130-7872. 16mm, b x w, sd., 15min.

Detailed account of the "Yankee Division" from August 1944 through the end of the European campaign.

2810. *Twenty-Ninth Infantry Division--"Let's Go."* U.S. Army, 1950, II, VI, CMF-130-7554. 16mm, b x w, sd., 19min.

Follows this outfit's combat operations in Normandy, St. Lô, Brest, and Germany.

2811. *Victory at Sea*. NBC/Encyclopaedia Britannica, 1966, IX. 16mm, b x w, sd., 79min.

A condensed version of the famous television series which reviews the highlights of the US naval war, including the Battle of the Atlantic and invasions in the MTO/ETO.

2812. *Victory at Sea--Beneath the Southern Cross*. NBC/U.S. Navy, 1953, V, VI, MN-7308-j. 16mm, b x w, sd., 30min.

Describes U.S. Navy operations in the South Atlantic.

2813. *Victory at Sea--D-Day*. NBC/U.S. Navy, 1953, V, VI, MN-7308-O. 16mm, b x w, sd., 30min.

Describes the naval phase ("Neptune") of the Normandy landings.

2814. *Victory at Sea--Design for War.* NBC/U.S. Navy, 1953, V, VI, MN-7308-a. 16mm, b x w, sd., 30min.

Describes the Battle of the Atlantic from 1939 to 1941, including America's undeclared war on the U-boat.

2815. *Victory at Sea--Killers and the Kill.* NBC/U.S. Navy, 1953, V, VI, MN-7308-p. 16mm, b x w, sd., 30min.

Describes the Battle of the Atlantic from 1943 to 1945, including the use of carrier hunter-killer groups.

2816. *Victory at Sea--Magnetic North.* NBC/U.S. Navy, 1953, V, VI, MN-7308-k. 16mm, b x w, sd., 30min.

Examines operations on the Murmansk convoy run.

2817. *Victory at Sea: Mare Nostrum.* NBC/U.S. Navy, 1953, V, VI, MN-7308-h. 16mm, b x w, sd., 30min.

Shows operations in the Mediterranean through 1941.

2818. *Victory at Sea: Roman Renaissance.* NBC/U.S. Navy, 1953, V, VI, MN-7308-n. 16mm, b x w, sd., 30min.

Portrays Allied naval operations at Sicily, Italy, and southern France.

2819. *Victory at Sea--Sea and Sand.* NBC/U.S. Navy, 1953, V, VI, MN-7308-i. 16mm, b x w, sd., 30min.

Reviews the USN role in the North African campaign, 1942-1943.

2820. *Victory at Sea--Sealing the Breach.* NBC/U.S. Navy, 1953, V, VI, MN-7308-c. 16mm, b x w, sd., 30min.

Recalls the Battle of the Atlantic from 1941 through the summer of 1943.

2821. *Victory at Sea--The Fate of Europe.* NBC/U.S. Navy, 1953, V, VI, MN-7308-v. 16mm, b x w, sd., 30min.

Describes various naval operations in the Mediterranean, Black Sea, and Near East.

2822. *Victory at Sea--The Mediterranean Mosaic.* NBC/U.S. Navy, 1953, V, VI, MN-7308-e. 16mm, b x w, sd., 30min.

Describes operations in the Mediterranean in summer 1942.

2823. *Victory in Europe.* CBS News/McGraw-Hill, 1958, VII. 16mm, b x w, sd., 30min.

Describes the military situation from December 1944 to May 1945, including those battles which brought an end to the Third Reich.

2824. *Work Horse of the Western Front--The 30th Infantry Division.* U.S. Army, 1950, II, VI, CMF-130-7585. 16mm, b x w, sd., 18min.

Follows the "Old Hickory" outfit from Normandy through St. Lô and into Belgium, Holland, and Germany.

2825. *World War II: G.I. Diary.* Time-Life Video, 1980, VIII. 16mm, b x w and color, sd., 30min.

A series of films using color location shots and archival clips to tell the war's stories through the memories of its veterans; those relevant include: (2) *G.I. Christmas*; (3) *Desert War*; (4) *The Double Strike (Schweinfurt/Regensburg, 1943)*; (5) *Anzio to Rome*; (7) *Americans in Paris*; (11) *The Bulge*; (12) *The Flying Fortress*; (15) *D-Day*; (18) *The Last Barrier: Crossing the Rhine*; (20) *Sicily*; (21) *Road to Berlin*; (22) *Nightmare at San Pietro*; and (24) *Hell in the Arctic*.

2826. *World War II, 1942-1945.* Coronet Instructional Films, 1963, XIII. 16mm, b x w, sd., 16min.

Traces events from the time America entered the conflict.

2827. *World War II--Twenty Years Later.* U.S. Army, 1965, II, VI, AFMR-648. 16mm, b x w, sd., 20min.

A chronological capsule review of military events.

APPENDIX: LIST OF JOURNALS CONSULTED

Introduction: Although the bibliography is comprised mostly of references to books, certain periodicals yielded one or more articles of interest. To assist those who may wish to check newer issues of those still published, this list is provided.

Aero Digest
Aerospace Historian
Air Aces
Air Classics
Air Force
Air Force and Space Digest
Air Force Law Review
Air Force Magazine
Air Pictorial
Air Power
Air University Quarterly Review
Air University Review
Airlift Operations Review
Airman
Airpower Historian
All Hands
American Aviation Historical Society Journal
American Committee on the History of the Second World War Newsletter
American Heritage
American Historical Review
American History Illustrated
American Legion Magazine
American Medical Women's Association Journal
American Mercury
American Opinion
American Society of Naval Engineers Journal
Antiaircraft Journal
Armed Forces and Society
Armed Forces Journal International
Armor
Armored Cavalry Journal
Army
Army Digest
Army Quarterly and Defence Journal
Atlantic Monthly
Aviation
Aviation Quarterly
Battles
British History Illustrated
British Journal of International Studies
Bulletin of Bibliography
Bureau of Ships Journal
Collier's
Commentary
Commonweal
Coronet
Current History
Diplomatic History
Engineer
Esquire
Field Artillery Journal
Flying
Foreign Affairs
Fortune
George Washington Law Review
Harper's
Historian
History Today
Hobbies
Infantry Journal
Infantry School Quarterly
Interavia
International Affairs (London)
Journal of American History
Journal of Contemporary History
Journal of Modern History
Journal of the Royal United Service Institute
Life
Look
Marine Corps Gazette
Military Affairs
Military Chaplain
Military Engineer

Military Journal
Military Medicine
Military Review
Military Surgeon
National Geographic Magazine
Naval War College Review
Navy
Navy Civilian Engineer
New York Times Magazine
New Yorker
Ordnance
Political Science Quarterly
Popular Mechanics
Popular Science
Prologue
Quartermaster Review
RAF Flying Review
Reader's Digest
Red River Valley Historical Review
Sandlapper
Saturday Evening Post
Saturday Review of Literature
Scale Modeler
Science Digest
Sea Classics
Sea Power
Ships and the Sea
Signal
Smithsonian
Soldiers
Southern Folklore Quarterly
Southwestern Historical Quarterly
Soviet Literature
Soviet Military Review
Steamboat Bill of Facts
Strategy and Tactics
Surface Warfare
TAC Attack
Tactical Air Reconnaissance Digest
Theater Arts
Translog
TV Guide
U.S. Army Aviation Digest
U.S. Army Combat Forces Journal
U.S. Coast Guard Academy Alumni Association Newsletter
U.S. Naval Institute Proceedings
U.S. News & World Report
Vital Speeches of the Day
Warship International
Washington Post Magazine
Wings
Wisconsin Magazine of History
World War II Journal
World War II Magazine

AUTHOR INDEX

SUBJECT INDEX

FOR USE
IN
LIBRARY
ONLY